FIFTH EDI

WALTER AERTS
PETER WALTON

Global Financial Accounting and Reporting: Principles and Analysis

CENGAGE

Australia • Brazil • Mexico • Singapore • United Kingdom • United States

Global Financial Accounting and Reporting: Principles and Analysis,
Fifth Edition
Walter Aerts and Peter Walton

Publisher: Annabel Ainscow

List Manager: Birgit Gruber

Marketing Manager: Sophie Clarke

Senior Content Project Manager:
   Phillipa Davidson-Blake

Manufacturing Manager: Eyvett Davis

Typesetter: Lumina Datamatics, Inc.

Text design: Lumina Datamatics, Inc.

Cover design: Jonathan Bargus

Cover Image:
   © Boumen Japet/Shutterstock

For product information and technology assistance, contact us at **emea.info@cengage.com**.

For permission to use material from this text or product and for permission queries, email **emea.permissions@cengage.com**.

British Library Cataloguing-in-Publication Data
A catalogue record for this book is available from the British Library.

ISBN: 978-1-4737-6712-6

Cengage Learning EMEA
Cheriton House, North Way,
Andover, Hampshire, SP10 5BE,
United Kingdom

Cengage Learning is a leading provider of customized learning solutions with employees residing in nearly 40 different countries and sales in more than 125 countries around the world. Find your local representative at: **www.cengage.co.uk**

Cengage Learning products are represented in Canada by Nelson Education, Ltd.

To learn more about Cengage platforms and services, register or access your online learning solution, or purchase materials for your course, visit **www.cengagebrain.com**

Printed in China by RR Donnelley
Print Number: 01   Print Year: 2019

BRIEF CONTENTS

CONTENTS

PREFACE

This book was conceived as a support for courses where the objective is to provide students with a working understanding of financial statements and the meaning of accounting numbers. Our intention is to place financial reporting in its business context, and to make it clear to managers how accounting reflects their work. We also aim to teach the conceptual foundation of accounting and how this translates into the financial statements of businesses. The book is aimed at future users of accounting information – managers and analysts – not at future auditors or accountants.

The book is sited emphatically in an intuitive approach to understanding accounting and concerns itself with the underlying logic of the corporate accounting system and its exploitation in the financial statements. It is not a bookkeeping course and we have used a spreadsheet for double entry, rather than T-accounts or debits and credits, since we believe that the latter are technically unnecessary and are practically an obstacle to non-specialists.

The book does not situate itself in an individual national context. It uses International Financial Reporting Standards (IFRS® Standards) as its basis. These have become the de facto global set of standards for financial reporting and reflect the rules followed by nearly all European listed companies and by an increasing number of Asian, African and American (non-US) companies. We rely extensively on the conceptual framework underlying the standards in order to explain basic financial reporting concepts. We also use current IFRS® terminology (e.g. statement of financial position, statement of profit or loss (and other comprehensive income)) in order to be consistent with the IFRS® extracts used in our book.

Walter Aerts
Peter Walton

ACKNOWLEDGEMENTS

This book has evolved out of teaching materials drawn from a wide range of teaching experiences in Belgium, France, the Netherlands, Switzerland, the UK and the USA. As a result, many people, both students and colleagues, have influenced the content indirectly, and we are grateful for their help and advice over the years. We should also like to thank Andrew Ashwin, Annabel Ainscow, Birgit Gruber and Phillipa Davidson-Blake for their support and commitment in producing a new edition, as well as the rest of the publishing team at Cengage Learning.

The text contains quotations from published material and we should like to thank the following for permission to use these: Trustees of the IFRS Foundation, Association of Chartered Certified Accountants (*Accounting & Business*), the International Federation of Accountants, the United Nations Conference on Trade and Development, the Organisation for Economic Cooperation and Development, the US Securities and Exchange Commission and the Institute of Chartered Accountants in England and Wales. We also thank the many companies whose financial statements have supplied illustrative material.

Reviewer acknowledgements

The publishers and author team would like to thank the following academics for their review comments which have helped shape this new edition:

Tersia Botha, University of South Africa

Chris Coles, University of Stirling

Karol Marek Klimczak, University of Navarra

Salma Vanker, University of KwaZulu-Natal

Laura Zoni, Università Cattolica del Sacro Cuore

STRUCTURE OF THE BOOK

The aim of this book is to provide a complete companion to financial reporting that will take business students with no knowledge of accounting from the mechanics of how financial records are structured through to being able to understand and analyze published consolidated financial statements. However, this is not to say that every course will want to devote as much time to financial reporting as this would take. The book is therefore structured into what we believe are separable building blocks.

Part 1 covers material that is often not taught as such in a course on accounting and financial statement analysis. It is about the environment within which financial reporting takes place – how it is regulated, what an accounting department in a company does, how the accounting records are checked. It also includes the main material on the International Accounting Standards Board (the Board). We think this is useful background, not least because students come to the course with different previous exposure to accounting and preconceptions as to what it is. However, it can be dispensed with, or can be set as pre-course reading.

Part 2 is the core introduction to financial accounting. We examine the basic accounting techniques used by a reasonably simple individual company and the preparation of annual financial statements from the accounting database. This presentation is based on using worksheets to show what is happening in the company's accounting database, rather than the formal bookkeeping techniques which involve the famous debits and credits. Most courses require this fundamental knowledge of the accounting equation, the iteration between the statement of profit or loss (income statement) and the statement of financial position (balance sheet) and accrual accounting.

Part 3 then provides a discussion about how financial statements are interpreted. Chapter 8 provides a thumbnail sketch of some of the finance theory that informs interpretation. Most accounting books do not contain such a chapter but we have included it on the basis that accounting is often taught before finance in an MBA or management course and this may help students get to grips with the purposes of analysis as opposed merely to the techniques. It can easily be dispensed with. Chapter 9 contains the basic material on accounting ratios and Chapter 10 introduces the statement of cash flows as a statement that analyzes the changes in opening and closing financial position. In our view, Parts 2 and 3 constitute a basic introduction to accounting for non-financial managers.

However, we are aware that most sets of published financial statements that a manager will want to review are likely to be consolidated financial statements, and our preference in our own teaching is to include some material, however limited, on group accounting. In Part 4, we show how groups of companies prepare consolidated financial statements to enable them to present a worldwide picture of their economic situation. Chapter 11 provides a little contextual analysis about the annual reports of multinational companies and their use and introduces the statement of comprehensive income. Chapter 12 provides the basics of how a consolidation is done.

A course could certainly stop there, but we provide two chapters with further technical issues. Chapter 13 aims to show that the consolidated statements are a confection of statements drawn up in different currencies and dealing with different activities. The chapter addresses segment reporting and foreign currency translation issues. Chapter 14 analyzes a selection of current technical issues, including a discussion of fair value and financial instruments. We think this may go beyond what some teachers are aiming to achieve at entry level but we also think students may find it useful to have such a discussion. Chapters 15 and 16 are offered in the general spirit of trying to address all major issues that intersect with financial reporting in order to provide a complete guide for the non-financial manager. Again, many courses may not want to spend time on this, but, by the same token, the student who buys and keeps the book will be able to refer back to it should the need arise.

Part 5 goes further into techniques of financial statements analysis and reviews those such as Z scores, shareholder value and growth calculations. It could be dropped entirely or taught with Chapter 9.

The fifth edition of this book addresses a number of current developments and changes in IFRS Standards, including changes in the IASB® *Conceptual Framework for Financial Reporting*, and the introduction of IFRS 9 *Financial Instruments* and IFRS 15 *Revenue from Contracts with Customers*.

Teaching & Learning Support Resources

Cengage's peer-reviewed content for higher and further education courses is accompanied by a range of digital teaching and learning support resources. The resources are carefully tailored to the specific needs of the instructor, student and the course. Examples of the kind of resources provided include:

 A password-protected area for instructors with, for example, a test bank, PowerPoint slides and an instructor's manual.

 An open-access area for students including, for example, useful weblinks and glossary terms.

Lecturers: to discover the dedicated teaching digital support resources accompanying this textbook please register here for access:
cengage.com/dashboard/#login

Students: to discover the dedicated learning digital support resources accompanying this textbook, please search for **Global Financial Accounting and Reporting: Principles and Analysis,** 5th Edition on:
cengage.com

BE UNSTOPPABLE!

Learn more at **cengage.com**

PART 1

The accounting and business environment

This first section of the book is intended to provide context and background to the world in which financial reporting takes place. Many management students may never previously have come across accounting or have any idea of the structures within which it operates. This section tries to provide background information that should help students understand the subject better in a real world setting. Chapter 1 introduces financial statements and the institutional framework within which International Financial Reporting Standards are developed. Chapter 2 talks about accountants and their different functions.

CHAPTER 1

Financial reporting and regulation

This chapter lays out the structure of the book, and the approach it takes to mastering accounting information. The first step is a review of what financial information is for, and how it is controlled by governments, the stock exchanges and other institutions. It introduces International Financial Reporting Standards (IFRS Standards) as the main technical reference in this book.

Chapter structure

- Introduction
- Using this book
- Annual financial statements
- Uses of financial statements
- Accounting choices
- Accounting regulation
- International Financial Reporting Standards
- IASB *Conceptual Framework for Financial Reporting*
- Summary
- Discussion questions

Introduction

The ultimate objective of this book is to enable you to use financial accounting information effectively. Accounting reports are the only way currently available of getting a picture of what a company is doing, how it is structured and so on. Photographs can show you the company's physical locations and, if it manufactures or sells physical products, what these look like. Words can describe the company and its products, but only accounting data can tell you about a company's profitability, its size and its financial structure in a format that is more or less comparable with other companies, and carries with it an assurance that this is the whole of the company, warts and all, that you are looking at, not just the good-looking parts. Whether you like numbers or not, if you want to be an effective manager, you need to understand what accounting can tell you.

Financial accounting is intimately linked with business and, as Karl Marx was the first to point out, business cannot exist, except in very primitive forms, without accounting. Accounting data make the business visible, measure its progress and make it possible to manage the business and understand it. Accounting enables the business to work in many locations, directed by a central team. Multinational companies can only work because accounting is there to control what is going on in distant places, to monitor this and to provide information back to centre.

If you look at developing countries and those in transition to a market economy, the lack of accounting skills and of reliable and independent auditors to verify data and ensure that resources are used as intended, are major obstacles to economic progress.

On the whole, most managers meet accounting in the form of financial reports, and are rarely concerned with the day-to-day running of the accounting department. However, they do interface with this in areas such as salaries, expense refunds, authorizing payment of invoices and so on. Financial reports and understanding them are the central issue in this book, although we will certainly pass by the accounting department to see what is going on there, as well as review audit, both internal and external. We will focus also on published financial reports. The calculation and dissemination of internal reports is itself a long and complicated subject, usually dealt with as *management accounting* or managerial accounting, and calling for adaptation of standard accounting data for internal purposes. In order to understand that, you need to know about standard accounting data and that is the purpose of this book. What you learn here will enable you to understand the annual financial statements published by companies but also the basis of most internal reports as well, since they use the same source data. Externally disseminated financial statements have to be drawn up by reference to a set of accounting rules. This book focuses on the rules issued by the International Accounting Standards Board (the Board), which are used by listed companies in many countries in the world, including the European Union (EU), South Korea, Brazil and Japan.

Using this book

The book is organized to take you into the accounting world in a series of steps; these do not involve your learning how to be an accountant. In Part 1, we will look at the environment within which financial reporting takes place – how it is regulated, what an accounting department in a company does, how the accounting records are checked. In Part 2, we will go on to examine basic accounting techniques used by a reasonably simple individual company and the preparation of annual financial statements from the accounting database. This presentation will be based on using worksheets to show what is happening in the company's accounting database, rather than the formal bookkeeping techniques that involve the famous debits and credits. Part 3 will then discuss how financial statements are interpreted.

We then move on to look at larger companies. In Part 4, we see how groups of companies prepare consolidated financial statements to enable them to present a worldwide picture of their economic situation. We will then go on to consider related issues of international taxation, auditing, corporate governance and dissemination of information to stock exchanges. Part 5 will come back to financial statement analysis and review more sophisticated techniques such as growth calculations, integrated ratio analysis, shareholder value and Z scores.

While the structure of the book has been designed to lead you logically through a potential minefield as comfortably as possible, you can, of course, choose to omit some chapters. Our intention is not merely to teach you to understand the nature of accounting information but also to enable you to understand the interactions between accounting and management in a wider sense and to see how intimately accounting links with the life of the company, both internally and in helping manage relations with the outside environment in which the company operates.

Annual financial statements

All commercial companies produce *annual financial statements* (also sometimes labelled as the annual report or the annual accounts – discussed in Chapter 11). Generally, these have to be filed with the government, either centrally or in regional offices, and they have to be sent to shareholders. In many countries, the government file is available to the public, so the financial statements are, in effect, public and available to competitors or customers or suppliers, and are regularly consulted by these. Equally there are credit information companies, such as Dun & Bradstreet, Standard & Poor's or Moody's Corporation, which collect financial information and sell it to interested parties.

Many small companies do not like this exposure, but large companies generally welcome it and indeed publish the data widely, including on their websites. Large companies are well aware that this is the only independently confirmed information on the company that is widely available, and is a major tool in engendering confidence in those with whom the company wishes to do business.

The annual financial statements typically consist of the following elements:

- *The statement of profit or loss* (also referred to as 'income statement' or 'profit and loss account') reports on the revenue, expenses and profit of the company for the financial year and consequently is the main performance indicator as far as profitability is concerned. The standard-setter has recently enlarged the scope of this financial performance statement and now calls it the 'statement of comprehensive income' (which is also sometimes described as the 'statement of profit or loss and other comprehensive income' referring to its two components).

- *The balance sheet* (the IASB® terminology is '*statement of financial position*') gives a picture at a given moment – the last day of the financial year – of how the company has been financed and how that money has been invested in productive capacity and other resources (plant, buildings, computers, inventories, cash, etc.).

- *The notes to the accounts* (in North America these are called 'footnotes') can be anything from two or three pages to 40 or 50 – the notes provide detailed analysis of some of the figures in the balance sheet and statement of profit or loss, such as the dates when loans fall due for repayment or the different constituents of the total inventory. Importantly, the notes also contain a statement of the accounting policies followed by the company. They are increasingly a means of conveying non-accounting information, such as contingent environmental liabilities, to interested outsiders. The notes are subject to audit.

- *The statement of cash flows* is an analysis of the main cash movements through the company in the financial year, such as cash created by the company through profitable operations, cash spent on acquiring new productive capacity, cash repaid to lenders and new borrowings. This statement is obligatory in most developed countries, but not all. It is mandatory under IFRS Standards.

- *The statement of changes in equity* is now, under IFRS Standards, a separate report that details dividend payments, issues of share capital and other transactions that change equity, including the net profit (net income) of the year.

- *The audit report* is the statement by the independent auditors of their opinion on the other statements.

For a large multinational, these reports are usually bundled together with a lot of voluntary disclosures about group activities. Typically, the published *annual report* of a company will start with a chairman's statement, thanking the management team and saying what a good (usually, but just occasionally bad or indifferent) year it has been and so on. This is followed by many pages of photographs of managers, products and plant, as well as lots of charts, graphs and other data that show how individual divisions in the group have behaved. None of these data is subject to independent checking – but it is nonetheless very useful information that no one should neglect. It very often gives a more detailed picture of the deeds behind the numbers and helps an analyst get a feel for the company.

We will discuss corporate governance issues in more detail in another chapter, but between the operating information and the hard accounting information, many companies put in disclosures, which stock exchanges and other regulators have encouraged or even made mandatory, about company policy in what are perceived as key areas – above all, future prospects, but also things like the company's continuing viability, the risks that it faces, the nature of the control systems which enable the management to believe that they know what is going on in the company worldwide, and how the company deals with sensitive issues such as relations between the management and the auditors, and the award of salary increases to senior management.

If you've never seen the hard copy of a company's annual report, you should have a look at one and, preferably, several. Generally, all you need do is go to the company's website and follow a link to 'investors' or 'investor relations'. In most cases, the full annual report is directly downloadable from the company website.

It may have occurred to you that publishing the annual report is an extremely expensive business – it is. Aside from the cost of creating the financial statements in the first place and indeed having them audited, the cost of producing the photographs, artwork and analytical copy, plus running them past your company lawyers and your public relations advisers, is very high before you even get into the cost of printing probably several million copies and having translations made if, like many multinationals, your report is available in several languages. Internally, the annual report will involve the accounting managers, the legal and company secretarial specialists, the investor relations staff and public relations – apart from the chief executive, chairman and the board. Also note that companies try to publish their annual report as soon as possible after the financial year-end – companies listed in the USA often aim at six to eight weeks after the year-end. More than 12 weeks is unusual and the EU specifies a maximum of four months for listed companies.

Uses of financial statements

It is a standard question to ask who uses company financial statements. Broadly, very many people inside and outside the company look at these documents – as we have said already, they constitute the only performance indicator that is publicly available and independently verified. So we can be confident that they are used. What no one has been able to prove incontestably, is how financial data are integrated into decision-making and how different accounting scenarios influence users. Accounting data are, or should be, only one of several sources of information about a company and its future prospects. They are concerned with past performance which is not in all circumstances a guide to future performance. Many people prefer to let a specialist (a broker, financial analyst or financial journalist) look at the data and then provide an opinion.

The standard-setter – of whom more later – says the following:

STANDARDS

 IASB CONCEPTUAL FRAMEWORK *(extracts)*

Objective of financial statements
1.2 The objective of general purpose financial reporting is to provide financial information about the reporting entity that is useful to existing and potential investors, lenders, and other creditors in making decisions relating to providing resources to the entity. Those decisions involve decisions about:

    (a) buying, selling or holding equity and debt instruments;
    (b) providing or settling loans and other forms of credit; or
    (c) exercising rights to vote on, or otherwise influence, management's actions that affect the use of the entity's economic resources.

Source: IASB, Conceptual Framework for Financial Reporting

The International Accounting Standards Board (the Board) stresses information needs of those who have to make decisions about providing funds to the company as the overall motive for external financial reporting. Those who provide funds to the company (current and potential investors, lenders and other creditors) are seen as the primary beneficiaries of what the Board calls 'general purpose financial statements'. They are 'general purpose' because they are directed to users who don't have the power to require a company to provide specific information directly to them. To the extent that suppliers, customers or other groups make decisions relating to providing funds to the company in the form of credit, they are considered finance (or funds) providers. Other parties (e.g. employees, government agencies, public at large) may also benefit from using the financial reports, but, according to the Board's view, financial statements are not primarily directed to those user groups.

While usefulness for decision-making by finance providers as the objective of financial statements makes sense, it needs to be put into context. There are two major different traditions in accounting that affect not only how accounting is regulated, but also how it is done and how it is used. These are the Anglo-Saxon tradition and the continental European tradition, and we will need to come back to these ideas time and again to explain how accounting works.

Anglo-Saxon accounting

The Board's position owes more to the Anglo-Saxon than to the continental tradition of accounting. Anglo-Saxon is the term widely used, but 'anglophone' would be more appropriate. In this tradition, countries (USA, UK, Australia, Canada, New Zealand, etc.) had in the early twentieth century no freestanding accounting regulations on their statute book (although they had criminal laws, tax laws, etc.). Instead, businesses were left to work out their own accounting rules (but alongside disclosure requirements enshrined in company or stock exchange law), and this often took place alongside the development of a powerful accounting profession. You could call this a market solution – to the extent that companies need to communicate understandably, such as to raise finance, they use understandable common measures, but no one obliges them to do so.

What has then happened is that the government has reinforced the market from time to time, so that the legal obligation to provide information has grown over time. The regulations have generally been made heavier following on from some market abuse – such as the Enron frauds in the USA or, further back historically, the Wall Street crash of 1929. This last was blamed on adventurous accounting, and the Securities and Exchange Commission (SEC), which is the world's leading stock market regulator, was created by the US government as a response.

Accounting regulation in the anglophone countries is a function of the legal vehicle used, not a function of the kind of activity carried on by the business (although there are often special rules for banks and insurance companies, which we do not address in this book). So if you are a US company that wants to be listed on the New York Stock Exchange, you will need to meet stringent SEC accounting requirements, but if you want to run the same business with no public offering of shares, there are hardly any formal accounting requirements that apply in the USA. Similarly, if you want to constitute your business as a public limited company (plc – not necessarily listed on the London Stock Exchange) in the UK, you will have to comply with many corporate accounting rules, but if you constitute it as a partnership, there are no statutory requirements for accounting.

STANDARDS

 IASB CONCEPTUAL FRAMEWORK *(extracts)*

Users of financial statements

1.5 Many existing and potential investors, lenders and other creditors cannot require reporting entities to provide information directly to them and must rely on general purpose financial reports for much of the financial information they need. Consequently, they are the primary users to whom general purpose financial reports are directed.

1.10 Other parties, such as regulators and members of the public other than investors, lenders and other creditors, may also find general purpose financial reports useful. However, these reports are not primarily directed to these other groups.

Source: IASB, Conceptual Framework for Financial Reporting

In an Anglo-Saxon accounting context, the financial statements are traditionally a function of the financing of the company. They derive from the Industrial Revolution when technology first transformed business and entrepreneurs started looking for vehicles through which they could raise capital to start industrial ventures. Prior to the Industrial Revolution most business investment was made by owner-managers and was inevitably relatively small scale. But from this point on, the managers of companies were less and less often the source of finance for those companies, and financial reports developed as a means of informing outside financiers (shareholders principally but also banks) as to what had been done with their money. We have the start of a split between management and capital: professional managers started to run 'companies' in which several investors, eventually many, had put money.

The annual accounts were a necessary means of informing the investors (shareholders) and creating an atmosphere of confidence, which, in turn, would encourage investors to reward the managers – in conditions of uncertainty, the investors would reduce the reward to managers, because they could not be sure that it had been earned. At the same time, the idea of independent audit developed as a means of increasing the degree of confidence that shareholders might have in the financial statements. In more recent times, companies have simply extended this principle to customers, suppliers, staff and the general public, as these have become more sophisticated in their understanding of financial data.

Continental Europe

The continental European accounting tradition has its roots much earlier in business history than Anglo-Saxon accounting. The main model for European systems started out in 1673 as a French government statute (known as the 'Savary Ordonnance'), which was borrowed by other countries in this form or in its later form as part of Napoleon's Commercial Code (1807). The French required all businesses (in whatever legal form, but companies as such were rare at that time) to calculate an annual 'inventory' – in effect, a statement of financial position (balance sheet). The French model was subsequently borrowed by many countries, one way and another, and in particular by Belgium, Spain, Germany and Italy (this is not to suggest that accounting regulation in those countries is still exactly the same now – regulation is constantly evolving).

The main reason for its introduction in France is believed to have been government regulation of the economy. The government was concerned at the large number of business bankruptcies. Apart from causing people to lose money, bankruptcies also damage confidence in the market, and this, you will appreciate, is essential if the market is to function correctly. Government concern to strengthen the operation of the market, and thus the national economy, is often a key trigger of regulation.

The effect in continental Europe has been to create a tradition where *all* businesses are subject to accounting rules (with extra rules for limited liability companies and listed ones), and where accounting regulation is primarily the concern of the government rather than the accounting profession or companies themselves. This remains broadly the case in these countries still.

Link with taxation

These different historical roots can probably also explain another important aspect of accounting regulation – the link between reporting performance for shareholders and measuring profits for tax purposes. This link is looser in Anglo-Saxon countries than in continental European ones. In the UK, income tax was introduced first in 1799 – well before there was any accounting regulation as such. There grew up a tradition, therefore, where measurement of profit for tax purposes was seen as a legal matter, with its own statutes and jurisprudence that were separate from company regulation. In continental Europe, however, income taxes were mostly introduced in the early twentieth century (Germany was a little ahead of this) but well after the introduction of accounting regulation by the State. Not surprisingly, measurement of profit for tax purposes became closely intertwined with other accounting needs, and the formal link between reporting to the tax authorities and reporting to shareholders is much closer than in Anglo-Saxon jurisdictions.

It should be said that the relationship between these two reporting streams is constantly evolving, and that the widespread use of consolidated accounts has introduced a new element into the equation. Consolidated financial statements (or consolidated accounts) are produced by large groups of companies for their shareholders. They consist, as we shall see later, of aggregate figures for all the individual companies making up the group. Tax assessment is done only through the individual companies, and the group financial statements therefore have no tax implications. This means that larger companies, at least, are able to separate out to some degree the measurement of profit for tax purposes, and the reporting of financial performance for shareholders and others. You will appreciate that, in theory, there should perhaps be no difference between the two concepts, but, in practice, governments distort economic behaviour through taxation, partly to counter tax avoidance and partly to give companies incentives to behave in a way that the government wishes to encourage (e.g. installing environmentally friendly processes, maintaining employment).

This usually means that tax considerations enter into company strategic choices (or should – individual companies differ quite widely in the extent to which they integrate tax into their planning) and also play a significant role in accounting regulation. For example, tax rules may well fix maximum limits on some expenses, and this will encourage companies to charge the maximum in their accounts. The rules may also refuse to accept other types of expenditure as a deduction from taxable profits, with the consequence that companies restrict some kinds of activity. We will look at this later in Chapter 15, on taxation.

The extent to which taxation impacts on company accounting is not only a function of the regulatory environment, but also depends on the ownership of the company, which is, in turn, an issue frequently linked to size. Many small and medium-sized companies do not operate as a group of companies and their ownership is in the hands of the managers, or of a family. This may mean that the shareholders do not depend on the annual financial statements as their only source of information about the company – they work in the company, or they can ask or even just go along and have a look.

This means that there is no point in producing sophisticated economic measurements for the shareholders. Annual financial statements of small and medium-sized companies are consequently influenced most heavily by tax considerations – reducing the profit in order to reduce tax becomes the main objective in making accounting choices. This may also mean that managers of small companies have only a hazy idea of their profitability, because they believe the reported figure to be artificially low as a result of tax manipulations yet have no means of knowing the extent of the difference. This is not particularly useful for management decision-making!

Accounting choices

Some people come to accounting believing that it is a set of precise rules that permit the exact determination of company profit and the value of the company. In fact, accounting rules are anything but precise, the calculation of profit can never be anything but an estimate and the accounts do not under any circumstances show what a company is 'worth' (we should also bear in mind that value is a subjective notion and must always be defined when used – for example, the value of something as between buyer and seller is usually different, there are different calculation bases such as economic value, cost, etc.).

You will soon appreciate as you go through this book that accounting is full of choices. We can distinguish between three types of encounter between choice and rules:

1. The rules are quite specific and there is no choice (maybe the law specifies what must be done or an accounting standard).
2. There are accounting rules, but we have freedom to make a choice between two or more alternative sets of rules, each of which is acceptable to regulators (the most common case).
3. There are no rules so we must decide for ourselves how to deal with a problem (maybe by reference to what other people in the same line of business generally do, or after consultation with our auditors).

The existence of these choices is something that makes accounting comparisons difficult within the same jurisdiction, and also leads to different accounting rules being used in different countries. Companies are generally required, therefore, to state clearly in their annual financial statements what choices they have made in key areas. Large companies typically have several pages devoted to 'accounting principles' alongside their financial statements.

The variability of accounting principles is often criticized by the financial press, and it is one reason why those who design MBA courses insist on a significant accounting component in the degree. As we advance through the accounting territory, we will highlight areas where there are choices and show how these impact the content of financial statements.

Profit as estimate

The 'real' profit of a company can only be determined absolutely when the company has ceased operations, all the company resources have been sold, its debts have been paid off and all its money has been distributed to its owners.

To illustrate, suppose a company builds a factory, equips it with sophisticated machinery and then uses it to manufacture a product that it sells. Say the factory and equipment cost €100m, and the factory closes down after 10 years and is sold for €10m; we can say that, in addition to raw materials, staffing, power and so on, the company had a net infrastructure cost of €90m (€100m to set up, less final exit receipt of €10m) for the factory, which should be taken into account in determining profit for each of the 10 years in which the factory was operating. We only know this net cost for sure when the factory has been sold (when the residual value of the factory facilities is realized). If, however, we ignore the cost of the factory in determining profit in the years when the factory is operating, we will be overstating the profit. Overstating the profit will mislead those who lend to or invest in the company, and potentially lead to paying out too much in tax and dividends so that the company eventually fails. To avoid this, we are obliged to include an estimate of this expense, so the annual profit during those years is necessarily based in part on an unprovable estimate.

Accounting regulation

The existence of choices in accounting is one very good reason to have regulation. Of course, choice is not of itself necessarily a bad thing: it is only a problem in accounting where some people use accounting choice to deceive others. This explains why governments become involved in accounting regulation. As tax collectors they naturally want reliable figures for (taxable) income. As managers of the national economy they want that economy to function efficiently and produce wealth. The economy's functioning, and particularly that of the capital markets, is at least slowed down – if not stalled entirely – if investors, customers and suppliers do not know whether they can rely on the financial statements of companies with which they wish to do business. Investors either do not invest or demand much higher returns to compensate for the uncertainty, clients may go elsewhere or be prepared to pay only a low price, while suppliers may refuse to supply on credit. If the financial stability of a company cannot be judged reliably, others are reluctant to deal with it.

This leads to another argument, which is that, given that the markets cease to function without reliable information, market pressures surely will force competitive companies to adopt reliable, comparable accounting in order to reduce financing costs and help business relations generally. This argument is also valid, and is supported by the way in which many large companies in the past have voluntarily adopted international financial reporting standards for their group financial statements and use an international audit firm to attest the validity of these. However, the market is not necessarily that efficient, and there are failures that, in part, derive from unclear accounting causing people to make wrong decisions.

The world functions on a complex mixture of regulation and market forces. Given that this book is intended to be used outside any one specific legal environment, we propose to present below the different types of regulation that are to be found. You should note that regulation can exist at an international level (for example IFRS Standards), at a regional level (for example EU directives and regulations) and at a national level. International managers should make a note that there will be a different mix of regulators in different countries and they may need to familiarize themselves with the local situation.

Types of regulation

It may be worth pointing out that the reasons why a change in regulation takes place are a fruitful field of research in accounting. The model that we will use here, known as a contingent model, suggests that, starting from an equilibrium position where there is no obvious pressure for change, there is a cycle:

1. Equilibrium
2. Shock (which destroys the equilibrium)
3. Search for an acceptable solution
4. Articulation of regulation
5. New equilibrium
6. Unexpected consequences of the change.

The shock to the system could come from any one of a multitude of sources. Individual financial scandals have, in the past, been a common source of disequilibrium (the Enron failure brought about significant changes in American and European regulation), but other possibilities are economic changes such as the introduction of new techniques (e.g. derivatives and financial instruments generally), legal changes in the national economy (e.g. joining the EU, moving from a communist regime to a market economy), economic phenomena (such as the subprime crisis and the credit crunch that followed) and so on. The search for a solution often involves seeking consensus, which will involve different people on different issues, leading to some inconsistencies in regulation. The method of articulating the solution is also subject to local cultural differences – some countries prefer legal regulation, others like codes of best practice and so on. The result of all this is that accounting rules are different in different countries in some of their details, even if the main lines tend to converge.

We would distinguish the following types of regulatory body:

- Government – for economic management
- Government – for tax purposes
- Stock exchange
- Private sector body
- Professional accountants
- Specialist industry organizations.

We should also emphasize that the regulation of the financial statements of banks and insurance companies, while typically linked to that of commercial companies, is nonetheless usually subject to separate rules, because governments wish to control the financial health of banks much more closely than that of commercial companies, and impose limits on their activities based on balance sheet figures. This book does not, however, address the financial statements of banks and insurance companies.

Government

As we have discussed, the government is interested in the efficient functioning of the economy, and this leads to regulation designed to ensure that the markets can operate as far as possible free from fraud and misrepresentation. This form of regulation may be articulated through laws that address accounting, through commercial codes and also government regulatory agencies. An example of this kind of approach would be France, where there are laws governing accounting but also government-sponsored committees that operate under the aegis of the Ministry of Finance and issue detailed regulations on specific accounting issues.

The government is also active in regulating accounting for tax purposes. This is often done through individual measures contained in annual finance laws or similar instruments. In some countries, jurisprudence, the decisions of tax courts on specific cases, can also be very important in determining some accounting issues. This is notably the case in Germany and, to a lesser extent, in the UK.

The stock exchange usually regulates the financial information that has to be provided by companies listed on it. In some countries, there is a government regulator that does this, such as the SEC in the USA, while the exchange itself is run by private sector bodies. In other countries, there is no split between those who run the stock exchange on a day-to-day basis (generally the members of the exchange) and those who regulate admission to it. This is the case, for example, in Switzerland, where the private sector regulates listed companies (although subject to a limited legal framework). In the EU, there has been a move to establish national regulators that are separate from the stock exchange. These are coordinated through the European Securities and Markets Authority (ESMA).

Private sector

In most countries, there is some input into accounting best practice from the private sector in the form of standard-setting committees of one kind or another. In the USA, although the SEC controls listings on the various stock exchanges, and is therefore responsible for specifying what accounting rules they should use, in practice, it leaves the task of writing detailed rules (accounting standards) to a private sector body, the Financial Accounting Standards Board (FASB). The FASB is financed by a levy on companies that are registered with the SEC and is a freestanding body without any special rights other than those it derives from the SEC's endorsement of its standards.

This is typical of the modern form of detailed rule-making – the rules do not have to go through a long drawn-out statutory process, and can be changed at any time if they appear to be ineffective or become irrelevant. The flexibility and rapidity of this form and the high level of technicality of its pronouncements are the major argument for using a private sector body rather than relying solely on statutes or government agencies, where accounting regulation would have to compete for parliamentary time with other important issues and be debated by those with no knowledge of accounting.

In many countries that have this kind of private sector regulatory body, it developed from advisory committees run by the accounting profession, and most developed professional accounting bodies have technical committees that make recommendations as to best practice. Such a committee may be the only private sector source of national standards in a particular country but, even so, it does not necessarily command the automatic acceptance of its pronouncements. An example would be the technical committee of the Ordre des Experts Comptables in France.

Another source of private sector rules is industry associations. Their activity varies very much from sector to sector and country to country, but sometimes such organizations agree special rules that apply to their members and are intended to address accounting for transactions specific to their industry, or that lead to a higher comparability in presentation or valuation of balance sheet and profit or loss items. Evidently such arrangements are voluntary but in some countries they may also be endorsed by official regulatory committees – the UK standard-setter approves 'statements of recommended practice', which are prepared by industry groups such as banks or insurers, and France's Autorité des Normes Comptables confirms industry-specific applications of its accounting plan.

Different combinations of these kinds of regulatory organization exist in each developed country, and the diverse sources of regulation are one reason why expert local advice is needed.

International

Apart from the national regulators, there are also international bodies that provide important rules. The most well known is the IASB (the Board). The Board is the world's leading accounting standard-setter. Since 2002 when its standards were mandated by the European Commission for use by all listed companies in Europe, there has been a rush in all major and many minor economies to use its standards. The Board itself says that its standards are either compulsory or allowed in more than 100 countries. It runs a database of the rules in 166 countries round the world to monitor adoption. This can be consulted on its website (www.ifrs.org). Australia and South Africa moved to IFRS Standards in 2005, followed shortly afterwards by New Zealand. Canada, Korea and Brazil moved in 2011. China issues its own standards modelled closely on IFRS Standards, and in 2015 the chairman of the IFRS Foundation (which runs the Board) announced that Chinese standards were virtually the same as IFRS Standards. Japan allows companies to adopt IFRS Standards voluntarily and a significant number of larger companies do so. Japan houses the only IFRS Foundation office other than its London base, and the country has issued Japanese International Standards as an interim step towards moving all listed companies to the international model. IFRS Standards are accepted by the SEC as the equivalent of US Generally Accepted Accounting Principles (GAAP) if used by foreign registrants.

What is the big attraction? Well, if we look at the European Commission's decision in issuing the Regulation 2002/1608, the main issue was that a fundamental objective of the EU is to create a single market with no barriers to movement within it. The Commission perceived that the slightly different financial reporting in each member state was an obstacle to the free flow of capital. If investors could compare one company with another, irrespective of where the parent company's main office was based, they could invest more efficiently and companies could raise finance more easily.

A second issue with the Commission was that if IFRS Standards were widely used outside the EU, this would also make it much easier for European companies to raise money on markets outside Europe. The big prize was access to the US markets. When the Commission made its decision, non-US companies listed on an American stock exchange had to provide additional information, including a reconciliation of their equity and earnings to what they would have been under US GAAP. In 2007 AXA, the European insurer, told the SEC that it estimated that preparing this cost them $20m a year, not including internal staff time. One of the Board's objectives from the start was to achieve parity with US GAAP and this happened in 2007. From 2008, companies using IFRS Standards as issued by the Board have not needed to provide this expensive reconciliation.

Generically then, we can say that using IFRS Standards means that companies can be directly compared with one another, irrespective of national origins. This should help the investor make better choices. It also helps companies to get more exposure than they otherwise would. They can more easily be listed on different stock exchanges and their financial statements are directly comparable. Using common rules is part of participating in a global investment market.

There are also things known as interpretations. These have the same force as IFRS Standards, and are included in the generic term IFRS Standards. They are issued by a special body, now the IFRS Standards Interpretations Committee, but previously the International Financial Reporting Interpretations Committee (IFRIC®), and prior to 2002 the Standards Interpretations Committee (SIC®). The Interpretations Committee receives queries as to how IFRS Standards should be applied in circumstances that are not specifically covered by a standard, or is asked to resolve apparent conflicts between standards.

Another problem for regulators is that some jurisdictions have been tempted to modify IFRS Standards slightly when adopting them. This results in there being slightly different versions in use. EU companies have to state that they use 'IFRS Standards as endorsed by the EU' (or a similar formula). The SEC only accepts the original IFRS Standards as a substitute for US GAAP when used by a foreign issuer.

There are no other bodies writing international accounting standards for private sector companies, but we should mention that the United Nations (UN) supports an intergovernmental working group devoted to accounting and auditing issues at the corporate level. This takes place under the auspices of the UN Conference on Trade and Development (UNCTAD) and is called the Intergovernmental Working Group of Experts on International Standards of Accounting and Reporting (ISAR for short). The ISAR group commissions research reports into current accounting problems. These are debated at an annual conference and recommendations are made to help governments develop their regulatory and professional structures. ISAR supports the Board and helps involve governments, particularly of developing countries, in discussions about the utility and implementation of IASB® standards.

There is also an international representative of the accounting profession: the International Federation of Accountants (IFAC), based in New York. We will come back to it in Chapter 2, on the accounting profession. It has committees which publish recommendations on auditing, education and other matters. It issues auditing standards through its International Auditing and Assurance Standards Board, and these are increasingly being used in Europe to give uniform audit alongside international accounting standards. However, the IFAC also hosts the International Public Sector Accounting Standards Board (IPSASB) which focuses on the accounting and financial reporting needs of national, regional and local governments, related governmental agencies and the constituencies they serve.

Public sector

This is probably a good point at which to mention that accounting in the public sector is generally very different from that in the private sector, although governments are beginning to turn to private sector techniques. Basically, private sector accounting is concerned with determining profit and the financial position of, and related sources of finance for, an enterprise. It produces annual reports, which are, in effect, a series of interim reports on a business that is intended to have long or limitless time horizons.

Public sector accounting, by way of contrast, has traditionally had short horizons where the object is primarily to explain what has been done with the money available to spend in any one year. Reports typically focus on a particular source of revenue (e.g. government grants for road improvement) and explain how it has been spent, or on a particular activity (e.g. primary school education). Any particular public sector unit, say a municipality or a government ministry, does not therefore present a single coherent report on its activities for the year, but rather a whole series of individual reports. Equally, the public sector makes little or no distinction between short-term (sometimes known as current) and long-term (sometimes called capital) expenditure – money in one particular year might be spent on building one hospital, and other money on paying the running costs of another hospital, but for traditional public sector accounting these are just two 'funds' like any others. The new hospital is, in effect, treated as a current year expense and does not appear on any kind of government 'balance sheet' as an asset.

In the 1990s the desire for performance evaluation measures in the public sector caused a number of countries, led by New Zealand, to move towards private sector techniques where long-lived purchases remain on the books, and where 'revenues' are determined or, to put it another way, outputs are assigned financial values, so that the efficiency of the use of resources can be measured. It would be a mistake to think that such a revolution in public sector accounting will be either widespread or rapid. First, it involves a desire on the part of government for transparency in their financial dealings, which is not something too many governments necessarily see as a policy objective. Second, the change over involves massive re-education, not only of accounting staff but also all those who use financial information, and also a complete reform of accounting systems, which is both costly and time-consuming.

For the moment it would be better to think of public sector accounting as a different subject from that of the private sector (and one which will not be taken further in this book), although changes can be expected. The IPSASB of IFAC plays an important catalyst role by issuing and promoting benchmark guidance, conducting educational and research programmes, and facilitating the exchange of information among accountants and those who work in the public sector. It develops International Public Sector Accounting Standards (IPSAS) for financial reporting by governments and other public sector entities. In general, IFRS Standards are used as the starting point in developing these standards.

International Financial Reporting Standards

The IFRS Standards, established by the IASB (the Board), are increasingly recognized as a mature and rigorous set of rules for the preparation of the financial statements of many large and multinational companies and are accepted by most security market authorities. The standards are also used as the basis for national accounting requirements (partially or in full) or as an international benchmark for countries that develop their own requirements.

The Board is a private sector body and is not responsible to any governmental organization, although it has an oversight body (Monitoring Board) drawn from market regulators.

The Board's objectives are set out in a constitution, the ultimate goal being the development and rigorous application of a single set of global accounting standards, which will produce high-quality financial information to help participants in the world's capital markets to make economic decisions. The Board has, however, no authority to enforce the correct use of its standards.

Table 1.1 gives an overview of the IFRS Standards as of January 2019. The table comprises both the main standards (IAS® Standards and IFRS Standards) and the interpretations of the successive Interpretations Committees. Over time the titles have evolved but the generic for all pronouncements is now IFRS Standards, and those standards issued before 2001 are known collectively as IAS Standards. The Board has also issued two practice statements that provide non-mandatory guidance. We will refer to these rules in this text in chapters covering the appropriate topic.

Table 1.1   List of IASB® pronouncements as of January 2019

Conceptual framework	
CF	Conceptual Framework for Financial Reporting
Main standards	
IAS 1	Presentation of Financial Statements
IAS 2	Inventories
IAS 7	Statement of Cash Flows
IAS 8	Accounting Policies, Changes in Accounting Estimates and Errors
IAS 10	Events after the Reporting Period
IAS 12	Income Taxes
IAS 14	Segment Reporting
IAS 16	Property, Plant and Equipment
IAS 19	Employee Benefits
IAS 20	Accounting for Government Grants and Disclosure of Government Assistance
IAS 21	The Effects of Changes in Foreign Exchange Rates
IAS 23	Borrowing Costs
IAS 24	Related Party Disclosures
IAS 26	Accounting and Reporting by Retirement Benefit Plans
IAS 27	Separate Financial Statements
IAS 28	Investments in Associates and Joint Ventures
IAS 29	Financial Reporting in Hyperinflationary Economies
IAS 32	Financial Instruments: Presentation
IAS 33	Earnings per Share
IAS 34	Interim Financial Reporting
IAS 36	Impairment of Assets
IAS 37	Provisions, Contingent Liabilities and Contingent Assets
IAS 38	Intangible Assets
IAS 40	Investment Property
IAS 41	Agriculture
IFRS 1	First-time Adoption of International Financial Reporting Standards
IFRS 2	Share-based Payment
IFRS 3	Business Combinations
IFRS 4	Insurance Contracts
IFRS 5	Non-current Assets Held for Sale and Discontinued Operations
IFRS 6	Exploration for and Evaluation of Mineral Resources
IFRS 7	Financial Instruments: Disclosures
IFRS 8	Operating Segments
IFRS 9	Financial Instruments
IFRS 10	Consolidated Financial Statements
IFRS 11	Joint Arrangements
IFRS 12	Disclosures of Interests in Other Entities
IFRS 13	Fair Value Measurement
IFRS 14	Regulatory Deferral Accounts
IFRS 15	Revenue from Contracts with Customers
IFRS 16	Leases
IFRS 17	Insurance Contracts

(Continued)

Interpretations

SIC 7	Introduction of the Euro (IAS 21)
SIC 10	Government Assistance – No Specific Relation to Operating Activities (IAS 20)
SIC 25	Income Taxes – Changes in the Tax Status of an Enterprise or its Shareholders IAS (12)
SIC 29	Service Concession Arrangements – Disclosures
SIC 32	Intangible Assets – Website Costs
IFRIC 1	Changes in Existing Decommissioning, Restoration and Similar Liabilities
IFRIC 2	Members' Shares in Co-operative Entities and Similar Instruments
IFRIC 5	Rights to Interests arising from Decommissioning, Restoration and Environmental Rehabilitation Funds
IFRIC 6	Liabilities arising from Participating in a Specific Market – Waste Electrical and Electronic Equipment
IFRIC 7	Applying the Restatement Approach under IAS 29 Financial Reporting in Hyperinflationary Economies
IFRIC 10	Interim Financial Reporting and Impairment
IFRIC 12	Service Concession Arrangements
IFRIC 14	IAS 19 – The Limit on a Defined Benefit Asset, Minimum Funding Requirements and their Interaction
IFRIC 15	Agreements for the Construction of Real Estate
IFRIC 16	Hedges of a Net Investment in a Foreign Operation
IFRIC 17	Distributions of Non-cash Assets to Owners
IFRIC 19	Extinguishing Financial Liabilities with Equity Instruments
IFRIC 20	Stripping Costs in the Production Phase of a Surface Mine
IFRIC 21	Levies
IFRIC 22	Foreign Currency Transactions and Advance Consideration
IFRIC 23	Uncertainty over Income Tax Treatments

Practice statements

PS1	Management Commentary
PS2	Making Materiality Judgements

Structure of the IASB

The Board operates under the IFRS Foundation (IFRSF), an independent organization with trustees representing all regions of the world and all groups interested in corporate financial reporting. The IFRS Foundation raises funds and has oversight of the Board. The trustees are subject in their turn to the oversight of the Monitoring Board. The Monitoring Board consists of representatives of the world's capital markets and is intended to provide additional public accountability to the organization.

The current standard-setting structure has the following components:

- Monitoring Board
- IFRS Foundation
- The Board

- IFRS® Advisory Council
- IFRS® Interpretations Committee.

A significant new development in 2013 was the creation of an additional advisory body called the Accounting Standards Advisory Forum (ASAF). This does not yet have the constitutional status of the IFRS Advisory Council, but plays a significant role in the evolution of standards.

The structure of the Board is outlined in Figure 1.1.

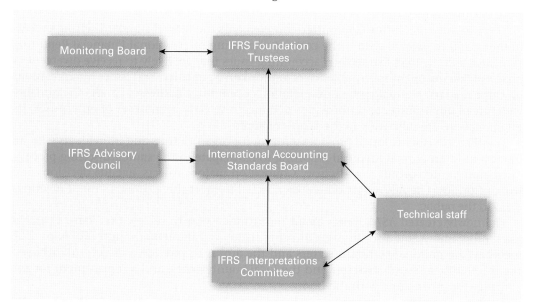

Figure 1.1 The structure of the Board

The trustees appoint the board members (as well as the members of the Interpretations Committee and the Advisory Council), exercise oversight and raise the funds needed. As an organization of an international scope, the geographical balance of the trustees is a sensitive issue. The current geographical balance is as follows: six from North America, six from Europe, six from the Asia/Oceania region and four from any area, subject to establishing overall geographical balance. There is also an appropriate balance to the professional backgrounds of the trustees, which include auditors, preparers, users, academics and other officials serving the public interest. Two will normally be senior partners of prominent international accounting firms.

All the appointments made by the trustees are subject to the approval of the Monitoring Board. The Monitoring Board was created in 2009 and included representatives of the SEC, European Commission, International Organization of Securities Commissions (two members), and the Japanese Financial Services Agency. The Basel Committee (bank supervisors) has observer status. The Monitoring Board was expanded in 2014 to include the financial market regulators from South Korea and Brazil. It is likely to be further expanded to include stock exchange representatives from more emerging markets.

The Board has sole responsibility for setting accounting standards. It develops and issues International Financial Reporting Standards and approves interpretations developed by the IFRS Interpretations Committee. It comprises 14 board members, each with one vote. The primary qualification criterion for membership is technical expertise. There is a balance of professional backgrounds (auditors, preparers, users and academics). Since 2009 there has been a geographical requirement in addition to that of technical expertise.

Although the Board has full discretion over its technical agenda, it would normally form working groups or other forms of specialist advisory groups to give advice on major projects. It can outsource detailed research or other work to national standard-setters. A key element of its strategy in its first decade was to converge its standards with those of the USA. Many international institutions, including the G20 governments, believe that it is essential that the sets of rules, which are used by nearly all the world's largest companies, should stay as close together as they can.

The IFRS Interpretations Committee complements the formal standard-setting process of the board. It reviews, within the context of existing International Financial Reporting Standards and the IASB Framework, accounting issues that are likely to receive divergent or unacceptable treatment in the absence of authoritative guidance, and issues interpretations on these matters. Normally, the Interpretations Committee addresses issues of reasonably widespread importance, and not issues of concern to only a small set of enterprises. Its interpretations are submitted to the Board for approval.

The IFRS Advisory Council provides a forum for organizations and individuals with an interest in international financial reporting to participate in the standard-setting process. The board has to consult the Advisory Council on major projects, agenda decisions and work priorities. The Advisory Council is expected to meet three times a year at meetings open to the public.

The newly created ASAF meets about four times a year to review the Board's current work programme and also discuss emerging issues and implementation problems. The members are national standard-setters and the aim is to provide a direct link between the international standard-setter and the local counterparts, and a replacement for the convergence programme with the USA.

The membership is on geographical lines, with three regions represented by organizations that liaise with smaller standard-setters:

- European Financial Reporting Advisory Group (EFRAG)
- Group of Latin American Standard-Setters (GLASS)
- Asian and Oceanian Standard-Setters Group (AOSSG).

There are eight national standard-setters directly involved, including the USA, Canada, France, the United Kingdom, Korea, China and Japan. The AOSSG and GLASS were set up relatively recently with the help of the IASB to encourage the involvement of small standard-setters, whereas EFRAG was created in 2001 as part of the formal endorsement process of IFRS Standards (discussed below).

Standard-setting due process

The Board's standard-setting procedures have to ensure that resulting International Financial Reporting Standards (including interpretations) are of high quality and are developed only after giving constituencies opportunities to make their views known at several points in the standard-setting due process. Due process is a keenly scrutinized issue that plays a key role in sustaining the legitimacy of the international standard-setter. It is an independent private sector body, and yet its rules have become law in a large number of countries. Due process is designed to ensure that standards are subjected to rigorous scrutiny and that all constituents have the opportunity to participate in some way in their elaboration.

The process for the development of a standard has become more complex over time and presently consists of the following stages (see also Figure 1.2):

Figure 1.2   Standard-setting due process of the Board

- A project proposal emerges after an idea coming from board members, the Advisory Council, the ASAF or others. If there is a strong indication that there is a financial reporting problem, a project opens up in the 'assessment stage' of the research programme. The technical staff then conduct research, sometimes with the help of national standard-setters, to look into the problem. They might issue a 'research paper' that sets out their findings. If the Board decides that a case has been made, the project moves to the 'development stage'. The staff work further on the problem and identify possible solutions and their likely effects. The end product will normally be a 'discussion paper' that sets out the issue and identifies the way the standard-setters think it should be solved.

- During the early stages of a project, the Board may establish an advisory committee, or working group, to give advice on the issues arising in the project. Consultation with the working group and the ASAF occurs throughout the project.

- The organization now conducts what it calls an 'agenda consultation' (the last one took place in 2015, and the next is likely in 2020) where it calls on constituents to review the different projects in its research programme and say how they should be prioritized, or if they should be abandoned, as well as suggest new topics.

- If the Board decides, following input from constituents, that a project should be followed through, it moves to the standard-setting agenda. It consults with the IFRS Advisory Council and the ASAF and then makes a recommendation to the trustees of the IFRS Foundation. The standard-setters then review the comments on the discussion paper and debate with the staff how to develop these into a standard. From that debate (which could easily take two years), the standard-setter publishes an exposure draft for public comment.

- Following the receipt and review of comments on that, the Board would issue a final Standard.

Publication of an exposure draft, a main standard or an interpretation requires approval by nine of the 14 members of the board. A full-blown due process including a preliminary views paper would likely take at least four years and often considerably more. When the standard-setter publishes a standard, it also publishes a 'basis for conclusions' to explain publicly how it reached its conclusions (including dissenting opinions) and to give background information that may help users of the standards to apply them in practice. The details of the organization's research and standard-setting programmes can be viewed on the website by clicking on 'standards development' on the home page (www.ifrs.org).

IFRS Standards in Europe

Since 2005 all listed companies have had to use IFRS Standards (apart from a few exceptions that came on stream in 2007). Historically, however, European accounting standards were established through company law directives, which aim at harmonizing company law across member states. Table 1.2 provides an overview of the main developments regarding financial accounting and reporting rules in the EU. European accounting rules are stipulated in the 2013 EU Accounting Directive, which replaces earlier statutes known as the Fourth and Seventh Directives. The EU Accounting Directive comprises the accounting rules for the preparation and presentation of financial statements of individual legal entities (individual accounts). It also sets the ground rules for the preparation and presentation of the financial statements of a company as an economic entity, usually a group of individual but economically interdependent legal entities (group or consolidated accounts). Member states were required to incorporate the directive into national legal requirements. Although this has succeeded in achieving a considerable degree of comparability between financial statements prepared in different member states, many differences remain. This is due to the fact that the accounting rules of the directives are not very detailed (only minimum rules that may be strengthened by national requirements), do not cover all relevant topics (for example foreign currency translation issues or deferred taxation) or leave choices to member states (alternative rules giving member states options).

Table 1.2   Financial reporting in the European Union – main developments

1978	Fourth Company Law Directive (individual financial statements)
1983	Seventh Company Law Directive (consolidated financial statements)
1995	Decision on new accounting strategy (adhering to IAS Standards instead of further development of specific European accounting rules)
2000	Announcement of plan to require IAS Standards for consolidated financial statements of listed companies by 2005
2001	Fair Value Directive [requiring/allowing for fair value measurement of specific balance sheet items (mainly financial instruments)]
2002	IAS® Regulation
2003	Modernization Directive
2005/2007	IFRS Standards mandatory for listed companies in European Union
2009	Publication Directive
2012	Capital Maintenance Directive
2013	Accounting Directive (replacing the Fourth and Seventh Company Law Directive)
	Within the European Commission financial reporting comes under the Directorate General for Financial Stability, Financial Services and Capital Markets Union (website: ec.europa.eu/finance/index_en.htm)

The EU Accounting Directive does not provide rules for listed companies. These, as mentioned earlier, have been required to follow IFRS Standards since 2005. IFRS Standards are, however, not automatically applicable in the EU when issued by the Board. An endorsement mechanism has been installed to ensure that the IFRS Standards conform with EU public policy concerns and meet the needs of European listed companies. The endorsement mechanism relies on a two-tier structure: a regulatory level (the Accounting Regulatory Committee, ARC) and an expert level (EFRAG). The ARC decides whether to recommend to the European Council of Ministers that it should adopt or reject a standard for application in the EU. EFRAG advises the European Commission on the technical assessment of individual IFRS Standards for application in the EU. Additionally, EFRAG is expected to play a proactive role in interacting with the standard-setter.

The IAS Regulation applies only to listed companies, and the European Commission left to member states the decision as to whether to extend IFRS Standards to non-listed companies. Most states allow unlisted companies a choice, although Germany requires national GAAP for all individual company statements and for the group statements of unlisted companies (see also Table 1.3).

Table 1.3 Effects of the IAS Regulation (EU)

	Individual financial statements	*Group/consolidated financial statements*
Listed companies	Member state option	IFRS Standards mandatory
Unlisted companies	Member state option	Member state option

This situation is likely to evolve in different ways. National rules are likely to change to become more like IFRS Standards anyway. The Board issued in 2009 an *IFRS for SMEs®* *Standard*. This is a simplified form of IFRS Standards that is intended for use with companies in which there is no 'public interest' (primarily are not listed on a public stock exchange). The Commission will not require adoption of this standard by member states, and different Member States view it with differing degrees of enthusiasm. The UK has adapted it for use by medium-sized private companies.

As mentioned earlier, a particular issue that impacts European companies is that the EU has not in fact endorsed all the IFRS Standards. As a result of pressure from French banks, the Accounting Regulatory Committee 'carved out' part of IAS 39 on the measurement of financial instruments. In stating the basis on which their accounts are prepared, European listed companies are required to specify that they have followed 'IFRS as endorsed by the EU'.

This created a number of problems, not least with the USA. The SEC has approved for use in the USA without a reconciliation only IFRS Standards as issued by the IASB. To qualify as equivalent to US GAAP, the company must state that it follows IFRS Standards as issued by the IASB, and the audit report must confirm this.

This specific problem disappeared in 2018 when IAS 39 was replaced by IFRS 9, *Financial Instruments*, but the idea that the EU might change an IFRS Standard remains a threat that politicians like to wave about when trying to persuade the standard-setter to follow a particular course of action.

IFRS Standards worldwide

As discussed already, a number of developed and developing countries have already moved to IFRS Standards or are intending to do so.

In South Africa, IFRS Standards are mandatory for all domestic listed companies. In Japan, listed foreign companies may use IFRS Standards (or any other national GAAP for that matter), but domestic companies are not allowed to use IFRS Standards. Canada, Brazil and South Korea have adopted IFRS Standards. Japan is planning to move to IFRS Standards.

China has developed its own standards in conjunction with the Board. In 2015 the organization pronounced that these are virtually identical to IFRS Standards and the Chinese government announced a new programme to extend the standards to smaller entities.

From October 2002 the FASB and the IASB committed to the convergence of US rules and IFRS Standards. Different initiatives were taken, such as a short-term convergence project aimed at removing a variety of individual differences between US GAAP and IFRS Standards, joint projects on significant accounting issues such as business combinations, revenue recognition and leasing. The convergence programme led in 2007 to the SEC accepting IFRS Standards as equivalent to US GAAP for the purposes of registration with the SEC. This very important concession meant that foreign companies listed in the USA and using IFRS Standards did not have to offer US investors a reconciliation of their figures to US GAAP. IFRS Standards therefore offer a relatively cheap way to being listed in the USA, and this has been significant in persuading countries to adopt IFRS Standards for all listed companies.

The financial crisis put many strains on relationships between the FASB and the IASB and their respective constituents, and they failed to converge on accounting for financial instruments (while remaining fairly close to each other in their requirements) despite exhortations from the G20 governments. A number of convergence projects were dropped during the crisis because of pressure on standard-setting time. Over this period the USA decided that there was no case for it to adopt IFRS Standards as such, and the convergence programme has ended.

The two boards still meet together from time to time, and believe it is important not to diverge fundamentally, but the focus for international technical co-operation has moved to the ASAF and multilateral convergence.

IASB *Conceptual Framework for Financial Reporting*

The IASB (the Board) developed a conceptual framework with high level principles that constitute the frame of reference for financial reporting under IFRS Standards. The *Conceptual Framework* sets out theoretical foundations of financial statements: the objective of financial reports, the qualitative characteristics of useful financial information, what should be included in financial statements and how it is to be measured, presented and disclosed. In its original form, it was issued in 1989 as the *Framework for the Preparation and Presentation of Financial Statements*. It was revised and re-issued in 2018 as the *Conceptual Framework for Financial Reporting*.

In what follows in this chapter, we will elaborate somewhat on the first two topics of the *Conceptual Framework*: the objective or main purpose of financial reports and the qualitative characteristics of useful financial information. In Chapter 3, we will continue discussing the conceptual framework – more specifically, the definitions of the building blocks of financial statements and their recognition and measurement features.

Objective of financial reporting

Recall that, according to the Board, the overall objective of financial reporting is: '*to provide financial information about the reporting entity that is useful to existing and potential investors, lenders and other creditors in making decisions relating to providing resources to the entity*' (IASB *Conceptual Framework*, para. 1.2). The targeted decisions are basically *resource allocation decisions*. These involve decisions about buying, selling or holding equity and debt instruments (e.g. shares and bonds) and providing or settling loans and other forms of credit, as well as decisions about exercising rights to vote on, or otherwise influence, management's actions. This is elaborated further as shown in the following box:

STANDARDS

 IASB CONCEPTUAL FRAMEWORK *(extracts)*

Usefulness of Financial Reporting in Assessing Cash Flow Prospects and Stewardship

1.3 The decisions described in paragraph 1.2 depend on the returns that existing and potential investors, lenders and other creditors expect, for example dividends, principal and interest payments or market price increases. Investors', lenders' and other creditors' expectations about returns depend on their assessment of the amount, timing and uncertainty of (the prospects for) future net cash inflows to the entity and on their assessment of management's stewardship of the entity's economic resources. Existing and potential investors, lenders and other creditors need information to help them make those assessments.

1.4 To make the assessments described in paragraph 1.3, existing and potential investors, lenders and other creditors need information about:

(a) the economic resources of the entity, claims against the entity, and changes in those resources and claims; and

(b) how efficiently and effectively the entity's management and governing board have discharged their responsibilities to use the entity's economic resources.

Source: IASB, Conceptual Framework for Financial Reporting

Basically, in order to be effective, financial statements need to provide users with information that helps them assess both:

- Prospects of future net cash inflows to the company, and
- Management's stewardship of the company's resources.

Although financial statements mainly report on the past, they are expected to deliver key inputs to enable assessments of the company's future returns and risks and of its ability to generate positive net cash flows in the future. Note that, in addition to helping to assess future cash flows, stewardship information is separately identified within the Board's view on the overall objective of financial reporting. *Stewardship* relates to management's accountability for the custody and safeguarding of the company's resources and for their efficient and profitable use. Stewardship responsibilities usually also affect a company's ability to generate future cash flows. In that regard, it is not a priori evident how information needed to assess the stewardship of management would be different from information needed to help users assess the prospects of future net cash inflows to the company.

The building blocks for financial reporting are identified as information about the resources of the company, the claims against those resources and how these change over time. No surprises here, as these constitute the basic components of the balance sheet and statement of financial performance, which we will further elaborate in Chapter 3. Moreover, these two statements are key in getting a view on efficiency and effectiveness issues with regard to management's use of the company's resources.

Qualitative characteristics of financial information

Qualitative characteristics are the attributes of financial information that underpin the decision-usefulness of financial reporting. As we have seen, the *Conceptual Framework* states that decision-usefulness is the overriding criterion on which to base financial reporting. The qualitative characteristics of financial information identify the types of information that are likely to be most useful to existing and potential users for making decisions on the basis of information in the company's financial reports. Making these explicit does not necessarily make it any easier for preparers and auditors to make accounting policy choices. It does, however, provide a framework for discussion and evaluation of priorities.

Figure 1.3 summarizes the qualitative characteristics of useful financial information and their ingredients. The framework distinguishes fundamental and enhancing characteristics and puts forward a pervasive cost constraint – the cost of the information provided should not exceed its benefits.

Figure 1.3   Qualitative characteristics of useful financial information

The *fundamental qualitative characteristics* are relevance and faithful representation. These are the essential ones – without these, financial information cannot be considered useful for decision-making.

Relevance refers to information's capability of making a difference in the decisions of providers of finance. Financial information is capable of making a difference in decisions if it has predictive value, confirmatory value or both. Information has *predictive value* if it helps form expectations of the future. It has *confirmatory value* if it confirms or changes expectations of the future made in the past. The predictive value and confirmatory value of financial information are often interrelated. For example, information on current year's sales can be used as the basis for predicting future sales, but can also be compared with projections of future sales that were made in past years. In that sense, the same information helps to correct and improve the processes that were used to prepare users' past predictions. *Materiality* is a company-specific aspect of relevance. Information is material if omitting it or misstating it could influence decisions of finance providers. Materiality of information depends on the nature or magnitude, or both, of the items to which the information relates in the context of an individual company's financial report. On the one hand, materiality is a relative matter. An amount of €10,000 is probably not material for a multinational company, but may be material for a small company. On the other hand, if the amount relates to the discovery of a €10,000 bribe, it may be a material issue even for a multinational.

Faithful representation is the second fundamental quality characteristic that makes financial information useful for decision-making. Financial reports depict economic phenomena in words and numbers. To be useful, financial information must not only represent all relevant phenomena, but it must also faithfully represent the phenomena that it purports to represent. A perfectly faithful representation would be a depiction that is complete, neutral and free from error. A *complete* representation contains all information a user needs to understand the phenomenon being depicted, including all necessary descriptions and explanations to support comprehension. A *neutral* representation is a depiction without bias in the selection or presentation of financial information so that no interested party is favoured over another. A faithful representation should be *free from error* (no errors or omissions in the description of the phenomenon and in the processing of those descriptions). Free from error does not mean perfectly accurate in all respects. Recall that accounting relies heavily on estimates of various types that build on management's judgements (remember 'accounting choices') and these are not error proof. An estimate will, however, be considered faithful if no errors have been made in selecting and applying an appropriate process for developing the estimate. A faithful representation also implies that business phenomena are reported according to their economic substance and not primarily according to their legal form (*substance over form*). For example, a company sells goods to a third party before the end of its financial year, but simultaneously agrees to buy the goods back after year-end. There would be two separate legal contracts (a sale agreement and a repurchase agreement), but one could very well argue that, economically, both agreements have to be considered as a single transaction in order to faithfully represent the economics of the deal.

The *Conceptual Framework* identifies four *enhancing qualitative characteristics*. These are verifiability, comparability, understandability and timeliness. The enhancing qualities distinguish more useful from less useful information. They are very desirable, but not as critical as relevance and faithful representation. They may never be invoked to override requirements set by the fundamental qualities of financial information.

Verifiability implies that different knowledgeable and independent actors could reach a consensus that a particular depiction is a faithful representation. If verifiability is not fully assured, users are likely to be more cautious because they may perceive greater risk that the information does not faithfully represent what it purports to represent.

Comparability increases usefulness as it enables users to identify and understand similarities in and differences among items. Comparability relates to time (similar information about the same company but about another period or moment in time) and space (similar information about other companies).

Understandability (classifying, characterizing and presenting information in a clear and concise manner) refers to users with a reasonable knowledge of business and the economics behind it and who are willing to analyze and review information diligently (sometimes with the aid of advisers). This means that information on complex economic transactions should not be avoided. But information that is difficult to understand should be presented and explained as clearly as possible

Timeliness refers to having information available in time to be capable of influencing decisions. Older information tends to be less useful than information based on more recent inputs. Timely information is, however, only useful if it is relevant and faithfully represented. It is likely to include estimates and other uncertainties and this may create tension with verifiability. Some would argue that timely information is most useful for prediction, whereas verifiable, certain, data are most useful for stewardship purposes (i.e. judging performance retrospectively). People drawing up financial statements will sometimes have to make accounting choices that will involve trade-offs between timeliness and verifiability.

Finally, there is the *pervasive cost constraint* in the sense that the benefits of the information provided must not exceed the costs of assembling, presenting and using it. Cost as such is not a qualitative characteristic, but it puts a rational economic barrier on the usefulness of financial information.

There are a number of major issues we can draw from the analysis of the qualitative characteristics of financial information as presented in the *Conceptual Framework*. One is the *substance over form* requirement for faithful representation. The financial statements should depict economic phenomena, but they should do so irrespective of the legal form. We will see later how this impacts on financial statements. Another major issue is that financial information must be capable of changing a decision, and this requirement is more critical than *verifiability*. In financial accounting, forward-looking estimates are considered important in providing relevant information (e.g. expected cash flows, useful lives, collectability assessments and salvage values), but they cannot be directly verified. However, excluding information using those estimates would make the financial reports much less useful. Again, we will elaborate later how estimates of the future form an essential part of the financial reporting process. It is better from the perspective of investor decision-making to publish data based on management's best estimate than to wait for uncertain outcomes to be resolved.

You may have an image of accounting as a process of tracking numbers, recording them, then summarizing them; a world in which there is no uncertainty and no drama. Some accounting is like that, but preparing financial statements often involves very difficult judgements and many estimates of future outcomes. It is a risky business, as the SEC's compliance division will confirm.

Summary

The objective of this chapter was to start to explain the environment of accounting. It has looked at the main financial statements published by companies and discussed the framework through which these are regulated. It has noted that governments need to regulate accounting to ensure the efficient running of the economy and the financial markets in particular, since business relies heavily on accurate information about other businesses. Government also wants to collect taxes and accounting is linked directly with the calculation of taxable profits. Apart from this, there are other bodies with an interest, notably stock exchanges, specialist standard-setting agencies and bodies organized by the accounting profession or industry sectors.

In the international field, there is a strong movement towards the use of International Financial Reporting Standards that are promulgated by the International Accounting Standards Board. These enable company reports to be compared across national boundaries and help smooth management decision-making in the context of global business. The standard-setter built an elaborate institutional setting to sustain the legitimacy of its work. Related to this, it developed a conceptual framework as a theoretical frame of reference for its current and future standards. The framework elaborates theoretical foundations of financial statements and assists users in understanding and interpreting financial reports.

Discussion questions

1. What is usually included in the annual financial statements of a company?
2. Contrast broadly the regulatory traditions in continental Europe as opposed to the anglophone countries.
3. Are the financial accounting requirements of entities in the public sector different from those of business in the private sector?
4. Compare and contrast the different types of accounting regulation that exist.
5. How is the IASB's organizational setting structured?
6. Explain what is meant by relevance, faithful representation and comparability and how they make financial information useful.
7. Elaborate the potential tension between timeliness and verifiability as characteristics of useful financial information.

CHAPTER 2

Accounting and accountants

This chapter discusses the work of the company accounting department and the system called 'internal control', which is used to provide reasonable assurance regarding the reliability of the corporate financial statements. It will also introduce independent accountants and the auditing profession, as well as discussing the external audit.

Chapter structure

- Introduction
- Accounting function
- Accounting database
- Recording transactions
- Organization of data within the general ledger
- Control and audit
- The accounting profession
- Summary
- Discussion questions

Introduction

We are going to start this chapter by looking at the accounting system within a company and how it maintains its records. If you want just to be able to read financial statements, you may prefer not to learn about the processes through which the data in them are collected. On the other hand, a successful manager in a multinational is bound to have responsibility at some point for a freestanding operating unit and therefore for oversight of its accounting system. In addition, understanding where the information comes from is always going to help understand the information itself, and this is, of course, true of that provided by financial statements.

This chapter introduces the systems such as internal control and internal audit that are there to safeguard the company's assets and underpin the accuracy of the records. It then looks at the audit performed by external independent accountants and introduces the wider field of corporate governance. A more detailed review of audit, internal control and corporate governance is to be found in Chapter 16.

Accounting function

All businesses need a financial accounting system that tracks all the economic transactions that the business undertakes, records them logically in a database, and provides reporting tools to communicate information to decision-makers. This system is a prime resource of the business and should provide:

- Controls to ensure that only legitimate expenses are paid

- Systems to ensure that debts to suppliers are well tracked and paid when due

- Systems to calculate salary payments to employees and deduct social security and other charges

- Controls to ensure that all customers are correctly invoiced, and that customers in turn pay what they owe

- Controls to safeguard the company's assets

- Information to management on a regular basis to enable them to run the business efficiently

- Information to the authorities to support payment of taxes

- Information to shareholders on the health of the company and to help determine dividends

- Information and measurements to others with whom the company has performance-related contracts (debt covenants, employee bonus schemes, joint ventures, franchises, licences, etc.)

- Information to those who lend money to the company and to suppliers

- Information that represents the company to all outside interests and all stakeholders.

Notice that while the first six objectives are wholly internal to the operation of the company, the other five involve providing information to those who are external to the company. We could describe the first six functions as being those of financial control and the others as those of financial reporting.

The accounting department of a company needs to meet these objectives, and this is mostly done through feeding the company's database, and then using the aggregate data to prepare reports about the company's activities. The nature of the accounting department will vary enormously depending on the size of the company. A very small business may simply use a part-time bookkeeper to process transactions and maintain the database, or use an outside accounting firm to do this. The largest global companies, acting as a group of legal entities, will have large accounting departments in each operating unit, together with an extensive head office unit to gather together data from throughout the group. In an international group, the management of the group is controlled mostly through uniform accounting systems that involve subsidiaries in sending data regularly to head office (or via regional offices) to enable central and regional management to know what is happening. In this sense, it would be impossible to manage an international group without accounting.

BETWEEN THE LINES

Different companies have different needs – in a large, publicly held company the shareholders will usually be remote from the management, whereas in a small, family company, the managers are often also major shareholders. We will generally assume that the typical company we are dealing with is a large multinational, but will point out differences for smaller businesses as we go along. In this case, a small, family business will often want to keep information secret, while a multinational will generally be keen to give information (accounting reports are normally on the group's website).

Usually such a group will have an internal accounting manual which lays out the procedures to be followed in accounting for typical transactions in order to ensure a uniform treatment of operations worldwide, without which management would have difficulty in interpreting the accounting information. The accounting manual may run to several volumes and is usually available in several languages.

In fact, global companies have problems because national accounting rules differ from country to country. The national rules should normally be followed for tax purposes, so the group has to have a reporting system that is capable of delivering uniform data worldwide for management purposes and for the group financial statements, while also providing potentially different data in each country to suit local tax requirements. This is one of the reasons that large companies welcome worldwide convergence on IFRS Standards. Potentially, group accounts and individual company accounts can use exactly the same rules. Too much should not be made of the existing differences, since they tend to centre on one or two areas of accounting and generally, therefore, the transition from one set of accounts to the other is not that complicated. At the same time, this is a problem that multinationals have to address, and one that is costly in terms of hiring professionals to deal with it. Very often a multinational will choose to have uniform internal systems, and then ask its accounting advisers in each country, who are familiar with the subtleties of the local regulations, to liaise with the local tax officials and prepare a revised set of accounts for local reporting purposes (see Figure 2.1).

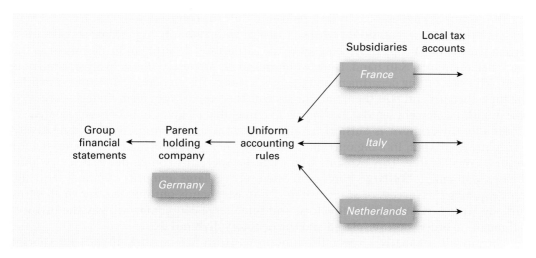

Figure 2.1 Group reporting flows

In principle, the company's accounting function should provide systems that capture all the transactions that the company undertakes. The main categories of this are:

- Sales

- Purchases

- Payroll

- Treasury

- Investment in long-term (productive) capacity.

These transactions involve an interaction with other departments, and the exact split of responsibility between the accounting function and the operating department will vary according to the nature of the business and the technology used.

In the *sales* area, there are many combinations possible. In a hotel, for example, the reception desk ('front office') generally also operates customer billing and cash collection, and then passes the transactions on to the accounting function ('back office'). In retailing, very often sales representatives call on retailers and take orders in person. The sales person then transmits the order to the company where the system captures it as an instruction to the warehouse and a linked instruction to the accounting department to issue an invoice. Increasingly companies are enabling their customers to access their intranet to place orders directly into the company system, which are then, through the computer, translated into delivery instructions and an invoice.

The accounting department will normally have a data file for each customer, will control credit levels and will send out monthly statements of account to the customer and track payment when that is due. The issue of credit control is occasionally a problematic one that gives liaison difficulties between accounting staff and sales staff. On the one hand, the accounting department will want to make sure that where credit is given, the customer does pay the bills in due course. The sales department, on the other hand, wants to sell as many units as possible, and easy credit helps them to do this, so they may be less demanding in their assessments of creditworthiness.

The capture of *purchases* has its own problems. Here the company will often have a system of purchase orders or requisitions where a manager with authority to purchase supplies must sign a requisition, a copy of which goes to the accounting department to alert them to the fact that a purchase is in hand. Later, when the goods are received, a delivery document is sent to the accounting department and then the invoice. The accounting department marries all these together and puts them into the system. The supplier data file is then checked with the monthly statement sent by the supplier to ensure that all invoices have been recorded.

Finally, the account is authorized and paid. In a small company, this is relatively straightforward, but, in a big operation, it can be very complicated and the potential for error is considerable. This explains why there are specialist companies that review purchases, particularly for large stores, and often recover large amounts of money. Equally, this explains the success of scams where a fraudster sends out invoices for small sums for, say, listing in an internet directory, and some large companies will pay the invoice, although no order was ever placed and the directory does not exist.

The *payroll* is usually a specialist function within accounting. It calls for special knowledge in that, in many countries, the employer is responsible for deducting social security charges from the employee, sometimes the employee's income tax is deducted by the employer, and then there may be pension schemes and other voluntary schemes, such as savings or membership of a staff social club, to which the employee contributes. This means that each employee's pay file is individual and probably quite complex. Small companies will often subcontract this function to an accounting firm or a specialist service company. The possibilities for error are considerable, and where government deductions are involved, there may be fines for making mistakes. The accounting involved is also quite complex in that the company deducts money from the individual's pay packet and then has to pay this to government departments, pension funds and so on.

The *treasury* function is one where all the others meet up: treasury controls all the receipts and payments into the company's bank accounts, as well as any cash tills that might exist (company accountants do not like cash floating around). Evidently this is the area in which authorizations are most stringently required and also where accurate coding of transactions is essential. The treasury unit works very closely with the company's bankers. Accessing the bank's accounting system in real time, the treasury knows exactly how much money is in each of the company's accounts at the close of banking business and then lends out any surplus, perhaps on the overnight market (yes, you can lend money just overnight, provided you have enough of it to do so in large quantities).

The accounting system is organized with separate data files for each bank account, so that the company's information can be checked directly against the statement put out by the bank. This provides a regular control on the accuracy of the company's records – all expenses and revenues that have gone through the bank should also be in the company's records. The company regularly (ideally at least once a month) prepares a 'bank reconciliation'. This is a document that compares the balance on the bank account as seen by the bank, with the balance on the corresponding data file within the company. These two will rarely agree because of time lags in transactions going through the bank account, but the differences can and must be identified as a check on the accuracy of both sets of records (in a large company this can involve cross-checking hundreds of transactions). One way of conducting a fraud is to make payments without entering them in the company's accounting records. These payments will show up as differences on the bank reconciliation, but if nobody reviews the reconciliation, they will stay outside the company records.

You can see that the accounting unit has a quite complex set of tasks and objectives. Its prime function is to capture information for the company and to ensure that customers pay their bills and that suppliers are paid – it is a service function to help the company to operate efficiently. However, most company frauds are going to involve obtaining money via the accounting department, so the staff and systems have to be organized to prevent this. Therefore they may seem less than keen on giving a service and rather too inclined to demand bits of paper, and signatures, that appear to be obstacles to the free running of the company.

Accounting database

Coming back to the central issue of accumulating information, a company's financial accounting system is organized to provide data for a central database (the *general ledger*), which is then used as the source of information used by management internally and for external reporting purposes. The accounting database normally looks as shown in Figure 2.2.

Figure 2.2 The financial accounting database

Recording transactions

Information flows into the database through several layers of processing that summarize and re-summarize individual transactions to build up to aggregates for the year's activities (Figure 2.3).

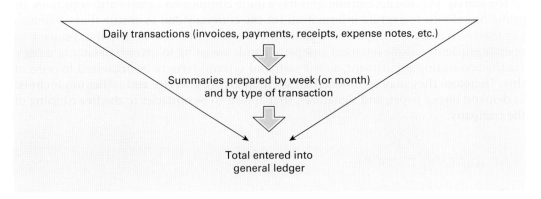

Figure 2.3   Building aggregates

Journals are used to build up the periodic summaries and feed aggregated data into the general ledger. The general ledger is then used as a source for the preparation of a periodic statement of profit or loss (income statement) and a statement of financial position (balance sheet). This kind of approach was particularly useful when all entries in the database were made by hand, and is still used even though virtually all systems in companies are computerized. The essential idea is that while aggregated data are needed in the ledger, to enable management summaries to be prepared, the system must be capable of being interrogated to confirm that a particular transaction has or has not taken place, so it must be possible later to go from the monthly figure in the ledger, for example, back through the journals to the individual transaction. This is both because accounting departments have regularly to deal with queries, and because the transactions are subject to checking by internal or external auditors. There must be what is called an *audit trail* to show the links and provide evidence that the initial transaction was authorized. Computerized systems may very well carry out the intermediate stage between the individual transaction (known as a 'prime entry' in the trade) and the ledger total. Once the first entry has been keyed in, the system will organize a batch of similar transactions and 'post' this to the ledger, but it is normally organized also to provide a printout of each batch, which becomes the bridge between prime entry and ledger. Of course, there could be several intermediate levels.

Some decisions have to be taken as to what level of detail is going to be useful within an accounting system. At one extreme, an accounting system might record every single transaction separately so that its annual profit and loss account is a detailed list of every transaction that has taken place over the year. At the other extreme, the profit and loss account could be one figure representing the net difference (profit or loss) of the whole year's revenues and expenses.

The exact point at which one makes a decision about the degree of detail to be kept will vary with the specific circumstances of each company, its size and the nature of the business being carried out. However, as guidelines, the final records should obviously, as a minimum, keep information aggregated for a whole accounting year on each of the separate categories (of the statement of profit or loss and statement of financial position) which will appear in the annual financial statements. Normally, however, the database will be much more detailed. It will need to be capable of delivering information about each individual operating unit within a company, so that an analysis showing the profitability of each unit for management purposes can be produced without difficulty. This information is aggregated for the purposes of the published financial statements.

The precise form taken by the general ledger and the journals, and the classification of items, will vary from one system to another. In some countries (e.g. France, Belgium, Greece, Spain), there is a State-mandated system, generally known as a *chart of accounts* or accounting plan. In other countries (e.g. Germany, Switzerland, Austria), there are widely used standard charts whose adoption is voluntary. Generally, anglophone countries do not use standard charts of this kind, but large companies with uniform systems worldwide must develop in effect their own chart of accounts. A nationally standardized chart has certain advantages in terms of staff training, lower audit costs and cheaper software, but has typically been rejected by anglophone professions as being too restrictive.

In large companies, the system may well be partitioned to enable the major operations (sales, purchases, treasury and payroll) to operate independently of one another – with links to the central ledger to ensure the integrity of the system. In this way, the specialist functions can operate dedicated systems that not only maintain the ledger, but issue invoices or bank transfers, issue monthly statements to customers, provide analysis of outstanding items, etc.

XBRL (eXtensible Business Reporting Language) is set to revolutionize accounting data handling and reporting in this context. Instead of treating accounting information as a block of text, XBRL provides an identifying tag for each individual item of information, such as individual accounts in a chart of accounts. These tags are computer readable and enable automated processing of accounting and related business information by computer software. The specific tags of individual data items are defined in taxonomies. These function as dictionaries. Different taxonomies can coexist and be linked for reporting purposes. This offers a viable solution to link IFRS Standards and national reporting taxonomies. Indeed, national jurisdictions may need their own taxonomies (like a standard chart of accounts and specific reporting formats) to reflect their local accounting regulations, but XBRL could automatically convert them in a generally accepted IFRS® taxonomy. Once the appropriate XBRL taxonomies are established and the data are gathered accordingly, different types of report using varying subsets of the data can be produced with minimum effort. The accounting department could, for example, quickly and reliably generate internal management reports, financial statements for publication, tax and other regulatory filings, as well as credit reports for lenders. XBRL would remove time-consuming and error-prone data-handling processes and improve data accuracy through automated data checks.

The International Accounting Standards Board (the Board) has developed an IFRS taxonomy, which it updates regularly. The Securities and Exchange Commission (SEC) requires US companies to file XBRL tagged data and offers free software to help investors manipulate the tagged data. An investor can, for example, compare sales in different companies by using this kind of system. They can, in effect, construct their own analysts' reports comparing companies in the same field. The European Commission is constructing a system that will link national stock exchanges through a single portal.

Organization of data within the general ledger

When the data about the accounting transactions of the company reach the general ledger, they will be stored according to a system which has been in existence for hundreds of years: the *double-entry system*. The first written account of the system appeared in 1494 (by Luca Pacioli) and the fact that the system is still in use today will give you some idea of its practical effectiveness.

First, the general ledger is organized into a series of 'accounts' – data files – each of which is used to record transactions of a particular type. For example, if your business is selling books, you would need one account in which to record sales, another to record the cost of the books sold and a series of accounts to record the various different types of expense incurred in the business (advertising, rent of premises, heat, etc.), as well as accounts for financing and investments in property and equipment, information systems, inventory, etc. (This is the minimum – if more analysis were useful, then more accounts would be used.)

Each account within the general ledger is organized in a particular way. The account has two columns for figures and some space to write in explanatory remarks and cross-referencing details. The left-hand column is always referred to as the *debit column* and the right-hand column is called the *credit column* (there seems to be no satisfactory explanation for the derivation of these words). Debit and credit are also used as verbs, so one says 'debit insurance expense' to mean a figure should be entered into the left-hand column of the insurance expense account. In formal, manual bookkeeping there are no plus or minus signs; the value of an account is the difference between the debit and credit columns, and can be either a debit balance (more left hand than right) or a credit balance (more right hand than left).

A traditional manual ledger account would look as shown in Figure 2.4.

Account number:		Account name:		
Date	*Narrative*	*Ref.*	*Debit*	*Credit*

Figure 2.4 Layout of a manual ledger account

A computerized printout often preserves the same format, but may also provide a running balance perhaps in a third column out to the right, or elsewhere on the printout.

The exact form in which the accounts are kept is not of essential interest for our purposes – what is important is how the figures are arrived at and what they mean, rather than the detail of the methodology of the data file. However, one normally comes across accounting statements, notably one's bank statement, from time to time, and knowledge of the notation system is useful to that extent. An example of a personal bank statement is shown in Figure 2.5.

If you were looking at a financial accounting textbook intended for accountants, then the whole of the discussion of accounting rules and techniques would involve notation involving debits and credits – making entries in left-hand and right-hand columns. This notation system is largely redundant for our purposes, and we will use non-specialist signs and tools such as worksheets to explain what is going on. Since you are not going to run an accounting system, a detailed knowledge of the notation is not useful and tends to divert attention from the reality of what is actually going on.

CREDIT SUISSE

Genève

Compte privé

Date	Narrative	In our favour	In your favour	Balance
170717	Balance brought forward			2,726.50
260717	Receipt IIM		348.00	3,074.50
270717	Credit Card settlement	1,791.65		1,282.85
280717	Receipt DIP		7,589.70	8,872.55
300717	Monthly payments	3,700.70		5,171.85
090817	Cash – ATM	500.00		4,671.85
160817	Cash – ATM	500.00		4,171.85

Credit = in your favour
Debit = in our favour

Figure 2.5   Example of a personal bank statement

Control and audit

The accounting system, as we have seen, fulfils a number of different functions, being both an *information system* and a *security or control system*. In both cases, it is essential that the system is efficient and effective. Without an effective system, central management (a) does not know reliably what is going on in the company, and (b) cannot safeguard the shareholders' interests. In recent years, this issue has come to be seen as more and more important – the well-known corporate embarrassments, such as the fall of Barings Bank, the large loss at the French Société Générale and the reporting problems of Royal Ahold, would almost certainly not have been possible with tighter systems – in the jargon, tighter internal control. Public concern has grown to the point where many companies publish a statement in their annual report to the effect that the directors are satisfied that they have in place an adequate system of internal control. One of the main objectives of the *internal control system* is to ensure the integrity of the information system and the security of the company's assets. In that sense, it is heavily relied on by external auditors in assessing the viability of the company's records. In this section, we will take a closer look at how a system of internal control operates and its links, through internal audit, to the external audit.

Internal control

Internal control has recently become more important because of the focus on corporate governance and the demands this places on boards of directors and executives to implement and demonstrate control over business operations. One of the most authoritative definitions of internal control comes from COSO (Report of the Committee of Sponsoring Organizations of the Treadway Commission).

Defining internal control

The COSO definition of internal control has become widely accepted and is referred to in other international control frameworks as well. According to COSO, internal control is broadly defined as a process, established, operated and monitored by those charged with governance and management of a company (board of directors, management and other personnel) to provide reasonable assurance regarding the achievement of objectives in the following categories:

- The effectiveness and efficiency of the company's operations
- The reliability of its financial reporting
- Its compliance with applicable laws and regulations.

As a process, internal control goes beyond policies and procedures and also includes factors such as corporate culture, systems and organizational structures. The COSO definition underscores the importance of the relationship of control and objectives. Without objectives, talking about control is meaningless. From a broad managerial perspective, the COSO report identifies three categories of control objective. The first category addresses a company's basic business concerns, including performance and profitability goals and safeguarding of resources (basically an efficiency concern). The second relates to the preparation of reliable financial statements and related financial data derived from such statements. The third deals with complying with those laws and regulations to which the company is subject. Within the COSO framework, financial reporting concerns are a basic objective of a system of internal control, although not an exclusive one.

Internal control: system components

According to COSO, a system of internal control consists of five interrelated components:

- *Control environment* – Attributes of the people conducting the company's activities and the environment in which they operate, influencing overall control consciousness
- *Risk assessment* – Identification and analysis of relevant risks as a basis for determining ways to manage those risks
- *Control activities* – Policies and procedures established and executed that enable management's directives to be carried out
- *Information and communication* – Identification, capture and exchange of information for the conduct and control of operations in a form and timeframe that enables people to carry out their responsibilities
- *Monitoring* – Assessing of performance of internal control over time and making modifications as conditions change.

These five interrelated components are relevant for each internal control objective. For example, accurate financial reporting builds on a supportive control environment with a strong ethical commitment of corporate management, identification of relevant threats and exposures (erroneous record-keeping, unacceptable accounting rules, unrecognized fraud and embezzlement of assets, loss or theft of data, etc.), efficient information gathering and processing routines, and appropriate control policies and procedures to manage financial reporting risks (good document design, accounting manuals, organizational measures, checks and balances, etc.).

STANDARDS

 COSO – COMPONENTS OF A SYSTEM OF INTERNAL CONTROL *(extracts)*

Control environment

The control environment sets the tone of an organization, influencing the control consciousness of its people. It is the foundation for all other components of internal control, providing discipline and structure. Control environment factors include the integrity, ethical values and competence of the entity's people; management's philosophy and operating style; the way management assigns authority and responsibility, and organizes and develops its people; and the attention and direction provided by the board of directors.

Risk assessment

Every entity faces a variety of risks from external and internal sources that must be assessed. A precondition to risk assessment is establishment of objectives, linked at different levels and internally consistent. Risk assessment is the identification and analysis of relevant risks to achievement of the objectives, forming a basis for determining how the risks should be managed. Because economic, industry, regulatory and operating conditions will continue to change, mechanisms are needed to identify and deal with the special risks associated with change.

Control activities

Control activities are the policies and procedures that help ensure management directives are carried out. They help ensure that necessary actions are taken to address risks to achievement of the entity's objectives. Control activities occur throughout the organization, at all levels and in all functions. They include a range of activities as diverse as approvals, authorizations, verifications, reconciliations, reviews of operating performance, security of assets and segregation of duties.

Information and communication

Pertinent information must be identified, captured and communicated in a form and timeframe that enables people to carry out their responsibilities. Information systems produce reports, containing operational, financial and compliance-related information, that make it possible to run and control the business. They deal not only with internally generated data, but also information about external events, activities and conditions necessary for informed business decision-making and external reporting. Effective communication also must occur in a broader sense, flowing down, across and up the organization. All personnel must receive a clear message from top management that control responsibilities must be taken seriously. They must understand their own role in the internal control system, as well as how individual activities relate to the work of others. They must have a means of communicating significant information upstream. There also needs to be effective communication with external parties, such as customers, suppliers, regulators and shareholders.

Monitoring

Internal control systems need to be monitored – a process that assesses the quality of the system's performance over time. This is accomplished through ongoing monitoring activities, separate evaluations or a combination of the two. Ongoing monitoring

(Continued)

> occurs in the course of operations. It includes regular management and supervisory activities, and other actions personnel take in performing their duties. The scope and frequency of separate evaluations will depend primarily on an assessment of risks and the effectiveness of ongoing monitoring procedures. Internal control deficiencies should be reported upstream, with serious matters reported to top management and the board.
>
> *Source: COSO, Internal Control – Integrated Framework, Executive Summary*

The internal control system is intertwined with a company's operating activities and exists for fundamental business reasons (see objectives to be accomplished by the system). Internal control is most effective when controls are built into the company's infrastructure and are a part of the essence of the company's operations: internal control should become part of the company's DNA. 'Built-in' controls support quality and empowerment initiatives, avoid unnecessary costs and enable quick response to changing conditions. From this perspective, an accounting information system functions as an integral part of an internal control system and is thus more than a bundle of co-ordinated information flows. In fact, accounting information flows are intertwined with risk assessment processes, hierarchical and horizontal (between different functional departments) communication routines and specific control activities to ensure both the validity, completeness and accuracy of financial reports and the integrity of the resources they report on.

Control activities

Control activities usually involve a *policy component* and a *procedures component*. A policy establishes what should be done, while procedures are the actions to implement policies. For example, a policy might call for a creditworthiness review before a customer order is formally accepted. The procedure is the actual credit check, performed in a timely manner and with attention given to the factors set forth in the policy, such as financial guarantees, the payment history of the client and the balances of outstanding orders and sales invoices due.

A common and useful way to classify control activities is in relation to the timing of their occurrence – preventive, detective and corrective controls. *Preventive controls* are policies and procedures designed to prevent an error or fraud from occurring. For example, a creditworthiness check on new customer orders prevents shipping goods and recognizing receivables in the balance sheet for which no full payment will be received. Preventive financial controls, such as validation and edit checks on the input of transactions before they are recorded, will prevent material misstatements in accounting records, whether by error or fraud, from occurring during transaction processing in the accounting system. *Detective controls* are policies and procedures that are designed to detect errors or fraud that might preclude the achievement of specific business or process objectives. Detective financial controls will be built into the accounting system to spot material misstatements that may occur in processing transactions. *Corrective controls* are usually linked to detective ones and aimed at correcting problems in a timely manner.

Strong preventive controls are essential to support the effectiveness of information and control systems. In an accounting system that processes a high volume of transactions, a lack of preventive controls on the input of transactions before they are recorded can render detective and corrective controls ineffective in detecting and correcting errors in a timely manner. Preventive controls can take myriad forms. Within the context of an accounting information system they can be programmed validity and edit checks, file transmission controls, automated posting to ledgers and automated summary checks and reports. These types of preventive application control are usually accompanied by preventive control measures of an organizational nature, such as an appropriate system of delegation and accountability, linked with a structure of formal approvals and what is known as 'separation of functions'.

While all accounting transactions are centralized ultimately on the general ledger, it is good management practice to split up the way the transactions are initiated, recorded and processed into different functional units, partly to allow for the development of specialist skills (division of labour) and partly to provide an environment where fraud becomes difficult. This is known as *separation of functions* (or *segregation of duties*). It calls for the separation of the four basic functions of transaction processing:

- Authorizing transactions

- Executing transactions

- Recording transactions

- Safeguarding resources resulting from consummating transactions.

A simple example would be that where a payment has to be made, the payment is authorized by one person, the cheque or transfer document drawn by another person, the cheque or transfer signed by a third and the general ledger entry made by a fourth. Each person is responsible for ensuring that they process nothing that is not correctly supported by documents and authorizations, and therefore, in theory at least, four people would need to be in collusion for a fraudulent payment to be made without a significant risk of detection. Equally, at least four people should have checked that the transaction is valid and has been correctly categorized. Separation of functions is a nice example of an efficient preventive control, in the sense that it simultaneously supports different types of control objectives: safeguarding of assets, ensuring the validity, completeness and accuracy of recorded information and compliance checking.

Separation of functions is obviously easier in a large company than in a small one, and it also has the effect of increasing the costs of each transaction. There is therefore a difficult trade-off between the costs and the level of assurance. But even in small companies with only a few employees it is usually possible to assign responsibilities in a way that achieves the necessary checks and balances. Alternatively, oversight of incompatible activities by the general manager can substitute functional diversification. Recall the payments example. In small companies, it is not uncommon that the general manager is the only person authorized to approve outgoing payments and that monthly (or daily) bank statements are to be delivered unopened directly to him or her for review of outgoing payments.

There is, however, the psychological problem that people get used to routines and after a while do not check effectively. Indeed, in a system where everyone knows there are five other people checking the transaction, each link in the chain may start to rely on someone else doing the job properly, leading to a general failure. This is one of the reasons why *monitoring activities*, involving assessment by appropriate personnel of the design and operation of controls on a timely basis, is a necessary component of an effective internal control system.

Even with strong preventive controls, detective and corrective controls remain necessary. The internal control system will typically include routine checks such as inspection of the monthly bank reconciliation and outstanding customer and supplier accounts, all of which provide areas where fraudulent items can be kept outside the system, but also where company records can to an extent be checked against the records of outside organizations with which the company deals. Many companies keep asset registers where lists of computers and desks and so on (to say nothing of cars, plant, etc.) are maintained and these should be checked periodically against the physical existence of these items. Equally, where staff have access to large quantities of goods (supermarket staff, factory workers, etc.) it is usual to have security systems that control what goods the employees are taking in and out of the business.

It should be clear, however, that a good system of internal control can provide only *reasonable* (not absolute) *assurance* regarding the achievement of the major control objectives, including the effectiveness of the accounting and reporting systems. Each system of internal control has its inherent limitations. Internal control heavily relies on human judgement in decision-making and this can be faulty. Control activities are bound by cost–benefit considerations due to resource constraints and they can break down as a result of a simple error or mistake. Internal controls can always be circumvented through the collusion of two or more people. Additionally, management usually has the ability to override the internal controls if that suits their personal interests better.

BETWEEN THE LINES

Why should you check goods being taken *into* a company? It is not always relevant, but a sophisticated fraud is easy to operate in something like a bar where the barman takes in, for example, a bottle of whisky, then, when a customer asks for a measure of whisky, the barman serves the customer from his private inventory and keeps the money. This way the customer is not cheated and the bar owner does not necessarily have any idea anything is wrong. The barman is robbing the business by using its infrastructure, but the main internal controls generally focus on the relationship between the value of sales and the value of the liquor consumed, and the barman is circumventing these controls by bringing in liquor.

The US Sarbanes–Oxley Act of 2002 (commonly referred to as SOX) made executive management responsible not just for establishing, evaluating and assessing over time the effectiveness of internal control over financial reporting and disclosure, but also for periodically asserting its effectiveness (see Chapter 16 for further details). In the European Union (EU), no equivalent of the SOX requirements on internal control currently exists. As to accounting system specifications, the EU Accounting Directive implicitly requires companies to maintain accounting records enabling them to prepare financial statements, but explicit requirements on form and content of the accounting records and related controls are left to national legislation. This has led to divergent national requirements in European countries, but none has legal requirements comparable to the SOX requirements to publicly disclose conclusions regarding the effectiveness of internal control with regard to financial reporting.

Internal audit

Most large companies have an internal audit department. The primary task of internal auditors should be to examine and evaluate the adequacy and effectiveness of the company's internal control system and the quality of performance in carrying out assigned responsibilities. In fact, the *internal audit function* can be considered to be part of the monitoring component of the internal control system. It should be stressed, however, that the primary responsibility for establishing and maintaining the internal control system does not belong to the internal audit function but to the chief executive officer (CEO), along with key management personnel. The internal audit function's primary responsibility is to evaluate the effectiveness of internal control and thus contribute to ongoing effectiveness.

One of the key issues for a proper functioning of an internal audit function is its *independence*: the internal audit department should be independent of the activities it audits. The independence of the audit department should be assured through its organizational position and authority within the company and through recognition of its objectivity. Of crucial importance is the reporting line: it is generally recommended that internal auditors report directly to either the (audit committee of the) board of directors, the CEO or a committee of top corporate executives.

The scope of internal auditing potentially covers all activities within the company. In some companies, internal auditors are heavily involved with operational controls, such as periodically monitoring production quality, testing the timeliness of shipments to customers or evaluating the efficiency of production processes (operational internal audit). In other companies, the internal audit function will focus primarily on compliance and financial reporting issues (financial internal audit). So, in practice, the scope of the activities of the internal auditors tends to vary considerably, depending on the company's management.

Typically (and we will focus now on responsibilities of the internal auditors that are related to financial reporting), the department consists of a team of several people whose job is to visit the group's different sites and check whether accounting policies and procedures (usually documented in a policies and procedures manual) and related controls are being followed correctly and remain effective. Partly the task is psychological: if people know that at any time in the year the internal audit department may call in to check the accounting transactions and see whether the procedures in the group manual have been followed, they are encouraged to apply the procedures more thoroughly and anyone who was contemplating fraud is discouraged . . . the internal audit department thus acts as a preventive control measure.

The internal audit department can help create a culture within the company that says the accounting function has a vital role to play and that members of it are valued for their technical knowledge and their skill in handling the sometimes difficult interpersonal situations that can arise. Equally, this department can provide important feedback about application problems to those who design and maintain the procedures. A difficulty in operating group-wide systems is that not all operating units are the same size (and therefore may have quite different accounting structures and personnel) and not all have the same type of operations.

By way of example of the problems that can arise when trying to install uniform systems, here is an actual example taken from a group that had both electronics and entertainment interests. Within the entertainment division was a subgroup that ran London theatres and produced live theatrical shows. The head office internal audit department was conducting an exercise to fix levels of expenditure authority within operating units, as part of the internal control structure. It said that the chief executive of this subgroup could sign contracts only up to an individual value of £500,000. Beyond that, he should seek authority from the chief executive of the entertainment division. The chief accountant of the theatrical subgroup said this was not possible because the group did not know the value of many contracts that were signed. The internal audit manager was dumbfounded – how could the chief executive sign contracts without knowing their value? Should he not be replaced at once (and maybe the chief accountant, too)?

The chief accountant explained that theatre contracts in the West End of London are usually open ended. They provide for a minimum weekly rental (generally against a percentage of sales) and, as long as this is exceeded, the contract can run indefinitely. Indeed, the object of the exercise is to find a single production that could potentially run for years. So while the minimum weekly rental might be (say) £50,000, the show could run for two or three years, or only two or three weeks, so the value of the contract could be anything from £200,000 to £20m or more. The internal audit manager then understood, but pointed out that the chief executive of the worldwide group could only sign contracts up to £10m without the approval of the board of directors. In the end, they agreed to write a special authority for the theatre subgroup, based on maximum weekly figures.

Getting the 'control environment' right is a very tricky problem in a large group. Ideally you want the accounting departments of the different units to be efficient and useful contributors to the team, who are willing to provide a high quality of service to help with the efficient running of the unit. However, the integrity of the group system and the necessity to provide inputs whose justification can be demonstrated, if necessary years after the event in a tax investigation, demand that accounting staff insist on the presentation of the appropriate paperwork and the required authorizations. Accounting staff in remote subsidiaries sometimes have a particularly difficult time since they have a line responsibility to the chief executive of their subsidiary, but a functional responsibility to the head office accounting managers. Locally employed staff, particularly in areas where unemployment is high, may fear losing their job if they upset the local chief executive, and may therefore not apply systems correctly.

The internal audit team should make frequent but unscheduled visits to subsidiaries to make spot checks on recent transactions but also to reinforce the local accounting unit if there are problems. The internal audit team should have a reporting responsibility within the head office, and not to local managers, although, of course, they should discuss local problems with operational management on site.

It follows from this that working in internal audit is not a particularly easy job. It is necessary to have a wide knowledge of the group's operations and information systems. A great deal of time is spent away from home visiting remote subsidiaries and often either working in foreign languages or with people who are obliged to use their second or third language, and who, of course, have different cultural backgrounds and therefore different understandings about their role and responsibilities. People in either accounting or operational roles often resent also what they perceive as an intrusion from head office, without understanding that without effective accounting systems the group cannot continue to exist for very long.

The Institute of Internal Auditors (IIA) has played a major role in the development of the internal auditing profession. Established in the USA in 1941, the IIA has grown into a highly respected international organization and has taken a leadership role in providing professional guidance for internal auditors. The IIA establishes ethical and practice standards, provides education and promotes professionalism through its worldwide network. It sponsors a certification programme leading to the designation of Certified Internal Auditor (CIA) for those who meet the examination and experience requirements. The IIA's Standards for the Professional Practice of Internal Auditing are divided in attribute standards for the internal auditor and the internal audit department and performance standards for the performance and reporting of internal audit activities.

STANDARDS

DEFINING INTERNAL AUDITING

Internal auditing is an independent, objective assurance and consulting activity designed to add value and improve an organization's operations. It helps an organization accomplish its objectives by bringing a systematic, disciplined approach to evaluate and improve the effectiveness of risk management, control and governance processes.

Source: Institute of Internal Auditors (www.theiia.org)

External audit

In most jurisdictions, the financial statements of medium and large companies must be submitted to an independent (external) audit. This is often referred to as *statutory audit* and is usually carried out by independent firms of auditors. *External audit* has evolved differently in different countries, and the object of the audit is not uniform. In some countries, the auditor has a quasi-legal role to check for the legality of the company's activities and its annual financial statements, whereas, in other countries, the auditor is checking the accounts on behalf of the shareholders. In both cases, the audit firm is usually appointed by the management of the company. The responsibility both for keeping accounts and for preparing the annual financial statements is that of the management of the company, not that of the external auditors whose function is purely to check.

The external auditor expresses an opinion on the *representational fairness* of the financial statements in conformity with generally accepted accounting principles. While the company's system of internal control should provide reasonable assurance regarding the reliability of financial statements, the external auditor brings the assurance to a higher level. It is, however, not the responsibility of the external auditors to detect fraud. While external auditors should certainly report fraud if they spot it and they will normally comment on the adequacy of the internal control system to prevent fraud, their job is not to search for fraud, even if many people think that it is. In a modern multinational, management is looking to the statutory auditor to provide reassurance to outside stakeholders that the financial statements of the company are a valid representation of the company's financial position and performance. This is part of the very broad role played by financial statements, and the fact that the information is independently verified is probably one reason why the role is so broad.

STANDARDS

INSTITUTE OF INTERNAL AUDITORS: STANDARDS FOR THE PROFESSIONAL PRACTICE OF AUDITING

Attribute standards

1000 Purpose, Authority and Responsibility. The purpose, authority and responsibility of the internal audit activity should be formally defined in a charter, consistent with the *Standards*, and approved by the board.

(Continued)

1100 Independence and Objectivity. The internal audit activity should be independent, and internal auditors should be objective in performing their work.

1200 Proficiency and Due Professional Care. Engagements should be performed with proficiency and due professional care.

1300 Quality Assurance and Improvement Program. The chief audit executive should develop and maintain a quality assurance and improvement program that covers all aspects of the internal audit activity and continuously monitors its effectiveness. The program should be designed to help the internal auditing activity add value and improve the organization's operations and to provide assurance that the internal audit activity is in conformity with the Standards and the Code of Ethics.

Performance standards

2000 Managing the Internal Audit Activity. The chief audit executive should effectively manage the internal audit activity to ensure it adds value to the organization.

2100 Nature of Work. The internal audit activity evaluates and contributes to the improvement of risk management, control and governance systems.

2200 Engagement Planning. Internal auditors should develop and record a plan for each engagement.

2300 Performing the Engagement. Internal auditors should identify, analyze, evaluate and record sufficient information to achieve the engagement's objectives.

2400 Communicating Results. Internal auditors should communicate the engagement results promptly.

2500 Monitoring Progress. The chief audit executive should establish and maintain a system to monitor the disposition of results communicated to management.

2600 Communicating the Acceptance of Risks. When the chief audit executive believes that senior management has accepted a level of residual risk that is unacceptable to the organization, the chief audit executive should discuss the matter with senior management. If the decision regarding residual risk is not resolved, the chief audit executive and senior management should report the matter to the board for resolution.

Source: Institute of Internal Auditors, 2016 (www.theiia.org)

Nearly all multinationals have their financial statements audited by one of the four international audit networks that dominate the business:

- PricewaterhouseCoopers
- KPMG
- EY (Ernst & Young)
- Deloitte.

These four firms are probably better known than many of their clients and one of their logos on the audit report (published within the financial statements) carries a high level of reassurance to users in general and the capital markets in particular. As a consequence, any company with ambitions is likely to use one of these firms. In addition, they have worldwide networks and are capable of delivering an audit anywhere in the world. This is quite important in that the multinational generally prefers to have a single firm responsible for all its subsidiaries, not least because this reduces the risk of lack of co-ordination between countries. This tends to reinforce the dominant position of the 'Big Four', as they are known, since other audit firms cannot generally offer the global service.

The basic statutory audit consists of two tasks:

1. Check that the accounting database effectively picks up all the company's activities and is correct.
2. Check that the financial statements drawn up from it are a correct representation of what is in the accounting database, use appropriate accounting policies and are a reasonable representation of the company's real state (but this last aspect may not always be part of local audit requirements).

The audit firm maintains a master file on the company and in this is collated all the relevant information necessary for the annual audit. This includes items left outstanding from the previous audit for subsequent management action and an analysis of the company's systems. When starting a new audit, the first requirement is to check the accuracy of the systems chart. Having established the current system and internal controls in place, the next step is to check how well these work. This is done by sampling the transactions of a particular (short) period. If this checking reveals that the internal control system is correctly applied, the auditor can go on to carry out verifications of things like inventory valuations, bank reconciliations (comparing the client's bank records with the statements provided by the bank), customer accounts, supplier accounts and so on. Only if the internal control system is thought to be ineffective, will more detailed checking be done.

Once satisfied with the database, the auditor looks at the financial statements and the interpretation of the database that has been made in these. The nature of the company's business does not necessarily change every year, so there need not be any queries at this point, but as new transactions appear, so there may well be disagreement about how these are represented. Such disagreements are usually resolved more or less amicably between the audit staff and the chief accountant, but occasionally there can be substantial disagreement – usually because a change in treatment would diminish profits (we will be looking at cases throughout this book). In such circumstances things can be very tense and large companies have been known to bring in legal opinion, or consult another firm of auditors, when trying to insist on their view of the financial statements. The auditor can, in some countries, even be replaced, but this generally sends a bad signal to the market. The auditor's only threat is to refuse to sign the audit report at all (very extreme) or (more normally) to say that they will be obliged to include a reservation in their audit report which details the matter in dispute.

In the past the public report of the auditor was formulaic and followed industry guidelines. The European Commission, among other bodies, has been trying to move towards a form of report that gives the reader more entity-specific information.

There is also usually a private report that is given to the management, and is known as a *management letter*. This, unlike the published audit report, does not follow any prescribed formula, but rather comments on the audit findings for the year, highlights potential areas of weakness and makes recommendations. This is something which the following year's audit will re-visit to see what action has been taken.

The conduct of the audit is regulated in three ways. First, the statutory audit, by definition, is mandated by a government statute (such as a company law or a commercial code) which will prescribe the objects of the audit and normally specify whether client confidentiality applies or not. In the second place, there will normally be a national professional association for auditors that will provide detailed audit regulations. Finally, the audit firm itself will have its own internal procedures which all of its staff follow – for reasons of efficiency and also to enable the firm's management to assess the degree of risk in the audit and similar issues.

The audit firm has a potentially difficult relationship with its client because, on the one hand, the outside world depends on the rigour of the audit firm to ensure that the company maintains proper accounts and gives adequate reports while, on the other, the audit firm is in effect appointed by the management, must negotiate with the management and, in many countries, hopes to be able to sell supplementary services such as tax advice and management consultancy to the audit client. This problem is part of the issue of *auditor independence*. Regulators are concerned that, since auditors are at the front line of corporate regulation, they should be independent of management and provide an appropriate control on management. Other aspects of the independence issue include restrictions on employment of former audit firm employees by the client and the necessity of auditor partner rotation over time.

Companies listed on the US stock markets are obliged to appoint an *audit committee* whose members liaise with the statutory auditors. The Sarbanes–Oxley Act requires that all members of the audit committee are independent. The company should also disclose whether or not the audit committee includes at least one member who is a financial expert. The idea is that the audit committee provides a knowledgeable forum free from the influence of operating management where shareholder representatives can discuss audit problems. SOX even requires that the audit committee appoint the firm of external auditors. The role of the audit committee is growing in a context where society is becoming more and more concerned with corporate governance issues.

COMPANY REPORT

NESTLÉ

Report of the Statutory Auditor on the Consolidated Financial Statements to the General Meeting of Nestlé S.A.

Opinion
We have audited the consolidated financial statements of Nestlé S.A. and its subsidiaries (the Group), which comprise the consolidated balance sheet as at 31 December 2017, the consolidated income statement, consolidated statement of comprehensive income, consolidated statement of changes in equity and consolidated statement of cash flows for the year then ended, and notes to the consolidated financial statements, including a summary of significant accounting policies.

In our opinion the consolidated financial statements (pages 64 to 142) give a true and fair view of the consolidated financial position of the Group as at 31 December 2017, and its consolidated financial performance and its consolidated cash flows for the year then ended in accordance with International Financial Reporting Standards (IFRS) and comply with Swiss law.

Basis for opinion

We conducted our audit in accordance with Swiss law, International Standards on Auditing (ISAs) and Swiss Auditing Standards. Our responsibilities under those provisions and standards are further described in the Auditor's Responsibilities for the Audit of the Consolidated Financial Statements section of our report. We are independent of the Group in accordance with the provisions of Swiss law and the requirements of the Swiss audit profession, as well as the IESBA Code of Ethics for Professional Accountants, and we have fulfilled our other ethical responsibilities in accordance with these requirements.

We believe that the audit evidence we have obtained is sufficient and appropriate to provide a basis for our opinion.

Other information in the annual report

The Board of Directors is responsible for the other information in the annual report. The other information comprises all information included in the annual report, but does not include the consolidated financial statements, the stand-alone financial statements of the Company, the compensation report and our auditor's reports thereon.

Our opinion on the consolidated financial statements does not cover the other information in the annual report and we do not express any form of assurance conclusion thereon.

In connection with our audit of the consolidated financial statements, our responsibility is to read the other information in the annual report and, in doing so, consider whether the other information is materially inconsistent with the consolidated financial statements or our knowledge obtained in the audit, or otherwise appears to be materially misstated. If, based on the work we have performed, we conclude that there is a material misstatement of this other information, we are required to report that fact. We have nothing to report in this regard.

Responsibility of the Board of Directors for the consolidated financial statements

The Board of Directors is responsible for the preparation of the consolidated financial statements that give a true and fair view in accordance with IFRS Standards and the provisions of Swiss law, and for such internal control as the Board of Directors determines is necessary to enable the preparation of consolidated financial statements that are free from material misstatement, whether due to fraud or error.

In preparing the consolidated financial statements, the Board of Directors is responsible for assessing the Group's ability to continue as a going concern, disclosing, as applicable, matters related to going concern and using the going concern basis of accounting unless the Board of Directors either intends to liquidate the Group or to cease operations, or has no realistic alternative but to do so.

Auditor's responsibilities for the audit of the consolidated financial statements

Our objectives are to obtain reasonable assurance about whether the consolidated financial statements as a whole are free from material misstatement, whether due to fraud or error, and to issue an auditor's report that includes our opinion. Reasonable assurance is a high level of assurance, but is not a guarantee that an audit conducted in accordance with Swiss law, ISAs and Swiss Auditing Standards will always detect a material misstatement when it exists. Misstatements can arise from fraud or error and are considered material if, individually or in the aggregate, they could reasonably be expected to influence the economic decisions of users taken on the basis of these consolidated financial statements.

(Continued)

As part of an audit in accordance with Swiss law, ISAs and Swiss Auditing Standards, we exercise professional judgment and maintain professional scepticism throughout the audit. We also:

- Identify and assess the risks of material misstatement of the consolidated financial statements, whether due to fraud or error, design and perform audit procedures responsive to those risks, and obtain audit evidence that is sufficient and appropriate to provide a basis for our opinion. The risk of not detecting a material misstatement resulting from fraud is higher than for one resulting from error, as fraud may involve collusion, forgery, intentional omissions, misrepresentations, or the override of internal control.
- Obtain an understanding of internal control relevant to the audit in order to design audit procedures that are appropriate in the circumstances, but not for the purpose of expressing an opinion on the effectiveness of the Group's internal control.
- Evaluate the appropriateness of accounting policies used and the reasonableness of accounting estimates and related disclosures made.
- Conclude on the appropriateness of the Board of Directors' use of the going concern basis of accounting and, based on the audit evidence obtained, whether a material uncertainty exists related to events or conditions that may cast significant doubt on the Group's ability to continue as a going concern, if we conclude that a material uncertainty exists, we are required to draw attention in our auditor's report to the related disclosures in the consolidated financial statements or, if such disclosures are inadequate, to modify our opinion. Our conclusions are based on the audit evidence obtained up to the date of our auditor's report. However, future events or conditions may cause the Group to cease to continue as a going concern.
- Evaluate the overall presentation, structure and content of the consolidated financial statements, including the disclosures, and whether the consolidated financial statements represent the underlying transactions and events in a manner that achieves fair presentation.
- Obtain sufficient appropriate audit evidence regarding the financial information of the entities or business activities within the Group to express an opinion on the consolidated financial statements. We are responsible for the direction, supervision and performance of the Group audit. We remain solely responsible for our audit opinion.

We communicate with the Board of Directors or its relevant committee regarding, among other matters, the planned scope and timing of the audit and significant audit findings, including any significant deficiencies in internal control that we identify during our audit.

We also provide the Board of Directors or its relevant committee with a statement that we have complied with relevant ethical requirements regarding independence, and to communicate with them all relationships and other matters that may reasonably be thought to bear on our independence, and where applicable, related safeguards.

From the matters communicated with the Board of Directors or its relevant committee, we determine those matters that were of most significance in the audit of the consolidated financial statements of the current period and are therefore the key audit matters. We describe these matters in our auditor's report, unless law or regulation precludes public disclosure about the matter or when, in extremely rare circumstances, we determine that a matter should not be communicated in our report because the adverse consequences of doing so would reasonably be expected to outweigh the public interest benefits of such communication.

Report on other legal and regulatory requirements

In accordance with article 728a para. 1 item 3 CO and the Swiss Auditing Standard 890, we confirm that an internal control system exists, which has been designed for the preparation of consolidated financial statements according to the instructions of the Board of Directors.

We recommend that the consolidated financial statements submitted to you be approved.

KPMG SA
Geneva, 14 February 2018

Source: Nestlé, Financial Statements, 2017

Corporate governance

In recent years, more and more government and shareholder attention has been given to the question of how management's freedom of action may be limited by outside interests – a topic known as *corporate governance*. Corporate governance issues arise whenever ownership of a company is separated from its management. There are many issues in this area which cause concern to investors and governments. Abuses by management are not necessarily widespread, but sometimes the remuneration of top executives seems out of all proportion to the effort put in; sometimes managers are either implicated in or unaware of frauds taking place within the company, or indeed of risk-taking by middle management. Some company bosses are thought to be able to operate virtually as dictators, with no effective monitoring of their activity within the company.

Criticism in this area, articulated for example in the financial press, has produced a number of different outcomes. At a general level, most companies are not insensitive to the views of the outside world and make at least a token response by disclosing in their annual report some details of their activities in sensitive areas. Notably, companies are increasingly making voluntary disclosures about their interaction with the environment, their involvement with their employees and the wider community, and their policy on issues such as the use of child labour by subcontractors. In addition, institutional investors such as insurance companies and pension funds, increasingly provide a checklist of corporate governance matters to the directors of the companies in which they plan to invest. Only if the board can satisfy them on these points will they go ahead and make an investment.

Many countries have specific rules, regulations and public guidance on corporate governance. Governance regimes tend to differ due to historical, economic and cultural influences. However, with the emergence of global markets national governance structures came under greater public scrutiny and these pressures resulted in a number of government or quasi-official reports (Viénot I and II in France, Cromme in Germany, from Cadbury to Higgs in the UK, OECD) and, more recently, in somewhat converging codes of conduct in most countries that tend to recommend the installation of supplementary controls on management and the distancing of management from the audit. The first plank of such an approach calls for companies to appoint a *chairman who is not also the chief executive*, and for the board to include 'non-executive' or *independent directors* who can bring experience and independence to the boardroom. The *non-executive directors*, aside from normal board meetings, are then called on to form at least two key committees: the *compensation committee* (which fixes executives' pay packages) and the *audit committee*. The audit committee should provide a forum in which external and internal auditors can discuss audit issues without line management being present. Sometimes there exists a third committee, the *nomination committee*, charged with the responsibility of proposing to the board any new executive or non-executive directors. It is generally recommended that a majority of the nomination committee members are non-executive directors.

The basic idea is that the non-executive directors have no role in the day-to-day running of the company, but are there to safeguard investors' interests and to provide ethical controls. Of course, for this to work, the individuals must be experienced in business matters and be willing to take a strong line within the board. It is not clear that this always works, not least because appointment of non-executive directors generally falls to the chairman or chief executive. However, in principle, the non-executives should be in a position to determine what a fair pay package is for senior executives by reference to market conditions. Equally, they should provide some protection for staff who wish to express concerns in the context of internal controls and audit. A problem frequently encountered in large companies is that even if staff are aware that some fraud or abuse is taking place, they are reluctant to report it because they fear that no action will be taken, but their position will be made untenable. The existence of an audit committee should make it possible for staff to raise issues that are passed up the audit chain and not discussed with operational management until an investigation has taken place.

In some countries, notably Germany and the Netherlands, large companies have a *two-tier board system* where a management board runs the company on a day-to-day basis, but this reports to a supervisory board. The supervisory board represents investors and staff, receives regular reports on corporate activity and can replace the management board if they wish.

In the USA, the Sarbanes–Oxley Act has been the main initiative to strengthen corporate governance after the Enron collapse. The SOX created the Public Company Accounting Oversight Board (PCAOB), strengthened auditor independence rules, increased accountability of company officers and directors, mandated top management to take responsibility for the company's internal control system, enhanced the quality of financial reporting and considerably increased white-collar crime penalties. We will come back to these developments in Chapter 16.

In Europe, the European Commission has made a number of initiatives to enhance corporate governance. In October 2004 it established the European Corporate Governance forum to encourage the co-ordination and convergence of national codes of corporate governance through regular high-level meetings. It increasingly mandates the disclosure of non-financial information in the annual report, particularly in the area of the relations between multinational companies and host states where subsidiaries do business.

The accounting profession

It is worth spending a few moments to look at the accounting profession as such. In the anglophone world, we tend to use the terms 'accountant' and 'auditor' interchangeably, and we tend not to distinguish very clearly between those people who operate independent public accounting firms and those who work for companies or in the public sector. Not the least reason for this is that there is no clear worldwide definition of what an accountant does and, indeed, the training and licensing arrangements and type of work done vary somewhat from country to country. For our purposes we will distinguish between the following categories:

1. Independent auditor
2. Independent accountant
3. Company accountant.

Independent auditors are specialists who work in audit firms and are licensed either directly or indirectly by the government to carry out the *statutory audit* (i.e. independent audit required by company law) of large companies. An individual who works in this way has generally completed a university degree and then studied for professional exams. These exams are typically under the supervision of a professional organization (e.g. American Institute of Certified Public Accountants) and a candidate must also spend at least three years as a student in a public auditing firm. In some countries, such as the UK, success in the professional examination, allied with the necessary practical experience, confers an auditing licence automatically and this is issued by the professional body. In other countries (e.g. Germany), the auditor must register with a government supervisory body.

In fact, many auditors leave public practice fairly early in their careers, either to undertake wider management careers or to work full time for a company. In anglophone countries, such accountants may well remain members of their professional body, but in many continental European countries, membership is linked to public practice and anyone leaving public practice leaves their professional body at the same time. This leads to professional bodies being quite different in size and nature. The Institut der Wirtschaftsprüfer (the only body for auditors of public companies in Germany) has approximately 18,000 members, while the Association of Chartered Certified Accountants (one of four bodies in the UK whose members may work as auditors) has more than 100,000 members.

The precise nature of the audit and the relationship between auditor and client vary from place to place. In France, the auditor has a public responsibility to report to the public prosecutor any evidence of a client's failure to comply with the law discovered during the audit. However, in most countries, the company's information must be kept confidential by the auditor. There are also differences as to what the auditor is commenting on in the audit report – sometimes it is simply conformity with local accounting rules, while sometimes the auditor is saying that the picture of the company given by the annual financial statements is not misleading. This difference is quite important since the user of the financial statements is being offered a different level of reassurance about the information.

It is relatively rare for audit firms to offer only an audit service, although France and Germany, in particular, say that the auditor, for reasons of independence, may only provide audit services to an audit client, even if they may offer other services to non-audit clients. Anglo-Saxon audit firms generally used to offer a wide range of consulting services to their audit clients and, indeed, provision of the audit was seen by some as the means of access to selling a wide range of consulting services. The Sarbanes–Oxley Act of 2002 put a stop to these practices, by prohibiting audit firms from providing a wide range of non-audit services to audit clients.

Independent accountants are a related branch of the profession. In some countries, a network of firms has developed that offer accounting services to (generally small) businesses. In France, there are, for example, the Experts Comptables and, in Germany, the Steuerberater. These firms specifically do not offer statutory audit for large companies and their principal role is in providing the accounting function for companies that are either too small to have an in-house service or that prefer to outsource the function. They may also provide tax and general business advice.

Company accountant, finally, is a function not necessarily covered by any professional organization, and indeed many company accountants do not have any specific accounting training. At the management end of company accounting, the larger companies tend to engage former auditors or others with specialized professional training to run their accounting function. However, it is commonplace in both North America and continental Europe for people to study business at university, perhaps with an accounting specialization, and then go directly into a company and work in the accounting, internal audit and finance areas, building up a store of practical experience in that way.

Professional accounting bodies exist in most countries, but their nature may vary quite a lot depending on the nature of the economy within which they operate. In the developed world, the standards of professional exams for auditors are comparable, and indeed in the EU are the subject of a harmonization statute (the EU Audit Directive, last updated in 2014), but in the developing world and in countries in transition to a market economy this is not necessarily so. Not all professional bodies have examination requirements for entry and not all are independent associations. For example, the Chinese Institute of Certified Public Accountants is an agency of the Chinese Ministry of Finance.

There are some regional bodies to which national bodies may belong, such as the Fédération des Experts Comptables Européens (now known as Accountancy Europe) or the Confederation of Asian and Pacific Accountants (CAPA). Finally there is, at a world level, the International Federation of Accountants (IFAC) which represents the profession worldwide and issues auditing standards and public sector accounting standards, as well as providing guidance on education and ethical matters.

Summary

In this chapter, we have looked at the functioning of the company accounting unit and seen that its objectives are to provide accurate financial data about the company but also to provide controls that prevent the possibility of fraud. The company runs a permanent accounting database into which all transactions are recorded, processed and summarized, and from which one may at any point produce reports about the company's performance and financial position. The processing of transactions follows the same principles irrespective of whether it is computerized or not, but computerized accounting information systems are widespread and permit efficient accounting and sophisticated analysis.

In larger companies, the accounting information system is an integral part of a 'system of internal control', which operates to safeguard assets, improve the reliability of accounting data, ensure compliance with applicable laws and contractual obligations and promote operational efficiencies. This system of internal control is usually backed up by an 'internal audit' function: dedicated staff checking that internal controls are applied and remain effective. Finally, all public companies, and many private ones, are subject to independent audit by external auditors. These professionals also rely on the internal control system and run sample checks on it in order to form an opinion on the accuracy of the company's financial records. They also give an opinion on the validity of the annual financial statements.

The external audit is a major part of a wider system of corporate governance, through which investors and other interested parties aim to monitor and control the behaviour of corporate managers, a subject that we will re-visit later in the book. This involves the use of disclosures, adherence to codes of behaviour and the use of board members who represent investor interests. The term 'accountant' or 'auditor' is used fairly freely and there are a number of professional structures and education patterns that occur in different countries. Generally, statutory auditors must be licensed by government and have completed suitable professional training and minimum periods of internship.

Discussion questions

1. What are the objectives that a company's accounting department should be aiming to achieve?
2. How is the company's accounting database organized and from where does it get its data?
3. How does the COSO report approach a 'system of internal control'?
4. Explain the difference between preventive, detective and corrective controls.
5. What is the relationship between internal control and internal audit?
6. What is the purpose of external audit, and who carries this out?

PART 2

Basic financial statements

Part 2 goes through the main techniques that are used to prepare the basic financial statements – the statement of profit or loss (income statement/profit and loss account) and the statement of financial position (balance sheet) – of individual companies. These are the core statements of a company's financial reporting.

Accounting concepts and the balance sheet equation

Chapter 3 introduces two of the main financial statements: the statement of profit or loss (income statement/profit and loss account) and the statement of financial position (balance sheet). It then goes on to explain the basic assumptions and conventions that are applied to financial accounting and that therefore provide the framework that both limits and informs accounting information. The chapter introduces the balance sheet equation, which represents the fundamental logic on which accounting is based. We will end this chapter with a closer look at how the International Accounting Standards Board (the Board) defines the basic components of a company's financial position and financial performance.

Chapter structure

- Introduction
- The balance sheet does not purport to show what the company is worth
- Company characteristics affecting financial reporting behaviour
- Content of the core financial statements
- The basics of a financial accounting system
- Generally accepted accounting principles
- Conventional measurement bases
- Accounting for transactions
- Elements of financial statements: definitions, recognition and measurement criteria

- ■ Summary
- ■ Discussion questions
- ■ Assignments

Introduction

In general terms, the *annual financial statements* produced by a business for external consumption (also known as the *annual accounts*) are the single public source of economic data on the company and they represent a prime form of communication between the company and its external stakeholders. The statements of larger companies are usually subject to verification by external experts (auditors) and are made available to shareholders. They form the starting point for corporate income tax assessment. They are usually of prime interest to all main business partners: banks, other lenders, suppliers of goods and services, major customers. They are often, particularly in large companies, an important device used to monitor contracts (bank covenants, profit shares in joint ventures, employee bonuses, royalties).

In most European jurisdictions, there is a requirement for the financial statements to be filed at a public registry so that, even if the company does not provide a copy of the financial statements directly to an interested party, access to them is still available (for example, in the UK, there is a single government office that holds all company files; in Belgium, they are held by the Banque Nationale de Belgique, but in Switzerland, access is restricted; while in Germany, many small and medium-sized companies deliberately do not file their financial statements – the fine is minimal). In the USA, the Securities and Exchange Commission (SEC) maintains a public register of listed companies, but there is no central filing system for private companies.

Listed companies usually put their financial statements on their website (in html or pdf format) – indeed, they see it as a major public relations document – while small, privately owned companies will give up information only when the law or their business interest decrees it.

Historically, the *balance sheet* and *the statement of profit or loss* have been the key financial statements, even though a modern corporation is now expected to publish a statement of financial position (balance sheet), a statement of profit or loss and other comprehensive income (statement of comprehensive income), a statement of changes in equity, a statement of cash flows and notes to the accounts. The statement of profit or loss is undergoing a period of change and the standard-setter now prefers to refer to a 'statement of profit or loss and other comprehensive income' (or, alternatively, 'statement of comprehensive income') as a kind of expanded statement of financial performance. This includes not only the results of operations as in an ordinary profit and loss account, but also changes in economic measurements based on current values (reported as 'other comprehensive income'). We will deal with that in Part 4 of this book, and, for the time being, will refer only to the more traditional statement of profit or loss. Indeed, at this point in the book, we will concentrate only on the balance sheet and the profit and loss account, since these are at the heart of the financial reporting system.

The statement of profit or loss sets out the result of the company's business operations for the accounting period (revenues less expenses for the period), while the balance sheet shows, at a given date, the company's financial position: what economic resources (assets), such as factories, equipment, inventory, cash and so on, the company controls and where the company's finance comes from (shareholders, banks, trade creditors). As providers of funds, the sources of finance represent claims against the company (equity claims and liabilities) and these are (by definition) equal to the company's assets.

The balance sheet does not purport to show what the company is worth

This issue crops up from time to time in MBA courses and is obviously a key question if one's main interest in looking at the annual financial statements is to form an opinion on the economic health and prospects of the company. Usually, when we ask what a company is 'worth', this means what would we have to pay to acquire the company and this, in turn, is linked to the value of the future benefits that one would gain by buying the company. If Company X will deliver a dividend (or net positive cash flow) of €10,000 a year for 10 years, a first estimate of its total value over 10 years is €100,000. Since, if you buy the company, you cannot enjoy all the benefits at once, you would normally be willing to pay less than €100,000 for it – you would deduct a discount to factor in the time value of money and the riskiness of the estimated cash flows. The price agreed is a compromise between the value to the purchaser and what the seller is willing to sell for. In fact, takeover situations typically arise because Company A believes that it can reorganize Company X (maybe there are savings to be made by combining operations) and deliver more than €10,000 a year from it. In this case, the owners of Company X will value it on the basis of €10,000 a year but Company A will make a bid at a higher price, so there is a basis for a deal.

The point is that *company value*, from a market perspective, is (a) based on *future* earnings and (b) these earnings may well be different in different situations. Financial statements give certain economic information about a company's *past* activities, drawn up according to a fairly flexible set of rules. They give partial information, and anyone wanting to make serious use of the statements needs to know (a) what are the rules, (b) to what extent are they flexible, and (c) how this impacts on interpretation of the information.

On top of that, anyone looking across national boundaries needs to know whether the company uses International Financial Reporting Standards (IFRS Standards) (figures comparable with other companies internationally), or whether it is using national accounting principles. If the latter is the case, one needs to know how the rules differ from one jurisdiction to another, where different flexibilities arise and so forth (which is much more complicated and is one reason why companies prefer IFRS Standards). Once the analyst has decoded the accounting information, then he or she can make a forecast of future earnings from that information about past performance (and related external factors) and come to a view about the company's worth.

Company characteristics affecting financial reporting behaviour

This brings us to another major point: while the bulk of accounting rules for commercial companies are the same in all developed countries, there are differences at a detailed level from one country to another (as discussed in Chapter 1). Also, the way the rules are applied may differ from one company to another within the same country. While the way companies record and track their transactions in their accounting systems does not vary substantially, the way these are presented in annual financial statements may be subject to significant variations. The rush to use IFRS Standards for listed companies is motivated by a desire to get away from the uncertainties caused by national differences.

However, differences in the accounting rule base used are not the only source of difference in financial statements. Looking first at companies within one country, there are many differences that impact on financial reporting, such as the nature of their ownership, their objectives, their legal form and their size.

Nature of ownership

Most European market economies are in fact mixed economies, with a large slice of activity in the hands of commercial companies but also with a significant element owned by the State. Where a business is owned by the State, its management may have different objectives from those of an ordinary commercial concern, for example, it may not be politically acceptable to show too much profit or the government may want to fatten the company up for privatization. State-owned enterprises may not operate under the same regulations as private sector firms.

In the private sector, it is easy to see two extremes: the large, multinational company listed on several stock exchanges and the small company owned entirely by its chief executive. A company whose securities are traded on the capital markets has a major concern in terms of maintaining the buoyancy of the share price and this is likely to lead the company either to release good news as soon as possible and hide bad news as long as possible, or to make an attempt to smooth profits so that the company appears to go from one successful year to another in a reliable progression. For these companies the capital market is a privileged user of their financial information and the rules are likely to be applied by such companies in ways that will influence the market reaction. The management of the company and its owners are separate and distinct from each other, and the financial statements play a significant role in the conduct of that relationship.

The small company, at the other extreme, has no external shareholders to whom to report. The manager is also the main shareholder and so the reporting pressures are likely to be different. Such a manager might be more concerned about keeping reported profits as low as possible in order to reduce tax liability. Or, if it is a family company, the manager may want to keep profits low so that relatives will not demand high dividends and cash can be kept in the business to finance expansion.

These are archetypes and there exist many variants. There are, for example, large, family-owned companies that are not listed on stock exchanges (e.g. IKEA, Bosch, Mars). There is a particularly large number of these in Germany and Switzerland and this gives rise to another issue, which is the extent to which the community calls for businesses of significant economic size to make financial disclosures purely because their size may cause them to impact on public interest.

Managerial objectives

The nature of a company's ownership generally impacts on its objectives. A State or other public sector entity probably has objectives other than profit generation, a listed company may want to angle towards maximizing declared short-term profits (or not – it depends on the culture of the capital markets in which it operates), a privately held company might want to minimize profits in order to minimize tax and dividends. By the same token, a privately held company that is planning to be listed on the capital markets in the future might choose to maximize profits. A commercial company listed on stock exchanges (a publicly held company) might be looking for long-term growth and be quite willing to take low profits while it builds market share. So while ownership and objectives are often closely interlinked, this is not always the case.

 WHY GLOBAL FINANCIAL REPORTING STANDARDS FOR SMALL AND MEDIUM-SIZED ENTERPRISES? *(extracts)*

BC36 Global financial reporting standards, applied consistently, enhance the comparability of financial information. Accounting differences can obscure the comparisons that investors, lenders and others make. By resulting in the presentation of high quality comparable financial information, high quality global financial reporting standards improve the efficiency of allocation and the pricing of capital. This benefits not only those who provide debt or equity capital but also those entities that seek capital because it reduces their compliance costs and removes uncertainties that affect their cost of capital. Global standards also improve consistency in audit quality and facilitate education and training.

BC37 The benefits of global financial reporting standards are not limited to entities whose securities are traded in public capital markets. In the Board's judgement, SMEs – and those who use their financial statements – can benefit from a common set of accounting standards. SMEs' financial statements that are comparable from one country to the next are needed for the following reasons:

(a) Financial institutions make loans across borders and operate multinationally. In most jurisdictions, over half of all SMEs, including the very small ones, have bank loans. Bankers rely on financial statements in making lending decisions and in establishing terms and interest rates.

(b) Vendors want to evaluate the financial health of buyers in other countries before they sell goods or services on credit.

(c) Credit rating agencies try to develop ratings uniformly across borders. Similarly, banks and other institutions that operate across borders often develop ratings in a manner similar to credit rating agencies. Reported financial figures are crucial to the rating process.

(d) Many SMEs have overseas suppliers and use a supplier's financial statements to assess the prospects of a viable long-term business relationship.

(e) Venture capital firms provide funding to SMEs across borders.

(f) Many SMEs have outside investors who are not involved in the day-to-day management of the entity. Global accounting standards for general purpose financial statements and the resulting comparability are especially important when those outside investors are located in a different jurisdiction from the entity and when they have interests in other SMEs.

Source: IFRS for SMEs Standard, Basis for Conclusions, July 2009

Nature of activity

Company activity is another variable affecting financial reporting. This is at its most obvious in regulations that affect banks and insurance companies. All jurisdictions have separate regulatory mechanisms for the accounting and disclosure requirements for financial institutions. These may relate to requirements for ordinary commercial companies (the European Union (EU) Accounting Directive – a major accounting statute of the European Union – has banking and insurance variants) but usually go beyond them because of the different nature of the assets and liabilities of such companies and the profound effects on society of the failure of financial institutions. In this book, we shall concentrate on the financial statements of ordinary commercial companies.

Legal form

Another significant variable in financial reporting within most countries is that of legal form. The major difference is generally between limited liability companies and entities that do not enjoy limited liability. For example, the EU Accounting Directive is based on legal form (and then size). Limited liability companies are those whose owners risk only the capital they put into a company – if the company makes a loss, the owners cannot be pursued for more money than they originally agreed to subscribe. Such limited liability vehicles are split in the EU Accounting Directive between public limited companies (which issue shares of equal value and may be listed on stock exchanges), such as the Aktiengesellschaft in Germany or the Société Anonyme in France, and private limited companies (Gesellschaft mit beschränkter Haftung, Société à responsabilité limitée, etc.) whose capital cannot be publicly traded and which do not necessarily issue shares as such.

In anglophone countries, absence of limited liability may also go with absence of regulation in financial reporting terms. In Britain, there are large auditing and consultancy firms employing thousands of people and with sales running into millions of pounds sterling that are constituted as partnerships where partners are personally liable for the full amount of all debts of the partnership, but there is no legal obligation to publish any accounts. The Church of England is probably the biggest landowner in the country, but publishes no financial statements.

Company size

In continental Europe, accounting regulations tend to run with the nature of the business (a commercial business follows the same basic accounting rules irrespective of size) but disclosures are modified according to size. The EU Accounting Directive recognizes four tiers of size, which are subject to change from time to time. These are:

- *Micro-entity* – must not exceed two out of the following: sales €0.7m, total assets €0.35m, number of employees 10.
- *Small company* – must not exceed two out of the following: sales €8.0m, total assets €4.0m, number of employees 50.
- *Medium-sized company* – must not exceed two out of the following: sales €40.0m, total assets €20.0m, number of employees 250.
- *Large company* – any listed entity, and all that exceed medium-size criteria.

Small companies may benefit from limited public disclosure and freedom from audit. These size criteria are built into reporting regulations within the EU and outside it. There is nothing self-evidently 'right' about the EU's criteria, but they do give recognition to the idea that small, privately held companies need not disclose as much as large companies, which is a view expressed in many countries, even if the precise cut-off between 'small' and 'not small' is necessarily arbitrary.

In overall terms, it is true to say that published financial statements are aimed at a wide range of potential users, including (actual or potential) shareholders, lenders, trade suppliers, tax authorities, customers, employees, etc. However, the company only provides one, general-purpose set of financial statements but where accounting rules provide any choices (and there may be many instances depending on the accounting standards used) different companies will choose measurements that give priority to different subsets of users. Some will maximize profit, others will minimize it and so on. These factors have to be considered when evaluating any particular company's financial statements.

Content of the core financial statements

The key financial reporting process involves preparing an annual statement of profit or loss and a statement of financial position (balance sheet). The statement of profit or loss brings together aggregated information about a company's financial performance during a 12-month period (most often, but not necessarily, the calendar year). The balance sheet shows the state of the company's financial position at the end of that period. Both statements are usually published with comparative data from the previous year (Figure 3.1).

Figure 3.1 Time periods covered by the statement of financial position and statement of profit or loss

The statement of profit or loss might be said to be reporting a 'flow' (business activities during a period), while the balance sheet is essentially a status report – a static inventory of the company's financial position according to two dimensions (the company's economic resources and the claims against the company) at a given moment (a 'snapshot' of an instant in time).

While the published data usually only show two years (although, in the USA, the SEC asks for three years of statements of profit or loss for publicly listed companies), analysts need data for a longer time scale and therefore build up collections of annual reports or use inputs from commercial company data services so that they can look at five and 10-year runs of data and get a wider picture of the progression of a company's economic state.

Obviously, we are going to look in some detail at the content of these statements during this course. However, the intention here is just to introduce them and you should concentrate on the broad lines and picking up the vocabulary.

Statement of profit or loss

The structure of a statement of profit or loss is as follows:

Statement of profit or loss for period 20X1

	€'000	
Sales (revenue)		5,356
Raw materials	1,739	
Salaries and wages	783	
Depreciation expense	462	
External services	873	(3,857)
Profit before interest and tax		1,499
Interest		(362)
Profit before tax		1,137
Taxation		(384)
Profit for the period, available for shareholders		753

You can see that this format can be split into three sections:

1. Operating result ('Profit before interest and tax')
2. Returns to providers of loan finance ('Interest')
3. Returns to government ('Taxation').

Looking at the operating result section, the approach to expenses shown in this format is known as the *expenses by nature* approach: it shows different types of input and outputs of the company's activities and enables the analyst to calculate the value added by the company in transforming raw materials into finished goods (assuming it is a manufacturing company) and selling them to outside parties. This is the most common approach in continental Europe.

The alternative approach to presenting operating performance data is that used more often in the UK and USA, which splits expenses not by type of expense, but by the activity to which the expense was assigned (in the technical jargon referred to as *expenses by function* approach). The Anglo-Saxon style of format looks like this:

Statement of profit or loss for period 20X1

		€'000
Sales (revenue)		5,356
Cost of sales		(2,601)
Gross profit (margin)		2,755
Distribution costs	382	
Administrative expenses	874	(1,256)
Profit before interest and tax		1,499
Interest		(362)
Profit before tax		1,137
Taxation		(384)
Profit for the period, available for shareholders		753

The function of expense method involves allocating raw materials, salaries, depreciation and other expenses against three functional areas: cost of sales (production), distribution (marketing, advertising, warehousing and other selling costs) and administration (accounting, legal, general management expenses). Note that the difference in format only relates to the operating result section. In our example, the 'operating' expenses are being presented in one of two ways:

Nature of expense	€'000	Function of expense	€'000
Raw materials	1,739	Cost of sales	2,601
Salaries and wages	783	Distribution costs	382
Depreciation expense	462	Administrative expenses	874
External services	873		
Total	3,857	Total	3,857

Opinions differ as to which is the more useful format for analysts. The IASB (the Board) says there is a case for providing both. Some would say that showing expenses by function enables a clearer comparison of efficiency between one company and another in the same industry. For example, if comparing two companies that both manufactured similar forklift trucks, you could compare cost of sales as a percentage of sales revenue to see which was manufacturing more cheaply – or which was making the larger difference (*gross profit margin*) between selling price and production cost. However, many companies do not have just a single product and so the opportunity for extremely precise comparisons does not usually occur. In addition, the allocation of expenses across functions must, up to a point, be subjective – if a canteen is used by both manufacturing and administrative staff, how much do you allocate to each function? Different companies might have different views. As information on the nature of expenses is generally perceived to be helpful for analysts when predicting future cash flows, the IASB requires additional disclosures in the notes on nature of expenses when the function of expense classification is elected for the statement of profit or loss.

In any event, this first part of the statement of profit or loss deals with a company's operating activities and provides a basis for comparisons with other years and other companies, irrespective of how those activities are financed. The lower part of the statement of profit or loss, by contrast, shows how the profit generated by the company's operations is split up:

- Interest (payment for the use of funds provided by loan (debt) finance)
- Taxation (tax on income due to government – society's share)
- Profit for the period, available for owners (to pay dividends to shareholders and to finance future expansion) and which is, in effect, the wealth generated by the company in that year.

The level of interest expenses is a function of the degree to which the company has been financed by debt. The taxes identified in both formats is tax on profits (or income) and does not include elements such as value-added tax (excluded from the statement of profit or loss), import taxes (included under relevant cost headings such as raw materials) and social security charges (included in salaries and wages).

Statement of financial position

The statement of financial position (balance sheet) presents a picture (as at the end of the financial year) of the company's economic resources (its 'assets' – factories, machinery, patents, inventories, cash, etc.) that it has acquired in the past and that have not yet been consumed within the business and, second, of how these assets have been financed. The presentation of information in the balance sheet follows precise rules, although the detail again may vary from one jurisdiction to another. The balance sheet can be presented according to two alternative formats. The format most commonly used is known as a *horizontal balance sheet* and looks as follows:

Assets €'000		*Equity and liabilities €'000*	
Intangible assets	943	Share capital	2,455
Tangible assets	1,988	Reserves	982
Investments	213	Retained earnings	947
Non-current (or 'fixed') assets	*3,144*	*Owners' equity*	*4,384*
Inventories	1,589	Provisions	520
Receivables	973	Financial liabilities	1,500
Cash and cash equivalents	881	Trade payables	359
Prepayments	176		
Total	6,763	Total	6,763

The left-hand side of the balance sheet shows the company's assets, split into those that will be used up over a period of more than one year (*non-current assets* or fixed/long-term assets) – typically physical plant (tangible assets), patents, brand names, licences (intangible assets) and investments (acquired shares of other companies or loans to other companies, often made for strategic purposes to cement a business relationship). The remaining assets (*current assets*) are usually constantly changing and are generated by the company's operating activities. Inventories are being diminished every day as sales take place, but also are being increased as new inventory is bought or manufactured. Amounts due from customers (receivables) would normally also be changing day-to-day: a company will normally always have inventories and receivables, but the individual items that make up the total are constantly changing. The amounts stated for each asset are expressed in currency units. Consequently, they include only those matters that can be measured in monetary terms.

The right-hand side of the balance sheet shows the company's sources of finance. This is split into *equity* (owners' equity) and *liabilities*. So, two broad sources of finance are distinguished: those related to the owners (equity) and those related to creditors (liabilities). As providers of funds, both groups have interests in the company and hold claims against the company, but with different priority. Figure 3.2 portrays the two dimensions of a company's financial position: the company's resources and its sources of finance; both views have to balance out by definition (balance sheet equation).

Figure 3.2 Balance sheet equation

Liabilities represent priority claims, while equity interests are residual claims against the company. From a legal point of view, the interests of the creditors precede those of the owners. Should the company go out of business, its assets would be liquidated (sold) and the proceeds from the sale of its assets would be used first to satisfy the claims of the creditors, while any remaining assets would go to the owners. That is the reason why owners are said to have a residual claim against (or residual interest in) the company's assets.

The equity section is further subdivided into *share capital* (contributed funds – money put into the company by the owners-shareholders, *shares* or, in the USA, *stock*) and accumulated profits attributable to owners (earned funds, *reserves* and *retained earnings*). Indeed, it is the owners who are exclusively entitled to the company's profit. So, equity has two origins:

- Funds contributed by the shareholders
- Funds generated by the company's own activities (accumulated profits, not distributed as dividends to the shareholders and in effect invested in the company for future growth).

Figure 3.3 presents equity as a residual interest and its two basic components: contributed funds and funds earned by the company through its operations.

Figure 3.3 Equity as residual interest

The liabilities section includes *provisions* (the company has a liability to pay something to third parties in the future, but the precise amount or timing is uncertain), *financial liabilities* (loans made by banks, the financial markets, etc.) and *trade liabilities* (*trade payables* or *trade creditors* – debts due to suppliers of goods or services). The liabilities will be further split into non-current and current liabilities according to whether the liabilities are expected to be paid after more than 12 months or earlier.

An alternative balance sheet format is the *vertical balance sheet*. This shows the same information, but presents it in a different way: liabilities are shown as a deduction from assets, and are split according to when they are due for payment, while the horizontal format shows them according to whether they are financing or trade related.

The balance sheet data presented in the vertical format would look like this:

	€'000	€'000
Intangible assets	943	
Tangible assets	1,988	
Investments	213	
Non-current assets		3,144
Inventories	1,589	
Receivables and prepaid	1,149	
Cash and cash equivalents	881	
Current assets	3,619	
Creditors due in less than one year	(359)	
Net current assets		3,260
Creditors due in more than one year		(1,500)
Provisions		(520)
		4,384
Equity		
Share capital		2,455
Reserves		982
Retained earnings		947
		4,384

In a published set of financial statements, the shareholders (and other users) receive not only this information, but several pages of explanatory notes which amplify the information and analyze certain categories such as non-current assets. Part of this extra detail is sometimes included in the basic statements themselves ('on the face of the accounts', as accountants would say). This additional information is regulated and many of the insights that an analyst wants from the annual financial statements are gained from a thorough review of the notes rather than of the primary statements.

For the most part, the same information is given in the balance sheet whichever way it is presented. The horizontal balance sheet focuses on presenting the company as a whole: total assets and the total sources of finance that have been used to acquire those assets. This is sometimes called an *entity approach*, treating the company as an economic whole and not distinguishing between different providers of finance. It also emphasizes that both dimensions of a company's financial position need to be 'in balance'. This is summed up as:

$$\text{Assets} = \text{Equity } and \text{ Liabilities}$$

This contrasts with the vertical presentation that focuses on the interest of the owners, and is known as a *proprietary approach*. This second approach says the owners' interest is measured by starting with the value of the assets and deducting loans and other payables from this amount:

$$\text{Assets } less \text{ Liabilities} = \text{Equity}$$

What is left is the owners' equity. This approach is often used in measuring personal wealth, but using a current market value: a family who bought a house with a loan might calculate (a) the current value of the house and (b) the amount of loan outstanding, and would arrive at the current value of their interest (equity) by deducting (b) from (a). Traditional accounting does not use current values, of course, so the value of the 'equity' number in the balance sheet does not equate to a current or market value of the company.

The general equilibrium between a company's resources and the claims against resources (sources of finance) is common to all accounting standards, but not necessarily the details of the component parts. What is included as assets or liabilities may differ among accounting standards. For example, not all assets under local accounting standards are accepted as assets under IFRS Standards (and vice versa). In this regard, the IASB *Conceptual Framework* provides strict definitions of assets, liabilities and equity. These definitions are important because an item should meet the criteria contained in the definitions to be eligible as an IFRS® balance sheet item. We will come back to these definitions later on in this chapter. At present neither the IASB nor the Financial Accounting Standards Board (FASB) prescribes a standardized format for the financial statements. They specify what minimum information must be given, but not how it should be presented.

The basics of a financial accounting system

In the next sections of this chapter we are going to review the basic accounting principles by which financial statements are prepared. We will do this by considering:

■ the underlying accounting assumptions and conventions

■ a review of the data recording process within companies

■ a further analysis of the balance sheet equation

■ a practical exercise in tracking transactions using the balance sheet equation

■ how simple financial statements are assembled.

Some knowledge of the accounts preparation process is essential for any sensible interpretation of the end product: the financial statements. The reason for this is that the statements are today highly technical documents that make many assumptions about the state of knowledge of the reader. It is quite impossible for an untrained reader to make much sense of financial statements. For example, just the technical terms (accruals? amortization? provisions?) immediately put the general reader at a disadvantage.

In fact, the problems go a lot further than that. Financial accounting does not purport to provide a comprehensive information system that gives a rounded economic picture of the company, even if the general public is inclined to believe that it does. The financial accounting system is based on a series of conventions that facilitate the recording and measurement process, but automatically limit the information taken into it. Preparers of financial statements use many estimates to contend with the uncertainties that surround business activities, such as the collectability of doubtful receivables, the probable useful life of plant and equipment and the outcome of pending litigation against the company. Such estimates will affect how the company's resources and commitments will be assessed and how revenue (income) and expenses will be allocated to one year rather than another. Overall, accounting is a subjective process, giving a partial picture that is highly conditioned by the accounting conventions used.

In a sense, the only absolutely accurate measure of profit is not available until the company has ceased to exist and its assets have been sold and its liabilities paid off – at that point you can calculate all the inputs to the business from its start-up to its final liquidation and arrive at a precise profit for its whole life. This, however, is not very useful in managing the company, and accounting is the art of estimating what proportion of the life profit of the company has been earned in a particular (usually 12-month) period. In order to arrive at this estimate the accountant has to make many assumptions about the future of the company and the uncertainties that surround it. While most accounting information is clear and exactly quantifiable, the published profit measure is essentially an estimate, not a matter of fact, and is subject to correction in subsequent years.

This does not mean that the information is of no use – quite the contrary – but it does mean that the user needs to be clear about what exactly is the nature of the information given in financial statements and therefore needs to understand the essentials of the underlying accounting process. It is rather like driving a car: you look most of the time at the road immediately ahead of you, because that is where the most important decisions lie. It is a convention that traffic driving in the opposite direction to you will use the opposite side of the road, so you need not watch that side so intently, even if, to have a complete picture, you should be looking at both sides, as well as behind you.

Accounting information is subject to constraints, which you need to know in order to interpret it and use it effectively, but it is also subject to estimate, which makes it flexible and open to manipulation.

Generally Accepted Accounting Principles

The foundation of financial accounting consists of a set of assumptions, conventions and rules referred to as *Generally Accepted Accounting Principles* or *GAAP*. According to the authority which establishes the principles, different GAAP sets can be discerned, like European GAAP (EU Accounting Directive) and related national GAAP, US GAAP and IFRS® GAAP. Although different GAAP sets have a lot of principles in common, significant degrees of freedom still exist. In this textbook, we use IFRS GAAP as our main frame of reference.

Most accounting regimes specify some general qualitative objective of financial accounting. The European Accounting Directive specifies two objectives: the financial statements should conform to GAAP and should give a *true and fair view* of the financial state of the company. IFRS Standards, however, require that the financial statements 'present fairly the financial position, financial performance and cash flows' (IAS 1 *Presentation of Financial Statements*). There is a UK legal opinion that says for the purposes of company law the IFRS Standards 'fairly present' means the same as 'give a true and fair view'.

The idea of a 'true and fair view' is a fundamental requirement of the European Accounting Directive. It is referred to in the audit opinion and derives from British accounting, but there is endless discussion about what it actually means – it has not been defined in law or by standard-setters. The unwary reader of financial statements might think that it means the financial statements are both true and fair, or perhaps that the financial statements are not misleading. This would be a dangerous position to take. The safer assumption is that the term merely means that the financial statements have been prepared by respecting all the technical rules in force at the time of their preparation. In theory, if application of the rules does not give a clear picture (or perhaps would be positively misleading), further explanation should be given in the notes.

If you think about it, for financial statements to be useful and comparable, they need to follow some kind of generally agreed rules. However, as soon as you start to measure according to pre-specified rules, you automatically limit what can be shown in the financial statements.

STANDARDS

The *Conceptual Framework for Financial Reporting* specifies the following:

1.2 The objective of general purpose financial reporting is to provide financial information about the reporting entity that is useful to existing and potential investors, lenders and other creditors in making decisions relating to providing resources to the entity. Those decisions involve decisions about:

(a) buying, selling or holding equity and debt instruments;
(b) providing or settling loans and other forms of credit; or
(c) exercising rights to vote on, or otherwise influence, management's actions that affect the use of the entity's economic resources.

Source: IASB, Conceptual Framework for Financial Reporting

For our purposes, you should be sceptical as to whether the existence of the true and fair view principle improves the quality of financial statements, and rely rather more heavily on the other European Accounting Directive requirement that the financial statements should use generally accepted accounting principles. The auditor's report will normally confirm that these have been followed. In the USA, the expression 'present fairly in accordance with GAAP' is to be interpreted in this sense.

The international rules actually confirm this pragmatic view. IAS 1 *Presentation of Financial Statements* puts forward the main premise that the application of IFRS Standards, with additional disclosure if necessary, is presumed to result in financial statements reflecting a fair presentation. Only in extremely rare circumstances in which management concludes that compliance with IFRS Standards would be so misleading that it would conflict with the objective of financial statements as specified in the *Conceptual Framework* (see extract), is a rebuttal of the basic full compliance assumption justified.

At a more applied level, financial accounting follows some key basic conventions:

- *Consistency*
- *Accrual basis*: accruals and related matching
- *Prudence*
- *Going concern*.

STANDARDS

 IAS 1 – PRESENTATION OF FINANCIAL STATEMENTS *(extracts)*

Fair presentation and compliance with IFRS Standards

15 Financial statements shall present fairly the financial position, financial performance and cash flows of an entity. Fair presentation requires the faithful representation of the effects of transactions, other events and conditions in accordance with the definitions and recognition criteria for assets, liabilities, income and expenses set out in the Framework. The application of IFRS Standards, with additional disclosure when necessary, is presumed to result in financial statements that achieve a fair presentation.

Source: IAS 1, Presentation of Financial Statements

Consistency

Consistency is fairly straightforward. It means that financial accounting practices should be used by a company consistently both from one year to another, and within the same year in relation to similar transactions.

Consistency helps to achieve *comparability*, an enhancing qualitative characteristic of financial information (see Chapter 1). It could be argued that, from an analyst's point of view, consistency is the most important characteristic needed in financial accounting. If the analyst is looking to put together several years' data to produce a forecast of future performance, each year needs to be prepared on a basis consistent with that in the other years. For predictive purposes, the rate and direction of change of the indicators is more important than their absolute values, so a set of indicators, even if only partial in terms of the overall economic picture, if it is produced consistently will provide useful information.

There may, however, be good reasons for a company to change financial accounting practices over time. Most jurisdictions require companies to explain any change in accounting methods in the notes to the financial statements and to provide, where a change takes place, alternative figures showing the effects of the change. However, there is often a grey area between, on the one hand, changing estimates or assumptions upon which allocations were based and, on the other hand, actually changing the accounting method.

For example, suppose it has been assumed that a certain piece of plant, costing €10m, will last for ten years and therefore its cost should be allocated against profits on the basis of €1m a year. After four years, the company decides that the plant will really last 20 years, so the annual charge goes down from €1m to €0.375m (spreading the remaining book value of €6m over the remaining useful life of 16 years). The retrospective annual charge of €0.5m goes further down to a prospective annual charge of €0.375m, since €4m have already been expensed in the first three years, while only €2m was appropriate under the new estimate. Generally, this manoeuvre would not be classified as a change in accounting policy, but only as a change in estimates, and would not call for any explanation in the notes, even though the profit in year five (and the following years) is inflated by the adjustment.

Consistency evidently has an important presentational dimension as well. IAS 1 *Presentation of Financial Statements* explicitly states that the presentation and classification of items in financial statements should be retained from one accounting period to the next. However, a significant change in the nature or scope of the operations of the company (for example through an acquisition, disposal or reorganization of operations) may justify a presentational change. In that case, comparative information must also be adapted on a consistent basis.

Accrual basis

Accruals is the name of the approach that distinguishes financial accounting from a simple record of cash transactions. The accruals convention is that accounting aims to depict business transactions and their effects on the company's resources and claims at the time they take place, rather than when cash changes hands. For example, a department store offers credit to its regular customers and is given credit by its suppliers. Suppose that the store agrees to take a special consignment of video cameras from a manufacturer. The cameras are delivered on 15 December. The store runs a special advertising campaign at 1 January. You go into the store on 10 January and buy a camera, charging it to your account. On 31 January, the store pays its camera supplier, and bills you. You settle your account on 26 February (see Figure 3.4).

Transactions:	15 December:	delivery by supplier to store
	10 January:	you buy camera
	31 January:	store pays supplier
	26 February:	you pay store

Figure 3.4   Sequence of trade transactions

Under a simple cash recording system there would be an inventory purchase on 31 January and a sale on 26 February, and yet we know that you actually went into the store and took the goods on 10 January. The accruals convention is that transactions are recorded as they take place, not only when there is cash involved. So the accruals system would log the incoming inventory on 15 December, the sale on 10 January, and so on. The *accruals basis of accounting* leads to financial statements that reflect not only information of past transactions involving the payment and receipt of cash, but also of obligations to pay cash in the future (arising when the new inventory is accounted for) and of resources that represent cash to be received in the future (recording a receivable when the sale is recognized on 10 January).

This brings us to the related principle of *matching*, or the simultaneous recognition of revenue and related expenses in the statement of profit or loss. This says that all costs and revenues associated with a particular transaction should be brought together when the sale takes place. This means that, in our example, when the store buys the inventory of cameras, they are treated as an asset (an item of value owned by the company) and shown in the balance sheet as inventory (not taken to the statement of profit or loss as an expense). Only when the individual camera is sold does it move from being inventory to being an expense. Otherwise, in the example, the expense would fall into December and the related revenue into January. If the store's financial year ended on 31 December, this would cause the first year's profit to be reduced and the second year's to be inflated. The matching principle requires us to put both revenue and expense in the same financial period (the one where the revenue was earned).

In the example, it is clear when each transaction takes place and there is no ambiguity about any of the transactions. However, there can be problems in this kind of area. For example, what if the camera turns out to be faulty and you return it, demanding your money back? Should the store not account for any sale until sufficient time has elapsed to be sure that the customer is satisfied? Ambiguities and uncertainties bring about conflicts with the next convention, that of prudence.

Prudence

Traditionally, the *prudence* convention requires that *revenues* (income) are only recognized in the financial statements when they are *certain*, while *expenses* should be recognized if they are *probable*. Related to this, revenues should only be recognized when *realized*, that is, when these are sufficiently concrete to be in cash or a form near to cash (an agreement to pay on which the company can go to court). Unrecoverable expenses, however, should be recognized even if not yet realized – for example, you have spent €5,000 working on a contract to design software for a client and you hear that the client may be having financial difficulties. *Matching* would require that you carry the costs forward (as a current asset) until you can invoice the client, but a prudent view would be to treat the work as a loss, because the client's ability to pay is open to question. This also has the effect of diminishing current year profit (and therefore tax), with the possibility of higher profit the following year. Tax management is mostly about deferring tax payments for as long as possible rather than escaping them altogether. While everyone would like to escape tax, if the accounts are accurate, this is generally not possible and the tax manager's objective is to defer tax as long as possible and thereby conserve the company's cash and reduce its financing needs.

At a theoretical level, there is a clear *conflict between the application of matching and that of prudence,* and the extent to which the one has priority over the other is one of the major differences in the application of accounting in national GAAP between one jurisdiction and another. Germany and Switzerland are famous for very prudent accounting (anticipating expenses, building secret reserves), while the UK is equally so for giving priority to the matching convention (deferring expenses, building hidden losses …).

At a practical level, the degree to which prudence is given a priority has also something to do with tax regulations. In the UK, tax rules only allow the recognition of an expense when that expense has become concrete – a prudent anticipation of an expense is disregarded for tax purposes, with the result that a company that follows very prudent accounting also appears to pay proportionately higher taxes. In France or Germany, some anticipation of expenses in the form of provisions is acceptable for tax, provided that it appears in the company accounts, thereby encouraging companies to be prudent in their accounting because that defers their taxes.

While *prudence* is a primary accounting convention in the EU Accounting Directive, its application in IFRS Standards is much more debated. The earlier standards will often reflect it, but the standard-setter now tends to the view that prudence in its traditional asymmetric interpretation ('asymmetric prudence' – losses would be recognized at an earlier stage than gains) would be inconsistent with the requirement that accounting information should be *neutral* (remember this to be essential for 'faithful representation', a fundamental qualitative characteristic of useful financial information). Tax considerations should also have much less impact under IFRS Standards than it often has on national GAAP.

In the *Conceptual Framework*, the meaning of prudence is restricted to an attitude of caution in the exercise of judgements when these are needed to arrive at estimates under conditions of uncertainty ('cautious prudence'). The framework warns that prudence should not lead to 'income smoothing', for example through the creation of undervalued assets or excessive provisions, deliberately understating assets or income and overstating liabilities or expenses.

Going concern

The going concern convention specifies that, in preparing the financial statements, it is assumed that the company will continue in business for the foreseeable future. This assumes that the company has no intention or need to liquidate or cease operations. This is a critical assumption because much of accrual accounting is based on allocating expenses over different future time periods, as we have already touched on. If the business is unlikely to be there in the future, this approach is not valid and prudence would require many items to be written off at once as valueless. This, of course, is often a bone of contention with auditors when a company whose financial statements they have signed, then goes out of business a few months later. People who have relied on the financial statements find the figures become meaningless when the company is no longer in business. The going concern assumption is used to justify the valuation procedures and is therefore a major assumption that should be considered by anyone analyzing the financial statements.

In fact, IAS 1 *Presentation of Financial Statements* requires management to make an assessment of the company's ability to continue as a going concern when it prepares the financial statements. If management is aware of material uncertainties related to events or conditions that may cast significant doubt on the company's ability to continue as a going concern, those uncertainties have to be disclosed. If it is concluded that the going concern basis is no longer appropriate, this would have a fundamental impact on the carrying value of assets and liabilities. These would have to be revised considering the need to cease operations and/or liquidate assets and liabilities.

Conventional measurement bases

In financial accounting, measurement means quantifying, in monetary terms, items that are recognized in financial statements. The observation that the balance sheet, as a status report of the company's financial position, is not a good representation of company value, is intrinsically linked with two measurement principles that still dominate current accounting practice: the historical cost principle and the monetary measuring unit convention. Measuring items in the context of financial statements requires the selection of a *measurement basis*, which can be either a historical cost measure or a current value measure. We will first elaborate on these measurement bases and then come back to the *monetary measuring unit convention*.

Historical cost

Financial accounting, as currently practised, is still mainly based on *historical cost*, i.e. the value of all (past) costs incurred to acquire an item on the date of acquisition. Historical cost accounting provides financial information on assets, liabilities, income and expenses using information that is derived from the transactions that created them. In essence, financial accounting works by tracking and recording all transactions of a company that have a financial value (bookkeeping) and then categorizing and processing these transactions according to different classes with specific economic characteristics (accounting), such as assets, liabilities, income, expenses. The categorizing and processing process often involves allocating the effect of transactions to different time periods.

As we have seen, financial accounting takes a starting statement of financial position (the balance sheet at the beginning of a year) and during the course of the year all economic transactions are recorded and classified. The classification will involve a first choice between the statement of profit or loss (revenues and expenses from operating activities during the year) and the closing balance sheet (statement of items owned and items owed to third parties). Thus the closing wealth is a summary of the effect of economic transactions of the year past rather than any independent valuation. The statement of profit or loss is a summary of business operations, whose net effect will be to increase or decrease the ending wealth.

The relationship between the statement of profit or loss and the statement of financial position is one that you will need to think about as you progress through the book. Under a pure historical cost regime, the statement of profit or loss is the key document in which revenues and expenses are stated, while the balance sheet value of assets is a residual of the profit measurement process. From this are deducted claims by third parties (liabilities) and what is left is equity.

This is a long way from an independent measure of value in an economic sense. For example, imagine that you bought shares in a listed company, say IBM, on 1 January for $50,000. During the year you receive dividend payments of $1,000. Under historical cost accounting, you have made a profit of $1,000 for the year, and your ending balance sheet will show assets of $50,000 (investment) and $1,000 (cash). However, it might be that the stock exchange valued your shares on 31 December at $55,000. Using market value as the measurement criterion, you are worth $56,000 (investment and cash) and your gain for the year is $6,000. Different measurement rules give different results, and historical cost accounting uses initial cost as the fundamental measurement criterion and only takes in 'realized' revenues – i.e. where cash or a reliable undertaking to pay cash has been obtained. In the example, the $5,000 gain in market value has not been realized – the shares have not been sold – so historical cost accounting disregards the gain. Of course, if you sold your shares at the end of the year, the gain would be part of your profit for the year – in the jargon the gain had been realized and could therefore be 'recognized'.

The big advantage of historical cost accounting is that historical cost is relatively easy to determine and can be verified. The main disadvantage is that subsequent to the date of acquisition, the continued reporting of historical cost-based values does not reflect any changes in market value.

IFRS Standards (and US GAAP for that matter) are not based exclusively on the historical cost principle. In fact, carrying amounts in an IFRS balance sheet are a mixture of historical costs, market values, net realizable values and discounted present values. That is why the measurement model underlying this balance sheet is often referred to as a *mixed-attribute model*. The mixture of different types of value makes the relationship between the statement of profit or loss and the balance sheet less straightforward than suggested following the historical cost model.

Current value

A valid alternative to the historical cost principle would be a current value measurement basis. A *current value* measure reflects current economic conditions at the reporting date and not the price of the transaction that gave rise to the asset or liability. In IFRS Standards, the most commonly used current value measure is called *fair value*. This is a term that is used in business to mean current (market) value. As a current value it is updated at reporting date to reflect economic conditions at that date. Because of the updating, current values capture any positive or negative changes in the factors included in the measurement of the reported items since the previous reporting date. The standard-setter has defined fair value more specifically as a current sale price (IFRS 13 *Fair Value Measurement* – we discuss this in detail in Chapter 14).

Under IFRS Standards, fair value is primarily used as a measurement basis for financial assets and liabilities. The argument is that, as with the IBM shares above, if there is a ready market on which such assets and liabilities can be sold, it is better information to reflect those values in the statement of financial position. Historically, the reason fair value accounting was introduced is that organizations were holding financial instruments whose risks and value they did not understand. They notched up sudden unexpected losses. Fair value is designed to protect against hidden losses and inform about hidden profits.

Fair value is not typically used for physical assets under normal circumstances. Companies mostly hold physical assets so that they can use them in the business, and their market value is less significant than their ability to generate cash flows from being used in the business. Financial assets and liabilities are not used in the same way, and are very near to being cash flows.

Fair value is also used in accounting where there is no observable monetary transaction from which the historical cost can be taken. This is the case in barter transactions, for example, which are not uncommon in international trade. A company might offer to exchange so many litres of palm oil against so many tractors. How would you account for this in the books? You would have to look at fair value – what is the market value of that many litres of palm oil or that many tractors?

It is used in a similar way to allocate between different components of a transaction. If you sell a new car with three years' free servicing, you have to allocate the price between the two components: the car itself and the three years' services. This will be done using the stand-alone selling prices (or fair value) of the two components.

In Part 2 of this book where we are dealing with the financial statements of relatively simple companies, the only financial instruments we will account for will be amounts due from customers (receivables) and amounts owed to suppliers (payables) or bank loans. In most cases, these would be at historical cost under IFRS Standards and so we will not re-visit fair value until Part 4 of the book. At the end of this chapter we will, however, come back briefly to what the *Conceptual Framework* has to say about current value measurement.

Monetary measurement unit

Financial accounting will record transactions as far as they can be expressed in monetary terms. Most transactions carried out by a company involve money, and therefore can be translated into money values easily, especially if the historical cost principle is applied. The use of money values to record business transactions has the advantage that money provides a common denominator by means of which heterogeneous facts and relationships can be expressed as numbers that can be added and subtracted. In fact, financial accounting uses money values to attach labels to economic events. The event of your buying a laptop computer becomes in accounting terms (from your perspective):

Assets:

Computers   + €900

Cash   − €900

So the physical item, the specific laptop with its specific design and operating characteristics, becomes asset €900.00.

While at a personal level you might regard the purchase as an 'expense', from an economic perspective, you presumably bought it in order to use it over a longer period (let's say over a three-year period), therefore it has a utility for you in the future and remains part of your wealth during that period. You have simply chosen to convert a cash asset into a computer asset, and, under a historical cost convention, we say that the initial accounting value of the computer is its cost value. Subsequently, the computer will gradually become an expense as it is used. This is how accounting works and, once the computer has no further use, it should have been fully expensed, but not before. This process is akin to that of language in tying word labels to objects and there are numerous analogies between the process of communicating by accounting and that of communicating by language.

Limitations imposed by measurement conventions

The use of money and historical cost as measurement conventions poses two problems: what happens to values that cannot be expressed in financial terms, and what happens when the value of the money itself changes?

Here too we can see the language analogy. There are some concepts that cannot be expressed by language, or indeed some concepts for which there is an expression in one language but not another. In accounting, there are some values not expressed – for example, a company may spend a lot of money advertising a new product. If the product is successful its trade name can become quite valuable in itself (Coca-Cola? Nestlé?) but the future sales value of an established trade name does not normally appear in the balance sheet since it was not bought. Similarly, efficient production depends to an extent on harmonious labour relations and good staff training, but neither value is expressed in financial accounting. It is difficult to say to what extent these omissions matter, but it is necessary to bear them in mind when reviewing balance sheet values. The measurement bases impose significant limitations on the scope of a balance sheet and a statement of profit or loss account. It is necessary to remember that the financial accounting data are organized on these measurement assumptions and values are not in any sense absolute, but are relative to a framework – change the framework and the values will change, too.

The other major problem in financial accounting is that of changes in the value of the measuring unit – inflation. Money is expressed in terms of its value at the time a transaction or event is recorded. The measurement system records a transaction at the nominal value in currency that is exchanged in that transaction. Subsequent changes in the purchasing power of the currency do not affect that amount. For example, supposing that we were measuring physical size, we could talk about something in terms of centimetres and metres. Two metres of cloth implies exactly the same length of cloth today as it did in 1900, but £5.00 worth of cloth is very much less today than it would have been in 1900 because the purchasing power of a pound, the measuring unit, is much smaller today than it was in 1900.

This means that the values expressed in historical cost accounting may not always be what they appear to be. For example, supposing a bookseller buys for inventory a book that cost him €37.50 and retails at €55.00 in 20X1. Over the next three years the publishers, reflecting the inflation of prices generally, increase their wholesale selling price to €45.00 and the retail price to €75.00. If the bookseller has not sold the copy he originally bought, it will appear in his accounts as inventory worth €37.50 – the historical cost. But if he wanted to buy another copy it would now cost €45.00. The book itself is virtually the same; it is the underlying value of the measurement unit that has changed (and as a consequence, if the book is sold for €75.00, it is not clear that the difference of €7.50 between the original inventory price and the replacement cost of the inventory should necessarily be treated as 'profit'). Many attempts have been made to deal with this change in the underlying purchasing power of the measurement unit, none so far with any lasting success.

Accounting for transactions

We are now going to focus in on the logic and procedures of accounting, with a view to establishing a simple model of how accounting works.

The balance sheet equation

One way of approaching this is to look at the company as an artificial and empty vehicle constructed to carry out a particular project. Finance is put into the vehicle and this is used to buy productive capacity (factories, warehouses, vehicles, computers, retail premises, offices, etc.). The production unit operates, its output is sold and profit is generated. The profit belongs to the owners of the company, and they will either take it out of the company as a dividend or leave it in as additional financing. The accounting unit must track what finance comes into the company and what is done with it and prepare periodic reports to the owners (Figure 3.5).

The nature of the vehicle is such that, at the beginning, it can only have as much 'value' as is put into it:

Owners' equity *and* Liabilities (sources of finance) = Assets (uses of finance)

This is called the *balance sheet equation* and is usually stated as:

Assets (uses of finance) = Owners' equity *and* Liabilities (sources of finance)

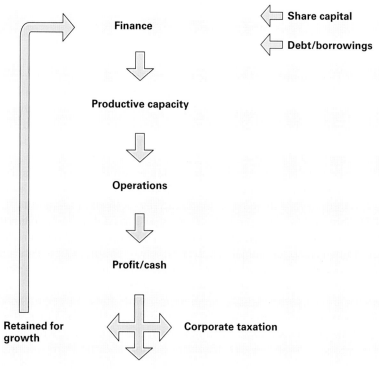

Figure 3.5 Tracking finance

In this view the left-hand side of the balance sheet equation is said to present the economic resources in which the company has invested the finance or funds available to it as of the balance sheet date. The right-hand side shows the sources of finance or the sources of the funds that are invested in the assets. Every euro invested in the company's assets at balance sheet date comes from either the company's owners (shareholders) or from its creditors (trade and other creditors and lenders), and every euro thus supplied is invested in some asset.

Any business transaction that will be recognized in the accounting system (we will refer to these as *accounting transactions*) will have a dual impact on the numbers in the company's accounting records. Any accounting for a transaction must preserve the equilibrium between sources and uses, and will involve either a change in both or a re-allocation within one side of the equation. This is the origin of the term 'double-entry accounting': any transaction must be reflected in (at least) two accounts.

Transactions that involve revenues and expenses fit in this fundamental equation approach, because revenues and expenses have a positive or negative effect on profit, and this belongs to the owners. Profit adds to the 'equity' part of the equation, while a loss will diminish the equity. By way of illustration, sale of inventory will diminish the inventory asset but will increase either cash or receivables assets. There will be a net change in assets, and the counterpart of this is a net change in equity (profit or loss).

BETWEEN THE LINES

Debt and equity

The sources of finance fall into two major categories: the finance put forward by the owners (equity), and the loans and other finance obtained from outside which do not attract an ownership share (liabilities/debt). The distinction between the two is that the owners take on all the risks of loss from the company's activities and gain from all profits, while loans are made purely in return for interest, which must be paid before arriving at any profit for the owners.

The difference between these two categories is fundamental. The suppliers of a loan are entering into a financial commitment with the company where the return they will receive, and therefore the cost to the company, is fixed in relation to the amount borrowed. The amount borrowed must be repaid at a fixed date and the lenders' risk is simply that the company may not have the means to repay, and bankers try to cover this kind of risk by asking for a legal link to company or shareholder assets – 'security' – in the event of default. The lenders' return is not affected by the company's profitability, except in the extreme of the company ceasing to trade.

The owners, by the same token, are the people with the last (residual) claim on the company's assets. They take the risk that the company will make a loss, but also reap the rewards if the company makes a profit. We can then recognize two basic categories of source of finance – that deriving from the owner, and that representing financial liabilities to outside people. The owners' interest is variable, because the owners accept final responsibility (remember, Assets − Liabilities = Equity).

Constructing a statement of financial position

The statement of financial position, or balance sheet, is the fundamental accounting statement in the sense that every accounting transaction can be analyzed according to its dual impact on the balance sheet. Let us take a practical example to illustrate how that works out. We will do this using a simple spreadsheet, and we will continue to use this spreadsheet as a means of analyzing accounting transactions. As indicated before, this is not how a bookkeeper or accounting software would make the entries; it does, however, reproduce the principles behind the bookkeeping, which are what are important. It is intended to simplify the learning process and put emphasis on the substance of the process rather than the form.

Note that the spreadsheet can have as many or as few rows as seems useful, but that overall it must be organized into two parts – assets and finance – and that, as the analysis proceeds, it is probably useful to split the assets side into 'cash' (i.e. bank account in accounting terms) and other assets, while other assets might equally split into short-term trading items and long-term ones (*current* and *non-current assets*). The financing side can also usefully be split between equity and liabilities, with liabilities subdividing into long-term debt (*non-current liabilities*) and trading liabilities (*current liabilities*), and equity into initial share capital and profits:

$$Assets = Equity \text{ and } Liabilities$$
$$(Cash + Short\text{-}term + Long\text{-}term \text{ assets}) = (Share \text{ capital} + Profit) + (Long\text{-}term \text{ debt} + Trading \text{ liabilities})$$

Example: supposing three friends decided to form a company called Reliable Runner SA that would sell cars. Jane put in €20,000, Alan put in €15,000 and Colin put in €15,000:

1. The initial financing, assuming the money was paid into a bank account, would be accounted for by showing (a) the (historical cost) value of money in the bank, and (b) the (historical cost) value of the shareholders' capital.

2. Next, the company obtained a bank loan for €30,000. Let us assume that this money is put into the company's bank account, so we have a similar transaction, increase in cash assets, increase in financing, but this time it is debt financing. The company now has total assets, all cash, of €80,000, while it has equity of €50,000 and liabilities of €30,000.

	1	2	3	4	Financial position
Assets					
Cash	+20,000 +15,000 +15,000	+30,000	−55,000	−18,000	7,000
Receivables					
Inventory				+18,000	+18,000
Property			+55,000		+55,000
Total	+50,000	+30,000	0	0	80,000
Liabilities/Equity					
Long-term debt		+30,000			+30,000
Trade payables					
Equity:					
Share capital	+20,000 +15,000 +15,000				50,000
Profit					
Total	+50,000	+30,000	0	0	80,000

3. Its next step is to buy a small office with a car lot for €55,000. Up until now we have been looking at transactions that affected both sides of the balance sheet equation, but the new transaction will affect one side only. The company is exchanging one asset, cash, for another asset, property. The total value it owns will remain the same, but the composition of the value will be different. Reliable Runner SA now has assets worth €80,000 in the form of property and cash, while it has liabilities of €30,000 (loan from the bank) and equity of €50,000 (owners' initial capital subscribed).

4. The next move is to acquire some inventory for trading, and the company buys €18,000 of second-hand cars for cash (i.e. by issuing a cheque – cash is usually used in accounting to mean liquid funds available immediately at the bank, not necessarily physical cash). Here again there is a swap between cash assets and other forms of asset – this time a current asset, inventory. It is assumed in accounting that inventories (which may be goods for resale, but also raw materials and work in progress) will be sold in less than one year. Of course, the longer the inventory turnover period the more financing is required by the company, and hence the emphasis in modern management of 'just in time' inventories.

The company is ready to start trading. If we drew up a balance sheet at this point (drawn from the company's accounting database above) it would look like this:

Assets		Financing	
Non-current assets		*Equity*	
Property	55,000	Share capital	50,000
Current assets		*Liabilities*	
Inventory	18,000	LT debt	30,000
Bank	7,000		
	80,000		80,000

Now we are ready to start trading and see what the effect of trading is on the balance sheet equation.

The owners' interest, or equity, represents initially the finance put into the company by the shareholders. That finance can be increased at any time during the company's life by the issue of new shares but, aside from that, it changes regularly as a result of the company's business activities. The shareholders are the ultimate recipients of the wealth generated or lost by the company. They bear all the risks of the company – if the company fails they will lose their investment – but they are also the people who benefit if the company is successful.

Gains or losses can arise in two main ways: first, through the operating activities of the company (any operating profit or loss will accrue to the benefit or cost of shareholders); second, through changes in the underlying values of the assets. For example, if a company has investments, and the value of these rises, then the shareholders own the increase in underlying values. An important difference between these two types of gain is that classical accounting only recognizes gains when they have been validated by a sale transaction (in the jargon, the gain must have been *realized* in order to be *recognized*). Consequently, many companies have value gains in their assets which are not reflected in the balance sheet (one form of hidden reserve). Operating activities though, by definition, involve a series of completed transactions.

If we concentrate on the business activities, it follows that as the shareholders are the ultimate recipients of any losses or profits, then business activities will have the effect of increasing or decreasing the shareholders' equity – in this sense, the statement of profit or loss is simply a summary of the business transactions which have occurred during a period, and is drawn up to explain the net change during a period in the value of the equity. (This linkage between the statement of profit or loss and the balance sheet is known as the *articulation* between the two, and is a central building block of financial reporting.)

Let us now move on to seeing how the business transactions work in a balance sheet context:

	Financial position A	5	6	7	Financial position B
Assets					
Cash	7,000	(a) +5,000			11,750
		(c) −250			
Receivables			(a) 7,000		7,000
Inventory	18,000	(b) −4,000	(c)−5,500	+12,000	20,500
Property	55,000				55,000
Total	80,000	+750	+1,500	+12,000	94,250
Liabilities/Equity					
Long-term debt	30,000				30,000
Trade payables				+12,000	12,000
Equity:					
Share capital	50,000				50,000
Profit		(a) +5,000	(b) +7,000		2,250
		(b) −4,000	(b) −5,500		
		(c) −250			
Total	80,000	+750	+1,500	+12,000	94,250

5. In our example, if a car were sold for €5,000 cash, we should be able to record the acquisition of a new asset (€5,000 cash) and also show an increase in equity of €5,000 (transaction 5a on the spreadsheet).

The sale increases the value of the owners' equity and the cash received increases the assets of the company. However, we have so far failed to record the other aspect of the transaction: the fact that we have given up part of our inventory. We need to record the reduction of our assets by one vehicle. We have gained a cash asset of €5,000, but we have given up a car asset, which, in this case, we had previously bought for €4,000 (part of our inventory of €18,000, which amount we need for profit measurement purposes to have allocated across the individual cars concerned – which could bring in an element of subjectivity). The real effect of the transaction is to create a profit of €1,000, and this is reflected in the accounts by *expensing* the inventory against the sale. We cancel the inventory value of the car sold by deducting this from the sale. In our balance sheet equation, we reduce inventory by €4,000 and reduce profit by €4,000 (transaction 5b).

This highlights the relationship between assets and expenses. When a company pays its electricity bill it is easy to see that the expenditure involved relates to something which has already been consumed in the business – the electrical energy. The payment therefore involves an immediate expense in the business operations of the company. It represents a value consumed. However, when a company makes a payment – as in the case of the acquisition of the car inventory in our example – the transaction is not always an expense. The car inventory represents an economic value (a resource) that will be consumed in the future by the company and remains in the balance sheet until it is consumed. And that is what has now happened in the case of the car sale in our example: an asset has been consumed, turned into an expense ('expensed') as a business transaction by the company.

Many assets represent simply a store of future economic value to be consumed by a business. Clearly, an inventory of goods for resale is going to be seen to be consumed relatively quickly. But, in the same way, assets such as equipment are used up over a period, albeit several years, and are consumed in the business. Equally, when a company pays in advance for something like insurance or rent, the expenditure is made initially to acquire a future economic benefit. That economic benefit expires as the company moves through the time period for which it paid in advance – the asset becomes an expense through the economic benefits being consumed by the company.

We should therefore distinguish between expenditure – where the company simply pays out money – and the classification of that expenditure as an expense of an accounting period, or as an asset to appear in the end-period balance sheet and be carried forward to become an expense in a future period.

Returning to the car example, let us also imagine that, as the new owner was driving away, a wing mirror fell off. The company arranged for a nearby repair shop to replace this and carry out one or two other minor repairs. Reliable Runner SA paid the repair shop €250 for this work. That expenditure would also be an expense since the car has been sold (transaction 5c).

During the course of the series of transactions we have just finished describing, the accounting value of the company has changed several times, so any balance sheet that we might have drawn up would also have changed as the transactions progressed. The net change in the equity over the period is, of course, the profit that has been made by the company during that period. Normally, this would be analyzed in the statement of profit or loss and only the net change shown in the published balance sheet within equity. A company can draw up a statement of profit or loss as often as it wishes; most companies do this monthly for internal management purposes, as well as annually for official reporting to shareholders and tax authorities.

Credit transactions

All the transactions that we have made so far have involved an exchange of cash. However, in business many transactions are made on credit, with the cash exchange following sometime later. The accounting treatment of such transactions follows exactly the same ideas that we have already explored: if a business sells some goods on credit, it gives up one asset in exchange for another; but where the asset received was cash in the earlier example, in a credit transaction the asset received will be a promise to pay. That promise or debt is just as valuable as the cash, as long as there is an expectation that the person who owes the debt will pay in due course (and why would you give credit in the first place if you were not sure you would be paid?). The account created is known as a receivable.

Suppose that Reliable Runner SA sells another car, this time for €7,000, and allows the customer credit. The transaction would appear in the balance sheet equation as an increase in equity and an increase in a new form of current asset, a receivable (transaction 6a in the spreadsheet). Let us say the allocated cost of the car sold was €5,500 so we have acknowledged through the balance sheet equation the expensing of another car from our inventory (transaction 6b).

Businesses also receive short-term credit from their suppliers – assets are purchased or other expenses incurred in exchange for a promise to pay in due course. In essence, this is a transaction very similar to the bank loan, with the difference that the finance is normally available only for a short period, so would be presented differently on the balance sheet. A credit supply consists of the receipt by a business of goods or services against a liability to pay later. The supplier and the debt which is owed are described as trade creditors or trade payables.

If our company now decided that it should expand its car inventory and bought two more cars for €12,000 but this time on credit, the company should record an increase in assets – the additional car inventory, and an increase in financing – the short-term credit given by the supplier (transaction 7). There is no limit to the number of rows that might be used – we are constrained slightly by the size of the printed page, but generally one would have as many rows as seemed useful in terms of enabling a relevant and efficient analysis of the figures into a statement of profit or loss and balance sheet.

If we were to draw up a statement of profit or loss for the whole period since the commencement of the business, it would now look like this:

	€	€
Sales		12,000
Expenses:		
Cars	9,500	
Repairs	250	9,750
Net profit		*2,250*

The statement of financial position or balance sheet at the end of the period would look like this:

Assets	€	Financing	€
Non-current assets		*Equity*	
Property	55,000	Share capital	50,000
Current assets		Profit for the year	2,250
Inventory	20,500	*Liabilities*	
Receivables	7,000	LT debt	30,000
Bank	11,750	Trade payables	12,000
Total	94,250	Total	94,250

This series of transactions represents the essence of how accounting tracks and reflects a company's financing and its operations. Essentially, the balance sheet is a financial model of the company – but based on the money value of transactions which have taken place. The statement of profit or loss is an analysis of the wealth-creating (or wealth-diminishing!) activities of the company. The statement of profit or loss can be drawn up for any period but is generally drawn up for one year for external reporting purposes and in businesses of any size, at least once a month for internal management purposes. Equally, a balance sheet, or statement of financial position, can be drawn up at any moment, but is published once a year for shareholders and others, while it is produced internally at least quarterly for management purposes.

The spreadsheet represents the company's accounting database. In reality this will consist of potentially hundreds of 'accounts' – data files – that are constantly being updated as the accounting department tracks the company's transactions and, indeed, participates in them with issuing invoices to clients, paying suppliers and so on. The balance sheet is in fact a highly aggregated summary of the data files in the accounting database and corresponds exactly with that database. The statement of profit or loss is also an aggregation of those data files that deal with the company's operations for a specific period. They represent a more detailed analysis than is provided by the one-line profit entry in the statement of financial position.

You can see in the example just examined how (a) the balance sheet is a presentation of the latest position in the company's accounting database, and (b) how the statement of profit or loss is an analytical document that gives the detail behind the net change in equity over the period (but excluding any new capital introduced by investors or dividends paid to them).

You should also note that the increase in company cash during the trading period (transactions 5–7) was €4,750, while the profit was €2,250. This is generally the case in accruals accounting, since we are trying to present an economic assessment and while this translates itself into cash flows in the end, there are timing differences. In this case, we can reconcile the two as follows:

Profit as calculated	*2,250*
Value of inventory consumed (paid earlier)	9,500
Amount owed by credit customer (will be received later)	−7,000
Change in cash during this period	*+4,750*

We will build on this model in subsequent chapters to see how it deals with more complex transactions and situations. But all the essentials of how accounting tracks company operations are contained in the example just examined. If you get stuck later on, you should always come back to this introduction to refresh your understanding of how accounting records company activity.

Elements of financial statements: definitions, recognition and measurement criteria

Having constructed a basic statement of financial position (balance sheet) and statement of profit or loss (profit and loss account) from a set of business transactions, we will now turn to some of the formal rules that the standard-setter has set to delineate the content of the building blocks of these financial statements. These formal rules are important as they sometimes depart from the traditional transactions-based view of accounting. The definitions and overall recognition criteria provide the general setting to which we will refer in later chapters.

Financial statement elements

The *Conceptual Framework* states that financial statements portray the financial effects of business events by grouping them into broad categories according to their economic characteristics. These characteristics are called the elements of financial statements. Five elements of financial statements are identified and defined: assets, liabilities, equity, income and expenses.

Assets, liabilities and equity are the elements that provide information about a company's financial position as portrayed in its balance sheet and are defined as follows:

- *Asset*: A present economic resource controlled by the entity as a result of past events. An *economic resource* is further defined as a right that has the potential to produce economic benefits.
- *Liability*: A present obligation of the entity to transfer an economic resource as a result of past events.
- *Equity*: The residual interest in the assets of the entity that remains after deducting all its liabilities.

Income and expenses are the elements of financial statements that provide information about the company's financial performance. These elements are defined as follows:

- *Income*: Increases in assets or decreases in liabilities, that result in increases in equity, other than those relating to contributions from holders of equity claims.
- *Expenses*: Decreases in assets or increases in liabilities, that result in decreases in equity, other than those relating to distributions to holders of equity claims.

Reading through these definitions, it becomes clear that they are not independent: primacy is given to the definitions of assets and liabilities, whereas the concepts of equity, income and expenses are defined in terms of the level of or changes in assets and liabilities. This is known as the *asset–liability approach* to financial statements.

The lack of independence in the definitions results from the necessity of *articulation* between the statement of profit or loss and the statement of financial position that we talked about earlier. Articulation requires a conceptual and mathematical correspondence between the statement of financial performance and the statement of financial position (between profit for the period and owners' equity) in order to preserve the interrelation and congruence of the flow of data between the financial statements. It results in financial statements that are fundamentally interrelated so that statements that show elements of the financial performance type depend on statements that show elements of financial position (or vice versa). Figure 3.6 illustrates the correspondence among the elements of financial statements.

The bulk of the IFRS Standards contain more specific rules with respect to the elements of financial statements. Besides additional definitions of the items specifically covered by a standard, these rules are typically oriented towards three aspects of financial statement elements: recognition, measurement and disclosure:

- *Recognition* is the process of capturing an item that meets one of the definitions above for inclusion in the financial statements. An item may meet the definition of, for example, an asset, but fail to meet specific asset recognition criteria and thus be kept off the balance sheet. In other words, meeting the definitions is a necessary but not a sufficient condition for inclusion in the financial statements.

Figure 3.6 Correspondence among financial statement elements

- *Measurement* is the process of quantifying in monetary terms information about an entity's assets, liabilities, equity, income and expenses. It will determine the monetary amount at which the elements of financial statements are to be recognized and carried in the balance sheet and statement of profit or loss.
- *Disclosure* refers to the process of additional information dissemination with regard to a financial statement element in the notes to the accounts.

Although IFRS Standards usually contain domain-specific recognition rules according to the nature of the elements involved (e.g. financial versus (in)tangible assets), the *Conceptual Framework* sets out some overall recognition criteria that have to be taken into account when deciding whether to include an element in the financial statements. These overall recognition guidelines are based on the qualitative characteristics of useful financial information. It states that *an item* that meets the definition of an asset or liability (and any related income, expense or change in equity) *should be recognized if it provides* users of financial statements with:

(a) *Relevant information* about the financial statement items
(b) A *faithful representation* of the asset or liability and of any resulting income, expense or change in equity.

Hence, not all assets and liabilities should be included (recognized) in the statement of financial position. For example, recognizing an asset may not provide relevant information if there is only a low probability that it will result in an inflow of economic benefits or recognizing a liability, if the existence of the item is difficult to ascertain (e.g. an obligation in a pending court case). Recognizing an item may also not lead to a faithful representation of the asset or liability if there is a high level of uncertainty when measuring the item. Such assessments may involve considerable judgement. The probability assessment, for example, refers to the degree of certainty that the future flow of economic benefits will materialize, and should take into account the information available when the financial statements are prepared. Also the cost or value of an item is not always readily available and must be estimated in many cases. The need for estimation does, however, not undermine relevance or faithful representation as long as the estimates can be reasonably justified.

Figure 3.7 summarizes the main issues regarding the process of including (information on) an item into the financial statements.

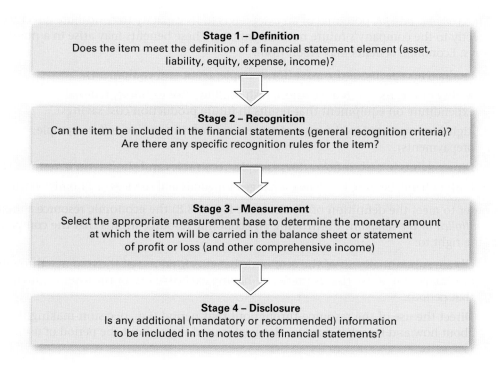

Figure 3.7   Considerations for including an item into the financial statements

Assets

A company's asset is an economic resource that it controls at reporting date as a result of past events. An economic resource is a right (or a bundle of rights) that has the potential to produce economic benefits.

Assets should be viewed as *rights*, rather than underlying physical or other objects. Such rights may take different forms: for example, rights arising from holding shares or debt instruments, rights over physical objects such as property and equipment, rights to receive goods and services, rights to benefit from the stand-ready obligations of other parties. Tangibility or physical substance is not an essential characteristic of an asset. Many assets will be intangible (such as licences) or monetary (such as trade receivables or loans granted).

The rights should have the *potential to generate* flows of *economic benefits*, but there is no minimum probability threshold for the related flows of benefits. There should, however, be at least one circumstance in which the economic resource would generate economic benefits.

Assets arise from *past transactions* or *past events*. A company would normally obtain assets through exchanges with third parties, by acquiring them in cash, credit or barter transactions (property, plant and equipment, inventory, investments), by selling goods or services (receivables) or by entering into arrangements that provide rights to future benefits (a loan to a third party). There might not always be an expenditure to recognize an asset: an item may be donated to the company free of charge, but if the item has the potential to generate future economic benefits, it meets the definition of an asset. By way of contrast, incurring expenditure may be indicative that future economic benefits are sought, but it is not conclusive proof that an asset has been acquired.

The *economic benefits* potential of an asset refers to its capacity to contribute directly or indirectly to the company's future net cash inflows. These benefits may arise in a number of ways. Economic benefits may result from:

- Productive capacity of the asset (for example, plant and equipment).
- Ability of the asset to reduce future cash outflows (for example, renewal expenditure on equipment that results in future production cost savings).
- Rights incorporated in the asset to receive services in the future (for example, prepayments).
- Direct claims to cash inflows (for example, receivables and short-term investments).
- Cash in hand, because it can be exchanged for goods and services (economic benefits).

In order to meet the definition of an asset (see Figure 3.8) the economic resource should be *controlled by the company*. Controlling an economic resource means that the company has the right to:

1. Obtain substantially all of the economic benefits from use of the resource throughout the period of use (for example, by having exclusive use of the asset throughout that period).
2. Direct the use of the resource throughout that period (i.e., decision-making rights about how and for what purpose the asset is used throughout the period of use).

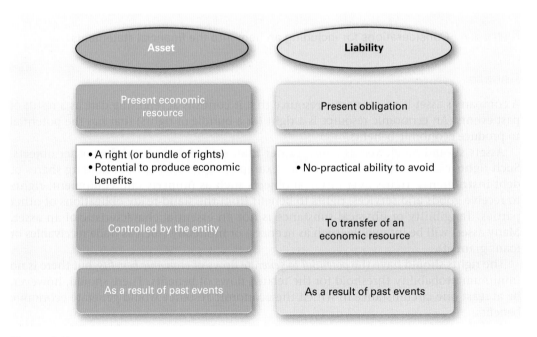

Figure 3.8   Definition of asset and liability

Control usually arises from legal rights of ownership, but an economic resource may satisfy the definition of an asset even where there is no legal ownership. To assess the control issue, it is important to analyze transactions in accordance with their substance and economic reality and not merely their legal form. The substance of business arrangements may give a company control over the economic benefits (and usually at the same time expose it to the risks) of a resource without specific ownership rights. A lease is a typical example of a situation where ownership and control do not coincide. A lease is a contractual arrangement between a customer (the lessee) and a supplier (the lessor) that conveys to the customer the right to use an asset for a period of time in exchange for consideration. Under a lease arrangement the owner of, for example, a plant transfers the control over the use of the plant (and over the future economic benefits of using the plant) to a lessee, although he or she (the lessor) retains legal ownership. Likewise, possession of an asset will usually indicate control but, even then, a company may hold inventory or cash as agent for another party and be restricted from using it in an exchange transaction, and hence does not control the asset. Moreover, the notion of an asset as a 'right' is kept broad and would, for example, also encompass any know-how that is controlled by keeping it secret.

Liabilities

A company's liability is a present obligation to transfer an economic resource as a result of past events.

A *present obligation* of a company refers to a present (at reporting date) duty or responsibility to act or perform in a certain way. The duty or responsibility obligates the company. The obligation implies the involvement of one or more third parties. A company will have a present obligation to transfer an economic resource if both:

1. The obligation has arisen from a past event (the obligating event), meaning that the company has received the economic benefits, or conducted the activities, that establish the extent of the obligation.
2. The company has no practical ability to avoid the transfer.

Three main types of obligation can be distinguished: contractual, imposed and constructive obligations. Most obligations are legally enforceable and arise under *contractual* arrangements for amounts borrowed (bank loans, corporate bonds), amounts owed for assets purchased or services obtained (trade payables). When advance payments have been received from third parties, there will be an obligation to provide goods or services. Obligations can also be *imposed* when grounded in legislation, such as obligations to pay income tax, the obligation to restore environmentally damaged sites and the obligation to pay damages under a lawsuit. Obligations can, however, also be *constructive*. A constructive obligation is created or inferred from a company's actions, such as its customary practices, published policies or public statements that create a valid expectation in a third party that the company will transfer the resource to the third party. For example, a company may have a published policy of refunding purchases to dissatisfied customers, indicating that it will accept responsibility for faulty goods beyond legal warranty requirements. The constructive obligation arises when the company has created a valid expectation with the customers of a rebate for anything faulty.

The purchase of goods and the use of services of third parties is an *obligating event* giving rise to trade payables (unless paid for in advance or on delivery). The signing of a bank loan contract is an obligating event that results in an obligation to repay the loan, probably with interest. In these cases, the obligation can be enforced by law. In the case of a constructive obligation to refund faulty goods, the obligating event arises when the goods are actually sold by the company. In these cases, the company will have no realistic alternative to settling the obligation created by the event, because the transfer of economic resources is legally enforceable, or because courses of action to avoid the transfer would cause significant disruption of its business and/or bring about adverse economic consequences far worse than the transfer itself.

There is, however, no such thing as 'voluntary liabilities', which are not based on commitments towards third parties, such as planned expenditure on repairs and maintenance of plant and equipment. In that case, the company has the alternative to cancel or postpone the expenditure or to sell the asset before the repairs and maintenance take place and, thus, avoid expenditure.

The liability will lead to a *transfer of an economic resource*. The actual settlement of the obligation could involve the payment of cash, the transfer of other assets, the replacement by one obligation with another, the rendering of services, etc. Uncertainty about the timing and amount of the transfer of resources is allowable. Liabilities with significant uncertainty of timing or amount of future transfers are known as 'provisions' (see Chapter 6).

Equity

Equity is defined as the residual interest in the company's assets after deducting its liabilities. The residual interest is the ownership interest and represents the shareholders' claim to the company's net assets. The logic of the definition of equity follows the balance sheet equation that assets minus liabilities equals equity. Both equity and liabilities represent (mutually exclusive) interests in a company's assets, but equity ranks after liabilities as a claim to those assets. This means that claims from liabilities must be met before a distribution can be made to shareholders in the event of liquidating the company.

Equity will usually be subdivided as follows:

- Funds contributed by shareholders
- Retained earnings
- Reserves.

Two main categories of reserves can be distinguished:

- Reserves representing income and expense items that were directly included in equity (instead of transiting through profit or loss)
- Reserves representing appropriations of retained profits.

In broad terms, equity comprises the funds that shareholders put into the company together with profits that the shareholders are entitled to, but have not yet received as dividends. Net profits that have not been distributed to shareholders are known as retained earnings. Equity may also include reserves such as gains on the revaluation of tangible fixed assets and gains and losses on the translation of assets and liabilities in foreign currency. These are, in effect, items of income and expense, but unlike retained earnings, they were not accounted for in the statement of profit or loss, but put directly in equity. The company is usually not allowed to treat them as available for distribution as dividends. Reserves may also come from appropriations of net profits for which legal or statutory requirements restrict the company's ability to distribute or otherwise use them.

Income and expenses

The definitions of income and expenses rely explicitly on the asset–liability approach of financial statements: they are defined as changes in assets and liabilities.

Income is increases in assets or decreases in liabilities. Income related to an increase in assets arises, for example, from the sale of goods or services that leads to an increase in cash or an increase in receivables (credit sale). However, if the sale proceeds include sales taxes (value-added tax VAT), the tax part would not be considered income, as it is owed to the tax authorities (creates a liability) and, thus, is not beneficial to the company's shareholders. Note that when a company issues new shares, the proceeds from the share issue would not be accounted for as income, because it is a contribution of shareholders, which increases equity directly and should not transit through profit or loss. Income will usually arise from business transactions, but may also be related to other events, such as a (positive) revaluation of pre-existing assets based on current values.

Expenses are decreases in assets or increases in liabilities. Examples of expenses related to decreased assets are numerous: cost of goods sold (depletion of inventory), advertising expenses (use of cash), depreciation (consumption of the resources embodied in long-term assets). Expenses as an increase in liabilities occurs, for example, when income taxes are recognized on profit but payment is deferred (payable as a liability). Expenses (losses) may also come from a negative (positive) revaluation of specific assets (liabilities) using current values. Note that, if expenditure on purchased services, for example, includes refundable VAT, the tax part would again not constitute an expense, as the purchase taxes can be reclaimed from the tax authorities (creates a receivable). Also, if a company pays cash dividends to its shareholders, assets (cash) would decrease, but no expense is recognized as it is a distribution to shareholders.

Measurement bases

The *Conceptual Framework* describes *measurement* as quantifying, in monetary terms, elements that are recognized in financial statements. Measuring those elements requires the selection of a measurement basis, which can be either a historical cost measure or a current value. Figure 3.9 elaborates on these measurement bases. The *Conceptual Framework* does not favour one basis over the other, but notes that under some circumstances one may provide more useful information than the other.

Figure 3.9   Measurement bases

Historical cost would typically reflect the cost of acquiring or creating an asset or taking on a liability, with both measures being adjusted for transaction costs. It is described as an entry value. Over time, historical cost is further adjusted to reflect, for example, the consumption of an asset or the fulfilment of a liability. An example of historical cost would be *amortized cost* (for some financial assets and financial liabilities) and historical *cost adjusted for depreciation and impairment* (for property, plant and equipment). Historical cost is sticky as it remains conditioned on the originating transaction and is not updated to reflect current acquisition prices. Historical cost can provide relevant information as, for example, expenses arising from consumption of an asset can be compared to related income to provide information about margins. Such margin information is often used to predict future cash flows.

A *current value* measurement basis on the other hand reflects conditions at the measurement date and not the price of the transaction that gave rise to the asset or liability. IFRS Standards use a number of current value measures with slightly different characteristics. *Fair value*, for example, reflects a price that would be received or paid for selling an asset or transferring a liability from the perspective of independent market participants. *Value in use* (for assets) and *fulfilment value* (for liabilities) on the other hand reflect the present value of future cash flows attached to these items and which are based on entity-specific assumptions (assumptions on how the company intends to use the asset or liability). Fair value, value in use and fulfilment value are described as exit values, whereas *current cost* (like historical cost) is an entry value. Unlike fair value, value in use and fulfilment value, current cost takes into account prices and transaction costs that would be incurred at the date the asset or liability is measured, based on the cost that an equivalent asset or liability would have. As current value is updated to reflect changes in prices and other factors, it tends to better reflect the amount, timing and uncertainty of expected future cash flows attached to the item.

The *Conceptual Framework* further explains that considering the objective of financial reporting, and the qualitative characteristics of useful information (relevance, faithful representation, other) is likely to lead to selecting different measurement bases for different types of assets and liabilities. This results in a *mixed-attribute measurement model*, with historical cost still being the leading measure for most industrial and commercial companies. It is, however, the individual IFRS Standards that will determine the final measurement options for specific types of assets and liabilities.

Summary

In this chapter we have taken a major step forward in looking at the technical basis of accounting. This has involved looking at the basic conventions of accounting, particularly historical cost as the valuation base, but also conventions such as accruals (accounts try to record all economic events affecting the company when they take place, not just cash movements), matching, going concern (allocations of costs to future periods are only valid if we think the company is going to continue to exist) and consistency (the comparability of data is limited if the basis on which it is prepared changes over time).

We dealt with the accounting database and its fundamental concepts that accounting information records both where finance came from and what was done with it (the balance sheet equation) and that therefore all movements within the database will involve at least two changes, since they must deal with both sources and uses of finance (double entry). We used a spreadsheet as a model of the accounting database and plotted a series of transactions through it. As a result, we were able to prepare a statement of profit or loss and a statement of financial position from the database.

Finally, we looked more closely at the official definitions of the elementary building blocks of financial statements. These definitions are governed by the asset–liability approach to financial statements. We also elaborated on the overall recognition criteria and measurement bases that are set by the *Conceptual Framework*. In order to properly understand the numbers presented in IFRS Standards financial statements, the analyst must be aware of these conceptual foundations.

Discussion questions

1. Discuss the shortcomings of a statement of financial position as a proxy for company value.
2. Critically assess the usefulness of fair value as a measurement attribute.
3. What is the link between a functional presentation and a presentation by nature of the statement of profit or loss? Provide a number of examples to illustrate your point.
4. Explain what is meant by relevance, timeliness and comparability and how they make financial information useful.
5. Elaborate the coherence (articulation) between a statement of financial position and a statement of profit or loss.
6. Which captions would one normally expect in the presentation of a company's equity?

Assignments

The following questions have answers on the lecturer side of the digital support resources for the book.

1. Jennifer decides that she will go into the tourist industry on Lake Geneva, and buy a concession to hire out canoes on the lake. She borrows CHF40,000 from her parents and puts in CHF20,000 herself. The arrangement with the Canton is that she pays CHF50,000 at the start for the concession, which runs five years, but must also pay an annual rental of CHF10,000 at the end of the season in October.

   She negotiates a deal with a canoe supplier, who sells her 20 canoes for CHF30,000 but agrees that she should pay CHF10,000 on delivery and the rest a year later.

   During the season she receives CHF90,000 (cash) in canoe rentals.

   Required:

   Making (and specifying) whatever assumptions you wish, you are asked to draw up a simple statement of profit or loss for the first year and statement of financial position at the end of the year.

2. On completing his MBA, James sees a possibility to make a profit selling computers. He has the opportunity to buy a job-lot of computers for €50,000, and he can buy a shop lease with two years to run for €5,000 and pay an annual rent of €6,000. He happens just to have inherited €60,000, so he starts a company and puts the money in as share capital.

During the first year, he sells €30,000 of computers for €45,000. During the second year he sells no computers at all, and at the end of the year he sells the remaining inventory for €1,000 and liquidates the company.

Required:

(a) Calculate his accounting profit for each of the two years of operations.

(b) Explain why the assumptions made at the end of the first year led to the wrong profit estimate.

(c) What are the consequences of the assumptions that proved to be incorrect?

3. A&S retail shop. Andy and Stewart met at a training course for young entrepreneurs. They decide to set up an enterprise to run a retail store at the centre of a small village. Andy recently received £9,000 as a donation from his rich aunt. He puts this money and another £3,000 of his savings into the business as share capital. Stewart puts in £12,000 of his own savings as share capital as well. A local bank grants them a three-year loan of £6,000. Every six months, they repay one-sixth of the bank loan and pay interest at a semi-annual rate of 3 per cent. The interest is recognized on a six-month basis. They rent a fully equipped store with sufficient storage space. They agree to pay a monthly rent of £700 (to be paid at the beginning of each month). Andy and Stewart pay themselves a salary of £600 each at month's end. They decide to use their initials to create the store's name A&S:

■ To announce the opening of the store on the first of April 20X1, A&S launches an advertising campaign that runs during the first week of April. This campaign costs £1,000 and is to be paid for on 7 April.

■ A&S purchases retail goods worth £7,000. The supplier agrees to grant a 10 per cent discount if A&S pays immediately on 1 April.

■ The first month turns out to be a success due to the advertising campaign. A&S is able to sell half its inventory for £4,900.

■ At the beginning of May, A&S purchases retail goods worth £5,000 in cash.

■ By the end of the May A&S manages to sell £3,500 of goods for £5,400.

■ In the month of June, A&S decides to provide several shopping carts to improve customer comfort. A&S buys 20 carts for only £1,200. The carts are delivered on 5 June and will be paid for mid-July. A&S estimates the expected life of the carts to be five years without any residual value.

■ In June, A&S sells £2,900 of goods for £4,500. A&S also buys retail goods for £5,000 and receives a promotional quantity discount of 7 per cent. The goods are paid for when delivered on 20 June.

■ The availability and convenience of shopping carts attract a broader range of customers. In the month of July, A&S sells £4,500 of retail goods for £7,200.

■ At the beginning of August, A&S buys £4,800 of goods and sells £3,800 goods for £5,800.

■ Eager to expand its business, A&S responds to an increasing demand for more customer convenience. In order to provide a home delivery service, A&S buys a second-hand motor van for £15,000 on 4 August. A&S estimates that the van will be used for five years, after which the van will have no residual value. A&S pays £12,000 immediately and agrees to pay the remaining balance before August 20X2.

■ A&S buy retail goods for £6,500 in September. A&S sells £3,500 of goods for £5,000 at the store. Furthermore, A&S delivers £750 of goods using the van and gets paid £1,200.

■ At the end of the month, A&S repays part of its borrowings and pays the interest to the bank.

■ In October, A&S experiences a slight downturn in sales. A&S manages to sell only £2,000 of goods for £3,400 at the store and delivers £750 of goods to customers at home for £1,200. Given this disappointing decrease in sales A&S buys only a minimum of goods and pays £1,250.

■ During the month of November, A&S grants promotional discounts to get rid of products near to their expiring dates. A&S sells in total £2,400 of goods at a price of £2,600.

■ At the beginning of December, A&S purchases a considerable quantity of goods to provide for the holiday shoppers. A&S buys £8,500 of goods and gets a 5 per cent discount for immediate payment.

■ December turns out to be a lucrative month. A&S temporarily hires a student on a part-time basis to help out in the store. A&S pays the student £300 at the end of the month. A&S sells £6,500 of goods for £9,900 at the store. On top of that, home deliveries (with a cost of £1,800) account for £3,200 in revenue.

■ A&S believes the owners have been working hard and rewards them with a new year's bonus of £300 each.

■ In January, A&S replenishes its inventory. A&S purchases £4,000 of goods. In January A&S sells £3,700 of goods for £6,300 altogether.

■ In February, A&S decides that the store requires a portable computer for administration purposes. A&S buys a portable computer at a price of £1,350. The computer is expected to last three years and to have no value afterwards.

■ At the beginning of February, A&S purchases £5,000 of goods. A&S sells £4,500 of goods for £7,850 at the store and another £850 of goods by delivery for £1,500.

■ In March, A&S relies on an accountant's services to help them with the preparation of their financial statements. A&S pays him £500. During this month A&S purchases another £5,000 of goods and succeeds in selling £4,600 of goods for £7,900.

■ At the end of the month, A&S repays part of its loan and pays the interest to the bank.

The fiscal year of A&S runs from 1 April 20X1 till 31 March 20X2.

You are asked to prepare for A&S a statement of financial position at the end of March 20X2 and draw up a statement of profit or loss for its first fiscal year.

4. George and Val set up a company together to trade as decorators. George owns a three-year-old van, which he puts into the company instead of cash for share capital. Val puts in €2,000 in cash and they agree the van is worth €2,000. They have no premises as such. Materials are stored in their home garage or left in the van. In the first month of business the following transactions take place:

(a) They get an order worth €600 to decorate a small flat. The customer pays €300 in advance.

(b) They buy materials worth €125 on credit from Cork Building Merchants which are used in this job.

(c) When the job is finished the customer pays a further €100 but says they will have to wait another month for the balance of €200.

(d) They get an order to decorate a large house for €1,200 plus materials. They buy €270 of materials on credit from the same builders' merchants.

(e) At the end of the month they have done 80 per cent of the work on the house-painting order and they pay themselves €500 each as salary.

Prepare a spreadsheet to show the transactions and then draw up a statement of profit or loss for the month and a statement of financial position as at the end of the month.

Next month:

(f) They complete the house job and receive €1,200 from the customer plus €270 for the materials.

(g) They get a job painting some shop premises – the price is €500 including materials. They buy materials on credit from the usual supplier for €80.

(h) They complete the job and receive €500 cash.

(i) The next contract is to decorate a flat and they agree to do the job for €800 plus materials. They obtain €180 of materials, but the supplier says that they must clear their outstanding account before he will release the goods. They pay what was due at the end of the previous month.

(j) The van breaks down and is repaired for €90 which is paid in cash.

(k) They complete the job and bill the customer for €980. The customer pays €600 and offers to pay the balance plus €20 interest if they will wait two months for it.

(l) They visit their first client because he hasn't paid the €200 outstanding, but he is not available and a neighbour tells them that he has just gone bankrupt.

(m) They do no further business that month and pay themselves €500 each as salary at the end of the month.

Update the spreadsheet and then draw up a statement of profit or loss for the month and a statement of financial position as at the end of the month.

CHAPTER 4

Accrual accounting

In this chapter, we go into the detail of how to apply accrual accounting in practice. We will look at credit transactions and the timing of transactions for accounting purposes in general. More specifically, we will address the issues of revenue recognition and of how items of inventory are transferred to the statement of profit or loss when the goods are sold and revenue is recognized.

Chapter structure

- Introduction
- Accrual basis of accounting
- Credit transactions
- Revenue recognition
- Period costs
- Inventories and profit
- Inventory accounting techniques
- Net realizable value
- Accruals and the working capital cycle
- Summary
- Discussion questions
- Appendices
- Assignments

Introduction

In Chapter 3, we looked at the balance sheet equation, how that works as the basis of the company's accounting database and how the company's transactions are captured and recorded within that database. In short, we dealt with the basic approach to recognition and measurement of transactions in financial accounting. In this chapter and the next one, we are going to go into this in more detail with a view to reaching the point where you can prepare basic financial statements, given a listing from the accounting database and information about the surrounding circumstances. It is important that you should know the relationship between the database and the financial statements that are published using its data, and that you should feel comfortable with the contents of the statement of financial position (balance sheet) and statement of profit or loss (income statement/profit and loss account).

Accrual basis of accounting

So far we have largely confined ourselves to looking at transactions in which goods were bought and sold for cash, but the real world of commercial trading includes many transactions in which cash changes hands at a different moment from that when the item or service is provided. Also, the classification of an item within a company's accounting system sometimes changes when the item is used up in the company's activities. To be useful, accounting needs to capture all the economic events that occur in a company when they take place, and the cash movement is usually only a part of the picture. The statement of profit or loss gives a picture of a company's operating performance over a period of time (for published financial statements the relevant period is commonly one year). In essence, that is a simple enough concept, but examined in detail, it poses questions as to which transactions of a company are properly taken in as being 'operating' and which transactions belong to which accounting period. In answering this question, accountants may well have to make allocations of expenses and revenues between different accounting periods, which brings in another subjective element in the preparation of financial statements.

To illustrate the point of accrual accounting and related allocation issues, let us imagine two cases for a company that makes up its statement of profit or loss for the year to 31 December:

- In case (a), it takes delivery of five washing machines (cost €300 each) on 15 December, and pays the supplier on 31 January. The machines are sold for €400 each during the first week of January.

- In case (b), the company obtains the washing machines on 15 December, pays the supplier in January, but sells the washing machines on credit on 20 December and receives payment from the customers in January.

Given that the months of December and January fall into different accounting periods, how should we deal with each set of transactions as far as the statement of profit or loss goes?

In case (a), the washing machines were acquired by the company in December, but paid for in January. Should they appear in the company's financial statements in December or January, and in what way should they appear (in accounting terms, how should they be 'recognized')? Should they be recognized as an expense in the statement of profit or loss for the year ended in December?

In case (b), the company acquired the goods and made the sale in December, but it paid for the goods and received the money for the sale in January. If we tie the goods and the sale together and put them in the same statement of profit or loss, should they go in the December figures or the January ones?

In order to resolve the dilemma, we should go back to first principles. What is the purpose of the information given in a company's financial statements? The answer is to provide decision-useful information for investors and creditors. If we put the expense in one statement of profit or loss and the revenue (the sale) in another, we are not actually recording the profit on the transaction within one statement of profit or loss, so the usefulness of both statements is impaired.

The IASB *Conceptual Framework* says the following about accruals:

> Accrual accounting depicts the effects of transactions and other events and circumstances on a reporting entity's economic resources and claims in the periods in which those effects occur, even if the resulting cash receipts and payments occur in a different period. This is important because information about a reporting entity's economic resources and claims and changes in its economic resources and claims during a period provides a better basis for assessing the entity's past and future performance than information solely about cash receipts and payments during that period.
>
> *Source: IASB, Conceptual Framework for Financial Reporting, para. 1.17*

Using these principles, we can resolve our two cases. First, transactions have to be recorded when they affect the company's economic resources and claims against those resources and according to how they affect those resources and claims. Second, revenue and expense (changes in resources and claims) relating to the same business transaction should be recognized in the same accounting period, and that is the period when the transaction took place.

Let us first consider case (a). When the washing machines were delivered the company was free to dispose of them in any way it wished up until the point at which a customer agreed to buy them. The company possessed the washing machines from the time of delivery, and a debt was owed to the supplier from that time. So, the purchase of the washing machines created, at delivery date, a resource for the company (an asset) and a claim of the supplier (liability) for an equivalent amount. There was, however, no net effect on the company's net wealth. At the end of December the company had not disposed of the washing machines, so they should therefore appear, in case (a), as an asset in the statement of financial position at 31 December (with a corresponding liability to the supplier). In January, the sale took place: the machines are no longer available as a resource to the company (the decrease in resources needs to be recognized as an expense at the moment of sale) and the selling price is owed by the customer (the trade receivable creates an increase in resources – revenue). Revenue (income) and expense will be recognized simultaneously because the sale transaction causes simultaneous changes in resources (although at different amounts). Payment of the supplier subsequently can be seen as settlement of a liability, just like the payment of any kind of debt.

In case (b), the customers agreed to buy the machines in December, but paid in January, so when did the transaction take place? The sale transaction took place at the moment when the customers agreed to buy the machines – legally, the machines were theirs, the company selling the machines no longer had the right to dispose of them and the customers had a legal obligation to pay the agreed selling price. The revenue from the sale relates to the moment the sale transaction took place, even though the cash receipt occurred at another time. The customers did not pay until January, but this did not affect the ownership rights of either party and, in economic terms, the deferral of the cash settlement is simply the selling company in effect making a loan for a period. In short, we can recognize a series of different states:

1. The company acquires the washing machines (an asset). It could exchange another asset (cash) for the machines, but is allowed to defer the cash settlement which creates a debt to the supplier (establishes a trade payable – a liability).

2. Some time later the company extinguishes the liability by payment of cash.

3. The company sells the washing machines, but again, instead of taking a cash asset in exchange, it accepts a debt asset (a receivable – the customer's promise to pay).

4. Later the customer settles his debt, cancelling the receivable in the company's statement of financial position in exchange for an increase in cash assets.

Of these four different elements, only the third relates to the statement of profit or loss, all the others are changes in balance sheet components. In case (b), no cash changes hands in either direction when the trading transaction takes place and this is a central element of profit determination through the accounting system – trading transactions are identified according to when they objectively take place, not according to when cash changes hands.

In this chapter, we are focusing on tracking and matching transactions in order to recognize them in the appropriate time period. We shall now go on to review how this problem is handled within the accounting system. We can break this down into four related areas:

1. Ordinary trade transactions on credit

2. Revenue recognition

3. Transactions where invoicing takes place periodically after the goods or services have been consumed and time-based expenses

4. Recognition of changed status where an asset is sold and therefore becomes an expense.

Generally speaking, credit transactions are such an integral part of day-to-day business activities that the data-recording system is designed to track these transactions as soon as they occur. Contrariwise, the other three types are frequently not built into the data collection system automatically and involve the preparer of financial statements in adjusting the figures produced by the recording system.

Credit transactions

The purchase of goods for resale by a company, and the sale of goods by the company frequently take place on credit, i.e. cash settlement follows after delivery, often with a delay of 30 to 60 days. Any trading company, as part of its management of cash resources, will try to obtain the maximum credit from suppliers of goods and give the minimum credit to customers. Of course, the offer of generous credit terms is one of the weapons that can be used in marketing a company's products, and is a point of tension between financial management and marketing. Equally, the correct assessment of the creditworthiness of customers is vital.

This kind of trading generally takes place in an environment where suppliers and customers have a continuing relationship with each other and regularly trade, and is known as trading on 'open account'. That is, a supplier company knows its customer well, knows the customer's reliability as regards ultimate payment and is therefore willing to supply goods on a simple understanding that the customer will pay. No special agreement is necessary for credit to be given on any particular order; there is a continuing flow of orders, goods and payment. In terms of accounting, we need to consider two kinds of transaction: the purchase of goods on credit and the sale of goods on credit.

Purchases on credit

When goods are purchased on credit, the company buying is gaining a new asset, but instead of exchanging the new inventory asset for a cash asset, the company is acquiring a new liability as the other half of the exchange. In terms of the balance sheet equation the supplier of the goods is making a loan (albeit a very short-term loan) to the company:

$$\text{Assets} = \text{Liabilities} + \text{Equity}$$
$$+ \text{Inventory } 100 = + \text{Payable to supplier } 100$$

Later on, when the company settles its debt to the supplier, it will cancel the short-term liability with an exchange for cash:

$$- \text{Cash } 100 = - \text{Debt settlement } 100$$

	1	2	Final
Assets			
Cash		−100	−100
Inventory	+100		+100
Liabilities			
Trade payables	+100	−100	0

In the long run, the inventory asset is being acquired in exchange for a cash asset, but in the short run, there are two stages in the transaction: (1) the acquisition of the asset together with a debt to the supplier; and (2) the cancellation of the debt against a cash payment.

The stage 1 recognition of the inventory and liability to the supplier means that the recording system will always be able to give an up-to-date picture of the amounts owed to suppliers and the amounts acquired for inventory, and will avoid the time delay in recognition that would occur under a system that only recognized cash transactions.

In terms of operating details, of course, a company usually has many suppliers, and while for a picture of the company's financial state of affairs the only important number would be the total owed short term to suppliers (representing something that it will shortly be necessary to settle in cash), for internal management purposes the company also needs to know how much is owed to each individual supplier.

What is often done, therefore, is that the *general ledger* carries an account that aggregates all the amounts owed to suppliers, but the company keeps a separate ledger that duplicates the movements on the total supplier account but holds a separate account for each supplier. The general ledger account then contains summary-level financial data, while the *subsidiary ledger* is used to record the detailed data for that account. The sum of all the balances of the individual accounts in a subsidiary ledger should equal the amount in the corresponding general ledger account. Each general ledger account that is supported by a subsidiary ledger is called a *control account*. The total supplier account in the general ledger will function as a control account for a subsidiary ledger with all the details of the credit purchase transactions.

Suppliers who provide goods on credit are called *(trade) creditors* and the amounts owed to them *(trade) payables*. So this subsidiary ledger is often called the *creditors' ledger* or *accounts payable ledger*. Again, although we describe this as a ledger, it is unlikely to be a book, but rather a computer file storing the details on disk and displaying management information on a screen or printing a hard-copy analysis of balances as required.

Sales on credit

The sale of goods on credit involves exactly the same type of transaction, but viewed from the opposite side. A company that sells on credit similarly needs to recognize the sale and the debt owed to it by its customer. The credit customer is known as a 'debtor' for accounting purposes, because he or she owes a debt to the company. The amount owed by the customer to the company is a 'trade receivable'. The International Accounting Standards, IFRS Standards (the Board and US GAAP) uses the term 'receivables' to refer to this type of financial asset, while the EU Accounting Directive typically uses the British English terminology and refers to 'debtors' as the corresponding balance sheet item.

Looking at the balance sheet equation, the company wants to recognize a sale (revenue that will increase the value of equity) and an asset (a receivable that is a promise to receive cash from the customer):

$$\text{Assets} = \text{Liabilities} + \text{Equity}$$

$$+ \text{Receivable } 200 = + \text{Revenue } 200$$

Subsequently, the debtor will settle the cash owed to the company, and this becomes an exchange between one asset (the promise from the customer) and cash:

$$- \text{Receivable } 200 + \text{Cash } 200 = 0$$

	1	2	Final
Assets			
Cash		+200	+200
Receivables	+200	−200	0
Equity			
Profit or loss			
Sales	+200		+200

BETWEEN THE LINES

What is a creditor?

A creditor is an individual or another company to whom the firm owes money. Another name for it is an *account payable*. Examples of creditors (or payables):

- *Trade creditors:* Suppliers of raw materials, other inventories, equipment and services that are purchased in the course of business for resale, for which payment has not yet been made.

- *Other creditors:* Amounts owing to outsiders for various other reasons, such as salaries, taxes and interest payable; usually routine recurring debts for services and supplies ancillary to trading operations.

In a statement of financial position, a common distinction is that between amounts due for settlement within 12 months and amounts due for settlement in more than 12 months. Trade creditors (or trade payables) would nearly always be for settlement in substantially less than 12 months.

In the general ledger a company would keep an aggregate account of all trade receivables, but here again the operating convenience of managing receivables is best served by a further subsidiary ledger in which all debtors have an individual, personal account. This subsidiary record is called the *accounts receivable ledger* or *debtors' ledger.*

As with the recording of creditors, the system is tracking the daily transactions of the company and therefore reflecting properly the full current financial state of affairs. In other words, the significance of the accruals principle is that the accounts reflect the real changes that have affected the firm's assets, liabilities, revenue and expenses, even though the cash has not changed hands.

The cumulative effect of the entries in the accounts that have just been described is that, at the reporting date, the general ledger shows the total amount owed to suppliers (with supporting detail in the subsidiary accounts payable ledger) and the amount receivable from customers (with detail in the subsidiary accounts receivable ledger).

The accounts receivable ledger function within the financial accounting unit of a company should use the data in its subsidiary ledger to monitor the amount of credit given to customers and the period of credit allowed. In that sense, the data in the subsidiary ledger are useful not only in terms of constantly updating the picture of the company's receivables, revenue and income but also in managing credit effectively and reducing the risk of non-payment. The data in the accounts payable ledger similarly monitor overall trade debts and costs, but also permit managing supplier accounts to take the maximum period of credit negotiated, making payments at due dates and checking supplier invoices against the delivery information. Both accounts receivable ledger and accounts payable ledger should be exploited to manage the company's short-term finances and to operate internal controls.

One of the crucial internal accounting controls is that the entries on the accounts in the general ledger balance with the summaries of the subsidiary ledgers. The balances of the so-called 'control accounts' in the general ledger for accounts receivable and accounts payable should always equal the total of the balances of the individual accounts in the respective subsidiary ledgers at reporting date. This control is crucial if the entries in the general ledger and in the subsidiary ledger are the result of separate inputs. Separate inputs of the same transaction data can be an important organizational measure to assure the validity, completeness and accuracy of the recording of events.

Revenue recognition

Revenue recognition is central to the financial accounting process and is at the core of accrual accounting. Put simply, revenue is the money value of goods supplied and services rendered that is attributable to the current accounting period. The aggregate value for revenue in an accounting period is also described as 'sales' or 'turnover' (in British English). Revenue does not include amounts collected on behalf of third parties, such as sales taxes or value-added tax (VAT), as these are not beneficial to the company's shareholders (they do not result in an increase in shareholders' equity but rather create a liability to government – recall the definition of 'income' from the *Conceptual Framework* – see Chapter 3).

Revenue is recognized in the statement of profit or loss when it is 'earned'. It is not enough merely to have a sales agreement signed by a customer, there has to be a sufficient degree of performance on the part of the seller as well. The timing of the recognition of revenue is quite important under accrual accounting, as it triggers the matching process where revenues are matched with related expenses to calculate the net effect of a transaction on the profit of the period. Remember that profit (or loss) is just a residual that emerges from the revenue and expense recognition process, as opposed to being independently measured, and that a correct profit figure requires that both revenue and related expenses are recognized in the same period (*matching principle*). This also implies that you need to have recognized revenue before a profit can be shown in the statement of profit or loss. This usually puts pressure on a company's management to recognize revenue as soon as possible and as much as possible.

Timing of revenue

A primary issue in accounting for revenue is determining when the 'earning' process underlying revenue recognition can be considered complete. Revenue will be recognized when a critical event in the sales process has taken place whereby the company satisfies its 'performance obligation' under the sales agreement. Identifying when the critical event for revenue recognition occurs is not always straightforward. To start with, let us look at a typical revenue cycle for the sale of goods containing the following stages:

1. Customer places order.
2. Sales order is recognized after credit approval of the customer and inventory check (a sales agreement is signed).
3. Goods ordered are shipped to customer.
4. Customer accepts delivery of goods.
5. Sales invoice is prepared and sent to customer.
6. Customer pays invoice after 30 days.

At which stage can the performance obligations of the supplier be considered to be satisfied? In principle, revenue will be recognized when the company satisfies its performance obligation by transferring goods or services to the customer. In other words, revenue is recognized at the point of delivery of the goods or service (stage four of the revenue cycle presented here – the customer signs a delivery note for acceptance of the goods). Revenue is not recognized when the customer places an order or when the sales order is formally acknowledged. Even though a customer contract exists at that time and the amount of revenue that will be earned could be reliably estimated, there has been no real performance of the contract on the part of the seller until the goods have been delivered to the customer. As a credit sale, receipt of payment on the sales invoice will change a receivable asset into a cash asset, but would not affect revenue. When a payment is received in advance from a customer (before delivery triggers revenue recognition), the company will recognize it as a liability, which is the obligation to deliver goods or render services in the future.

Revenue recognition under IFRS Standards

IFRS 15 *Revenue from Contracts with Customers* establishes a comprehensive framework to determine *when* to recognize revenue and *how much* revenue to recognize. The core principle is that a company will recognize revenue to depict the transfer of promised goods and services to customers in an amount that reflects the consideration to which the company expects to be entitled in exchange for those goods and services.

IFRS 15 *Revenue from Contracts with Customers* sets out a revenue model that requires companies to apply a *five-step process*. In order to identify the timing and amount of revenue to recognize, the company has to go through five steps:

1. Identify the contract with the customer.
2. Identify the separate performance obligations in the contract.
3. Determine the transaction price.
4. Allocate the transaction price to the separate performance obligations in the contract.
5. Recognize revenue when (or as) the company satisfies a performance obligation.

The five steps of the revenue model are illustrated in Figure 4.1. A *performance obligation* is a promise in a contract to provide goods or services to a customer. The promise may relate to the *supply of goods*, the *supply of services* (such as maintenance and consulting) and *permitting use of the company's assets* such as intellectual property (royalties) and property plant and equipment (rent).

IFRS 15 *Revenue from Contracts with Customers* starts from the premise that a contract with a customer exists (see extract from the Standard). More specifically, the contract should relate to the supply of goods or services that are an output of the company's ordinary activities in exchange for payment. A contract is necessary as it specifies the promises made and the terms of the transaction. Without a contract, it would be hard to identify the performance obligations or to determine the transaction price, two key elements of the five-step revenue model. Customer contracts need not be written, they may be oral, as long as the rights and obligations created by the contract are enforceable by legal means. The contract must have commercial substance (it must have a valid business purpose and affect the company's net cash flow prospects) and the collectability of the consideration to which the company will be entitled, should be probable. Collectability refers to the customer's *credit risk* – the risk that the customer will not be able to pay his debt under the contract. Once the creditworthiness of the customer has been approved (assessment that it is probable that the customer will pay), subsequent collecting problems would not affect the amount of revenue recognized from the contract.

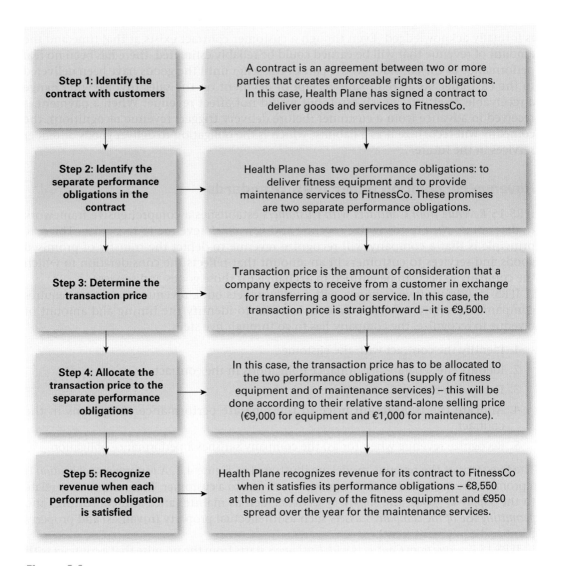

Figure 4.1 Revenue recognition model

Let us consider the following example to illustrate the five-step revenue model of IFRS 15. Health Plane is a company that manufactures and sells fitness equipment. In addition to selling equipment, Health Plane also offers its customers the possibility of entering into a servicing agreement for maintenance of the equipment. It also provides maintenance services and equipment sales separately. Health Plane enters into an agreement with FitnessCo to provide fitness equipment together with a one-year maintenance package for €9,500. The price of similar maintenance contracts is €1,000 a year, and the purchase price of the equipment when sold separately, is €9,000.

STANDARDS

IFRS 15 – REVENUE FROM CONTRACTS WITH CUSTOMERS – CUSTOMER CONTRACTS *(extracts)*

9. An entity shall account for a contract with a customer that is within the scope of this Standard only when all of the following criteria are met:

(a) the parties to the contract have approved the contract (in writing, orally or in accordance with other customary business practices) and are committed to perform their respective obligations;

(b) the entity can identify each party's rights regarding the goods or services to be transferred;

(c) the entity can identify the payment terms for the goods or services to be transferred;

(d) the contract has commercial substance (ie the risk, timing or amount of the entity's future cash flows is expected to change as a result of the contract); and

(e) it is probable that the entity will collect the consideration to which it will be entitled in exchange for the goods or services that will be transferred to the customer. In evaluating whether collectability of an amount of consideration is probable, an entity shall consider only the customer's ability and intention to pay that amount of consideration when it is due. The amount of consideration to which the entity will be entitled may be less than the price stated in the contract if the consideration is variable because the entity may offer the customer a price concession.

10. A contract is an agreement between two or more parties that creates enforceable rights and obligations. Enforceability of the rights and obligations in a contract is a matter of law. Contracts can be written, oral or implied by an entity's customary business practices. The practices and processes for establishing contracts with customers vary across legal jurisdictions, industries and entities. In addition, they may vary within an entity (for example, they may depend on the class of customer or the nature of the promised goods or services). An entity shall consider those practices and processes in determining whether and when an agreement with a customer creates enforceable rights and obligations.

Source: IFRS 15, Revenue from Contracts with Customers

Health Plane delivers and installs the fitness equipment on 1 October 20X1. At that time, FitnessCo pays a deposit of €2,000. The remaining balance is payable in accordance with Health Plane's normal credit terms (60 days). Health Plane has a 31/12 financial year-end.

Figure 4.1 applies the five-step revenue model of IFRS 15 to this revenue-generating contract.

Step 1: Health Plane has signed a *contract* to deliver goods and services to FitnessCo. The contract represents an *agreement between the two parties that creates enforceable rights or obligations*. The contract has commercial substance (both are established companies with business models for which the exchange makes sense), specifies the exchange of goods and services and identifies the payment terms. Health Plane will first check FitnessCo's creditworthiness before entering into a contract with the customer.

Step 2: The contract specifies the promised goods and services: the fitness equipment and the maintenance services. Health Plane has to determine whether these are *separate performance obligations*. This would be the case if 1) the *goods and services* in the contract are *capable of being distinct* (in our case, the company regularly sells the fitness equipment and the maintenance services separately), and 2) the promises for the goods and for the services *are separable from other promises within the contract*. In our case, the goods and services are not highly dependent on one another as FitnessCo could purchase (or not purchase) the fitness equipment or the maintenance services without significantly affecting the other. This would mean that Health Plane has to consider the supply of equipment and the supply of maintenance services as separate performance obligations and these will have their own revenue recognition pattern.

Step 3: The *transaction price* has to be determined as the *amount of consideration to which a company expects to be entitled in exchange for transferring promised goods or services* to the customer. In our case, the transaction price would be €9,500. There is no controversy here, but the determination of the transaction price could be more challenging if, for example, part of the transaction price is variable or if the customer pays in a form other than cash (e.g. barter transactions). *Variable consideration* would exist if the amount to be received depends on the occurrence or non-occurrence of future events. For example, the amount of consideration would be variable if a performance bonus would be awarded to the seller when the performance obligations are satisfied within a specific timeframe or on the achievement of a specified milestone. Variable consideration would also occur if the company grants the customer the right to return goods for various reasons (such as dissatisfaction with the goods) and receive a refund or another product in return. In those cases, the amount to which the company expects to be entitled has to be estimated (e.g. considering the probability of attaining the specified milestone or of the expected returns). The assessment of the transaction price is crucial in the revenue model of IFRS 15 as it will determine the amount of revenue that can be recognized when the performance obligations are satisfied. It means that, for example, for sales with a right of return revenue would not be recognized for the goods expected to be returned.

Step 4: The company has to *allocate the transaction price to each identified performance obligation*. This will normally be done using the *relative stand-alone selling price method*: the allocation will be based on the proportion of the stand-alone selling price of the performance obligation to the sum of the total stand-alone selling prices of all performance obligations of the contract. In our case, the sum of the stand-alone selling prices would be €10,000 with a relative allocation of 90 per cent for fitness equipment (9,000 divided by 10,000) and 10 per cent for maintenance services (1,000 divided by 10,000). Therefore, the transaction price of €9,500 will be allocated for an amount of €8,550 to the equipment component of the contract and for €950 to the maintenance component. In fact, this means that the discount within the contract (€500) will be allocated proportionally to the separate performance obligations. If a stand-alone selling price is not directly available, it would have to be estimated. Often this is done using the *cost plus margin approach*: the company forecasts the expected costs of the promised good or service and then adds an appropriate profit margin for the good or service.

Step 5: The company can only *recognize revenue* when it *satisfies an identified performance obligation* by transferring a promised good or service to a customer. The transfer of a good or service is assumed to occur *when the customer obtains control over the promised good or service*. So, under IFRS 15, the earning process of revenue is considered complete when control over a promised good or service passes to the customer. Recall the importance of the notion of 'control' in the IASB® definition of an asset (see Chapter 3). Control is expected to exist when the customer can direct the use of, and receive the benefits from, the good or service, and prevent others from doing the same. This will have to be assessed for each identified performance obligation separately. A performance obligation can be satisfied *at a point in time* (e.g. at delivery of a promised good) or *over time* (e.g. providing weekly cleaning services). In our case, revenue for the sale of goods will be recognized for an amount of €8,550 on 1 October 20X1 when the fitness equipment is delivered and installed by Health Plane. The maintenance promise of Health Plane is a promise to stand ready for a period of time (by making maintenance services available), rather than providing maintenance only when FitnessCo requires it. Consequently, revenue for the maintenance services will be spread over time, with one-quarter of the €950 services amount recognized in fiscal year 20X1. Note that the payment arrangements offered by Health Plane do not affect revenue recognition of the contract (although it will definitely affect other assets – cash and receivables).

Long-term contracts

In many cases, it is relatively easy to determine when a performance obligation is satisfied, but some cases require careful thought – for example, where goods are delivered (or services provided) over a relatively long time period. A ship may take several years to build – does the ship building company only recognize revenue when the ship is actually handed over to the customer? A legal case may take many months going through the courts – does a solicitor only recognize the revenue in the accounting year when the case is settled? In both examples, it would be normal for the client to make payment in a series of instalments, but if the cash value of the instalments were taken to revenue, that would not be an objective assessment of what had been supplied or 'earned'.

IFRS 15 *Revenue from Contracts with Customers* requires that for transactions involving the rendering of services over a longer time period (more than one accounting period), revenue should be recognized by reference to the stage of completion of the transaction at the reporting date, provided that progress toward satisfaction of the performance obligations can be reasonably estimated. This method is often referred to as the *percentage of completion method* (in contrast to the *completed contract method*, which is more common under tax-sensitive accounting regimes). It means that the company recognizes revenue and gross profits in each accounting period based on the progress of the work performed. The application of the percentage of completion method in practice will be based on a professional valuation of the amount of services performed within the single accounting period as a percentage of total services to be performed and using that as a base for allocating revenue, irrespective of cash payments. The method most popular to determine the progress to work completion is the *cost-to-cost measure*. Under this method, the company measures the percentage of completion by comparing costs incurred to date with the most recent estimate of the total costs required to complete the contract.

Revenue versus gains

Keep in mind that revenue is only one part of 'income' as defined in the IASB *Conceptual Framework* (although usually by far the most important one). Revenue is income that arises in the course of the ordinary activities of the company. Throughout this chapter, we assume that revenue is associated with the sale of the company's goods and services, but the company can realize income through other means. For example, if a company sells marketable securities (which figure on its statement of financial position as financial assets) for more than their book value, it realizes economic benefits that increase shareholders' equity, but this is not revenue (unless the company is in the business of selling securities). This type of income is called *gains*, to distinguish it from revenues from selling goods, rendering services or performing other ordinary business activities.

Similarly, decreases in assets during the period that result in decreases of equity (except dividends or other distributions to shareholders) for reasons not associated with the ordinary activities of the company are referred to as 'losses', and these are sometimes distinguished from expenses. Loss of assets through natural disasters as well as losses arising on the disposal of non-current assets, such as buildings or equipment, are typical examples. While revenues and expenses are reported as gross amounts, gains (losses) are often reported net of related expenses (income).

Period costs

It is worth mentioning here that there are expenses that are time based and not necessarily transaction based. Some items of expense are associated with a certain accounting period even though they cannot be traced to any specific revenue generating transactions occurring in that period. Rent of premises is an obvious example where the expense is incurred irrespective of whether any physical use is made of the premises or not. These time-based expenses are called *period costs*. In general, they are the cost of being in business. In a retail chain, for example, the overhead costs of head office activities and the costs of operating the retail stores during the period are expenses that cannot be traced directly to the specific merchandise sold.

An accounting recognition issue that is closely related is the recognition within one accounting period of expenses that have not yet been invoiced and where supply is on a continuing basis, such as the supply of electricity and telephone. No physical delivery takes place, and unless invoicing to the company using these facilities coincides exactly with the company's accounting period there will be some adjustment required to ensure that this kind of expense is also properly allocated to the appropriate accounting period. When there is no direct means to connect expenses and revenues, costs should be allocated in a systematic way among the accounting periods in which the business benefits from the costs. However, let us first look at an area where the application of a direct cause-and-effect relationship seems less problematic.

Inventories and profit

An important part of the routine capturing of economic transactions within the system and matching revenue to expenses is the treatment of inventories. As we have seen, when a company buys goods to resell (or manufactures goods to sell, which we will also look at in this chapter) their value is treated as an asset by the company (i.e. a resource that will generate future economic benefits (positive cash flows) for the company). But when the goods are actually sold, the economic benefits of the resource are realized and the cost of the goods has to be set against it – the inventory has to be 'expensed'.

First, we should note that in British English the term used for inventory is 'stock', but in American English 'stock' means shares in a company – quite confusing. As noted before, throughout this book we will use IFRS Foundation terminology (actually a mix of British and American English) and, thus, the label *inventory*. Let us start just with an assumption that the business buys finished goods for resale, so that we only have one category of inventory that is not processed in any way by the company.

The value of this inventory has a key role to play in the calculation of profit. The cost of goods sold is the amount paid by the retailer to buy the goods that are deemed to have been sold in the current accounting period. The difference between the sales revenue and the cost of goods sold is known as *gross profit* or *gross margin*. It is an important piece of data that can be used by management as a test of a company's efficiency and represents the amount available to a company to meet its operating expenses. The gross margin of two businesses of the same size and selling the same goods should be comparable, and any difference is worth investigation.

Under IFRS Standards, IAS 2 *Inventories* deals with the recognition of inventory as an asset, specific measurement rules and disclosures about inventories in the notes to the financial statements.

Cost of goods sold

The cost of goods sold is the amount paid by the company for the goods it sold to customers in the accounting period. When goods are bought for resale they become an asset – inventory – which is subsequently expensed when the goods are actually sold. In order to calculate the profit, a value has to be arrived at for the cost of the goods sold. Of course, this might be done by expensing each item when the transaction takes place, and some systems operate that way. But, in practical terms, this is often not worthwhile except where the company sells a very small number of items of high value – say, Rolls-Royce cars, Rolex watches, etc. Usually the measurement may be made just as accurately in terms of the cost for the year (or for a month or a week) by simply calculating the value of goods available for sale during the year and then deducting those that are on hand at the end of the year:

Inventory available at 1/1/20X1	XXX
plus Goods purchased during year 20X1	XXX
Goods available for sale in year 20X1	XXX
less Cost of inventory on hand at 31/12/20X1	XXX
= Cost of goods sold during year	XXX

Figure 4.2 illustrates the relationship between the elements taken into account when monitoring the inventory cost flow. Within the data collection system there are various ways of handling the inventory and purchases of goods for resale (or, for that matter, transfers into finished goods from the manufacturing process). The simplest way is to leave the opening inventory account untouched and accumulate new acquisitions of goods for resale in a 'purchases' account. Logically, purchases are made to replenish inventories of goods that have been sold so, in a broad sense, purchases could be expected to approximate to cost of goods sold over a period. At the point where one wants an accurate measure, one measures inventory currently on hand

and compares this with the opening inventory value. Any difference is then adjusted against purchases. Supposing opening inventory were €2,400, purchases during the period were €5,000 and inventory at the end were €2,600, the adjustment would be to reduce purchases by €200, which is the increase in inventory, and add that to the existing inventory figure.

Figure 4.2   Inventory monitoring flow

A more formal way of doing things is to move the opening inventory into the cost of goods sold or similar account, and then remove the closing inventory at the end of the period. The procedures are not really something you need to worry about. As with many things in accounting there are several different ways of doing it, and the company decides in the light of its information needs. For the purposes of exercises within this book, we will always use the method whereby the inventory remains in a separate account and is adjusted at the end of the reporting period.

Taking a practical example, let us say that a company started the year with an inventory of goods for resale that had cost €3,000. During the year it receives further deliveries: April €5,000, July €5,000 and November €6,000. The total value of goods available for sale in 20X1 was €19,000. Supposing that during the year-end stock-take, it was recorded that the goods still on hand had an original purchase cost of €4,500, the cost of goods sold figure derived (€14,500) will appear in the statement of profit or loss. Supposing that the sales revenue in this case was €25,000, the statement of profit or loss would then show:

	€
Sales	25,000
Cost of goods sold	−14,500
Gross profit	10,500

But note that the published statement of profit or loss might also be presented:

Materials purchased	16,000	Sales	25,000
Gross profit	*10,500*	Increase in inventories	1,500
	26,500		*26,500*

In terms of the company's accounting database, the adjustment would appear as follows:

	Closing balances	Inventory adjustment	Statement of profit or loss	Balance sheet
Assets				
Inventory	3,000	+1,500		4,500
Financing				
Sales	25,000		25,000	
Purchases	−16,000	+1,500	−14,500	
Profit				10,500

Calculation of inventory value

You may be able to see at once that the question of the inventory flow and valuation has critical importance in determining the profit of any particular accounting period and has implications for other accounting periods. The closing inventory at the end of the period is a component in determining the cost of goods sold (and therefore gross margin) for two periods: the one ending with that inventory measurement and the one beginning with that inventory measurement.

This can probably best be seen with an example. Let us suppose that a company in its first two years of trading has the following figures:

	Year 1	Year 2
	€	€
Sales	20,000	25,000
Purchases	17,000	21,000
Closing inventory value	(a) 2,000	4,000
	(b) 3,000	

As you see, we have included two alternative inventory figures at the end of Year 1: figure (a), €2,000, is the one the owner has calculated, but the auditor thinks the owner has undervalued the inventory and proposes figure (b), €3,000. The company was sold at the end of Year 2, with an inventory figure of €4,000 agreed by all parties. We have computed the gross profit for the two years, using the owner's and the auditor's inventory figures as at the end of Year 1:

Year 1	Using inventory (a) owner's view €	Inventory (b) auditor's view €
Sales	20,000	20,000
Cost of goods sold		
Opening inventory	0	0
Purchases	17,000	17,000
Goods available	17,000	17,000
Closing inventory	(2,000)	(3,000)
Cost of goods sold	15,000	14,000
Gross margin	5,000	6,000
Gross margin to sales ratio	25%	30%
Year 2	(a) €	(b) €
Sales	25,000	25,000
Cost of goods sold		
Opening inventory	2,000	3,000
Purchases	21,000	21,000
Goods available	23,000	24,000
Closing inventory	(4,000)	(4,000)
Cost of goods sold	19,000	20,000
Gross margin	6,000	5,000
Gross margin to sales ratio	24%	20%

If you study the figures, it will become apparent that where the closing inventory at the end of Year 1 has a higher value – column (b) – the gross profit was higher than (a), reflecting the impact of inventory on the cost of goods sold measurement. But the closing inventory is carried forward to become the opening inventory in Year 2 and, since it was higher in (b) than (a), the cost of goods sold in Year 2 for (b) is higher than for (a), so reversing the Year 1 position. By looking at the gross margin percentages you can also see how the inventory figure can distort the measurement of performance.

Of course, if you add the results for the two years together, you will find that the gross profit in aggregate is the same:

	(a)	(b)
	€	€
Year 1	5,000	6,000
Year 2	6,000	5,000
Two-year aggregate gross margin	*11,000*	*11,000*

So you can see that, over the complete life cycle of the company, the inventory measure will have no importance; total profits will be the same. The importance of the inventory measure is that it allocates cost between years and therefore allocates profit between years. Companies trying to minimize profits (say for tax purposes) would be inclined to undervalue inventory, while those trying to maximize profit would maximize inventory valuation.

Your response to this may be that the whole question is irrelevant in that the value of the inventory is surely something that can be empirically proved: you have ten items in inventory and purchase invoices show that these ten cost €X each, so the closing inventory value is €10X. In practice, companies can rarely identify individual items of inventory against the purchase price – neither for that matter would they necessarily find it worth the time and effort to identify individual purchases even if it were possible.

There is also the question of changing prices. In times of inflation, prices are generally changing, although rarely in step with one another, and in a global economy many items are sourced in different currencies. The prices of some items, particularly those reflecting rapid technological change, linked to prime commodities (such as oil, coffee beans, wheat, etc.) or priced in another currency, can fall dramatically or fluctuate quite widely in a short time. It follows that the prices a retailer will pay for items coming into inventory will not normally be level or uniform during any one accounting period.

If identification of individual items is not possible, and prices are not stable, we are left with the major problem of how to ascribe a cost to inventory on hand at the end of the year (or of any other accounting period).

The solution to this problem is that, since individual costs cannot normally be attached to individual items, the accounting measurement can be determined by using assumptions about inventory movements, which need not necessarily coincide exactly with the actual inventory movements since we cannot be certain about the movement of individual items. Indeed, accounting principles such as prudence may call for valuation approaches that differ from physical inventory flow patterns. Later in this chapter, we will go on to look at the various methods available to ascribe an accounting cost to inventory using various assumptions about inventory utilization patterns.

Relevant costs

We must also consider whether the purchase price is in itself the appropriate reflection of the inventory asset. There are two considerations here: on the one hand, we should consider whether we have added any value to the goods since they were first purchased and, on the other hand, prudence demands that we do not use an inventory measure that overstates the value of the inventory.

The first issue relates to the amount of cost that has to be recognized as an inventory asset and carried forward until revenue is recognized from a sale. It may be that, in most cases, a retailer, for example, buys goods wholesale, puts them on display and sells them, without in any way changing them. But if the retailer is involved in any costs that improve the product or change it in some way (e.g. a PC supplier buys processors, flat screens, keyboards and DVD devices from separate suppliers and sells them together as a workstation), it could be argued that these costs (assembling and repackaging) are part of the inventory asset since they represent an aspect of the cost in bringing the goods to the condition where they can be sold to the customer. The problem may perhaps be more clearly seen in relation to a second-hand car dealer. Supposing the dealer buys a car in bad condition after a crash but then repairs it, resprays it and generally restores it to a better condition. The item that is finally put on display and sold is not the same item that was bought in the first place. Should its inventory value be the purchase price alone or should it reflect the purchase price and the costs of renovating it?

If the inventory value were only the purchase price, this would ignore the extra costs associated with bringing the car to a saleable condition so, arguably, it would not match that cost and the subsequent profit on sale, which is what accounting tries to do. The general principle should now be clear: all the costs associated with creating a particular asset should be expensed at the same time as the asset is consumed (sold to the customer), in order to match revenues with expenses. Until the item is sold the costs should accumulate as part of the value of the asset, subject to the rule of being carried at the lower of cost or net realizable value (see later).

IAS 2 *Inventories* requires that the 'cost of inventories' comprises *all costs involved in bringing the inventories to their current location and condition* (at reporting date). These costs include costs of purchase, costs of conversion and other costs incurred in bringing the inventories to their present location and condition (IAS 2, para. 10). The *purchase cost* of inventory comprises the purchase price, import duties and other non-recoverable taxes, and transport and handling costs directly attributable to the acquisition of the inventory items. Trade discounts and rebates are deducted in determining the purchase cost. *Conversion costs* relate to manufacturing processes (production costs) and will be commented on later in this chapter (see the appendix on manufacturing accounts). The cost of inventories should, however, not include wastage, administrative overheads and selling costs. *Storage costs* are not included except if storage is essential in the production process, for example, processing in different stages with intermediate storage.

Costs that are not included in the inventory value are immediately expensed as period costs.

STANDARDS

 IAS 2 – INVENTORIES – COST OF INVENTORIES *(extracts)*

6. Inventories are assets:

    (a) held for sale in the ordinary course of business;
    (b) in the process of production for such sale; or
    (c) in the form of materials or supplies to be consumed in the production process or in the rendering of services.

10. The cost of inventories shall comprise all costs of purchase, costs of conversion and other costs incurred in bringing the inventories to their present location and condition.

11. The costs of purchase of inventories comprise the purchase price, import duties and other taxes (other than those subsequently recoverable by the entity from the taxing authorities), and transport, handling and other costs directly attributable to the acquisition of finished goods, materials and services. Trade discounts, rebates and other similar items are deducted in determining the costs of purchase.

12. The costs of conversion of inventories include costs directly related to the units of production, such as direct labour. They also include a systematic allocation of fixed and variable production overheads that are incurred in converting materials into finished goods. Fixed production overheads are those indirect costs of production that remain relatively constant regardless of the volume of production, such as depreciation and maintenance of factory buildings and equipment, and the cost of factory management and administration. Variable production overheads are those indirect costs of production that vary directly, or nearly directly, with the volume of production, such as indirect materials and indirect labour.

15. Other costs are included in the cost of inventories only to the extent that they are incurred in bringing the inventories to their present location and condition. For example, it may be appropriate to include non-production overheads or the costs of designing products for specific customers in the cost of inventories.

16. Examples of costs excluded from the cost of inventories and recognised as expenses in the period in which they are incurred are:

  (a) abnormal amounts of wasted materials, labour or other production costs;
  (b) storage costs, unless those costs are necessary in the production process before a further production stage;
  (c) administrative overheads that do not contribute to bringing inventories to their present location and condition; and
  (d) selling costs.

Source: IAS 2, Inventories

When a company values its inventories at historical cost, there is still a risk of overstating inventory values when goods become obsolete because of competitive or technological pressures or when prices fluctuate rapidly. For example, a British importer of a commodity may have ordered 1m tonnes at $28.00, while the £/$ 'exchange rate' was £1 = $1.20, giving rise to a historical cost of £23.33m. Assuming that the commodity was held in stock, but that the £/$ rate moved to £1 = $1.50, although the price of the commodity in dollars might remain fixed, the market value of the 1m tonnes in sterling would drop from £23.33m to £18.67m. Is it then reasonable to continue to value the inventory at £23.33m?

Accounting principles with regard to inventory measurement commonly apply the *lower of cost or market* – or LOCOM rule. It requires that if an asset is held for resale in the ordinary course of business and its historical cost exceeds the market value, the *asset value* should be *written down* (i.e. reduced) to the lower value in order to reflect the unrealized loss. Under IAS 2 *Inventories*, 'market value' is further specified as *net realizable value* – that is, what the company could obtain by selling the inventory in the normal course of business, less any future costs necessary to complete and sell the goods. We will come back to this issue later in this chapter.

It is also worth mentioning at this point that a manufacturing business will have a number of different components to its inventory. Aside from the inventory of *finished goods*, it will also have inventory of *raw materials* and probably a value for *work in progress* (sometimes labelled as 'work in process'). The latter value simply acknowledges that, where the production cycle takes some time, there will at any given reporting date be products that are only part completed.

Inventory accounting techniques

Having reviewed the problems underlying the accounting measurement of inventory value, we still have to cope with the fact that the unit costs of inventories tend to change over time. For example, the historical cost of purchased merchandise may well be different for each separate purchase. In this area, we can identify two categories of practice:

1. Continuous inventory with specific identification, where individual items are identified and traced for accounting purposes.
2. Periodic inventory practices that rely on assumptions about inventory movements.

Continuous inventory

Although in most industries it is impractical to attach to individual goods the cost of acquiring them and continuously track them, there are some cases where either the nature of the business or the technology used to control inventory allows *specific identification* and valuation.

If a business deals in a small volume of high-value items that are not homogeneous, as, for example, does a dealer in fine art, it is perfectly possible to keep records of the cost of each individual item of merchandise, so no assumptions need to be made about inventory movements. Each item can have its acquisition cost recorded and this can be expensed individually when the item is sold, leaving a closing inventory value that relates quite specifically to the items still in hand.

In short, what is called a *continuous inventory system* records all inventory movements on an individual basis (both incoming and outgoing movements), tracks all changes as they occur and enables determination of the amounts of inventory sold or consumed by consulting its records. It has considerable management benefits in a sophisticated retail business. One advantage may be the ability to calculate an actual cost of goods sold. Computer technology has also made possible the treatment of individual inventory items at their actual purchase cost, because the ability of a computer to deal with an enormous volume of data means that there is a facility for keeping this information available. However, such techniques are still costly and unlikely to be used simply so that inventory can be on an actual basis – generally, it is part of the management information system to monitor levels of inventory (for reordering and checking how fast individual items are moving) and to keep a check on buying prices to be sure that selling prices achieve the required gross profit margin on an item-by-item basis.

Periodic inventory using assumptions about inventory movements

A *periodic inventory system* records only additions to inventory on a continuous basis and uses methods based on assumptions about inventory movements to periodically allocate the costs of the incoming inventory between the cost of goods sold and the inventory asset carried forward to the next year. In a periodic inventory system, the quantity of inventory on hand is only tracked periodically (a physical count of closing inventory).

The allocation methods used in a periodic system would be applicable to any retailing business and to the retailing side of a manufacturing business. For example, going back to our used-car dealer, once cars had been refurbished they would come into inventory at a figure that included initial costs plus refurbishing costs. These systems deal with the subsequent transfer of those costs to expense at the time of sale and are therefore equally applicable whether the company is buying finished goods in from outside and simply reselling them, or whether it is adding value in some way by processing before selling. These systems come into play once the good is ready for resale and enters the retailing system.

There are three generally recognized systems for accounting for inventory within a historical cost framework: LIFO, FIFO and weighted average:

1. *LIFO* ('Last In, First Out') assumes that the first item of inventory to be sold will be the last item delivered into the stores. It allocates an accounting value to the cost of goods sold that uses the most recent purchase of goods into the stores.

2. *FIFO* ('First In, First Out') assumes that inventory will be rotated in an orderly manner consistent with good housekeeping: newly delivered items will go to the back of the shelf and the oldest items will be the first sold.

3. *Weighted average*, by way of contrast, ascribes a cost to sold units based on the average cost of all the items of that type that were on hand at the time of sale. A new average is computed each time a sale takes place.

Common-sense physical inventory control tends to follow FIFO principles: inventory would be rotated so that the oldest inventory is sold first. But there may be good reasons why, for accounting purposes, we should make the opposite assumption.

In periods of rising prices (and if we disregard temporary fluctuations and goods where technological change has affected their manufacturing cost, the trend for the past hundred years has been for prices to rise), LIFO will provide the lowest inventory value and the lowest profit, making it popular for tax purposes in some countries. FIFO, however, provides a higher inventory value and consequently a higher profit number. Weighted average provides a compromise solution to inventory valuation problems insofar as it always produces a final value between FIFO and LIFO. Note that the physical flow of goods does not necessarily correspond with the accounting assumptions on inventory movements: a retailer may apply FIFO for physical inventory management, but apply the weighted average method when valuing inventory for accounting purposes.

The EU Accounting Directive and US GAAP allow the three inventory accounting methods. In the UK, the vast majority of companies use FIFO for inventory valuation. Practice in other countries is more mixed. Weighted average is popular in continental Europe, whereas a significant number of US companies use LIFO.

IAS 2 *Inventories* does not, however, allow the use of LIFO to measure the cost of inventories, arguing that it is generally not a reliable representation of actual inventory flows. Consequently, companies obliged to follow IFRS Standards do not have the opportunity to use the LIFO assumption. It has become, therefore, a noticeable difference with US GAAP.

Note that the principle of consistency does not allow a company to switch inventory valuation methods from one year to another.

Later, when comparing one company's performance with another, you should check inventory valuation methods used to see that they are equivalent. Note also that US companies, if they use LIFO, are required to state the FIFO value of their inventories in the notes to the financial statements.

Net realizable value

Even when we arrive at a historical cost measure of the inventory on hand at reporting date using one of the major inventory flow assumptions, our efforts may not end there. In fact, IAS 2 *Inventories* requires that inventory is valued at *historical cost* unless its *net realizable value* is lower. The net realizable value of inventory items is the net amount that a company expects to realize from the sale of inventory in the ordinary course of business. Figure 4.3 illustrates how net realizable value is determined: one estimates the expected selling price under normal business conditions and subtracts estimated incremental production costs to make it a saleable product and estimated marketing, selling and distribution costs.

Figure 4.3   Net realizable value

If net realizable value is lower than historical cost, the inventory value should be written down below cost to the lower amount. So, the general inventory measurement rule under IFRS Standards states that inventories are measured *at the lower of cost and net realizable value*. This measurement rule is consistent with the more general view that assets should not be carried in excess of amounts expected to be recovered from their sale or use. It is, however, a first major departure from the historical cost principle.

Writing down the inventory may become necessary for a number of reasons. For example, the inventory has become damaged, obsolete or its market price has declined. Additionally, the costs to complete a saleable product (e.g. energy and labour costs) or the estimated costs to be incurred to make the sale (e.g. distribution costs) may have risen to levels such that the costs of inventory may no longer be recoverable from sale.

STANDARDS

 IAS 2 – INVENTORIES – NET REALISABLE VALUE *(extracts)*

6. Net realisable value is the estimated selling price in the ordinary course of business less the estimated costs of completion and the estimated costs necessary to make the sale.

9. Inventories shall be measured at the lower of cost and net realisable value.

34. When inventories are sold, the carrying amount of those inventories shall be recognised as an expense in the period in which the related revenue is recognised. The amount of any write-down of inventories to net realisable value and all losses of inventories shall be recognised as an expense in the period the write-down or loss occurs. The amount of any reversal of any write-down of inventories, arising from an increase in net realisable value, shall be recognised as a reduction in the amount of inventories recognised as an expense in the period in which the reversal occurs.

Source: IAS 2, Inventories

If there are established selling prices for the inventory items, the comparison of cost and net realizable value can be straightforward. In most cases, however, considerable judgement will be necessary to arrive at an accurate comparison. Note that net realizable value is an *entity-specific value*: estimates of it have to take into consideration the specific purpose for which the inventory is held in the ordinary course of business of the company. For example, if inventory items are designated to satisfy specific sales contracts, the estimate of the net realizable value should be based on the contract price and not on general selling prices, or if it is an inventory of materials held for use in the production of finished goods, the materials inventory will not be written down below cost if the finished goods in which they will be incorporated are expected to be sold above their cost.

The amount of any *write-down of inventories* to net realizable value will be recognized as an expense in the period the write-down occurs. The write-down to net realizable value is thus not governed by the revenue-matching principle that triggers the cost of goods sold calculation.

Accruals and the working capital cycle

We have seen that the use of accruals in accounting leads to a number of short-term assets and liabilities in the statement of financial position which are linked to the operating (trading) activities of the company. They are linked to one another because they are part of an *operating cycle*, even if the presentation of the balance sheet splits the liabilities from the assets. Conventional thinking in this area talks about the concept of 'working capital' and the working capital cycle (Figure 4.4). The *working capital cycle* models the operating activity of the company as a continuous chain of events:

- Purchase of raw materials for production (or goods for resale) gives rise to trade payables (or creditors) and inventories.
- During production raw materials are converted into finished goods inventories.

- Finished goods are sold to customers, which reduces inventories and creates receivables.
- Customers pay their invoices, which reduces receivables and increases cash.
- Cash is used to pay creditors and a residual cash balance is left, representing the profit (assuming a profit has been made in the operating process!).

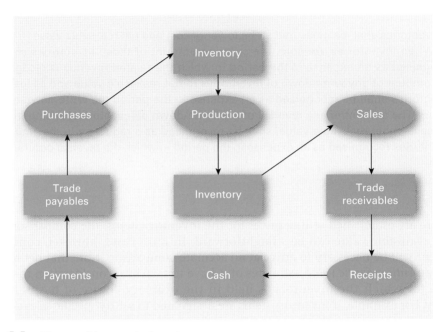

Figure 4.4 The working capital cycle

The working capital cycle (or operating cycle) can be defined as the average time it takes to acquire materials, services and labour, manufacture the product, sell the product and collect the proceeds from customers. It is a useful management model for showing the interrelationships of short-term resources and elements of finance tied up in the operating cycle, and some Anglo-Saxon statements of financial position present current assets (inventories, cash and trade receivables in Figure 4.4) and current liabilities (trade payables) together, to emphasize that they are economically linked. The working capital cycle is a central concept in any framework for the analysis and interpretation of financial statements. (See Chapters 8 and 9 on introductory financial statement analysis.) Investigating the working capital cycle is also useful in analyzing how cash flows through the company, although it does not exactly explain the cash balance in a company, which is essentially a residual that also includes short-term elements of financing and investing activities. (We will come back to this in Chapter 10 on the statement of cash flows.)

You should see that, because accounting tries to capture data when there is an economic event, and not just a cash transaction, the operating cycle involves a series of changes in working capital before a particular cycle is complete and the operation has been completed and a net inflow or outflow of cash has occurred. If a company stopped operating, this part of its statement of financial position would disappear, since it is only concerned with short-term operating events and, equally, when we wish to explain why, over a year, the profit does not equal net cash flow, changes in working capital are a significant part of the answer.

NOKIA – INVENTORIES *(extracts)*

Notes to consolidated financial statements – 2. Significant Accounting Policies: Inventory
Inventories are stated at the lower of cost or net realizable value. Cost is determined using standard cost, which approximates actual cost, on a first-in first-out ("FIFO") basis. Net realizable value is the amount that can be realized from the sale of the inventory in the normal course of business after allowing for the costs of realization.

In addition to the cost of materials and direct labor, an appropriate proportion of production overheads is included in the inventory values. An allowance is recorded for excess inventory and obsolescence based on the lower of cost and net realizable value.

Source: Nokia, Annual Report, 2017

Summary

In this chapter, we have dealt with that part of the company's accounting system that captures sales and expense 'events' as they happen and keeps track of amounts due to suppliers and amounts owed by customers. The timing of the recognition of sales revenue is crucial as it triggers the recognition of expenses, from which the profit emerges as a residual. Regular trading also involves constant changes in the inventories of purchased or manufactured goods that are held for sale. We have seen that companies usually do not transfer the costs for sold goods into the statement of profit or loss on a transaction-by-transaction basis, but rather calculate the cost of goods sold by adding up the value of all goods available for sale and calculating the value of goods still unsold, so that the difference between these two is the accounting value of goods sold. If the historical cost of the remaining inventory exceeds its net realizable value, the asset value should be written to the lower value. The operating cycle (goods being obtained on credit, put into inventory, being sold on credit giving rise to receivables and then finally turning into cash) links together these economic events in the accounting system and is known as the working capital cycle.

Discussion questions

1. Explain the link between accrual accounting and the concept of working capital.
2. Explain the crucial role of identifying performance obligations in the five-step revenue model.
3. Describe the issues of revenue recognition and profit determination relating to long-term construction contracts.
4. Elaborate how the concept of accruals is applied in accounting for inventory.
5. What is the primary difference between a periodic inventory system and a continuous inventory system?
6. A company usually reports on different types of inventory. Elaborate these and explain how they are different.
7. What is the meaning of a net realizable value test?

Appendices

1. Applying LIFO/FIFO and average cost assumptions to inventory

A detailed knowledge of each basis of measuring inventory is not necessarily useful for non-accounting management, but in order to see how each system works in practice, there follows a very simple set of inventory transactions. You can follow these through, if you wish, to see how they can acquire a different accounting value according to each of the three methods.

Imagine a student who spends his summer selling cold drinks on the beach in the south of France. He buys his inventory from a wholesaler and sells individual cans on the beach. During the summer his inventory turnover works out like this:

	Buys	*Sells*
June	100 crates @ €1.00	90 crates
July	150 crates @ €1.20	120 crates
August	150 crates @ €1.30	160 crates
Total	400 (cost €475)	370

At the end of August, therefore, he has on hand 30 crates of drinks and in order to determine a profit figure, he needs to work out a cost of goods sold for the 370 crates sold, and an inventory value for the remaining 30 crates.

Notice that:

1. We are not concerned with the selling price of his goods. We are trying to measure the cost of those goods, which is entirely independent of what he received when they were sold. Of course, we need to know in due course what the sales revenue was, in order to deduct cost of goods sold and arrive at a profit figure.

2. The wholesale price is rising throughout the period. If the buying price were stable, then the cost of goods sold would be the same under all three methods. It is only under conditions of changing prices that there is a problem about allocating cost in this context.

LIFO

The LIFO model charges out withdrawals from inventory at the value of the most recent invoice, subject to the constraint of quantities. If the inventory withdrawal is for 100 units and the last invoice was for 120, that price is used; but if the last delivery was 80, then the excess of 20 will be costed at the price of the next to last delivery and so on.

Use of the LIFO system has made the following allocations:

	€
Cost of goods sold (€90 + €144 + €207)	441.00
Closing inventory	34.00
Total goods purchased	475.00

Notice that the original inventory at the end of June is still part of the accounting value of inventory, and this is a particular feature of LIFO. Unless a business actually runs out of inventory, the accounting measure of inventory is likely to be at a very old rate (imagine a company that is still selling the same goods after 50 years), while the cost of goods sold will be a recent purchase cost:

	Cost of goods in	Cost of goods out	LIFO inventory
June			
	100 × €1.00	90 × €1.00 = €90.00	10 × €1.00 = €10.00
July			
	150 × €1.20	120 × €1.20 = €144.00	10 × €1.00 = €10.00
			30 × €1.20 = €36.00
			Total = €46.00
August			
	150 × €1.30	150 × €1.30 = €195.00	10 × €1.00 = €10.00
		10 × €1.20 = €12.00	20 × €1.20 = €24.00
		Total = €207.00	**Total = €34.00**

Note that in July the delivery was in excess of the withdrawal, so the July price was used for the withdrawal, while in August the withdrawal was greater than the delivery, so the withdrawal was costed at a mixture of the August delivery plus the balance from the July delivery remaining in the inventory valuation.

FIFO

The FIFO model assumes that all transfers out of inventory are made from the oldest goods in store at that time. Using our cold drink figures as for LIFO, this would give us the allocations between cost of goods sold and inventory which are shown here:

	Cost of goods in	Cost of goods out	FIFO inventory
June			
	100 × €1.00	90 × €1.00 = €90.00	10 × €1.00 = €10.00
July			
	150 × €1.20	10 × €1.00 = €10.00	40 × €1.20 = €48.00
		110 × €1.20 = €132.00	
		Total = €142.00	
August			
	150 × €1.30	40 × €1.20 = €48.00	30 × €1.30 = €39.00
		120 × €1.30 = €156.00	
		Total = €204.00	

The system has allocated the cost of the deliveries as follows:

	€
Cost of goods sold (€90 + €142 + €204)	436.00
Closing inventory	39.00
Total goods purchased	475.00

Notice that, in this case, the closing inventory value is at the most recent price. Where prices are rising, this means that FIFO will give the highest closing inventory figure – and therefore the lowest cost of goods sold. But if prices are falling, the opposite will hold good.

Weighted average

The weighted average method adjusts the average price of all units in inventory each time there is a new purchase. For example, if the existing inventory is ten units with an average cost of €7.00 and then five more units are delivered at a cost of €8.00 each, any subsequent withdrawal will be costed at:

$$(10 \times €7 + 5 \times €8)/15 = €7.33 \text{ per unit}$$

The allocations made by the weighted average using our original example are:

	Cost of goods in	Cost of goods out	Weighted average inventory
June			
	100 × €1.00	90 × €1.00 = €90.00	10 × €1.00 = €10.00
July			
	150 × €1.20	150 × €1.20 + 10 × €1.00 = €190	40/160 × €190 = €47.50
		120/160 × €190 = **€142.50**	
August			
	150 × €1.30	150 × €1.30 + €47.50 = €242.50	30/190 × €242.50 = €38.30
		160/190 × €242.50 = **€204.20**	

The allocation of the purchases under this method works out as follows:

	€
Cost of goods sold (€90 + €142.50 + €204.20)	436.70
Inventory at end of period	38.30
Total goods purchased	475.00

The main disadvantage of this method is that it can be quite cumbersome in use, given that the average has to be recalculated every time there is a new delivery of merchandise.

Impact on gross profit

The next stage in considering the use of different inventory valuation systems is to see what impact the choice of method has on the state of the financial affairs of the company.

If we say that the sales revenue achieved by our student selling cola was €740, his results would look like this:

	LIFO €	FIFO €	Weighted average €
Sales	740.00	740.00	740.00
Cost of goods sold	(441.00)	(436.00)	(436.70)
Gross profit	299.00	304.00	303.30
Balance sheet:			
Value of inventory	34.00	39.00	38.30

The choice of inventory measurement system provides a choice of profit figures. In our particular example, the difference between each of the three is not great, but then the quantities involved are not substantial. In a major company the inventory on hand could run to several million euros, therefore a method that results in a 10 per cent difference in cost of goods sold could have a significant impact on the company's financial performance.

2. Manufacturing accounts

We would regard it as beyond the scope of this book to examine in great detail how a manufacturing business (or any business that processes goods before resale) accounts for and allocates costs between expenses and the asset value of the finished goods (this is a complex and relatively controversial question normally dealt with in the context of management (cost) accounting). However, a general picture is certainly germane to your understanding of financial accounting.

As we have discussed, the matching principle calls for revenues and expenses that relate to the same transaction to be recognized in the statement of profit or loss of the same period. It follows that all the costs of manufacturing a product should therefore be expensed at the moment when the product is sold. Typically, a manufacturing concern buys raw materials, processes them and then sells them. The actual amount of time taken for the production cycle to be completed will vary from one industry to another, but may last many months between the initial delivery of raw materials and the finished goods moving into the warehouse.

Until the goods enter the warehouse, all the costs associated with producing them are accumulated and treated as an asset. However, the problems arise in defining exactly what are the costs associated with producing the finished goods.

We can easily distinguish between two broad categories of cost: *direct cost* and *overhead*. Direct costs are those costs arising directly from the manufacture of the product – for example, the raw materials, the cost of the workers who actually produce the good, packaging, etc. These can be seen quite clearly to form part of the inventory asset.

Where we run into problems is in the area of overheads where the cost cannot be so easily allocated. Typical overheads might be:

- Supervisory production staff
- Cost of machines used in production
- Cost of energy used in production
- Cost of factory building (rent, maintenance, rates, etc.)
- Cost of product design team
- Cost of accounting department
- Cost of general management.

As you go down the list, the costs become more remote from the production of the finished good, and it is difficult to pinpoint where exactly the line is drawn between costs that should be allocated to the finished product (*product costs*) and costs that should be immediately expensed as part of the general operating expenses (*period costs*).

The answer differs from one company to another, and indeed this is another factor which is influenced by national characteristics and the tax environment. Where tax measurement is linked closely to the company accounts, there is an incentive to carry the minimum of costs in the accounting value of manufactured goods and pass as many costs as possible immediately into expense, to defer tax. As a rule of thumb, expenses such as those of operating the factory (where they can be separated) might be allocated to the asset, while general business operating expenses, such as office staff, would not be treated as part of the asset. However, some companies may well treat only direct costs such as direct labour and raw materials as part of the asset and expense the rest immediately. One side effect of this is that where two companies in the same industry make different allocations, their financial statements will not be directly comparable: what is an operating expense in one may be treated as an asset in the other and expensed in the next period.

By way of a simple example, let us suppose that a small factory produces ashtrays. It buys plates of stainless steel that are then stamped out by a press into the shape of an ashtray. The factory is operated by four people; three are directly employed producing the ashtrays while the fourth manages the business and handles sales. The monthly payroll is €2,800, of which €1,000 goes to the manager. The factory is rented and costs €1,000 a month; the building includes the offices in which the manager works and these occupy one-tenth of the floor space. During the month of August the electricity bill is €100 and the raw materials consumed were worth €1,210. We might allocate the costs as follows:

	Total costs (€)	Product costs (€)	Period costs (€)
Payroll	2,800	1,800	1,000
Rent	1,000	900	100
Electricity	100	90	10
Raw materials	1,210	1,210	—
Totals	5,110	4,000	1,110

You can see that even in so simple an example the allocations are problematical: Does the manager not supervise production in any way? Is it reasonable to allocate the electricity bill on the basis of floor area when the machines probably use proportionately more than the office?

The main point is, however, that €4,000 would be treated as costs incurred in producing the finished goods. If the production in the month were 2,000 ashtrays, these would appear in the balance sheet at an inventory value of €2 each (€4,000 divided by 2,000 units) and would pass into the retail part of the business (the equivalent of 'purchases') as being delivered at €2 each. You can see that, if the rent, for example, were treated as a period cost and not allocated to the product, the average product cost would decrease to about €1.50. It follows that, for internal management purposes, it is vital to understand fully how costs are allocated within the company's system. Ignorance could lead to wrong decisions, such as how great the unit profit margin is. The €1,110 would be expensed immediately as operating expenses. The ashtrays, however, would be expensed only when they were sold – and at a value that depended on whether LIFO, FIFO or weighted average was in use.

Recall that IAS 2 *Inventories* requires that the (product) cost to be taken into the measurement of the inventory value of (semi-) finished goods comprises 1) costs of purchase, 2) costs of conversion, and 3) other costs incurred in bringing the inventories to their present location and condition. Following IAS 2, conversion costs include both *direct production costs* (mainly materials, labour and services) and *production-related overhead costs* (such as indirect materials and labour (e.g. maintenance and supervisory personnel), production-related depreciation expense, insurance, rent, heat and electricity). Non-production overheads (such as cost of accounting department and cost of general management from our list above) would not be part of product cost, neither would storage costs for finished goods awaiting sale. Product design costs could be an example of the third cost category included in inventory cost ('other costs'), to the extent that the product design efforts are specific for the inventory in its present location and condition.

In the end, IAS 2 *Inventories* allows much less variation in calculating product cost than many local GAAP varieties would, although it should be clear that procedures for allocating indirect costs will inevitably include significant room for discretion.

Assignments

The following questions have answers on the lecturer side of the digital support resources for the book.

1. Allocate revenue between different accounting periods in the following cases:

    (a) Carolyn works as a freelance journalist. In November 20X1, she wrote an article for a magazine. The article appeared in the February 20X2 issue and she was paid in March 20X2. She draws up her financial statements to 31 December.

    (b) Beker Industries manufactures and installs specialized telecommunications equipment at the premises of customers on behalf of Teleworks, a network operator. On 15 December 20X5, Teleworks placed an order with Beker Industries to manufacture and install 210 specialized equipment items at the plant sites of its customers. Beker Industries had the items on inventory and shipped them to the customers' plants on 28 December 20X5. Beker Industries expects to install the equipment by 5 January 20X6. Payment is due 14 days after installation of the goods. The financial year-end is 31 December.

(c) Standard International runs a small chain of bookshops. During the month of December 20X6 it sold books for an amount of €800,000. It also sold €100,000 worth of gift certificates, 5 per cent of which were redeemed by customers for merchandise in the same month. The financial year-end is 31 December.

(d) Merseyside Shipbuilding receives an order to build a small cargo ship. The work starts on 1 July 20X2. The company measures progress to completion on a cost-to-cost basis. At 31 December 20X2, the ship is assessed to be 20 per cent complete. At 31 December 20X3, it is 70 per cent complete and the ship finally leaves the yard on 30 June 20X4. During this period Merseyside Shipbuilding received the following payments from the client: 31 July 20X2 €500,000; 1 January 20X3 €500,000; 30 June 20X3 €500,000; 31 December 20X3 €500,000; 30 June 20X4 €750,000; 1 January 20X5 €1,250,000 (final instalment). Payments are non-refundable unless Merseyside Shipbuilding fails to perform as promised. Merseyside's financial year-end is 31 December.

(e) PrintCo manufactures and sells a range of laser printers. It usually sells its top level printer on credit at a price of €6,000 each. The cost (production cost) of that type of printer is €3,000. PrintCo also offers its customers the possibility to enter into a servicing agreement for maintenance of the printers. On 1 July 20X1, PrintCo enters into a combined agreement with a customer to provide ten of its top-level printers at €7,200 for each printer. The combined contract includes the printers and maintenance cover for two years. Customers could purchase separate maintenance cover for two years from PrintCo (or from other suppliers) at a rate of €2,000 per printer. PrintCo's cost of supplying maintenance for one printer is €500 a year. PrintCo has a 31 December financial year-end.

(f) Wirral Electrical sells electric appliances wholesale. The retail customers have a right to return the goods within 60 days. Any unused electrical devices returned within the 60-day period will get a full refund. In November 20X1, it sold 20 fan heaters at €15 each to a retailer (Meols Stores) and on 5 December 20X1 a further 30 at €15 each to the same customer. The cost of each of these heaters is €10. On 2 January 20X2, Meols Stores pays its outstanding account, subject to deduction of €30 for two heaters that it returned at the same time. In April 20X2, Meols Stores sends back a further heater, demanding a refund because the heater was defective. Wirral Electrical has a 31 December financial year-end.

2. Review the following revenue-related transactions with regard to a fiscal year-ending on 31 December 20X8:

■ On 30 June 20X8, Borlo AG recognized revenue on a sale of its products for €30m. The terms of the sale include free after-sales service for a period of two years. Borlo also offers after-sales service contracts separately. Borlo offered a similar contract but with no free after-sales service to other customers for €25m. The cost to Borlo AG of the after-sales service is estimated to be €2m per annum and a reasonable profit margin on the service would be 20 per cent.

■ On 20 December 20X8, Bamil SA sold goods and recognized revenue on delivery of the goods. The goods had a manufacturing cost of €10m and were sold at a gross profit margin of 20 per cent. The goods were supplied with a right to return up to and including 28 February 20X9. Bamil SA has significant experience in estimating returns for the goods supplied and estimates that 95 per cent of the goods will not be returned. The costs of recovering the returned goods are immaterial and the returned goods can normally be resold at a profit.

- On 1 December 20X8, Teleservices Ltd entered into a customer contract with another company to provide bundled telecom services. It charged £35,000 for initial connection and activation to its network and two ongoing services – access to the network for 1 year (starting on 1 December 20X8) and on-call troubleshooting advice for that year. The customer pays the £35,000 upfront, on 1 December 20X8. At that date, the connection to the network is established and Teleservices Ltd recognized the amount received immediately as revenue. Teleservices Ltd determines that, if it were to charge a stand-alone selling price for each service if sold separately, the selling price would be: connection and activation fee: £5,000, access fee £12,000 and troubleshooting fee £23,000.

3. Wirral Electrical had the following statement of financial position as at 31 December 20X1:

	€
Assets	
Inventories	400
Trade receivables	2,500
Cash	1,500
	4,400
Liabilities and equity	
Payables	3,200
Equity	1,200
	4,400

During 20X2 the following business was done:

	€
Cash sales	8,500
Credit sales	14,000
Receipts from clients	13,250
Payments to creditors	17,500
Purchases of goods on credit	18,400
Overheads paid cash	3,000

You are asked to:

(a) Enter the opening statement of financial position of Wirral Electrical and subsequent transactions on a spreadsheet (or any other working paper).

(b) Prepare a statement of profit or loss and statement of financial position for Wirral Electrical as at 31 December 20X2 (closing inventory was €600).

4. The inventory of Lowhill Gravel Company on 30 April 20X4 shows 500 tons of gravel at €7.00 per ton. A physical inventory on 31 May 20X4 shows a total of 600 tons on hand. Revenue from sales of gravel for May 20X4 totals €18,000. All sales took place after the purchases for the month of May were made. The following purchases were made during May 20X4:

Purchase date	Tons	€/ton
5 May	1,000	8.00
15 May	250	9.00
25 May	300	10.00

You are asked to:

(a) Compute Lowhill Gravel's inventory value as of 31 May 20X4, using (i) FIFO; (ii) LIFO; and (iii) the weighted average inventory valuation method.

(b) Compute the gross profit using each method.

5. The owner of Mansfield Supply Co. Ltd is considering a change of accounting policy as regards closing inventory valuation. For the first three years of the business, the company has used FIFO but the owner is now considering a change to weighted average. The condensed financial statements of Mansfield Supply Co. are given below. The relevant year-end inventory valuations according to the new method would be 31 December 20X1 €7,400, 31 December 20X2 €9,800, 31 December 20X3 €6,900.

You are asked to provide alternative financial statements based on the new inventory valuation figures:

Statement of profit or loss for the period ended:	31 Dec. 20X1		31 Dec. 20X2		31 Dec. 20X3	
	€	€	€	€	€	€
Sales		120,000		150,000		110,000
Opening inventory	—		6,300		8,100	
Purchases	68,000		82,900		63,400	
Closing inventory	6,300		8,100		6,700	
Cost of goods sold		61,700		81,100		64,800
Gross profit		58,300		68,900		45,200
Distribution/admin. expenses		59,100		64,800		44,800
Net profit/(loss)		(800)		4,100		400

Statement of financial position as at:	31 Dec. 20X1 €	31 Dec. 20X2 €	31 Dec. 20X3 €
Non-current assets (net)	36,000	32,000	28,000
Inventory	6,300	8,100	6,700
Cash	2,700	10,900	13,300
Total	45,000	51,000	48,000
Share capital	40,000	40,000	40,000
Reserves		(800)	3,300
Profit/(loss) for year	(800)	4,100	400
Equity	39,200	43,300	43,700
Trade payables	5,800	7,700	4,300
Total	45,000	51,000	48,000

6. The accounting records of RobinHood SA show the following inventory, purchases and sales data for the month of April:

Inventory			
	1 April	90 units @ €4	€360
Purchases			
	2 April	60 units @ €3.50	€210
	15 April	40 units @ €6	€240
	27 April	80 units @ €4.50	€360
Sales			
	7 April	70 units	
	18 April	30 units	
	24 April	40 units	

The company uses a periodic inventory system.

The physical inventory count on 30 April amounts to 130 units of inventory.

Required:

Determine the cost of inventory on hand at 30 April and the cost of goods sold for April under (a) the FIFO method; (b) the LIFO method; and (c) the weighted average method.

7. Complete the missing figures:

	A	B	C	D	E
Opening inventory	...	236	647	9,375	5,296
Closing inventory	12,200	110	...	8,760	5,820
Purchases	110,500	937	5,122	76,420	...
Cost of goods sold	108,950	...	4,928	...	33,996

8. The following transactions took place at a wholesale wine merchants during the
    month of August:

01 August	Opening inventory	72 crates @ €20
02 August	Purchase	20 crates @ €21
04 August	Sale	40 crates @ €30
05 August	Purchase	60 crates @ €23
09 August	Sale	60 crates @ €30
12 August	Sale	35 crates @ €30
13 August	Purchase	40 crates @ €24
17 August	Sale	10 crates @ €32
20 August	Purchase	50 crates @ €25
22 August	Sale	30 crates @ €32
23 August	Sale	30 crates @ €32
24 August	Purchase	45 crates @ €26
28 August	Sale	40 crates @ €32

You are asked to:

(a) Compute the closing inventory according to FIFO, LIFO and weighted
     average assumptions.

(b) Compute gross profit under each assumption.

9. Pino Fabrics manufactures three main products and provides the following data (cost
    data and selling price are per unit) with regard to its year-end inventories:

	Product A	Product B	Product C
Product cost	400	180	240
Selling price	600	240	440
Additional cost to enable sale (estimated)	—	40	160
Marketing costs (estimated)	140	40	40
Number of items	20,000	18,000	10,000

Required:

(a) Apply a net realizable value test to the inventory of Pino Fabrics.

(b) Propose inventory value adjustments.

10. Digit Industries manufactures telecommunication equipment in three production
    stages. There is a market for its semi-finished products (Stage 1 and Stage 2 product),
    but the company typically only sells finished products (Stage 3 product).
        Product cost per unit and (potential) selling price per unit is as follows:

Inventory category	Product cost/unit	Selling price/unit
Stage 1	300	240
Stage 2 – conversion costs	+ 80	
	380	420
Stage 3 – conversion costs	+ 120	
	500	560

The conversion costs stand for the incremental production cost of Stage 2 and Stage 3 processes. Estimated marketing and selling costs are assumed to be immaterial.

You are asked to calculate the net realizable value of Stage 1 semi-finished product of Digit Industries.

CHAPTER 5

Non-current assets and depreciation

In this chapter, we are going to look at how non-current assets are accounted for in the financial statements. Non-current assets are assets that are available for use by a company for more than one annual reporting period. These non-current (or long-term) assets can be of a tangible (property, plant and equipment), intangible (software, intellectual property) or financial nature (shares or bonds as investments). The chapter starts with an overview of the general valuation principles of long-term assets. More specifically, we will elaborate how the costs of productive facilities that are used up by the business are passed through the statement of profit or loss as part of a cost allocation process called depreciation. We then consider the main categories of non-current assets and their specific recognition and measurement characteristics.

Chapter structure

- Introduction
- General valuation principles of non-current assets
- Expensing non-current assets
- Accounting for depreciation
- Disposal or retirement of a long-term asset
- Specific valuation principles by type of non-current assets
- Intangible assets

- Tangible assets
- Investments
- Summary
- Discussion questions
- Assignments

Introduction

We have earlier used the model of the company as an empty shell into which finance is put, the finance is used to buy productive capacity (i.e. long-term assets such as factories, warehouses or machinery) and then profits are made (one hopes) by using this productive capacity in the company's ordinary activities. However, the *productive capacity of long-term assets* has a *finite life span*. Their service potential as an economic resource is used up over time in a company's operations. Accordingly, the *consumption of service potential* of the long-term assets will be *recognized as an expense* in the statement of profit or loss and adjustments made to the value of those assets in the statement of financial position (balance sheet). The profit figure each year would be an overestimate, if no attempt were made to match the using up of the productive capacity with the revenues that are derived from its use.

Just as the inventory of finished goods is consumed and expensed in the course of a company's operations, many other assets are also consumed – although they are frequently consumed at such a slow pace that it may not at first be evident that they should be considered as an expense. Indeed, in the nineteenth century, early companies such as the railways took the view that their non-current assets had such a long potential life that only repairs required to maintain them at the appropriate level should be expensed – no reduction in accounting value from the original cost was provided.

However, most long-lived assets are eventually consumed. For example, a simple retail operation might take place in a shop on the main street of a town. If the business owns the premises outright, you might ask whether the premises are in any way consumed during business operations. Well, the shop front will deteriorate in condition (wood or aluminium has a finite life) but, perhaps more important, the business may well depend on an attractive, modern presentation to attract customers and therefore it will be necessary to modernize the shop front every five years or so. In either case, there is some limitation on the life of a long-term asset and it will ultimately have to be replaced. If the asset is replaced by a new one, it follows logically that the old asset has been consumed and this expense should be recognized.

For some long-term assets the consumption may be clearer: a business that uses vans for distributing its product or cars for its salesforce to visit the customers has assets whose life is limited. Say a van is bought for €30,000, is used in the business for two years and then sold for €10,000: it is quite clear that in those two years the business has consumed €20,000 worth of van. For the accountant there is a problem: there is an expense of €20,000 covering two years which (a) must be recognized in the statement of profit or loss as such, (b) reflects a diminution of asset value that should therefore be reflected in the value of the asset in the statement of financial position, and (c) needs to be matched with the revenue generated by the operations and therefore should be allocated across two years of operations.

Looked at from another point of view, *every non-current asset is an unexpired expense* and at every accounting date a company must review to what extent each individual asset has been consumed during the financial year. The expense must be recognized (brought into the accounts), offset against revenue for a more accurate measure of net profit and the revised value of the asset shown in the statement of financial position. In principle, all assets can be regarded as a bundle of goods or services that are held by the company for subsequent use in the business. As the goods or services are used, some expense must be recognized and the unexpired expenses carried forward (this is, in fact, an important point about asset values under historical cost accounting: they are simply expenses of future periods; they do not represent any independent valuation of the asset's 'worth' in any external sense).

BETWEEN THE LINES

IASB CONCEPTUAL FRAMEWORK – DEFINITION AND RECOGNITION OF AN ASSET

Recall that the *Conceptual Framework* defines an asset as a present economic resource controlled by a company as a result of past events. An economic resource is further defined as a right that has the potential to produce economic benefits. The point here is that an asset represents an economic resource with potential of generating economic benefits and this service potential will be gradually consumed through the use of the resource in the company's operations. Depreciation stands for the consumption of the economic resource that constitutes the asset.

Applied to a van, this means that, provided that the van is useful in the company's operations as a resource to help generate positive net cash flows in the future and its acquisition cost can be reasonably estimated, it should be treated as an asset. As the van is used, its capacity to generate economic benefits will decline. Such a decline will negatively affect its value as an economic resource (it will decrease the value of the asset) and this will be accounted for as an expense – the depreciation charge.

We can divide the main accounting issues with regard to the *valuation of non-current assets* into two parts:

1. *Acquisition cost* – How do we determine the appropriate value of an asset at the point of acquisition?
2. *Cost allocation (depreciation) schedule* – How do we then systematically recognize the consumption or expensing of the asset period by period? (The deduction of the expense from the opening value will provide a revised value in the statement of financial position at the end of each period.)

IAS 16 *Property, Plant and Equipment* addresses these questions both in general and more specifically for tangible assets. Property, plant and equipment are tangible assets held for more than one accounting period (in this sense they are 'non-current', 'fixed' or 'long term') and used in the production or supply of goods and services, for rentals to others or for administration. Note that the EU Accounting Directive typically refers to non-current assets as 'fixed assets'.

General valuation principles of non-current assets

Non-current assets are *initially* recorded *at cost* that includes all expenditure to get the item ready for use (its *historical cost* or *acquisition cost*). At first sight, there might not seem to be any difficulty about the initial valuation of an asset. When a company buys a van, for example, a price is agreed and paid and that surely is the cost of the asset and the value at which it will initially enter the accounting system. In essence, that argument has much to support it but, if we look a little closer, we will see that there is a need to define more carefully what the asset has cost – or rather what aspect of the cost is an asset, and what an expense.

Supposing the van purchase was invoiced to the company (as is usually the case) at an 'on the road' price of €30,000, the invoice would then be made up of a number of items, as shown below:

Van supply	€
Basic vehicle	29,300
Special gearbox	1,300
Petrol	50
Annual vehicle tax	250
	30,900
less Discount	−900
Net payable	30,000

Should the van enter the books at the invoice price of €30,000? To answer that we have to consider whether all the items paid for on the invoice are really non-current assets, i.e. does everything included within the €30,000 purchase price have a life longer than the end of the current accounting period? In this case, there are two items, the petrol and the annual tax, that are ordinary running expenses that will be consumed within the current accounting year, so we should immediately treat those as an expense for operating the van. The discount may also be a problem. Clearly in this case, the amount of discount has been given to arrive at a round sum price, so arguably the expensed element, petrol and tax, should be reduced by some of the discount. Against that, it is unlikely that the dealer intended to offer discounts on petrol or tax, and there is a strong argument for applying the discount to the asset value alone. In this case, the costs would be allocated as shown below:

Van asset	€
Basic	29,300
Gearbox	1,300
less Discount	−900
Long-term asset:	*29,700*
Operating expenses:	
Petrol	50
Annual tax	250
Total invoiced	30,000

Let us consider one further complication: suppose that the company then employs a sign-writer to paint some advertising on the side of the van and this costs a further €500. Should that be treated as an expense or part of the cost of the asset? Is there any difference in nature between what the sign-writer contributed to the final product and what the vehicle manufacturer contributed? The answer has to be 'no', since both are costs associated with providing the van in the form required by the company. The final asset value of the van in the company's books would therefore be €30,200: €29,700 being the cost from the dealer and €500 being other costs associated with reaching the desired final asset.

Would it make any difference to the asset value if the sign-writing on the van had been done by the company's own staff? Suppose the €500 consisted of €100 for paint and €400 for staff wages, would that influence the asset value? Logically, the source of the cost should have no bearing, and that is indeed the case here. If a company uses some of its own resources in creating an asset, the cost of those resources becomes part of the cost of the asset. This is the same principle as that applied in manufacturing accounts (see Chapter 4) – just as wage and other costs were allocated to the value of the inventory of manufactured goods, so here the cost of bringing the van to the condition in which it will be used is added to its accounting value.

We can therefore go some way to defining what we understand by the *acquisition cost* of the asset. It consists of *all the costs associated with creating the asset in the form required by the company to start productive use.*

This principle applies in general to the measurement of all assets in the framework of historical cost accounting. The total asset value recorded can include not only costs paid to a supplier, but also extra items that have all contributed to the bringing into service of the asset. For example, a manufacturing company might well buy some machine tools that are installed in its factory by its own maintenance staff. In that case, the asset value at the point where they come into service will include the amount (exclusive of any expenses to do with operations) paid to the supplier, cost of delivery on site, cost of installation including maintenance staff wages and so on.

The basic test in allocating cost between asset value and expense is thus: was the cost a part of bringing the asset into service? If so, it would be allocated to asset value. *Subsequent expenditure* is added to the cost of an existing asset only if it will produce economic benefits beyond its originally assessed performance, for example:

- Extending the useful life or capacity of a plant
- Upgrading a machine to substantially improve the quality of its output
- Adopting new processes to substantially reduce production costs.

Subsequent expenditure on day-to-day servicing of the long-term asset, including the cost of small repair parts (often referred to as costs of repair and maintenance), is recognized in profit or loss as incurred.

Normally, then, the initial value of an asset will be its cost, but this is subject to a limitation as in the case of inventory valuation. For assets that are held for use in the business (as opposed to being held for resale), the rule is that they should be held at whichever is the lower of cost and recoverable amount. Prudence requires that asset values should not be overstated in the statement of financial position. The *recoverable amount* of an asset is the amount that the company expects to recover either by using the asset or by selling it. If the asset cost is higher than the recoverable amount, there is an *asset impairment* issue. For non-current assets, recoverable is normally taken to mean through use in the business. To use our van example, the fact that the van had been painted with advertising on the side would immediately reduce its resale value, but the company was not intending to resell it. The intention was to keep the van and use it in the business for deliveries etc. – so its cost will be primarily recovered through being operated as part of the business.

Nonetheless, non-current assets are subject to special write-downs when there has been some 'permanent impairment' of their value. This might occur if, for example, a company built a factory for manufacturing microchips, only to find that demand falls away – the cost of the factory is unlikely to be recovered through manufacturing the chips and its value should be reduced. We will come back to the issue of impairment testing of assets in Chapter 6.

STANDARDS

 IAS 16 – PROPERTY, PLANT AND EQUIPMENT – ELEMENTS OF ACQUISITION COST (extracts)

15. An item of property, plant and equipment that qualifies for recognition as an asset shall be measured at its cost.

16. The cost of an item of property, plant and equipment comprises:

(a) its purchase price, including import duties and non-refundable purchase taxes, after deducting trade discounts and rebates;

(b) any costs directly attributable to bringing the asset to the location and condition necessary for it to be capable of operating in the manner intended by management; and

(c) the initial estimate of the costs of dismantling and removing the item and restoring the site on which it is located, the obligation for which an entity incurs either when the item is acquired or as a consequence of having used the item during a particular period for purposes other than to produce inventories during that period.

17. Examples of directly attributable costs are:

(a) costs of employee benefits arising directly from the construction or acquisition of the item of property, plant and equipment;

(b) costs of site preparation;

(c) initial delivery and handling costs;

(d) installation and assembly costs;

(e) costs of testing whether the asset is functioning properly, after deducting the net proceeds from selling any items produced while bringing the asset to that location and condition (such as samples produced when testing equipment); and

(f) professional fees.

Source: IAS 16, Property, Plant and Equipment

Expensing non-current assets

A company acquires non-current assets in order to generate profits by their use in its operations over a number of periods. The service potential of these operating assets has, however, a finite life span and will be consumed by the business over time: machines wear out. The *acquisition cost* of these assets must therefore be *expensed in a systematic and rational way to the periods expected to benefit from the use of the assets.*

Although that may seem potentially quite a complex operation, in fact, systems have been evolved that deal with it pragmatically. In the first place, it should be made clear that the problem is again one of allocation. That is, accountants are not concerned primarily with assessing the reducing value of the asset in external terms, rather they are concerned with allocating the historical cost of the asset over the period of its use. The term *depreciation* is used to reflect that cost allocation process.

You should note that accounting doctrine distinguishes between two different kinds of reduction in the accounting values of assets: there is (1) systematic expensing of the cost of an asset over the periods that benefit from its use – *depreciation* or *amortization* – which takes place routinely every year; and (2) special write-downs where, usually at reporting date, all assets should be considered for *impairment* and their depreciated accounting value compared with their *recoverable value* (see also earlier). Any excess must be removed, but this is an unusual event.

Depreciation factors

Three basic factors are involved in elaborating a *depreciation schedule* for an asset:

1. The depreciable amount of the asset
2. The useful life of the asset
3. The method of cost apportionment (depreciation method).

The *depreciable amount* of an asset depends on two elements: the acquisition cost of the asset and its residual value. The asset has a value at the point where it comes into the company (*acquisition cost*) and when the company has finished with the asset, it may also have a resale or scrap value at that time (*residual value*). The difference between the acquisition cost and the residual value is the depreciable amount, or the expense that has to be recognized and allocated in some reasonable way across the periods when the asset remains in use. The residual value of an asset is sometimes referred to as its salvage value. This is another significant estimate in the financial statements where we can only say for certain what costs really were when an asset is sold, sometimes many years after it entered service.

The *useful life* of an asset refers to the period that the asset is expected to be used by the company. The useful life of an asset can be shorter than (but no longer than) its total economic life (the period over which an asset is expected to be economically usable by one or more users). Where the asset has a useful life that is shorter than its economic life, it is likely to have a substantial residual value.

The *depreciation method* refers to the systematic and rational manner in which the depreciable amount is expensed over time. Accounting standards generally require that the depreciation method used should reflect the pattern in which the asset's future economic benefits are expected to be consumed by the company. A variety of depreciation methods can be used to allocate the depreciable amount of an asset on a systematic basis over its useful life. These methods include the straight-line method, the diminishing balance method and the units of production method.

The allocation of the cost of non-current assets (applying the depreciation schedule) has significant effects on measured profitability, which, in turn, may impact taxation. In some jurisdictions (the Netherlands, UK, USA), depreciation for tax purposes is calculated separately from that for financial reporting purposes. However, in most mainland European countries, the rate of depreciation charged in the financial statements according to local GAAP rules is heavily influenced by tax considerations. In France, for example, the tax authorities will look at what is charged in the annual financial statements as the upper limit of what can be charged for tax purposes. So, when assessing depreciation schedules you should be aware that there is a strong link with taxation in many countries, and therefore accountants may be tempted to look at the agreed tax rates rather than apply accounting rules. Put another way, the accounting standards are sufficiently flexible for it to be possible to comply with both tax and accounting rules, but the possibility of deferring tax by using high depreciation rates will cause a company to be perhaps more prudent in its estimates than might otherwise be the case.

STANDARDS

 IAS 16 – PROPERTY, PLANT AND EQUIPMENT – DEPRECIATION ACCOUNTING *(extracts)*

6. Useful life is:

   (a) the period over which an asset is expected to be available for use by an entity; or
   (b) the number of production or similar units expected to be obtained from the asset by an entity.

50. The depreciable amount of an asset shall be allocated on a systematic basis over its useful life.

53. The depreciable amount of an asset is determined after deducting its residual value. In practice, the residual value of an asset is often insignificant and therefore immaterial in the calculation of the depreciable amount.

55. Depreciation of an asset begins when it is available for use, ie when it is in the location and condition necessary for it to be capable of operating in the manner intended by management.

56. The future economic benefits embodied in an asset are consumed by an entity principally through its use. However, other factors, such as technical or commercial obsolescence and wear and tear while an asset remains idle, often result in the diminution of the economic benefits that might have been obtained from the asset. Consequently, all the following factors are considered in determining the useful life of an asset:

   (a) expected usage of the asset. Usage is assessed by reference to the asset's expected capacity or physical output;
   (b) expected physical wear and tear, which depends on operational factors such as the number of shifts for which the asset is to be used and the repair and maintenance programme, and the care and maintenance of the asset while idle;
   (c) technical or commercial obsolescence arising from changes or improvements in production, or from a change in the market demand for the product or service output of the asset; and
   (d) legal or similar limits on the use of the asset, such as the expiry dates of related leases.

57. The useful life of an asset is defined in terms of the asset's expected utility to the entity. The asset management policy of the entity may involve the disposal of

(Continued)

assets after a specified time or after consumption of a specified proportion of the future economic benefits embodied in the asset. Therefore, the useful life of an asset may be shorter than its economic life.

60. The depreciation method used shall reflect the pattern in which the asset's future economic benefits are expected to be consumed by the entity.

61. The depreciation method applied to an asset shall be reviewed at least at each financial year-end, if there has been a significant change in the expected pattern of consumption of the future economic benefits embodied in the asset, the method shall be changed to reflect the changed pattern.

73. The financial statements shall disclose, for each class of property, plant and equipment:

(a) the measurement bases used for determining the gross carrying amount;
(b) the depreciation methods used;
(c) the useful lives or the depreciation rates used;
(d) the gross carrying amount and the accumulated depreciation (aggregated with accumulated impairment losses) at the beginning and end of the period; and
(e) a reconciliation of the carrying amount at the beginning and end of the period.

Source: IAS 16, Property, Plant and Equipment

Reverting to our example of a van, bought for €30,000 and sold for €10,000 two years later, the expense is €20,000 (difference between entry and exit values) and the decision to be made is how to allocate that expense over the two years to match the use of the van with the revenues generated by its use. (It is always a temptation to think that depreciating an asset has something to do with approximating the balance sheet value to a declining second-hand value. This is not the case in traditional historical cost accounting: depreciating is a cost allocation process, which equally is why assets in the balance sheet should be thought of largely as unexpired expenses rather than values – even if some of them have substantial resale potential.)

Of course, the accountant cannot know precisely how many years an asset will remain in use, or its precise residual value, at the time when a decision has to be made on allocating the expense. These, therefore, have to be estimated and corrections made (sometimes years later) if the estimates prove to be wrong. (Remember that the process of measuring the annual profit is in any event one of estimation – a question of trying to work out what proportion of the firm's lifetime profit was earned in that 12-month period.)

Depreciation methods

There are several depreciation methods used to allocate the cost of non-current assets on a systematic basis to the periods benefiting from their use. Broadly, these fall into one or other of two kinds: those that allocate over time and those that try to match depreciation to usage. We shall look first at these methods, and then at the way in which depreciation is reported in the financial statements.

Straight-line method

The *straight-line depreciation method* schedules depreciation as a function of time rather than as a function of usage. It is the one most favoured by companies, probably because it is the simplest and easiest to use. The straight-line method, as its name implies, assumes that the use of the asset is uniform throughout its useful life, and therefore allocates the expense accordingly.

The annual depreciation expense is found simply:

$$\frac{\text{Depreciable amount}}{\text{Estimated useful life}} = \text{Annual depreciation expense}$$

For example, supposing a company buys desks and other office furniture for €5,000, and estimates that they will be used for 10 years and have no scrap value. The annual depreciation would be charged as follows:

$$\text{Annual depreciation charge: } \frac{5,000}{10} = \text{€500}$$

This method is most appropriate to assets whose consumption takes place in a uniform manner. Examples of this would be assets such as a shop front, a building, a lease premium, furniture and so on.

Diminishing balance method

A method that allocates a high proportion of expense in the early life of the asset is the *diminishing balance method* (also called *reducing balance method*). This uses a method that gives a geometric reduction in the charge in succeeding years. A basic difference is that the annual depreciation charge is calculated by applying a percentage not to the depreciable amount but to the asset value after deduction of all previous years' depreciation. The net value of the asset after deduction of the accumulated depreciation might be called the balance of the asset, which diminishes year by year, hence diminishing balance. (The net value after depreciation is also known as *net book value* or *net carrying value*.)

There is a mathematical formula for calculating the depreciation rate to be used:

$$d = 1 - \sqrt[n]{\frac{R}{A}}$$

with: d = depreciation rate
n = number of accounting periods
R = residual value
A = acquisition cost

This rate is then applied each year to the balance of the asset at the beginning of the year in order to arrive at the annual depreciation expense.

To take a concrete example, suppose that an asset was acquired for €1,050 and was expected to have a five-year useful life and a scrap value of €50; the annual rate would be 45.6 per cent. This is applied to the asset's net value each year as follows:

	Net book value start of year €		Depreciation expense €	Net book value end of year €
1	1,050 ×	45.60%	= 479	(1,050 − 479 =) 571
2	571 ×	45.60%	= 260	(571 − 260 =) 311
3	311 ×	45.60%	= 142	(311 − 142 =) 169
4	169 ×	45.60%	= 77	(169 − 77 =) 92
5	92 ×	45.60%	= 42	(92 − 42 =) 50

The diminishing balance method allocates a high proportion of expense to the early years of the asset's useful life. It is therefore suitable for assets whose future service potential is subject to uncertainty, such as computer hardware or software, or which have a high maintenance cost in a later part of their useful lives. At a practical level, the diminishing balance method is not used very widely by companies and normally, where it is used, the annual depreciation rate is approximated (in the above example a company would probably accept 45 per cent as the rate). Very often, diminishing balance is used when the tax authorities allow it (governments like to collect taxes but they also sometimes use tax to influence behaviour, and high initial depreciation encourages companies to invest and therefore keep up with technology and create employment in the industries which make equipment).

COMPANY REPORT

LUFTHANSA – TANGIBLE ASSETS *(extract)*

Notes to the consolidated financial statements
Property, plant and equipment
Tangible assets used in business operations for longer than one year are valued at cost, less regular straight-line depreciation. The cost of production includes all costs directly attributable to the manufacturing process as well as appropriate portions of the indirect costs relating to this process. Borrowing costs in close connection with the financing of the purchase or production of a qualifying asset are also capitalised.

Key components of a tangible asset that have different useful lives are recognised and depreciated separately. Seats and in-flight entertainment systems installed in civilian aircraft are recognised separately. If costs are incurred in connection with regular extensive maintenance work (e.g. overhauling aircraft), these costs are recognised as a separate component insofar as they meet the criteria for recognition.

The following useful lives are applied throughout the Group:

T073 USEFUL LIVES OF PROPERTY, PLANT AND EQUIPMENT

Property, plant and equipment	Useful life
Buildings	45 years
New commercial aircraft and reserve engines	20 years to a residual value of 5%
Technical equipment and machinery	8 to 20 years
Other equipment, operating and office equipment	3 to 20 years

Source: Lufthansa Group Annual Report, 2017

Tax depreciation

As we have noted, tax rules can have a potentially distorting effect on the application of depreciation rules and consequently on comparisons between companies. Take the following example where the profit after all expenses but before depreciation is €20,000 and the tax rate is 25 per cent. A company buys a vehicle for €30,000; the tax rules say that this may be depreciated at 40 per cent diminishing balance without regard to residual value, and the company estimates it will use the vehicle for four years, when it can be sold for an estimated €10,000. The two approaches would give the following results:

	Profit before depreciation	*Annual depreciation*	*Profit after depreciation*	*Tax at 25%*
Tax method				
Year 1	20,000	(12,000)	8,000	2,000
Year 2	20,000	(7,200)	12,800	3,200
Year 3	20,000	(800)	19,200	4,800
Year 4	20,000	—	20,000	5,000
Totals	80,000	(20,000)	60,000	15,000
Straight-line/economic				
Year 1	20,000	(5,000)	15,000	3,750
Year 2	20,000	(5,000)	15,000	3,750
Year 3	20,000	(5,000)	15,000	3,750
Year 4	20,000	(5,000)	15,000	3,750
Totals	80,000	(20,000)	60,000	15,000

This illustrates fairly well what tax planning is about – both sequences give the same four-year total deductions, but the tax method reduces early profits and pushes tax payments towards later in the life of the asset, so the company is getting the maximum benefit in financing the asset. Of course, from a management perspective, the tax is distorting the quality of the information, turning a stable situation (same before-depreciation profit each year) into the appearance of a company which is becoming more profitable year on year (after-depreciation profit gets bigger over the four years).

This said, the distortion is mitigated in a large company because this will have a portfolio of assets, some of which are changed each year. A company with four vehicles, one of which is replaced each year, will have the same total annual depreciation (€20,000 every year) whichever method is used. Another point is that while in some jurisdictions accelerated methods of depreciation are available to help companies, they must be used for the shareholder accounts. However, as we shall see later in the book, if these companies are part of a group, the group financial statements can be prepared using normal economic methods such as straight line.

BETWEEN THE LINES

Special tax method

It may be useful to know that in some countries, notably France and Germany, the tax authorities use a depreciation method that is a combination of diminishing balance and straight-line methods. The problem with diminishing balance is that it cannot, by definition, depreciate an asset to zero, and the method if applied indefinitely leaves a very long tail of small annual charges. The tax authorities get around this by permitting a combination method where the company uses declining balance in the early years and then switches to straight line once this gives a higher annual charge, and this is applied without regard to any salvage value:

Year	Opening book value	Rate	Annual depreciation charge	Closing book value	Remaining useful life
1	50,000	40%DB	20,000	30,000	4 years
2	30,000	40%DB	12,000	18,000	3 years
3	18,000	40%DB	7,200	10,800	2 years
4	10,800	50%SL	5,400	5,400	1 year
5	5,400	50%SL	5,400	—	0

The depreciation calculation switches from diminishing balance (DB) to straight line (SL) in year 4 in this case. This is because at that point the diminishing balance calculation would give a lower annual depreciation charge (€10,800 × 0.4 = 4,320). Applying straight line to the asset value as it stands at that point (€10,800) gives two years at €5,400 and enables the asset to be depreciated to zero, whereas the strict application of diminishing balance would leave the asset with a value of €3,888 at the end of the fifth year.

There are other time-based methods, but these are the two that are classically used. There are potentially many usage-based methods. For example, it would be relatively simple to allocate depreciation on a van according to the number of kilometres travelled in the year. In practice, such methods are rarely used except by companies that extract minerals, particularly oil companies.

Units of production method

Mineral resource companies usually expense the mineral asset as it is extracted for sale – this is called the *units of production method* or the *depletion method*. Supposing a company acquires a quarry for extracting ore, and the acquisition cost is €5m, the unexpired expense represented by this asset would be the unmined ore available on the site, and it is relatively simple to allocate the acquisition cost on the basis of the amount of ore extracted. If the engineers estimated that the quarry contained 10m tonnes of ore, the cost of the quarry could be divided over the resource:

$$\frac{\text{€5m acquisition cost}}{\text{10m tonnes ore in quarry}} = \text{Depreciation of €0.50 per tonne}$$

As the ore was extracted, the quarry asset could be expensed in direct relation to the ore. So if extraction was as follows:

Year	Tonnes extracted
1	500,000
2	1,200,000
3	1,400,000
etc.	

the annual charge for depreciation would be:

Year	Annual depreciation
1	(500,000 × €0.50) €250,000
2	(1,200,000 × €0.50) €600,000
3	(1,400,000 × €0.50) €700,000
etc.	

Clearly, the accuracy of the units of production method depends on the accuracy of the estimate of the ore in the quarry, and this method is only suitable for assets where such estimates of the resource are possible and the utilization of the resource can be monitored in that way. However, it is a method of allocating expense that most closely follows the economic use of the asset, rather than working on an assumed utilization pattern.

Components approach

A long-term asset may be composed of several component parts with different useful lives or with significantly different patterns of consumption of economic benefits. This would imply the use of different depreciation rates and methods for each component. IAS 16 *Property, Plant and Equipment* requires that the company records its property, plant and equipment in sufficient detail to recognize those components separately, allocate the initial cost of the asset to its major components and depreciate each such component separately over its useful life. Subsequent expenditure that is incurred to replace or renew a separately recognized asset component will be treated as the acquisition of a new component.

The overall useful life of an electricity plant, for example, can be estimated to be 30 years, but one of its major component parts, a steam generator, has to be replaced every 10 years. The steam generators will therefore be recognized separately and depreciated over a 10-year period, while the other plant facilities will be depreciated over a 30-year period. When the steam generator is replaced after 10 years, the replacement is recognized as a new (component) asset and depreciated over the next 10-year period. In this regard, it is useful to note that, with some exceptions such as quarries and sites used for landfill, land has an unlimited useful life and therefore is not depreciated, while buildings constructed on the land are (we will come back to this later in this chapter).

Excess depreciation as a hidden reserve

Depreciation is also one of the ways in which companies that wish to follow highly 'prudent' accounting may reduce their profitability. This is done simply by charging excess depreciation against assets and profit. The consequence is that the company appears to have fewer assets than are actually in use, and these are one form of hidden reserve. In fact, accelerated depreciation for tax purposes (offered by governments as an incentive to companies to invest) has the effect of writing off assets while they are still in use, but some companies (rarely if ever those listed on stock exchanges!) go further than that.

Accounting for depreciation

Every year part of the asset cost is expensed in the statement of profit or loss and the statement of financial position shows a reduced net value for the asset (net book value or net carrying amount). In record-keeping terms, however, the net value of the asset is preserved through two accounts: opening (acquisition) cost and accumulated depreciation. As depreciation is expensed, the asset account is not reduced directly. Rather a separate, linked account is opened to accumulate the value written off. In the published statement of financial position a company must disclose both the original cost of an asset and the cumulative amount written off (this detail is usually found in the notes rather than directly in the balance sheet, but that does not change the principle). This disclosure is facilitated if the information is kept on two separate data files in the records – in a large company it would be impossible to give the information without taking that kind of precaution.

If we take a tangible asset with an acquisition cost of €15,000, an expected useful life of five years and no residual value, it would be depreciated at a rate of €3,000 a year on the straight-line basis. The following table shows how the book value of the asset would appear over the years:

Year	Annual depreciation charge €	Acquisition cost €	Accumulated depreciation €	Net book value €
20X1	3,000	15,000	3,000	12,000
20X2	3,000	15,000	6,000	9,000
20X3	3,000	15,000	9,000	6,000
20X4	3,000	15,000	12,000	3,000
20X5	3,000	15,000	15,000	0

For 20X1, the depreciation charge would be accounted for as follows:

Statement of profit or loss	−3,000 (reduce equity)
Accumulated depreciation	−3,000 (reduce assets)

The net book value of the tangible asset is the sum of the tangible asset account and the accumulated depreciation account relating to that asset at any given point:

Asset – gross cost	15,000
Accumulated depreciation	−3,000
Net book value at end 20X1	12,000

It follows from this that the accounting records are likely to have two accounts involving depreciation in any one year: the expense in the statement of profit or loss through which the appropriate part of the asset value is charged against profits in the year, and the reduction of the book value of the asset that is accumulated in a separate data file from the asset and accumulates over the useful life of the asset the total amount by which it has been charged against profits at any given moment.

The accumulated depreciation is simply the reduction of the asset value, but it is held in a separate account in order to facilitate disclosure. It always represents amounts that have already been expensed. Most corporate disclosure rules require that the business shows both the original cost of the assets and the accumulated depreciation. This also applies under IFRS Standards (see IAS 16 extracts box). The Nestlé company example shows how the gross (acquisition) value of the major components of it property, plant and equipment and the related accumulated depreciation (and impairments) are presented separately in the notes to the financial statements.

In some sophisticated accounting systems, the regular depreciation expense is recognized on a month-by-month basis and is written into a monthly accounting programme within a computerized system, so that it takes place automatically. However, in general terms, it is an adjustment to the financial records that must be made at every reporting date to recognize the consumption of some of the unexpired expenses that the company's assets represent.

Note that the management accounts of a company should normally make a deduction for depreciation in arriving at monthly profit and loss figures for operating units. A unit that makes a 'profit' before depreciation, but not enough to absorb the depreciation, is still making some contribution to the company's overheads, but in the long term is obviously not making sufficient money to repay its investment, let alone add to the value of the company. At the same time, the basis on which the depreciation charge is calculated should be checked because, as we have seen, this may not accurately represent the economic consumption of the assets concerned, which therefore distorts the performance measure.

We have dealt with depreciation as simply a question of absorbing the costs of the company's productive capacity as it is consumed in its operations. This is generally how depreciation is regarded these days, but you may come across alternative notions that are not necessarily incompatible.

NESTLÉ – RECONCILIATION DETAILS ON NET CARRYING AMOUNT OF PROPERTY, PLANT AND EQUIPMENT *(extracts)*

Notes to the consolidated financial statements

8. Property, plant and equipment

In millions of CHF

	Land and buildings	Machinery and equipment	Tools, furniture and other equipment	Vehicles	Total
Gross value					
At 1 January 2017	**17 380**	**30 166**	**7 653**	**731**	**55 930**
Currency retranslations	(96)	(17)	106	(27)	**(34)**
Capital expenditure[a]	1 031	2 061	799	43	**3 934**
Disposals	(94)	(499)	(494)	(100)	**(1 187)**
Reclassified (to)/from held for sale	(215)	(568)	(47)	(17)	**(847)**
Modification of the scope of consolidation	42	(20)	1	—	**23**
At 31 December 2017	**18 048**	**31 123**	**8 018**	**630**	**57 819**
Accumulated depreciation and impairments					
At 1 January 2017	**(5 727)**	**(16 708)**	**(5 472)**	**(469)**	**(28 376)**
Currency retranslations	(44)	(51)	(23)	18	**(100)**
Depreciation	(480)	(1 584)	(724)	(65)	**(2 853)**
Impairments	(166)	(177)	(17)	(6)	**(366)**
Disposals	63	454	474	83	**1 074**
Reclassified to/(from) held for sale	109	400	35	11	**555**
Modification of the scope of consolidation	2	17	3	—	**22**
At 31 December 2017	**(6 243)**	**(17 649)**	**(5 724)**	**(428)**	**(30 044)**
Net at 31 December 2017	**11 805**	**13 474**	**2 294**	**202**	**27 775**

[a] Including borrowing costs.

Source: Consolidated Financial Statements of the Nestlé Group, 2017

For example, in the past some accountants considered depreciation rather as a means of building up a replacement fund to buy new equipment when the old is worn out. This leads to the idea that instead of reducing the cost of the asset year by year in the statement of financial position, you create a kind of reserve in the financing side that will be used to buy the new asset. The snags with this are that:

a. The user has no way of knowing how old the assets are because in the asset side of the statement of financial position they are all shown at original cost, no matter how old they are, and there is no direct link with the replacement reserves in the financing side of the balance sheet.

b. Would the company necessarily want to replace a particular asset at the end of its life? Business changes rapidly.

c. Would the same asset still be available?

d. How do you know what it would cost? (This argument also leads to the argument that one should use replacement cost as the basis of depreciation.)

Another argument is that depreciation is the repayment, either to shareholders or to lenders of the money used to buy the equipment. Of course, the depreciation charge does not involve any cash movement – it is purely a paper adjustment of values within the accounting database. However, it should be realized that if no depreciation were charged in calculating profit, and all the profit were paid out in tax and dividend, the original capital would have been lost; so depreciation, by restricting profit, reduces tax and dividends and preserves the original capital.

This question of not involving a cash movement is also important in recognizing the difference between a company's profits for the year and its cash flow – the cash flow will be systematically higher than the profit by the amount of the depreciation expense.

Worked example

The figures below represent the data in the company's accounting database as at 31 December 20X1. As you can see, the company has the following non-current tangible assets: land €120,000 (not depreciated, considered to have an infinite life), buildings €80,000 (policy is to depreciate on a straight-line basis over 40 years – i.e. 2.5 per cent per annum) and plant €45,000 (being depreciated at 25 per cent diminishing balance – note that the figure consists of several components bought at different times). We have to update the accounting database for the annual depreciation charges, prior to issuing the annual financial statements. We need to depreciate the buildings and plant:

$$\text{Buildings } €80,000 \times 0.025 = €2,000$$

$$\text{Plant } (€45,000 - 18,000) \times 0.25 = €675$$

(we deduct the accumulated depreciation which has been charged in previous years to find the net book value and then apply the diminishing balance rate)

$$\text{Total charge for 20X1} = €8,750$$

Database	Adjustment	Statement of profit or loss	Statement of financial position
Assets			
Land	120,000		120,000
Buildings	80,000		80,000
Accumulated depreciation	−14,000	−2,000		−16,000
Plant	45,000			45,000
Accumulated depreciation	−18,000	−6,750		−24,750
Inventory	19,500			19,500
Receivables	17,250			17,250
Cash at bank	8,340			8,340
Totals	258,090	−8,750		249,340
Equity and Liabilities			
Share capital	80,000			80,000
Reserves	62,100			62,100
Profit for the year				16,040
Debt	75,000			75,000
Trade payables	16,200			16,200
Statement of profit or loss			
Sales	200,000		200,000	
Cost of goods sold	−82,310		−82,310	
Personnel	−61,200		−61,200	
Other expenses	−26,700		−26,700	
Interest	−5,000		−5,000	
Depreciation expense		−8,750	−8,750	
Totals	258,090	−8,750	16,040	249,340

Notice that the profit or loss data has been thrown into a separate column to identify it separately from the statement of financial position, but of course the net profit of €16,040 also appears in the statement of financial position.

Disposal or retirement of a long-term asset

A long-term asset will be removed from the company's statement of financial position (derecognized) on disposal or when no future economic benefits are expected from its use or disposal. At derecognition date, the non-current asset item disappears from the statement of financial position and a gain or loss on disposal is included in the statement of profit or loss. The gain or loss from the retirement or disposal is the difference between the net disposal proceeds and the net book value of the asset at the disposal date. Note that gains on disposal of long-term assets are not classified as revenue, but are included in other income.

Let us revert again to the example of a van, bought for €30,000 and expected to be used for two years with a residual value of €10,000. After one year of use the company receives a nice offer and decides to sell the van for €23,000. On disposal date, the net book value would be €20,000 (acquisition cost minus one year depreciation charge), leading to a gain on disposal of €3,000 to be included in the statement of profit or loss.

In the accounting records the disposal or retirement will have an impact on both the acquisition cost account and on the accumulated depreciation account. Both accounts will be reduced for the full amount related to the long-term asset disposed of. This will be reflected in the notes to the financial statements where the different types of change in the net book value of the non-current assets are disclosed (see the Nestlé company example).

Specific valuation principles by type of non-current assets

We did not want to get involved within the general presentation of non-current assets and depreciation with a discussion of particular types of asset. However, we now present a number of different kinds of long-term asset and discuss their particular attributes for accounting purposes.

As we discussed in the early part of the chapter, the value that a company will use for its long-term assets will incorporate the full cost of bringing the asset into service ('bringing the asset to the location and condition necessary for it to be capable of operating in the manner intended by management' according to IAS 16 *Property, Plant and Equipment*, para. 16). We have not examined the implications of this in respect of major categories of non-current assets or their specific recognition features, and we shall therefore now review some of the more frequently encountered types of non-current asset and the accounting practices normally followed. The EU Accounting Directive calls for non-current ('fixed') assets to be split between intangible assets, tangible assets and investments, with different valuation rules for each. Although not formally required, this split also makes sense for non-current assets under IFRS Standards.

Intangible assets

So far, discussion of assets has been confined to physical productive assets such as buildings or machinery, but companies also have other assets that are not physical in nature; these are called *intangible assets*. Intangible assets reflect intangible resources such as scientific or technical knowledge, development of new processes or systems, intellectual property, privileged customer relationships, etc. Typical intangible assets would be research and development, brand names, copyrights, computer software, licences, patents.

Intangible assets are increasingly important to companies and are a continuing source of accounting problems. It is very difficult to attach a historical cost to some intangibles, such as brand names, which are built up slowly over years. Even if one could attach a cost to the asset, there is still the question of estimating its useful life and related amortization. Note that the term depreciation is typically used for physical assets, whereas the term *amortization* is used as a depreciation synonym for intangible assets.

IAS 38 – INTANGIBLE ASSETS – DEFINITION *(extracts)*

8. An intangible asset is an identifiable non-monetary asset without physical substance.

9. Entities frequently expend resources, or incur liabilities, on the acquisition, development, maintenance or enhancement of intangible resources such as scientific or technical knowledge, design and implementation of new processes or systems, licences, intellectual property, market knowledge and trademarks (including brand names and publishing titles). Common examples of items encompassed by these broad headings are computer software, patents, copyrights, motion picture films, customer lists, mortgage servicing rights, fishing licences, import quotas, franchises, customer or supplier relationships, customer loyalty, market share and marketing rights.

10. Not all the items described in paragraph 9 meet the definition of an intangible asset, ie identifiability, control over a resource and existence of future economic benefits. If an item within the scope of this Standard does not meet the definition of an intangible asset, expenditure to acquire it or generate it internally is recognised as an expense when it is incurred.

12. An asset is identifiable if it either:

    (a) is separable, ie is capable of being separated or divided from the entity and sold, transferred, licensed, rented or exchanged, either individually or together with a related contract, identifiable asset or liability, regardless of whether the entity intends to do so; or

    (b) arises from contractual or other legal rights, regardless of whether those rights are transferable or separable from the entity or from other rights and obligations.

Source: IAS 38, Intangible Assets

IAS 38 *Intangible Assets* defines an intangible asset as 'an identifiable non-monetary asset without physical substance' (IAS 38, para. 8). This definition contains three essential characteristics of intangible assets:

    a. They are assets – present economic resources controlled by the company as a result of past events.

    b. They lack physical substance.

    c. They are identifiable.

A major problem with intangible assets is that of the *level of uncertainty surrounding the future economic benefits* that arise from expenditure of this nature. This uncertainty relates to both the amount of future economic benefits and the ability to control the future economic benefits flowing from the intangible items and restrict the access of others to those benefits. For example, if a company spends money training its staff, the object is to improve future operations and, one hopes, profitability. However, the improvement is not certain and the staff may leave at some future point, taking their improved efficiency with them. Similarly, advertising is done to generate future sales, but the long-term effects are generally impossible to estimate and are not under the control of the company.

The *identifiability* characteristic of the definition of an intangible asset is met when it is *separable* (capable of being separated from the company and sold, licensed, rented, etc.) or when it arises from *contractual or other legal rights*. This characteristic is essential to distinguish intangible assets from the more general concept of goodwill.

The *useful life* of an intangible asset can be *finite or indefinite*. The useful life of the intangible asset is usually assessed based on the expected cash flow streams associated with the asset. According to IAS 38 *Intangible Assets*, an intangible asset can be regarded as having an indefinite useful life when there is no foreseeable limit to the period over which the asset is expected to generate net cash inflows for the company. This means that, under IAS 38, it is possible to recognize some intangible assets without having to depreciate them at all.

Intangible assets can be acquired externally or generated internally, although current practice imposes limitations on internally generated intangible resources such as research and development.

Research and development

In some sense research and development (R&D) expenditure is the archetypal intangible asset and raises a number of basic questions when assessing whether the costs incurred in research and development activities qualify for asset recognition. These issues relate to determining whether and when an identifiable asset exists that will generate probable economic benefits for the company and how the cost of such an asset is measured with sufficient reliability.

Where a company has invested in researching and developing new products, it does not seem unreasonable that the cost of creating a new product should be considered an asset, provided that the new product will lead to a commercial exploitation. Very often it is relatively late in the R&D process that one can be reasonably certain that an asset (in the sense of something that will bring future economic benefits) has been created.

In defining the costs associated with creating the new product, there is the problem of the treatment of the costs of unsuccessful research. For example, supposing a chemist sets out to create a new headache tablet and takes four years, during which he tries five alternative bases, of which only the last is wholly satisfactory. Does the R&D asset include the costs only of the research into the alternative that was ultimately accepted? Or should the process of defining the unsuccessful alternatives be considered as part of finding the usable alternative, and therefore all the costs should be treated as an R&D asset?

In the USA, the difficulty of finding a suitable definition together with the operation of prudence have led to a situation where all R&D costs must be expensed as they are incurred. In Europe, the treatment in national accounting rules is generally more flexible: general research must be expensed immediately, but research involved in refining and developing a specific product may be treated as an asset and expensed over its useful life (although many companies expense all R&D expenditure immediately anyway, not least because it qualifies immediately as a deduction for tax purposes).

IAS 38 *Intangible Assets* focuses on the *distinction between the research phase and the development phase* of an internal project, whereby research costs should be expensed as incurred, but development costs may qualify for recognition. The IASB argues that at the research phase of a project, a company is unable to demonstrate that an intangible asset exists that will generate probable future economic benefits. In the development phase of an internal project, however, activities are focused on the application of research findings or other knowledge to a plan or design of new products or systems and circumstances that may enable the company to identify an intangible asset and demonstrate the probable future economic benefits flowing from these development activities. IAS 38 includes specific recognition criteria for development costs (and internally generated intangible assets in general) that expand on the general recognition criteria for assets (see extracts of IAS 38). If these criteria are met, an intangible asset arising from development should be recognized.

Estimating the useful life of internally generated intangible assets will usually be done on a prudent basis. As with patents, there is a strong economic argument for spreading this over the whole expected commercial exploitation of the project. But again there is the problem of uncertainty – can one reasonably expect that a new headache tablet, for example, might be exploited for as long as 20 years? The amortization method used should reflect the pattern in which the asset's future economic benefits are expected to be consumed by the company. If that pattern cannot be determined reliably, the straight-line method will be used. The residual value of an intangible asset with a finite useful life is generally assumed to be zero.

A detailed analysis of the intangible assets, divided into major classes and showing original cost and accumulated amortization, has to be disclosed and is usually shown in the notes to the accounts.

Brand names

In many bulk product areas where there are several competing products with very similar characteristics (coffee, chocolate, cars, washing machines, etc.), it has become increasingly understood by management that what is important to the success of a business is not so much its manufacturing capacity (or not exclusively its manufacturing capacity), but also its ability to sell the products. Very often this is associated with the creation and maintenance of brand names. Ownership of a brand name may be described as a right to a future economic benefit (and therefore potentially an accounting asset), but having that brand name appear in the statement of financial position is problematical.

STANDARDS

 IAS 38 – INTANGIBLE ASSETS – RESEARCH AND DEVELOPMENT *(extracts)*

8. Research is original and planned investigation undertaken with the prospect of gaining new scientific or technical knowledge and understanding.
Development is the application of research findings or other knowledge to a plan or design for the production of new or substantially improved materials, devices, products, processes, systems or services before the start of commercial production or use.
52. To assess whether an internally generated intangible asset meets the criteria for recognition, an enterprise classifies the generation of the asset into:

   (a) a research phase; and
   (b) a development phase.

53. If an entity cannot distinguish the research phase from the development phase of an internal project to create an intangible asset, the entity treats the expenditure on that project as if it were incurred in the research phase only.
54. No intangible asset arising from research (or from the research phase of an internal project) shall be recognised. Expenditure on research (or on the research phase of an internal project) shall be recognised as an expense when it is incurred.

57. An intangible asset arising from development (or from the development phase of an internal project) shall be recognised if, and only if, an entity can demonstrate all of the following:

(a) the technical feasibility of completing the intangible asset so that it will be available for use or sale;

(b) its intention to complete the intangible asset and use or sell it;

(c) its ability to use or sell the intangible asset;

(d) how the intangible asset will generate probable future economic benefits. Among other things, the entity can demonstrate the existence of a market for the output of the intangible asset or the intangible asset itself or, if it is to be used internally, the usefulness of the intangible asset;

(e) the availability of adequate technical, financial and other resources to complete the development and to use or sell the intangible asset; and

(f) its ability to measure reliably the expenditure attributable to the intangible asset during its development.

71. Expenditure on an intangible item that was initially recognized as an expense shall not be recognised as part of the cost of an intangible asset at a later date.

Source: IAS 38, Intangible Assets

Where a company buys a brand name from another company, there is no problem – a clear historical cost emerges from the transaction. But where a company creates a brand name – very similar to creating a new product – there are the problems of how early in the expenditure programme it becomes reasonable to categorize the costs as being an asset and how to reliably measure the cost of the brand name. Expenditure on internally generated brands (like advertising campaigns) is in most cases indistinguishable from the cost of developing the business in general.

A further issue that has arisen is the question of amortization of brand names acquired in company takeovers. Many large companies that carry brand names argued that the regular advertising and promotion budget maintains the value of the brand, and depreciation is therefore unnecessary and represents a double charge. The standard-setter has been receptive to these kinds of argument by allowing intangible assets with indefinite useful lives to be accounted for without systematic amortization.

Patents

Patents are, in effect, a legal protection of an invention that prevents anyone using the invention without permission. As such, they are sometimes costly to establish, but once established they do have a future economic use to the company (either from making or using the product or from licensing others to use it), provided that there is a demand for the particular invention.

Assuming that a patent does represent future economic benefits to the company, it should be recognized at cost and then the cost will be expensed over the expected useful life of the asset in the normal way. Where a company buys a patent, its historical value is clear, but where it invents the subject of the patent, the problem of identifying the related costs and the application of the specific recognition criteria for internally generated intangible assets come into play. The exact depreciation pattern could be a matter for debate, but unless exploitation can be foreseen with a high degree of certainty, patents are a good candidate for methods that load depreciation into the early years.

Purchased goodwill

Sometimes companies expand by 'buying' customers from other suppliers, and when this happens a company is said to be buying 'goodwill'. For example, a solicitor who was planning to retire could sell the goodwill of her practice to another solicitor. Her clients would presumably still need a solicitor, and although they cannot be forced to move to the alternative selected, she can write to them recommending a specific alternative. The person recommended would have paid a fee for this to happen, and would have an excellent chance of retaining the customers.

Should the figure paid by an entity that acquires customers in this way be treated as an intangible asset? In the absence of legal rights to protect the client relationship or their loyalty, there is usually insufficient ground to establish real control over these items to meet the definition of an intangible asset. Nevertheless, exchange transactions for the same or similar non-contractual customer relationships may provide evidence that the company is able to control the expected future benefits flowing from the customer relationships even in the absence of legal control. The existence of such exchange transactions also provides evidence that customer goodwill is separable, a necessary condition to meet the definition of an intangible asset. As such, exchange transactions are rare, this kind of goodwill is not frequently encountered in company accounts. However, if recognized, the purchased goodwill must be expensed in the usual way. Views differ as to the appropriate length of the period and the tendency is towards a short useful life on the basis that once the customers have tried the alternative service it is the quality of the alternative that will determine whether they remain customers or not.

STANDARDS

 IAS 38 – INTANGIBLE ASSETS – EXCLUSIONS *(extract)*

63. Internally generated brands, mastheads, publishing titles, customer lists and items similar in substance should not be recognised as intangible assets.

Source: IAS 38, Intangible Assets

IAS 38 *Intangible Assets* explicitly prohibits the recognition of internally generated goodwill as an asset, because it is not an identifiable (separable) resource controlled by the company that can be measured reliably at cost.

There is a third type of goodwill (goodwill arising on consolidation), which is a product of accounting for groups of companies and will be discussed in that context in Chapter 12.

Tangible assets

Historically, tangible long-term assets have been the major assets of companies. IAS 16 *Property, Plant and Equipment* covers the main non-current tangible assets. Property, plant and equipment are tangible assets held for more than one accounting period and used in the production or supply of goods and services, for rentals to others or for administration.

TOMTOM – INTANGIBLE ASSETS *(extract)*

Accounting policy – Other intangible assets

Other intangible assets includes both assets that have been acquired, either through individual asset acquisitions or through business combinations, and assets that have been generated internally, such as the group's core technology and geographical content database.

Internally generated intangible assets

Internal development costs for core technology are recognised as an intangible asset if, and only if, all of the following have been demonstrated:

- The technical feasibility to complete the project;
- The intention to complete the intangible asset, and use or sell it;
- The ability to use or sell the intangible asset;
- How the intangible asset will generate probable future economic benefits;
- The availability of adequate resources to complete the project; and
- The cost of developing the asset can be measured reliably.

Internally generated databases are capitalised until a certain level of map coverage is reached and ongoing activities focus on maintenance. At this point, capitalisation is discontinued.

Internal software costs relating to development of non-core software with an estimated average useful life of less than one year and engineering costs relating to the detailed manufacturing design of new products, are expensed in the period in which they are incurred.

The amount initially recognised for internally generated intangible assets is the sum of the expenditure incurred from the date when the intangible asset first meets the recognition criteria listed above. All expenditures on research activities are expensed in the income statement as incurred.

Acquired intangible assets

Definite-lived intangible assets acquired separately are initially recognised at cost. The cost of assets acquired separately includes directly attributable costs to bring the asset to its intended use. Intangible assets acquired in a business combination are identified and recognised separately from goodwill where they satisfy the definition of an intangible asset and their fair values can be measured reliably. The cost of such intangible assets is their fair value at the acquisition date.

Subsequent to initial recognition, all intangible assets [other than goodwill] are carried at cost less accumulated amortisation and accumulated impairment losses.

The amortisation of other intangible assets is recorded on a straight-line basis over the following estimated useful lives as follows:

- Map content and mapmaking platform: 4-20 years;
- Internally generated core technology: 3–7 years;
- Customer relationships: 5–13 years;
- Computer software: 2–5 years;
- Acquired technology: 4–5 years;
- Brand names: 5 years.

Customer relationships include customers for maps; there is a high cost involved in changing map providers and historically there is a high customer retention.

Source: TomTom International BV, ©2017 Annual Report

A detailed analysis of these assets, divided into major classes and showing original cost (or valuation) and accumulated depreciation, has to be shown and is usually given in the notes to the accounts (see the Nestlé company example).

Land and buildings

In general terms, a company would recognize such an asset as land or buildings at a value that was based on the purchase price and any other ancillary costs. A simple case would be where a company buys a ready-built factory and may only have ancillary costs for professional fees such as for a surveyor and the solicitor who drew up the contract. Both the purchase price and the fees would be capitalized in the acquisition cost of the asset – the fees represent an integral part of the cost of bringing the asset to the location and condition necessary for it to be capable of operating in the manner intended by management.

A more complicated case might be where a company buys a plot of land on which there is a derelict building, demolishes the building, clears the site and builds a new factory. The value of the factory in the company's accounting records would include all those costs, as well as perhaps architect's fees and so on.

The aggregation of these elements provides a base cost, but the accounting problems and depreciation approach will depend on the legal means whereby the land is held. A company may either acquire a lease – a licence to use the land for a specific number of years – or it may own the land outright. Under a lease, the problem is that the company's right to use the land will cease after a specified period, but the implications of that depend on the length of the period. If the lease is for a relatively short period, say five years, the asset must be expensed over that period. However, leases are also issued for much longer periods, occasionally as long as 999 years, in which case the cessation of the company's right to use the land is so remote as not to be worth considering. Leased property is usually depreciated over the life of the lease, with a maximum depreciation period for buildings of around 50 years.

Land that is owned outright provides a different problem because of the trend for land prices to rise. This means that in the classic approach to depreciation, the depreciable amount (acquisition cost less estimated residual value) may actually be negative. Supposing you acquired a piece of land for a project limited to 10 years and that the land cost €500,000, it could be that with the rise in land prices expected over the 10 years the residual value would be (say) €600,000, giving a negative depreciable amount of €100,000.

Land usually has an indefinite useful life and therefore is not depreciated. That still leaves the question of the buildings that may stand on the land. Buildings, by way of contrast, have a limited useful life and therefore are depreciable assets. The traditional approach would be to arrive at separate values for the land and buildings (perhaps by asking a professional valuer to give estimates of each and then applying the proportion to the historical cost) and then depreciate the buildings separately from the land – usually over 50 years on a straight-line basis. Here again, some companies argue that there seems little justification for depreciating buildings whose value may also rise but which, in any event, sit on land whose value is rising in the long term.

An issue that has not really presented itself very strongly yet is the question of creating provisions for the eventual reinstatement of land to its natural state. This has surfaced, for example, in respect of the decommissioning costs of nuclear power stations. It can be argued that any company that builds a factory should make provisions for the ultimate removal of the factory when its useful life has ended and include the corresponding cost as part of the acquisition cost of the asset. In this vein, IAS 16 requires that when a company incurs an obligation to dismantle and remove the tangible asset and restore the site on which it is located, it should estimate the associated costs and include the initial estimate in the acquisition cost of the asset (we will come back to the issues involved in Chapter 14). The capitalized decommissioning costs will be depreciated alongside the other acquisition costs to match the costs to the asset's revenue-earning period.

Plant and equipment

Here again, the purchase price of the plant may well be only a part of the total costs of bringing the plant into service. Ancillary costs to be capitalized might include elements such as site preparation, engineers' time in assembling and testing the plant on site, cost of transport to the site, etc. Sometimes a company's own workforce may be involved in the preparation of the asset. The fact that the company's workforce is involved does not change the basic concept – their wages etc. should be treated as part of the installation cost.

Leased assets

Sometimes a company acquires plant and equipment or other assets on a lease agreement, rather than buying them outright. The increasing use of this method of financing has highlighted a particular accounting problem. If a company acquires an asset under a lease agreement and, in effect, has the use of the asset throughout its useful life, should that asset be recognized in the statement of financial position? Should the obligation under the lease to make payments to the lessor be recognized as a liability?

If, for example, a company borrows €100,000 to buy some plant worth €100,000, both the plant asset and the debt liability would appear in the statement of financial position. When a company hires equipment on a lease for substantially the whole of its useful life, the company is in effect acquiring the asset's economic value while incurring a liability to pay for it in instalments. The instalments would include both an element of interest and an element of repayment of the value of the asset. Is this situation different in principle from that where the company borrows the money and buys the asset in two separate transactions?

The USA, UK and IASB all have standards requiring that where a company acquires substantially all the risks and rewards of ownership of an asset under a lease, that asset should be recognized in the statement of financial position as well as the liability to the lessor, irrespective of the fact that legal title of ownership to those assets is not transferred to the company. IAS 17 *Leases* (which was effective until 1 January 2019 and as a consequence would generate disclosures about the change in Standards in the 2019 financial statements) defines a lease as an arrangement whereby the lessor conveys to the lessee, in return for a payment or series of payments, the right to use an asset for an agreed period of time. The type of lease whereby substantially all the risks and rewards of ownership of an asset are transferred, is called a *finance lease* (as opposed to an *operating lease*). Accounting for finance leases is a typical example of the application of the 'substance over form' principle whereby the accounting rules act on economic substance and not on legal form.

It is not particularly useful in the context of an introductory financial accounting course to analyze in detail the methods that are used for arriving at a precise value of the asset and splitting the total amounts payable under the lease into repayment of the loan and interest charges. In principle, the asset is valued at fair value (its purchase price if bought on the open market) and this value is recognized as an asset. A balancing liability for the same amount is recognized as an obligation to the lessor. The amount payable over the length of the lease will normally be more than this, since it includes an interest element. The interest element is allocated over the length of the lease, ideally in relation to the outstanding value of the lease liability.

Take a simplified example where a company leases a machine for five years at a rate of €10,000 a year. If the company had bought the machine on the open market it would have cost €35,000. Accordingly, the machine will appear in the statement of financial position at €35,000 and there will also be a balancing lease liability of €35,000. This means that the difference between the fair value assumed and the total of the lease payments (€10,000 × 5 years = €50,000) is €15,000 and this represents the implied interest charge on the transaction.

The €15,000 needs to be allocated over the life of the asset in proportion to the amount of the loan outstanding, and this can be done accurately with a computer program or there are simplified approximations to work out the effective rate of interest being charged. If we simplify in this case and say that the implied rate of interest is 10 per cent, then the first annual payment of €10,000 would be split for accounting purposes as €3,500 interest charge (€35,000 lease liability × 10 per cent) and €6,500 as repayment of the lease liability, leaving €28,500 outstanding at the start of the second year.

In the second year the interest charge is 10 per cent × €28,500 = €2,850 and the balance of the annual payment, €7,150, is used to further repay the lease liability. This continues until the lease liability is extinguished. The leased asset is depreciated in the same way as assets which are owned once a value has been arrived at.

The distinction between operating leases and finance leases disappeared on 1 January 2019 when IFRS 16 *Leases* came into force. Under this standard all leases are accounted for as finance leases, and the operating lease category disappears (but you will still find it in accounts for years before 2019, of course). IFRS 16 says that all leases should involve the recognition of a 'right-of-use' asset and a lease liability.

There is an exemption for leases with less than one year to run, and low value items, in order to simplify application. The US has issued a similar standard developed alongside the IFRS Standards.

Investments

Investments represent the third main category of non-current asset: *long-term assets of a financial nature*, such as investments in another company's equity (shares) or in another entity's debt (bonds, loans). It is important to note from the start that, unlike tangible and intangible assets, investments are not subject to a depreciation regime. Instead, they are measured at historical cost (sometimes adjusted as 'amortized cost') or at fair value. (In what follows, we will refer to equity investments – shares of other companies; debt securities will be commented on in Chapter 14.)

Companies may make investments on both a short-term and a long-term basis. Short-term investments are often made in liquid securities when a company has a temporary excess of cash. These are sometimes called *treasury investments* and appear as a current asset, often as part of cash at a bank (cash equivalents).

Where a company makes an investment for strategic purposes, which it intends to hold for some length of time, this will appear as financial assets in the non-current or fixed asset category. Companies may invest in other companies for a number of reasons – to secure a relationship with a major customer or supplier; to participate in a new development but spread the risk with other interested parties; as a forerunner to a takeover. Where a company has a substantial equity stake in another (less than 50 per cent of the shares outstanding, but large enough, for example, to be given a seat on the board) this is called an investment in an *associated company* (the technique for accounting for associated companies is dealt with in Chapter 12). Where companies set up joint ventures (for example, oil companies sometimes jointly own pipelines) these are often shown as an investment in an associate.

According to the EU Accounting Directive, such investments are valued at acquisition cost, subject to any permanent impairment of value. If their current value falls below historical cost, then the investment should be written down (and the expense would normally appear in the financial result part of the profit and loss account). In some jurisdictions, if the current value exceeds historical cost, this information would be disclosed as a note to the accounts.

Under IFRS Standards, equity investments are measured at fair value (in accordance with IFRS 9 *Financial Instruments*). Fair value is defined as 'the price that would be received to sell an asset or paid to transfer a liability in an orderly transaction between market participants at the measurement date' (IFRS 13 *Fair Value Measurement*, para. 9). Essentially, fair value is a proxy for current market value. The effect of investments measured at fair value on profit will depend on how they are classified on initial recognition.

IFRS 9 *Financial Instruments* prescribes that equity investments are to be measured at fair value with the *default recognition of gains and losses in profit or loss*: the changes in fair value of the financial assets (unrealized holding gains or losses) are to be recognized in profit or loss in the period in which they occur. Only if the equity investment is not held for trading (an assumption not uncommon for strategic equity investments) can an irrevocable election be made at initial recognition to measure it at fair value through other comprehensive income (OCI) with only dividend income recognized in profit or loss (see also Chapter 12).

COMPANY REPORT

BEKAERT – LEASES *(extract)*

Notes to the consolidated financial statements
Standards and Interpretations that have not been early adopted
As at 31 December 2017, the Group has operating lease commitments for a nominal amount of € 90.3 million. A preliminary assessment indicates that these arrangements will meet the definition of a lease under IFRS 16, and hence the Group will recognize a right-of-use asset and a corresponding liability in respect of all these leases unless they qualify for low value of short-term leases upon the application of IFRS 16. The new requirement to recognize a right-of-use asset and a related lease liability is expected to have a significant impact on the amounts recognized in the Group's consolidated financial statements and the Group is currently assessing its potential impact. It is not practicable to provide a reasonable estimate of the financial effect until the review is complete.

Source: Bekaert, Annual Report, 2017

Summary

In this chapter, we first looked at the question – central to profit calculation – of the treatment of the costs of using up the company's productive capacity. We have seen that where an asset has a determinable useful life within the company, the cost of using up the asset must be allocated over its useful life, and impacts the estimate of profit for each accounting period. We have seen that there are several conventional bases for measuring depreciation and these do not necessarily reflect economic consumption patterns when there are tax considerations involved. We have noted that the depreciation charge reduces profit but does not cause any cash flow, thereby introducing another systematic difference between profit and cash flow on a period-to-period basis. When a long-term asset is disposed of, both gross acquisition value and accumulated depreciation are offset against disposal proceeds and a gain or loss on disposal is included in the statement of profit or loss.

We have also considered the accounting treatment and valuation specifics of the main long-term asset categories. Specific recognition and measurement rules with regard to intangible assets, tangible assets and investments have been reviewed.

Discussion questions

1. What is included in the acquisition cost of a long-term tangible asset? Give examples of at least four costs that would be included in the acquisition cost of a new production line.
2. What are the most common causes of the depreciation of a long-term tangible asset?
3. Under what conditions will the disposal of a long-term tangible asset lead to a loss? How will the sale of a long-term asset affect the financial statements?
4. Discuss the recognition rules for research and development costs.
5. Contrast the accounting consequences of financing the acquisition of a building through a bank loan or as a finance lease.

Assignments

The following questions have answers on the lecturer side of the digital support resources for the book.

1. Profit forecasts
    A company is considering investing in a project with a five-year useful life. The project involves paying €75,000 for a licence to manufacture a new product and equipping a production line at a cost of €300,000. The product is expected to have a useful life of five years only and at the expiry of that time the production line will be sold and should yield a salvage value of €50,000. In order to launch the product the company plans a three-month advertising campaign that will cost €100,000.

    Required:

    Assuming that in each year the expected sales are €1,000,000 and expenses other than those detailed above are €800,000, draw up two alternative series of statements of profit or loss for the project using (a) straight line, and (b) diminishing balance depreciation of 30 per cent per annum, for the plant, while treating the other expenses consistently in each set.

    If, for policy reasons, the company wished to maximize profits in the first two years of operation, what accounting choices could be made (within the terms of generally accepted accounting principles) to achieve this?

2. Depreciati Limited purchased a truck for long-distance deliveries in Europe on 3 January 20X7. The acquisition cost of the truck amounts to €100,000. The truck is expected to have a salvage value of €20,000 at the end of its eight-year useful life.

    Required:

    (a) Prepare a depreciation schedule for the truck using the straight-line method.
    (b) Prepare a depreciation schedule for the truck using the diminishing balance method.

3. On 1 January 20X7, Nyvice Limited purchases a specialized machine tool for €20,000. The useful life of the machine tool is estimated to be five years. The residual value at the end of its useful life is expected to be zero. On 1 January 20X8, Nyvice purchases another machine tool for €4,000. The second machine tool has an expected useful life of four years and a residual value of €400. On 31 December 20X9, the company unexpectedly sells the first machine tool for €6,000. Nyvice uses the straight-line depreciation method for its equipment.

Required:

Show how the statement of financial position and the statement of profit or loss of Nyvice Limited are affected by the purchase of the machine tools for the years 20X7, 20X8 and 20X9.

4. Zetis SA had the following situation in its accounting database at 31 December 20X1:

Assets	
Land	150,000
Buildings (at cost)	50,000
Accumulated depreciation on buildings	−4,000
Plant and equipment (at cost)	46,800
Accumulated depreciation on plant and equipment	−19,300
Vehicles	52,500
Accumulated depreciation on vehicles	−27,300
Inventory at 1 January	9,400
Trade receivables	17,300
Cash	24,600
Equity and Liabilities	
Share capital	100,000
Retained earnings	189,300
Trade payables	5,400
Sales	247,200
Purchases	−69,600
Salaries	−131,000
Other expenses	−41,300

You are asked to draw up a statement of profit or loss and statement of financial position of Zetis SA after making the following adjustments:

(a) Provide depreciation on the following assets: buildings, 2 per cent straight line; plant and equipment, 15 per cent straight line; vehicles, 40 per cent diminishing balance.

(b) Closing inventory at 31 December was 10,650.

5. A company decides to replace one of its production lines with new machinery. All the costs associated with the exercise are grouped together by the accountant in the same account, pending later analysis. The items appearing in the account after three months are:

	€
Removal of old machinery	2,800
Installation of new power lines	350
Resurfacing factory floor	825
Purchase of new machines	62,100
Transport of machines to factory	3,200
Hire of crane to position new machines	450
Servicing after first month's production	375
Replacement of conveyor damaged in production	580
Engineer's fee to check installation	250

In addition to the above items, the payroll records show that the company's maintenance crew spent 300 hours installing the machines. The usual charge-out for labour is €5.75 per hour.

Please indicate which of the above items should be part of the acquisition cost of the new machinery.

6. Bramen NV, a Dutch engineering company, decided to replace an older machine with a new one because of efficiency concerns and higher quality requirements. The machine was purchased in Canada, transported to Schiphol Airport by plane and subsequently transported to Haarlem by road. The new machine replaces the old one, which is dismantled.

Please indicate which of the following expenditure items will be included in the acquisition cost of the new machine:

	Yes	No
1. Air transportation costs		
2. Seven per cent trade discount on gross purchase price		
3. Production losses in start-up phase		
4. Twelve per cent overhead charge		
5. Installation costs paid to external crew		
6. Personnel costs of employees involved with pre-operational testing		
7. Investment grant of the Dutch government		
8. Three per cent financial discount if payment received within 30 days		
9. Value-added tax (VAT) paid at import		
10. Training costs of personnel		
11. Insurance of transport from Canada to Haarlem		

7. On 2 January 20X1 Machinery Unlimited purchased a second-hand trailer at a price of €63,000. Before placing the trailer in service, the company spent €2,200 painting it, €800 replacing tyres and €4,000 overhauling the chassis. Machinery Unlimited management estimates that the trailer will remain in service for six years and have a residual value of €14,200. The trailer's annual mileage is expected to be 18,000 miles in each of the first four years and 14,000 miles in each of the next two years. In deciding which depreciation method to use, the general manager requests

a depreciation schedule for each of the following depreciation methods: (a) straight line and (b) units of production.

You are asked to:

(a) Prepare a depreciation schedule (i.e. for the six-year period) for each depreciation method, showing asset cost, depreciation expense and asset book value.

(b) For income tax purposes, Machinery Unlimited wishes to use the depreciation method that minimizes income tax payments in the early years of asset use. Identify the depreciation method that meets this requirement.

8. On 1 January 20X5 Jolly SA purchases production equipment for its new production line and pays €25,000. Additional installation costs with regard to the acquired equipment amount to €2,800. The equipment will be depreciated over a three-year useful life using the diminishing balance method. The residual value of the equipment is estimated at €6,000.

On 1 July 1,20X5, Jolly SA acquires a small office building for €600,000. Additionally, Jolly SA pays a 10 per cent registration fee on the building. The office building has an estimated useful life of 30 years and a residual value of €120,000.

Required:

(a) Prepare a depreciation schedule for both assets (more specifically, over the three-year period for the production equipment and for the first and the last two years of the useful life of the office building), showing asset cost, annual depreciation expense and the net book value of the asset. The company's financial year ends on 31 December.

(b) Assume that on 1 January 20X7 the company receives an offer to sell the production equipment (after two years of productive use) for €12,000. What will the impact on the statement of financial position and on the statement of profit or loss of Jolly SA be if the company decides to sell the equipment for the amount offered?

(c) What will be the impact on the statement of financial position and on the statement of profit or loss if the offer is cut to €8,000?

9. Intange NV has to take some final decisions on issues regarding its intangible assets. The company attracted a new staff member for the accounting department and confronted her with the following matters during the preparation of the draft financial statements of Intange NV for the financial year ending 30 June 20X9:

(a) In March 20X9, Intange NV paid €1m for a television advertising campaign for its products that will run for six months from 1 April 20X9 to 30 September 20X9. The directors of Intange NV believe that increased sales as a result of the publicity will continue for two years from the start of the advertisements.

(b) On 1 December 20X8, Intange NV started research work with a view to the eventual development of a new processor chip. By 30 June 20X9 Intange had spent €1.6m on this project. Intange has a past history of being particularly successful in bringing similar projects to a profitable conclusion. As a consequence, the directors of Intange would like to treat the expenditure to date on this project as an intangible asset in the statement of financial position.

(c) On 2 January 20X8 Intange NV started a project to elaborate a more efficient production process. Expenses relating to the project of €2m were charged in the statement of profit or loss in its financial year ended 30 June 20X8. Further costs of €1.5m were incurred in the three-month period to 30 September 20X8.

On that date it became apparent that the project was technically feasible and commercially viable. Further expenditure of €3m was incurred in the six-month period from 1 October 20X8 to 31 March 20X9. The new process, which began operating on 1 April 20X9, was expected to generate cost savings of at least €600,000 per annum over the 10-year period commencing 1 April 20X9.

(d) Intange NV spent €200,000 sending its staff on training courses during the first six months of the year ended 30 June 20X9. Although these courses have been expensive, they have led to a marked improvement in production quality and staff now need less supervision. This in turn has led to an increase in revenue and cost reductions. The organizer of the course has stated that the benefits from the training should last for a minimum of four years. The directors of Intange argue therefore that the cost of the training should be treated as an intangible asset and that six months' amortization should be charged in the statement of profit or loss based on the date on which the training courses were completed.

(e) On 1 January 20X9, Intange NV renewed its licence to extract minerals that are needed as part of its production process. The cost of renewal of the licence was €200,000 and the licence is for a five-year period starting on 1 January 20X9. The directors of Intange NV estimated that at 30 June 20X9 the net disposal value (fair value less costs of disposal) of the licence was €175,000. They further estimated that over the remaining 54 months of its duration, the licence would generate net cash flows for Intange NV that had a present value, at 30 June 20X9, of €185,000.

(f) Intange NV was commissioned by a customer to research and, if feasible, produce a new electronics component of the graphic systems manufactured by the customer. At 30 June 20X9, Intange had spent €2.4m on this project, but at this date it was uncertain as to whether the project would be successful. The directors of Intange argue that the €2.4m should be treated as an expense in the statement of profit or loss.

Required:

For each of the above items (a) to (f), how should the new accounting staff of Intange NV treat the items in the financial statements for the financial year ending 30 June 20X9, in order to be consistent with IFRS Standards?

(ACCA adapted)

10. On 1 January 20X5, Alder Repair Company leases a highly specialized machine tool from Top Equipment Incorporated, the manufacturer of those tools. The lease agreement specifies the fair value of the specialized machine tool on 1 January 20X5 ($309,250), the lease term (three years) and the annual lease payments ($120,000) payable at the end of each year. The specialized machine tool has a three-year economic life and is expected to have zero residual value. The interest rate implicit in the annual lease payments amounts to 8 per cent. The lease payments do not include extra fees for services provided by Top Equipment. If needed, these supplementary services would be charged separately. Similar machine tools are depreciated on a straight-line basis by Alder Repair Company.

Required:

Show how the statement of financial position and the statement of profit or loss of Alder Repair Company are affected by the lease agreement for the years 20X5, 20X6 and 20X7. Treat the lease agreement as a finance lease, but also compare with how the financial statements would look if it were accounted for as an operating lease.

CHAPTER 6

Refining the accounting system

In this chapter, we are going to look at other areas where the accountant intervenes in the accounting database to refine the information, usually as part of the process of preparing the annual financial statements and with a view to giving a more precise profit estimate and a more accurate representation of the company's financial position. We are going to look at accruals and deferrals of expenses and revenue, provisions to anticipate future expenditure related to past events, as well as impairment testing for loss of value in assets. We will end this chapter with a closer look at the structure of the financing side of the balance sheet and the components of a company's equity.

Chapter structure

- Introduction
- Accruals and deferrals of expenses and revenue
- Provisions
- Asset impairment
- Bad debts and doubtful receivables
- Hidden reserves
- Capital structure
- Summary
- Discussion questions
- Assignments

Introduction

The routine accounting system works very well for things like delivery notes and invoices to customers and recording deliveries from suppliers. However, there are transactions that fall slightly outside this convenient framework and need to be brought into it or aligned with it, in order to accurately depict the company's financial position and performance for the period. For example, we consume electricity and gas, use telephones and are invoiced afterwards; generally, company lawyers or auditors do not send in monthly bills, but rather invoice us at the end of delivering a series of services that frequently do not correspond to our accounting year. In a number of areas, the company accountant has to intervene and form a judgement as to which economic events (and their consequences in terms of expenses and income) have not been brought into the accounting database yet, but should be incorporated into the financial statements to faithfully represent the company's financial condition and performance. These considerations are typical for accrual accounting and give rise to adjustments in the accounting database such as accrued expenses, accrued revenue, provisions and impairments. Similarly, some economic events and transactions already posted in the database will have to be matched with next period's revenue and, thus, have to be deferred. Such period matching may be necessary for revenue as well.

Accruals and deferrals of expenses and revenue

Accrued expenses and accrued revenue (sometimes just called *accruals*) are previously unrecorded expenses and revenue that need to be adjusted at the end of the accounting period to reflect the amount of expenses incurred or revenue earned during the accounting period. Deferred expenses and deferred revenue (sometimes called *deferrals*) are previously recorded (and probably paid/received) expenses and revenue that have to be adjusted at the end of the accounting period by deferring part of them to the following accounting period.

Accrued and deferred expenses and revenue are the near cousins of payables/creditors and receivables/debtors. These are items where the economic transaction takes place at a different time from the cash transaction, but where the volume or frequency of the transactions does not warrant a continuing record in the basic accounting system, or where the invoice or similar document that is used to record the economic event arrives sometime after the expenses are incurred or the revenue earned – or sometime in advance of this. We have a *timing difference between the notification of the item* (used as an entry in the accounting database) *and the economic event,* so the accountant must make adjustments when preparing the annual financial statements. (Note that a highly sophisticated accounting database that is used for preparing monthly internal accounts may well make monthly adjustments for accruals and deferrals, or use standard charges or some other device to bring these time-based items regularly into the database. For our purposes, the first need is simply to be aware of this type of transaction; later we will need to take these into account when preparing annual financial statements.) Figures 6.1 and 6.2 outline the accounting consequences of accruals and deferrals of expenses and revenue respectively. In these figures A, L and E refer to assets, liabilities and equity respectively. They are shown to indicate the impact of accruals and deferrals on the balance sheet equation.

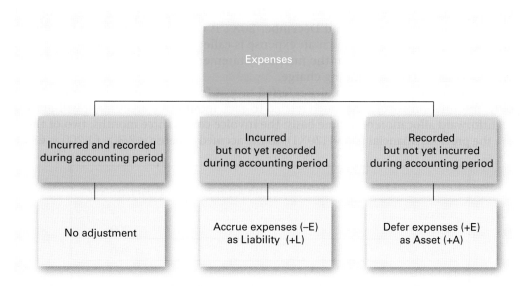

Figure 6.1   Accruals and deferrals of expenses

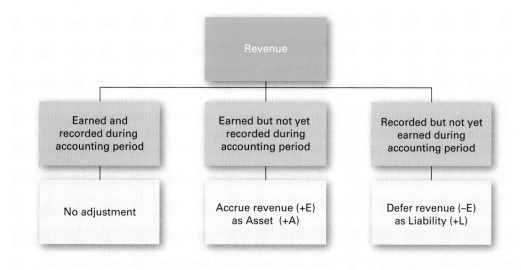

Figure 6.2   Accruals and deferrals of revenue

Accrued expenses

Accrued expenses represent amounts for goods or services that have been received or supplied by third parties, but have not yet been invoiced, paid or formally agreed with the supplier at year-end. Typical transactions in this area would be invoices for items such as telephone, gas or electricity, where the bill is received after the service or product has been consumed. For example, supposing a business prepares financial statements to 31 December each year, but receives in February 20X2 a gas bill for the months of November 20X1, December 20X1 and January 20X2. The proportion of the bill relating to November and December 20X1 is an expense of the financial year ended on 31 December 20X1. Such an expense is called an 'accrued expense' and calls for an adjustment to be made in the financial statements for the year to 31 December 20X1 to recognize the outstanding charge.

Supposing in this case the invoice referred to was for €1,200. In the absence of any specific information about how much related to each month, the accountant will make a straightforward allocation on a time basis: the invoice covers three months, two of those are in the previous financial period (20X1), so the accrued expense is 2/3 × €1,200 = €800:

	Year-end adjustment	Following year
Assets		
Cash		−1,200
Totals	0	−1,200
Liabilities		
Accrued expenses	+800	−800
Equity		
Profit for year 20X1	−800	
Profit for year 20X2		−400
Totals	0	−1,200

This adjustment would be inserted in the accounting system in order to allocate the expense across the appropriate years. The €800 expense would be deducted from profit in year 20X1, while the corresponding liability would be put in a temporary account and appear in the 20X1 statement of financial position as a short-term liability. In the following accounting period (20X2), when the €1,200 bill was paid, only €400 would be treated as an expense, while €800 would extinguish the year-end liability. The operation of the accrual account ensures that the actual payment of the bill automatically expenses the correct portion into the operating expenses of the following year as well as cancelling the accrual.

Not all accruals fall across two accounting periods. For example, there would be a major accrual each year for the audit fee, which is conventionally treated as an expense of the year being audited (on a matching basis), although the work is carried out in large part in the following year. Accrued vacation pay is another significant accruals category: expensed when personnel services are rendered, but usually paid in the following calendar year.

A further point to note is that not all accruals are for known amounts. That is, when the accountant is drawing up the financial statements, he or she may not have received an invoice such as the gas bill examined above. Part of the exercise in drawing up the annual statements (sometimes called *the year-end exercise*) involves checking expense accounts to see whether all charges for the year have been received. If they have not, the precise details of the charge may not have arrived and the accountant will be obliged to estimate – based on previous year charges or current trends as appropriate (just one of the many instances where the data in the annual financial statements are not a matter of indisputable fact).

Deferred expenses

Deferred expenses (also called *prepaid expenses*) are the opposite of accrued expenses – they are payments made or invoices received in one financial year for expenses which relate to a subsequent year. Some items and services, such as rent and insurance (also prepaid mobile phone cards), are paid in advance. Such prepaid services represent an economic resource (future service potential) and should be recognized as an asset at the time of payment – they only become an expense as time elapses and the service or good is used up.

In practice, the accounting information system does not automatically recognize such prepaid services as assets since, in practical terms, they start to be used up immediately. Usually, such transactions are accounted for as expenses when the invoice or payment enters the accounting records and later on, as a further part of the year-end exercise, the accountant will examine such expense categories to check whether the whole of the asset has indeed expired and was properly an expense. Frequently there is an unexpired portion since rental periods, for example, rarely coincide exactly with a company's financial year and, in order to match the transaction to the correct financial periods, the expense needs to be diminished and an asset recognized at balance sheet date, representing the unexpired portion of the expense.

If we take an insurance premium as an example, suppose an annual premium is paid on 1 April 20X1 and the company's financial year runs to 31 December. Nine-twelfths of the premium should be expensed in the year of payment and three-twelfths recognized as an asset at 31 December 20X1 – to be expensed in the following year (20X2).

Assuming that the premium was €2,400 and that it was initially treated as an expense, three-twelfths (€600) should be recognized as an asset at the year-end:

	Original payment	Year-end adjustment	Following year
Assets			
Cash	−2,400		
Prepaid expenses		**+ 600**	**−600**
Totals	−2,400	+600	−600
Equity			
Profit for year 20X1	−2,400	+ 600	
Profit for year 20X2			−600
Totals	−2,400	+600	−600

The use of the temporary prepaid expenses account allows the part of the expense which relates to the following year to be carried forward to the expenses for that year.

Deferred revenue

Deferred revenue (also called *precollected* or *unearned revenue*) is revenue that has been recognized before it is actually earned. At year-end, part of the recorded revenue that has not been earned yet is deferred or carried forward to the following year. The deferred revenue represents a liability that arises because the company has received advance payment for a service it has agreed to render in the future. A typical example from the publishing industry is unearned subscription revenue that represents journal subscription payments received in advance, for which the publishing company agrees to deliver issues of its journal during some future period.

Assuming that a publishing company receives an annual subscription fee of €1,400 at the start of the annual subscription period (1 April 20X1) and that the subscription fee is initially treated as full revenue, three-twelfths (€350) of the revenue will be deferred and recognized as a short-term liability at the year-end:

	Original receipt	Year-end adjustment	Following year
Assets			
Cash	+1,400		
Totals	1,400	0	0
Equity			
Profit for year 20X1	+1,400	−350	
Profit for year 20X2			+350
Liabilities			
Deferred revenue		+350	−350
Totals	1,400	0	0

Again, the use of the temporary deferred revenue account allows the part of the revenue that relates to the following year to be forwarded to the revenue of that year.

Note that 'deferred revenue' is one of those peculiar liabilities that do not imply expected future cash outflows. It meets the definition of a liability in the sense that the future economic benefits to be sacrificed refer to services or goods to be delivered, not cash to be paid.

Accrued revenue

Accrued revenue is the reverse of unearned revenue: revenue will be recognized in the statement of profit or loss before actual receipt of cash (or before recording of a formal revenue notification).

Assume that on 1 September 20X1 a financial company loans €100,000 to another business that will repay the loan in one year. The company charges interest on the loan at an annual interest rate of 9 per cent to be paid at the end of the loan term. The company prepares its annual financial statements for the period ending 31 December 20X1. In this case, the borrower does not actually pay the interest in the year in which the loan was provided. But even if the interest payment is not made until next year, the company has earned interest revenue (or interest income) this year for a period of four months. The amount earned but unpaid as of the end of 20X1 (one-third of €9,000) will be shown on the balance sheet of the loan provider as an asset. The accrued interest revenue (interest income) is similar to a short-term receivable.

	Year-end adjustment	Following year
Assets		
Accrued revenue	+3,000	−3,000
Cash		+9,000
Totals	3,000	6,000
Equity		
Profit for year 20X1	+3,000	
Profit for year 20X2		+6,000
Totals	3,000	6,000

The operation of the accrued revenue account ensures that the actual receipt of the interest cash flow in 20X2 will cancel out the accrual and leads to the recognition of a net interest revenue for the year of €6,000 in the 20X2 statement of profit or loss.

COMPANY REPORT

VODAFONE – ACCRUED AND DEFERRED REVENUE (extracts)

The Group principally obtains revenue from providing mobile and fixed telecommunication services including: access charges, voice and video calls, messaging, interconnect fees, fixed and mobile broadband and related services such as providing televisual and music content, connection fees and equipment sales. Products and services may be sold separately or in bundled packages.

Revenue for access charges, voice and video calls, messaging and fixed and mobile broadband provided to contract customers is recognised as services are performed, with unbilled revenue resulting from services already provided accrued at the end of each period and unearned revenue from services to be provided in future periods deferred. Revenue from the sale of prepaid credit is deferred until such time as the customer uses the airtime, or the credit expires.

Revenue for the provision of televisual and music content is recognised when or as the Group performs the related service and, depending on the nature of the service, is recognised either at the gross amount billed to the customer or the amount receivable by the Group as commission for facilitating the service.

Customer connection revenue is recognised together with the related equipment revenue to the extent that the aggregate equipment and connection revenue does not exceed the fair value of the equipment delivered to the customer. Any customer connection revenue not recognised, together with any related excess equipment revenue, is deferred and recognised over the period in which services are expected to be provided to the customer.

Source: Vodafone, Annual Report, 2018

Provisions

A *provision* is an amount charged against profit or loss (*provision expense*) and carried forward in the statement of financial position as a liability (*provision liability*) in anticipation of a future expenditure (of uncertain timing and/or amount) that derives in some way from current circumstances (i.e. the event generating the future expenditure has already taken place in the current period). Typically, a provision is characterized by *considerable uncertainty* about the exact amount and the moment when the future expenditure will crystallize, so a provision is created for an *estimated amount*.

Generally, a provision is recorded where some current event is likely to have future consequences that will create an outflow of company resources (a potential future expense). Accrual accounting would require that these future consequences are accounted for in the period in which the originating economic event occurs and not in the period in which payment or settlement of its consequences will eventually take place. Taking the provision expense in the period in which the causal economic event occurs is consistent with the principles of prudence and matching. The provision can always be released back to the statement of profit or loss (*provision reversal*) at some future time if the future expenditure does not materialize.

Suppose that a company guarantees the product that it manufactures under a warranty agreement. Under the terms of the product warranty, the company undertakes to repair or replace manufacturing defects that become apparent within one year from the date of sale. On past experience, it is likely that in future periods a material amount of costs will be incurred in replacing or repairing the products sold in the current period. Both the prudence and the matching principles require that the profit of the period in which the revenue is recognized be adjusted for the future (expected) replacement and repair costs. At the time of the sale, the exact amount of warranty expense is still uncertain. The company can, however, estimate the number of warranty claims and the future repair and replacement costs based on past experience.

Other common examples of this kind of situation are where a company agrees to pay a pension in the future to employees based on their current employment services or where a company decides to restructure or close down an operation. The adverse impact of business activities on the environment could also create a remediation obligation that has to be provided for.

From an accounting perspective, the provision is created by reducing profits (provision expense) and increasing liabilities:

	Create provision
Equity	
Profit for the year	−15,000
Liabilities	
Provisions	+15,000

Note that the provision is accounted for in the statement of financial position as part of liabilities (although generally separated clearly from debt). Taking into account the estimated timing of the expected future expenditure, it can be a long or a short-term liability.

Provisions should be reviewed at each reporting date and adjusted to reflect the current best estimate of the liability amount. When the expenditures for which the provision has been created actually occur, the provision will be used:

	Use provision
Assets	
Cash	−15,000
Liabilities	
Provisions	−15,000

The actual expenditure for which the provision has been set up does not give rise to an additional expense, but extinguishes (part of) the provision. If it is no longer probable that an outflow of company resources will be required to settle the obligation, the provision should be reversed. The reversal will be credited to income:

	Reverse provision
Equity	
Profit for the year	15,000
Liabilities	
Provisions	−15,000

Provisions can appear, at first sight, to be rather a fluid subject. Students tend immediately to think that provisions must give company accountants a splendid opportunity to manipulate profits, by reducing profits in booming years and boosting them in lean years (see also 'hidden reserves' later in this chapter). This is true to a certain extent. For example, the concept of provisions as conceived by the EU Accounting Directive gives companies a fair amount of flexibility in deciding how to make use of provisions. However, tax authorities are well aware of this and strictly control what provisions, if any, are accepted in calculating the taxable profit. Moreover, the International Accounting Standards Board (the Board) has introduced quite restrictive recognition and measurement rules with regard to provisions with the effect of restraining manipulative use of provision accounting.

IAS 37 *Provisions, Contingent Liabilities and Contingent Assets* defines a provision as a *liability of uncertain timing or amount* (IAS 37, para. 10). As a liability, a provision should meet the definition and recognition criteria of a liability, but the main difference with an ordinary liability is the uncertainty of the timing or the amount (or both). The *main characteristics* of a provision according to IAS 37 can be described as follows:

- It reflects a present obligation (at reporting date) as a result of a past event that will probably (i.e. more likely than not) lead to a future outflow of company resources (usually cash) to settle the obligation.
- The *timing or amount* of the future outflow of resources is however still *uncertain*.
- The *obligating event* (the cause of the obligation) lies in the past and should not refer to a future cause.

- The *obligation* can be *legal* (i.e. enforceable by law) *or constructive*. A constructive obligation is an obligation that derives from a company's past actions whereby it has indicated to third parties that it will accept certain responsibilities; this may be by a pattern of past practice or by some form of public statement.

- The obligation exists only where the company has no reasonable alternative but to settle the obligation. The company has *no ability to avoid a future transfer of resources* (settlement of the obligation) if action necessary to avoid it would cause significant business disruption or have economic consequences significantly more adverse than the settlement itself.

- Although the amount and/or timing of future payments are uncertain, it should be possible to arrive at a *reliable estimate* of the amount of the obligation.

STANDARDS

 IAS 37 – PROVISIONS, CONTINGENT LIABILITIES AND CONTINGENT ASSETS
(extract)

14. A provision shall be recognised when:
    (a) an entity has a present obligation (legal or constructive) as a result of a past event;
    (b) it is probable that an outflow of resources embodying economic benefits will be required to settle the obligation; and
    (c) a reliable estimate can be made of the amount of the obligation.

If these conditions are not met, no provision shall be recognised.

Source: IAS 37, Provisions, Contingent Liabilities and Contingent Assets

IAS 37 offers a decision tree that is quite helpful in deciding on the recognition of provisions. The decision tree is shown in Figure 6.3. Note that the left-hand side of the decision tree leads to the recognition of a provision in the statement of financial position and of a corresponding provision expense in the statement of profit or loss.

In the case of a product warranty, the obligating event is the sale of the product with a warranty, which gives rise to a legal obligation. A history of claims can be compiled in order to determine the probability of warranty claims and the probable amount of claims related to the sales for a given period can be estimated. In this case, all three recognition criteria have been met and a provision for warranty claims will be recognized in the financial statements. Lawsuits are another area for which provisions can be significant. However, it may not always be clear that a present obligation exists in a lawsuit. Generally one does not wait for the final court decision to recognize a liability, but ponders all available evidence (including the opinion of legal experts) in deciding whether a present obligation exists. If available evidence brings the legal experts to the opinion that it is likely that the company will be found liable, a provision will be recognized for the best estimate of the amount needed to settle the obligation.

Pensions are often a special case, and we will come back to those later in the book in more detail, but you can see that where, for example, the company gives long service awards, the right to the award is gained by (say) 10 years of service and is therefore being earned during the 10 years and is strictly a cost of those 10 years, but it is difficult to predict how many employees will qualify for these at any given time. This is a classic provision – the company is contractually committed to pay such awards, but does not know how many people will eventually claim them, nor when, so it is a case for a provision.

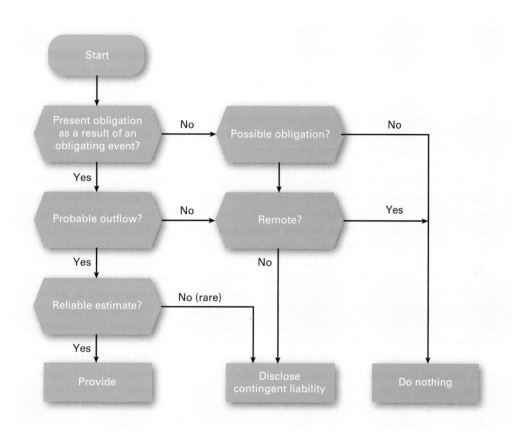

Figure 6.3 Decision tree – recognizing a provision

Once it is established that a provision needs to be recognized, the company has to come up with a *measurement* of the provision. IAS 37 *Provisions, Contingent Liabilities and Contingent Assets* states that the amount recognized should be the *best estimate of the expenditure required to settle the present obligation*. This is again a significant judgement issue on the part of the company's management. Where the provision being measured involves a population of items (e.g. a product warranty provision with many potential returns), the estimate will be based on an *expected value* approach: the provision is estimated by weighting all possible outcomes by their associated probabilities. Where the provision involves a single item (e.g. the outcome of a litigation case), the provision will be made for the *most likely outcome*.

Figure 6.3 also illustrates the borderline between provisions and contingent liabilities. A *contingent liability* refers to (IAS 37, para. 10):

1. A *possible obligation* that arises from past events and *whose existence will be confirmed only by the occurrence or non-occurrence of one or more uncertain future events* not wholly within the control of the company; or

2. A *present obligation* that is not recognized because the *future expenditure is not probable* or the *obligation cannot be measured with sufficient reliability.*

NOVARTIS – PROVISIONS FOR PRODUCT LIABILITIES, GOVERNMENT INVESTIGATIONS AND OTHER LEGAL MATTERS *(extracts)*

Novartis has established provisions for certain product liabilities, governmental investigations and other legal matters where a potential cash outflow is probable and Novartis can make a reliable estimate of the amount of the outflow. These provisions represent the Group's current best estimate of the total financial effect for the matters described below and for other less significant matters. Potential cash outflows reflected in a provision might be fully or partially off-set by insurance in certain circumstances.

Novartis has not established provisions for potential damage awards for certain additional legal claims against its subsidiaries if Novartis currently believes that a payment is either not probable or cannot be reliably estimated. In total, these not-provisioned-for matters include more than 1000 individual product liability cases and certain other legal matters. Plaintiffs' alleged claims in these matters, which Novartis does not believe to be entirely remote but which do not fulfill the conditions for the establishment of provisions, currently aggregate to, according to Novartis' current best belief, approximately USD 1.5 billion. In addition, in some of these matters there are claims for punitive or multiple (treble) damages, civil penalties and disgorgement of profits that in Novartis' view are either wholly or partially unspecified or wholly or partially unquantifiable at present; the Group believes that information about these amounts claimed by plaintiffs generally is not meaningful for purposes of determining a reliable estimate of a loss that is probable or more than remote.

A number of other legal matters are in such early stages or the issues presented are such that the Group has not made any provisions since it cannot currently estimate either a potential outcome or the amount of any potential losses. For these reasons, among others, the Group generally is unable to make a reliable estimate of possible loss with respect to such cases. It is therefore not practicable to provide information about the potential financial impact of those cases.

There might also be cases for which the Group was able to make a reliable estimate of the possible loss or the range of possible loss, but the Group believes that publication of such information on a case-by-case basis would seriously prejudice the Group's position in ongoing legal proceedings or in any related settlement discussions. Accordingly, in such cases, information has been disclosed with respect to the nature of the contingency, but no disclosure is provided as to an estimate of the possible loss or range of possible loss.

Source: Novartis, Annual Report, 2017

The difference between a provision and a contingent liability is quite important as to its reporting consequences: a *contingent liability* is not recognized in the statement of financial position and statement of profit or loss and *will only be disclosed in the notes to the accounts*.

Pending litigation for which available evidence does not indicate that it is more likely than not (but still reasonably possible) that the company will be found liable is an example of a possible obligation to be disclosed as a contingent liability. If the probability of any settlement is regarded as slight (remote), no action is taken. A financial guarantee is an example of the second type of contingent liabilities. If a company guarantees payment of a loan made to a third party, there is definitely a legal obligation. However, as long as there is no available evidence that the borrower has or probably will default, no provision should be recognized in the financial statements. However, as the granting of a guarantee makes the company contingently liable, the nature and the amount of the financial guarantee must be disclosed in the notes to the accounts.

COMPANY REPORT

PHILIPS – CONTINGENT LIABILITIES *(extracts)*

Guarantees
Philips' policy is to provide guarantees and other letters of support only in writing. Philips does not stand by other forms of support. The total fair value of guarantees recognized on the balance sheet amounts to EUR nil million for both 2016 and 2017. Remaining off-balance-sheet business and credit-related guarantees provided on behalf of third parties and associates decreased by EUR 11 million during 2017 to EUR 17 million (December 31, 2016: EUR 28 million).

Source: Philips, Annual Report, 2017, Reproduced by Courtesy of Royal Philips

When looking at national accounting regimes, the extent of the use of provisions is one of the areas where Anglo-Saxon practice is noticeably different from practice in continental Europe, and as usual this is driven by tax considerations. Many European tax authorities are more sympathetic to provisions than their anglophone counterparts, which leads to a greater use of them, since they reduce profit. The IAS 37 definition of a provision (see earlier) requires there to be a firm commitment to make a payment, but in many national accounting regimes (including the EU Accounting Directive) a provision is already justified if there is simply a possibility of making a payment.

Finally, it is worth noting that the *borderline between provisions and accrued expenses* is not always that evident. Recall that accrued expenses are liabilities to pay for goods or services that have been received or supplied but have not yet been invoiced or paid. Sometimes the amount or timing of these accruals has to be estimated, but the uncertainty involved in estimating accruals is generally considered to be much less than for provisions. Moreover, accrued expenses are often not reported separately in the statement of financial position; they may be included in trade or other payables, whereas provisions are reported separately with extensive disclosures in the notes to the accounts.

Asset impairment

Periodically, assets that have already been recognized on the statement of financial position should be reviewed for potential impairment. An *asset impairment* occurs if the economic value of the asset drops below its carrying amount (net book value). The general idea is that a company acquires an asset because it believes the expected future economic benefits to be generated by that asset exceed its cost. Subsequently, if the asset's remaining expected future benefits drop below its carrying value, that asset is considered to have become impaired. In that case, the carrying value of the asset will be adjusted downwards for an *impairment loss*. Like a provision, it is created by making a *deduction from profit or loss*, but where the opposite entry for a provision goes into the financing side of the statement of financial position as a liability, the asset impairment adjustment is a *deduction from the asset value* (somewhat comparable with depreciating an asset).

Asset impairment rules generally prescribe an *impairment test* in which the carrying value of the asset is compared to some threshold value level to determine whether an impairment has occurred and a write-down must be made. If the threshold level has been triggered, the amount of the impairment loss must be determined and recorded.

These issues are covered by IAS 36 *Impairment of Assets*. IAS 36 requires that assets are not to be carried at values in excess of their *recoverable amount* (the threshold value). An asset is regarded as impaired if its carrying amount exceeds the recoverable amount (IAS 36, para. 1). Basically, the recoverable amount of an asset is the *amount the company can recover either through using the asset in the future* ('value in use' – see later) *or selling the asset now*.

Assets have to be reviewed for indications of possible impairment at the end of each reporting period (IAS 36, para. 9). Impairment indicators may relate to either the assets themselves (e.g. machinery gets damaged by a fire) or to the economic environment in which they are used (e.g. low oil and gas prices reducing the utility of a coal-fired power plant). They include both external sources (such as market interest rates, significant adverse changes in technological, market, economic or legal environment in which the company operates) and internal sources (such as internal restructurings, evidence of obsolescence or physical damage of an asset). If there is an indication that an asset may be impaired, a detailed calculation of the recoverable amount is made and the carrying value will be reduced accordingly.

COMPANY REPORT

NOVARTIS – IMPAIRMENT OF GOODWILL AND INTANGIBLE ASSETS *(extracts)*

Novartis applies the fair value less costs of disposal method for its impairment assessment. In most cases, no directly observable market inputs are available to measure the fair value less costs of disposal. Therefore, an estimate is derived indirectly and is based on net present value techniques utilizing post-tax cash flows and discount rates. In the limited cases where the value-in-use method would be applied, net present value techniques would be applied using pre-tax cash flows and discount rates.

Fair value less costs of disposal reflects estimates of assumptions that market participants would be expected to use when pricing the asset or CGUs, and for this purpose, management considers the range of economic conditions that are expected to exist over the remaining useful life of the asset.

The estimates used in calculating the net present values are highly sensitive and depend on assumptions specific to the nature of the Group's activities with regard to:

- Amount and timing of projected future cash flows
- Long-term sales forecasts
- Actions of competitors (launch of competing products, marketing initiatives, etc.)
- Sales erosion rates after the end of patent or other intellectual property rights protection and timing of the entry of generic competition
- Outcome of R&D activities (compound efficacy, results of clinical trials, etc.)

- Amount and timing of projected costs to develop IPR&D into commercially viable products
- Probability of obtaining regulatory approval
- Future tax rate
- Appropriate royalty rate for the Alcon Brand name
- Appropriate terminal growth rate
- Appropriate discount rate

Source: Novartis, Annual Report, 2017

BETWEEN THE LINES

Illustration – impairment of a long-term asset

Assume a company acquired on 2 January 20X1 a specialized machine for €1,500,000, expecting to use it to produce a specific product for 12 years. The equipment was depreciated on a straight-line basis. By the end of 20X4 demand for the specific product has dropped so much that the company expects that the net cash flows the product would generate over the remainder of its product life cycle would be less than the machine's net carrying value (€1,000,000). The value in use was estimated at €800,000, while the estimated net selling price on 1 January 20X5 was €750,000. In that case, the equipment is written down to €800,000, its estimated value in use and the impairment loss is recognized in the 20X4 statement of profit or loss.

Recoverable amount

The *recoverable amount* is the *higher of an asset's 'fair value less costs of disposal' and its 'value in use'* (IAS 36, para. 18) (Figure 6.4).

Figure 6.4   Recoverable amount

The IASB defines *fair value* as *'the price that would be received to sell an asset or paid to transfer a liability in an orderly transaction between market participants at the measurement date'* (IFRS 13 *Fair Value Measurement*, para. 9). The fair value definition is very near to current market price. This means that the 'fair value less costs of disposal' essentially equals the net selling price of the asset. However, if the asset is not traded in an active market, a reliable estimate should be made of the amount obtainable from an arm's length sale between knowledgeable, willing buyers and sellers, less expected costs of disposal. In that case, the outcome of recent transactions for similar assets within the same industry would be considered good evidence. Costs of disposal are the incremental costs that would be directly attributable to the disposal of the asset, such as transaction taxes and legal costs, but also costs of removing the asset.

Value in use is to be distinguished from market value and fair value. It typically reflects the value to a particular user rather than to the market in general, recognizing the extent to which the asset contributes to the specific business and performance of the company. IAS 36 *Impairment of Assets* defines value in use as the present value of estimated future cash flows from continued use of the asset and eventual disposal at the end of its useful life. Being based on present value calculations, discounting will be an essential part in measuring value in use. Basically, estimating the value in use of an asset involves two essential steps (IAS 36, para. 31):

(a) Estimating the future cash inflows and outflows to be derived from continuing use of the asset and from its ultimate disposal.
(b) Applying the appropriate discount rate to those future cash flows.

IAS 36 provides detailed guidance to apply these rules (see box below for some headlines of the calculation guidance).

It is not always necessary to determine both the fair value less costs of disposal and the value in use. If either of the values exceeds the carrying amount of the asset, the asset is not impaired and it is not necessary to estimate the other amount. So, in practice, one will probably start with determining the fair value less costs of disposal (or the net selling price). If this value proves to be lower than the asset's carrying amount, the more complex calculation of value in use will become necessary. Figure 6.5 illustrates the typical sequence of steps of an impairment test process.

STANDARDS

 VALUE IN USE – CALCULATION HEADLINES

In calculating an asset's value in use, one should use:
1 Estimates of the future cash flows the entity expects to derive from the asset and expectations about possible variations in the amount and timing of those future cash flows; the estimates should include all estimated future cash inflows and cash outflows except for cash flows from financing activities and income tax receipts and payments.
2 Cash flow projections based on assumptions that reflect the asset in its current condition (without considering future restructurings or improvements) and represent management's best estimate of the set of conditions that will exist over the remaining useful life of the asset.
3 A pretax discount rate that reflects current market assessments of the time value of money and the risks specific to the asset; the discount rate should not reflect risks for which the future cash flows have been adjusted.

Source: Adapted from IAS 36, Impairment of Assets, paras 30–57

Figure 6.5 Impairment test

Individual assets versus cash-generating units

In principle, an asset's recoverable amount is determined at the individual asset level (IAS 36, para. 66). However, assets are often used in combination with other assets and not in isolation. Individual long-term assets usually do not generate cash flows independently. It is their utilization together with other types of asset that generates cash flows. Hence, if the cash flows necessary for the calculation of value in use are not generated by individual assets but by a combination of assets being used together, it is only sensible to estimate value in use in total for groups of assets. These groups are referred to as *cash-generating units*. So, if an asset does not generate cash inflows that are largely independent of those from other assets, the recoverable amount will be determined at a higher level – the cash-generating unit to which the asset belongs.

A cash-generating unit (CGU) is the *smallest identifiable group of assets that generate cash flows that are largely independent of the cash flows from other assets or groups of assets*. IAS 36 *Impairment of Assets* insists that a CGU should be identified for the lowest level of aggregation of assets possible. Identifying the lowest level of independent cash inflows for a group of assets will not always be straightforward and could involve considerable judgement. The independence of cash flows will be indicated by the way management monitors the company's operations, for example by product lines, businesses or geographical locations. Management's analysis will probably reflect the independence of cash inflows in its reporting structures and formats. IAS 36 specifically stipulates that the existence of an active market for the output produced by an asset or group of assets, constitutes primary evidence that cash flows are independent. Such an asset or group of assets will, therefore, be a CGU. Examples of outputs from assets for which an active market exists include oil, electricity, marketable subassemblies, etc.

STANDARDS

IMPAIRMENT RULES – INDIVIDUAL ASSETS VERSUS CASH-GENERATING UNITS (examples)

1. A mining entity owns a private railway to support its mining activities. The private railway could be sold only for scrap value and it does not generate cash inflows that are largely independent of the cash inflows from the other assets of the mine.

   It is not possible to estimate the recoverable amount of the private railway because its value in use cannot be determined and is probably different from scrap value. Therefore, the entity estimates the recoverable amount of the CGU to which the private railway belongs, i.e. the mine as a whole.

2. A bus company provides services under contract with a municipality that requires minimum service on each of five separate routes. Assets devoted to each route and the cash flows from each route can be identified separately. One of the routes operates at a significant loss.

   Because the entity does not have the option to curtail any one bus route, the lowest level of identifiable cash inflows that are largely independent of the cash inflows from other assets or groups of assets is the cash inflows generated by the five routes together. The CGU for each route is the bus company as a whole.

   Source: IAS 36, Impairment of Assets, paras 67 and 68

The recoverable amount of the asset's CGU is determined in the same way as an asset's recoverable amount. The principles to determine the CGU's fair value less costs of disposal and its value in use are the same as those applicable for an individual asset. The carrying amount of the CGU should include all assets that generate the future cash inflows at the CGU level. Sometimes it will be necessary to include allocations of the carrying amount of corporate assets (such as a research centre, a central IT department or the corporate head office) when they contribute to the generation of cash inflows of the CGU.

Annual impairment test requirements

IAS 36 *Impairment of Assets* (para. 10) requires that intangible assets with indefinite useful lives be tested for impairment annually, irrespective of whether there is any indication that these may be impaired. The same applies to capitalized goodwill (see Chapter 12 on consolidated financial statements), which is not subject to systematic annual depreciation, but should be tested for impairment annually (according to IFRS 3 *Business Combinations*). An annual impairment test is also required for intangible assets that have not yet been brought into use, due to their higher intrinsic uncertainty.

By their nature, goodwill and intangibles will necessarily be tested for impairment at the level of CGUs. These impairment tests can be performed at any time during an annual period, provided that the tests are scheduled at the same time every year.

ILLUSTRATION – IDENTIFICATION OF A CASH-GENERATING UNIT IN A RETAIL STORE CHAIN

Store Downtown belongs to Alphaline, a retail store chain. Downtown makes all its retail purchases through the central purchasing centre of Alphaline. Pricing, marketing, advertising and human resources policies (except for hiring Downtown cashiers and sales staff) are decided at corporate level. Alphaline also owns five other stores in the same city as Downtown (although in different neighbourhoods) and 20 other stores in other cities. All stores are managed uniformly.

In identifying a CGU in this context, one should consider, for example, whether internal management reporting is organized to measure performance on a store-by-store basis and whether the business is run on a store-by-store profit basis or on a region/city basis. Although the stores of Alphaline are managed at a corporate level, they are all located in different neighbourhoods and probably have different customer bases. Downtown generates cash inflows that are largely independent of those of the other stores of the retail chain and, therefore, it is likely that Downtown is a CGU.

Source: Adapted from IAS 36 – Illustrative Examples

Impairment loss

If an asset's carrying amount exceeds its recoverable amount, it will be written down and an impairment loss recognized as an expense in the statement of profit or loss.

If the impairment loss is determined at the level of a CGU, the CGU's impairment loss has to be allocated between the assets of the CGU. If goodwill has been allocated to the

ILLUSTRATION – IDENTIFICATION OF A CASH-GENERATING UNIT IN A SINGLE PRODUCT COMPANY

Company Unique produces a single product and owns plants A, B and C. Each plant is located in a different continent. A produces a component that is assembled in either B or C. Alternatively, plant A's products can be sold in an active market. The combined capacity of B and C is not fully utilized. Unique's products are sold worldwide from either plant B or C. For example, plant B's production can be sold in plant C's continent if the products can be delivered more quickly from plant B than from plant C. Utilization levels of plants B and C depend on the allocation of sales between the two sites.

As there is an active market for plant A's products, A could sell its product in that market and so generate cash inflows that would be largely independent of the cash inflows from plants B or C. Therefore, it is likely that plant A is a separate CGU, although part of its output is used by plants B and C.

Although there is an active market for the products assembled by plants B and C, cash inflows for B and C depend on the allocation of production across the two plants. It is unlikely that the future cash inflows for plants B and C can be determined individually. This brings us to conclude that plants B and C together are the smallest identifiable group of assets that generates cash inflows that are largely independent.

Source: Adapted from IAS 36 – Illustrative Examples

asset base of the CGU, the impairment loss is allocated first to reduce the carrying amount of goodwill. Second, the remaining impairment loss is allocated to the other assets of the CGU pro rata, on the basis of their carrying amounts in the CGU.

An impairment loss should be reversed (and income recognized) when there has been a change in the estimates used to determine an asset's recoverable amount since the last impairment loss was recognized. However, an impairment loss should only be reversed to the extent the reversal does not increase the carrying amount of the asset above the carrying amount that would have been determined for the asset (net of amortization or depreciation) had no impairment loss been recognized.

Bad debts and doubtful receivables

Probably the most commonly occurring asset impairment adjustment is that relating to collectability of company receivables. A company's suppliers will naturally expect to be paid in full, but, at the same time, the company may not expect to collect all its receivables. At first sight, that might seem a little odd, but there are various reasons why this may be:

1. *A customer may be a bad risk*: it is difficult to assess creditworthiness, so mistakes are made and credit given to those who cannot pay or, by way of contrast, a company with a good credit record may suddenly hit bad times.

2. *A customer might be disputing the amount of the invoice you sent*: perhaps he or she thinks the price charged was higher than that agreed or the quantity greater than that delivered.

3. *A customer may have refused to accept some of the goods because they were faulty* or may be planning to send some faulty goods back, but this has not yet been picked up by the accounting system.

So, there are many reasons why the receivables' balance at any given point is unlikely to be collected in full. If the full accounting value was used in the statement of financial position, it would therefore overstate the value of the asset and of the profit for the period.

There are two separate aspects of assessing a 'prudent' value for outstanding receivables (or 'debtors' in British English). First, there is the case of specific receivables that, on the evidence available, are not likely ever to be paid and, second, there is a more general assessment of the collectability of all receivables.

In the first case, it is a routine part of credit management to inspect all outstanding receivables and particularly those that have been outstanding a long time. What exact length of time is appropriate depends on the normal terms of credit in a particular industry – in most cases, if a receivable has not been paid within 60 days of the issue of the invoice (or perhaps by the end of the month following the month of issue), the credit manager will regard the receivable as overdue and in need of follow-up. After 90 days the receivable is a source of concern and normally a credit manager would be in touch directly with the debtor at that point to discover why payment has not been made. After six months the credit manager and the accountant should consider the receivable together with whatever information the credit manager has gleaned from the customer (or indeed the salesforce) to decide whether the receivable is likely to be settled. It may be that the client is going into liquidation or disputes the bill and refuses to pay and a decision has to be taken about recoverability. If it is decided that the amount is not recoverable, then the receivable becomes categorized as a bad debt and should be removed from the receivables' total. Note that, in practice, the phrases *bad debts* and *doubtful debts* are quite common, although it would be more accurate to use the labels *bad receivables* and *doubtful receivables*.

The bad debt, although it derives originally from a sale, is considered to be an expense. After all, the original sale took place; it is the settlement of the receivable that has not happened. Accordingly there is a simple transfer to decrease the receivable account (and therefore cancel the amount outstanding) and decrease the profit and loss account for the same amount. This evaluation of individual receivables should take place routinely throughout the year, but in any event it will also be a part of the exercise undertaken in preparing financial statements to ensure that no bad debts are included in the receivables' total.

COMPANY REPORT

BP – SIGNIFICANT ACCOUNTING POLICIES, JUDGEMENTS, ESTIMATES AND ASSUMPTIONS *(extract)*

Determination as to whether, and by how much, an asset or group of CGUs containing goodwill is impaired involves management estimates on highly uncertain matters such as future commodity prices, the effects of inflation on operating expenses, discount rates, production profiles and the outlook for global or regional market supply-and-demand conditions for crude oil, natural gas and refined products. Judgement is required when determining the appropriate grouping of assets into a CGU or the appropriate grouping of CGUs for impairment testing purposes.

The estimated future level of production in all impairment tests is based on assumptions about future commodity prices, production and development costs, field decline rates, current fiscal regimes and other factors.

As disclosed above, the recoverable amount of an asset is the higher of its value in use and its fair value less costs of disposal. Fair value less costs of disposal may be determined based on similar recent market transaction data or, where recent market transactions for the asset are not available for reference, using discounted cash flow techniques. Where discounted cash flow analyses are used to calculate fair value less costs of disposal, judgements are made about the assumptions market participants would use when pricing the asset, CGU or group of CGUs containing goodwill and the test is performed on a post-tax basis. Assumptions made in impairment tests in 2017 relating to discount rates, oil and gas properties and oil and gas prices are discussed below. Changes in the economic environment or other facts and circumstances may necessitate revisions to these assumptions and could result in a material change to the carrying values of the group's assets within the next financial year.

Discount rates

For value-in-use calculations, future cash flows are adjusted for risks specific to the cash-generating unit and are discounted using a pre-tax discount rate. The pre-tax discount rate is based upon the cost of funding the group derived from an established model, adjusted to a pre-tax basis. Fair value less costs of disposal calculations use the post-tax discount rate.

The discount rates applied in impairment tests are reassessed each year. In 2017 the discount rate used to determine recoverable amounts based on fair value less costs of disposal was 6% (2016 6%). The discount rate used to determine recoverable amounts based on value in use was 9% (2016 9%). In both cases, where the cash-generating unit is located in a country which is judged to be higher risk an additional 2% premium was added to the discount rate (2016 2%).

(Continued)

Oil and natural gas properties

For oil and natural gas properties, expected future cash flows are estimated using management's best estimate of future oil and natural gas prices and production and reserves volumes. The estimated future level of production in all impairment tests is based on assumptions about future commodity prices, production and development costs, field decline rates, current fiscal regimes and other factors.

Reserves assumptions for value-in-use tests are restricted to proved and probable reserves.

Source: BP Annual Report 2017

The second consideration is that of taking a prudent view of the likely value to be received from the current receivables' balance at reporting date. As we noted, there are many reasons why the total of accounts receivable may not be ultimately converted to cash, but most of the problems on individual receivables only come to light after the debt has aged a little. Consequently, as the bulk of the receivables outstanding at any one moment will be current, there is no way of knowing which will cause problems.

The prudent response to this is to set aside an 'allowance for doubtful receivables'. This is an amount expensed in the statement of profit or loss, but simply held as a credit balance in the general ledger against the day when any of the receivables outstanding at balance sheet date is classified as bad.

The object of making this general allowance for doubtful receivables is to show a prudent value of total receivables. Exactly how much should be set aside in the allowance is a matter for consideration in the context of the business of each company. In general terms, a company might be guided by:

- Industry practice generally

- Average percentage of actual bad debts experienced by the company in previous years

- An estimate consisting of a high proportion of receivables outstanding more than (say) three months plus a low proportion of current receivables.

The precise amount will be a matter of the opinion of the accountant preparing the statements and the auditor.

It may be helpful to look at the impact of such an allowance in the context of a statement of profit or loss and statement of financial position. Let us say that Wholesale Merchants Ltd has total receivables in its general ledger of £115,000 and that in preparing the annual financial statements the accountant has decided that £1,000 of receivables should be treated as definitely bad, while a further £1,300 should be set aside as an allowance for doubtful debts.

The impact of this will be to create an expense of £2,300 and reduce the published balance sheet value of receivables by the same amount. Within the company's records, the transactions would be:

	Write off bad debt	Create allowance
Assets		
Receivables	−1,000	
Valuation allowance		−1,300
Equity		
Profit for the year	−1,000	−1,300

The carrying amount of the receivables goes down by £1,000 directly and in the published statement of financial position the receivables figure would also be reduced by the valuation allowance, although in the general ledger the allowance will be held in a separate account, and in practical terms all the 'live' receivable accounts will continue to be followed up with monthly statements etc.

Normally, a company will set aside an allowance for doubtful receivables each year, and in the next set of statements will simply add to or subtract from the existing allowance to reach the required figure. For example, a company with an un-utilized balance on the allowance of £500 brought forward from the previous year would determine the required allowance for the current statement, let us say £750, and then expense the difference (£250) needed to bring the valuation allowance up to the required amount.

It is important to realize that the allowance for doubtful receivables is an adjustment made in order that the published financial statements show a reasonably prudent view. Notice that none of the individual accounts of the customers is credited. They still record the full amount due. The allowance will be used during the following year, as the bad debts materialize. This ensures that the bad debts do not affect the expenses (and hence the profit) of the year in which they prove to be bad, but rather the year in which the business was done.

Hidden reserves

Hidden reserves (also known as *secret reserves* or *silent reserves*) refer to accounting adjustments that lead to under-reporting of the company's real assets and over-reporting of its liabilities. They usually result from deliberate deductions from reported profit, commonly justified by prudence considerations. For example, a company may deliberately undervalue its tangible assets, inventories, receivables or overvalue its provisions. They are hidden in the sense that the value discrepancies are not overtly visible in the statement of financial position and the accounting adjustments do not appear separately in the statement of profit or loss when charged. (The term *reserve* might be somewhat confusing here, as it has a specific connotation in technical accounting jargon (as discussed later in this chapter) and will appear in the statement of financial position as a component of owners' equity. Hidden reserves are rather different.)

Although hidden reserves do not represent available funds, they are a *store of future profits*. For example, undervalued inventory will lead to lower cost of goods sold (and higher profit) when the consumption of the inventory asset is charged against revenue in subsequent periods. Property, plant and equipment that has been depreciated much more quickly than an economic consumption pattern would justify will underestimate the economic depreciation expense in subsequent periods and may bring about excessive disposal gains when sold before the end of its useful life. In general, future profits can be inflated by transferring amounts out of the hidden reserves.

To have hidden reserves, the company must have reduced earlier profits (in better times) by accounting entries that lead to lower reported profits and lower (undervalued) net assets.

The main sources of hidden reserves are:

- Writing down assets excessively
- Creating provisions for fictitious risks or future events (provision recognition issue)
- Overstating allowable provisions (provision measurement issue)
- Overstating financial liabilities.

Less strict provision accounting can lead to significant hidden reserves. Clearly, provisions may provide great scope for reducing profits under a 'prudent' accounting regime, even though they are not necessarily considered to be an 'allowable' (i.e. accepted by the tax authorities) expense for calculating the tax base. A typical example of provisions that used to be popular for these purposes and that are still allowed in the EU Accounting Directive (and in numerous other local GAAP regimes) are the 'deferred maintenance' provisions.

COMPANY REPORT

SIEMENS – ALLOWANCE FOR DOUBTFUL TRADE RECEIVABLES (extract)

Trade and other receivables
Impairment losses on trade and other receivables are recognized using separate allowance accounts. The allowance for credit risks involves significant management judgement and review of individual receivables based on individual customer creditworthiness and current economic trends. Generally, valuation allowances are based on customer ratings provided by SFS, which are centrally determined based on customer information as well as information from external rating agencies. The customer ratings also consider the country-specific component of country credit ratings. As of September 30, 2018 and 2017, Siemens recorded a valuation allowance for trade and other receivables (including leases) of €1,176 million and €1,391 million, respectively.

Source: Siemens, Annual Report, 2018

Provisions for maintenance and repairs usually relate to installations and equipment that require substantial expenditure every few years for major refits or refurbishment and the replacement of major components. Suppose a power plant has a useful life of 25 years, but the steam generators need to be replaced every eight years. Utility companies used to account for this type of replacement programme by building a maintenance provision over a period of eight years up to the estimated replacement cost. The provision is then used when the steam generator is actually replaced. IAS 37 *Provisions, Contingent Liabilities and Contingent Assets* does not allow this kind of provision, because at balance sheet date there exists no obligation to replace the steam generator independently of the company's future actions. Even the actual intention of the company to effectively replace the steam generator after the eight-year period does not create a present obligation as the company can always decide not to replace the steam generator or avoid the future expenditure by selling the power plant during the eight-year period. In fact, IAS 16 *Property, Plant and Equipment* clears this point with its guidance on allocating expenditure on an asset to its component parts where these components have different useful lives or provide benefits in a different pattern. Instead of a provision being recognized, the depreciation of the steam generator has to be scheduled over eight years (and not the 25-year periods of the power plant as a whole). The replacement costs of the steam generator then incurred have to be capitalized and depreciated over the subsequent eight years.

It should be clear that, in the aggregate, the 'deferred maintenance' type of provisions (and similar 'intentional' or even more general provisions for potential risks) can be used to even out the trend of profits over several accounting periods or projecting a trend of modestly rising profits over the years (what shareholders generally expect), when true underlying profits may be quite volatile. Provisions that have been created with a view to concealing profits or storing them for the future (the Securities and Exchange Commission talks about 'cookie jar' provisions) would be hidden reserves.

By way of illustration, suppose that in 20X1 a company reported profits of €100m with financial analysts adjusting their forecasts accordingly. The position might be:

	20X1 €m	20X2 €m	20X3 €m
Reported profit	100		
Market expectations		120	140

Market participants tend to project future earnings based on the company's historical track record. In 20X2 the draft financial statements show a profit of €150m but the company does not expect to be able to sustain that level of profitability in the future, as the current profit was largely due to favourable, but exceptional, operating conditions. If it reports that profit, the situation would be:

	20X1 €m	20X2 €m	20X3 €m
Reported profit	100	150	
Market expectations			225

So the company sets up an 'opportunistic' provision and recognizes the corresponding provision expense in the current year:

	20X1 €m	20X2 €m	20X3 €m
Draft profit		150	
Provision (expense)		−30	
Reported profit	100	120	
Market expectations			*140*

The following year is particularly bad, but by reversing the unused provision reported profit can be enhanced considerably:

	20X1 €m	20X2 €m	20X3 €m
Draft profit			110
Release provision			+30
Reported profit	100	120	140

In the end, reported profit shows a steadily increasing trend, which is usually preferred by investors as it suggests continued growth and a lower risk profile.

Pressure on immediate profitability in the international capital market means that such provisions are used less often than they used to be, but it is not unusual for companies to try to even out profit flows a little by matching windfall profits with extra expenses (known as *income smoothing*).

Hidden reserves are generally more common in accounting regimes where prudence is a dominant accounting principle than when IFRS Standards are applied. In fact, many of the international rules (and IAS 37 *Provisions, Contingent Liabilities and Contingent Assets* is an obvious example of this) are inspired by a quest to bring down hidden reserves, as their existence would not be consistent with the principle of faithful representation (and neutrality). Recall that prudence is not part of the qualitative characteristics of useful information according to the *Conceptual Framework*, whereas it remains a key principle in the EU Accounting Directive and in many local accounting regimes. Clearly, while hidden reserves may be defended on the grounds of prudence, they provide endless opportunities for disguising the true state of a company's profit and financial position.

Capital structure

A company's *capital structure* refers to how it finances its overall operations and growth by using different sources of funds. It is a jargon term to indicate the composition of the financing side of a company's financial position. Broadly, companies are financed externally with a *mixture of equity capital and debt capital*.

Equity (capital) are funds owned by shareholders (owners) and consist of: (a) *contributed funds* (the money that shareholders originally invested in the company in exchange for shares), and (b) *internally generated (earned) funds*, which mainly comprise profits from prior years that have not been distributed to shareholders and have been retained by the company in order to finance future operations and expansion. Equity *participates fully in the risks and rewards of ownership* – it has no guaranteed return, but no upper limit either. Companies have limited liability so the equity holder's downside risk is limited to the amount of his or her investment. The equity is only ever repaid to the individual investor in the event of liquidation. Ordinarily, investors realize the equity investment by selling the shares they own to someone else, although in restricted circumstances companies can buy back their own shares.

Debt (capital) refers to borrowed funds that are at work in the company. Debt is usually advanced to the company for a *fixed period*, earns a *fixed return* (although the interest rate may be variable if it floats in line with market rates) and must be repaid at the end of that period. The debt may be for the short, medium or long term, may be in foreign currency and can derive from a variety of sources. Many large companies obtain debt by issuing bonds or debentures that are bought and sold on the international financial markets. This traditional distinction between equity capital and debt capital has broken down somewhat as a result of *financial engineering* – banks compete with each other for corporate clients by devising ever more complicated debt instruments that incorporate characteristics of equity.

Equity and debt each has its own advantages and drawbacks and the decision as to what proportion of debt and equity to use in a company is a major corporate finance issue: company management is challenged to find the *optimal capital structure* in terms of risk/ reward payoff for shareholders. In principle, a company that uses a high proportion of debt (a highly geared company) has the possibility of enhancing the return to shareholders at the cost of making the return more volatile and more risky to the shareholder (see 'financial leverage' as discussed in Chapter 17). The ratio of debt to equity is one of the key metrics reviewed by analysts in this regard and some companies put a lot of effort into massaging this ratio.

Generally, companies have a target debt/equity ratio around which they operate, but that they do not usually achieve in practice. Issuing new equity can be expensive (professional fees, underwriting, etc.) and therefore companies tend to use internally generated funds and debt to finance new projects in the first instance and then every few years issue new equity to move back closer to their target gearing.

Components of equity

The main ingredients of equity are:

- Ordinary shares
- Preference shares
- Retained earnings
- Reserves.

The holders of *ordinary shares* are the ultimate owners of the company and all other forms of finance rank ahead of these when it comes to the ultimate payment of their claims. Their interest in the company is a *residual claim* – what is left after all other calls have been met. Ordinary shares have a *nominal (face or par) value*. When companies are created, legal documents are drawn up that specify the upper limit on the number of shares that can be issued. Companies are not obliged to issue all these, and their effective voting share capital is the *issued share capital*. Note that sometimes companies have different classes of ordinary shares – 'A' shares, 'B' shares, etc. – often this is to give different voting rights to different groups of shareholders, a practice not entirely popular with the market.

Ordinary shares are rarely issued at par value and the difference between issue price and nominal value is also part of equity. It is called *share premium*. Costs of issuing shares are offset against share premium.

Preference shares attract a *fixed return* (hence '7 per cent preference shares') and holders do not routinely have voting rights, so they have the characteristic of debt. By the same token, the preference dividend may not be paid if there are no profits and does not qualify as a deduction before tax. Usually, if no dividend is paid preference shareholders are enfranchised. Typically preference shares are *cumulative* – if the dividend is not paid, the right to receive it accumulates against future profits. Dividends cannot be paid to ordinary shareholders ahead of preference shareholders. It is a matter of opinion as to whether preference shares should be treated as debt or equity for the purposes of calculating gearing.

Retained earnings are accumulated profits earned in prior years that have not been distributed to shareholders, but are eligible to be paid over to shareholders by way of dividend.

Reserves can be split in two main categories: (a) reserves representing *appropriations of retained profits*, and (b) reserves representing *accumulated other comprehensive income (OCI)*, resulting from income and expense items that were directly included in equity (instead of transiting through profit or loss). The first category refers to reserves that result from appropriations of accumulated prior profits for which legal or statutory requirements restrict the company's ability to distribute or otherwise use them (*legal reserves*; *statutory reserves*). The second main category of reserve includes items such as gains on the revaluation of tangible fixed assets and gains and losses on the translation of assets and liabilities in foreign currency. These are, in effect, items of income and expense, but unlike retained earnings, they are not accounted for in the statement of profit or loss, but are put directly in equity (as *OCI* – see also Chapter 11). The company is usually not allowed to treat them as available for distribution as dividends.

Convertibles

Convertible securities – either preference shares or debt (convertible debentures) that can be converted at some point in the future into ordinary shares – are another form of debt that was particularly popular at the end of the twentieth century. The merit of convertible securities is that the initial fixed return status means that there is little risk to the lender, while the possibility of converting to equity in the longer term means that if the company does well, the holder can convert to equity and participate in the company's growth. For the issuer, it means a finer issue price and, if converted, a relatively cheap way to issue equity. For the analyst, there is a problem as to whether convertible debt should be treated as debt or equity for analytical purposes.

In recent years, companies have issued all sorts of complex financial instruments that combine both elements of debt and elements of equity. The earliest instruments were probably convertible debentures or preference shares, where companies might argue that they should be considered to be part of the equity component rather than debt. Variants on this might be debt (sometimes called *mezzanine debt*) that ranked behind other debt for repayment and received a return based on profitability of the company. More recent developments are capital bonds and perpetual loan notes. If a loan is never to be repaid, it can be argued that it is more like equity than debt.

Summary

In this chapter, we have dealt with year-end adjustments, including accruals and deferrals (of expenses and revenue) and provisions. We specifically outlined the more subjective aspects of provision accounting and the borderline with contingent liabilities. We have introduced and discussed the concept of impairment testing of asset values, which has become a primary procedural issue in preparing financial statements at year-end. The underlying idea of the impairment test requirement is that an asset should not be carried on the statement of financial position at more than the company will be able to recover either from using or selling the asset. Adjusting the carrying amount of receivables for bad or doubtful debts is a specific application of the recoverability analysis of asset values. We have also visited briefly the structure of the financing side of the balance sheet and the major components of equity.

Discussion questions

1. Accurately accounting for accruals and deferrals is a major issue in preparing financial statements. Discuss what constitutes an accrual and a deferral and give appropriate examples of the main categories one can discern.
2. Explain why and how deferred revenue is recognized in the statement of financial position.
3. In what sense is provision accounting a specific application of the principle of accrual accounting?
4. Explain the meaning of the word 'impairment' within the context of IFRS Standards and discuss why it can be difficult to apply the concept to individual assets.
5. Identify and discuss the main categories of equity that you would find in an IFRS® statement of financial position.
6. A company that grants defined pension benefits to its employees usually shows in its statement of financial position a net liability representing the difference between the obligation to pay pension benefits and the fair value of the assets included in the pension fund. Explain why it is not enough to expense the company's yearly contributions to the pension fund and eventually include an overview of the relevant assets of the pension fund (that is a separate entity) as an addendum in the notes.

Assignments

The following assignments have answers on the lecturer side of the digital support resources for the book.

1. The following balances were extracted from the accounting records of Arlington SA as at 31 December 20X1:

	€
100,000 Ordinary shares	100,000
10% Preference shares	50,000
12% Debenture (Long-term debt)	50,000
Premises	130,000
Motor vehicles (gross cost €48,000)	36,000
Purchases	219,700
Administration expenses	73,200
Distribution costs	102,600
Sales	476,900
Trade receivables	39,250
Trade payables	23,600
Inventory at 1 January 20X1	21,250
Bank balance (asset)	70,420
Investments (at cost)	45,800
Reserves	48,220
Debenture interest	3,000
Preference dividend	2,500
Ordinary dividend	5,000

You are required to draw up a statement of profit or loss and a statement of financial position for Arlington SA as at 31 December 20X1, after taking into account the following adjustments *(note that expenses have been analyzed by function, not by type, in this example)*:

(a) The closing inventory (31 December 20X1) was valued at €19,300.

(b) Preference and ordinary dividends were paid halfway through the year, as well as debenture interest, but an accrual should be made for the balance of the debenture interest for the year. The company proposes a final dividend of €8,000 on ordinary shares.

(c) The audit fee has been agreed at €5,000.

(d) Insurance (included in administrative expenses) has been paid in advance and €950 relates to 20X2.

(e) Accrued expenses of €480 for telephone services (included in administration expenses) and €620 for light and heat (included in distribution costs) have not yet been taken into account.

(f) The trade receivables balance includes €1,200 of bad debts, which should be written off.

(g) Depreciation of 25 per cent on a straight-line basis should be charged on the motor vehicles (which are vans used in distribution activities).

(h) The market value (fair value) of the investments at 31 December 20X1 amounts to €44,100.

(i) It is estimated that the income tax charge for 20X1 will be €20,000.

Before drawing up the financial statements, set up a table using the format below and analyze the effect of each of the adjustments on the financial statement categories indicated.

Adjustments	Assets	Liabilities	Equity/Profit for the period
(a)	+/−	+/−	+/−

(*Comment*: This question is presented in an unhelpful way! You should reorganize the information from the database onto a spreadsheet in a way with which you are comfortable and then deal with the adjustments. You will not have come across one or two adjustments, and should just suggest a way of dealing with them based on what you know so far.)

2. Critically assess the following cases within the context of the IAS 37 requirements for provision accounting:

(a) Company A offers a one-year warranty for the products that it manufactures. Yearly revenue subject to product warranty amounts to €3,000,000. In past years on average 3 per cent of the products proved defective. Defective products are replaced or reimbursed.

(b) Company B produces and sells phosphate fertilizers that are used to grow grains. The process of extracting the raw materials from the land that the company owns has a major impact on the natural environment. At reporting date, estimates of environmental remediation costs amount to €5,000,000.

(c) A lawsuit claiming damages has been filed against Company C. The company foresees a reasonable possibility of losing the lawsuit. The company's legal advisers have estimated potential settlement costs at €350,000.

(d) Company D runs an airline. The company is required by law to overhaul its aircraft once every three years. The future overhaul and maintenance costs are estimated at €2,500,000.

(e) Company E decides to close down one of its divisions. Before the end of its financial year, a detailed plan for closing down the division was communicated to the division's works council and termination notices were sent to all employees affected by the closure of the division. Company E estimates that it will have €900,000 in restructuring costs.

(f) Company F has a policy of refunding purchases of dissatisfied customers even though it has no legal obligation to do so. The refunds policy is published in its semi-yearly product catalogue, which is widely distributed and accessible on the company's commercial website.

3. Greenfield Dynamics manufactures and sells golf carts with a product warranty. The warranty provides for the replacement or repair of manufacturing defects discovered within the first year after manufacture. During fiscal year 20X5 Greenfield sold 5,000 vehicles under warranty. Greenfield's repairs department estimates that 85 per cent of the golf carts sold will have no defects, 10 per cent will require a minor repair

(costing €500 per vehicle) and 5 per cent of the golf carts sold will require a major repair (costing €900 per vehicle). The company's chief accountant estimates that the minimum amount of the provision expense for the product warranty will be €200,000 and the maximum will be €600,000. Greenfield is also involved in a tax dispute with the tax authorities. At the end of fiscal year 20X5 the company's legal counsel are convinced that the most likely outcome is that Greenfield will lose the dispute and have to pay €100,000. The estimated minimum expenditure for a settlement is €2,000 and the maximum amount is €500,000.

Required:

Calculate the amount to be provided by Greenfield Dynamics in its 20X5 financial statements in respect of warranty claims and the tax dispute.

4. On 2 January 20X3, Dinasus Ltd purchased a specialized machine tool for £3,000,000. The straight-line depreciation schedule established an annual depreciation charge of £600,000 over a five-year useful life. Changes in market demand brought the company to carry out an impairment test at the end of accounting period 20X6. The impairment test was executed by external valuation experts and they concluded that (a) the machine tool suffered permanent impairment of its operational value, (b) the original useful life was still appropriate, (c) the net present value calculation of the cash flows to be generated by the machine tool amounted to £800,000 and (d) £950,000 is a reasonable estimate of the net selling price of the machine tool at the time of the impairment test.

Required:

What are the accounting effects of this impairment test for accounting period 20X6?

5. At 31 December 20X3, Biaz Company carries out a review for impairment of a machine shop, acquired at the beginning of 20X1 for £20,000. The useful life of the machine shop was estimated at five years with a zero residual value. The machine shop is depreciated on a straight-line basis. Taking into account the impact of technological advances on operating conditions, the recoverable amount of the machine shop is estimated at £6,000, with a remaining useful life of two years.

Required:

Determine if any impairment loss is to be accounted for by Biaz Company at the end of 20X3. What would be the book value of the machine shop at the end of 20X4 (if no further impairment during 20X4)?

6. On 1 April 20X0, Teleconstruct acquired a production plant at a cost of €800,000 in order to produce and package microchip devices. The plant had an estimated residual value of €50,000 and an estimated life of five years. Teleconstruct applies the straight-line depreciation method. On 31 March 20X2 Teleconstruct was informed by a major customer (who regularly ordered microchips produced by the plant) that it

would no longer be placing orders with Teleconstruct. Even before this information was known, Teleconstruct had been having difficulty finding work for this plant. The company now estimates that net cash inflows earned from operating the plant for the next three years will be:

Year ended:	€
31 March 20X3	220,000
31 March 20X4	180,000
31 March 20X5	170,000

On 31 March 20X5, the plant is still expected to be sold for its estimated residual value. Teleconstruct has assessed that there is no market in which to sell the plant at 31 March 20X2 and that it was not able to reliably estimate the plant's fair value at that date. Teleconstruct's cost of capital is 10 per cent and the following values should be used to calculate the present value of the future net cash inflows and establish the plant's value in use:

Value of 1€ at:	€
End of Year 1	0.91
End of Year 2	0.83
End of Year 3	0.75

Required:

Calculate the carrying amounts of Teleconstruct's plant at 31 March 20X2 after applying any impairment losses.

7. See assignment Traduct SA in Chapter 12 for an exercise on impairment issues including goodwill.

CHAPTER 7

Preparing financial statements

In this chapter, we are going to reach the end of our journey to the first major objective, which is to gain the ability to put together a simple statement of profit or loss and statement of financial position. The techniques we have been using are not those used directly by accountants, but the object is to understand the principles, in order to be able to use financial statements better as managers. This chapter will serve to bring together and review the different allocations and adjustments we have discussed so far, and should consolidate the techniques learned.

Chapter structure

- Constructing financial statements
- Accounting adjustments
- Additional adjustments for interest and taxation
- Uses of financial statements
- Summary
- Assignments

Constructing financial statements

The basic technique for the preparation of a statement of profit or loss (income statement/ profit or loss account) and a statement of financial position (balance sheet) consists of taking the aggregate transaction data from the accounting records as at the end of the financial year, quantifying the adjustments necessary to convert the data to reflect Generally Accepted Accounting Principles (GAAP), then putting the base data and the adjustments together in the approved statement format.

There is no prescribed way of carrying out this exercise, but most accountants prepare working papers on the basis of what is called an extended trial balance. This is not exactly the method we shall use, but we will discuss it here for your information.

The base data with which the accountant starts are the *trial balance* as at the end of the financial year, that is, the *listing of all the balances on all the general ledger accounts at the end of the period*. The accountant must then refine these data by adjusting for unrecorded expenses, revenue invoiced but not yet earned, depreciation, bad debts, provisions, impairment losses, etc. This may seem a potentially limitless exercise involving a major investigative activity, but, in fact, the accountant always starts off with the previous year's adjustments and then checks to see what has changed subsequently, so that the 'year-end exercise' is built up incrementally as the business develops.

The adjustments that are calculated at this stage are put into working papers in the first instance and a draft set of statements is prepared. These will form the basis of discussion with management and auditors, since usually they will involve taking a position about open transactions and other uncertainties (and will also impact on issues like taxation and profit-related bonuses).

The traditional extended trial balance working paper consists of four sets of debit and credit columns, which will be added across to give the final picture. You will recall that, formally speaking, the accounting database is constructed with two columns for each account (see Chapter 2) although we have not replicated that presentation, since our object is to understand how the figures work rather than run an accounting function:

Ledger balances		+	Adjustments	=	Profit or loss		or	Balance sheet	
D / C			D / C		D / C			D / C	
€	€		€	€	€	€		€	€

Mathematically, the ledger balances and adjustments are added together horizontally. Each adjusted balance will have its place in either the statement of profit or loss or statement of financial position (balance sheet) and the adjusted total is entered in the appropriate column. The total debits and credits in the first column will equal each other, as will those in the adjustments column, but the statement of profit or loss and balance sheet columns must be added together to get balancing totals. For our purposes, we shall continue to work with single-column spreadsheets, and we will add across to the right as we put in adjustments and so on.

The adjustments consist typically of all the elements we have looked at in the preceding sessions and which are necessary to provide financial statements that fully comply with GAAP. Specifically, these *adjustments* involve the following:

1. *Calculation of cost of goods sold*: Insertion of closing inventories to arrive at the measurement of the cost of the goods sold during the period.

2. *Adjustment for accruals/deferrals*: Bringing into the accounts details of expenses and revenues relating to the period but unrecorded at reporting date; carrying forward the unexpired expense for payments made that relate to future periods and deferring revenues received but yet unearned at reporting date. (The information for this in a practical situation comes from examining individual ledger accounts to

check the periods covered by payments/receipts, and examining payments/receipts after the reporting date.)

3. *Charging annual depreciation*: Debiting the operating expenses and crediting accumulated depreciation (or amortization) to reflect the expensing of long-term assets consumed during the year.

4. *Updating provisions*: Adjusting existing provisions for uses and reversals and adding new provisions.

5. *Reviewing assets for potential impairment*: If an impairment test evidences an impairment loss, the asset value will be decreased (credited) while the impairment loss will be accounted for in the statement of profit or loss as an operating expense (debiting an expense account).

The easiest way to see what happens in practice is if we now take an example, and work through the adjustments individually.

Worked example

The trial balance of Mornington Crescent Emporium SA as at 31 December 20X1 was as follows:

Mornington Crescent Emporium SA
Trial balance as at 31 December 20X1

	€
Assets	
Premises	30,000
Equipment (at cost)	15,000
Accumulated depreciation	−4,500
Inventory at 1 January 20X1	13,250
Trade receivables	23,000
Bank	18,560
	95,310
Equity and liabilities	
Share capital	50,000
Retained profits	10,500
Trade payables	16,850
Sales	193,000
Purchases	−145,000
Salaries and wages	−15,325
Rent	−10,000
Insurance	−2,500
Legal and professional expenses	−1,250
Telephone	−345
Light and heat	−620
	95,310

In reviewing the accounting transactions both before and after the reporting date (balance sheet date), the following information comes to light:

1. The value of the inventory of goods for resale at 31 December 20X1 was €14,150.
2. Rent is payable quarterly in advance and rent for the three months January to March 20X2 was paid in December 20X1.
3. An insurance premium of €1,000 was paid in September 20X1, covering the period October 20X1 to March 20X2 inclusive.
4. A telephone bill of €120 was received in February 20X2 and related to the three months ending 31 January 20X2.
5. An electricity bill (the most recent one paid) for the three months up to the end of November 20X1 for €150 was paid in December 20X1.
6. The financial statements must be audited and the estimated cost of the audit is €2,000.
7. At year-end the company received a notification that a lawsuit was filed against it for injuries due to defects of goods sold. The company's legal counsel believes that an unfavourable outcome is probable and that a reasonable estimate of the settlement is €1,000. Settlement is expected to occur at the beginning of May 20X2.

The accountant normally provides depreciation on a straight-line basis for the equipment owned by the company (note that there is already accumulated depreciation in the trial balance) on the basis that it will have a nil salvage value and a useful life of 10 years. There are no indications that assets might be impaired.

The above details represent the accountant's blueprint for action. She or he will set out the trial balance information on the extended trial balance worksheet we have described, and will then set out to incorporate the adjustments that are required on the worksheet, in order to calculate a draft set of statements.

We will not go through the formalities of the extended trial balance as such but will use a spreadsheet. While managers are unlikely to have to prepare a set of financial statements themselves, they need to understand the mechanics of the process, since they may well be involved in making decisions about year-end adjustments and in any event need to know what are the areas of certainty and uncertainty that are concerned with the accounting process and, ultimately, with reported profit. Generally, some hands-on practice at drawing up statements fixes the basics more clearly in the mind!

Accounting adjustments

a. Inventory of goods

The trial balance already contains an 'inventory' figure – the opening inventory at the beginning of the year. The value of the inventory at the end of the year (independently established either by the company or by outside stock-takers) is €14,150. Inventory levels have increased by €900 and this must be reflected in the final statement of financial position. As we have discussed previously, this also fixes the cost of goods sold, and we can adjust the trial balance as follows:

Inventory of goods available for sale	+900 (+Assets)
Purchases (becomes 'cost of goods sold')	– 900 (+ Equity)

b. Rent prepayment

The information outside the trial balance shows that the €10,000 expenses recorded in the rent account include a payment for the first three months of 20X2. The rent account must therefore be adjusted to show the 20X1 expense only and recognize that at reporting date there is an asset, the unexpired rent expense for three months. From the information given, the rent account balance represents 15 months' rent, so the unexpired element must be three-fifteenths, or €2,000. Therefore the expense account is reduced by €2,000 and a new asset must appear:

Rent expense	− 2,000 (+ Equity)
Prepaid expenses	+ 2,000 (+ Assets)

c. Insurance prepayment

The accountant also knows that the last insurance paid (€1,000) referred to a six-month period of which only half was in 20X1, so here again he or she has to recognize an unexpired expense. The last payment related half to 20X1 and half to 20X2, so €500 (1/2 × €1,000) should be recognized as an asset (prepaid insurance services). Again the expense account is reduced and prepaid expenses increased:

Insurance expense	− 500 (+ Equity)
Prepaid expenses	+ 500 (+ Assets)

d. Telephone accrual

The telephone bill paid in 20X2 included elements that related to 20X1 and are therefore expenses for 20X1. They must be incorporated in the 20X1 statement of profit or loss and recognized as current liabilities in the statement of financial position at year-end 20X1. The proportion of the bill relating to 20X1 was two-thirds – the months of November and December, so two-thirds of the bill should be accrued (€80). Telephone expenses for 20X1 are increased and another new balance sheet account opened up, this time accrued expenses:

Telephone expense	+80 (− Equity)
Accrued expenses	+80 (+ Liabilities)

e. Electricity accrual

The electricity account also needs adjusting for accrued expenses, but the basis of calculation this time is different. The accountant has discovered from the ledger that the electricity account includes charges only up to the end of November, but no invoice for December charges has yet come in. Notwithstanding, he or she has to make an accrual, and must base the calculation on something else. Sometimes this is done by taking the previous year's figure and making an allowance for inflation, sometimes by taking a proportion of the most recently paid bill. In this case, the most recent bill was for three months, so using that as a basis an accrual of one-third of the earlier bill (1/3 × €150 = €50) is made. You may think this is a rather crude approximation, which it is, but the amount in relation to overall expenses is not material so a more precise approach is not necessary. As before, the light and heat expense account is increased and the accrued expenses are equally increased:

| Light and heat expense | +50 (− Equity) |
| Accrued expenses | +50 (+ Liabilities) |

f. Accrued audit expense

The cost of the annual audit (although the actual work may in part take place after the reporting date) is considered to be part of the operating expenses for 20X1 and this accrued expense should also be recognized. The figure in this case is €2,000 and a new expense line is created for it. The adjustment is:

| Legal and professional expense | +2,000 (− Equity) |
| Accrued expenses | +2,000 (+ Liabilities) |

g. Provision for litigation

From the advice of the legal experts it is likely that the company will be found liable for the injuries caused by defective products sold in the past. The accountant concludes that there is a present obligation arising from a past event and that a future settlement payment is probable (around May next year). Although the settlement expenditure is still uncertain, the legal experts are able to provide a reliable best estimate. All three recognition criteria for a provision have been met and a corresponding liability will be recognized in the statement of financial position.

An expense line is created for the provision as an operating expense and a new liability account is inserted in the statement of financial position. The adjustment is:

| Provision expense | +1,000 (− Equity) |
| Short-term provision (liability) | +1,000 (+ Liabilities) |

h. Depreciation

The company's equipment appears in the statement of financial position at €15,000 original cost and must be depreciated over 10 years on a straight-line basis. The annual expense will therefore be:

$$\frac{15,000}{10} = 1,500$$

This is entered by creating a new expense line for the annual charge to operating expenses and crediting the other side of the transaction to the accumulated depreciation account to reflect the reduced value of the asset:

| Depreciation expense | +1,500 (− Equity) |
| Accumulated depreciation | +1,500 (− Assets) |

The classic problem with the adjustments is to have non-balancing adjustments, with the effect that although one starts from a database where assets equal liabilities and equity, this equilibrium is destroyed by the adjustments. Of course, computerized worksheets build in control of this nature to avoid the problem. MBA students in an exam context have less luck, generally.

Worksheet	Trial balance	Adjustments	Statement of profit or loss	Balance sheet
Premises	30,000			30,000
Equipment (at cost)	15,000			15,000
Accumulated depreciation	−4,500	(h) −1,500		−6,000
Inventory	13,250	(a) +900		14,150
Trade receivables	23,000			23,000
Bank	18,560			18,560
Prepaid expenses		(b) +2,000		2,500
		(c) +500		
Totals	**95,310**	**11,900**		**97,210**
Share capital	50,000			50,000
Retained profits	10,500			10,500
Profit for year				(i) 16,730
Trade payables	16,850			16,850
Sales	193,000		193,000	
Purchases	−145,000	(a) +900	−144,100	
Salaries and wages	−15,325		−15,325	
Rent	−10,000	(b) +2,000	−8,000	
Insurance	−2,500	(c) +500	−2,000	
Legal and professional expenses	−1,250	(f) −2,000	−3,250	
Telephone	−345	(d) −80	−425	
Light and heat	−620	(e) −50	−670	
Accrued expenses		(d) +80		2,130
		(e) +50		
		(f) +2,000		
Short-term provision		(g) +1,000		1,000
Provision expense		(g) −1,000	−1,000	
Depreciation expense		(h) −1,500	−1,500	
Profit			(i) −16,730	
Totals	**95,310**	**11,900**		**97,210**

Note: Letters in brackets refer to the adjustments previously discussed.

Since we are splitting out on the worksheet a separate column for the statement of profit or loss, the balance sheet sections will not balance internally – the profit is missing from the equity section. In order to correct this and 'prove' the balance sheet, we need to calculate the profit figure and enter it into the balance sheet [*entry (i)*].

You have now completed working papers for the statement of profit or loss and statement of financial position as they would appear in the company's books, and all that remains is to set them out in an acceptable format for publication:

Mornington Crescent Emporium SA

Statement of profit or loss for the year ended 31 December 20X1 (format for use internally)

	€	€
Sales		193,000
Cost of goods sold		(144,100)
		48,900
Salaries and wages	15,325	
Rent	8,000	
Insurance	2,000	
Light and heat	670	
Depreciation expense	1,500	
Provision expense	1,000	
Legal and professional expense	1,250	
Telephone	425	
Audit fee	2,000	(32,170)
Profit for year 20X1		**16,730**

Statement of profit or loss for the year ended 31 December 20X1 (published format)

	€	€
Revenue		193,000
Cost of goods sold		(144,100)
		48,900
Personnel costs	15,325	
Other operating expenses (excluding depreciation and provision expense)	14,345	
Depreciation expense	1,500	
Provision expense	1,000	(32,170)
Profit for year 20X1		16,730

Note: The profit figure in the worked example up to now is somewhat simplified as it does not include interest expense or taxation (but see below for further elaboration).

Statement of financial position as at
31 December 20X1

	€	€
Non-current assets		
Premises		30,000
Equipment (at cost)	15,000	
less accumulated depreciation	(6,000)	9,000
		39,000
Current assets		
Inventory	14,150	
Trade receivables	23,000	
Prepaid expenses	2,500	
Bank	18,560	58,210
Total assets		97,210
Equity		
Share capital		50,000
Retained earnings	10,500	
	16,730	27,230
		77,230
Current liabilities		
Short-term provisions		1,000
Trade payables		16,850
Accrued expenses		2,130
Total equity and liabilities		97,210

Additional adjustments for interest and taxation

In preparing annual financial statements, we have so far dealt only with the operating result. We now need to add to that adjustments for interest payments and taxation, and consider the dividend.

Interest is usually paid in arrears (sometimes monthly, or quarterly or every six months – customs differ between countries and types of borrowing) and will often need to be considered when calculating year-end accruals.

Taxation also varies from country to country. Tax on company profits may be levied at a national level only, or at both national and regional level. It is rarely found at local municipality level. In some countries, it is paid after the accounting year, once annual profits have been determined; in many countries, companies make payments on account based on their own estimate of the profit for a quarter year or half year. At the year-end, there will normally be an amount to be accrued.

The deduction of interest and tax expense normally figures separately in the statement of profit or loss:

Profit before interest and tax	*XXXXX*
Finance costs (interest expense)	(XXXX)
Profit before tax	*XXXXX*
Income tax expense	(XXXX)
Profit for the period (available for shareholders)	XXXX

There remains after that the question of dividends to shareholders. Large listed companies will usually pay a dividend every six months and this will be charged directly against accumulated profits in shareholders' equity (companies listed on the New York Stock Exchange have to produce figures every quarter and some pay a dividend every quarter as well). The amount of the final, year-end dividend has to be approved by the shareholders in a general meeting, which takes place when the financial statements have been finalized, as they too are approved at that meeting.

In some national accounting regimes, this final dividend is also shown within the statement of profit or loss as a deduction from the profit for the period (although not as an expense but as an appropriation of net profit!) and in the balance sheet as a liability, but treatment varies from country to country. More often the dividend is shown simply as a deduction from retained earnings once it has been paid. The IFRS Standards, however, are very explicit on this point: in accordance with IAS 10 *Events after the Reporting Period* dividends declared after the reporting date may not be recognized as a liability because they do not constitute a present obligation yet at the date of the statement of financial position – instead, they will be disclosed in the notes to the accounts.

Worked example (continued)

In order to demonstrate how the adjustments would look, let us return to the financial statements we prepared in the worked example and rework them on the basis of a different capital structure. We can also include an allowance for doubtful receivables and a current income tax accrual.

The share capital in the original example was €50,000. Let us now substitute a different capital structure:

	€
Ordinary shares	40,000
5% Long-term debenture	10,000
Total capital structure	50,000

The company would need to make the following adjustment for the yearly interest on the debenture liability (interest expense reduces equity and interest is accrued as a liability):

Debenture interest (5% × €10,000)	+500 (− Equity)
Accrued expenses	+500 (+ Liabilities)

The total trade receivables outstanding was €23,000. If the company wanted to take into account an allowance for doubtful receivables of 1 per cent, this would involve a charge of €230 against profits and a reduction of the asset value, in this case, by the same amount:

Doubtful debt expense	−230 (−Equity)
Trade receivables	−230 (−Assets)

Assuming an income tax rate of 30 per cent, the company would also need to set aside €4,800 as an income tax accrual (original profit was €16,730; deduction of €230 doubtful debt allowance and €500 debenture interest would leave €16,000, 30 per cent of which is €4,800).

Current tax expense	−4,800 (−Equity)
Taxes payable	+4,800 (+Liabilities)

Assuming that you are using the same working papers as before, the adjustments are entered into the adjustment column and then extended across horizontally into the statement of profit or loss and statement of financial position.

The adjusted financial statements are as follows:

Mornington Crescent Emporium SA
Statement of profit or loss for the year ended 31 December 20X1

	€	€
Revenue		193,000
Cost of goods sold		(144,100)
		48,900
Personnel costs	15,325	
Other operating expenses	14,345	
(excluding depreciation, impairment and provisions)		
Depreciation expense	1,500	
Provision expense	1,000	
Allowance for doubtful receivables	230	(32,400)
Profit before interest and tax		*16,500*
Interest expense		(500)
Profit before tax		*16,000*
Income tax expense		(4,800)
(Net) Profit for the period		*11,200*

Mornington Crescent Emporium SA
Statement of financial position as at 31 December 20X1

	€	€
Non-current assets		
Premises		30,000
Equipment (at cost)	15,000	
less accumulated depreciation	(6,000)	9,000
		39,000
Current assets		
Inventory	14,150	
Trade receivables	23,000	
less impairment allowance	(230)	
Prepaid expenses	2,500	
Bank	18,560	57,980
Total assets		96,980
Equity		
Share capital		40,000
Retained earnings	10,500	
	11,200	21,700
		61,700
Non-current liabilities		
Long-term debenture		10,000
Current liabilities		
Short-term provisions		1,000
Trade payables		16,850
Accrued expenses		2,630
Taxes payable		4,800
Total equity and liabilities		96,980

Uses of financial statements

This is by way of recapitulation of some of the issues that we considered at the beginning of this book. It is a major problem of financial reporting that a single set of numbers is expected to satisfy diverse objectives:

- Measure how much dividend might be paid
- Provide reassurance of a company's financial strength to creditors
- Provide a basis for measuring future growth for stock market analysis
- Measure management performance in a principal/agent context

- Provide the basis of taxation of the company
- Give employees an idea of the company's strength.

Moreover, it needs also to be understood that the large, listed company, which has operations in many parts of the world, sees its annual report as a public relations document for trumpeting the group's strength and viability. A private, family-controlled company, may see its financial statements as something secret, to be disclosed to as few people as possible, and where profit is minimized in order to keep taxation low and to retain as much cash as possible in the company. We focused on these different perspectives in Chapter 1 of this book.

It will be clear to you that (a) some of the objectives mentioned above are contradictory; and (b) accounting (GAAP) leaves open some choices that can affect how these objectives are met. But recall that, for the International Accounting Standards Board (the Board), current and potential investors, lenders and other creditors are seen as the primary beneficiaries of the IFRS® financial statements. Some of the objectives just examined are consistent with the overall objective of financial reporting according to the Board, but others are not. Tax measurement rules, for example, may well affect national accounting rules, but should not drive accounting choice in an IFRS® context (although tax consequences are real economic consequences for a company and should be accounted for accordingly – see Chapter 15 in this book). Employees, customers, government agencies and the public at large may benefit from using the financial reports, but financial statements are not primarily directed to those user groups.

Summary

In this chapter, we have demonstrated the technique used to prepare annual financial statements from the accounting database. This involves extracting a trial balance and then using that as a working paper in which we incorporate adjustments for revenues and expenses that fall at either side of the year-end, for provisions, impairments, interest and income taxes. This should result in general purpose financial statements published in a format accessible to external users

Assignments

The following questions have answers on the lecturer side of the digital support resources for the book.

1. The trial balance of Arénières Inc. at 31 December 20X4 shows the following:

	€
Land	82,100
Buildings (at cost)	120,000
Accumulated depreciation – buildings	−36,000
Equipment (at cost)	89,500
Accumulated depreciation – equipment	−53,700
Bank account	83,200
Trade receivables	91,300
Inventory at 1 January 20X4	214,300
Share capital	100,000
Retained earnings	185,600
7 per cent debenture	50,000
Trade payables	184,800
Sales	942,700
Purchases	−398,100
Salaries	−343,600
Other operating expenses	−102,200
Interest expense	−3,500
Interim dividend	−25,000

The following additional information is provided:

(a) The closing inventory at 31 December 20X4 was €216,300.

(b) No depreciation has been provided for 20X4. The company assumes zero residual values and uses the following straight-line rates: buildings 2 per cent and equipment 20 per cent.

(c) The audit fee for 20X4 is expected to be €20,000.

(d) The company estimates that it had telephone expenses of €1,200 and energy expenses of €1,350 outstanding at the year-end.

(e) Included in 'other operating expenses' is a business insurance policy, which costs €3,000 and which runs for the year from 1 April 20X4.

(f) The company decides, on the recommendation of its auditors, that it would be prudent to create a provision of €10,000 against a claim for damages resulting from faulty merchandise.

(g) Corporate income tax for 20X4 is estimated at €15,000.

Required:

Draw up a statement of profit or loss and a statement of financial position for Arénières Inc. for its fiscal year ended 31 December 20X4.

2. The trial balance of Ansermet SA at 31 December 20X6 was:

	€
Land	155,000
Buildings (at cost)	560,000
Accumulated depreciation – buildings	−112,000
Plant (at cost)	1,890,200
Accumulated depreciation – plant	−1,039,610
Share capital	750,000
Share premium	220,000
Retained earnings	254,790
Long-term debt	600,000
Inventory at 1 January 20X6	619,300
Trade receivables	414,700
Bank	208,100
Payables	336,800
Sales	2,740,500
Purchases	−1,247,000
Personnel expenses	−691,300
Other operating expenses	−268,100

Supplementary information:

(a) The closing inventory was valued at €584,600.

(b) The audit fee with regard to the 20X6 financial statements is agreed at €50,000.

(c) The company paid outstanding December 20X6 travel expenses for various staff in January 20X7 – total value €2,750.

(d) No interest had been paid at 31 December 20X6 on the long-term debt, which was contracted on 1 January 20X6 at 7 per cent.

(e) Depreciation should be provided at a rate of 2 per cent straight line for the buildings (assuming no residual value) and 30 per cent diminishing balance for the plant.

(f) The company is facing litigation from an employee who has left and its legal advisers think it is likely that the company will lose the case; consequently, management decides to recognize a provision against legal costs of €20,000.

(g) The tax advisers suggest that the company will have to pay about €60,000 tax on the 20X6 profit.

Required:

Draw up a statement of profit or loss and a statement of financial position for Ansermet SA for the year ended 20X6.

3. You are asked to prepare the statement of financial position and statement of profit or loss of Agrestic Corp for the year ended 31 December 20X4.

The trial balance of Agrestic, extracted from the company's accounts at 31 December 20X4, is shown below (all amounts in €):

	€
Land	200,000
Buildings (at cost)	630,000
Accumulated depreciation – buildings	−84,000
Equipment (at cost)	108,000
Accumulated depreciation – equipment	−27,610
Trade receivables	253,800
Cash and cash equivalents	120,730
Inventory at 1 January 20X4	685,260
Share capital	800,000
Retained earnings	65,000
Trade payables	95,420
Long-term debt	300,000
Provision (liability)	50,000
Sales	2,465,300
Purchases	−1,258,000
Salaries	−420,800
Other operating expenses	−210,740

You receive the following additional information:

(a) The value of the inventory on hand at 31 December 20X4 was €558,460.

(b) No depreciation has been provided for 20X4. The company uses the following depreciation rates: 30 years' straight line for the buildings and 30 per cent diminishing balance for the equipment. Residual values are assumed to be zero.

(c) The provision (liability) in the trial balance has been set up in 20X3 to pay for probable legal costs in pending litigation. The company received the final court decision on the litigation case on 28 December 20X4. The court decision set the indemnification at €46,000. The original estimate of the litigation costs amounted to €50,000. At year-end, the court decision was not yet included in the accounts and management decides to record the amount due under the heading 'Other payables'.

(d) The company decides to recognize a new provision of €80,000 for decontamination of land.

(e) The audit fee for the 20X4 financial statements has been agreed at €20,000.

(f) At 31 December 20X4 the interest of 5.5 per cent on the long-term debt has not been paid yet. The long-term debt was contracted on 1 September 20X4.

(g) The company estimates that 2 per cent of the total amount of the trade receivables will be irrecoverable.

(h) In December 20X4 Agrestic paid rent on operating leases covering the period December 20X4 to February 20X5 for a total amount of €3,000.

(i) The company's tax adviser estimates 20X4 income tax to be €120,000.

(j) Agrestic's board of directors proposes a dividend of 50 per cent of the 20X4 net profit to be distributed in May 20X5.

4. The trial balance of Mare's Nest, as extracted from the company's accounting database at 31 December 20X4, is shown below (all amounts in €):

	€
Land	450,000
Buildings (at cost)	1,320,000
Accumulated depreciation – buildings	−640,000
Equipment (at cost)	1,652,000
Accumulated depreciation – equipment	−495,600
Trade receivables	489,000
Long-term receivables	65,000
Cash and cash equivalents	365,200
Inventory (raw materials and consumables) – 1 January 20X4	896,600
Share capital	1,500,000
Retained earnings	185,000
Trade payables	854,000
Long-term debt	1,000,000
Provision (liability)	250,000
Sales	4,638,500
Cost of sales	−2,805,000
Other operating income	126,500
Distribution costs	−897,800
Administrative expenses	−690,800
Interest expenses	−58,200

The following supplementary information is also provided:

(a) On 25 October 20X4, the company recorded and paid tuition fees (€10,000 – 100 per cent administration) for an in-house course on the new accounting information system. The course was scheduled to be equally spread over the period from 1 November 20X4 to 28 February 20X5.

(b) The audit fee pertaining to 20X4 is negotiated at €125,000.

(c) Depreciation should be provided straight line at a rate of 10 per cent for the equipment, while the buildings have an estimated useful life of 33 years (no residual values assumed). Buildings, land and equipment are allocated as follows: 60 per cent production, 20 per cent distribution and 20 per cent administration.

(d) The closing inventory at 31 December 20X4 was €1,133,800.

(e) The company paid a consultant €3,200 for a review of the production cycle administrative controls. The consultant's invoice has been accounted for as 20X4 expenses, but the invoice was in fact an advance invoice for review services to be performed during 20X5.

(f) Mare's Nest received €24,000 of advance fees ('Other operating income') from concessionaires on 1 July 20X4, covering marketing services to be delivered over a one-year period (ending on 30 June 20X5).

(g) The company granted a loan of €60,000 to an employee for a five-year period at an annual interest rate of 4 per cent. The employee has to pay the interest charge semi-annually. The agreement started at 1 December 20X4. Interest received will be accounted for as finance income.

(h) The tax advisers estimate the company's 20X4 income taxes to be €100,000.

Required:

Draw up a statement of profit or loss and a statement of financial position for Mare's Nest 20X4 fiscal year.

5.   The following end-of-year balances (in €) were extracted from Gearcorp's accounting information system at 31 December 20X1:

	€
Land	250,000
Buildings (acquisition cost)	1,250,000
Accumulated depreciation of buildings	−437,500
Equipment (acquisition cost)	595,000
Accumulated depreciation of equipment	−178,500
Share capital	650,000
Retained earnings	230,000
Long-term debt	960,000
Inventory at 1 January 20X1	260,490
Trade receivables	280,300
Cash and cash equivalents	1,040,000
Trade payables	675,900
Sales	1,810,410
Purchases	−627,360
Salaries	−482,630
Other operating expenses	−120,530
Interest expense	−36,000

Additional information at year-end:

(a) The value of the closing inventory at 31 December 20X1 was €320,550.

(b) So far, no depreciation has been provided for 20X1. As far as buildings are concerned, the company assumes a zero residual value and applies a 5 per cent straight-line depreciation rate. The equipment is depreciated using the diminishing balance method. The equipment has an estimated useful life of five years and a residual value of €100,000.

(c) The company rents a building in which the offices of its administrative personnel are located. The monthly rent amounts to €5,000. Currently, the trial balance includes the payment of the rent relating to January 20X2, since that rent was prepaid in December 20X1.

(d) The audit fee pertaining to 20X1 is agreed to be €110,000.

(e) The company's tax advisers estimate that Gearcorp will have to pay about €72,000 corporate income tax on the 20X1 profit.

(f) Included in other operating expenses is a business insurance policy which cost €4,800 and runs for the year from 1 April 20X1.

(g) The company is facing litigation from a former employee and considers it appropriate to recognize a provision against legal costs of €30,000.

Required:

Use the above information to make the necessary accounting adjustments and draw up Gearcorp's statement of profit or loss for the 20X1 fiscal year as well as its statement of financial position at 31 December 20X1.

PART 3

An introduction to financial statement analysis

The object in this part of the book is to start to develop some ideas about what financial statement analysis is for and how it is done. Up until now we have been looking at the nuts and bolts of preparing financial statements, essentially so that you understand the fairly strict framework within which accounting data are produced. Now we move on to ask why analysts look at financial statements (Chapter 8) and then we start to use some of the traditional tools (Chapter 9).

A framework for interpretation

In this chapter, we look at the fundamental questions an analyst is asking and review some of the management models that guide companies and against which we measure their performance. This section of the book is intended to deepen your understanding of financial statements in terms of interpreting the data disclosed in them, rather than, as previously, in terms of understanding the rules of recognition and measurement. However, it should be remembered that the material in this chapter is usually addressed much more fully in a corporate finance course. The chapter is provided as a link between the two subject areas.

Chapter structure

- Introduction
- Financial structure
- Sources of finance
- Dividend policy
- Working capital management
- Performance assessment
- Summary
- Discussion questions

Introduction

In interpreting financial statements, it is necessary to make assessments of how a company has behaved in relation to how it might have been expected to behave. In order to have a framework of expectations, it follows that one must have theories about how companies should behave, and it is this area that we will discuss in this chapter. You will, of course, have your own views about how companies should behave, and other courses within your programme will also have provided many other insights. The reason for raising the issue of company behaviour is that you cannot make assessments of a company's performance without some idea of how you expect it to perform. Inevitably, the treatment here will address first principles: the objective is to provide a basic set of ground rules against which to judge company behaviour, rather than giving any detailed discussion of the theoretical background. You should extend this yourself. You need to bring to financial analysis a mixture of accounting, finance and strategy.

Financial analysis mainly concerns itself with *two areas of inquiry*:

1) Evaluation of the financial structure and policy of a company
2) Evaluation of corporate management's performance.

A potential lender to the company will be assessing slightly different aspects from those assessed by a potential investor (or perhaps the same aspects but with a different weighting), but both areas of inquiry are commonly taken into account as they are interrelated.

The first question to evaluate is that of *financial risk*. This question primarily relates to a company's *financial structure and financial position* . A key issue involves the composition of its sources of finance – equity versus debt (see also the concept of 'capital structure' in Chapter 6). The more borrowing a company already has, the more risky it is to lend more. As we discussed earlier, the level of borrowing also impacts the variability of profit (interest on borrowings is often a fixed expense that will not decrease in periods when business does not go well and revenue declines). A potential investor will need to assess the degree of financial risk in order to decide whether the profit prospects of the company are sufficiently attractive. Business is about taking risks, so investors (and lenders) do not shun 'risky' investments, but they do expect a higher potential return as compensation for a higher degree of risk. Note that financial risk constitutes only part of a company's risk profile – it also includes operational or commercial risk which is inherent in its business activities (e.g. a company may have high commercial risk when it is producing products for a saturated or declining market). Financial statement analysis will be instrumental in evaluating financial risk, but will be much less useful for commercial risk assessment.

The second main area of inquiry relates to an *assessment of management performance*: how efficient and effective is management in using the company's funds and assets? Such an assessment focuses on the return side of the investor's decision and is needed *to predict future returns* from investing in the company (prospects for future profits and future net cash inflows).

For the investor, there is a link between financial structure and position (financial risk) and management performance (return – future potential profits). The return that an investor wants should be sufficient to:

a. Compensate for inflation
b. Equal the return available from no-risk investments
c. Provide compensation for the risk.

The *risk/return relationship* is represented graphically in Figure 8.1 (below). The risk/return relationship holds good for both shareholders and lenders: they all strive for a reasonable balance between risk and potential benefits of an investment.

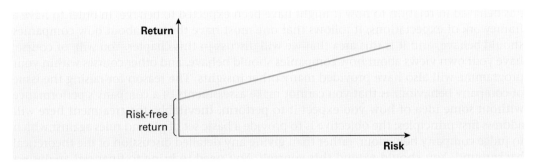

Figure 8.1 The risk/return relationship

Investors need information on risk and potential return in order to decide on their investment. They will use different sources of information. Part of their inquiry will be of a qualitative nature, e.g. by developing a feeling for industry trends and by trying to get a good picture of the capabilities and integrity of management. Other assessments will be of a quantitative nature, and these will rely extensively on information embedded in the company's financial statements and focus on the areas elaborated above.

The interdependency of risk and return is behind the analytical approach that looks at financial structure and management performance: the first to assess financial risk, the second as a basis for forecasting future returns so that the financial decision can be made. We will now take a look at considerations in financial structure (including dividend policy and working capital management) and management performance.

Financial structure

A company's financial structure is narrowly related to its balance sheet as the depiction of the company's financial position at a moment in time. It is therefore worth revisiting the balance sheet of a company and re-examining it by analyzing its major components. You will remember that the company is simply a legal vehicle into which investors have put money. This, in turn, has been used to buy productive capacity, which is used to conduct operations and generate profits.

In Figure 8.2, the statement of financial position is structured in such a way as to show how the company has dealt with a number of strategic issues. It enables the analyst to see clearly the long-term financing structure, the investment in productive capacity and the different components of working capital and their relationship to each other. In Figure 8.3, the same building blocks of the statement of financial position are labelled according to accounting terminology.

The issues in relation to the basic structure are, first, that of the *proportion of debt to equity* (often known as gearing) and then, within debt, the *term structure or maturity mix* (when does the debt fall due for repayment?). Other questions that arise are the security ranking of different debt sources, and, in the case of a multinational, the currency makeup.

As regards the basic *gearing* of a company, there is no satisfactory guide as to what a 'good' debt/equity mix is. Of course, in general terms higher debt may both increase the return and increase the risk of a company. What is usually found is that there are industry patterns that reflect other aspects of risk. For example, high-technology companies have a high operational risk and tend to have little financial gearing as a result.

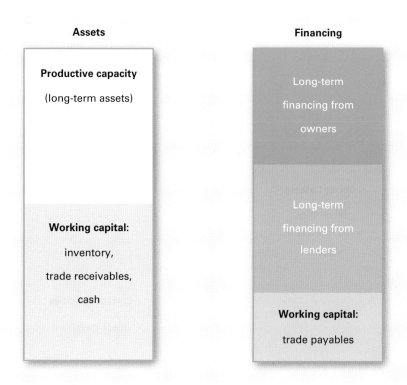

Figure 8.2 Financial structure

Size and ownership are also factors in explaining the debt structure. Family-held or director-controlled businesses typically try to avoid issuing equity to outsiders because of the loss of management control that this might bring, so they tend to prefer to borrow. Small and medium-sized companies therefore often have higher gearing than their larger competitors.

Gearing has the additional benefit that, under tax law, interest is deductible as an expense in arriving at taxable profit, while the return to the shareholder is after tax. Therefore, given a tax rate of 30 per cent, the real net cost of a 10 per cent interest rate is 7 per cent when compared with the return to equity.

There are no real guidelines as to the appropriate ratio between debt and equity in any industry. Gearing varies enormously from one industry to another and in assessing the gearing in any one company the safest approach is a comparison with the gearing in similar companies. An examination of the statement of financial position of a company will reveal its gearing, and comparison of several balance sheets over a period of time will reveal the trend of that particular company.

Most companies work to a notional debt/equity target ratio. But when raising new finance, they do not automatically split the financing requirement between equity and debt. Normally, they borrow for specific needs and then every few years have a major share issue to restore the debt/equity ratio.

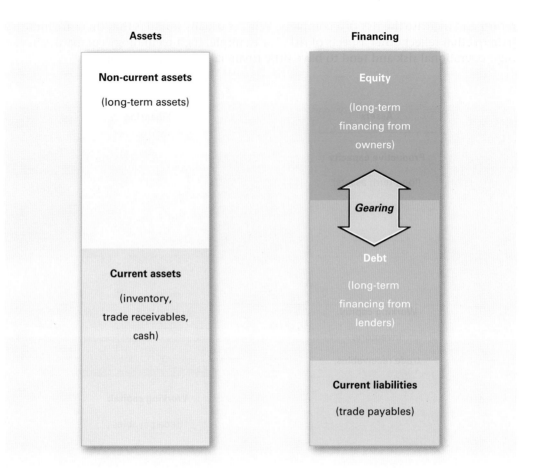

Figure 8.3 Gearing

Sources of finance

Share issue

When an existing company wants to raise more equity capital, it will usually ask its existing shareholders to subscribe more (companies listed on a stock exchange are generally obliged to offer new shares to existing shareholders first). This is done by means of what is called a *rights issue*. If, for example, a company has 1m shares already issued, the current price on the stock exchange is $3.00 per share and the company wants to raise approximately $1.25m in new finance, it could give existing shareholders the right to buy one new share for every two held, and at a price of $2.50 a share.

The reduction (discount) between the market price and the price of the new share would reflect an expectation that the future profits would have to be split between more people, albeit in the longer term the extra profits created by the expansion of the company would compensate for this. The shareholder may then either buy the shares or sell his or her right to them on the stock exchange.

Normally, a company would have the share issue underwritten, that is, specialist institutions would guarantee to the company to buy all unsold shares at a predetermined price. The *underwriter* receives a large fee for accepting this risk, and this is one reason why share issues are not undertaken frequently. Any share issue has to be accompanied by detailed statements (a *prospectus*) about the company's past performance and future expectations. This involves the use of experts to check and confirm the information and is another reason for the high cost of raising equity.

An alternative to issuing rights is to *issue shares on a different capital market*. This has the advantage of opening up new sources and not obliging the company to sell the new shares at a discount, as well as potentially bringing in *finance denominated in a foreign currency*. This is not a common tactic and most stock exchanges require that existing shareholders are at least given the right to participate in any future issue of shares, but is likely to become more frequent among large companies as the market becomes ever more global and companies want to have the many strategic advantages of being listed on several stock exchanges. It is evident that companies with multiple listings tend to be strong supporters of IFRS Standards as global reporting standards.

Loans

Loan finance can be obtained in a number of ways, either through *financial institutions* or *directly through the public markets*. Typically, many small and medium-sized companies arrange long-term loans from their commercial banks or from merchant banks, in a single direct transaction. However, very large companies can also arrange 'syndicated loans', where the finance is provided by a group of banks or other lending institutions. *Syndicated loans* are commonly arranged by governments or state agencies for financing development or budget deficits, but they are also sometimes provided for special transactions by commercial companies such as the purchase by an airline of a new fleet of aircraft.

The *rate of interest* chargeable on such loans is usually a *floating rate* that goes up and down in accordance with a market interest rate indicator. Central banks fix a minimum lending rate and loans are usually expressed as X per cent over minimum lending rate – in Europe, the European Central Bank's interest rate is considered to set the basis for commercial borrowing and lending rates. Although actual rates offered to a customer are fixed individually by the banks, there is usually no difference in the rate between banks.

Bonds

Companies also raise large blocks of finance by *issuing debt directly to the capital market*, known as *bonds*. Frequently such bonds are issued at a *fixed interest rate*. Bonds, like shares, can be taken up in small quantities by individuals: so bond debt could be raised from a large number of sources. Medium-sized family companies in Europe are often quite active in raising finance on the bond market since that offers public financing and a stock exchange listing but without dilution of control, since only debt is listed and not equity.

Leasing

Another possible source of finance is *leasing*. Here the company in effect rents an asset with finance often supplied by the supplier of the asset. This has the advantage of avoiding the need to raise finance separately when buying new assets. As discussed in Chapter 5, the accounting requirements now ensure that theoretically liabilities under leases appear in the statement of financial position in the same way as other sorts of finance.

Other aspects of debt management

Other aspects of debt management are maturity mix, currency and interest rates. The *maturity mix* is the scheduling of repayment of debt – has the company borrowed in such a way that all its borrowings will fall due at the same time? It may be expensive to carry out a massive refinancing in one exercise and it is usual to spread out the maturity dates of debt.

This also impacts on *interest rates* – raising long-term debt at fixed interest rates means locking the company into a high interest charge for a long period if such a manoeuvre takes place when the market rates of interest are high. Borrowing on floating rate agreements can be expensive if made when the market is low but then it subsequently rises. The ideal is to borrow long-term on fixed rates when the market rates are low, and to borrow on floating rates when the market is high.

Hedging

For a continental European company that wishes to raise finance in a currency other than the euro, a further element of financial strategy is involved. This is the question of *hedging foreign investments*. The existence of the euro may well reduce the amount of borrowing done in foreign currencies by European companies, but the *currency mix* can be an important issue and is something normally to be disclosed by companies.

When a French company buys a US subsidiary, if it provides the cash from its home resources, it has debt raised in euro and an investment denominated in US dollars. There is, therefore, a transactional exchange exposure: the exchange rate between the euro and the US dollar fluctuates regularly.

A company investing in a foreign currency risks two things:

(a) *Commercial risk* – that the investment will of itself yield a suitable return

(b) *Currency risk* – that the exchange rate will not vary so widely as to make the loan finance more costly over a period of time.

To illustrate the problem with our US/France example, suppose a French company buys for US$100m a small US company that subsequently achieves annual profits of a steady $15m – an acceptable return of 15 per cent. The purchase is financed by a domestic loan and at the time of purchase the exchange rate was $1.00 = €1.00. The French company would therefore have borrowed €100m, and let us say that the interest rate was 7 per cent. To illustrate the exchange risk, if we ignore the commercial risk of the investment itself and assume profits remain steady at $15m, the euro out-turn of the investment will also depend on the exchange rate. Table 8.1 shows the situation at the time of the initial investment, and the impact of rate changes in both directions.

Table 8.1 Impact of exchange rate changes

Investment = $100m
Annual return = 15%
Exchange rate $1 = €1 (at date of acquisition of subsidiary)
French loan €100m – interest rate = 7%

US profit ($)	Rate $1 = (on reporting date) (€)	French profit (€) (pre-tax)	Interest (€)	Net result (€)
15m	1	15m	7m	8m
15m	0.80	12m	7m	5m
15m	1.30	19.5m	7m	12.5m

As you can see from Table 8.1, the result in terms of the French parent's receipts can vary widely as a result of the exchange exposure. The exposure, of course, extends to the value of the investment as well: if the exchange rate went to $1 = €0.80, the euro equivalent of the original investment drops from €100m to €80m, giving an additional balance sheet 'loss' of €20m.

This kind of problem was a major contributor to the Southeast Asian financial crisis of the late 1990s. A number of indigenous companies borrowed heavily in US dollars to finance expansion in the area. When their exchange rates started to slide, this meant that the local currency value of their debt increased enormously, as also did the relative cost of interest. At a stroke the companies became loss making and had rapidly worsening debt/equity ratios at the same time.

A decision has to be made as to whether a company wishes to accept both the commercial risk and the exchange risk, and usually the answer will be negative. The exchange risk can be minimized by raising the finance in the country in which the investment is made. So, in our example above, if the French parent company had borrowed $100m on the US capital market, both the investment and the associated loan and interest would be denominated in the same currency, thereby cancelling one risk with another. The company would have hedged its investment and the exposure would be limited to the difference between the US return and US interest payment.

A look at the debt analysis provided in the annual financial statements and the investment analysis will give some indication of the extent to which any particular company hedges its foreign investments with foreign borrowing – although precise details of the investment in subsidiaries are rarely provided as such.

Dividend policy

If it is assumed that the major preoccupation of the managers of a company is to maximize the gain for their shareholders, a major question will be how, in practice, this is best achieved. Shareholder *gains from an equity investment* arise in two ways:

(a) *Dividend* – through the receipt of dividends
(b) *Market appreciation* – through the increase in the stock market price of the shares (also referred to as 'capital appreciation').

Note in passing that although the creation of profit should help in both these aims, it is not the creation of profit in itself that is the objective.

Following on from the identification of these two types of gain, there arises the question of what importance to give each aim in relation to the other. Is the shareholder indifferent as to whether the gain comes from dividend or market appreciation, or does he or she prefer dividend at the expense of growth in share price or vice versa?

One school of thought is that the dividend is unimportant – if a company retains the bulk of its profits in order to finance new profit-making opportunities, the market price of the shares should rise in anticipation of the higher levels of profit to be earned in the future (remember, as we have discussed before, that the market price of shares is determined by expectations of future performance). The shareholder benefits by an increase in market price. If the shareholder needs cash flow from the investment, then he or she can independently convert the market gain into cash flow by selling some of the shares.

However, other theorists say that shareholders give a priority to receiving an assured cash flow from dividends. They hold the shares, not for long-term price appreciation, but for short-term, continuing cash flows. Therefore, if the company does not pay a dividend these shareholders are disenchanted, sell the shares and the share price falls because expectations of future dividend cash flows are low. Management is therefore failing in both aspects of maximizing shareholder wealth.

In practice, some companies apparently see a need to pay a continuing cash flow to shareholders irrespective of profit, while others are influenced in determining the amount of a dividend by the current profit. In looking at published financial statements, a comparison of net profit after tax with the dividend payments will show whether the dividend is determined independently of the profit level.

Some theorists point out that in all probability it is incorrect to assume that all shareholders are looking for the same type of return – some may want dividends, others prefer price appreciation. Consequently, there may be no discernible pattern in shareholder preferences: those who want high dividends will invest in companies that offer high dividends, while those who want price appreciation will invest in the companies that offer that possibility. This is called the *clientele effect* – companies acquire the clientele that prefers their particular approach to the question.

There is no overall best practice in this area against which to evaluate individual companies, but the question of *dividend policy* is an integral element of financial management because of its *potential effect on shareholder wealth* (the main objective of management) and subsequently because of the *effect on the company's cash flows and its financing*. A company with high dividends will have that much less cash available from internal operations – but, depending on which theory you prefer, may find it easier to issue new shares. In any event, internally generated cash flows are an important part of a company's financing and dividend payments a major use of that finance.

Working capital management

A company's *working capital cycle* consists of a *continuous flow of value-relevant items to sustain operations* and keep the company's business going. We have already reviewed working capital movements and their impact on cash flows in Chapter 4. Their essential nature in many companies is represented in the simplified diagram shown in Figure 8.4. The company has a cash position that it has obtained from shareholders, lenders or from past profitable operations. These funds are used to acquire inventories, either by purchasing goods from third parties or by producing them itself. Other operating costs are also incurred. Trade payables (and other types of current liabilities) intervene between the incurrence of these costs and the actual outgoing cash flows (payments). The company sells the goods to customers, who either pay cash or buy on credit. If the company sells on credit, trade receivables intervene between the recognition of the revenue and the incoming receipts. When the customer pays, the cash position is replenished.

Basically, in a manufacturing company the working capital affects the following components of the statement of financial position (see rectangles in Figure 8.4):

1. Raw material inventory
2. Work in progress inventory
3. Finished goods inventory
4. Trade receivables (debtors)
5. Cash (equivalents)
6. Trade payables (creditors).

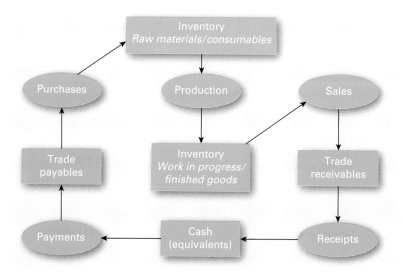

Figure 8.4 The working capital cycle

Working capital needs demand a net investment of funds: *net working capital*. The net investment in working capital amounts to the difference between working capital assets (current assets) and working capital liabilities (trade creditors/current liabilities). It is the net investment of funds needed to keep the working capital cycle going. This is illustrated in Figure 8.5b where net working capital is displayed as the differential (overlap) between current assets and current liabilities as originally shown in Figure 8.5a. Net working capital represents a permanent investment of funds over and above the funds needed to keep up the company's long-term infrastructure assets.

Figure 8.5a Gross working capital

Figure 8.5b   Net working capital

   The investment in net working capital tends to increase with sales and may be a hurdle for young fast-growing companies when they neglect to properly finance their growth.

   Financial management in this area consists, on the one hand, of keeping to a minimum the cash tied up in working capital, while, on the other hand, preserving sufficient cash or readily convertible current assets to meet payment needs. In general terms, cash flows are benefited by withholding payment to creditors for as long as possible, while keeping inventories at the various stages of production and debtors to a minimum. However, restriction of cash outflows is not the only objective of management, and there are interactions between the commercial success of a company and these working capital elements:

1. *Inventories of raw materials.* The unit cost of raw materials may be reduced by bulk buying, and maintenance of inventory at very low levels risks the possibility of production being halted by a late delivery of an essential item.

2. *Inventories of finished goods.* High inventories of finished goods allow sales always to be satisfied quickly – a sudden increase in demand can be supplied instantly. Sales may be lost because of delays in supply to the customer.

3. *Receivables.* Every company, in the interests of cash management, wishes to buy on credit and have as long a credit period as possible. Customers therefore will take into account the credit available from each supplier when deciding between competing supplies of uniform products.

4. *Payables.* When buying supplies it may be that the supplier who offers the best unit price or the best value for money in terms of product quality is also the supplier who offers the least credit (since they have a competitive edge).

It follows that each company has to determine its working capital management in the light of the *trade-offs* between the ideal *financial management policy* and the ideal *commercial policy*. What exactly these trade-offs amount to will depend on the circumstances of each company and the nature of the industry within which it operates. *Just in time* inventory management, developed in particular by Japanese manufacturers, says that tight management control of inventory levels should eliminate production stoppages or failure to supply customers, while keeping inventories at a minimal level and reducing capital requirements. Suppliers are expected to maintain inventories and deliver to the customer 'just in time'.

It is impossible to suggest any general guidelines as to what is appropriate. In evaluating the working capital policy of any particular company, it is essential to compare its policy with that of other companies in the same field or industry norms. The only overall guidelines are that companies should, on the one hand, keep their working capital levels at a minimum consistent with commercial policy while, on the other hand, ensuring that they are generating sufficient short-term cash flows (from inventory and receivables) to meet their requirements for settling amounts due to creditors and other payments (i.e. that they are sufficiently 'liquid').

Liquidity is another major aspect of working capital management and is usually picked up by the analyst to assess *liquidity risk*, the short-term component of a company's financial risk profile. As a concept, liquidity is easy to grasp – simple domestic management proceeds smoothly as long as cash is available to meet bills as they fall due for payment. Liquidity as applied in a particular company is a rather more difficult matter to grasp because of the extreme variability of circumstances for each company.

In essence, each company needs to plan its cash outflows and its cash inflows and try to time them so that they coincide with one another. If inflows are large but at infrequent intervals (for example, in large-scale civil engineering contracts), the company is likely to need to maintain high inventories of cash or overdraft facilities, whereas if inflows are regular (for example, in food retailing), cash balances may be kept low and surplus funds invested in the short-term money market.

We can sum up the factors that affect working capital management as follows:

1. *Length of production cycle.* If it takes a long time to move from delivery of raw materials to completion of the finished product, inventories of raw materials and work in progress will be high.

2. *Variability of demand/flexibility of production.* If demand levels fluctuate, high inventories of finished goods may be required, except where the production cycle is short and the volume of production can be changed rapidly.

3. *Scale of credit sales.* In some industries, all sales are on credit, in others, virtually none. The length of credit demanded will also vary. A high proportion of credit sales and long credit periods will mean a high volume of trade receivables.

4. *Frequency of sale transactions.* A company that sells a high volume of units, each having a relatively low unit price, will tend to have a regular cash inflow. One selling a small number of high-value objects will have an irregular cash inflow. Cash levels will be low where there are regular inflows, but higher where inflows are irregular.

5. *Frequency of payments.* Where outflows are high and infrequent, cash levels may be kept low between outflows, but this pattern is relatively rare since basic running expenses such as wages and overheads form a fairly large and regular component of outflows.

By way of example, one would expect a company in the heavy capital goods industry, say, one that manufactured turbines to order, to have a long production cycle and infrequent cash inflows. It could therefore be expected to have a high level of inventories, receivables and cash, and therefore a high proportion of current assets to current liabilities.

At the other extreme, a retail organization such as a hypermarket would experience frequent, high-volume sale transactions and no credit sales (although the trend towards retailers issuing in-store credit cards is changing that pattern slightly). Its inventories, trade receivables and cash balances would, therefore, be very low. The relationship between current assets and current liabilities would be in a completely different proportion.

Generally, however, this relationship should be stable. As sales increase or decrease, the absolute value of inventories, trade receivables and trade payables should normally fluctuate in proportion to sales but remain constant in their relationship towards one another. Any marked shift in this relationship means that something has changed in the way the company is managed. One would also expect the relationship between the elements of working capital to be broadly comparable as between companies which work in the same business sector.

In the next chapter, we shall be looking at financial statement analysis, and one of the measures used for evaluating a statement of financial position is the proportion of current assets to current liabilities (known as the *current ratio*). You will realize from the discussion of working capital that the nature of the current ratio can be expected to vary from one industry to another and care should be exercised in evaluating it!

Performance assessment

While the financial statements provide considerable information about the financial position of the company, they do not really do the same for a wider *appreciation of management performance*. Of course, one major dimension of management performance is *profitability* (financial performance), and the financial statements will give that in a number of different forms, but *other areas of management performance* are not covered. By way of example, a particular UK company published its business objectives in the annual report and these were:

1. Maximize use of existing assets (rather than diversify).
2. Increase market share.
3. Build on strong personnel traditions.

Only the first objective can be related to the financial statements as such, although the company usually includes a lot of information about the other aspects in the management commentary section of its annual report (see also Chapter 11). Evaluation of performance involves many considerations other than those that are visible from the annual financial statements. However, our concern here is the information available in the published financial statements.

In its financial objectives the same company stated that its target return is 25 per cent on the assets used and this, of course, can be evaluated from the financial statements themselves. The financial objectives are also expressed as a 5 per cent increase in real terms in earnings per share, and this, too, can be evaluated by reference to the financial statements.

But notice certain characteristics of the targets for evaluating performance: the absolute profit figure, for example, is not mentioned – the important measures are profit in relation to assets, and net earnings in relation to the individual share (after adjusting for inflation). You cannot judge performance in an absolute sense, but only in relation to another aspect of the company's structure. So, a target of (say) profit before tax of €200m is meaningless, whereas a target of 25 per cent return on assets can be compared usefully with other companies.

Improving *shareholder value* is one possible target for company management to aim for. We will come back to the subject later and look at what this means, but it can be taken to be not only making current profits but ensuring that future profits are better as well. The target of increasing market share cited above is one example of a strategy that should yield not only current profits but future profits as well. For example, increased marketing expenditure is probably necessary to boost market share, causing a short-term decline in profitability; but, once that share has been achieved, it can probably be maintained with less marketing, and the higher volume of business should reduce average unit costs, thereby increasing profit both by increasing sales and by reducing average costs.

Summary

Corporate finance and its management is a very wide subject, and, in this chapter, we have made a very short examination of some of the major areas. Within such confines, it is impossible to be other than superficial, but at the same time a total ignorance of corporate finance issues makes analysis and interpretation of financial statements a less productive exercise.

We have examined the structuring of company finance between debt and equity: this will influence both the volume and variability of the return to the shareholders. Equity is normally raised through the home stock exchange, although flotation on foreign exchanges is both possible and increasingly popular. Usually equity on the home market will be raised by first offering new shares to existing holders. However, issuing shares is an expensive exercise and is not, therefore, done at short intervals.

Debt finance may be obtained from a variety of sources, both individual lenders and capital market issues. The possibility of raising debt on foreign markets allows companies making foreign investments to hedge their investment – to limit their exposure to exchange rate fluctuations.

A major policy decision for companies is their approach to dividend payments to shareholders. Theorists are not agreed as to the best policy and some companies try to maintain a steady flow to shareholders irrespective of profit performance, while others gear their dividend to profits. The effect on share price of the dividend policy is not certain and it is possible that different shareholders have different preferences, buying shares in those companies whose policy most nearly satisfies their preference.

Working capital management is an important aspect of finance, but the composition and best policy towards working capital will be influenced by commercial considerations and the actual circumstances of the individual company within an industry. Some industries require very high levels of current assets, while others need very little. Policy, therefore, has to be evaluated in relation to the individual company.

Performance assessment has implications wider than purely assessing profit, although profitability is clearly an important measure. Profitability can most easily be stated by expressing it in relation to another aspect of the company's structure, such as assets employed in the business.

Discussion questions

1. Why does an analyst need to take a view about the riskiness of a company as well as its profitability?
2. Distinguish between debt and equity and explain the importance of the distinction between these sources of funds in financial statement analysis.
3. What is the working capital cycle, and what are the likely conflicts in managing this from a financial point of view as opposed to a sales or production point of view?
4. Explain why net working capital tends to be industry specific.
5. How does high liquidity affect the risk/return relationship?

CHAPTER 9

Financial statement analysis I

This is the first chapter to address the tools for conventional financial statement analysis. It introduces the ratio, the classical working tool, and explains how the ratio facilitates comparisons and what key ratios are particularly useful in gaining a quick insight into company performance and financial position.

Introduction

Although this chapter is entitled 'Financial statement analysis', to an extent that is misleading because, of course, the whole book is about financial statement analysis. The preceding chapters, dealing as they do with the preparation of financial statements, are intended to give insights into the recognition and measurement framework within which financial statements are prepared and the limitations of that framework. The chapters that follow will look at more variables in financial statement preparation and how these impact on interpretation of financial statement information.

Given that framework, we are now going to look at some technical elements used in the process of evaluating the financial statements of individual companies in order to arrive at conclusions about the company. We are going to examine financial statements through the eyes of users of financial information and, in particular, look at the tools that are used to aid analysis and extract useful information about the company.

The purpose of financial statement analysis

There are many potential users of financial statements, but for the purpose of financial statement analysis we are going to focus primarily on the needs of equity investors (shareholders) and to a lesser degree those of suppliers of credit. Such users will each be interested in different aspects of the company and will also have differing levels of technical expertise available to them to interpret what they see. This is an underlying problem in the preparation of financial statements – they should contain information to enable sophisticated users to make good investment decisions, while at the same time they should not obscure the broad picture with so much detail that the less sophisticated user cannot understand them. However, financial statements are becoming increasingly complex and it is doubtful whether they are at all meaningful to those with no special training. Many companies include a section in their annual report (usually entitled 'Highlights from the year' or something similar) that gives a synopsis for the user who is not equipped to undertake a detailed analysis of the figures.

The tools of analysis that we are going to examine in this chapter are those used by the sophisticated user, and we should consider their objectives in making the analysis to see the relevance of the tools to that purpose. Stockbrokers and investment analysts examine financial statements in order to advise on investments in the shares – or bonds – of commercial companies. The investment might be made by a private individual or an institutional investor such as a pension fund, insurance company or unit trust. The trend in most markets is away from *individual investors* and towards *institutional investors*. Many people prefer to make their investments by way of a collective investment vehicle, such as a mutual fund or a policy with a life assurance company, so stock exchange investment is increasingly professionalized. However, the internet offers an alternative approach through the use of online brokers by individuals. Some people apparently like to get up early in the morning, check what the financial reports on television, radio or internet are saying, and then buy and sell shares. They then go to work, and when they get home in the evening check out the internet to see how their investment plays have worked out.

As we discussed in Chapter 8, users of financial statements are primarily interested in answering *two basic questions*:

1. How well did the company perform?
2. How strong is the financial position of the company?

BETWEEN THE LINES

Value of financial statements

The main features may be summarized as:

- Acting as a significant landmark in the cycle of business information
- Prompting questions and indicating trends
- Providing a basis for decision-makers to create their own model of the company
- Giving reassurance because the financial statements are subject to regulation and to audit and there is awareness that auditors at least cast an eye over the non-statutory sections of the annual report, and
- Providing progressively greater detail, such as segmental information, for those who wish to probe the various aspects of the business.

Their purpose in posing these questions, however, will differ, as will the relative importance of the one question to the other. Investment analysts are mainly interested in assessing future performance of the company. They are, therefore, only interested in the financial statements as a predictor of the future. The information about what the company did last year has no value of itself; its only relevance is as to whether it will do better or worse next year and whether the expected return is adequate for the expected level of risk.

Typically, such analysts are specialists in a particular industry and their investment advice is based on an assessment of the likely performance of the industry in the future, combined with an appreciation of which company within the industry is most likely to perform well within the anticipated economic environment. The performance of any individual company will be affected by the economic environment within which it operates: it is affected by general levels of economic activity, changes in exchange rates, commodity prices, the introduction of new technology, inflation levels, etc.

Management cannot control these external forces that will affect all companies within a particular industry in the same way. But the best management will be able to minimize the impact of negative external forces and maximize the impact of positive external forces. Financial statement analysis provides one method of assessing how well managements perform from one company to another in the same industry.

The emphasis for the lender making a credit decision is likely to be different. Lenders do not participate in success in that the return they receive is not geared to profit. In addition, payment of interest will take place irrespective of the level of profit, so the lenders' concern in future performance is merely that there should be sufficient cash flow for the company to stay in business and pay the interest (*interest cover*).

The greater concern for lenders is the financial strength of the business. The lenders' main risk is that the company should fail and be unable to repay the loan (*default risk*). Future performance will, of course, have an impact on this, but the stability of the company's finances is the first concern, the marketability of the company's assets the second. The debt/equity gearing will therefore be a key issue, as will the relationship of the company's assets to its liabilities and the external value of the assets. For example, if it costs €100m to open a microchip factory, this asset is useful while there is a profitable market for microchips, but if the company failed following a slump in demand for microchips, a lender would find it difficult to raise €100m on the factory. Recall that the asset impairment rules touch this external value issue through the notion of the recoverable amount of assets.

If we look at the nature of the questions themselves (performance, financial position), it can be seen that each is the sum of a number of different issues. Management performance might be measured according to growth in assets, profit generated in relation to assets used or success in reducing tax liability, or extent of cash inflows, etc. The relevance of each detailed question will vary from one company to another, since no two companies are exactly the same and no two industries require the same proportion of long-term (non-current) assets to current assets, current assets to liabilities, debt to equity, etc.

What may be a useful and relevant measure of success in one industry may be totally irrelevant in another industry. For example, the ratio of sales to assets may be useful when comparing one retail company to another since it says something about the efficiency with which their premises are employed. But such a ratio would be meaningless in relation to an advertising agency, where perhaps a better measure of efficiency would be sales in relation to staff numbers or staff cost. This point should be borne in mind when considering the application of the analytical tools.

Traditional financial statement analysis

Financial statement analysis has been carried out ever since financial statements existed, but the methods of analysis have become more sophisticated over the years and, in particular, the development of computers has permitted the use of complex statistical analysis and the development of financial models. In this chapter, we shall look at the longer established methods and review recent developments later in the book.

The basis of traditional analysis is *comparison*. An absolute number has little information value: to say that Nestlé made €995m last year means very little. If we say Nestlé made €995m but a similar company (say Danone) made only €750m then the information begins to fit into a framework and have more use. But an important point in analysis is the relevance of the comparison. To say Nestlé made €995m but British Airways lost €500m tells us nothing about either company, merely what we already know: that their operations and objectives are quite different.

The framework for comparison may be either the company's own performance in other years, the performance of another company in the same industry or an industry average. Comparison over a period of years is known as a *time series analysis* (or *intertemporal comparison*), while that with a different entity or an industry average is called a *cross-sectional analysis* (or *intercompany comparison*).

Time series analysis

At a simple level, *time series analysis* (also referred to as *horizontal analysis*) would compare for a single company the figures for one year with those of the preceding year. But this is not very sound from a statistical point of view because such a short period may not reveal trends or may have been distorted by individual events. Analysts therefore, and particularly when making predictions, use at least a five-year base and often prefer a ten-year base. Companies usually provide a five or ten-year summary of principal figures within their annual report. Such a timeframe allows trend analysis.

Trend percentages can be used to follow changes in financial statement items over a longer period. They are computed by selecting a base year and setting the amounts of the items of the financial statements of that base year equal to 100 per cent. The corresponding amount for each following year is stated as a percentage of the base amount. Trend percentages of total sales for a five-year period will be computed as follows:

Trend percentages of total sales (20X3 = 100%)						
	20X8	20X7	20X6	20X5	20X4	20X3
Sales (€m)	617	583	492	413	627	445
Sales – trend %	139	131	111	93	141	100

A long time base may raise questions about the impact of inflation – a 5 per cent inflation rate will lead to a 40 per cent loss of value in the measuring unit over ten years. The impact of inflation on the numbers must therefore be considered in time series analysis. If it is thought to be significant, a simple remedy is to convert the measurement unit to a common value by use of the retail price index – although where property revaluations have taken place during the series, care should be taken in the interpretation.

Cross-sectional analysis

Cross-sectional analysis involves making a comparison with other companies in the same industry for the same year. Potentially, this may yield insights if the companies have very similar products, since differences will be the result of different management strategies in the face of the same problems.

Useful comparisons can still be made even if the companies are not exactly similar in their product line, but in evaluating the figures produced it is necessary to make allowances for the differences between the companies. This can become particularly difficult in relation to comparisons with companies that have diversified activities. For example, if one were doing an analysis of listed international media companies, one would find Walt Disney, Fox and Netflix. However, while Walt Disney, Netflix and Fox all make films, and all three have significant television activities, only Disney and Fox have conventional TV channels and make films for release through cinemas. Walt Disney, of course, also has theme parks and resorts.

Useful comparisons can still be made, but the interpretation must take account of the differences between the companies. A general point to remember is that analysis rarely offers very exact comparisons: you can often only say 'X is worse than (better than) Y as regards such and such an attribute', not 'X performed 22.58 per cent more badly (better) than Y'.

The other possibility in cross-sectional analysis is the use of *industry averages*. Many industries have trade associations that collect and publish such data, and some specialist financial data companies also compile this type of information for sale. These can provide some useful comparisons but here again interpretation must be cautious because the 'average' may be distorted by a number of factors. Because many companies have peripheral activities or more than one product, they may be included in an industry average for their main product, but their accounts will include the results of the other operations, leading to some distortion. Again the definition of the industry grouping may be so wide as to make comparison useless. Sometimes the grouping is dominated by one or two large companies, as would be the case with media companies in Germany, dominated by Bertelsmann, so it may be that the national 'industry average' reflects heavily the structure of one or two companies.

Tools of analysis

A simple approach to analysis would be to compare one component of the statement of financial position (balance sheet) or statement of profit or loss of a company with the same component of the statement of financial position or statement of profit or loss of another company. However, in cross-sectional analysis this would not be very helpful if the two companies being compared were of different sizes. The size problem is overcome by standardizing financial statements and by the use of financial ratios. Moreover, financial ratios, as we will see, are a powerful tool to measure and compare fundamental aspects of the risks and returns which drive investor decisions.

Common-size financial statements

Common-size financial statements allow the comparison of companies with different levels of total assets or sales by introducing a *common denominator*. In a common-size balance sheet each component of the statement of financial position is expressed as a percentage of total assets. For example, a company's statement of financial position could be restated as follows:

	Published €m	Common size %
Assets		
Non-current assets		
Tangible assets	113.9	22.4
Investments	8.6	1.7
Current assets		
Inventories	53.2	10.5
Receivables	218.6	43.0
Bank	114.3	22.4
Totals	508.6	100.0
Liabilities and equity		
Trade and related liabilities	111.6	22.0
Short-term borrowing	201.3	39.6
Long-term borrowing	3.1	0.6
Provisions	24.1	4.7
Equity	168.5	33.1
Totals	508.6	100.0

In a common-size statement of profit or loss each item is expressed as a percentage of sales. This might look like the following:

	Published €m	Common size %
Sales	5,356	100.0
Cost of sales	(2,601)	(48.6)
Gross margin	*2,755*	*51.4*
Distribution costs	(382)	(7.1)
Administrative expenses	(874)	(16.3)
Profit before interest and tax	*1,499*	*28.0*
Interest	(362)	(6.8)
Profit before tax	*1,137*	*21.2*
Taxation	(384)	(7.1)
Net profit for the period	*753*	*14.1*

Common-size financial statements are not only useful to cross-sectional analysis (comparing operating and financing characteristics of two companies of different size in the same industry), but also for (internal) *structural or vertical analysis* of the financial statements of a company. A common-size statement of financial position reveals the relative magnitude of the major categories of assets, equity and liabilities. The same proportioning procedure can be repeated within the major asset, equity and liabilities categories to reveal the relative importance of subcategories, for example inventories relative to total current assets, the capital structure of the company (debt relative to equity) and the debt structure (long-term relative to short-term borrowing). If multi-period common-size financial statements are available, the structural perspective can be usefully combined with horizontal analysis for pointing out important changes in the relative weight of financial statement components from one year to the next.

Use of financial ratios

Financial ratios standardize financial statement data in terms of mathematical relationships expressed in the form of percentages or times. Instead of comparing absolute amounts from financial statements, a ratio is used to *express the relationship between two elements of financial data that are logically linked*, and *compares that relationship in time or with the same relationship in another company*. That is more easily understood in relation to an example.

Suppose we wished to compare the profit performance of two companies and had the following data about each company:

	Company A €	*Company B* €
Sales	100,000	200,000
Net profit	10,000	15,000

Assuming that their products and activities are similar, a straight comparison would yield the information that Company B had more sales than A and made more profit than A. In other words, Company B is bigger than A – but that is easy to see and tells us very little about their relative efficiency.

However, a test of efficiency would be possible if we converted the information given to a ratio of profit to sales, which would then tell us which company had the lower costs per unit of sales. This ratio is commonly used, and is sometimes called the 'net profit margin ratio':

$$\text{Net profit margin ratio} = \frac{\text{Net profit}}{\text{Sales}}$$

Applied to our example companies this yields:

$$\text{Company A} \quad \frac{10{,}000}{100{,}000} \times 100 = 10\%$$

$$\text{Company B} \quad \frac{15{,}000}{200{,}000} \times 100 = 7.5\%$$

By using a ratio we eliminate the size difference (the ratio expresses a relationship internal to each company) and are then able to make a meaningful comparison. We can see that Company A has a better performance than B; it makes a higher profit from its sales, so is more efficient than B, although smaller. Note that common-size financial statements are a form of ratio analysis, with total assets as a common denominator for balance sheet categories and sales for income statement items.

A practical point to bear in mind here is that the comparison is warped if the content of the numbers used is not exactly the same. For example, if in the above comparison the Company A profit was before tax, and the Company B profit was after tax, the comparison of ratios would not be valid. The *golden rule* is that *like must always be compared with like.*

The use of just the one ratio would not be sufficient to make a final assessment of either company. We should certainly look for other ratios to indicate other perspectives on performance, such as sales to capital employed. It could be that A is more capital intensive than B, so that would qualify the efficiency assessment in the first ratio. In essence, a good analyst will look for as many ratios as are meaningful, in order to build up a complete picture of the companies being examined.

Ratio analysis permits many comparisons, depending on the degree of detail available from the source data, and in general the analyst should always be free to construct whatever ratios seem appropriate in the context of the companies under review. However, some ratios are more commonly used than others and the ratios we will review in this chapter are generally useful for most companies. Note that many companies include a selection of ratios in their annual report. For example, Ericsson publishes ratio data in a 10-year summary section (see Company Report).

COMPANY REPORT

ERICSSON

Financial highlights – Ten-year summary *(extracts)*

SEK million	*2017*
Alternative performance measures	
Gross margin	22.1%
Operating margin	−18.9%
EBITA margin	−10.7%
Cash conversion	−58%
Free cash flow	5,109
Capital employed, SEK million	158,230
Return on equity	−29.4%
Return on capital employed	−22.0%
Equity ratio	38.4%
Capital turnover	1.2
Working capital, SEK million	59,779

Source: Ericsson, Annual Report, 2017

Management performance ratios

Assessments of management performance will usually start with a focus on *profitability ratios* and, in a second stage, extend profitability analysis to *asset utilization ratios*. We have grouped the common management performance ratios in Table 9.1. To an extent these ratios are self-explanatory. They all answer different aspects of the question as to how well management has performed.

Profitability ratios

Profitability is a primary measure of the overall success of a company. Earning a satisfactory profit is the fundamental goal of most businesses.

The *net profit margin* is a first candidate measure of overall profitability. The net profit margin is also referred to as *return on sales* (with the term 'return' used as a synonym of 'profitability'). It shows (in its change from year to year, or compared to another company) how successful management is in creating profit from a given quantity of sales.

Table 9.1   Management performance ratios

A. Profitability ratios

Net profit margin $= \dfrac{\text{Profit after tax}}{\text{Sales}}$

Gross operating margin $= \dfrac{\text{Sales less Cost of sales}}{\text{Sales}}$

Net operating margin $= \dfrac{\text{Profit before interest and tax}}{\text{Sales}}$

Return on equity (ROE) $= \dfrac{\text{Profit after tax}}{\text{Equity}}$

Return on assets (ROA) $= \dfrac{\text{Net profit before interest}}{\text{Total assets}}$

$= \dfrac{\text{Profit after tax} + (\text{Interest} \times (1 - \text{tax rate}))}{\text{Total assets}}$

Return on capital employed (ROCE) $= \dfrac{\text{Net profit before interest on long-term debt}}{\text{Equity} + \text{Long-term debt}}$

Earnings per share (EPS) $= \dfrac{\text{Profit after tax}}{\text{Number of shares outstanding}}$

B. Asset utilization ratios

Total asset turnover $= \dfrac{\text{Sales}}{\text{Total assets}}$

Long-term asset turnover $= \dfrac{\text{Sales}}{\text{Long-term assets}}$

Inventory turnover $= \dfrac{\text{Cost of sales}}{\text{Inventories}}$

Receivables turnover $= \dfrac{(\text{Net credit}) \text{ Sales}}{\text{Receivables}}$

Net and gross operating margin ratios narrow down the analysis to operating profitability. *Gross operating margin* (sometimes referred to as *gross margin* or *gross profit margin*) shows control of manufacturing or purchasing costs (depending on the activity of the company). It represents the percentage of total sales (revenue) that is left over above production-related expenses. It is the preferred ratio to measure operating efficiency. *Net operating margin* additionally includes (control over) selling, general and administrative overheads. By taking into account all operating expenses, it shows what is left over from total sales to cover interest and taxes and enable a profit. It is sometimes referred to as *EBIT margin* (earnings before interest and tax). Gross and net operating margin are typically used together to monitor the inherent profitability of a business. The gross operating margin tracks the relationship between unit selling prices and product cost per unit, while the net operating margin is used to track the impact of supporting selling, administrative and general expenses on profitability. Margin ratios are very useful for trend analysis and intra-industry comparisons. It is, however, very difficult to compare margin ratios for companies in different industries, as they tend to be *industry specific*. For example, food retailers operate with low profit margins, while profit margins are generally high in the clothing industry. Both types of business can generate nice profits, because a high sales volume can compensate for a low profit margin in food retail companies.

Net (operating) profit, considered by itself or as a percentage of sales, does not take into account the investment needed to generate the profit. A return on investment (ROI) ratio does. Depending on what is meant by 'investment', different ROI ratios can be used: return on equity (ROE), return on assets (ROA) and return on capital employed (ROCE).

ROE measures how much the company has earned on the funds invested by its shareholders. Funds invested by shareholders are set equal to equity and thus imply both directly invested funds and funds invested indirectly through retained profit. Obviously, the ROE ratio reflects a shareholder perspective. ROE is a slightly dangerous figure in that it is not a 'real' return and should not be compared with, for example, the rate of interest paid on a bank deposit account. It can be used in time series analysis to show whether profitability is improving or declining, viewed from the equity perspective, as opposed to all finance.

ROA reflects how much the company has earned on the investment of all the funds committed to the company. In this ratio, the investment base is set equal to the sum of equity and all liabilities – the total sources of funds invested in the company's assets. The ROA shows how well the company has used its funds, irrespective of the relative magnitudes of the sources of those funds (short-term liabilities, long-term liabilities, equity). As the ROA ratio brings in the debt element of the company as well, it affords a comparison between the efficiency of companies with different debt/equity ratios. The ROA ratio is used to evaluate management performance both at corporate level and at individual business unit level (divisions within the company). The business unit manager usually has significant influence over the assets used in the business unit, but has little control over how those assets are financed. The business unit manager usually has no impact on the relative roles of external creditors and shareholders in financing his or her assets, because financing decisions are in most cases taken at corporate level and not at business unit level.

Taken in conjunction with the ROE ratio, the ROA ratio shows whether the return to shareholders is changing better or more badly than the return on overall financing.

Return on capital employed shows how much the company has earned on invested long-term funds (also called *permanently employed capital*). Shareholders' equity and long-term debt (non-current liabilities) are funds entrusted to the company for a relatively long period of time and can be considered quasi-permanent capital. Figure 9.1 shows that *capital employed* is also *equal to non-current assets plus net working capital*. In fact, the statement of financial position equivalency (as presented in Figure 9.1) indicates that capital employed is expected to finance non-current assets and the portion of current assets that is not financed by current liabilities (or net working capital).

The three ROI ratios differ not only with regard to the denominator (the investment base), but also in the *calculation of the numerator* (the profit figure used). The calculation of the *ROE* ratio is straightforward: net profit after tax is by definition the residual *net profit attributable to the funds invested by shareholders*. In arriving at this net profit figure, part of the cost of finance – the interest on debt financing – was subtracted as an expense. Using the same net profit figure in calculating *ROA or ROCE* would in fact understate the earnings generated by total funds or long-term funds available. Thus, when including interest-bearing debt in the investment base, the *interest expense* should be *added back to the net profit figure* to arrive at an earnings level that is not affected by the relative use of equity or debt financing.

Figure 9.1 Capital employed

Because the interest expense is tax deductible, it also affects taxation in the statement of profit or loss. This means that the amount of the adjustment of the net profit figure in the calculation of ROA or ROCE should be the after-tax interest expense. The *after-tax interest expense* is the interest expense multiplied by the complement of the tax rate. For example, if the corporate tax rate on income is 30 per cent and the gross interest expense amount to €10,000, the after-tax interest expense would be €10,000 × (1 − 0.3) or €7,000.

The different ROI measures each reflect the earnings generated by a specific pool of funds, excluding the costs of the specific funds considered. In practice, the interest adjustments are sometimes ignored by analysts because they add complexity to calculating the ROA and ROCE ratios.

Earnings per share (EPS) is another way of checking whether profitability is growing from a shareholder-only perspective. EPS is calculated as net profit for the period (net income or net earnings) divided by the average number of shares outstanding during the period. It shows how much of a period's net profit has been earned by each ordinary share. This ratio is given great importance by Anglo-Saxon companies and analysts. It has taken on a major significance in the investment industry and is the single most commonly used measure to compare companies' performance. It usually appears on the face of the statement of profit or loss of listed companies (a regulatory requirement in some jurisdictions). Many accountants, however, deplore its use as being too simplistic – it reduces a complex information set to a single figure, thereby destroying much of the message. The basic calculation of earnings per share is relatively easy. EPS calculation can, however, become more complicated if there is significant fluctuation of shares outstanding throughout the year and if there are different types of share or extra share rights. There is even a separate standard dealing with it – IAS 33.

IAS 33 *Earnings per Share* requires that listed companies disclose both *basic EPS* and *diluted EPS* on the face of the statement of comprehensive income (or of the statement of profit or loss if this is presented as a separate statement). IAS 33 considers the basic EPS ratio insufficient if a company has issued share options, share warrants or convertible securities that can be converted into ordinary shares at the option of the holders of those securities. These types of financial instrument (equity instruments) are called *potential ordinary shares*, as they entitle their holder to acquire ordinary shares. If these potentially ordinary shares are actually exchanged for ordinary shares, they may have the effect of reducing (diluting) the earnings accruing to pre-existing shareholders, through the fact that the number of shares outstanding will increase and through the effect of the conversion on net profit available to ordinary shareholders. IAS 33 sets the rules for calculating both basic and diluted earnings per share and provides a basis for quantifying the impact of the conversion of issued equity instruments into ordinary shares in the future.

Analysts also talk about *'quality of earnings'* as well as the absolute number as being important (how sustainable are the profits?; what activities are they derived from?). This is a question which needs further consideration in the light of accounting and other devices that are discussed later. The key question is the extent to which current profits are affected by special circumstances (e.g. asset sales) and to what extent they can be expected to continue for the foreseeable future.

The EPS number is used as an input to a market ratio, the *price/earnings* or *P/E ratio*:

$$\text{Price/Earnings} = \frac{\text{Market price per share}}{\text{EPS}}$$

The P/E ratio involves an amount not directly controlled by the company: the current market price of an ordinary share. It reflects how the market judges the company's performance. The P/E ratio is another form of rate of return ratio, albeit inverted. The numerator is today's market price and the denominator the EPS for the most recent 12 months. Thus, the P/E ratio varies throughout the year and the major financial newspapers and websites usually display a company's P/E ratio along with the daily market prices of its ordinary shares. The P/E ratio is also called the *earnings multiple*. It reflects the market's expectations about the company's performance and measures how much the market is willing to pay for a share in the company's potential future earnings. Basically, a high P/E ratio indicates that investors expect that the company's earnings will grow rapidly. Growth expectations will be linked to the industry to which the company belongs. As the relative rate of expected growth in earnings differs significantly among industries, so will the typical P/E ratios for industries tend to vary. In this vein, it makes more sense to compare the P/E ratio of Peugeot SA to the P/E of Volkswagen AG than to the P/E of Microsoft Inc. A decline of the predictions of general economic conditions generally has a negative effect on the overall level of P/E ratios, because the market takes it as an indication that the earnings of virtually all companies will be affected. We will come back to the P/E ratio later.

Investors generally expect two kinds of return: appreciation of the market price of a share and dividend income. Investors who like to receive dividend income will look at the *dividend yield ratio*. It reflects the relationship between the dividends per share paid to shareholders and the current market price of a share. The ratio measures the percentage of a share's market value that is returned (annually) in cash to the shareholders.

$$\text{Dividend Yield} = \frac{\text{Dividend per share}}{\text{Market price per share}}$$

Dividend yields vary widely, from 0 per cent to 5–6 per cent. Young, high growth companies usually are reluctant to pay cash dividends, as they need the funds to finance further growth. Companies with high dividend yields are usually older, established companies. The major sources of financial news publish dividend yields of listed companies daily.

Asset utilization ratios

Asset utilization ratios focus on the relationship between the results of operations (e.g. sales or cost of sales) and the (specific) resources used by the business. They measure *how efficiently management uses the company's assets*. This is typically assessed through asset turnover ratios. The concept of a *turnover ratio* can be explained best with regard to inventory turnover: if the company keeps an inventory of only one unit and sells 50 units during the accounting period, the inventory must completely turn over and be replaced 50 times (assuming we want to keep the ending inventory equal to the beginning inventory). If the inventory were 50 units and 50 units are sold, the inventory must turn over and be replaced only once.

Total asset turnover shows how efficient a company is in using its total asset base. It measures the company's success in keeping the total asset base active, with sales as the activity measure of reference. But again, the absolute ratio has little meaning; it is the comparison from one year to another or one company to another similar company which yields the interesting measure of efficiency. For example, does the company make less and less use of capacity? If so, it might indicate a dying market for the product, even if inflation were pushing up the sales price and the profits.

Long-term asset turnover focuses only on the use of non-current assets. The ratio is often narrowed down to the turnover of property, plant and equipment. It shows the level of sales the company was able to generate for each euro invested in property, plant and equipment. The long-term asset turnover ratio is sometimes referred to as (the inverse of) the *capital intensity ratio*. This label better reflects the industry-specific nature of the ratio. A steel company is a typical example of a company with a high level of long-term tangible assets (highly capital intensive) and, thus, a low long-term asset turnover ratio. Companies with low long-term asset turnover tend to have a lot of fixed costs, which makes them particularly vulnerable to cyclical fluctuations in business activity. When business activity declines and sales drop, they may be unable to cover the fixed costs. Conversely, companies that are not capital intensive, like many service companies, usually have much more flexibility to reduce their costs when sales decline.

STANDARDS

 IAS 33 – EARNINGS PER SHARE *(extract)*

Presentation of basic and diluted earnings per share

66. An entity shall present in the statement of comprehensive income basic and diluted earnings per share for profit or loss from continuing operations attributable to the ordinary equity holders of the parent entity and for profit or loss attributable to the ordinary equity holders of the parent entity for the period for each class of ordinary shares that has a different right to share in profit for the period. An entity shall present basic and diluted earnings per share with equal prominence for all periods presented.

67. Earnings per share is presented for every period for which a statement of comprehensive income is presented. If diluted earnings per share is reported for at

least one period, it shall be reported for all periods presented, even if it equals basic earnings per share. If basic and diluted earnings per share are equal, dual presentation can be accomplished in one line on the statement of comprehensive income.

67A. If an entity presents items of profit or loss in a separate statement as described in paragraph 10A of IAS 1 (as amended in 2011), it presents basic and diluted earnings per share, as required in paragraphs 66 and 67, in that separate statement.

68. An entity that reports a discontinued operation shall disclose the basic and diluted amounts per share for the discontinued operation either in the statement of comprehensive income or in the notes.

68A. If an entity presents items of profit or loss in a separate statement as described in paragraph 10A of IAS 1 (as amended in 2011), it presents basic and diluted earnings per share for the discontinued operation, as required in paragraph 68, in that separate statement or in the notes.

69. An entity shall present basic and diluted earnings per share, even if the amounts are negative (i.e. a loss per share).

Source: IAS 33, Earnings per Share

The *inventory turnover* ratio is based on the relationship between the inventory and the volume of goods sold during the period. It shows how many times on average the inventory was acquired and sold during the period. A high inventory turnover indicates that the company is able to sell its inventory quickly. This suggests efficient inventory management, but it can also be troublesome if it means that the company does not keep enough inventory on hand, which could lead to fewer sales if the company cannot fill incoming customer orders. Note that we use cost of sales as the numerator in the ratio and not sales revenue as such, because both inventory and cost of sales are measured at cost.

The *receivable turnover* ratio reflects the relationship of receivables to (credit) sales during the period. A high receivable turnover ratio suggests that the company efficiently manages the funds tied up in credit-granting and is effective in its credit collection activities. In practice, the amount of credit sales is not always known and, if so, total sales will be used as a rough approximation. While a low receivable turnover ratio suggests that significant funds are tied up in unproductive assets, a very high receivable turnover could mean that the company has an overly stringent credit policy that could lead to lost sales.

Inventory turnover and receivable turnover are important *indicators of working capital management*. They are measures of both operating efficiency and liquidity (see next section). Tensions between operating efficiency and liquidity needs are typical for the trade-offs to be made in working capital management.

In this section, we have covered the major management performance ratios, albeit not the only ones. The definitions given are ones commonly found, but are not the only definitions possible – when discussing ratios it is sensible to check exactly what definition is being used. The need to check ratio definitions before comparing is never more true than with the debt/equity or gearing ratio (see next section).

Financial strength ratios

Financial strength ratios indicate the strength of the company's financial position from different points of view. While profitability ratios highlight the return side of the basic risk/return relationship, financial strength ratios mainly focus on the financial risks associated with the company's financial structure and financial position. Basic financial risk concerns are typically assessed using long-term solvency ratios and short-term liquidity ratios. The most common financial strength ratios are shown in Table 9.2.

Table 9.2   Financial strength ratios

A. Long-term solvency risk ratios

Gearing (Debt/equity ratio)	$=$	$\dfrac{\text{Debt}}{\text{Equity}}$

This ratio is also frequently computed on the basis of debt to total finance:

Gearing (Total finance)	$=$	$\dfrac{\text{Debt}}{\text{Debt} + \text{Equity}}$
Interest cover	$=$	$\dfrac{\text{Profit before interest and tax}}{\text{Net interest charges}}$
Dividend cover	$=$	$\dfrac{\text{Earnings per share}}{\text{Dividend per share}}$

B. Short-term liquidity risk ratios

Current ratio	$=$	$\dfrac{\text{Current assets}}{\text{Current liabilities}}$
Acid test (or quick ratio)	$=$	$\dfrac{\text{Current assets} - \text{Inventories}}{\text{Current liabilities}}$

Days outstanding of working capital components (see text)

Solvency refers to the ability to generate cash internally or from external sources in order to meet long-term financial obligations. Solvency ratios mainly focus on the relative size of debt in the financial structure of the company. *Liquidity* refers to the company's ability to generate cash to meet its short-term obligations (essentially working capital needs and immediate debt repayment needs). Liquidity tests focus on the size of and relationships between current assets and current liabilities (working capital components).

Long-term solvency risk ratios

The *debt/equity ratio* is the solvency ratio found most frequently in the financial press and reflects the relationship between loan finance and shareholders' funds. Debt financing introduces risk because debt implies fixed commitments in the form of interest payments and principal repayment. Recall that default risk refers to potential failure to satisfy the fixed payments associated with debt that will ultimately result in bankruptcy. A lesser financial risk is that a heavily indebted company will have difficulty in obtaining additional debt financing when needed or will have to pay significantly higher interest rates.

A high debt/equity ratio indicates high financial risk because it implies substantial interest charges and an exposure to interest rate movements: if interest rates are rising, this will imply lower profitability in the future. The existence of debt means that ultimately repayment must take place and a glance at the schedule of outstanding debt given in the notes to the accounts will indicate how early this may take place. Most agreements for the provision of long-term finance include stipulations as to the maximum debt/equity ratio the company may have (*loan covenants*) – and this sort of covenant has been the driver of a certain amount of creative accounting designed to improve the debt/equity ratio.

The debt/equity ratio is sometimes computed in slightly different ways, for example debt as a proportion of total capital employed. Sometimes the computation of debt will include all liabilities, both short term and long term. Occasionally, debt repayable within one year is mixed in within short-term trade and operational creditors, thereby mixing a financing element with working capital. When computing the liability ratios, it is logical to look at the analysis of the short-term creditors and include the pure financing element (normally indicated as 'borrowings' or debt in the note that analyzes short-term creditors) in the debt/equity ratio and the rest of the short-term creditors (trade creditors, taxes payable, dividends payable, etc.) as part of the working capital.

Although *debt financing* implies financial risk, it also holds the *potential for an additional return to shareholders*. When debt is used successfully – if the company is able to earn more on the external funds provided than the cost of debt – the return to shareholders is magnified through *financial leverage*. Thus, the impact of debt financing on the trade-off between risk and return is not that straightforward. We will elaborate on the subject of financial leverage in Chapter 17.

The *interest cover ratio* is often used as a surrogate for the debt/equity ratio, or in addition to that ratio. This is partly as a response to creative accounting schemes that have reduced the reliability of the debt/equity ratio. Interest cover indicates the safety margin between profits and interest charges. In good times, bankers and others like to see interest 'cover' of five times, but it is not unusual to see cover drop to as low as three times.

Short-term liquidity risk ratios

Short-term liquidity problems arise because current cash inflows don't match current cash outflows. Take another look at Figure 8.4. The working capital cycle runs on a proper matching of cash receipts and cash payments. Liquidity problems arise when cash receipts from sales lag behind the cash payments to suppliers, employees, tax creditors, etc. Additionally, the working capital cycle should be able to generate sufficient cash to service short-term debt payments. The main liquidity ratios focus on the makeup of working capital and the activity level of its components.

The *current ratio* and *acid test ratio* (called the *quick ratio* in the USA) are the most common liquidity tests. They measure in a crude way the relationship between assets that will shortly mature to cash, and liabilities that will require cash settlement within one year or one operating cycle. The acid test excludes inventory on the basis that in some industries inventory turns over very slowly and therefore should not be looked to for very quick maturity into cash. Inventory is indeed the least liquid current asset and the most likely to suffer from losses if it has to be liquidated at short notice.

As we discussed in Chapter 8, when looking at working capital management, interpretation of these ratios should be made with care since the working capital structure of companies varies considerably from one industry to another. Hotels and retail businesses often have acid test ratios of less than one (i.e. their short-term monetary assets are smaller than their short-term monetary liabilities), because (a) they have very few credit sales, so few receivables and (b) they generate immediate cash from sales and have no need to keep large amounts of cash available at the bank to pay creditors.

As so often in ratio analysis, what is important is not the absolute number, but the direction and rate of change from one year to another. If a company's activity does not change, its working capital ratios should not change either. A sudden move in the working capital ratios means that something in the company's structure has changed, and further questions should be asked as to why this is – for example, an increase in the current ratio may be generated by an increase in inventories, so one should ask: Why have inventory levels risen? Has there been a sudden fall-off in demand for the company's products?

Another way of examining individual components of working capital is to compare their balance sheet value with the annual sales or the cost of sales figure (gross margin components). *Days inventory outstanding* provides information on how liquid the inventories are. For example, for a retail company, the ratio of inventory on hand at the year-end to annual cost of sales will tell you how many days' business would be required to sell the inventory:

$$\text{Days inventory outstanding} = \frac{\text{Inventories}}{\text{Cost of sales}} \times 365 \text{ days}$$

Similarly:

$$\text{Credit given} = \frac{\text{Receivables}}{\text{(Credit) Sales}} \times 365 \text{ days}$$

$$\text{Credit obtained} = \frac{\text{Trade payables}}{\text{Cost of sales}} \times 365 \text{ days}$$

Credit given tells you how many days' credit are given to customers (but note that you need to know either that all sales are on credit or that a substantial proportion of them is on credit). Where a company is buying goods for resale, *credit obtained* – the ratio of trade payables to cost of sales – will show the days' credit obtained or taken from suppliers.

These ratios can also be useful even if you do not know that there is a high proportion of credit sales, or where most of the company's products are manufactured (so purchases from suppliers are only a small part of cost of sales), because while the absolute number of days is no longer a meaningful figure, a significant (say, more than 10 per cent) shift in the figure from one year to another will indicate a change in credit arrangements.

Averaging balance sheet figures in ratios

It is not uncommon for ratios including balance sheet figures to be calculated by using an average of the balance sheet element during the period. This is usually done by taking one half of the sum of the beginning and ending balance of the item, although it could be meaningful to take into account the timing of specific movements in the balance sheet items over the period. In the illustrations and examples in this book, we will, however, use ending balance sheet amounts that can be more easily traced down to the figures on the face of the balance sheet.

Analyzing financial statements

It is very easy for people approaching ratios for the first time to go through a series of reactions, initially seeing the calculation of the ratios as an end in itself and then later asking what use the ratios are. Essentially, analysis is about decoding the messages that are built into financial statements and using them to 'tell the story' of the company. Ratios are a means of throwing light on certain aspects of a company, but not all ratios will be important for all companies and often the calculation of ratios leads to a question rather than an answer. You must remember that ratio analysis (even if important) is only part of the investment appraisal process, and investors need to look at economic variables, information about the company's future plans, etc., as well as decoding the information in the financial statements.

So how does one set about analyzing a set of financial statements? The first question you must ask yourself is why you are making the analysis – is it for lending purposes or for investing? Is it for a long-term or short-term involvement? In other words, what is the nature of the decision you need to make?

Having identified your analysis objective, you should gather what general information is available to you about the nature of the company and its activities – this will depend on whether you have a full annual report that will include much non-financial information and under what circumstances you are carrying out the analysis.

Only then can you look at the financial statements and start work on calculating ratios. A normal process would be to compute a number of standard ratios that we have discussed already, for as long a time series as you have information available. Any one set of financial statements will include previous year comparative figures, but in an ideal situation you would have more than one set of statements so that you could compile a longer time series.

Having computed your ratios, you should look to see if there are any patterns – which ratios are stable, which are changing? If ratios are changing, you need to ask why they are doing so. This may be obvious from the financial statements. For example, if the return on equity ratio increases, this might be because of an increase in profit, an increase in sales or a reduction in equity. If the net profit margin ratio (net profit/sales) has gone up (say from 10 to 12 per cent), and you see that sales have remained static, this means that the amount of profit per euro of sales has increased, which probably means that the company is controlling its costs more efficiently but, by way of contrast, that poses questions as to why sales have not increased.

It may be that a picture gradually emerges of the activities of the company, and what you have to do is attempt to 'tell the story' of the company based on what is available from its figures.

The next step is to do some cross-sectional analysis, if you have the necessary information – either data from another company in the same field or industry data. You can then compare ratios and there may be further insights into your company from this process. If Company A has a gross operating margin of 35 per cent, why does Company B, in the same year and carrying out the same activities, have a gross margin of 40 per cent?

Worked example

In order to help put the use of ratios into some context, we will carry out basic analysis on a three-year time series of company data – note that we are not given any background information about the company's activities, so that will limit how far we can make deductions about what is going on, and we do not have any material for cross-sectional analysis. Also, the financial statements are simplified to the extent that we do not have a breakdown of non-current assets and all debt is long-term. The company pays a dividend of 20 (unchanged over the years). Interest relates to long-term debt. The applicable tax rate is 30 per cent:

Financial statements:

	20X7	20X8	20X9
	€'000	€'000	€'000
Statement of profit or loss:			
Sales	620.0	745.0	762.0
Cost of sales	−217.0	−245.8	−266.7
Gross margin	*403.0*	*499.2*	*495.3*
Distribution costs	−204.6	−260.7	−266.7
Administrative expenses	−95.1	−97.2	−101.4
	103.3	*141.3*	*127.2*
Interest	−10.0	−30.9	−37.5
	93.3	*110.4*	*89.7*
Taxation	−32.7	38.9	−31.4
Net profit	60.6	71.5	58.3
Statement of financial position:			
Non-current assets (net)	312.0	532.0	495.0
Inventories	43.4	49.2	66.7
Receivables	62.0	74.5	91.4
Cash	67.0	70.3	58.0
Total assets	484.4	726.0	711.1
Ordinary shares (€1)	120.0	120.0	120.0
Retained earnings	195.5	267.9	315.2
	315.5	*387.9*	*435.2*
Debt (long-term)	100.0	250.0	200.0
Trade payables	36.2	49.2	44.5
Taxes payable	32.7	38.9	31.4
Total equity and liabilities	484.4	726.0	711.1

Before starting on the ratios, let us just see if there are any trends visible from the financial statements as such. We can see that sales increased substantially from 20X7 to 20X8 (20 per cent) but the increase dropped to 2 per cent from 20X8 to 20X9. Profits increased in 20X7/X8, as you would predict from the sales, but dropped off in 20X9. An obvious explanation of this is the rapid increase in interest expense: from €10,000 in 20X7 to €30,900 in 20X8 and €37,500 in 20X9. Looking at the statement of financial position, you can see debt going from €100,000 to €250,000 and then dropping to €200,000 (given the rising interest cost, it may well be that interest rates rose steeply during this period). We can see that long-term assets rose sharply as well, so already we can see some sort of story here: a company seems to have expanded capacity substantially in 20X8, leading to borrowing but also higher sales. In 20X9 sales growth has not continued at the same pace and interest rates have risen, causing the company's profits to fall.

Let us calculate the key ratios and see how this story is fleshed out:

	20X7	20X8	20X9
Management performance ratios			
A. Profitability ratios			
ROE	60.6/315.5 = 19.21%	71.5/387.9 = 18.43%	58.3/435.2 = 13.40%
ROA	$(60.6+(10\times(1-0.3)))/$ $484.4 = 13.96\%$	$(71.5+(30.9\times(1-0.3)))/$ $726 = 12.83\%$	$(58.3+(37.5\times(1-0.3)))/$ $711.1 = 11.89\%$
ROCE	$(60.6+(10\times(1-0.3)))/$ $(315.5+100) = 16.27\%$	$(71.5+(30.9\times(1-0.3)))/$ $(387.9+250) = 11.55\%$	$(58.3+(37.5\times(1-0.3)))/$ $(435.2+200) = 13.31\%$
EPS	60.6/120 = 50.50	71.5/120 = 59.58	58.3/120 = 48.58
Gross operating margin	(620−217)/620 = 65.00%	(745−245.8)/745 = 67.01%	(762−266.7)/762 = 65.00%
Net operating margin	103.3/620 = 16.66%	141.3/745 = 18.97%	127.2/762 = 16.69%
Net profit margin	60.6/620 = 9.77%	71.5/745 = 9.60%	58.3/762 = 7.65%
B. Asset utilization ratios			
Total asset turnover	620/484.4 = 1.28	745/726 = 1.03	762/711.1 = 1.07
Long-term asset turnover	620/312 = 1.99	745/532 = 1.40	762/495 = 1.54
Inventory turnover	217/43.4 = 5.00	245.8/49.2 = 5.00	266.7/66.7 = 4.00
Receivables turnover	620/62 = 10.00	745/74.5 = 10.00	762/91.4 = 8.34
Financial strength ratios			
A. Long-term solvency risk ratios			
Gearing	100/315.5 = 31.70%	250/387.9 = 64.45%	200/435.2 = 45.96%
Gearing (Total finance)	100/(100+315.5) = 24.07%	250/(250+387.9) = 39.19%	200/(200+435.2) = 31.49%
Interest cover	103.3/10 = 10.33	141.3/30.9 = 4.57	127.2/37.5 = 3.39
Dividend cover	60.6/20.0 = 3.03	71.5/20.0 = 3.58	58.3/20.0 = 2.92
B. Short-term liquidity risk ratios			
Current ratio	(43.4+62167)/ (36.2+32.7) = 2.50	(49.2+74.5+70.3)/ (49.2+38.9) = 2.20	(66.7+91.4+58.0)/ (44.5+31.4) = 2.85
Acid test	(62+67)/ (36.2+32.7) = 1.87	(74.5+70.3)/(49.2+38.9) = 1.64	(58.0+91.4)/(31.4+44.5) = 1.97
Days inventory outstanding	(43.4/217)×365 = 73.00	(49.2/245.8)×365 = 73.06	(66.7/266.7)×365 = 91.28
Credit given	(62/620.0)×365 = 36.50	(74.5/745)×365 = 36.50	(91.4/762)×365 = 43.78
Credit obtained	(36.2/217.0)×365 = 60.89	(49.2/245.8)×365 = 73.06	(44.5/266.7)×365 = 60.90

Growth	20X7/X8	20X8/X9
Sales	20.16%	2.28%
Profit	19.47%	−7.04%
Capital employed	53.53%	−0.42%
Net long-term assets	70.51%	−6.95%

Interpretation

Overall, this looks like a company that has gone for a major expansion/replacement of capacity in 20X8 (long-term assets increased by 70 per cent), financed largely by an increase in debt. This has resulted in increased sales and improved operating margins in 20X8, but in 20X9 the expansion of sales has not continued and the company has also been hit by higher interest expense.

The effect of the heavy investment is to reduce return on assets from 13.96 to 12.83 per cent, and reduce asset turnover from 1.28 to 1.03 although a return to sales growth would easily correct this in the following year. The impression is that the market for the company's product slowed down in 20X9, causing an increase in unsold inventory (days inventory outstanding up from 73 to 91 days). Receivables turnover has also slipped, suggesting that the company may be chasing sales with extended credit offers (or its customers may be similarly hit by slowdown). Gross operating margin has also slipped, which suggests that the company may have cut sales prices in order to boost business.

The company has sensibly used its internal cash flow to contribute to financing the 20X8 investment (debt increased by €150,000 while long-term assets increased by €220,000 – although credit obtained moved from 61 days to 73) and subsequently to reduce borrowing in 20X9. The gearing ratio (on total finance) moved from an unremarkable 24 per cent (10 times the interest cover) to a rather more risky 39 per cent, although interest cover remained reasonable at 4.6. In 20X9 the repayment of €50,000 brought gearing down to 31 per cent but the higher interest rates and lower profits caused interest cover to decline further to 3.4. If the market does not drop further the company should be able to continue to reduce borrowing and diminish the exposure to interest costs, showing an improved return.

Overall, this looks like a company that has set out on a relatively ambitious expansion plan, financed by borrowing and internal cash flows, and that has hit some difficulties with a slowdown in demand. While its gearing rose quite sharply in the expansion phase, the company looks as though it has a sensible policy of retrenching and reducing debt. It should be able to continue to trade satisfactorily and generate further cash to further reduce gearing.

Summary

Financial analysts, lenders and other users of financial statements are concerned to measure both the efficiency of a company's management and the financial strength of the company. They do this by extracting data from the published financial statements and either making comparisons or feeding the data into financial models.

The traditional approach to financial analysis involves making comparisons of a company's results over several years (time series) or comparisons between one company and another (cross-sectional). In order to make the analysis more meaningful, various devices are used to take away the disparity in size between companies.

The chief of these is the use of financial ratios, which express one accounting number in relation to another (economically linked) number. When making comparisons using ratios, it is necessary to be sure that the ratios being compared have been calculated from the same basis, and that the companies being compared do, indeed, have broadly similar characteristics.

An examination of the patterns of ratios and the financial statements themselves can lead the analyst to deduce what the company has been doing without any further non-financial information, although investors would normally take into account not only the results of financial statement analysis but also any other available information about the economy generally, the industry in which the company works, etc.

Assignments

The following questions have answers on the lecturer side of the digital support resources for the book.

1. The following is the statement of profit or loss and statement of financial position of company Gamma.

Statement of profit or loss	
Sales	145,600
Cost of sales	−64,200
Other operating expenses	−49,400
	32,000
Interest expense	−17,500
Taxation	−4,500
Net profit	10,000

Statement of financial position

Assets		Financing	
Tangible assets	149,000	Share capital (€1)	50,000
Accumulated depreciation	−17,500	Retained earnings	63,000
Inventories	82,300	Debt (long-term)	100,000
Cash at bank	56,300	Trade payables	57,100
	270,100		*270,100*

Required:

Calculate a standard set of accounting ratios (e.g. return on equity, return on assets, gross operating margin, net operating margin, current ratio, gearing ratio) and supply the definition you have used with your answer. Tax rate = 30 per cent.

2. The following figures are drawn from the statement of financial position of Medmove:

	20X1 €'000	20X2 €'000	20X3 €'000
Long-term assets (net)	2,350	2,900	3,800
Current assets			
Inventories	150	160	160
Receivables	310	300	310
Cash	55	0	235
Total assets	2,865	3,360	4,505
Financing			
Trade payables	220	600	200
Debt (long-term)	0	0	1,500
Total liabilities	220	600	1,700

No fresh shares were issued during the period. The industry has an organization which publishes average financial data.

The industry average statement of financial position is:

Long-term assets	75	Equity	70
Inventories	10	Debt (long-term)	20
Receivables	10	Payables	10
Cash	5		
Total	100	Total	100

You are asked to:

a) Calculate whatever ratios you think may be useful in analyzing Medmove's figures (but including current ratio, debt/equity). Tax rate = 30 per cent.

b) Using the analytical data that you have just computed, and the industry average statement of financial position, comment on the company's position and development.

3. Company RATIS had the following financial statements:

	20X2 €'000	20X3 €'000	20X4 €'000
Statement of profit or loss			
Sales	620.0	745.0	762.0
Cost of sales	−217.0	−245.8	−266.7
Gross margin	403.0	499.2	495.3
Distribution costs	−204.6	−260.7	−266.7
Administrative expenses	−95.1	−97.2	−101.4
	103.3	141.3	127.2
Interest	−10.0	−30.9	−37.5
	93.3	110.4	89.7
Taxation	−32.7	−38.9	−31.4
Net profit	60.6	71.5	58.3
Statement of financial position			
Long-term assets (net)	312.0	532.0	495.0
Inventories	43.4	49.2	66.7
Receivables	62.0	74.5	91.4
Cash	67.0	70.3	58.0
Total assets	484.4	726.0	711.1
Ordinary shares (€1)	120.0	120.0	120.0
Retained earnings	195.5	267.9	315.2
	315.5	387.9	435.2
Trade payables	36.2	49.2	44.5
Taxes payable	32.7	38.9	31.4
Debt (long-term)	100.0	250.0	200.0
Total equity and liabilities	484.4	726.0	711.1

Required:

(a) Compute whatever ratios you think will be useful in analyzing the above figures (but including EPS, ROCE, gearing, current ratio, total asset turnover, gross operating margin, net operating margin). Tax rate = 30 per cent.

(b) Comment on the company's development and activity during the period covered by the financial statements.

4. Ratio puzzle 1

The following statement of financial position for year-end 20X4 relates to company Theta:

Assets		Equity and liabilities	
Long-term assets	10,000	Share capital	35,000
Cash	30,000	Retained earnings	5,000
Receivables	? (a)	Trade payables	20,000
Inventories	? (b)	Long-term borrowing	? (c)
Total	? (d)	Total	? (d)

As you can see, the figures for some balance sheet items are missing – items (a), (b), (c), (d). In addition, the following ratio data have been provided for company Teta:

- Current ratio = 3.5
- Acid test ratio = 2.5
- Gearing = 0.5

These ratios are based on Theta's financial position at year-end 20X4.

Required:

Complete the statement of financial position of company Theta using the ratio data.

5. Ratio puzzle 2

The following data are based on company Leta's financial statements at year-end 20X7:

Equity	3,600
Interest expense	413
Net operating margin	24%
Return on equity	22%
Income tax rate	10%

You are asked to use these data to complete company Leta's statement of profit or loss for its financial year ending 31 December 20X7, using the following format:

Sales	...
Cost of sales and other operating expenses	...
Profit before interest and tax	...
Interest expense	...
Profit before tax	...
Income tax expense	...
Profit for the period	...

6. Gunge AG and Guntzel AG are both wholesale companies working in the same business segment. Given the information embedded in a number of ratios that we collected (see table below), they seem, however, to take a different customer approach to their business.

Ratio	Gunge AG	Guntzel AG
Return on capital employed	14%	15%
Credit given	59 days	19 days
Credit obtained	50 days	47 days
Gross operating margin	42%	17%
Current ratio	2.4	1.3
Net operating margin	11%	11%
Days inventory outstanding	50 days	21 days

Required:

Explain what the ratios reveal with regard to the operating approach of Gunge AG and Guntzel AG. Take into account price competitiveness and customer service level.

7. The managing director of Bavarian Hypermarkets has been approached by the chief executive and majority shareholder of Black Forest Supermarkets, a medium-sized supermarket chain operating in southern Germany. Black Forest is looking for a partner: it feels it cannot grow any further without outside capital, and would like to sell 40 per cent of its shares to a larger supermarket operator who could inject more capital and provide management expertise to expand the supermarket chain further. Black Forest is quite willing to contemplate selling a majority stake in due course.

Bavarian Hypermarkets is quite interested in the deal, because they think that the two businesses would be a good fit in operational terms. They hire your firm to carry out an analysis of Black Forest, and you are given the following financial statements, on which you are asked to comment:

Black Forest Supermarkets

	20X6 €'000	20X5 €'000	20X4 €'000
Statement of profit or loss			
Sales	3,674	2,987	1,643
Cost of sales	−2,718	−2,151	−1,133
	956	836	510
Distribution costs	−412	−392	−242
Administrative expenses	−183	−190	−86
	361	254	182
Interest	−315	−243	0
	46	11	182
Taxation	−15	−3	−65
Net profit	31	8	117
Statement of financial position			
Non-current assets			
Intangible assets	2,100	2,200	0
Tangible assets	4,446	4,220	2,085
Investments	0	0	240
Current assets			
Inventories	301	255	105
Receivables	38	42	29
Cash at bank	68	54	73
Total assets	6,953	6,771	2,532
Financing			
Ordinary shares (€1)	1,200	1,200	1,200
Retained earnings	1,241	1,210	1,202
	2,441	2,410	2,402
Long-term debt	4,000	4,000	0
Trade payables	512	361	130
Total equity and liabilities	6,953	6,771	2,532

Required:

Provide a report commenting on the financial statements of Black Forest Supermarkets. Your report should identify and comment on all strengths and weaknesses of the company as revealed by its figures. The tax rate = 30 per cent.

8. You work for the financial analysis section of a merchant bank and are asked to prepare a report on the following figures, which relate to a clothing retailer, who is looking to the bank to take a share stake:

	20X3 €m	20X4 €m	20X5 €m
Statement of profit or loss			
Sales	589.4	601.2	604.1
Cost of sales	−206.3	−222.4	−235.6
	383.1	*378.8*	*368.5*
Distribution costs	−22.7	−18.5	−32.1
Administration expenses	−241.9	−254.0	−266.7
Profit/(loss) before interest and tax	*118.5*	*106.3*	*69.7*
Interest expense	−49.5	−63.0	−72.0
Profit/(loss) before tax	*69.0*	*43.3*	*–2.3*
Taxation	−22.8	−14.3	0.8
Net profit/(loss)	46.2	29.0	−1.5
Statement of financial position			
Non-current (tangible) assets			
Land and buildings	620.0	620.0	620.0
Fittings and equipment	72.4	72.4	72.4
Accumulated depreciation	−37.2	−44.4	−51.6
	655.2	*648.0*	*640.8*
Current assets			
Inventories	143.9	152.0	179.5
Receivables	5.7	6.1	5.9
Bank	12.7	7.3	0.0
Total assets	817.5	813.4	826.2
Ordinary shares (€1)	120.0	120.0	120.0
Retained earnings	166.4	165.4	133.9
	286.4	*285.4*	*253.9*
Long-term debt	450.0	450.0	450.0
Trade payables	58.3	63.7	95.4
Taxes payable	22.8	14.3	0.0
Bank overdraft	0.0	0.0	26.9
Total equity and liabilities	817.5	813.4	826.2

You are asked to prepare:

(a) Key ratios that are relevant to the analysis of this company. Tax rate = 30 per cent.

(b) A report that attempts to explain what has been happening to the company over the last three years, using ratios and trends as appropriate, makes recommendations as to the desirability of becoming involved and makes suggestions for the future management of the company.

9. Who is who?

The following six ratio sets refer to real-life listed companies (consolidated statements). These are:

1) An investment company (venture capital)
2) A brewery
3) A supermarket chain
4) A restaurant chain
5) A publisher (weekly publications and printing business)
6) A steel company.

	A	B	C	D	E	F
Debt/equity ratio	0.21	0.90	1.52	3.46	0.26	1.74
Current ratio	2.6	0.95	1.06	1.38	0.63	0.91
Acid test ratio	2.57	0.90	0.39	0.58	0.63	0.86
Inventory turnover	25.12	63.39	11.73	3.33	N/A	185.32
Credit given	70.00	79.00	8.00	38.00	73.00	3.00
Asset turnover	0.94	0.87	2.35	0.97	0.01	3.25
Return on equity	0.11	0.05	0.04	0.01	0.16	0.02

Required:

Identify which company is represented in columns A to F.

CHAPTER 10

Statement of cash flows

Financial analysts make considerable use of cash flow information in their evaluation of companies. This chapter introduces the statement of cash flows and its preparation. It starts out by reviewing the relationship between profits and cash flow, then introduces the format, structure and content of the statement of cash flows and finally shows how to construct one.

Chapter structure

- Introduction
- Usefulness of cash flow information
- Cash flow cycles
- Format and structure of the statement of cash flows
- Cash flows from investing and financing activities
- Cash flows from operating activities
- Direct method for reporting operating cash flows
- Constructing a statement of cash flows 1
- Disposal of long-term assets
- Constructing a statement of cash flows 2
- Interpretation
- Presentational differences
- Summary
- Discussion questions
- Assignments

Introduction

Our focus so far has been on the preparation of the statement of financial position (balance sheet) and the statement of profit or loss (income statement), but in this chapter, we are going on to consider another essential component of annual financial statements, the *statement of cash flows*. We first introduced this statement in Chapter 1 – it analyzes the company's cash flows during the period covered by the statement of profit or loss. It presents information about the cash flows associated with the period's operations (with the statement of profit or loss reporting on the economic results of those operations), but also about the cash flows associated with the company's investing and financing activities of the period.

The statement of cash flows shows, for example, the cash generated by the company from its operating activities during the year, the company's investment in new non-current assets (increase in or renewal of its productive capacity) and the changes in the company's external financing from one statement of financial position to the next. The statement of cash flows *complements the other primary statements* and functions in conjunction with both the statement of profit or loss (performance dimension) and balance sheet (financial position).

Although company law generally does not require the disclosure of a statement of cash flows, many accounting standards do. Internationally, corporate practice has settled more or less on what was originally the US model of presentation, which served as the main source of inspiration for IAS 7 *Statement of Cash Flows*.

Usefulness of cash flow information

Financial analysts have long used cash flow as a useful indicator of company performance to complement profit measures and not least when making comparisons between companies operating in different countries. One of the advantages of a cash flow measure is that it disregards charges such as non-cash depreciation or provisions, which may be applied differently by different companies, and focuses on actual revenue flowing in and costs being paid out. In this sense, it filters out some of the differences that arise from accounting practices rather than operating practices.

The statement of profit or loss concentrates on measuring the economic result of the company's operations, irrespective of whether the associated cash changed hands during the accounting period or not. The statement of cash flows shows what cash transactions did take place and what the *net cash effect of the company's operations* was. This information is important to investors, whose return (dividends) is in part dependent on cash flows, and to various creditors who depend on the company's ability to generate adequate cash flows to fulfil its financial obligations.

While the balance sheet shows the financial position of a company at a specific instant of time, the statement of cash flows reflects the *change in financial position* between two balance sheet dates. It provides information that enables users to evaluate the changes in the company's assets and in its financial structure. Whereas liquidity and solvency tests are mainly based on static financial position information, cash flow information may be used to highlight the *dynamics of the short-term liquidity and long-term solvency* characteristics of the company: a statement of cash flows offers details to explain why liquidity and solvency ratios have changed between consecutive statements of financial position.

At a more generic level, cash flow information is also important as an essential *input for economic decision models*, which require an evaluation of a company's ability to generate cash and the timing and certainty of the cash flows. In that context, historical cash flow information is used as an indicator of the amount, timing and certainty of future cash flows. Bankers, when lending to any size company, generally ask for a cash flow projection as part of any loan proposal.

Cash flow cycles

In discussing the structure of a statement of financial position, we have treated cash as being part of working capital, but, of course, the cash in the bank is simply the residual of a great number of different types of cash flows, not only operating cash flows but also purchases and sales of long-term assets, receipt of financing, reimbursement of old debt, etc.

In the statement of cash flows, the net change in cash balances is the figure we are trying to explain, in terms of different types of cash flow cycle that generate or use cash. In fact, cash flows through the company continuously in a number of *short-term and long-term conversion cycles*. Figure 10.1 shows the short-term and long-term cash flow cycles and their interaction with the company's cash position.

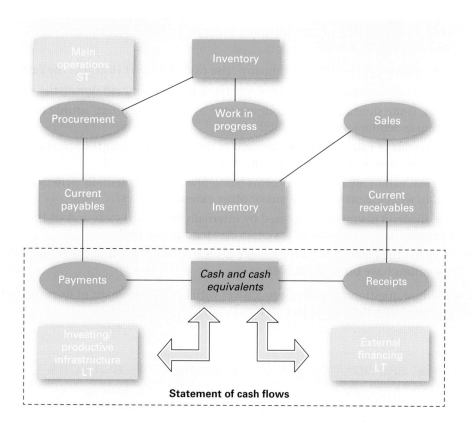

Figure 10.1   Long-term and short-term cash flow cycles

During the course of a year a company will be generating cash flows from its main business operations, which will be used not only for materials, labour and other periodic costs but also for purchasing new productive assets or to pay off debt. It might also borrow fresh funds, sell off old assets and so on. The working capital cycle (also called 'operating cycle') is the main short-term cash conversion cycle, while the investing and financing cycle are typically longer term (they relate to non-current sources and uses of funds).

The investing cycle involves the acquisition, renewal and disposal of intangible and tangible productive infrastructure, while the financing cycle refers to the long-term sourcing of funds through share capital issuance and borrowings. The investing and financing cycles set the framework, which supports a smooth functioning of the operating cycle. Like the working capital cycle, the long-term cash conversion cycles are both a source and a use of cash.

The different cash conversion cycles all bring about a change in the cash position of the company (and in the various components of the statement of financial position for that matter), and the statement of cash flows specifically analyzes the changes in the company's cash position according to the main drivers of the changes.

The *cash flow analysis* gives important insights into the company's success and strategy. It shows what cash has been created (or used) by the company's operations in a year – an important measure of performance, in an absolute sense, but also key to the company's potential for internally generated growth. What the company does with its cash (investing in productive capacity, paying off debt, paying dividends, etc.) provides useful *indicators of corporate strategy*. Some of the questions that can be addressed using the statement of cash flows are the following:

- From which sources did the company raise cash last year? How was the cash used?
- Was the operating cycle capable of satisfying its need for cash during the year?
- If not, is the shortage of cash compensated by new borrowings, issuing new share capital or selling long-term assets?
- Is a surplus of cash used for repayment of debt, for investments in productive assets, retirement of shares or for the distribution of dividends?
- To what extent are new investments being financed by internally generated cash and to what extent by new loans or other external sources?
- Are dividend payments supported by internally generated cash or does the company have to borrow to maintain dividend payments?
- Why has the balance of cash available decreased, knowing that the company's operations have been profitable?

These kinds of question are difficult to answer with only a statement of financial position and/or a statement of profit or loss on hand.

Format and structure of the statement of cash flows

In the statement of cash flows, the net change in cash balances is the figure to be explained. The net change in cash will be aggregated from cash flows regrouped in three major categories: operating activities, investing activities and financing activities. The *basic structure of the statement of cash flows* looks as follows:

Cash flows from operating activities
+ Cash flows from investing activities
+ Cash flows from financing activities
_____
Net change in cash during period
+ Beginning cash balance
_____
= Ending cash balance

Operating activities are defined (in the negative) to be all transactions that are not investing or financing activities. They are primarily the revenue-generating activities of a company. Operating cash flows include the cash inflows associated with revenue and cash outflows associated with operating expenses. IAS 7 *Statement of Cash Flows* provides the following examples of *cash flows from operating activities*:

a. Cash receipts from the sale of goods and the rendering of services
b. Cash receipts from royalties, fees, commissions and other revenue
c. Cash payments to suppliers for goods and services
d. Cash payments to and on behalf of employees
e. Cash receipts and cash payments of an insurance entity for premiums and claims, annuities and other policy benefits
f. Cash payments or refunds of income taxes unless they can be specifically identified with financing and investing activities
g. Cash receipts and payments from contracts held for dealing or trading purposes.

Operating cash flows of a period generally result from transactions and other events that enter into the determination of profit of that period.

Investing activities relate to the acquisition and disposal of long-term (tangible and intangible) assets and financial investments. Note that changes in current receivables and inventory are not treated as investment activities – changes in current assets are typically included in operating activities.

Financing activities are activities that result in changes in the size and composition of the contributed equity and borrowings of the company. Again, changes in current payables are part of operating activities and are not included in financing activities. Note also that changes in equity reflect financing activities only to the extent that they relate to the issuance or retirement of share capital. Changes in equity that result from retained profits are part of the profit-generating operating activities.

Cash equivalents

In a statement of cash flows the change in cash balances to be explained covers a concept of cash that is somewhat broader than cash on hand and demand deposits. Many companies, when they have any temporary excess cash, lend this out short term on the money market or buy short-term securities for periods of as few as one or two days. These short-term investments are sometimes called 'treasury' investments and are regarded as being so liquid as to be the same as cash (they are referred to as *cash equivalents*).

For purposes of the statement of cash flows, 'cash' means the sum of actual cash and *cash equivalents*. IAS 7 defines *cash equivalents* as 'short-term, highly liquid investments that are readily convertible to known amounts of cash and which are subject to an insignificant risk of changes in value' (IAS 7, para. 6).

STANDARDS

 IAS 7 – CASH AND CASH EQUIVALENTS *(extracts)*

7. Cash equivalents are held for the purpose of meeting short-term cash commitments rather than for investment or other purposes. For an investment to qualify as a cash equivalent it must be readily convertible to a known amount of cash and be subject to an insignificant risk of changes in value. Therefore, an investment normally qualifies as a cash equivalent only when it has a short maturity of, say, three months or less from the date of acquisition. Equity investments are excluded from cash equivalents unless they are, in substance, cash equivalents, for example in the case of preferred shares acquired within a short period of their maturity and with a specified redemption date.

8. Bank borrowings are generally considered to be financing activities. However, in some countries, bank overdrafts which are repayable on demand form an integral part of an entity's cash management. In these circumstances, bank overdrafts are included as a component of cash and cash equivalents. A characteristic of such banking arrangements is that the bank balance often fluctuates from being positive to overdrawn.

Source: IAS 7, Statement of Cash Flows

In this chapter, we will look first at the more straightforward issues of investing and financing activities and then look at cash flow from operations, before going on to preparing a statement of cash flows.

Cash flows from investing and financing activities

In discussing the statement of financial position, we have pointed out that it is a basic tenet of financial management that long-term assets should generally be bought with long-term finance, in order to match the expected cash inflows from use of the asset with the outflows to repay the finance. Sometimes companies borrow short-term and arrange new finance when the short-term debt expires (*roll over the borrowing*), but this involves two risks: first, that finance may be difficult to obtain in the second phase and, second, that interest rates may have increased, making the cost of borrowing uneconomic in relation to the asset purchased. The cost of capital is normally an important factor in evaluating an asset purchase and companies expose themselves to an interest rate risk if they do not match the borrowing to the investment cash flows. Matching investment with the borrowing is known as *hedging the interest rate risk*, and the decision whether to do this or not is part of the company's financial strategy.

A company will generate long-term finance by retaining cash generated by its operations (increasing its equity through retained profits), but it would not necessarily wish to restrict its investments in new activities (or expanding existing ones) to the rate at which cash is generated internally. It will therefore often borrow outside finance or issue new shares.

Typically, a company will wish to preserve a balance between the amount of funds borrowed and that obtained by issuing shares. That is, it will have a target balance between debt and equity. However, as we mentioned in Chapter 8, issuing shares is a costly business, so what companies often do is finance new projects purely from internal cash flows and borrowing and then once every few years issue a major block of shares which reduces the debt/equity ratio and enables them to pay off (*retire*) some existing debt. Equally, a company might sell off part of its operations that it no longer wants, as part of a rationalization programme.

A company that is expanding will also be buying new long-term assets regularly, as well as selling off old ones that are worn out or that have been superseded by new technology. There will therefore be a pattern of regular change.

The long-term changes to be expected can be summarized as follows:

- Uses of finance:

    Purchase of new long-term assets

    Retirement of existing debt

- Sources of finance:

    Issue of new shares

    New long-term borrowing

    Sale of long-term assets.

In a statement of cash flows, these would be presented as:

- Cash flow from investing activities:

    Purchase of long-term assets (*outflow*)

    Sale of long-term assets (*inflow*)

- Cash flow from financing activities:

    Issue of new shares (*inflow*)

    Payment of dividend (*outflow*)

    New borrowing (*inflow*)

    Retirement of debt (*outflow*).

Note that we have slipped in the payment of dividends here in the financing section. We will discuss this later, but IAS 7 *Statement of Cash Flows* sees payment of dividend as an adjustment of equity, although some jurisdictions prefer it to be presented elsewhere in the statement of cash flows, such as in cash flow from operations, as a distribution of the cash generated. (Where exactly it appears in the statement of cash flows is not as important as checking when making comparisons that it is treated the same way in all statements being compared.)

Cash flows from investing and financing activities are usually identified indirectly through an analysis of changes for the period in the non-current balance sheet categories. Direct identification of these cash flows through an analysis of the movements (transaction by transaction) in the cash (equivalent) accounts would be a more direct way, but the accounting database usually lacks the detail to proceed in that fashion.

IAS 7 – INVESTING AND FINANCING ACTIVITIES *(extracts)*

16. The separate disclosure of cash flows arising from investing activities is important because the cash flows represent the extent to which expenditures have been made for resources intended to generate future income and cash flows. Only expenditures that result in a recognized asset in the statement of financial position are eligible for classification as investing activities. Examples of cash flows arising from investing activities are:

    (a) cash payments to acquire property, plant and equipment, intangibles and other long-term assets. These payments include those relating to capitalized development costs and self-constructed property, plant and equipment;

    (b) cash receipts from sales of property, plant and equipment, intangibles and other long-term assets;

    (c) cash payments to acquire equity or debt instruments of other entities and interests in joint ventures (other than payments for those instruments considered to be cash equivalents or those held for dealing or trading purposes);

    (d) cash receipts from sales of equity or debt instruments of other entities and interests in joint ventures (other than receipts for those instruments considered to be cash equivalents and those held for dealing or trading purposes);

    (e) cash advances and loans made to other parties (other than advances and loans made by a financial institution);

    (f) cash receipts from the repayment of advances and loans made to other parties (other than advances and loans of a financial institution);

    (g) cash payments for futures contracts, forward contracts, option contracts and swap contracts except when the contracts are held for dealing or trading purposes, or the payments are classified as financing activities; and

    (h) cash receipts from futures contracts, forward contracts, option contracts and swap contracts except when the contracts are held for dealing or trading purposes, or the receipts are classified as financing activities.

17. The separate disclosure of cash flows arising from financing activities is important because it is useful in predicting claims on future cash flows by providers of capital to the entity. Examples of cash flows arising from financing activities are:

    (a) cash proceeds from issuing shares or other equity instruments;

    (b) cash payments to owners to acquire or redeem the entity's shares;

    (c) cash proceeds from issuing debentures, loans, notes, bonds, mortgages and other short or long-term borrowings;

    (d) cash repayments of amounts borrowed; and

    (e) cash payments by a lessee for the reduction of the outstanding liability relating to a finance lease.

Source: IAS 7, Statement of Cash Flows

CAPGEMINI – CONSOLIDATED STATEMENT OF CASH FLOWS

4.2.4 Consolidated statement of cash flows

in million of euros	Notes	2016	2017
Profit for the year attributable to owners of the Company		921	820
Non-controlling interests		(13)	(12)
Depreciation, amortization and impairment of fixed assets		299	301
Change in provisions		(5)	(9)
Losses on disposals of assets		6	15
Expenses relating to share grants		54	64
Net finance costs	9	104	18
Income tax expense	10	94	303
Unrealized gains on changes in fair value and other		(11)	32
Cash flows from operations before net finance costs and income tax (A)		1,449	1,532
Income tax paid (B)		(167)	(139)
Change in accounts and notes receivable and advances from customers and amounts billed in advance		(45)	(113)
Change in capitalized costs on projects		13	(12)
Change in accounts and notes payable		128	55
Change in other receivables/payables		(59)	7
Change in operating working capital (C)		37	(63)
NET CASH FROM OPERATING ACTIVITIES (D=A+B+C)		1,319	1,330
Acquisitions of property, plant and equipment and intangible assets	13–14	(197)	(241)
Proceeds from disposals of property, plant and equipment and intangible assets		21	15
		(176)	(226)
Cash inflows (outflows) on business combinations net of cash and cash equivalents acquired		(23)	(238)
Cash outflows in respect of cash management assets		(36)	(16)
Other cash (outflows) inflows, net		(16)	(54)
		(75)	(308)
NET CASH USED IN INVESTING ACTIVITIES (E)		(251)	(534)
Proceeds from issues of share capital		–	320
Dividends paid		(229)	(262)
Net payments relating to transactions in Capgemini SE shares		(315)	(531)
Proceeds from borrowings		505	7
Repayments of borrowings		(1,004)	(97)
Interest paid		(115)	(86)
Interest received		43	62
NET CASH USED IN FINANCING ACTIVITIES (F)		(1,115)	(587)
NET INCREASE (DECREASE) IN CASH AND CASH EQUIVALENTS (G=D+E+F)		(47)	209
Effect of exchange rate movements on cash and cash equivalents (H)		(31)	(91)
CASH AND CASH EQUIVALENTS AT BEGINNING OF YEAR (I)	21	1,948	1,870
CASH AND CASH EQUIVALENTS AT END OF YEAR (G+H+I)	21	1,870	1,988

Source: Capgemini Group, Consolidated Financial Statements, 2017

Cash flows from operating activities

The statement of profit or loss and the statement of financial position are based on the accrual principle, which could be summed up as trying to present an economic analysis of profit by recording transactions when any relevant economic event takes place (sales, expenses, using up of assets, etc.). Cash flows are only one type of event recorded and, while a company must manage its cash flows, it cannot manage the business just on cash flow information – it needs to know about economic profit and profitability.

For example, a company might have more cash coming in from sales than going out on expenses, but if it is not also recording the consumption of its non-current assets (depreciation), it could be making an economic loss even though generating a cash surplus in the short to medium term. Consequently, management focus has traditionally been on profits but, in a healthy company, the reinvestment of cash generated is the main source of internal growth and management should be looking at how best to allocate this resource to increase the profitability of the company.

The statement of cash flows helps to show what wealth is being generated. Of course, over the life of the company the total of profits will equal the total of cash flows generated, but on a period-to-period basis, this is not the case because of allocations of asset costs (depreciation) and timing differences from credit operations.

Again, the simplest way to get at the operating cash flows for the year would be to look at the company's cash (equivalent) accounts or the cashbook (a journal that records all receipts and payments) and remove cash flows relating to long-term assets and financing. This can be done if the accounting records keep details on the types of activity involved, and in the jargon this is known as the 'direct' way of calculating cash flows. However, while this probably is easy enough for a small company, and may be the easiest way also for the small entrepreneur to envisage cash flows, in large companies it is arguably easier and more efficient to calculate the operating cash flow by manipulating the statement of profit or loss and statement of financial position. This is known as the 'indirect' method. In fact, most companies present the information using the indirect method, so that is the one we will use.

The *indirect method of calculating operating cash flows* consists of taking the net accounting profit for the year and then making *three types of adjustment*:

1. Adjustments for non-cash income and non-cash expenses
2. Timing differences arising from the working capital cycle
3. Adjustments for non-operating items.

Non-cash income and non-cash expenses are items that enter into the determination of profit or loss, but do not imply a cash flow (e.g. depreciation, provisions, impairment adjustments, etc.).

Non-cash profit or loss items

As we have seen already, the process of preparing annual financial statements involves several kinds of adjustment: refinements to the profit to anticipate revenues and expenses that have not been included in the accounting database (such as accrued expenses and accrued revenue) and to defer previously recorded revenue and expenses to the following period (deferred revenue and deferred expenses), recognition and derecognition of provisions and periodic and incidental adjustments to asset values (reflecting the using up of productive assets and extraneous value changes in assets).

In the case of accruals and deferrals, these are short-term timing differences between profit or loss items and cash flows but, in the case of asset value adjustments, the associated cash flow (purchase of an asset) has already taken place and we are simply showing that, economically, it has lost some value that should be taken into consideration when estimating the economic position of the company. From a statement of cash flows perspective, the cash outflow on non-current assets appears under 'investing activities' and is reported when the asset is acquired. Therefore, when depreciation is charged, the investing cash flow has by definition already been reported. There is no operating cash outflow associated with depreciation or impairment charges for loss of value. Consequently, any charge to the statement of profit or loss for the year for these items should be added back to arrive at the underlying cash flow.

Provisions may turn into cash flows in due course, but their fate is uncertain and they too are added back here. Equally, where a provision is released, this will have the effect of increasing profit without increasing cash flows. Such releases must therefore be deducted from profit in calculating operating cash flow.

We can summarize as follows. The statement of profit or loss includes some items that do not reflect current cash outflows or cash inflows. These non-cash income and non-cash expenses should be used to adjust the accounting profit in order to arrive at a first, although rough, approximation of the net operating cash flow:

Net profit or loss after tax	xxxx
Add back:	
Depreciation charge for the year	xxx
Impairment loss for the year	xxx
Provisions created in the year	xxx
Deduct:	
Provisions released in the year	(xxx)
'Cash flow proxy'	xxxx

If no statement of cash flows is available, analysts frequently calculate this proxy figure, which is relatively easy to derive from the basic financial statements. It does not reflect the short-term timing differences that derive from credit operations, neither does it filter out investment and financing related items, but it is often used as an approximation of cash flows from operations. In the absence of directly available cash flow information, it has the advantage, in making comparisons between companies and particularly across national boundaries, that it excludes the most subjective elements of annual profit estimations, thereby providing more directly comparable figures.

Working capital movements

Working capital is generated by the operations of a company (see discussion in Chapter 4) and builds on a short-term cash conversion cycle in that a company buys materials (creating inventory and creditors), processes the materials (in a manufacturing environment), pays the creditors, sells the finished goods on credit (creating receivables) and finally the debtors settle in cash, completing the cycle. The exact needs of any business for working capital are dependent on the nature of the business. Some retailers, particularly supermarkets, keep very low inventories and have little or no credit sales, so their net working capital could even be negative. On the other hand, a manufacturing concern may have a long production cycle that takes many months for raw materials to progress through manufacturing and be sold as finished goods. Such companies will have extensive inventories as well as receivables and payables.

Movements in working capital items other than cash will affect cash flow from operating activities: increased trade receivables will mean that the cash from those sales will be received in the next accounting period; increased trade payables means that the cash outflow to suppliers has been deferred to the next period. The statement of cash flows will therefore need to take account of changes in working capital (excluding cash, which is the pivotal figure around which the statement of cash flows is organized and whose changes we are trying to explain) in order to show the cash generated during the year from operations.

Let us just look at an example of how that works. Supposing that in its start-up year a company had no initial share capital but had sales of €10,000, and had purchased €8,000 of goods for resale. Its inventory at year-end was worth €1,000, it owed €5,000 to its suppliers and its credit clients owed €2,000. The business had, therefore, the following statement of profit or loss:

	€
Sales	10,000
Cost of sales	−7,000
Profit	3,000

Its statement of financial position at the end of the period was:

Assets	€
Inventory	1,000
Receivables	2,000
Cash	5,000
	8,000
Financing	
Equity – Profit	3,000
Payables	5,000
	8,000

The business has made a profit of €3,000, but its cash generated was €5,000. How was this possible? The answer is in the movements in non-cash working capital:

	€
Cash owed to suppliers	5,000
Cash held in inventories	−1,000
Cash not yet paid by clients	−2,000
Non-cash working capital	2,000

The €2,000 difference represents *timing differences* and, if the business stopped trading and disposed of its inventories, its cash position would in a few weeks equal its profit as clients paid their accounts and the company paid its suppliers.

If we now move forward into the second accounting period, we can show how the change in net working capital affects cash flows. Let us say that the business has grown by 50 per cent and that the statement of profit or loss for period 2 gives the following result:

	€
Sales	15,000
Cost of sales	− 10,500
Profit	4,500

Assuming that credit sales and purchases had grown proportionately, receivables at the end of period 2 would be €3,000, inventory €1,500 and payables €7,500. We can display the statement of financial position at the ends of periods 1 and 2 alongside each other and see not only how the cash position has changed, but also how the other balance sheet components have moved at the same time:

	End period 1 €	End period 2 €	Uses of finance €	Sources of finance €
Assets				
Inventory	1,000	1,500	500	
Receivables	2,000	3,000	1,000	
Cash	5,000	10,500	5,500	
	8,000	15,000		
Financing				
Payables	5,000	7,500		2,500
Equity				
Accumulated profit	3,000	7,500		4,500
	8,000	15,000	7,000	7,000

In the two right-hand columns we have analyzed the change in each balance sheet component that has taken place during the second year. If you look at the changes, you can see that the inflow of cash is related to the accounting profit through the changes in the other elements of working capital:

	€
Accounting profit	4,500
less Uses of finance:	
▪ increase in receivables	− 1,000
▪ increase in inventory	− 500
plus Sources of finance	
▪ increase *in payables*	2,500
Increase in cash	5,500

The example given is much simplified in order to highlight the changes in working capital – in many companies, the increase in payables would not be so high as to finance the increase in receivables and inventory entirely, and there would, of course, be some share capital subscribed to start with. Accrued or deferred expenses and revenue (or similar items) have been ignored, but would be included here.

Non-operating items

Transactions and events that enter into the determination of profit are not exclusively limited to operating activities. Investing and financing activities may affect the statement of profit or loss as well.

For example, when a company sells an item of plant or equipment, this will give rise to a gain or loss that is included in the statement of profit or loss, to the extent that the selling price is different from the net carrying value of the item sold. Such non-operating items affecting the profit figure should not be included in the net operating cash flow.

Let us assume that the company sells an item of equipment with a net book value of €60,000 (acquisition cost €100,000 and accumulated depreciation of €40,000) for €90,000. This sale will give rise to a gain on disposal of €30,000 that is included in the operating result. From a statement of cash flows perspective, the transaction is an investing activity (a disposal of a long-term asset) and the inflow from the sale proceeds (€90,000) is to be accounted for in full as an investing cash flow. The gain on disposal is part of the cash flow from investing activities and should therefore be excluded from the net operating cash flow.

Indirect calculation model

After the three types of adjustment, the indirect calculation model of the net operating cash flow would roughly look like the following:

Net profit after tax	XXXX
Add back	
Depreciation for the year	XXX
Impairment loss of the year	XXX
Provisions created	XXX
Deduct	
Provisions released	(XXXX)
Gain on asset disposal	(XXXX)
Net change in non-cash working capital	(XXXX)
Cash flow from operating activities	XXXXX

Direct method for reporting operating cash flows

Although most companies use the indirect method for calculating and reporting operating cash flows, IAS 7 *Statement of Cash Flows* encourages companies to use the direct method to report operating cash flows.

Under the *direct method*, major classes of gross cash receipts and gross cash payments relative to operating activities are presented. This kind of information could be extracted from the cashbooks (not very feasible for most companies) or constructed by adjusting sales, cost of sales and other items in the statement of profit or loss for:

1. Changes during the period in inventories and operating receivables and payables
2. Other non-cash items
3. Non-operating items.

The direct method results in a more straightforward presentation that is intuitively understandable by users with little accounting knowledge. The information it provides (and which is not available under the indirect method) may also be useful in estimating future cash flows.

By the same token, the *indirect method* (also referred to as the *reconciliation method*) has the advantage that it helps the analyst to understand the reasons for the difference between the period's net profit figure and the period's net operating cash flow. If the direct method of presentation is used, IAS 7 does not require the presentation of such a reconciliation.

STANDARDS

IAS 7 – DIRECT METHOD STATEMENT OF CASH FLOWS (extract)

		20X2
Cash flows from operating activities		
Cash receipts from customers	30,150	
Cash paid to suppliers and employees	(27,600)	
Cash generated from operations	2,550	
Interest paid	(270)	
Income taxes paid	(900)	
Net cash from operating activities		1,380
Cash flows from investing activities		
Acquisition of subsidiary X, net of cash acquired	(550)	
Purchase of property, plant and equipment	(350)	
Proceeds from sale of equipment	20	
Interest received	200	
Dividends received	200	
Net cash used in investing activities		(480)
Cash flows from financing activities		
Proceeds from issue of share capital	250	
Proceeds from long-term borrowings	250	
Payment of finance lease liabilities	(90)	
Dividends paid*	(1,200)	
Net cash used in financing activities		(790)
Net increase in cash and cash equivalents		110
Cash and cash equivalents at beginning of period		120
Cash and cash equivalents at end of period		230

* This could also be shown as an operating cash flow.

Source: IAS 7, Statement of Cash Flows – Illustrative examples

The direct method and the indirect method are two models of a statement of cash flows as exhibited in IAS 7. The two models refer to the same raw accounting data. Note that the method chosen does not affect the presentation of investing and financing cash flows and that both methods necessarily result in the same net operating cash flow figure. Note that IAS 7 requires that interest and dividend paid and received and taxes paid should always be disclosed separately on the face of the statement of cash flows (in both presentation models).

STANDARDS

IAS 7 – INDIRECT METHOD STATEMENT OF CASH FLOWS (extract)

	20X2	
Cash flows from operating activities		
Profit before taxation	3,350	
Adjustments for:		
Depreciation	450	
Foreign exchange loss	40	
Investment income	(500)	
Interest expense	400	
	3,740	
Increase in trade and other receivables	(500)	
Decrease in inventories	1,050	
Decrease in trade payables	(1,740)	
Cash generated from operations	2,550	
Interest paid	(270)	
Income taxes paid	(900)	
Net cash from operating activities		1,380
Cash flows from investing activities		
Acquisition of subsidiary X, net of cash acquired	(550)	
Purchase of property, plant and equipment	(350)	
Proceeds from sale of equipment	20	
Interest received	200	
Dividends received	200	
Net cash used in investing activities		(480)
Cash flows from financing activities		
Proceeds from issue of share capital	250	
Proceeds from long-term borrowings	250	
Payment of finance lease liabilities	(90)	
Dividends paid*	(1,200)	
Net cash used in financing activities		(790)
Net increase in cash and cash equivalents		110
Cash and cash equivalents at beginning of period		120
Cash and cash equivalents at end of period		230

* This could also be shown as an operating cash flow

Source: IAS 7, Statement of Cash Flows – Illustrative examples

Constructing a statement of cash flows 1

Let us now work a practical example. The working method is to take two consecutive statements of financial position, calculate the difference between them and analyze these into inflows and outflows of cash. The scheme shown in Figure 10.2 can be used as a rule of thumb to designate balance sheet movement as cash outflows or cash inflows.

An increase of assets (for example buying a car or inventory) and a decrease of equity or liabilities (for example paying a dividend to shareholders or retiring debt), generally imply a use of cash. An increase of equity or liabilities (for example selling new shares, making a profit, getting a new bank loan) and a decrease of assets (for example depreciating long-term assets, selling inventory), imply a source of funds:

	20X2	20X1	Δ	Outflow	Inflow
Assets					
Non-current tangible assets (at cost)	980	740	240	240	
Acc. depreciation	−350	−265	85		85
Inventories	180	171	9	9	
Trade receivables	115	98	17	17	
Cash	92	110	18		18
	1,017	854			
Financing					
Equity					
Share capital	600	600	—		
Reserves	90	90	—		
20X2 profit	50	—	50		50
Liabilities					
Trade payables	62	59	3		3
Long-term debt	215	105	110		110
	1,017	854		266	266

In the current example, the first step may be redundant, but this is useful where the analyst has to research more data to complete the analysis, as we shall see later. The cash difference is the figure we are trying to explain, and is entered onto the worksheet to ensure that one can make a mathematical control of the differences – when taking one statement of financial position from another, the difference must be in equilibrium, since the two original statements are in equilibrium.

The cash figure is entered on the basis that an increase in assets is an outflow and a decrease of assets is an inflow, even though this is obviously counterintuitive. It should be thought of simply as the balancing difference.

Figure 10.2 Classifying balance sheet movements as inflows or outflows of cash

Having calculated the inflow/outflow data, we can proceed to lay it out according to the type of activity with which the cash flow is associated (operating, investing and financing activities), as follows:

Operating activities	
Net profit after tax	50
Add back depreciation	85
	135
Changes in non-cash working capital	−23
Net cash flow from operations (A)	112
Investing activities	
Purchase of tangible fixed assets (B)	−240
Financing activities	
New long-term debt (C)	110
Net change in cash (A+B+C)	−18
Cash balances	
At beginning of year	110
At balance sheet date	92
Difference	−18

Taking the statement of cash flows line by line, the net profit figure is the profit for the year in the statement of financial position (and in the statement of profit or loss, of course). The depreciation charge for the year is the difference between accumulated depreciation at the beginning and end of the year. The change in non-cash working capital is:

Increase in inventories	−9
Increase in trade receivables	−17
Increase in trade payables	+3
Net change in non-cash working capital	−23

All that is left after that is the increase in non-current tangible assets of 240 and the increase in long-term debt of 110. You should check off the differences identified in the worksheet against the statement of cash flows to be sure you see where the information comes from.

Having drawn up this statement, the next question is: *what useful information does the statement of cash flows provide us about the company?*

Essentially here the message is simple – the company has acquired a substantial new non-current tangible asset, and has financed it approximately half by the cash flow it has generated in the year and half by increasing its long-term debt.

The increase in productive capacity is a good sign indicating increased future profits (provided the company can manage the tangible asset successfully, of course). The degree of debt financing is out of line with the company's prior debt/equity ratio. In 20X1 the ratio was 105/690 or 15 per cent, and the financing of a new long-term asset 50 per cent by long-term debt must change this significantly. In fact, the new debt/equity ratio is 215/740 = 29 per cent. Of course, the company may be planning to reduce the debt in 20X3 when it has generated more cash from operations, or may simply have decided to adopt a more aggressive financing stance.

Disposal of long-term assets

The use of raw balance sheet data in constructing a statement of cash flows is more complicated when there are both inflows and outflows under the same caption of the statement of financial position in the course of the year. This is frequently the case with long-term assets, like property, plant and equipment (PP&E), where companies are not only expanding capacity, but are replacing old equipment with new.

As regards the statement of cash flows, *long-term asset disposals lead to two adjustments:*

1. To separate out the disappearing book value of the old long-term asset from the newly acquired assets

2. To remove the gain or loss on disposal from the operating profit and put it into the investing section, since all non-current asset acquisitions and disposals should appear there.

Suppose that a company had non-current tangible assets at cost of 540 and accumulated depreciation of 235 at the beginning of the year. During the year it sold for 135 some equipment that had cost 275 and had accumulated depreciation of 160. It replaced this with a tangible asset that cost 400. The depreciation charge for the year was 132.

The analysis of the statement of financial position would give the following picture:

	20X2	20X1	Δ	Outflow	Inflow
Non-current tangible assets	665	540	125		
Accumulated depreciation	−207	−235	28		

On the face of it, the company has acquired a new tangible asset that cost 125, and there was a depreciation credit for the year instead of a charge. This is, of course, hardly likely and would send the analyst immediately to the notes to the accounts for an analysis of movements on tangible assets, where it would quickly be discovered that there had been a disposal and an acquisition. Consequently, the analysis can be completed more fully:

	20X2	20X1	Δ	Outflow	Inflow
Non-current tangible assets	665	540	125	400	275
Accumulated depreciation	−207	−235	28	160	132

On the tangible assets line, the 125 represents the difference between the acquisition at 400 and the original cost of the asset disposed of, 275. For the purposes of the analysis, we will put both the gross cost and the accumulated depreciation of the asset that has been sold into our worksheet, so that it is clear what is happening. The accumulated depreciation on this asset was 160, which, taken with the difference of 28 between balance sheet dates, means that the charge for the year was 132 (160 − 28 = 132).

The analysis, therefore, now includes all the elements that have intervened during the year: sale of a long-term tangible asset, acquisition of another one, and depreciation charge for the year.

In the statement of cash flows the depreciation charge of 132 will be added back to profit in the calculation of operating cash flows. The purchase of the new tangible asset at 400 will appear under investing activities, and there too we must put the asset sold. The book value of 115 (275 − 160) should go there, but it should be adjusted by the amount of the gain or loss. In this case, it is a gain of 20 (135 − 115), which we should remove from operating cash flows and add to the book value of the asset in investing activities. We would therefore have 'asset disposal 135' (115 + 20), which is the cash flow arising from the sale of the long-term asset.

Had the resale price received been (say) 100, this would have resulted in an accounting loss of 15. This loss of 15 should be removed from the operating result and be deducted from the disposal under investing activities: 'asset disposal 100' (115 − 15).

We can restate our indirect calculation model for operating cash flow as:

Net profit after tax	XXXXXXXXX
Add back	
Depreciation expense/Impairment loss	XXXXXX
Provisions created	XXXXXX
Loss on disposal of assets	XXXXXX
Deduct:	
Provisions released	(XXXXXX)
Gains on disposal of assets	(XXXXXX)
+/− Change in non-cash working capital	(XXXXXX)
Net cash flow from operating activities	XXXXXXXXX

Constructing a statement of cash flows 2

Unlike the preparation of the statement of profit or loss and statement of financial position, there is no one tried and tested way of preparing a statement of cash flows any more than there is a unique format for presenting the data.

We shall continue to use the system of comparing opening and closing statements of financial position. This direct comparison has the merit that it produces a table of differences where (given that the two statements of financial position do balance to start with) the differences in outflows will equal the differences in inflows. It gives a good starting point by providing a framework of change for that particular company.

Let us do a new example. The statement of profit or loss follows and the statement of financial position has been laid out as a working paper:

Connecticut River Co. Ltd
Statement of profit or loss

Sales		500
Materials used	148	
Salaries	105	
Depreciation	116	
Other operating expenses	95	−464
		36
Gain on disposal of asset		3
Interest expense		−9
		30
Taxation		−11
Net profit after tax		19

Connecticut River Co. Ltd
Statements of financial position

	20X2	20X1	Δ	Outflow	Inflow
Land	105	105	—		
Buildings	235	235	—		
Accumulated depreciation	−113	−107	6		
Plant	441	397	44		
Accumulated depreciation	−356	−282	74		
Inventory	82	75	7		
Trade receivables	243	216	27		
Cash	73	62	11		
Trade payables	190	195	5		
Debt	160	150	10		
Share capital	200	200	—		
Reserves	141	156	15		
Profit for the year	19	—	19		

The worksheet shows the crude differences between the two years' statements of financial position, and the next step is to go in search of explanations of these differences.

The first one is an increase of accumulated depreciation on buildings. There is nothing inherently unusual in this – presumably this is the depreciation charge for the year, which we can verify in a real-life situation from the analysis of non-current assets given in the notes. The statement of profit or loss shows us that the total charge for the year was 116, so there remains another 110 to explain. This 6, anyway, can be put into the inflow column as part of cash flow from operations.

Moving on to plant, there is a net difference of 44. However, there is an asset disposal in the statement of profit or loss (gain on disposal of 3). As there is no change in any non-current assets other than plant, this disposal must occur here, so the difference of 44 must be the difference between an acquisition and a disposal. The non-current asset analysis in the notes to the accounts will reveal that the company bought a new plant asset for 85, and disposed of one whose original cost was 41, which enables us to reconcile the difference:

Plant acquired	85
Plant sold	−41
Balance sheet difference	44

We will, therefore, complete the plant assets line by showing an outflow of 85 and inflow of 41. Of course, this sale will impact on the depreciation line for plant as well, since the accumulated depreciation on the plant that has been sold must be removed. The net difference on depreciation is 74, but we know from the other depreciation lines that the depreciation charge for plant during 20X2 was likely to be 110 (116 in statement of profit or loss, less 6 depreciation on buildings). This would give the following:

Depreciation for the year on plan	110
Balance sheet difference	74
Depreciation on plant sold	36

We should be able to verify this from the non-current assets analysis in the notes, in a real-life case. We would show 110 as an inflow, being part of the net cash flow from operations, and 36 as an outflow. Of course, the 36 is not an 'outflow' in a real sense, but it is a deduction from the book value of the asset that was sold and it is arithmetically convenient to note it here in this way, bearing in mind it is a deduction from an inflow. The 41 gross cost less 36 accumulated depreciation represents the accounting disposal value of the plant that has been sold (5) to which we will eventually add the gain of 3 (from the statement of profit or loss) to arrive at the sale proceeds which must have been 8.

After that we have routine increases in receivables and inventories, analyzed as outflows. The difference in cash is 11, and we will analyze this as an outflow, to preserve the balance sheet equilibrium (in effect, it is the difference between the inflows and the outflows, of course).

If you are unhappy with this treatment of the cash difference, another way to deal with it is just to leave it out. If you do that, when you add up the inflows and outflows you will obviously have a difference, which will be the amount of the cash difference. If these two differences agree, your analysis is arithmetically correct; if not there is a problem.

The trade payables have actually reduced from 20X1 to 20X2, which is fairly unusual (but not impossible) where the inventories and trade receivables have increased, since these three are all linked in an operational sense to the same variable – sales – and therefore should tend to move together. From an analytical perspective, a decrease in trade payables is a decrease in financing and therefore an outflow.

The debt line shows an increase of 10. A review of the notes to the accounts will in many jurisdictions show a breakdown of debt, and, in this case, we understand that a new debt has been taken out for 70. This means therefore that an old debt has been retired, if the net variation is only 10:

New debt	70
Retirement of old debt	−60
Net movement on debt	10

The new debt is an inflow, repayment of the old debt an outflow.

There is no change in share capital, but reserves have gone down by 15. The most obvious explanation for this would be the payment of a dividend, which in most jurisdictions flows directly from retained profit reserves. A review of the analysis of movements on equity in the statement of changes in equity (or in the notes to the accounts if the separate statement is not available) would confirm this. This is then analyzed as an outflow.

The final difference is the profit for the year of 19. This will start off our statement of cash flows, but we must bear in mind that it includes a disposal gain of 3, which must be reallocated in the statement of cash flows to the investment section. The completed worksheet with the analyses looks like this:

Connecticut River Co. Ltd
Statements of financial position

	20X2	20X1	Δ	Outflow	Inflow
Land	105	105	—		
Buildings	235	235	—		
Accumulated depreciation	−113	−107	6		6
Plant	441	397	44	85	41
Accumulated depreciation	−356	−282	74	36	110
Inventory	82	75	7	7	
Trade receivables	243	216	27	27	
Cash	73	62	11	11	
Trade payables	190	195	5	5	
Debt	160	150	10	60	70
Share capital	200	200	—		
Reserves	141	156	15	15	
Profit for the period	19	—	19		19

We can now proceed to lay out the statement of cash flows in the formal way:

Connecticut River Co. Ltd
Statement of cash flows for the year ended 31 December 20X1
Operating activities

Net profit for the year	19	
Add back		
Depreciation	116	
Deduct		
Gain on asset disposal	−3	
	132	
Net change in non-cash working capital	−39	
Net cash flow from operating activities		93
Investing activities		
Purchase of plant	−85	
Disposal of plant	8	
Net cash flow from investing activities		−77
Financing activities		
Loan received	70	
Retirement of debt	−60	
Dividend paid	−15	
Net cash flow from financing activities		−5
Net change in cash during year		11
Cash balance 1 January 20X2	62	
Cash balance 31 December 20X2	73	

Notes:
1. The net change in non-cash working capital is the total of inventory (outflow 7), trade receivables (outflow 27) and trade creditors (outflow 5).
2. The figure for disposal of fixed assets is the book value of the plant sold (gross cost 41 less accumulated depreciation 36) plus the gain on disposal of 3 moved down from operating activities.

Interpretation

The statement of cash flows is an interesting summary of a company's changes in financial position during the course of a year and can often give clues to business strategy that are not so readily apparent from the statement of financial position or the statement of profit or loss. The format of the statement of cash flows with the basic distinction between operating, investing and financing activities is intended to aid in this type of analysis.

Different elements will have more or less importance from one company to another, but major considerations that should be taken into account when interpreting company statements are:

1. How successful is the company at generating cash from operations? To what extent does this internally generated cash flow provide finance for expansion and to what extent is it used up in providing dividends for shareholders?

2. Is the company disposing of many long-term assets? If so, does this mean a rundown of the business? Are assets being renewed or are new assets being acquired for expansion?

3. Is the company borrowing extensively and, if so, for what purpose? Is it restructuring its debt by replacing old debts with new; is it borrowing for new expansion; is it issuing new equity?

4. Is there any hidden message in the changes in working capital? For example, is a company acquiring higher inventories and higher receivables without any corresponding increase in trade payables? Or, conversely, are payables growing very quickly while other working capital elements are stable (possibly implying a cash shortage or at least an attempt to delay outflows)? Has there been a sudden drop in cash?

The statement of cash flows can potentially provide a useful picture of the structural changes that a company is undergoing and it should be examined with care for any hidden messages.

If we look at the statement of cash flows we have just constructed, the messages there are relatively simple.

Most of the company's operating cash flow comes from depreciation; the profit is relatively small in percentage terms. The main outflow has been on the purchase of new long-term assets, but these – at 85 – are less than the depreciation of 116. In a crude sense, this means that the company's total assets are getting smaller. This would prompt an analyst to ask the company if this is significant. It may not be. The company may depreciate its assets very quickly, for tax or prudence reasons, but it is curious.

The increase in working capital is relatively high in relation to profits as well, and one should check (the figures are not given here) whether there has been a substantial increase in sales to justify the change in working capital or, if not, what is going on. The increase in working capital is twice the net profit, which means that profits are being swallowed up to finance expansion. This may be a good thing, which will give a better return the next year, but, at this point, it looks a bit doubtful.

The company seems to have 'rolled over' debt by repaying some but replacing it. Again, this is perfectly normal. On the whole, the statement of cash flows reveals that the company is investing in working capital more than long-term assets. This may be a good sign, meaning higher sales the next year and more efficient use of plant, but an analyst would be looking for further information to explain this. Aside from the growth of working capital, the picture is one of little change.

Some analysts will want to know the amount of *free cash flow*. The concept of free cash flow refers to the operating cash flow that can be freed up for new investment initiatives. Free cash flow can be calculated as the *net operating cash flow minus three items*:

1. Cash needed for planned investing activities (like replacements of long-term assets to maintain existing productive capacity)

2. Scheduled debt repayments

3. Normal dividend payments.

A large amount of free cash flow means that there is a lot of discretionary room for expansion and new opportunities, extra retirement of debt or dividend increases. If free cash flow is negative, it would indicate that extra financing is needed just to maintain the current level of business activity (and the related commitments). If a negative free cash flow continues for several years, this becomes troublesome if sources of extra cash (new debt, new share issues, selling assets) dry up. Note that some analysts will only take into account net operating cash flow and planned net capital expenditures to calculate free cash flow.

Additionally, analysts will use cash flow information to construct some extra liquidity and solvency ratios, such as net operating cash flow to current liabilities (*liquidity test*) or net operating cash flow to current liabilities plus long-term debt (*solvency test*). This last ratio is typically used by credit officers in evaluating a company's creditworthiness for long-term debt.

Presentational differences

There are sometimes differences at the level of detail as to how a statement of cash flows is presented. In particular, our model here assumes that interest payments and taxation are part of the net operating cash flow (as they are included in the net profit measure), while dividends are treated as a financing item. Not everyone agrees with that presentation. IAS 7 allows some choice in this matter. It suggests that interest paid can be classified under either operating or financing activities, and interest and dividends received can be included in either operating or investing cash flows. Dividends paid can be interpreted as a cost of obtaining external finance and included in the financing cash flow or they can be treated as a component of the net operating cash flow.

Some companies start from the net operating result instead of from the net profit before or after taxes in the indirect net operating cash flow model. This is not prohibited, but it will naturally affect the content of the different types of adjustment that have to be made to arrive at the net cash flow from operating activities.

A cash flow statement will be accompanied by a significant number of extra disclosures in the notes to the accounts. IAS 7 *Statement of Cash Flows* contains a lot of specific disclosure requirements in this matter. These notes are usually cross-referenced in the statement of cash flows.

Some investing and financing activities do not imply cash flows at all (or only in part), such as the conversion of convertible debt into ordinary shares or acquiring an item of equipment through a finance lease. These non-cash transactions should be excluded from the statement of cash flows, although additional disclosures in the notes would be expected.

In all cases, the analyst should either make or adjust his or her own statement of cash flows on a uniform base, or read the notes to the accounts carefully to see how the company has been constructed and take care over items such as dividends so that the statement can be adjusted to be comparable with others.

Summary

Most companies produce a statement of cash flows as well as the statement of profit or loss and statement of financial position. The statement of cash flows analyzes the changes in financial position from one balance sheet to the next for their effect on the company's cash position. The International Accounting Standards Board (the Board) formats of a statement of cash flows that analyzes cash flows between operating, investing and financing activities, have become generally accepted.

Companies generate funds internally from their profit-making activities, but the extent of these funds differs from accounting profit insofar as the accounting profit includes non-cash adjustments such as depreciation and provisions and to the extent that there have been changes in the working capital of the company derived from trading.

Companies' finances are also affected by the acquisition of new long-term assets, the sale of old assets, the borrowing of funds and the issuing of new shares. The payment of dividends and taxes is another drain on company cash flows. The statement of cash flows regroups all these elements of change for the information of shareholders and other financial statement users. The statement of cash flows provides useful information about the company's financial management and underlying changes in financial position and strategy.

There are no special rules for the workings necessary to construct a statement of cash flows, but we have approached this using one specific method. The method used depends on an analysis of the net change in position between one statement of financial position and the next. This basic analysis provides a framework from which one may systematically extend the full outflows and inflows by correcting for net movements in each of the important balance sheet categories.

Discussion questions

1. Explain briefly the incremental utility of the statement of cash flows to external users of financial statements.
2. The statement of cash flows contains three major sections. What are these sections and what kind of information is contained in each?
3. Why does only a small minority of companies use the direct method to elaborate the statement of cash flows?
4. Discuss the different types of adjustment needed to derive a net operating cash flow figure from net profit after tax. Provide an example of each type of adjustment.
5. What is the logic of analyzing components of the statement of financial position when constructing a statement of cash flows?

Assignments

The following questions have answers on the lecturer side of the digital support resources for the book.

1. Seurat AG commenced business on 1 January 20X1, having acquired an existing trading concern. The company's opening statement of financial position was:

	€
Property, plant and equipment	5,000
Inventory	1,200
Cash	1,800
	8,000
Share capital	8,000

During the year it traded successfully and had the following statement of profit or loss:

	€
Sales	25,000
Cost of goods sold	−17,500
	7,500
Other operating expenses	−4,500
Net profit after tax	3,000

Its statement of financial position as at 31 December 20X1 was as follows:

		€
Property, plant and equipment		5,000
Accumulated depreciation		−1,000
Non-current assets		4,000
Current assets:		
Inventory	1,800	
Trade receivables	2,300	
Cash	4,300	8,400
Total assets		12,400
Share capital		8,000
Retained profit		3,000
		11,000
Trade payables		1,400
Total equity and liabilities		12,400

Required:

Calculate Seurat's cash flow from operations for 20X1, and reconcile this with the company's net profit figure (assuming there is no taxation or dividend for 20X1).

2. During 20X2 Seurat AG (see question 1) continued to trade successfully, and also expanded. It acquired new equipment for €8,000, and borrowed €5,000 in order to help finance the transaction. Its statement of profit or loss for 20X2 is shown below and its statement of financial position as at 31 December 20X2 was as follows:

Statement of profit or loss 20X2	€	
Sales	57,500	
Cost of goods sold	−36,300	
	21,200	
Other operating expenses	−11,000	
Profit before tax	10,200	
Taxation	−3,000	
Net profit after tax	7,200	
Statement of financial position at 31 December 20X2	€	€
Property, plant and equipment		13,000
Accumulated depreciation		−2,800
Non-current assets		10,200
Current assets:		
Inventory	4,400	
Trade receivables	2,900	
Cash	11,900	19,200
Total assets		29,400
Share capital		8,000
Retained profit		10,200
		18,200
Trade payables		3,200
Taxes payable		3,000
Long-term borrowing		5,000
Total equity and liabilities		29,400

You are asked to prepare Seurat's statement of cash flows for 20X2.

3. Seurat AG (see questions 1 and 2) continued to develop in 20X3. It acquired new equipment for €15,000 and sold its original equipment for €3,500 (the equipment sold had a net book value of €3,000 at the time of sale). The company also paid off its bank loan and paid a dividend of €2,000. Its trading results for 20X3 are given below and its statement of financial position as at 31 December 20X3 was as follows:

Statement of profit or loss 20X3	€
Sales	69,700
Cost of goods sold	−41,300
	28,400
Other operating expenses	−13,500
	14,900
Gain on sale of equipment	500
Net profit before tax	15,400
Taxation	−4,620
Net profit after tax	10,780

Statement of financial position at 31 December 20X3	€	€
Property, plant and equipment		23,000
Accumulated depreciation		−3,100
Non-current assets		19,900
Current assets:		
Inventory	4,800	
Trade receivables	3,200	
Cash	7,400	15,400
Total assets		35,300
Share capital		8,000
Retained profit		18,980
		26,980
Trade payables		3,700
Taxes payable		4,620
Total equity and liabilities		35,300

Required:

(a) Prepare Seurat's statement of cash flows for 20X3.

(a) Comment on the company's financial position.

4. You are given below successive statements of financial position for a company (as at 31 December 20X6 and 20X7) and are asked to prepare a statement of cash flows for 20X7:

	20X6	20X7
	€'000	€'000
Property at valuation	2,350	3,850
Plant and equipment	980	1,560
Accumulated depreciation	−423	−572
	2,907	4,838
Inventories	841	923
Receivables	1,213	1,297
Cash	106	73
Total assets	5,067	7,131
Share capital	430	460
Share premium	802	892
Revaluation reserve	435	935
Retained earnings	551	771
	2,218	3,058
Trade payables	1,432	1,675
Taxes payable	217	198
Long-term creditors	1,200	2,200
Total equity and liabilities	5,067	7,131

You are advised that no long-term tangible assets were disposed of during 20X7 and that taxation (€217,000) and dividends (€105,000) which related to 20X6 were paid out during 20X7.

(*Comment*: You should note that this case includes long-term assets held at valuation rather than historical cost. A valuation change does not involve any cash flows.)

PART 4

The financial statements of multinational companies

In Part 4, we switch from an approach anchored in the financial statements of individual companies to one where the focus is the multinational group of companies as a reporting entity. In the remainder of this textbook, we will refer to such a group of companies that operate under a unified management structure as a multinational company (MNC). While all the accounting and reporting rules that we reviewed in the earlier parts of this textbook hold good, there are additional factors that need to be taken into account to understand the content of the financial statements of a multinational company. In particular, as the statements are the result of aggregating the financial position and activities of a number of individual companies, knowledge of additional accounting and disclosure rules is necessary to appropriately analyze and understand the figures of a multinational company. Equally, there are public interest issues such as transparency and controls on management behaviour that come into play when looking at a group employing thousands of people and whose actions affect many different economies.

CHAPTER 11

The annual report

This first chapter of Part 4 reviews briefly the annual report of the multinational company. It summarizes its main components and considers its use as a publicity document. Additionally, this chapter elaborates on the notion of comprehensive income and on how it relates to the traditional statement of profit or loss (income statement/profit and loss account).

Chapter structure

- Introduction
- Content of the corporate annual report
- Publicity document
- Statement of comprehensive income
- OCI and the IASB *Conceptual Framework*
- Analyzing the annual report
- Summary
- Discussion questions

Introduction

As we discussed in Chapter 1, it is widely recognized that there are at least two quite different types of company in any developed economy: small and medium-sized enterprises (SMEs) and large, listed multinationals (MNCs). Where exactly one draws the line between the two is not clear and, in any event, probably varies from economy to economy, but we can identify two models that represent the contrasting poles. First, the SME is a company whose shares are held by a small number of individuals and are not publicly traded. The managers of an SME are usually shareholders. The SME employs relatively few people, its financing is oriented towards bank loans and the main users of its annual financial statements are the tax authorities, the management and the bank.

The opposite pole is the MNC, which may be listed on several stock exchanges. The MNC has no one shareholder with a significant proportion of its equity, has professional managers, is active in many countries and employs thousands of people. Its main objective is to generate returns for shareholders, which it does by generating ever larger profits and trying to increase the share price. Generally, its annual report will have to satisfy a wide range of users: the analysts in the financial markets, so that they can encourage institutional funds to buy the shares; the general public, in the sense of creating a public image of responsibility; and governments, to reassure them that the company is honest and meets its commitments (and does not need further statutory surveillance). Transparency in reporting is essential because uncertainties lead investors to demand higher returns and generate tensions with governments and the general public.

From a financial reporting perspective, the two types are quite different animals. The SME has narrow reporting needs, closely linked to taxation, and rarely if ever enters into complex transactions, while the MNC has a wide audience and needs to use the annual report and its financial statements as a major publicity tool both to inform and reassure the world about the activities of the company. Equally, the scope of activities is different: the SME typically has few lines or, indeed, only one line of business, its scale of activity is small and it is usually based in one country; therefore it is relatively easy to see what is going on from its financial statements. The MNC, on the other hand, has many different activities, works in many different currencies and many languages and may well have extremely complex financial and other transactions. A kind of report is needed that can make some attempt to bring together all these different elements and convey some impression of them to users – technically a very demanding challenge!

In terms of regulations, the difference between SME accounting and MNC reports is usually most visible through the difference between individual financial statements and group financial statements (although you should not forget that many small or micro-businesses are not organized as limited liability companies and may only have the most rudimentary of accounts, while some SMEs may operate as groups and have to produce group financial statements). An MNC is usually a combination of very many individual entities, often in a range of product areas and in different countries, operating under some kind of unified management structure. Typically, such a group has sophisticated accounting systems that are capable of providing detailed internal information on a timely basis for management purposes, while maintaining all the usual functions of a financial reporting system as well.

Each individual company in a group has to prepare single company or statutory financial statements that are used, among other things, for tax purposes, and then the group prepares what are called 'consolidated' or group financial statements, which aggregate the data from the individual companies. These consolidated financial statements are what we shall look at from here on. They reflect the financial position, performance and cash flows of an economic entity, not of a legal one. Consolidated financial statements serve the purpose of giving an economic picture of the reporting entity, which is not used for taxation and is therefore free of constraints imposed by tax rules. In many countries, the rules for drawing up consolidated financial statements are separate from those for individual financial statements (although they build on these). In international circles, the accounting rules used are now primarily IFRS Standards – which we use here – although there are, of course, many American MNCs and foreign companies listed in the USA that use those of the US capital markets (the Financial Accounting Standards Board or FASB – US GAAP).

The consolidated financial statements are published each year, generally in a glossy document often running to 100 pages or more. They are usually reproduced on the corporate website as well, sometimes as a complete pdf document but also sometimes as individually accessible sections. This document includes both legally required information and public relations material. It is often known as the *annual report* or the *corporate report*.

Content of the corporate annual report

The contents of the annual report will differ from one company to another – as a result of the non-regulatory parts – but, in general, and you should make sure you study some examples to see this, the average annual report contains the following:

1. *Corporate publicity material.* This is not statutory and not checked by the external auditor. Often this is described as a review of operations and contains a chairman's statement or president's letter. It might run to 50 or more pages, will have lots of photographs and is designed to present a good image of the company. This information should not be discarded by the user – much of it is highly informative and relevant – you should just not expect it to contain too much bad news, even though some companies do try to be much more transparent than others.

2. *Management report.* This can be very confusing, because the publicity material may also include items that are described as a management report. The IFRS Foundation refers to this type of narrative reporting as *management commentary*.

   Take into account, however, that different countries have different regulations and different traditions about narrative disclosures alongside the financial statements. Companies listed in the USA have to provide a 'Management's discussion and analysis' (MD&A), which discusses the year's results in relation to the previous year and future prospects. Some companies listed in the USA include this in the annual report document. Similarly, in the UK large companies are required to prepare an 'Operating and financial review' (OFR).

   In 2010, the International Accounting Standards Board (the Board) issued the practice statement *Management Commentary*, providing a broad, non-binding framework for the presentation of this type of reporting. It is seen as a narrative report that offers a context within which to interpret the performance, position and progress of the company. Management should provide its perspective on the business and its analysis of the interaction of the elements to help users to understand the company's financial statements and to understand management's objectives and strategies for achieving those objectives. The management commentary report should supplement and complement the financial statements with explanations of the financial statement figures and the conditions and events that shaped that information. The standard-setter's practice statement suggests that the management commentary should cover the following essential areas:

   a. Nature of the business

   b. Management's objectives and related strategies

   c. Key resources, risks and relationships

    d. Results of operations and prospects

    e. Critical performance measures and indicators that management uses to evaluate progress in meeting its objectives.

It should be noted, however, that the practice statement is not a mandatory standard. Consequently, companies are not required to comply with the practice statement, unless specifically required by their jurisdiction.

    The EU Accounting Directive also requires companies to publish a formal management report, including a narrative review of the development of the company's business and of its position, together with a description of the principal risks and uncertainties that it faces. Where appropriate, the EU management report should include non-financial key performance indicators relevant to the particular business, including information relating to environmental and employee matters.

    The European Commission's Transparency Directive has extended these disclosures for listed companies with a corporate governance statement in which companies disclose information about their corporate governance practices. Auditors have to verify that the information provided in the management report is consistent with the annual financial statements for the same financial year. However, some EU member states have gone beyond this requirement and made the management report subject to a full audit requirement.

3. *Statement of financial position.* This is as you would expect from your studies to date, but when we extend the concept of financial position of an individual company to that of an international group of companies, a layer of additional issues arises. We will examine these additional issues in the next chapters.

4. *Statement of comprehensive income (or statement of profit or loss and other comprehensive income).* We are already familiar with the statement of profit or loss (income statement/ profit and loss account), but there are extra ramifications of this that are relevant to large companies with a portfolio of subsidiaries and more complex transactions. We will elaborate the extension of the statement of profit or loss later in this chapter.

5. *Statement of changes in equity.* Although this statement is not formally required in all jurisdictions, it is under IFRS Standards. It is a bringing together of information to help the shareholder better understand the changes in equity over the years. IAS 1 *Presentation of Financial Statements* specifies that an analysis should be provided of changes in equity during the year, to include payment of dividends, details of all classes of equity and any changes in these, the net profit or loss for the period and any expenses or income taken directly to equity without passing through the statement of profit or loss. Note that the last are also included in the statement of comprehensive income (statement of profit or loss and OCI).

    Figure 11.1 documents changes in equity and presents them as originating either from transactions with shareholders in their capacity as owners (new share issues, dividend payments, buy-back of shares (treasury shares)) or from transactions with others than shareholders in their capacity as owners (wealth creation by the company's operations). Both transaction types bring about changes in the different classes of equity (share capital, share premium, retained earnings, reserves or accumulated OCI) and these changes are detailed in the statement of changes in equity. There is a definite link with 'comprehensive income', which we will elaborate in the next section.

6. *Statement of cash flows.* As introduced in Chapter 10, this statement shows how the company has generated cash during the period and where that cash has gone. The

statement of cash flows is a very useful analytical tool and is required as a primary statement by IAS 7 *Statement of Cash Flows*. In a multinational group the statement of cash flows will report incoming and outgoing cash flows at the group level.

7. *Summary of significant accounting policies*. Actually a statutory note to the financial statements, but often placed separately by large companies, usually in close proximity to the statement of profit or loss and statement of financial position. Essential first reading when an analyst looks at a set of financial statements because this specifies what set of rules (e.g. IFRS Standards, US GAAP, etc.) have been followed in preparing the financial statements.

8. *Notes to the accounts* (also referred to as 'Notes to the financial statements'). The notes provide essential further analysis of main statement items (including those of the statement of cash flows). For large companies a lot of very useful information is to be found in the notes and they should always be read very carefully.

9. *Auditor's report*. This is sometimes found at the beginning of the financial statements, sometimes at the end, but should always be checked first in case there is anything unusual.

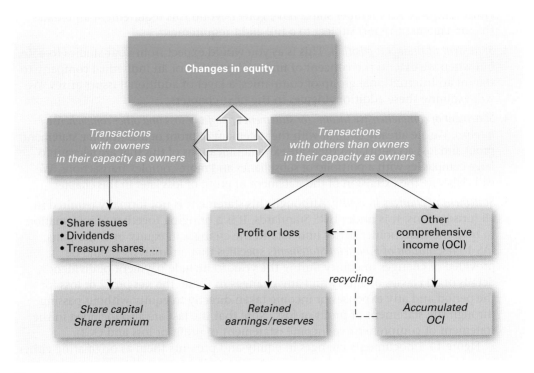

Figure 11.1 Changes in equity

It would be a good idea to look at some examples of corporate reports and try to split them up into these categories – identify the different components – just to make sure you can do so. If you are able to locate the annual report of an SME, this would be a helpful comparative tool. In many countries, the SME has much lighter disclosure requirements than the MNC and most SMEs prefer not to show their financial statements to anyone. In France, Belgium and the UK, any limited company has nonetheless to file a copy of its annual financial statements with a public registry, and so they are in theory available to anyone who wants to look (although late filing is endemic among SMEs). In Germany, SMEs are supposed to file but many do not, while in Switzerland, the file is not open to the public. Generally, therefore, SME financial statements are much more difficult to find and, when you have them, contain much less detail than the financial statements of multinationals.

Publicity document

For the MNC, however, the annual report fulfils a quite different role. As far as statutory and contractual requirements are concerned, the MNC has obligations to publish because of its economic importance and usually because it is listed on one or several stock exchanges. These obligations are typically very stringent. Thereafter, the MNC wishes to influence investors and any signs of opacity or failure to disclose what is regarded as key information will cause investors to become suspicious. When they get suspicious they either do not invest or demand a higher return for their money to compensate the increased risk that is attached when there is uncertainty surrounding the company. For example, if an MNC has potentially polluting manufacturing activities but says nothing about its pollution control in the annual report, investors may fear that there is bad news awaiting in the future with, say, a big bill to clean up a polluted river or compensate a poisoned community.

The annual report of an MNC has come to be a major publicity document. It has great authority as the major formal communication between the group and the outside world, and MNCs build on that to use it to present the company in as positive a light as possible and to explain what the company is doing. In some ways, it represents the company's passport. Aside from its statutory and investor role, the annual report is widely used when making major sales pitches to potential clients, when talking to governments, even when taking on new staff – it is a way of establishing the company's identity, its size, its range of activities, its financial strength.

The annual report is a key document and many large companies automatically include it on their website. This last is potentially a trap for the analyst or student. For the moment there is no regulation as such of financial information on corporate websites. While company law usually requires that, say, income statements and balance sheets are never published without the audit report and the accompanying explanatory notes about accounting policies and so on, it is not always clear that these constraints apply to the internet. Some companies may put only extracts of key financial data on the internet and the analyst should be wary of missing information; and, if in doubt, obtain the published hard copy. That said, of course, the internet is a great way of obtaining corporate data rapidly. You can even access MNCs' filings with the Securities and Exchange Commission (SEC) in the USA which are all made available on the SEC's EDGAR database (www.sec.gov). This gives access not only to the annual report information but also all other data required by the SEC, including MD&A. For a detailed review of a US-listed company, this is a good tool.

Statement of comprehensive income

As we have discussed earlier in this book, there are potentially two ways of approaching the *articulation* between the statement of financial position and the statement of profit or loss. In what we will call the *operating approach*, you measure the company's revenue and deduct from that the expenses incurred (including using-up of assets), and that gives you net income (net profit/net earnings) and the statement of financial position consists of the historical cost of the assets less the amounts deemed to have been used up, and the liabilities incurred to finance them.

In the other approach, which we will call the *asset–liability approach*, you measure the assets and liabilities in the balance sheet, and the sum of all the changes from one balance sheet to the next (other than transactions with shareholders in their capacity of owners, e.g. to issue new shares or pay dividends) is set equal to the income for the period (also called *comprehensive income*).

Note that the resulting income figures under both approaches will not be the same. While the comprehensive income yielded by the asset–liability approach will include the net income under the operating approach, it will also include changes in value of the assets and liabilities that are not derived from operations. For example, if a company owned shares in, say, Apple, which at the earlier balance sheet date were worth $10m at their market price, and at the subsequent balance sheet date the market price had gone up to $12m, this would give an increase in balance sheet values of $2m. This increase would be recognized under comprehensive income, but not in net income under the operating approach.

You should be aware also that when using an asset–liability approach, a measurement basis such as fair value will indeed likely give rise to valuation changes from one balance sheet to the next. IFRS Standards use fair value for some financial instruments which we will look at in Chapter 14.

In the past it had come to be the practice to allow some changes in value not to pass through the statement of profit or loss, but rather to go straight to equity. A significant example of this is the *foreign currency translation difference*. We will look at this in detail in Chapter 13, but the issue is that when you prepare consolidated financial statements, you have to add together the financial statements of companies that may be using different currencies. They all have to be converted ('translated') to a single 'reporting' currency. If exchange rates have moved during the year, this means that there will be a value difference (gain or loss) that has nothing to do with the underlying assets and liabilities, and is essentially temporary and a product of the financial reporting process. These differences were placed directly in equity.

Another example of changes in value going straight to equity are changes in revaluation surplus of tangible non-current assets. This comes from IAS 16 *Property, Plant and Equipment* which allows companies to periodically remeasure such assets at fair value and balance an increase in value of those non-current assets with an increase of the revaluation surplus account in equity, even if in practice companies rarely use this option.

Over time, standard-setters came to feel that although these differences were visible in the financial statements, they were not presented clearly or necessarily in the same place. IFRS Standards now require that value changes that do not pass through profit or loss should be shown immediately after the traditional statement of profit or loss, by adding a section called 'Other comprehensive income' (OCI) so that the two together would add up to total comprehensive income.

Figure 11.2 presents the basic structure of a statement of comprehensive income and highlights its link with the statement of changes in equity. The components of OCI are enumerated in the extract from IAS 1 *Presentation of Financial Statements* (see below).

Figure 11.2 Statement of comprehensive income

IAS 1 *Presentation of Financial Statements* allows a presentation option for the *statement of comprehensive income* (renamed in 2011 as the statement of profit or loss and OCI, although the use of the new terminology is not mandatory):

(a) a single continuous statement, or

(b) two separate but consecutive statements.

Whichever presentation is chosen, the distinction is retained between items recognized in profit or loss and items recognized in OCI. The only difference is that, for the *two-statement approach*, a total is struck in the separate statement of profit or loss at 'profit for the year' (this is the same amount as is presented as a sub-total under the *one-statement approach*). This 'profit for the year' is then the starting point for the statement of profit or loss and OCI, which needs to be presented immediately following the statement of profit or loss.

IAS 1 additionally requires companies to group and present items in OCI on the basis of whether they might at some point in time be reclassified from OCI to profit or loss. Note that Figure 11.1 refers to this reclassification issue as 'recycling'.

So, irrespective of which presentation method is selected, the items of OCI should be classified by nature and grouped into those that:

(a) will not be reclassified subsequently to profit or loss

(b) may be reclassified subsequently to profit or loss when specific conditions are met (in accordance with other IFRS Standards).

This additional presentation requirement makes the potential effect of items of OCI on profit or loss in future periods clearer. The following extracts provide illustrative examples of the alternative presentation formats. They include the split in presentation of OCI according to the reclassification issue.

OTHER COMPREHENSIVE INCOME – DEFINITION

Other comprehensive income comprises items of income and expense (including reclassification adjustments) that are not recognised in profit or loss as required or permitted by other IFRS Standards.

The components of other comprehensive income include:

a. changes in revaluation surplus (see IAS 16 *Property, Plant and Equipment* and IAS 38 *Intangible Assets*);
b. remeasurements of defined benefit plans (see IAS 19 *Employee Benefits*);
c. gains and losses arising from translating the financial statements of a foreign operation (see IAS 21 *The Effects of Changes in Foreign Exchange Rates*);
d. gains and losses from investments in equity instruments measured at fair value through other comprehensive income in accordance with paragraph 5.7.5 of IFRS 9 *Financial Instruments*; d(a) gains and losses on financial instruments measured at fair value through other comprehensive income in accordance with paragraph 4.1.2a of IFRS 9;
e. the effective portion of gains and losses on hedging instruments in a cash flow hedge and the gains and losses on hedging instruments that hedge investments in equity instruments measured at fair value through other comprehensive income in accordance with paragraph 5.7.5 of IFRS 9; and
f. for particular liabilities designated as at fair value through profit or loss, the amount of the change in fair value that is attributable to changes in the liability's credit risk (see paragraph 5.7.7 of IFRS 9).

Source: IAS 1, Presentation of Financial Statements, Extract from para. 7

 PRESENTATION OF PROFIT OR LOSS AND OTHER COMPREHENSIVE INCOME IN ONE STATEMENT

XYZ Group – Statement of profit or loss and other comprehensive income for the year ended 31 December 20X7

(illustrating the presentation of profit or loss and OCI in one statement and the classification of expenses within profit or loss by function)

(in thousands of currency units)	20X7	20X6
Revenue	390,000	355,000
Cost of sales	(245,000)	(230,000)
Gross profit	145,000	125,000
Other income	20,667	11,300
Distribution costs	(9,000)	(8,700)
Administrative expenses	(20,000)	(21,000)
Other expenses	(2,100)	(1,200)
Finance costs	(8,000)	(7,500)
Share of profit of associates	35,100	30,100
Profit before tax	161,667	128,000
Income tax expense	(40,417)	(32,000)
Profit for the year from continuing operations	121,250	96,000
Loss for the year from discontinued operations	—	(30,500)
PROFIT FOR THE YEAR	121,250	65,500
Other comprehensive income:		
Items that will not be reclassified to profit or loss:		
Gains on property revaluation	933	3,367
Investments in equity instruments	(24,000)	26,667
Remeasurements of defined benefit pension plans	(667)	1,333
Share of gain (loss) on property revaluation of associates	400	(700)
Income tax relating to items that will not be reclassified	5,834	(7,667)
	(17,500)	23,000
Items that may be reclassified subsequently to profit or loss:		
Exchange differences on translating foreign operations	5,334	10,667
Cash flow hedges	(667)	(4,000)
Income tax relating to items that may be reclassified	(1,167)	(1,167)
	3,500	5,000
Other comprehensive income for the year, net of tax	(14,000)	28,000
TOTAL COMPREHENSIVE INCOME FOR THE YEAR	107,250	93,500
Profit attributable to:		
Owners of the parent	97,000	52,400
Non-controlling interests	24,250	13,100
	121,250	65,500
Total comprehensive income attributable to:		
Owners of the parent	85,800	74,800
Non-controlling interests	21,450	18,700
	107,250	93,500
Earnings per share (in currency units):		
Basic and diluted	0.46	0.30

Alternatively, items of OCI could be presented in the statement of profit or loss and OCI net of tax.

Source: IAS 1, Presentation of Financial Statements, Extracts from Implementation Guidance

PRESENTATION OF PROFIT OR LOSS AND OTHER
COMPREHENSIVE INCOME IN TWO STATEMENTS

XYZ Group – Statement of profit or loss for the year ended 31 December 20X7

(illustrating the presentation of profit or loss and other comprehensive
income in two statements and the classification of expenses within profit or
loss by nature)

(in thousands of currency units)

	20X7	20X6
Revenue	390,000	355,000
Other income	20,667	11,300
Changes in inventories of finished goods and work in progress	(115,100)	(107,900)
Work performed by the entity and capitalised	16,000	15,000
Raw material and consumables used	(96,000)	(92,000)
Employee benefits expense	(45,000)	(43,000)
Depreciation and amortisation expense	(19,000)	(17,000)
Impairment of property, plant and equipment	(4,000)	—
Other expenses	(6,000)	(5,500)
Finance costs	(15,000)	(18,000)
Share of profit of associates	35,100	30,100
Profit before tax	161,667	128,000
Income tax expense	(40,417)	(32,000)
Profit for the year from continuing operations	121,250	96,000
Loss for the year from discontinued operations	—	(30,500)
PROFIT FOR THE YEAR	121,250	65,500
Profit attributable to:		
Owners of the parent	97,000	52,400
Non-controlling interests	24,250	13,100
	121,250	65,500
Earnings per share (in currency units):		
Basic and diluted	0.46	0.30

XYZ Group – Statement of profit or loss and other comprehensive income for the year ended 31 December 20X7

(illustrating the presentation of profit or loss and OCI in two statements)

(in thousands of currency units)

	20X7	20X6
Profit for the year	121,250	65,500
Other comprehensive income:		
Items that will not be reclassified to profit or loss:		
Gains on property revaluation	933	3,367
Investments in equity instruments	(24,000)	26,667
Remeasurements of defined benefit pension plans	(667)	1,333
Share of gain (loss) on property revaluation of associates	400	700
Income tax relating to items that will not be reclassified	5,834	(7,667)
	(17,500)	23,000
Items that may be reclassified subsequently to profit or loss:		
Exchange differences on translating foreign operations	5,334	10,667
Cash flow hedges	(667)	(4,000)
Income tax relating to items that may be reclassified	(1,167)	(1,667)
	3,500	5,000
Other comprehensive income for the year, net of tax	(14,000)	28,000
TOTAL COMPREHENSIVE INCOME FOR THE YEAR	107,250	93,500
Total comprehensive income attributable to:		
Owners of the parent	85,800	74,800
Non-controlling interests	21,450	18,700
	107,250	93,500

Alternatively, items of OCI could be presented, net of tax.

Source: IAS 1, Presentation of Financial Statements, Extracts from Implementation Guidance

OCI and the IASB *Conceptual Framework*

The IASB *Conceptual Framework* has something to tell about the statement of comprehensive income as well. Although it does not express a preference for a one-statement or two-statement approach for reporting financial performance (one single statement with a separate section of profit or loss or two separate statements), it does, however, describe the *statement of profit or loss* as the primary source of information about a company's financial performance. Furthermore, the *Conceptual Framework* puts forward two additional constraints that limit discretion in putting income and expenses straight to equity:

1. All *income and expenses are presumed to be included in the statement of profit or loss,* unless the Board has reason to decide that excluding certain income and expenses and instead including them in the statement of other comprehensive income provides more relevant and/or more faithfully represented information.

2. Only income and expenses arising from *changes in assets and liabilities that are measured using current values* can be accounted for in OCI.

The assumption that all income and expenses are (eventually) included in the statement of profit or loss means that *income and expenses included in OCI will normally be reclassified* ('recycled') to profit or loss in a future period. Only in exceptional circumstances may the standard-setter decide that such income and expenses will not be reclassified to profit or loss, for example, if there is no clear basis for recycling. This would be done in the individual IFRS Standards. The *Conceptual Framework* views on OCI are brought together in Figure 11.3.

Figure 11.3 Profit or loss and OCI

Analyzing the annual report

Generally speaking, when you first look at a company's report with a view to analyzing the financial statements, we would suggest that you follow this routine:

1. Read the publicity material to get an idea of the company's activities and how it sees them.
2. Check the auditor's report to see if there are any warnings. There are not usually any, because disagreements have been worked out before finalizing the financial statements or the auditors have made sure that adequate information is available elsewhere.
3. Read the summary of the significant accounting policies to see which set of accounting principles has been used and whether there is anything special you should note about the methods used. If you are looking at a European company, remember to check if the company uses IFRS Standards as issued by the IASB or as endorsed by the European Union (EU).
4. Look at the main statements: Statement of profit and loss and OCI, Statement of financial position and Statement of cash flows to get the overall accounting picture.
5. Look at the Statement of changes in equity and the Notes to the statements to get more detail.

Figure 11.4 wraps up the relationships between the primary financial statements and related concepts.

What the practice statement *Management Commentary* recommends as essential areas of management discussion of the company's situation (see earlier in this chapter) is quite a good guide to what the analyst is trying to do – to flesh out the company's strategy, the risks it faces, its investment stance, etc. The analyst should be trying to provide this kind of strategic overview by analyzing the financial statements and related material.

Figure 11.4 Relationships between primary financial statements

Summary

This chapter is a short introduction to the world of the financial information of large, multinational companies listed on the main stock exchanges. These companies use the annual report as a major publicity document; it also has to satisfy many legal disclosure requirements. While the basic financial statements that you already know are still at the core of their financial information package, the MNC publishes 'consolidated' figures – which bring together the sum of all its subsidiaries – to give a world overview. We will look at the techniques for putting these together in the next chapter. Their annual reports include a statement of comprehensive income which comprises value changes that have not passed through the traditional statement of profit or loss. The reports also include much more supplementary information both by way of detail behind the financial statements and of other matters concerning company strategy and activities.

Discussion questions

1. Identify the users and uses of a multinational group's financial statements as opposed to those of a small company.
2. Explain how a management report supplements and complements a company's financial statements.
3. Explain how the concept of comprehensive income is related to profit of the year.
4. Provide four examples of 'OCI' and explain how they meet the definition criteria of income and expense.

CHAPTER 12

Consolidated financial statements

This chapter introduces the concept of consolidated financial statements – also known as group accounts or group financial statements – which are the basis of figures published by multinational corporations. The chapter deals successively with issues such as consolidating wholly owned subsidiaries, goodwill and its measurement, non-controlling interest and the accounting treatment of associates and joint arrangements.

Chapter structure

- Introduction
- Rationale for consolidated financial statements
- Control as trigger for consolidation
- Consolidation basics
- Acquisition method
- Goodwill and its subsequent measurement
- Non-controlling interest
- Consolidated statement of profit or loss
- Associates and joint arrangements
- Additional disclosure on interests in other companies
- Summary
- Discussion questions
- Assignments

Introduction

As discussed in Chapter 11, multinational companies (MNCs) publish an annual report whose accounting numbers are *consolidated financial statements*, often referred to as *group accounts* or *group financial statements*. These are an attempt to represent the whole economic entity, which is the MNC. In effect, they are based on the assumption of an Anglo-Saxon pyramid style of management structure. That is to say, there is a 'head office' management team at the top of a chain of command that extends to the furthest subsidiary. The central management's authority must be respected in all the companies owned by the group.

In practice, modern group structures do not always correspond to this model in all their arrangements. In individual operations, they may have all sorts of shifting arrangements with other companies. There are often alliances with other groups in particular areas. For example, oil companies may form alliances with each other to exploit oil wells or build pipelines, while fighting it out with each other in the high street for retail sales of petrol. These kinds of involvement mean that, at the margin, group financial statements have some difficulty in reflecting the economic realities, but they are still the best implement we have for measuring MNC activities.

Your strategy and economics courses will, if they have not already done so, give you ideas about why companies are organized in groups. However, it is worth just reviewing quickly the main practical reasons.

Group structures

Groups can be organized and structured in different ways. Traditional theory notes that companies tend to develop on either a horizontal or vertical basis. Companies with a vertical basis typically have a production chain for a product that involves:

1. Extraction of raw materials
2. Transport to manufacturing centres
3. Manufacture of products
4. Distribution through wholesale outlets
5. Retailing to consumers.

The description 'vertical' relates to the progress from basic raw materials to final retailing to the consumer. In theory, a company in the manufacturing sector might well expand its activities up and down to control both its raw materials and its retailing, and this would be called a *vertical group*. Examples of this are the major oil companies, which not only extract the oil but also own tanker fleets, refineries and filling stations.

A *horizontal group*, by comparison, expands into different industries united by some similar process or product. For example, a company might manufacture plastic mouldings for motor manufacturers and thus might expand sideways by moving into the manufacture of plastic mouldings for the toy industry. Oil companies may sprout chemical offshoots to exploit the by-products of the oil-refining process.

These two directions are natural lines of development for companies that wish to expand. However, there is a third type of group, the *conglomerate*. The conglomerate diversifies into non-related fields, with the aim of building up a profitable group that draws strength from the fact that it consists of many diverse elements operating in different economic environments. (Finance theory has the concept of a portfolio where diversification across a minimum number of different investments reduces the overall risk of the total holding.)

The advantage to a group of being in several different areas is that when one product is having a bad year, other products should not be so badly affected. A particular disadvantage of the vertical group is that if demand for its final product is depressed, it follows that the whole chain of production is similarly depressed. However, it should be noted that while the diversified conglomerate looks like a good idea on paper, there are few managements that have been equally successful at managing all parts of such groups. But, again, this is a question to pursue within your strategy courses.

Building a group

If a company is going to expand, there are *three main ways* in which the group may be built up: 1) the *development of new subsidiaries* by a company, 2) the acquisition by *takeover* of other companies, and 3) *mergers* between companies. Expansion by takeover has long been a common practice among Anglo-American companies and is also much more common now in Europe, even if the rules in different countries are sometimes an obstacle. There has for some time been a polarization of business with large companies needing to become gigantic in order to compete on a global scale. The 'global' business can command lower costs than smaller, national businesses, through economies of scale.

It does also happen that companies form *joint ventures* with other companies. For example, Sony Ericsson Mobile Communication AB was a joint venture established in 2001 by the Japanese consumer electronics company Sony Corporation and the Swedish telecommunications company Ericsson to produce and market mobile phones. The stated reason for this venture was to combine Sony's consumer electronics expertise with Ericsson's technological leadership in the communications sector. The joint venture operated for more than a decade, but ceased to exist when Sony acquired Ericsson's 50 per cent stake in the joint venture in February 2012. A joint venture like this provides a different kind of vehicle and has its own special accounting rules.

Companies have a need to find new products – business theory suggests that products and businesses have a life cycle. When a company's main product is at a 'mature' stage (when the market is static or beginning to decline, and margins have been pared to the limit), it is time for the company to use the cash the product has generated to look for new products or it will decline and disappear. Large, international companies are therefore constantly buying new companies that either help to build global market share or represent an attempt to find growth products.

COMPANY REPORT

THE ACQUISITION OF REGAL CINEMAS BY CINEWORLD GROUP *(extracts)*

- The Acquisition will create a globally diversified cinema operator across ten countries and allow Cineworld to access the attractive North American cinema market, which has the largest box office market in the world with an industry box office of greater than US$10 billion in each year since 2008 and stable admissions in excess of 1.25 billion in each year over the same period.
- Following completion of the Acquisition ("Completion"), Cineworld and Regal (together, the "Enlarged Group") will have a combined 9,542 screens across the United States and Europe making it the second largest operator in the world (by number of screens).

- Attractive financial effects of the Acquisition:

  - Expected to be strongly accretive to earnings in the first full year following Completion (FY 2019);
  - Cineworld's return on invested capital associated with the Acquisition expected to meet its cost of capital in the first full year after Completion;
  - The Cineworld Board expects to be able to maintain Cineworld's existing dividend policy following Completion, underpinned by the future prospects of the Enlarged Group; and

- The Cineworld Board estimates that, following Completion, the Enlarged Group will be able to achieve annualised pre-tax combination benefits of US$100 million and additional annual structuring benefits of US$50 million.

- Since Cineworld's combination with Cinema City Holding B.V. ("Cinema City") in 2014 (the "Cinema City Combination"), the Cineworld management team has grown EBITDA and revenue in the period FY 2013 to FY 2016 by a compound annual growth rate of 10.2 per cent. and 6.7 per cent., respectively, with an increase in EBITDA margin over the same period. This growth has been achieved by enhancing the customer experience, successfully acquiring new sites, diversifying multiplex offerings, implementing loyalty schemes and adopting a highly disciplined approach to cost. The Cineworld Board believes that the Cineworld management team can replicate this success with the Enlarged Group by implementing similar initiatives within the Regal business to further enhance shareholder value.

Source: Cineworld Group announcement, 5 December 2017

Creating a new subsidiary

The simplest case of group expansion is where a company forms a subsidiary to expand its operations. This may be done for a variety of reasons. For example, it may be that the holding company wants to take on borrowing specifically for a project, and that can most easily be done by putting the project's assets and the associated lending within a separate subsidiary. It gives the lender a clearer sight of the project independently of the rest of the group.

It is often quite useful for management purposes to organize business operations into separate subsidiaries, since one can delegate management responsibility by making the manager of a specific project a director of that subsidiary, thereby giving him or her the legal power to operate the subsidiary effectively; whereas, if there were no subsidiary, the manager would have to be a director of all the group's activities, extending his or her legal authority beyond the required point.

Once a company extends its operations beyond its home country base there are other powerful reasons for forming new subsidiaries in foreign countries. Where a company has a foreign operation it will be subject to foreign tax on the earnings of the foreign operation. That in itself is a highly complex issue but, if there is no local subsidiary, the question of the profit attributable to that operation is even more complex. In a foreign environment, the limitation of liability is still more important and, since the operation is likely to be more remote than a domestic subsidiary, the necessity for clear lines of management responsibility is even stronger. A foreign operation will have to keep records of its transactions in the local currency, and this is sometimes more easily done through a chain of subsidiaries.

Taking over another company

The more noticeable development of groups occurs when one company takes over another pre-existing operation. The reasons for a company to do this are also many and various. If a company is bent on rapid expansion, and has the finance available, there are obvious advantages in acquiring another company that is already trading in the field rather than starting up a totally new company. By takeover, the expanding company gains in one stroke an established market position, working assets and experienced management in that field. Against that it may have to pay a premium to persuade the shareholders of the acquired company that they would benefit from the takeover.

An established public company with a good profit record can frequently take over another company simply by offering to give the shareholders of the acquired company shares in the public company in exchange for their existing shares. If it succeeds in persuading them that this is worthwhile, it has only to issue more shares rather than actually raise additional finance – a very effective way of expanding.

Merging companies

The third form of expansion is that of a *merger*. Since this is the least common form, we will not devote a great deal of time to considering it, but it differs in an essential way from acquisition. Under an acquisition, Company A buys Company B. In effect, it is simply acquiring a new asset in the same way as it might buy a new factory, but at the same time this raises all the usual questions about the valuation of the asset. Under a merger, Company A and Company B are combining their assets to form, in effect, a new, expanded company whose assets and liabilities are the sum of A and B.

It should be mentioned already that, for accounting purposes, the International Accounting Standards Board (the Board) and also the FASB do not accept the existence of a true merger – they claim that it is always possible to identify an acquirer and an acquiree.

Control and levels of influence in a group

We have implied so far that when a company expands, the new companies it acquires will be fully under its control. However, this is not necessarily the case. A company may have different levels of influence over another company in which it has invested.

If Company A buys more than 50 per cent of the shares of Company B, the implication is that, since the shareholders elect the directors and the directors run the company, Company A can fully control Company B by exercising its majority vote. It follows from this that 'control' can exist well short of having 100 per cent ownership of the shares in a subsidiary.

It also follows, however, that if Company A has only 40 per cent of the shares in Company B and the remaining 60 per cent are owned by Company C, Company A may well have no influence at all, since Company C has a voting majority. By contrast, if Company A had 40 per cent, but the remaining 60 per cent was widely dispersed with no one having more than 2 or 3 per cent, Company A would have effective control except where all the other shareholders joined together to frustrate A, which rarely happens in practice.

At the other extreme, Company A might have only a token shareholding of 10 per cent and have no effective influence whatsoever on Company B. You can see that outside a situation where an investor company owns a clear majority of the shares in a second company, the question of the degree of influence exerted by one company over another is difficult to assess.

ROCHE – ACCOUNTING POLICIES *(extract)*

Consolidation policy

Subsidiaries are all companies over which the Group has control. The Group controls an entity when the Group is exposed to, or has rights to, variable returns from its involvement with the entity and has the ability to affect those returns through its power over the entity. Companies acquired during the year are consolidated from the date on which control is transferred to the Group, and subsidiaries to be divested are included up to the date on which control passes from the Group. Inter-company balances, transactions and resulting unrealised income are eliminated in full. Changes in ownership interests in subsidiaries are accounted for as equity transactions if they occur after control has already been obtained and if they do not result in a loss of control. Associates are companies over which the Group exercises, or has the power to exercise, significant influence, but which it does not control and they are accounted for using the equity method.

Source: Roche Group, Finance Report, 2018

Rationale for consolidated financial statements

If we take the basic case of a group that has wholly owned subsidiaries – the most common situation – the question arises: 'What is the purpose of producing group financial statements?'

The main argument for consolidated financial statements is that, although a group may operate through a whole network of theoretically independent legal entities, the fact of real control by a central holding company means that, economically, there may well be only one real entity. (Note, however, that the rationale for consolidated financial statements depends on the pyramid concept of management structure where there is centralized control. It does not work for groups of linked companies with no central economic control, such as Japanese keiretsu.)

It follows that to appreciate the strength of this economic entity it is not sufficient to look only at the holding company: one must look at the total assets and liabilities under the unified control and disregard the legal entities.

A potential investor who looks only at the holding company financial statements might very easily be misled as to the strength of the group. To take a very simple case, Company H, a holding company, might be constituted so that all its trading operations are channeled through a single subsidiary, Company X, which also contains all the operating assets and liabilities. The statement of financial position below shows how the balance sheet of the two companies might look.

	Company H €'000	Company X €'000	H Group €'000
Property, plant and equipment	500	1,000	1,500
Investment in subsidiary	500	—	—
Current assets	250	350	600
Total assets	1,250	1,350	2,100
Share capital	500	500	500
Retained earnings	300	(50)	250
	800	450	750
Long-term debt	300	700	1,000
Trade payables	150	200	350
Total equity and liabilities	1,250	1,350	2,100
Debt/equity ratio	37.5%	155%	133%

If a potential investor looks only at Company H's statement of financial position, he or she could have no idea of the underlying asset and liability structure. The company has a 37.5 per cent debt/equity ratio, so the potential investor would probably regard it as a relatively low-risk company. However, if the financial statements are consolidated (and in essence this just involves adding together the statements of all the companies in the group: the investment cost of the subsidiaries in the parent company statement of financial position is replaced by the assets and liabilities actually acquired), and the 'investment in subsidiary' of €500,000 is replaced by the assets and liabilities of Company X, the statement of financial position looks very different. From the consolidated financial statements, the investor could see that in fact the group is very highly geared; that is, it has a large amount of debt outstanding, and the losses made by Company X are reflected in the group profit and loss.

The view that an investor might have of Company H is quite different according to whether it is the consolidated financial statements or simply those of the holding company that are seen, and this is the reason for preparing consolidated financial statements. They give a picture of the economic entity rather than the legal entity: they provide information that is more useful in investment decision-making.

The technique of consolidated accounting for groups was not put forward until the early part of the twentieth century, by contrast with much of basic company accounting, which stems from the second half of the nineteenth century. In the European Union (EU), rules for consolidated financial statements are set by the EU Accounting Directive. One commonly finds that the annual report of a European company includes two sets of financial statements: the consolidated financial statements and the parent company's statutory financial statements, with the latter still largely influenced by tax rules.

Meanwhile, with the spread of IFRS Standards, consolidation practices of listed companies have become globally harmonized to a large extent. The main rules governing the preparation of consolidated financial statements are covered in IFRS 10 *Consolidated Financial Statements* and in IFRS 3 *Business Combinations*.

Control as trigger for consolidation

IFRS 10 *Consolidated Financial Statements* identifies 'control' as the basis for consolidation. A company (as investor) is required to consolidate an investee (the investment), if it controls the investee. IFRS 10 provides the following definition of *control*: 'An investor controls an investee when the investor is exposed, or has rights, to variable returns from the involvement with the investee and has the ability to affect those returns through its power over the investee' (IFRS 10, para. 6). Control gives rise to a *parent-subsidiary relationship*.

The IFRS 10 definition of control comprises *three essential criteria* (see also Figure 12.1):

1. *Power to direct* – Does the investor have the current ability to direct activities that significantly affect an investee's returns?
2. *Exposure*, or rights, *to variable returns* from an investee.
3. *Linkage between power and returns* – Ability of the investor to use its power to affect its returns of the investee.

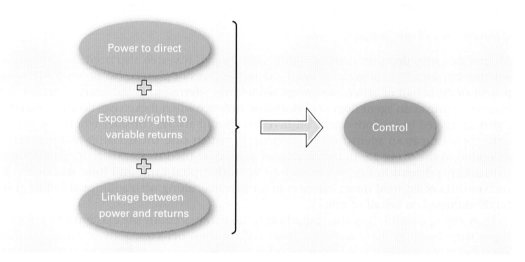

Figure 12.1 Elements of the definition of control

Power

An investor has power over an investee when the investor has existing rights that give it the *current ability to direct* the so-called *relevant activities*, i.e. the activities that significantly affect the investee's returns. Power arises from rights. Assessing power can be straightforward, such as when power over an investee derives directly and solely from the *voting rights granted by shareholdings* (control will exist when an investor holds > 50 per cent of an investee's voting rights). In other cases, the assessment will be more complex and require more than one factor to be considered, such as when power results from *contractual arrangements*. For example, a contractual agreement may enable an investor to direct enough other shareholders on how to vote in order to obtain relevant power. In another context, an investee could be designed so that voting rights are not the dominant factor in decision-making, such as when any voting rights relate to administrative tasks only and the relevant activities are directed by means of contractual arrangements. Large minority holders may also engender power when other shareholdings are widely dispersed, and an investor holds significantly more voting rights than any other shareholder or group of shareholders.

Returns

An investor is exposed, or has rights, to *variable returns* from its involvement with the investee when the investor's returns from its involvement have the potential to *vary as a result of the investee's performance*. The investor's returns can be positive or negative. Returns can be synergistic as well as more direct such as dividends or changes in the value of an investment.

Linkage between power and returns

An investor controls an investee if the investor not only has power over the investee and exposure or rights to variable returns from its involvement with the investee, but also has the ability to use its *power to affect the investor's returns* from its involvement with the investee.

Control – other issues

An investor with decision-making rights regarding an investee also needs to determine whether he/she acts as *principal or agent* – does the investor exercise his power for its own benefit or on behalf of others (a concept sometimes referred to as 'fiduciary control'). An investor acting as an agent does not control an investee when it exercises decision-making rights delegated to it. Conversely, an investor should always consider whether another entity is acting as an agent for the investor, in which case the decision-making rights delegated to the agent are to be considered as held by the investor directly. This issue is particularly relevant to businesses such as venture capital firms and fund managers, as such entities often hold direct interests in an investee, along with additional holdings in funds managed on behalf of others.

In assessing control, it is also important to take into account the existence of *potential voting rights*, such as share warrants, share call options, debt or equity instruments that are convertible into ordinary shares, or other similar instruments that have the potential, if exercised or converted, to provide the investor incremental voting power or reduce another party's voting power with regard to the investee's relevant activities.

IFRS 10 *Consolidated Financial Statements* requires that consolidation of an investee starts from the date the investor obtains control of the investee and ceases when the investor loses control. IFRS 10 is applicable to all types of investee, including structured entities (also called 'special purpose vehicles') in which the relevant activities are mainly directed by contractual arrangement (and not through voting right mechanisms) and more conventional voting interest entities, to determine which are to be consolidated.

Consolidation basics

The essence of consolidation as accounting treatment is that the assets and liabilities of the holding company and its subsidiaries should be treated as though they were a single entity. The rationale is that, if the holding company controls the assets and liabilities of other companies, then the difference between the individual legal entities should be set aside and the economic whole should be treated as though it were a single company.

This means that instead of showing in the holding company's statement of financial position the amount invested in a subsidiary, we substitute the assets and liabilities of the subsidiary companies. In essence, this is simple enough, but it gives rise to certain problems where the holding company's investment is different in value to the net worth (net value of assets less liabilities) in the subsidiary, or where the holding company owns less than 100 per cent of the shares in the subsidiary.

We will illustrate the accounting solutions in a series of examples that will deal with the individual aspects of different situations and will concentrate on the balance sheet effects (and deal with the consolidated profit or loss later). First, let us look at the basic case, where the holding company's (Holding) investment in the subsidiary (Sub) exactly coincides with the value of the net assets (or equity) in the subsidiary. This would happen where the holding company has formed a subsidiary and subscribed to all the subsidiary's shares.

In order to prepare consolidated financial statements, the *investment by the holding company* is *eliminated and replaced by the assets and liabilities of the subsidiary*. In the example below, a parent company (Holding) has an investment of €25m in a subsidiary (Sub). This investment is represented by €30m of assets and €5m of current liabilities which are in Sub's statement of financial position. For consolidation we put Sub's assets and liabilities into Holding's statement of financial position to replace the investment asset. We look through the investment to the assets and liabilities it represents. In calculating consolidated statements of financial position this is usually done by putting the balance sheets alongside each other, eliminating the parent company's investment against the subsidiary company's equity, and then adding the remaining balance sheet items across (see below):

	Holding €m	Sub €m	Elimination €m	Group €m
Property, plant and equipment	100	20	—	120
Investment in subsidiary	25	—	(25)	—
Current assets	30	10	—	40
Total assets	155	30	(25)	160
Share capital	70	25	(25)	70
Retained earnings	30	—	—	30
	100	25	(25)	100
Current liabilities	15	5	—	20
Long-term liabilities	40	—	—	40
Total equity and liabilities	155	30	(25)	160

The elimination column shows how the investment in Sub has been cancelled out against the net worth of the subsidiary (in this case entirely represented by the share capital of the subsidiary) and then the assets and liabilities have been added across – thus effectively substituting the assets and liabilities of Sub, which have a net value of €25m, for Holding's investment in Sub of €25m. This kind of working paper is classic for consolidation – of course, it lends itself easily to a computer spreadsheet application.

Presenting a financial picture of a group as if it were a single entity, also means that *intragroup transactions* and *intra-group balances* need to be eliminated (cancelled) as part of the consolidation process. For example, if one company within the group sells its products to another company of the same group, the seller will record the sale in its revenue and the same amount will end up in the cost of sales of the buyer. Moreover, if the invoice has not been paid yet, the buyer will have a trade payable and the seller a trade receivable in its statement of financial position. Another example would be where a parent company provides an interest-bearing loan to a subsidiary. In this case, the parent will treat the loan as a financial investment with any interest received accounted for as income, whereas the subsidiary will show the loan as a financial liability and interest paid as a finance expense. From the point of view of the group as a single entity, these transactions do not exist and have to be eliminated: intra-group balances at reporting date of receivables and liabilities will be eliminated in the consolidated statement of financial position and related income, expenses and profits in the consolidated statement of profit or loss (see more later in this chapter).

These consolidation basics have been further developed in a set of rules known as the *acquisition method*. The IFRS® acquisition accounting rules are covered in IFRS 3 *Business Combinations*. These complement the consolidation requirements as found in IFRS 10 *Consolidated Financial Statements*.

Acquisition method

The *acquisition method* (or *purchase method*) is the accounting method to be used for business combinations – when a company acquires another company (or another business) and the separate businesses have to be brought together in one set of consolidated financial statements for the first time.

A *business combination* is defined as an event in which an acquirer obtains control of another business (the acquiree). Because a business combination always subsumes an acquirer and an acquiree, it is accounted for as the acquisition (or purchase) of a set of net assets. Note that these net assets do not necessarily have to constitute a legal entity, but they have to represent an economically viable bundle of assets and related activities (a separate business).

An essential element of a business combination is the *transition of control* (as defined in IFRS 10 *Consolidated Financial Statements* – see above). A business combination implies the transition of control over a business from one party to another, with the acquirer being the one who obtains control. The timing of the transition of control is also essential in establishing when exactly the acquisition takes place (the *acquisition date*).

The core principle of IFRS 3 is that the acquirer of a business recognizes the assets and liabilities of the acquired business at their fair values at acquisition date and discloses information that enable users to evaluate the nature and the financial effects of the acquisition. We will explain the main recognition and measurement rules of the acquisition method building on a basic example.

Consolidation difference at acquisition date

The primary example of a business combination is the classic takeover, where one company buys the shares of another and takes over the management of the acquired company.

From a consolidation perspective, this may lead to a technical issue when eliminating the acquisition cost of the shares in the parent company's accounts. In the example above, the value of the 'investment in subsidiary' in the parent company agreed with the initial capital of the subsidiary, because the parent started the subsidiary and supplied its share capital. However, when a company buys the shares of an existing company, it is usually paying the existing shareholders to hand over their shares – the money does not go to the acquired company and there is no link between the value of the investment as it appears in the parent's statement of financial position and the book value of equity in the subsidiary. They will be different amounts, and that leaves us with a difference between the two which is a core issue in preparing consolidated financial statements.

STANDARDS

IFRS 3 – DEFINITION OF A BUSINESS *(extract)*

A business is an integrated set of activities and assets that is capable of being conducted and managed for the purpose of providing goods or services to customers, generating investment income (such as dividends or interest) or generating other income from ordinary activities.

Source: IFRS 3, Business Combinations

When one company takes over another, it usually pays a price for the shares that is related to its expectations of future profit potential and not to the book value of the shares. Consequently, the book value is usually different from the purchase price and an adjustment is required when preparing group financial statements to deal with this difference. It is known as *consolidation difference*, or goodwill arising on consolidation.

The acquiree's equity value has to be assessed at acquisition date, including reserves and accumulated profits until that date. When a holding company buys another company, the latter will usually have accumulated reserves and retained earnings in its equity at acquisition date. These equity components of the acquired company are called *pre-acquisition reserves* and must be offset against the investment in the subsidiary in preparing the consolidated financial statements.

In the following example, we have the statements of financial position of the Holding company and its subsidiary Sub at the acquisition date. Holding has paid €38m for 100 per cent of the shares in Sub whose net assets value (or equity value) is €25m. The consolidation adjustments are as follows:

	Holding €m	Sub €m	Elimination €m	Group €m
Property, plant and equipment	100	20	—	120
Investment in subsidiary	38	—	(38)	
Goodwill	—	—	13	13
Current assets	17	10	—	27
Total assets	155	30	(25)	160
Share capital	70	20	(20)	70
Retained earnings	30	5	(5)	30
	100	25	(25)	100
Current liabilities	15	5	—	20
Long-term liabilities	40	—	—	40
Total equity and liabilities	155	30	(25)	160

Note that the €13m 'goodwill' figure is simply the difference between the investment in the subsidiary at its worth in the parent company's financial statements and the carrying value of the equity of the subsidiary in its statement of financial position at the time of acquisition. Note also that the €5m of retained earnings included in equity at acquisition date are frozen for group accounting purposes at that moment as pre-acquisition reserves. Retained earnings generated later from profits of the subsidiary after acquisition will flow through to the consolidated statement of financial position and increase group retained earnings, but the €5m at the moment of acquisition will always disappear in the consolidation adjustment.

STANDARDS

 IFRS 3 – THE ACQUISITION METHOD *(extracts)*

4. An entity shall account for each business combination by applying the acquisition method.

5. Applying the acquisition method requires:

   (a) identifying the acquirer;
   (b) determining the acquisition date;
   (c) recognising and measuring the identifiable assets acquired, the liabilities assumed and any non-controlling interest in the acquiree; and
   (d) recognising and measuring goodwill or a gain from a bargain purchase.

6. For each business combination, one of the combining entities shall be identified as the acquirer.

8. The acquirer shall identify the acquisition date, which is the date on which it obtains control of the acquiree.

10. As of the acquisition date, the acquirer shall recognise, separately from goodwill, the identifiable assets acquired, the liabilities assumed and any non-controlling interest in the acquiree. (…)

18. The acquirer shall measure the identifiable assets acquired and the liabilities assumed at their acquisition-date fair values.

32. The acquirer shall recognise goodwill as of the acquisition date measured as the excess of (a) over (b) below:

   (a) the aggregate of:

      (i) the consideration transferred measured in accordance with this IFRS Standard, which generally requires acquisition-date fair value;

      (ii) the amount of any non-controlling interest in the acquiree measured in accordance with this IFRS Standard; and

      (iii) in a business combination achieved in stages, the acquisition-date fair value of the acquirer's previously held equity interest in the acquiree.

   (b) the net of the acquisition-date amounts of the identifiable assets acquired and the liabilities assumed measured in accordance with this IFRS Standard.

Source: IFRS 3, Business Combinations

Recognition and fair value adjustments of acquired assets and liabilities

At this stage of our basic example, we calculated goodwill based on the carrying value of the acquiree's net assets as they figure in the individual financial statements of the acquired company at acquisition date. IFRS 3 does, however, demand some preliminary adjusting of the acquiree's net asset position before the consolidation process can effectively take place.

When first preparing the accounts of the new subsidiary for consolidation, the parent must review the individual assets and liabilities of the acquired company and make *two kinds of adjustment of the acquired company's assets and liabilities*:

1. Recognize any additional assets and liabilities that are not carried on the acquiree's statement of financial position but represent economic substance to the acquirer (IFRS 3, para. 10).

2. Adjust the carrying amounts of the acquiree's assets and liabilities to their fair value at acquisition date (IFRS 3, para. 18).

Through these additional adjustments, parts of the consolidation difference that we determined in the previous section will be allocated to identifiable assets and liabilities of the acquired company.

Recognizing additional assets and liabilities

Part of the consolidation difference may relate to intangible assets, such as a brand name, a patent or a customer relationship, that the acquiree did not recognize as assets in its financial statements because it developed them internally and charged the related costs to profit or loss. Recognizing an additional intangible will, however, affect goodwill.

For example, company Alfa pays €200m for company Beta whose book value of net assets at acquisition date is €100m. Company Beta has a single product, HHH, which is a household name. As a first approximation, the goodwill might be set at €100m. However, if Alfa recognizes the HHH brand as an asset in the consolidated statement of financial position at €75m, this means goodwill becomes €200m less net assets €100m less brand €75m or €25m.

In determining whether, at the acquisition date, an item not previously recognized by the acquiree but deemed to have economic substance, has to be recognized as part of the business combination, one should first check whether the item meets the definitions of assets and liabilities in the IASB *Conceptual Framework*.

For example, reorganization expenses that the acquirer expects to incur in the future to affect its plan to exit an activity of an acquiree or to terminate the employment of or relocate employees, is a typical item that tends to pop up in acquisitions. However, if the acquirer is not obliged to incur such reorganization expenses, there is no present obligation at acquisition date and thus no extra liability. Therefore, the acquirer cannot recognize those expected costs as an additional reorganization provision in the business combination.

Adjusting acquired assets and liabilities to their fair value at acquisition date

What this remeasurement requirement means is that the bundle of acquired assets and liabilities is valued as at the date of the takeover, and that only the remaining difference between the revalued identifiable net assets and the investment by the parent will finally be accounted for as goodwill.

The rationale for revaluing the acquired assets and liabilities is that they are being purchased by the new parent company and historical cost, viewed from the parent, runs from the date the parent acquired them, not the date at which they were acquired by the company which the parent has acquired. This seems perfectly reasonable. Recall that fair value is a concept near to current market value.

Note that both kinds of consolidation adjustment can only appear in the consolidated financial statements; they are not entered into the accounting records of the subsidiary. This means that they have to be reassessed and re-entered whenever subsequent consolidated financial statements are prepared. Moreover, some of these adjustments need a close follow-up in time.

For example, if a new intangible with a useful life of five years has been recognized as part of the business combination, the intangible (existing only in the consolidation files) has to be amortized over its useful life, with the periodic amortization expense to be accounted for as an extra consolidation adjustment.

As another example, assume that one of the fair value adjustments relates to a depreciating tangible asset (like PP&E). In the post-acquisition period the depreciation of the acquired tangible asset must be based on its fair value at acquisition date. However, in the subsidiary's own (individual) financial statements, depreciation will go on based on the original historical cost of the asset. So, in the consolidation files both the fair value adjustment and a fair value depreciation adjustment are required.

To pursue the mechanics of this with our basic example, let us assume that the consolidation adjustments at acquisition date involve recognizing an intangible asset worth €8m and increasing the value of the non-current tangible assets to a fair value of €22m. This would give the adjustments shown below:

	Book value of Sub €m	Adjustment €m	Fair value balance sheet €m
Non-current assets			
– Intangibles	—	8	8
– Property, plant and equipment	20	2	22
Current assets	10	—	10
Total assets	30	10	40
Share capital	20	—	20
Retained earnings	5	10	15
	25	10	35
Current liabilities	5	—	5
Total equity and liabilities	30	10	40

When the revised figures are built into the consolidated financial statements with the holding company, this will give rise to an adjusted goodwill value. It is this figure that will finally end up in the consolidated financial statements as goodwill:

	Holding €m	Revised Sub €m	Elimination €m	Group €m
Non-current assets				
– Goodwill	—	—	3	3
– Other intangibles	—	8	—	8
– Property, plant and equipment	100	22	—	122
Investment in subsidiary	38	—	(38)	—
Current assets	17	10	—	27
Total assets	155	40	(35)	160
Share capital	70	20	(20)	70
Retained earnings	30	15	(15)	30
	100	35	(35)	100
Current liabilities	15	5	—	20
Long-term liabilities	40	—	—	40
Total equity and liabilities	155	40	(35)	160

Goodwill and its subsequent measurement

It should be clear by now that *goodwill is a residual*: it arises as the residual portion of the purchase price of the investment and cannot be individually identified. Being a residual, the question remains as to whether the goodwill figure can really be regarded as an asset (i.e. does it meet the definition of an asset and the recognition criteria?) and, if it is an asset, whether it should be systematically depreciated or periodically tested for impairment.

One could take the view that there is no relationship between the cost of the investment (the cost that the new parent incurred in buying the subsidiary) and the accounting value of the subsidiary, so that goodwill is a meaningless figure. It is almost as though you said the distance from Zurich to Vienna is 600 kilometres, while the distance from Zurich to Geneva is 400 kilometres, so what is the difference of 200? Whatever it may be, it is not the distance between Geneva and Vienna. If goodwill is just a meaningless difference, then it should be labelled as such in the statement of financial position, perhaps, and left alone.

However, the standard rationale for accounting for goodwill is that the purchase price of the new subsidiary's shares represents the cost of acquiring a bundle of assets and liabilities. This cost should be allocated over all identifiable assets acquired and liabilities assumed and, if there is an excess, this is goodwill and represents 'intangible' assets such as know-how, client goodwill, etc. to which no accounting value can be reliably attributed. In this vein, IFRS 3 *Business Combinations* defines goodwill as *future economic benefits arising from the acquired assets that are not capable of being individually identified and separately recognized*. Its value stems mainly from the synergies of the net assets of the acquiree and from the expected synergies and other benefits from combining the net assets of the acquired company with those of the acquirer. This 'core goodwill' represents resources from which future economic benefits are expected to flow to the entity.

The second question is whether, having identified goodwill as an intangible asset, it should be subject to a systematic amortization scheme or to a periodic impairment test.

Initially, IFRS Standards opted for an *amortization approach*, with acquired goodwill to be amortized on a systematic basis over the best estimate of its useful life. There was a rebuttable presumption that its useful life did not exceed 20 years from initial recognition. However, systematic amortization of goodwill has been an annoying accounting rule for companies with an aggressive acquisition strategy. Clearly, if goodwill is capitalized and amortized, an aggressive company will find that its measured profits from an acquisition are being reduced by the amortization charge. This is not popular with managements who are trying to justify a takeover by showing enhanced profitability (research into takeovers actually shows that practically all acquirers pay too much money and the people who gain most are the original shareholders in the acquired company). The amortization approach has the advantage of being a well-understood practice, due to its simplicity and transparency but, by the same token, it has the awkward side-effect of creating too much rigidity in subsequent accounting for the effects of goodwill on profit or loss.

IFRS 3 *Business Combinations* abandoned the amortization requirements and introduced an *impairment approach* – goodwill is to be tested for impairment annually or more frequently if events or changes in circumstances indicate that it might be impaired. Consequently, goodwill is measured at cost less any accumulated impairment losses. Note, however, that the EU Accounting Directive and related national GAAP have not been affected by these changes and still require goodwill to be amortized over its useful life.

The impairment approach for goodwill introduces quite a fastidious and recurrent impairment testing process. We introduced impairment testing in Chapter 6. Impairment testing requirements are covered by IAS 36 *Impairment of Assets*. They call for a comparison of the carrying value of the asset with its recoverable amount. Where the carrying amount of the asset is higher than its recoverable amount, the asset is impaired.

Because goodwill, by its nature, does not generate cash flows independently from other assets or groups of assets, the recoverable amount has to be determined at the level of the cash-generating unit (CGU) to which it belongs. This means that goodwill should first be allocated to particular CGUs. If this cannot be done on a consistent and reasonable basis, the goodwill will be identified with a group of CGUs. The goodwill will then be part of the total carrying amount of the group of CGUs, which will be compared with the recoverable amount at the same organizational level.

An impairment charge should be recognized if the carrying value (including the allocated goodwill) is higher than the recoverable amount of the group of CGUs. An impairment charge calculated at the CGU level will first be allocated to the goodwill associated with the CGU (or group of CGUs) and, second, to the other non-monetary assets existing at that level in proportion to their carrying amounts.

For example, a CGU for which the recoverable amount has been estimated at €48m, comprises the following (allocated) assets:

	Carrying value €m
Goodwill	10
Property	40
Plant and equipment	20
	70

After impairment testing the net carrying values of these assets will become:

	Goodwill €m	Property €m	Plant and equipment €m	Total €m
Carrying value before impairment	10	40	20	70
Impairment loss	(10)	(8)	(4)	(22)
Carrying value after impairment	0	32	16	48

The impairment loss of €22m (i.e. the difference between the recoverable amount of the CGU and its carrying value) is first allocated to goodwill (reduced to zero) and next to the carrying amount of the other assets pro rata the relative carrying value of each asset. The reductions in the carrying amount of the individual assets are treated as an impairment loss. However, the carrying amount of any individual asset should not be reduced below the highest of its fair value less costs of disposal, its value in use and zero. If this is the case for an individual asset, the impairment loss not allocated to the individual asset will be allocated on a pro rata basis to the other assets of the CGU.

The costs of such impairment reviews are likely to be high compared to a relatively straightforward amortization procedure. Especially determining the recoverable amount and, more specifically, the value in use of a CGU may be an extensive and time-consuming exercise. While the amortization method is quite successful in targeting the acquired goodwill and making management accountable for its expenditures on goodwill, the impairment-only method is more a valuation approach rather than an accountability approach.

The impairment approach is arguably inconsistent with the general position of IAS 38 *Intangible Assets* that internally generated goodwill should not be recognized. Across the impairment test, it will be quite impossible to separate the acquired goodwill from the internally generated goodwill of the acquiring company at the acquisition date and from the internal goodwill of the business combination built up after the acquisition date. Also, acquired activities are often reorganized and combined into existing activities of the acquiring company, making any distinction difficult. If a clean separation is not possible, different kinds of goodwill will be mixed, probably leading to cushions against recognizing impairment losses that have in fact occurred in respect of the acquired goodwill. If the consumption of the acquired goodwill is not accounted for, this engenders a situation where in fact internally generated goodwill is recognized as an asset up to the amount of the initially recognized acquired goodwill. Moreover, if a business combination is so successful that the recoverable amount of a CGU to which goodwill has been allocated continues to exceed its carrying amount, the goodwill allocated to that unit will continue indefinitely to be recognized at its fair value at the acquisition date.

If the impairment test of goodwill proves positive, the impact of the impairment on the consolidated statement of profit or loss has to be taken at once. At the time of the bursting of the internet bubble, some groups had to take massive write-offs. After impairment testing of the goodwill that had arisen when AOL and Time Warner combined, the company had to take a $100bn impairment loss against its goodwill account, basically admitting that the acquisition had been severely overpriced and that AOL had nearly no value.

Non-controlling interest

In preparing our consolidations so far we have used an example where the holding company owns 100 per cent of the shares of its subsidiary (company Sub). Although this is often the case, it is not always so – companies may sometimes have less than 100 per cent of the shares in the subsidiary. The reason might be political: in some foreign countries the government insists that where a multinational wishes to set up a local operation it should be done in partnership with either the foreign government or with local business people. Another reason might be operational – the company wishes to work in partnership with someone else in order to have access to their technical expertise etc.

As far as accounting treatment goes, ownership of less than 100 per cent of the shares presents a problem. If the basic idea is to present an economic picture which gives an overview of the group activities, consolidating 60 per cent of a factory where one owns 60 per cent of the company that runs it, does not really give the whole picture. Showing that the factory is part of the group but is financed in part by outside shareholders gives a more complete picture of the situation.

Accounting standards take the view that where a company has control of another, then it has effective control of all the assets and liabilities, even though the ownership of some part of the company is in other hands. Accordingly, the procedure is that the holding company consolidates all the assets and liabilities, but acknowledges the outside interest with a separate component of group equity, called *non-controlling interest* or *minority interest*.

But then the question pops up whether the non-controlling interest should affect goodwill or not. In this respect, IFRS 3 *Business Combinations* allows two alternatives: the 'partial goodwill' method and the 'full goodwill' method. Under the *partial goodwill method*, the non-controlling interest is recognized at its share of the identifiable net assets and does not include any goodwill. The non-controlling interest is recorded by reference to its share of the fair value of the assets and liabilities of the acquired entity at acquisition date. If any recognition or fair value adjustments are booked in the consolidation process, the non-controlling interest takes part in these adjustments. The *full goodwill method* on the other hand will recognize goodwill for the non-controlling interest in a subsidiary as well as the controlling interest. The full goodwill method implies that the non-controlling interest and the goodwill are both increased by the goodwill that relates to the non-controlling interest.

Let us first apply the *partial goodwill method* (which has been the standard method in the past). Assuming that the acquiring company L had bought only 80 per cent of the subsidiary M, paying €600,000 and no additional fair value adjustments, the consolidation would be:

Pre-acquisition equity in the subsidiary is worth €400,000, so company L's share is €320,000 (80 per cent) and the non-controlling interest is worth €80,000 (20 per cent), based on the split of share ownership. Company L actually paid €600,000, so it must recognize goodwill of €280,000 (€600K − €320K). In the consolidation adjustments we cancel the pre-acquisition equity of company M as usual, but the counter-adjustment is to create a new line called non-controlling interest of €80,000, as well as offsetting L's part of the equity against its investment.

Under the *full goodwill method*, one would add the difference between the fair value (at acquisition date) of the non-controlling interest and the amount established under the partial goodwill method to goodwill and to the value of the non-controlling interest. Measuring the non-controlling interest at fair value may prove difficult in practice. It does not suffice to extrapolate partial goodwill to 100 per cent of the outstanding shares, as the fair value of the controlling interest usually includes a control premium whereas the fair value of the minority interest does not. Sometimes an acquirer will be able to measure it on the basis of active market prices for the equity shares not held by the acquirer. In other situations, however, an active market price for the equity shares will not be available and other valuation techniques will have to be used:

	Company L €'000	Company M €'000	Elimination €'000	Group €'000
Goodwill	—	—	280	280
Property, plant and equipment	1,200	300	—	1,500
Investment in M	600	—	(600)	—
Current assets	550	225	—	775
Total assets	2,350	525	(320)	2,555
Share capital	800	300	(300)	800
Retained earnings	1,150	100	(100)	1,150
Non-controlling interest			80	80
	1,950	400	(320)	2,030
Current liabilities	200	125	—	325
Long-term liabilities	200	—	—	200
Total equity and liabilities	2,350	525	(320)	2,555

Note that under US GAAP, the non-controlling interest must always be measured at fair value, and full goodwill is always recognized.

Consolidated statement of profit or loss

We have so far concentrated primarily on the statement of financial position, since this is perhaps the more difficult aspect of consolidated financial statements to understand, but the *consolidated statement of profit or loss* (consolidated income statement/consolidated profit and loss account) also has its own technical challenges. In preparing a consolidated statement of profit or loss, *consolidation-specific items* of income and expense have to be added, while *intra-group items* of income and expense have to be eliminated.

You will have seen that the consolidated statement of profit or loss includes charges such as depreciation of fair value adjustments or impairment losses on goodwill that do not appear in the financial statements of the individual companies making up the group. At the same time, the consolidated statement of profit or loss excludes a number of expenses and revenues that are to be found in the individual companies – essentially all those that involve trading with another company within the group.

Most groups have quite a large number of transactions that are with other members of the same group. If these were not eliminated, the consolidated financial statements would potentially include the same transaction many times over. Imagine a vertically integrated company growing cocoa beans in subsidiary A, manufacturing chocolate in subsidiary B and then selling this through wholesaler C in another country. You might have the following figures:

	Expenses	Revenue	Profit
Subsidiary A			
Expenses	1,200	—	—
Sales to B	—	1,500	—
Profit	—	—	300
Subsidiary B			
Purchases from A	1,500	—	—
Other expenses	5,000	—	—
Sales to C	—	7,500	—
Profit	—	—	1,000
Subsidiary C			
Purchases from B	7,500	—	—
Other expenses	500	—	—
Sales to retailers	—	8,500	—
Profit	—	—	500
Totals	15,700	17,500	1,800

If you aggregate the figures, you will have a consolidated statement of profit or loss like this:

Revenue	17,500
Expenses	15,700
Profit	1,800

However, a large part of the revenue and the expenses are within the group and are double counted:

Sales from A to B	1,500
Sales from B to C	7,500
Total	9,000

These appear both in the aggregate expenses and the aggregate revenue, so are artificial from the perspective of the group as a single economic entity. Had the group been a single legal entity, the internal transactions would have no meaning. It is only the external transactions that should be retained in the consolidated statement of profit or loss. This should be:

Revenue (outside the group)	8,500
Expenses (outside the group)	6,700
Profit	1,800

Notice that this does not change the profit, just the revenue and expenses. From the perspective of an outsider, the internal transactions have no meaning and result in a false set of figures. For example, the profit margin before eliminations would be:

Profit	1,800
Sales	17,500
Margin	10.3 per cent

After elimination of intra-group transactions:

Profit	1,800
Sales	8,500
Margin	21.2 per cent

The intra-group transactions only exist because of the group structure, and they cause the double-counting problem. If they were not eliminated, they would mislead investors (some famous frauds have been engineered this way) and analysts would have difficulty comparing figures between groups.

Note that for the financial statements of the individual companies the revenue and expenses are valid and for tax purposes, the profits are still dealt with as part of the individual companies. Subsidiary A would be taxed on 300, subsidiary B on 1,000 and subsidiary C on 500, which is a factor we shall come back to in relation to taxation of groups later (see Chapter 15).

You can see that the group financial accounting system must be able to distinguish between transactions with fellow subsidiaries and transactions with outside parties, so that the internal transactions can be included in the individual company accounts but excluded from the group financial statements.

Harmonization adjustments are another type of adjustment that should be made to ensure that the accounting policies used for the consolidated financial statements are also applied in the financial statements of the individual companies that make up the group – the *consistency principle* applies to group financial statements.

When a group has subsidiaries in different countries, they will be subject to different tax rules, which may, in turn, influence policies such as depreciation or provisions. Equally, all the subsidiaries in the same country may not necessarily follow the same rules, although they usually do. This sometimes results in a situation where, in the consolidation process, the depreciation rates and other aspects of measurement in individual companies have to be adjusted so that the same accounting principles are applied consistently throughout the group. To keep this process as simple as possible and ensure comparable figures for management purposes throughout the group, some companies apply uniform accounting rules worldwide, and then prepare local variants for tax purposes.

In broad terms, the preparation of the consolidated financial statements (which can be done on a spreadsheet) involves the stages shown in Figure 12.2.

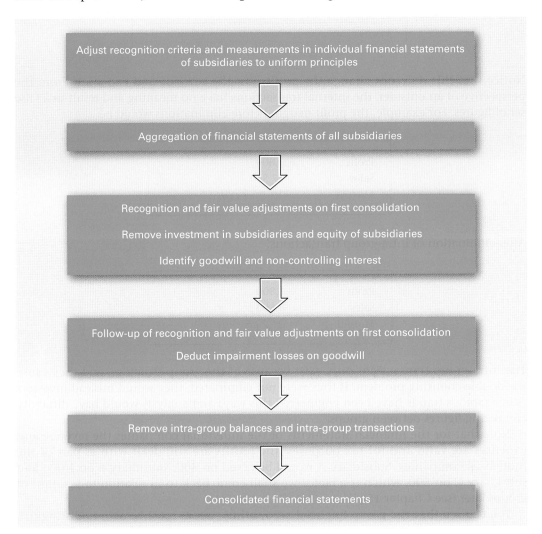

Figure 12.2 Process of preparing consolidated financial statements

The accounting principles used in the consolidated financial statements are traditionally those of the parent company. This aligns with the idea that the consolidated financial statements have the effect of treating all transactions as though they have been carried out within the parent. However, the influence of taxation and the pressure to align group accounting on the principles used in the major financial markets means that in many countries a multinational may, in fact, draw up the consolidated financial statements on principles different to those used in the parent; in that case, the measurement adjustments ('restatement' of figures in the jargon) may be substantial and sophisticated information systems are required to permit the collection of the necessary data.

Associates and joint arrangements

At the beginning of the chapter, we pointed out that there are different kinds of relationship possible between an investor and a company it has invested in (the investee). The *different types of inter-company relationship* are presented in Table 12.1. Accounting regulation recognizes three different categories:

1. The investor has a controlling or *dominant influence*: i.e. the investor can dictate the strategy of the investee, appoint its management and so on. In this situation, the investee is consolidated, as we have just examined.

2. The investor is not able to determine strategy, but has *significant influence*: i.e. the investor's views are considered in determining the investee's strategy. This could, for example, be effected through representation on the investee's board of directors.

3. The investor is not able to determine strategy and has *no influence* whatsoever.

Table 12.1   Inter-company relationships

Type of inter-company relationship	Amount of voting rights	Qualification of shareholdings
1 Control	> 50%	Subsidiary
2 Significant influence	≥ 20%	Associated company
3 No real influence	< 20%	Financial investment

The second column of Table 12.1 indicates the relative amounts of voting rights that are presumed to lead to a specific type of inter-company relationship. It should be noted, however, that the distinctions between these categories are not always very clear cut, and depend a lot on the surrounding circumstances. As we have discussed, a shareholding representing 40 per cent of the outstanding voting rights could put the investor in a dominant position if there are no other major concentrations of ownership. However, it would be more likely to put the company in a position of significant influence.

The type of relationship between the investor and the investee will determine the way the shareholdings are accounted for in the investor's financial statements. The link between the type of inter-company relationship and the accounting method used under IFRS Standards is documented in Table 12.2.

Financial investments

Financial investments are shareholding where the investor has *no real influence* and which are primarily held to *benefit from price changes*. This is presumed to be the case when an investor holds an interest of less than 20 per cent. Technically, these are the easiest to account for, although the accounting treatment can be different according to the applicable accounting regime.

Table 12.2   Inter-company relationship and accounting consequences

Type of inter-company relationship	Qualification of shareholdings	Accounting method (IFRS Standards)
1 Control	Subsidiary	Full consolidation (acquisition method)
2 Significant influence	Associated company	Equity method
3 No real influence	Financial investment	Fair value method

■ *Under IFRS Standards*, financial investments are treated as financial instruments and are measured in the statement of financial position *at fair value*. IFRS 9 *Financial Instruments* covers the appropriate accounting rules. As financial assets, the equity investments are to be measured at fair value with the default recognition of gains and losses in profit or loss: the changes in fair value of the financial assets (unrealized holding gains or losses) are recognized in profit or loss in the period in which they occur. Only if the equity investment is not held for trading can an irrevocable election be made at initial recognition to measure it at fair value through other comprehensive income (OCI) with only dividend income recognized in profit or loss. So, by default, IFRS 9 *Financial Instruments* presumes that equity investments are held-for-trading (to profit from price changes of the shares) although, in practice, purposes other than trading may motivate holding a financial investment. For example, a company may acquire an equity investment in order to cement a strategic (longer term) commercial relationship with another company, without the intent of exercising significant influence on its management. In that case it would make sense to allow unrealized gains and losses to bypass profit or loss. Note that the classification of a financial investment as not held-for-trading is irrevocable in order to create consistency and discipline over time.

COMPANY REPORT

ROCHE – CONSOLIDATION *(extract)*

The Group periodically undertakes transactions that may involve obtaining control or significant influence of other companies. These transactions include equity acquisitions, asset purchases and alliance agreements. In all such cases management makes an assessment as to whether the Group has control or significant influence of the other company, and whether it should be consolidated as a subsidiary or accounted for as an associated company. In making this assessment, management considers the underlying economic substance of the transaction in addition to the contractual terms.

Source: Roche Group, Finance Report, 2018

■ *Under the EU Accounting Directive*, financial investments are measured *at cost* – equity investments without significant influence are held in the investor's books at historical cost subject to any impairment of value. If the investment's current value falls below historical cost, then the investment should be written down (and the expense would normally appear in the financial result part of the statement of profit or loss). In some jurisdictions, if the current value exceeds historical cost, this information would be disclosed as a note to the accounts. If the investor receives a dividend from the investee company, then this is treated as financial income.

Associated companies

Associates are companies where the investor has *significant influence* over the investee. The case of associated companies has historically been more controversial with regard to its accounting consequences.

For example, suppose you are a French company that sells bottled non-alcoholic beverages and you want to expand in Russia. The market is difficult, the risk high, so you decide to go into a joint venture with another soft drink company and a Russian entrepreneur. You each take a one-third stake in a new bottling plant in Moscow, which will be managed by the Russian partner with technical assistance from the two multinational partners. How is this going to appear in your consolidated financial statements?

Since you do not own or run the plant, it will not be consolidated. By way of contrast, you have a significant input into the decision-making and a significant investment, which impacts on the future expansion of your company in that market. You could certainly just treat the investment as a financial asset, but this does not convey the much closer economic relationship you have in it. What can you do?

Essentially, there are two basic methods to account for associates: the *equity method* and the *proportionate consolidation method*. Under the equity method, the investor shows its investment in its consolidated financial statements at the accounting value of that investment in the investee's books. If, for example, the investor has 25 per cent of the shares in the investee, it shows that investment at 25 per cent of the book value of equity in the investee's financial statements and not at historical cost to the investor or at fair value. Under the proportionate consolidation method, the investor takes a proportion of all assets and liabilities of the investee into the consolidated financial statements.

These two different approaches are probably best understood through a detailed example. Suppose that Company A buys 20 per cent of Company C, whose statement of financial position at the moment of acquisition is as follows:

	€m
Assets	
Property, plant and equipment	600
Current assets	300
Total assets	900
Financing	
Shares	400
Retained earnings	50
	450
Debt	250
Payables	200
Total equity and liabilities	900

The book value of C's equity in C's accounting records is €450m; A owns 20 per cent of that, which is therefore worth 450 × 0.2 = €90m. Under the equity method, the investment in C that appears in A's consolidated financial statements should therefore be €90m, and any difference between that and the historical cost of the investment is considered as goodwill. The adjustments to bring C into A's consolidated financial statements at equity value would be as follows:

	Company A	Company C	Group
Assets			
Goodwill	—	+60	60
Property, plant and equipment	1,050	—	1,050
Cost of investment in C	150	−150	—
Equity value of investment in C	—	+90	90
Current assets	420	—	420
Total assets	1,620	—	1,620
Financing		—	
Shares	300	—	300
Retained earnings	420	—	420
	720	—	720
Debt	600	—	600
Payables	300	—	300
Total equity and liabilities	1,620	—	1,620

Under IFRS Standards, the goodwill should be reviewed for impairment in the normal way. On subsequent consolidations, the book value of C would normally have changed, and all changes must also be reflected in A's financial statements. So if, for example, C made a net profit of €50m in the year after A had acquired its 20 per cent stake, A would show 'income from associates' of €10m as a separate line item in its statement of profit or loss and would increase the carrying value of its investment in C in its statement of financial position by €10m. Any subsequent dividend would decrease the carrying value and increase cash at bank.

If, however, C were dealt with on a proportional basis, the consolidation would look like this:

	Company A	Company C (20%)	Adjust	Group
Assets				
Goodwill	—	—	+60	60
Property, plant and equipment	1,050	120	—	1,170
Cost of investment in C	150	—	−150	—
Current assets	420	60	—	480
Total assets	1,620	180	−90	1,710

Financing				
Shares	300	80	−80	300
Retained earnings	420	10	−10	420
	720	*90*	*−90*	*720*
Debt	600	50	—	650
Payables	300	40	—	340
Total equity and liabilities	1,620	180	−90	1,710

Under the proportionate consolidation method, a part of the underlying assets and liabilities of C appears in A's statement of financial position, as in a normal consolidation, and in future years any profits or losses post-acquisition will flow through to the consolidated statement of profit or loss.

Both methods have their critics. Critics of the equity method point out that only the book value of the equity is shown, and this may conceal a company that is heavily indebted. Indeed, associated companies have been used as a means of shifting debt off the main balance sheet. In addition, the method involves recognizing income from the associated company that has not been paid to the investor and over which the investor does not exercise control – something an analyst would be wary of (see 'quality of earnings' in Chapter 17). Critics of proportionate consolidation, by the same token, say that a mathematical fraction of assets and liabilities has no economic significance – an investor cannot sell 20 per cent of a factory in case of difficulty, for example – and that the resulting consolidation is meaningless.

It is clearly a difficult issue because the relationship between the investor and its investment may be highly significant (e.g. the investors in a joint venture may draw significant economic benefit from that relationship but none has a majority holding) and should therefore not be missing from the group financial statements. From an analyst's perspective, the equity method is easier to decode because profits and losses are separately identified ('income from associates') in published financial statements and can therefore be considered on their own merits in relation to the particular company. Evaluating the effect of proportionate consolidation on the financial statements is not usually possible.

STANDARDS

 IAS 28 – INVESTMENTS IN ASSOCIATES AND JOINT VENTURES *(extracts)*

Significant influence

5. If an entity holds, directly or indirectly (e.g. through subsidiaries), 20 per cent or more of the voting power of the investee, it is presumed that the entity has significant influence, unless it can be clearly demonstrated that this is not the case. Conversely, if the entity holds, directly or indirectly (e.g. through subsidiaries), less than 20 per cent of the voting power of the investee, it is presumed that the investor does not have significant influence, unless such influence can be clearly demonstrated. A substantial or majority ownership by another investor does not necessarily preclude an investor from having significant influence.

(Continued)

6. The existence of significant influence by an entity is usually evidenced in one or more of the following ways:

   (a) representation on the board of directors or equivalent governing body of the investee;
   (b) participation in policy-making processes, including participation in decisions about dividends or other distributions;
   (c) material transactions between the investor and the investee;
   (d) interchange of managerial personnel; or
   (e) provision of essential technical information.

   Source: IAS 28, Investments in Associates and Joint Ventures

IFRS Standards require the use of the equity method for associated companies and prohibits the use of proportionate consolidation. The rules are covered by IAS 28 *Investments in Associates and Joint Ventures*. Associated companies are defined as those where the investor has 'significant influence', which is assumed to be the case where the investor holds at least 20 per cent of the voting rights of the investee. However, the IASB also has a standard that specifically addresses joint ventures – IFRS 11 *Joint Arrangements* – and the requirements of that intersect with those for associates.

Joint arrangements

The standard-setter defines a *joint arrangement* as 'an arrangement of which two or more parties have joint control' (IFRS 11, para. 4). The parties involved are bound by a contractual agreement that provides joint control of the arrangement to two or more of those parties. *Joint control* is 'the contractually agreed sharing of control of an arrangement, which exists only when decisions about the relevant activities require the unanimous consent of the parties sharing control' (IFRS 11, para. 7). Joint arrangements are quite common in companies operating in the extractive industries, property and construction sectors. This might be the case, for example, where two or three oil companies build a pipeline for shared use.

Joint arrangements take many different forms and structures. IFRS 11 *Joint Arrangements* recognizes *two kinds of joint arrangement*:

1. *Joint operations.* A joint operation is a joint arrangement whereby the parties that have joint control of the arrangement (i.e. joint operators) have rights to the assets and obligations for the liabilities, relating to the arrangement. Here the joint operators each devote certain assets (and related liabilities) to a joint exploitation but retain direct ownership of those assets and liabilities. In most cases, no special legal vehicle is created.

   Revenues from the sale of the joint product and any expenses incurred in common, are usually split – for example, when two airlines both operate on the same route and agree to share revenues.

   A joint operator recognizes and measures the assets and liabilities (and the related revenues and expenses) in relation to its interest in the arrangement in accordance with relevant IFRS Standards applicable to the particular assets, liabilities, revenues and expenses.

2. *Joint ventures.* A joint venture is a joint arrangement whereby the parties that have joint control of the arrangement (i.e. joint venturers) have rights to the net assets of the arrangement.

Joint ventures are usually structured through a legal entity. But the existence of a legal structure in a joint arrangement does not automatically mean that it qualifies as a joint venture. They will have to be assessed to determine whether the venturers' rights and exposures are to the entity's net assets, or to its underlying (gross) assets and liabilities. The latter category will be classified as joint operations because this better reflects the economic substance of the arrangement.

A joint venture intersects with associates – a company or other legal vehicle is created, the venturers make investments in this entity, which, in turn, owns assets and undertakes operations.

A joint venturer recognizes its investment in a joint venture and accounts for it using the equity method. IFRS 11 prohibits the use of the proportionate consolidation for joint ventures, although other accounting regimes (e.g. EU Accounting Directive) do allow it.

Additional disclosure on interests in other companies

IFRS 12 *Disclosure of Interests in Other Entities* specifies minimum disclosures with regard to interests in subsidiaries, joint arrangements, associates and unconsolidated structured entities. The required disclosures aim to provide information in order to enable users to evaluate (1) the nature of, and risks associated with, the reporting entity's interests in other entities; and (2) the effects of those interests on the group's financial position, financial performance and cash flows.

Special attention will go to *structured entities* (also called 'special purpose vehicles' – see also extract from IFRS 12). It should be clear what a structured entity is in the context of the operations of the group and how judgement is applied in assessing whether the group is 'involved' with a structured entity. Material involvement in structured entities may broaden the transactions and relationships to which the disclosures may apply, especially for those who sponsor, or perhaps even transact with, but are not considered as having control over the structured entities.

STANDARDS

 IFRS 12 – DISCLOSURE OF INTERESTS IN OTHER ENTITIES *(extracts)*

Structured entities
B21 A structured entity is an entity that has been designed so that voting or similar rights are not the dominant factor in deciding who controls the entity, such as when any voting rights relate to administrative tasks only and the relevant activities are directed by means of contractual arrangements.
B22 A structured entity often has some or all of the following features or attributes:

(a) restricted activities.
(b) a narrow and well-defined objective, such as to effect a tax-efficient lease, carry out research and development activities, provide a source of capital or funding to an entity or provide investment opportunities for investors by passing on risks and rewards associated with the assets of the structured entity to investors.
(c) insufficient equity to permit the structured entity to finance its activities without subordinated financial support.

(Continued)

(d) financing in the form of multiple contractually linked instruments to investors that create concentrations of credit or other risks (tranches).

B23 Examples of entities that are regarded as structured entities include, but are not limited to:

(a) securitisation vehicles.
(b) asset-backed financings.
(c) some investment funds.

B24 An entity that is controlled by voting rights is not a structured entity simply because, for example, it receives funding from third parties following a restructuring.

Source: IFRS 12, Disclosure of Interests in Other Entities

Summary

In this chapter, we have reviewed the techniques of preparing consolidated or group financial statements. A core theme is the determination and measurement of goodwill arising on consolidation, with related issues such as the bringing into the statement of financial position of intangibles such as brands that are typically missing from individual company balance sheets, the fair valuing of newly acquired assets and liabilities and the incorporation of non-controlling interests. We have noted the necessity of removing transactions within the group since these will distort performance figures and ratios and the necessity of ensuring that accounting policies are harmonized. The consolidated financial statements give a wider economic picture than separate company financial statements. The financial statements of a single subsidiary of a group are always open to distortion.

Group structures may also include associated companies, joint arrangements and financial investments without significant influence. These types of investment require a different kind of accounting treatment to subsidiaries which are under control of a group's parent company.

Discussion questions

1. Discuss the differences of the concepts of company, business and business combination within the context of IFRS 3.
2. Does a controlling interest always imply majority ownership? Does one need to know the exact level of ownership in a subsidiary in order to prepare consolidated financial statements?
3. In order to account for investments in other companies, it is common to distinguish different degrees of ownership or influence. Describe these and explain the reasoning for the distinctions made. What are the related accounting consequences?
4. At acquisition date, the net assets of the acquired subsidiary are included in the consolidated financial statements at their acquisition date fair value. However, most of the parent's assets and liabilities are measured on a historical cost basis. Is this consistent?
5. Describe the different types of joint arrangements and their respective accounting treatment.

Assignments

The following assignments have answers on the lecturer side of the digital support resources for the book.

1. Dickens Enterprises formed a new subsidiary in March 20X4, called Great Expectations (GE). At 31 December 20X4, the statements of financial position of the two companies were as shown below. During 20X4 no intra-group transactions have been recorded.

    You are asked to prepare a work sheet for the consolidated financial statements of Dickens Enterprises as of 31 December 20X4:

	Dickens	GE	Elimination	Group
Property, plant and equipment	5,200	750		
Investment in GE	500	—		
Inventories	700	49		
Trade receivables	800	60		
Cash	1,200	25		
Total assets	8,400	884		
Share capital	3,000	500		
Retained earnings	1,900			
Profit for 20X4	700	31		
	5,600	531		
Long-term borrowings	1,000	300		
Short-term liabilities	1,800	53		
Total equity and liabilities	8,400	884		

2. Alpha Company has set up a subsidiary to deal with the distribution of its products by mail and internet order. At 31 December 20X6, their respective statements of financial position were:

	Parent	Subsidiary
Property, plant and equipment (net)	980	340
Investment in subsidiary	180	—
Loan (long-term) to subsidiary	50	—
Current assets	360	195
Total assets	1,570	535
Share capital	800	180
Retained earnings	360	—
Loan from parent	—	50
Long-term borrowings	300	250
Current liabilities	110	55
Total equity and liabilities	1,570	535

Required:

Draw up a consolidated statement of financial position of Alpha Company at 31 December 20X6.

3. Company Earduster acquired 50 per cent of the share capital of company Talebearer on January 20X6. These shares were acquired at the foundation of company Talebearer.

   During the first year after the acquisition there have been no transactions between Earduster and Talebearer.

   The condensed statement of financial position and statement of profit or loss of both companies at 31 December 20X6 are as follows (all amounts in €):

	Earduster	Talebearer
Property, plant and equipment	4,100,000	300,000
Investment in Talebearer	250,000	—
Other financial assets	100,000	—
Inventories	2,250,000	900,000
Trade receivables	900,000	400,000
Total assets	7,600,000	1,600,000
Share capital	2,000,000	500,000
Retained earnings	2,000,000	—
Profit for the year	400,000	60,000
Short-term debt	—	400,000
Trade payables	2,300,000	440,000
Other payables	900,000	200,000
Total equity and liabilities	7,600,000	1,600,000
Statement of profit or loss		
Revenue	11,000,000	3,600,000
Cost of sales	–10,000,000	–3,000,000
Gross profit	*1,000,000*	*600,000*
Other operating income	1,000,000	300,000
Other operating expenses	–1,600,000	–840,000
Profit for the period	400,000	60,000

Required:

Prepare the consolidated financial statements of the Earduster group as at 31 December 20X6:

(a) Using the full consolidation method (combined with the partial goodwill method).

(b) Using the proportionate consolidation method.

(c) Using the equity method.

4. On 1 July 20X5, Omega Company purchased 90 per cent of the outstanding shares of Beta Company for 1,000,000. Immediately after the acquisition, the separate statements of financial position of both companies appeared as follows (all amounts in €):

	Omega	*Beta*
Property, plant and equipment	1,500,000	880,000
Investment in Beta Company	1,000,000	—
Other financial assets	50,000	160,000
Inventories	900,000	520,000
Trade receivables	650,000	240,000
Cash	263,200	48,000
Total assets	4,363,200	1,848,000
Share capital	2,000,000	800,000
Retained earnings	563,200	48,000
Long-term debt	1,000,000	600,000
Current payables	800,000	400,000
Total equity and liabilities	4,363,200	1,848,000

Beta Company's other financial assets represent a long-term investment in Omega's long-term debt. The debt was purchased for an amount equal to Omega Company's carrying amount of the debt. On 1 July 20X5, Omega Company owes Beta 100,000 for services rendered.

Required:

(a) Prepare a consolidated statement of financial position of Omega Company as of the acquisition date (using the partial goodwill method).

(b) What is the effect on the consolidated statement of financial position of Omega if, on the acquisition date, the fair value of the property, plant and equipment of Beta Company were 980,000?

5. On 1 January 20X5, Invigilator Enterprises acquired 100 per cent of the shares of Lemma Company.

The separate condensed statements of financial position immediately after the acquisition appeared as shown below (all amounts in €):

	Invigilator Enterprises	Lemma Company
Intangible assets	—	2,000
Property, plant and equipment	490,000	80,000
Investment in Lemma	600,000	—
Inventories	230,000	360,000
Trade and other receivables	400,000	240,000
Total assets	1,720,000	682,000
Share capital	1,000,000	200,000
Retained earnings	140,000	100,000
Provisions	20,000	30,000
Current liabilities	560,000	352,000
Total equity and liabilities	1,720,000	682,000

Additional information (at acquisition date):

(a) Lemma owns a patent for the production of a new product. Lemma did not recognize the patent in its separate financial statements. The estimated fair value of the patent at acquisition date amounts to €80,000.

(b) The fair value of Lemma's main corporate offices is €130,000 (net book value of €50,000).

(c) The fair value of Lemma's inventories amounts to €320,000.

(d) On 1 January 20X5, Invigilator Enterprises still has to pay an invoice (€100,000) for services rendered by Lemma Company in December 20X4.

Required:

(a) Prepare the consolidated statement of financial position of the Invigilator Group as at 1 January 20X5.

(b) Prepare the consolidated statement of financial position of the Invigilator Group as at 1 January 20X5, assuming that the investment in Lemma represents only 90 per cent of the outstanding shares of Lemma Company (apply the partial goodwill method).

6. On 1 July 20X4, Dabster Company acquired 100 per cent of the share capital of Saltus Company.

At the date of acquisition the balances of the equity accounts of Saltus were as follows:

Share capital	400,000
Retained earnings	300,000
Profit for the year (interim)	40,000

The condensed statements of financial position of both companies at 31 December 20X4 are as follows (all amounts in €):

	Dabster	Saltus
Property, plant and equipment	1,550,000	500,000
Investment in Saltus	800,000	—
Inventories	300,000	200,000
Trade receivables	150,000	200,000
Cash and cash equivalents	50,000	100,000
Total assets	2,850,000	1,000,000
Share capital	1,500,000	400,000
Retained earnings	500,000	300,000
Profit for the year	100,000	100,000
Current liabilities	750,000	200,000
Total equity and liabilities	2,850,000	1,000,000

Additional information:

(a) At acquisition date, the fair value of Saltus Company's corporate offices (with a remaining useful life of 20 years) shows a surplus value of €50,000 over the carrying amount.
(b) During the fourth quarter of 20X4, Dabster sells some of its inventory to Saltus for €125,000, which represents cost plus a mark-up of 25 per cent. Half of these goods are still in the inventory of Saltus at the end of 20X4.
(c) At 31 December 20X4, goodwill recognized on the acquisition turns out to be impaired. An impairment loss of 10 per cent should be taken into account.

Required:

(a) Prepare the consolidated statement of financial position of Dabster Group as at 31 December 20X4.

(b) Prepare the consolidated statement of financial position of Dabster Group as at 31 December 20X4, assuming that the investment in Saltus represents 80 per cent of the outstanding shares. Apply the partial goodwill method.

(c) What would be the impact on the consolidated statement of financial position if the full goodwill method is applied for the 20 per cent non-controlling interest?

7. You work in the mergers and acquisitions department of a merchant bank and have spotted what you consider to be an attractive acquisition. Northeast Foods plc is a small, listed food manufacturer based in Leeds. It has for many years sold a well-established range of tinned speciality foods. The market regards it as rather sleepy and lacking the management edge necessary to convert to modern technology, bring in new products and compete generally. The company is slowly losing market share as supermarkets bring in own-label products of the kind that were Northeast's strength. The €1 ordinary shares currently trade at €5.25.

You have also identified Wearside Products plc, a relatively young company, which grew rapidly as a result of the success of its tortilla chips. It has broadened its product range but is hungry for more brands and needs to grow to be able to compete more effectively in international markets. Northeast would be a good fit for Wearside, and is reasonably cash rich.

You are about to have a meeting with the chairman of Wearside to discuss mounting a takeover. You are going to suggest that Wearside offers one of its €1 ordinary shares (market value €4.50) plus €1.50 cash for each Northeast share, giving Northeast shareholders a profit of 75 cents at present prices. You are prepared to take less than 100 per cent if necessary but would regard a 60 per cent stake as the minimum acceptable. For 60 per cent you would be willing to offer one Wearside share plus €1.20 cash:

	Wearside	Northeast
	€m	€m
Non-current assets		
Intangibles	200.1	—
Property, plant and equipment	180.2	67.1
Investments	—	10.5
Current assets		
Inventories	37.4	20.2
Receivables	41.8	19.3
Cash	5.9	39.2
Total assets	465.4	156.3
Share capital (€1 ordinary shares)	68.5	24.0
Retained earnings	123.9	79.7
	192.4	103.7
Current liabilities	48.3	21.6
Non-current liabilities	224.7	31.0
Total equity and liabilities	465.4	156.3

Required:

(a) Draw up a post-takeover statement of financial position for the group in order to illustrate the effects of the proposed takeover, assuming that Wearside would borrow short term to meet the cash element of the bid (and subsequently repay from Northeast's cash reserves). You should draw up alternative statements of financial position on the basis of:

  (i) No extra recognition or fair value adjustments

  (ii) Recognizing a brand worth €40m

  (iii) Recognizing a brand worth €20m and fair value adjustments of tangible non-current assets worth €20m.

(b) Draw up a statement of financial position on the basis of taking only 60 per cent of the shares, without additional asset recognition, using historical cost as fair value and applying the partial goodwill method.

(*Note*: This is a fairly tough case and is designed to introduce you to the realities of mergers and acquisitions thinking.)

8. Traduct SA produces dictionaries of ancient languages such as Latin and Greek. The company has two divisions, Uno and Duo, which constitute two separate cash generating units. Uno operates as a legal entity and was acquired by Traduct SA at the beginning of 20X4. The goodwill arising on the acquisition of Uno has been allocated to the CGU of Uno.

Near the end of 20X4, a flooding destroys the paper inventory of Uno and damages its machinery and equipment. At 31 December 20X4, the directors of Traduct SA decide to carry out a review for impairment of the net assets of Uno.

The net assets of Uno immediately before the impairment review (which took place on 31 December 20X4) consist of the following:

Net assets of Uno	Carrying value prior to impairment test €m
Goodwill arising on acquisition	25
Land	40
Buildings	90
Machinery and equipment	18
Inventory – paper	10
Inventory – other	30
Net current assets (other than inventory)	65
Total	278

The following information is relevant to the impairment review:

■ Discounted cash flow calculations (budgeted future cash flows expected to arise from the continuation of Uno's activities) show that the value in use of Uno can be estimated at 228.
■ Uno could be sold on 31 December 20X4 for 190.
■ The recoverable value of the paper inventory of Uno is zero.
■ The recoverable value of the machinery and equipment of Uno amounts to two-thirds of its book value.
■ Due to rising land prices, the market value of the land is higher than its book value.
■ The net current assets (other than inventory – paper) are stated at the lower of cost and fair value less costs to sell.

Required:

(a) Compute the amount of impairment of the net assets of Uno arising from the impairment review.

(b) Allocate the impairment loss between the components of the net assets of Uno.

(c) Show the values of each of the components of the net assets of Uno after the necessary adjustments resulting from the impairment review.

CHAPTER 13

Operating segments and foreign operations

This chapter looks into problems arising from multinational operations, including the issues of segment reporting and foreign currency translation. Segment reporting complements consolidated financial statements in that it disaggregates group level data into information by business line, geographical area and/or customer type. Company segments often reflect different risk and return profiles, which cannot be determined from the aggregated consolidated financial statements. In this chapter, we also address the special accounting problems of working in several currencies. Up until now we have assumed that the financial statements of a group's subsidiaries were all kept in the same currency, but this is rarely the case for a multinational. The analyst does not necessarily need to be able to convert financial statements for consolidation purposes and, in any event, cannot break out conversion effects from published financial statements. However, conversion or translation from several currencies potentially brings in a number of distortions, of which the analyst should be aware. In addition, year-on-year comparisons are likely to be affected by value shifts in currencies in which a multinational has major operations, assets and liabilities. Often companies will bring these to the attention of the analyst.

Chapter structure

- Introduction
- Stock exchange requirements
- Segment reporting

- Foreign currency transactions and foreign operations
- Primary (translating foreign currency transactions in the functional currency) and
- Secondary translation (translating foreign currency financial statements in a group's presentation currency)
- Alternative accounting methods for secondary translation
- Functional currency and type of foreign operation
- Hedging a net investment in a foreign currency
- Summary
- Discussion questions
- Assignments

Introduction

The modern multinational corporation typically is present in many countries of the world, often operates different lines of business and trades in many currencies. While consolidated financial statements have the advantage of measuring and presenting the economic group as a whole, they also have the disadvantage of providing highly aggregated data, which may be difficult to interpret when a group has several disparate types of business activity and works in several different economies. This problem is addressed by segment reporting requirements – requiring companies to disclose information by operating segments.

Usually a multinational will have subsidiaries in many foreign countries and will also have raised finance outside its national base. Quite often multinationals not only borrow money outside their home market, but are also listed on several stock exchanges in different parts of the world. When preparing consolidated financial statements, it is obviously necessary that all items are expressed in a single presentation currency. Given that the values of a group's assets and liabilities may be stated in foreign currencies, and that the exchange rates between currencies are changing constantly, there is therefore a considerable accounting problem in converting (*translating*) amounts expressed in foreign currencies into the presentation currency. In addition, different stock exchanges may have different reporting rules.

Clearly, this situation is bound to pose a number of problems, both in interpreting such aggregated data and in expressing annual consolidated financial statements in a single currency. We shall look first at the problems of being listed on several stock exchanges, then at the provision of further analysis of company activities and finally at the accounting problems of converting to a single currency.

Stock exchange requirements

Multinational companies often see a stock exchange listing on different regional markets as a strategic issue, not necessarily connected with the company's financing. A listing gives local credibility, increases awareness of the company and its products and enables it to make takeover bids which involve share exchange rather than necessarily cash. There is also an issue of the market being able to evaluate a company accurately – for example, many tech and internet companies are drawn to the US NASDAQ system because there are lots of similar companies there, and such companies believe their cost of capital will be lower. National markets may also be relatively illiquid so companies are drawn to the regional leaders.

Over time the effect of internationalization has been to drive both markets and then companies to attempt to harmonize the kind of financial statements that they use and the information disclosures. IFRS Standards, which we are using in this book, are accepted by most stock exchanges and are as a consequence used by many multinational companies.

However, the major exception to this harmonization is still the USA. Although the Securities and Exchange Commission (SEC) has given a major concession to foreign companies reporting under IFRS Standards and that wish to be listed on any of the US exchanges, domestic US companies are still not allowed to use IFRS Standards for US filing purposes. Foreign issuers registered with the SEC have to either use US principles or provide reconciliations, both of which are costly, but foreign companies using IFRS Standards are exempt, which provides a major incentive to use these. Currently there are about 600 foreign companies that are listed in the USA and use IFRS Standards. Analysts, when making international cross-sectional comparisons, need to check whether companies are using IFRS Standards or US GAAP for their financial statements, and decide on which basis of accounting they want to make their comparison.

Segment reporting

Multinational companies usually have a number of products or business lines, operate in diverse geographical areas and serve different customer classes. They manage different *operating segments* and these may vary significantly in terms of rates of profitability, growth opportunities, risks and future prospects. For example, PSA Peugeot Citroën is well known for its passenger cars but the company actually operates in three distinct business segments: Automotive (the design, manufacture and sale of passenger cars and light commercial vehicles); automotive equipment (vehicle interior systems, automotive seating, emission control technologies, etc.); and finance companies (retail financing to customers and wholesale financing to dealers). Many large automobile companies have very large finance divisions, which may be bigger than the manufacturing subsidiaries.

While consolidated financial statements aggregate accounting data bottom up to present a picture of the financial position, performance and cash flows of the economic group as a whole, they tend to disguise differing risk and return profiles of group components and, thus, may be difficult to interpret when a group has several disparate types of business activity and works in several different economies. This problem is addressed by requiring companies to disclose information by operating segment.

The core principle of IFRS 8 *Operating Segments* is that an entity should disclose information to enable users of its financial statements to evaluate the nature and financial effects of the types of business activity in which it engages and the economic environments in which it operates. Information about the different types of product and service provided, possibly in combination with different geographical areas in which it operates and/or different customer types, should help users of financial statements better assess the company's risks and returns and make more informed judgements about the company as a whole.

A disaggregation of financial statement data by lines of operations can indeed provide significant information on different risk and return profiles, not determinable from the aggregated consolidated financial statements. For example, segment data could reveal that the larger part of net income is earned by a small high performing product group, that only one out of three business lines is profitable and thus subsidizes the other two, or that important geographical areas have not yet been penetrated, hinting at continued growth opportunities.

Operating segments

Disaggregation of consolidated financial statements into operating segments should follow the way that management analyzes the company to make operating decisions. IFRS 8 *Operating Segments* requires operating segments to be identified on the basis of internal reports about components of the company that are regularly reviewed by the chief operating decision-maker (CEO, chief operating officer or a group of executive officers) in order to allocate resources to the segment and to assess its performance. Disaggregated performance appraisal (implying the existence of segment revenues, expenses and assets) drives the identification of operating segments. Although segmentation would usually be organized by business or product lines, management can also organize it by geographical area, by customer type, by legal entity, or on another basis. For example, internal management reporting may be structured solely by legal entity, resulting in internal segments composed of groups of unrelated products and services. The Nestlé Group (see www.nestle.com) applies a combination of a geographic and a product perspective, through three geographic zones and several globally managed businesses. Nestlé's reportable operating segments (see Nestlé Group Company Report in this chapter) are: Zone Europe, Middle East and North Africa, Zone Americas, Zone Asia, Oceania and sub-Saharian Africa, Nestlé Waters, Nestlé Nutrition, other (mainly Nespresso, Nestlé Health Science and Nestlé Skin Health).

COMPANY REPORT

GROUPE PSA (PEUGEOT CITROËN/OPEL VAUXHALL) – SEGMENT INFORMATION

Note 4 – Segment information

In accordance with IFRS 8 – Operating Segments, segment information is presented in line with the indicators used internally by management to measure the performance of the Group's different business segments. The Group's main performance indicator on the segments is Recurring Operating Income.

For internal reporting, the full data of the Finance segment is given at 100%. It represents the consolidation of all the entities of the Finance divisions by global integration or at equity, before the impact of IFRS 5. The 'Reconciliation' column provides a link with the presentation given in the consolidated income statement.

4.1 Business segments

The columns for each segment shown in the table below are on a stand-alone basis. All intersegment balance sheet items and transactions are eliminated and, for the purposes of reconciliation with the Group's financial statements, are shown under the heading 'Eliminations and reconciliations' together with unallocated amounts. Faurecia and Banque PSA Finance publish consolidated financial statements and segment information for these two businesses is therefore presented down to the level of net profit. For the other segments, as cash positions and taxes are managed jointly in some countries, only operating income and share in net earnings of equity-accounted companies are presented by segment.

All intersegment commercial transactions are carried out on an arm's length basis on the same terms and conditions as those applicable to the supply of goods and services to third parties.

The 100% column under Finance companies represents the data on full consolidation of the companies in partnership with Santander and BNP Parìbas. These columns coupled with the 'Reconciliation' column make it possible to piece together the consolidated contribution of finance companies, with the share in net earnings of companies at equity in partnership with Santander and BNP Paribas.

(Continued)

| 2017 (in million euros) | Automotive | | | Finance companies | | Réconciliation | Eliminations and unallocated [1] | Total |
	Peugeot Citroën DS	Opel Vauxhall	Automotive Equipment	Other Businesses	100%			
Revenue								
* third parties	40,281	6,864	17,947	2	1,347	(1,231)	—	65,210
* intragroup, intersegment	454	374	2,235	88	129	—	(3,280)	—
Total [2]	40,735	7,238	20,182	90	1,476	(1,231)	(3,280)	65,210
Recurring operating income (loss)	2,965	(179)	1,170	23	632	(618)	(2)	3,991
Non-recurring operating income	176	2	4	20	3	—	—	205
Restructuring costs	(426)	(440)	(86)	1	(1)	1	—	(951)
Impairment of CGUs, provisions for onerous contracts and other	(96)							(96)
Other non-recurring operating income and (expenses), net	(11)	(38)	(13)	3	(14)	11	—	(62)
Operating income (loss)	2,608	(655)	1,075	47	620	(606)	(2)	3,087
Interest income			12		—	—	30	42
Finance costs			(114)		—	—	(94)	(208)
Other financial income			—		5	(1)	121	125
Other financial expenses			(31)		(1)	—	(165)	(197)
Net financial income (expense)	—	—	(133)	—	4	(1)	(108)	(238)
Income taxes expense			(262)		(204)	194	(429)	(701)
Share in net earnings of companies at equity	(55)	—	35	11	17	209	—	217
Other expenses related to the non-transferred financing of operations to be continued in partnership	—	—	—	—	—	—	—	—

Consolidated profit (loss) from continuing operations			715		437	(204)		2,365
Profit (loss) from operations to be sold or continued in partnership	—	—	(7)	—	—	—	—	(7)
Consolidated profit (loss) for the period			708	—	437	(204)		2,358
Capital expenditure⁽³⁾ (excluding sales with a buyback commitment)	2,717	169	1,217	—	30	(13)		4,120
Depreciation provision	(1,877)	−25	(722)	—	(19)	7		(2,636)

(1) The 'Eliminations and unallocated' column includes eliminations of intersector sales between the Finance companies and the other sectors (€106 million).
(2) Of which a turnover of €39,076 million for manufacturer's activity of the Automotive Division Peugeot Citroën DS.
(3) The capital expenditure of the Peugeot Citroën DS and Opel Vauxhall segments relates to capital expenditure incurred for the production of Peugeot Cltroën DS and Opel Vauxhall vehicles.

In 2017, on a fully consolidated basis, Banque PSA Finance (Finance Companies segment) generated net banking revenue of €1,145 million. Net provision expense (cost of risk) amounted to €64 million.

4.2 Geographical segments

The indicators provided by region are revenue broken down by customer marketing area and property, plant and equipment broken down by geographic location of the consolidated companies.

(in million euros)	Europe	Eurasia	China & South–Asia	India Pacific	Latin America	Middle East & Africa	North America	Total
2017								
Revenue	47,762	481	3,439	1,287	4,719	2,985	4,537	65,210
Property, plant and equipment	11,538	143	478	123	582	73	341	13,278
2016								
Revenue	38,959	339	3,191	916	3,781	2,323	4,521	54,030
Property, plant and equipment	9,686	160	407	118	472	62	388	11,293

Source: Groupe PSA, Annual Report, 2017

NESTLÉ GROUP

Segment reporting

Operating segments reflect the Group's management structure and the way financial information is regularly reviewed by the Group's Chief Operating decision maker (CODM), which is defined as the Executive Board.

The CODM considers the business from both a geographic and product perspective, through three geographic Zones and several Globally Managed Businesses (GMB). Zones and GMB that meet the quantitative threshold of 10% of total sales or trading operating profit for all operating segments, are presented on a stand-alone basis as reportable segments. Even though it does not meet the reporting threshold, Nestlé Waters is reported separately for consistency with long-standing practice of the Group. Therefore, the Group's reportable operating segments are:

- Zone Europe, Middle East and North Africa (EMENA);
- Zone Americas (AMS);
- Zone Asia, Oceania and sub-Saharan Africa (AOA);
- Nestlé Waters;
- Nestlé Nutrition.

Other business activities and operating segments, including GMB that do not meet the threshold, like Nespresso, Nestlé Health Science and Nestlé Skin Health, are combined and presented in Other businesses. Following a change of business structure, effective as from 1 January 2017, Nestlé Professional has been managed as a Regionally Managed Business instead of a Globally Managed Business and consequently reported as part of Zone EMENA, Zone AMS and Zone AOA. 2016 comparatives have been restated.

As some operating segments represent geographic Zones, information by product is also disclosed. The seven product groups that are disclosed represent the highest categories of products that are followed internally.

Segment results (Trading operating profit) represent the contribution of the different segments to central overheads, unallocated research and development costs and the trading operating profit of the Group. Specific corporate expenses as well as specific research and development costs are allocated to the corresponding segments. In addition to the Trading operating profit, Underlying Trading operating profit is shown on a voluntary basis because it is one of the key metrics used by Group Management to monitor the Group.

Depreciation and amortisation includes depreciation of property, plant and equipment and amortisation of intangible assets.

No segment assets and liabilities are regularly provided to the CODM to assess segment performance or to allocate resources and therefore segment assets and liabilities are not disclosed. However the Group discloses the invested capital, goodwill and intangible assets by segment and by product on a voluntary basis.

Invested capital comprises property, plant and equipment, trade receivables and some other receivables, assets held for sale, inventories, prepayments and accrued income as well as specific financial assets associated to the segments, less trade payables and some other payables, liabilities directly associated with assets held for sale, non-current other payables as well as accruals and deferred income.

Goodwill and intangible assets are not included in invested capital since the amounts recognised are not comparable between segments due to differences in the intensity of acquisition activity and changes in accounting standards which were applicable at various points in time when the Group undertook significant acquisitions. Nevertheless, an allocation of goodwill and intangible assets by segment and product and the related impairment expenses are provided.

Inter-segment eliminations represent inter-company balances between the different segments.

Invested capital and goodwill and intangible assets by segment represent the situation at the end of the year, while the figures by product represent the annual average, as this provides a better indication of the level of invested capital.

Capital additions represent the total cost incurred to acquire property, plant and equipment, intangible assets and goodwill, including those arising from business combinations. Capital expenditure represents the investment in property, plant and equipment only.

Unallocated items represent items whose allocation to a segment or product would be arbitrary. They mainly comprise:

- corporate expenses and related assets/liabilities;
- research and development costs and related assets/liabilities; and
- some goodwill and intangible assets.

Source: Nestlé Group, Annual Report, 2017

The *management approach* to identifying operating segments has the advantage that it builds on the company's internal organization, highlighting the risks and opportunities that management believes are important. The *internal reporting focus* probably enhances a user's ability to predict actions or reactions of management that can significantly affect the company's prospects.

Operating segments can be vertically integrated (think of, for example, highly integrated international oil companies). According to IFRS 8, operating segments are not limited to those that earn (a majority of) their revenue from external customers. An operating segment can be a component of a company that sells primarily or even exclusively to other segments of the company. Different stages of vertically integrated operations can become separate reporting segments if the company is managed that way.

Not all operations of a company will necessarily be part of an operating segment. For example, the corporate headquarters or some functional departments may not earn revenues or they may earn revenues that are only incidental to the activities of the company. These would not be operating segments.

IFRS 8 – OPERATING SEGMENTS *(extracts)*

5. An operating segment is a component of an entity:

(a) that engages in business activities from which it may earn revenues and incur expenses (including revenues and expenses relating to transactions with other components of the same entity);

(b) whose operating results are regularly reviewed by the entity's chief operating decision-maker to make decisions about resources to be allocated to the segments and assess its performance;

(c) for which discrete financial information is available; and

(d) may engage in business activities for which it has yet to earn revenues, for example, start-up operations may be operating segments before earning revenues.

Source: IFRS 8, Operating Segments

Reportable segments

Not all operating segments have to be reported, however. To be reportable, an operating segment must be significant; that is, it must meet at least one of the following *quantitative thresholds* (IFRS 8, para. 13):

■ Its *reported revenue*, from both external customers and intersegment sales or transfers, is 10 per cent or more of the combined revenue, internal and external, of all operating segments.

■ The absolute measure of its *reported profit or loss* is 10 per cent or more of the greater, in absolute amount, of (i) the combined reported profit of all operating segments that did not report a loss, and (ii) the combined reported loss of all operating segments that reported a loss.

■ Its *assets* are 10 per cent or more of the combined assets of all operating segments.

If the total external revenue reported by operating segments constitutes less than 75 per cent of the company's revenue, additional operating segments must be identified as reportable segments (even if they do not meet the quantitative thresholds set out above) (IFRS 8, para. 15). Two or more operating segments may be aggregated into a single operating segment if the segments have similar economic characteristics and are similar in respect of nature of products and services, nature of production and distribution processes, type or class of customer, and (if applicable) nature of regulatory environment, for example, banking, insurance or public utilities (IFRS 8, para. 12).

IFRS 8 grants companies a lot of discretion in determining operating segments, limited only by internal reporting practices. This discretion entails, however, the need to explain to the public how and why reportable segments are identified as they are. In this vein, the company has to disclose the factors driving the segmentation, including the basis of organization (for example, whether management has chosen to organize the entity around differences in products and services, geographical areas, regulatory environments or a combination of factors). Moreover, for each reportable segment, the company has to indicate the types of products and services from which it derives its revenue (IFRS 8, para. 22).

Segment information content

Complete segment financial statements are not required, but for each reportable segment, information must be provided on *segment revenue*, *segment profit or loss*, *segment assets* and *other related segment information*, such as a split between external and internal revenue, depreciation and amortization, liabilities, etc. if such information is regularly provided to the chief operating officer.

IFRS 8 does not, however, define the segment information items (revenues, expenses, result, assets, liabilities), neither does it require that accounting policies to be used for segment reporting are necessarily the same as those applied in the consolidated financial statements. In the end, internal reporting procedures will determine the measurement basis of segment information. In this vein, segment reporting rules and practices (with regard to both definition/recognition and measurement) may be highly entity specific, and, thus, jeopardize the usefulness of segment information for cross-sectional (inter-company) analysis.

In the case of the PSA group (including Peugeot, Citroën, Opel and Vauxhall) (see Company Report extract) 'recurring operating income' is the main performance indicator to assess segment performance. For each of the segments the following main information items are available: revenue (external and internal), (recurring) operating income, non-recurring operating items, capital expenditure, depreciation and amortization. There is however no information on segment assets and segment liabilities. Groupe PSA only displays non-current assets for its condensed display on geographical segments. Segment assets and liabilities are only required if they are regularly provided to the chief operating decision-maker, but they are useful for comparative segment ratio analysis (see Chapter 17). The Nestlé Group uses a performance metric labelled 'trading operating profit', that is, operating profit before impairment of goodwill and other operating income/expenses. Nestlé does provide segment assets and segment liabilities information.

Although the format of segment reporting is entity-specific, in the end the segment financials have to add up into the consolidated financial statements. That's why the company has to provide reconciliations of the total of the reportable segments' revenues, measures of profit or loss, assets and liabilities (if applicable) to the corresponding group level figures in the consolidated financial statements.

Finally, IFRS 8 requires companies to present analyses of revenues from external customers and certain non-current assets by geographical area and even to disclose revenues/assets by individual foreign country (if material), irrespective of the identification of operating segments. In addition, information about the external revenues for each product and service and about the extent of the company's reliance on its major customers, has to be disclosed.

In practice, segment disclosures tend to vary considerably from company to company. Note that national accounting rules are usually much less exigent on segment disclosures than IFRS Standards or US GAAP. Even the EU Accounting Directive only calls for disclosure of sales by product and geographical area, but many companies used to go beyond that. However, the EU is expanding some disclosures for political reasons. It now requires companies operating in the extractive industries and logging to disclose payments in host countries on a country by country basis.

IFRS 8 – OPERATING SEGMENTS *(extracts)*

Information about profit or loss, assets and liabilities

23. An entity shall report a measure of profit or loss for each reportable segment. An entity shall report a measure of total assets and liabilities for each reportable segment if such amounts are regularly provided to the chief operating decision-maker. An entity shall also disclose the following about each reportable segment if the specified amounts are included in the measure of segment profit or loss reviewed by the chief operating decision-maker, or are otherwise regularly provided to the chief operating decision-maker, even if not included in that measure of segment profit or loss:

(a) revenues from external customers;
(b) revenues from transactions with other operating segments of the same entity;
(c) interest revenue;
(d) interest expense;
(e) depreciation and amortisation;
(f) material items of income and expense disclosed in accordance with paragraph 97 of IAS 1 Presentation of Financial Statements (as revised in 2007);
(g) the entity's interest in the profit or loss of associates and joint ventures accounted for by the equity method;
(h) income tax expense or income; and
(i) material non-cash items other than depreciation and amortisation.

An entity shall report interest revenue separately from interest expense for each reportable segment unless a majority of the segment's revenues are from interest and the chief operating decision-maker relies primarily on net interest revenue to assess the performance of the segment and make decisions about resources to be allocated to the segment. In that situation, an entity may report that segment's interest revenue net of its interest expense and disclose that it has done so.

Source: IFRS 8, Operating Segments

When analyzing the financial statements of multinational companies, it is well worth trying to assemble as long as possible a time series of segment data to work out growth trends by business. This will then provide a picture of which businesses are expanding, which contracting and so on.

Analysts would like more segment data. They complain that it is very difficult to forecast future profits of companies if they do not know the relative profitability of different product lines, and are unable to judge what proportion of sales is generated by each. Companies, however, do not like giving too much detailed analysis because they feel it gives away competitive advantage, and some argue that analysts do not understand the artificiality that can be induced by segment analysis. Where a company trades across the world, there are many transactions between subsidiaries, and these take place at relatively artificial prices which are fixed by the company.

For example, if a new product is developed by the French parent company, but the product is manufactured in South Africa, does the African subsidiary pay a royalty on the development cost to the French parent? How do you allocate worldwide advertising costs? If you have several different product lines, how do you allocate all the costs of running the head office, including preparation of group financial statements, stock exchange listing costs, investor relations, etc.? There are many factors that impinge on these decisions, including tax, and the resulting allocations of cost are not necessarily economically meaningful (see Chapter 15 on taxation).

Analysts should look closely at the segment data provided by a company, but remember that allocations distort the overall picture and that no two groups necessarily make their allocations in the same way. Segment data are probably more useful for time series analysis than cross-sectional.

STANDARDS

 IFRS 8 – OPERATING SEGMENTS *(extracts)*

Information about products and services
32. An entity shall report the revenues from external customers for each product and service, or each group of similar products and services, unless the necessary information is not available and the cost to develop it would be excessive, in which case that fact shall be disclosed. The amounts of revenues reported shall be based on the financial information used to produce the entity's financial statements.

Information about geographical areas
33. An entity shall report the following geographical information, unless the necessary information is not available and the cost to develop it would be excessive:

(a) revenues from external customers (i) attributed to the entity's country of domicile and (ii) attributed to all foreign countries in total from which the entity derives revenues. If revenues from external customers attributed to an individual foreign country are material, those revenues shall be disclosed separately. An entity shall disclose the basis for attributing revenues from external customers to individual countries.
(b) non-current assets other than financial instruments, deferred tax assets, post-employment benefit assets, and rights arising under insurance contracts (i) located in the entity's country of domicile and (ii) located in all foreign countries in total in which the entity holds assets. If assets in an individual foreign country are material, those assets shall be disclosed separately.

The amounts reported shall be based on the financial information that is used to produce the entity's financial statements. If the necessary information is not available and the cost to develop it would be excessive, that fact shall be disclosed. An entity may provide, in addition to the information required by this paragraph, subtotals of geographical information about groups of countries.

Information about major customers
34. An entity shall provide information about the extent of its reliance on its major customers. If revenues from transactions with a single external customer amount to 10 per cent or more of an entity's revenues, the entity shall disclose that fact, the total amount of revenues from each such customer, and the identity of the segment or segments reporting the revenues. The entity need not disclose the identity of a major

(Continued)

customer or the amount of revenues that each segment reports from that customer. For the purposes of this IFRS Standard, a group of entities known to a reporting entity to be under common control shall be considered a single customer. However, judgement is required to assess whether a government (including government agencies and similar bodies whether local, national or international) and entities known to the reporting entity to be under the control of that government are considered a single customer. In assessing this, the reporting entity shall consider the extent of economic integration between those entities.

Source: IFRS 8, Operating Segments

Foreign currency transactions and foreign operations

Any group that operates in different countries is likely to operate in several different currencies. Indeed it may be that most of a group's subsidiaries operate in currencies other than those of its parent (e.g. how many of Nestlé's subsidiaries operate using the Swiss franc?). This of course means that there is a foreign currency conversion question to be resolved when preparing consolidated financial statements.

It is worth considering the behaviour of exchange rates briefly in order to understand the environment within which the accounting decisions have to be made. In the early part of the twentieth century, exchange rates were relatively stable and governments attempted to reinforce this stability by promoting 'fixed parities' between currencies or against the price of gold. Later, economic pressures, particularly inflation, made it very difficult to maintain such fixed exchange rates. One solution was to go for 'pegged' rates, where currencies were allowed to move within a narrow tolerance, but this too proved impossible in the economic conditions of the 1960s and 1970s.

Today we have a situation where most currencies are allowed to 'float'; that is, they have no fixed exchange rate and can change rapidly from one day to another. This creates a number of severe financial management problems, as well as accounting problems, and these are not the least of the reasons for the introduction of the euro. As we will show in this chapter, having to deal in many currencies introduces very many measurement problems into accounting, quite apart from uncertainties in decision-making because values are not stable.

For example, a German company buys an asset in the UK. The asset can be bought for £10,000 one day when £1 = €1.40, and can be stated at €14,000 in the German accounts, but next day the rate might move to £1 = €1.20. Is the asset then worth €12,000 and if the rate goes to £1 = €1.10 the day after, do you change the asset once more to €11,000? Rates do not normally move quite as dramatically as in the example, but they do move quickly and the movements are not necessarily consistently in one direction. A sharp drop in value one day does not mean that next day or two years later the value will not gain.

Our purpose in addressing these questions is to consider their impact on the financial statements of public companies. This impact can be seen in two different areas:

1. Translation of foreign currency transactions and related individual assets and liabilities which are denominated other than in the own reporting currency

2. Translation of the financial statements of foreign subsidiaries for inclusion in consolidated financial statements.

These topics are covered in IAS 21 *The Effects of Changes in Foreign Exchange Rates*. We will address the questions above with this Standard as our reference, except when noted otherwise.

Primary and secondary translation

When a multinational group, as a reporting entity, prepares consolidated financial statements, each individual entity included in the reporting entity first has to determine its specific measurement currency (the *functional currency*) and measure its results and financial position in that currency. The functional currency is not necessarily the local currency of the individual entity's country of residence, but in most cases it is. A multinational group will probably comprise individual entities with a number of functional currencies and, thus, will have to consolidate a number of individual financial statements in different reporting currencies.

If an individual entity within the group entered into foreign currency transactions (i.e. transactions that are denominated or require settlement in a currency other than the functional currency of the entity), the foreign currency items first have to be translated into its functional currency. This is the *primary translation* process (i.e. translation of transactions).

Once the individual entities within a reporting entity (the multinational group made up of a parent and one or more foreign subsidiaries and investments in associated companies) have prepared their financial statements in their functional currency, these have to be translated into the currency in which the reporting entity presents its consolidated financial statements. If the functional currency of the individual entity is not the same as the presentation currency of the group, a *secondary translation* process (i.e. translation of financial statements) has to be carried out. The sequence of the currency translation processes and their relationship with the consolidated financial statements is presented in Figure 13.1.

In most cases, the functional currency of the parent will be chosen as the presentation currency of the group financial statements, but this is not a general requirement.

Functional currency

The functional currency concept is central in the translation requirements. Functional currency is defined as 'the currency of the primary economic environment in which the entity operates' (IAS 21, para. 8). The primary economic environment in which an entity operates is normally the one in which it primarily generates and expends cash. The functional currency is determined separately for each individual entity within a group. There is no such thing as a 'group functional currency'.

IAS 21 provides specific guidance on how to determine a functional currency (see IAS 21 extracts). It comments on the factors that an entity must consider in determining its functional currency.

It should be clear that determining the functional currency is not a free choice and sometimes will ask for professional judgement when evaluating the relevant indicators. In general, greater emphasis is given to the currency of the economy that determines the pricing of transactions than to the currency in which transactions are denominated (e.g. in the oil industry the US dollar will be considered as functional currency for crude oil revenue, even if actual sales are denominated in another currency).

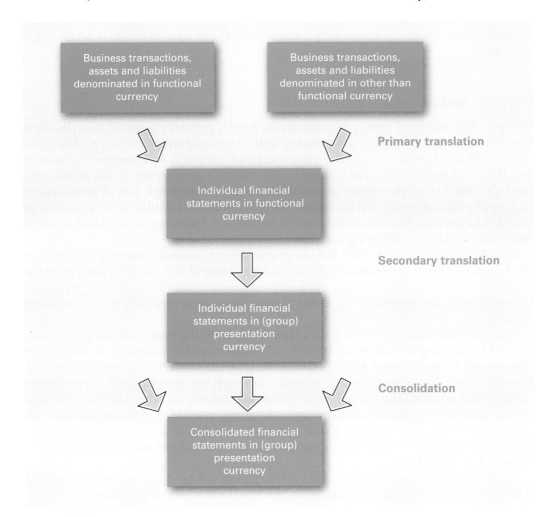

Figure 13.1 Primary and secondary translation

If the individual entity is a foreign operation, additional indicators have to be considered when determining the functional currency of that entity. A *foreign operation* is defined as 'a subsidiary, associate, joint venture or branch of a reporting entity, the activities of which are based or conducted in a country or currency other than those of the reporting entity' (IAS 21, para. 8).

Primary translation

Translating foreign currency transactions in the functional currency

A foreign currency transaction is simply a business transaction that is denominated or requires settlement in a foreign currency. Examples include a German company buying or selling goods and services on credit for a price expressed in US dollars, or a Norwegian company taking out a bank loan denominated in euro.

IAS 21 – THE EFFECTS OF CHANGES IN FOREIGN EXCHANGE RATES *(extracts)*

Functional currency

9. The primary economic environment in which an entity operates is normally the one in which it primarily generates and expends cash. An entity considers the following factors in determining its functional currency:

(a) the currency:
   (i) that mainly influences sales prices for goods and services (this will often be the currency in which sales prices for its goods and services are denominated and settled); and
   (ii) of the country whose competitive forces and regulations mainly determine the sales prices of its goods and services.

(b) the currency that mainly influences labour, material and other costs of providing goods or services (this will often be the currency in which such costs are denominated and settled).

10. The following factors may also provide evidence of an entity's functional currency:

(a) the currency in which funds from financing activities (i.e. issuing debt and equity instruments) are generated.

(b) the currency in which receipts from operating activities are usually retained.

11. The following additional factors are considered in determining the functional currency of a foreign operation, and whether its functional currency is the same as that of the reporting entity (the reporting entity, in this context, being the entity that has the foreign operation as its subsidiary, branch, associate or joint venture):

(a) whether the activities of the foreign operation are carried out as an extension of the reporting entity, rather than being carried out with a significant degree of autonomy. An example of the former is when the foreign operation only sells goods imported from the reporting entity and remits the proceeds to it. An example of the latter is when the operation accumulates cash and other monetary items, incurs expenses, generates income and arranges borrowings, all substantially in its local currency.

(b) whether transactions with the reporting entity are a high or a low proportion of the foreign operation's activities.

(c) whether cash flows from the activities of the foreign operation directly affect the cash flows of the reporting entity and are readily available for remittance to it.

(d) whether cash flows from the activities of the foreign operation are sufficient to service existing and normally expected debt obligations without funds being made available by the reporting entity.

Source: IAS 21, The Effects of Changes in Foreign Exchange Rates

On initial recognition of the foreign currency transaction, the transaction will be recorded in the functional currency by applying the spot exchange rate at the date of transaction, i.e. multiplying the foreign currency amount by the spot exchange rate between the functional currency and the foreign currency at the date of the transaction. But what happens next at subsequent reporting dates?

The most important single category here is borrowing in foreign currencies – loans may be negotiated for a period of several years and need to be restated in several statements of financial position between initial receipt and final repayment. For example, suppose a UK company borrowed $5m on the eurodollar market for five years, and the current value of the liability moved as shown in Table 13.1. The accounting question that arises is: what value should be given to the loan liability in the interim statement of financial position between receiving the loan (1.1.20X1) and repaying it (31.12.20X5)? In this transaction, the company has to repay more than it borrowed and the difference will also need to be recognized as a loss at some point. How and when should the loss be recognized?

Table 13.1   Movements in value

Reporting date	Exchange rate £=	Sterling equivalent
01.01.20X1	$1.60	3.125m
31.12.20X1	$1.55	3.226m
31.12.20X2	$1.40	3.571m
31.12.20X3	$1.25	4.000m
31.12.20X4	$1.30	3.846m
31.12.20X5	$1.40	3.571m

In terms of providing useful information for shareholders, the only really useful information is the final repayment value and the total loss over the loan period. However, this information is only available at the end of the period. Should the exchange differences be recognized only at that point?

Potentially, there could be a number of responses to the question, but IAS 21 takes the view that such items should be translated at the current rate on each reporting date (the closing rate) and the resultant difference be taken to the statement of profit or loss. The rationale for this is that the current rate provides the best available (if poor) approximation of the future repayment date and represents the best available information. In fact, accounting for foreign currency transactions according to IAS 21 depends on the type of asset acquired or liability incurred. More specifically, the treatment of foreign currency items depends on whether the item is monetary or non-monetary.

Monetary items are 'units of currency held and assets and liabilities to be received or paid in a fixed or determinable number of units of currency' (IAS 21, para. 8). Monetary items such as cash, accounts receivable and loans outstanding derive their value from the number of monetary units into which they are convertible.

Non-monetary items, such as inventory, equipment, land, buildings and cars, derive their value primarily from supply and demand. In our example, the UK company incurred a monetary liability and will show it in the financial statements at its sterling equivalent using the exchange rate in effect at the reporting date (date of the statement of financial position). Monetary assets (like accounts receivable) are similarly translated using the exchange rate in effect at reporting date. Foreign currency non-monetary assets (and liabilities) are translated using the historical rate of exchange that was in effect at the time the item was acquired or incurred.

One particularly interesting aspect of IAS 21 is that the Standard requires that exchange differences arising on translating monetary items at rates different from those at which they were translated on initial recognition during the period, or in previous statements of financial position, shall be recognized in the statement of profit or loss of the period in which they arise, irrespective of whether it is a loss or a gain. Such gains are unrealized until the monetary item is settled (in our example, until the loan is repaid), and this recognition of them in profit or loss is one of the few cases where an unrealized gain is taken to the income statement.

(Note that in the rather exceptional case that non-monetary items are measured at fair value in a foreign currency (for example in application of IAS 40 *Investment Property*), these should be translated using the exchange rates at the date when the fair value was determined. Exchange differences resulting from revaluation of non-monetary items carried at fair value will be recognized directly in equity or in profit or loss according to the treatment of the original fair value adjustments.)

Hedging foreign currency transactions

By way of background information in this area, we should also mention other aspects of dealing in foreign currencies that affect profit measurement but which are less immediately germane to an understanding of corporate reports.

One of the ways in which companies minimize the risk of changes in exchange rates causing losses is to take out 'hedges' against individual transactions. For example, where a UK company wants to buy (say) a French machine tool for €10,000 and places the order at a time when the exchange rate is £1 = €1 for delivery in six months' time, there is a risk that the rate could move to (say) £1 = €0.8 by the time delivery takes place, with the result that the expected sterling cost rises from £10,000 to £12,500. The company can avoid the risk by buying euro in advance (*buying forward*) and so fixing the rate actually paid. This sort of technique is known as *hedging*. When such a transaction takes place, the asset would be recognized in the buyer's books at the exchange rate built into the forward contract, not at the rate ruling when the asset was delivered.

In the absence of a hedge, individual transactions are translated at the rate ruling when the transaction took place. Suppose the French machine was delivered on 30 June, when the rate was £1 = €0.8, but three months' credit was allowed. Settlement was made on 30 September when the rate was £1 = €0.85. The accounting transactions would be:

1. Recognize asset 30 June at £12,500 and create creditor.
2. Settle creditor 30 September at £11,765 and recognize in profit or loss an exchange gain of £735.

If hedged by a forward exchange contract, the value of the asset would be adjusted for the fair value of the forward contract on delivery date (a value that approximates the difference on the contract amount between the spot exchange rate on 30 June and the forward rate).

Secondary translation

Translating foreign currency financial statements in a group's presentation currency

The need for secondary translation arises when a multinational group has to consolidate the financial statements of individual entities with different functional currencies.

ANGLOGOLD ASHANTI – FOREIGN CURRENCY TRANSLATION

Functional currency

Items included in the financial statements of each of the group's entities are measured using the currency of the primary economic environment in which the entity operates (the 'functional currency'). The functional currency of the parent company is South African Rands.

Transactions and balances

Foreign currency transactions are translated into the functional currency using the approximate exchange rates prevailing at the dates of the transactions. Foreign exchange gains and losses resulting from the settlement of foreign currency transactions and from the translation at the reporting period exchange rate of monetary assets and liabilities denominated in foreign currencies are recognised in the income statement.

Group companies

The results and financial position of all group entities (none of which has the currency of a hyperinflationary economy) that have a functional currency different from the presentation currency are translated into the presentation currency as follows:

- share capital and premium are translated at historical rates of exchange at the reporting date;

- retained earnings are converted at historical average exchange rates;

- assets and liabilities for each statement of financial position presented are translated at the closing rate at the date of that statement of financial position;

- income and expenses for each income statement presented are translated at monthly average exchange rates (unless this average is not a reasonable approximation of the cumulative effect of the rates prevailing on the transaction dates, in which case income and expenses are translated at the rates prevailing at the date of the transaction); and

- all resulting exchange differences are recognised in other comprehensive income and presented as a separate component of equity (foreign currency translation).

Exchange differences arising from the translation of the net investment in foreign operations, and of borrowings and other currency instruments designated as hedges of such investments, are taken to other comprehensive income on consolidation. On repayment or realisation, permanent loans and investments are recycled from FCTR to the income statement. For the company, the exchange differences on such monetary items are reported in the company income statement.

Source: Extract from 'Summary of significant accounting policies', AngloGold Ashanti,
Notes to the Financial Statements, 2017

The financial position and results of each individual entity within the group have to be expressed in a common currency (presumably the functional currency of the parent company) so that consolidated financial statements can be presented in the group's presentation currency.

IFRS 10 *Consolidated Financial Statements* defines consolidated financial statements as the financial statements of a group presented as those of a single economic entity. In other words, we remove the separate legal status of each individual entity in the group and treat them as one company.

One implication that we might draw from this is that we should treat all the transactions of the foreign subsidiary as though they had been carried out by the parent company. That would indeed be treating the group as a single entity. If we did that, we should then look at the individual assets and liabilities of the subsidiary as though they were part of the parent and, logically, we should use the exchange rate for each which we would have used if the transactions involved had been carried out directly by the parent. The approach would be something like that shown in Table 13.2.

Table 13.2   Consolidation exchange rates

Balance sheet item	Rate
Assets	
Property, plant and equipment	Rate at time of acquisition
Receivables	Closing rate at reporting date (best estimate of likely proceeds)
Inventory	Rate at time of acquisition
Cash	Closing rate at reporting date
Financing	
Equity	
Share capital	Rate at time of subscription
Retained earnings	Rate ruling at successive reporting dates when each slice of retained earnings was added to the statement of financial position
Liabilities	
Trade and other payables	Closing rate at reporting date (best estimate of likely payments)
Long-term borrowings	Closing rate at reporting date

This arrangement seems quite logical – it treats every element as though the transaction had been carried out by the parent and converted into parent company currency as though the parent had bought foreign currency to meet each transaction. Of course, it means that, since different rates are used for different elements of the statement of financial position, this statement will not balance. A new item, *translation difference*, has to be added.

That in itself poses a further problem: is the translation difference (gain or loss) something that should flow through the consolidated statement of profit or loss? If the result is a gain, this must be an unrealized gain because the parent still owns the subsidiary and prudence requires that this should not be recognized in the statement of profit or loss. Against that, unrealized gains on long-term liabilities are recognized.

Then again, is this translation adjustment truly a gain or loss? Insofar as rates of exchange may fluctuate both up and down, there is no real reason to suppose (on first principles) that the translation difference may not be purely temporary, an accident caused by the timing of the statement of financial position.

For example, if the rate of exchange at reporting date is £1 = €1.30 and the next week £1 = €1.40, how valid would it be to recognize a gain or a loss as at reporting date, when the position has already changed at the time the statements are being prepared? If the gain or loss is temporary, then is it useful to include it in the statement of profit or loss? You can see that there are some close analogies here with inflation accounting; both issues pose questions of valuation of assets and liabilities, and whether or not changes in value should be recognized in the statement of financial position and in the statement of profit or loss.

The other question that we must pursue is whether the agreeably logical solution of translating the statement of financial position of the foreign subsidiary as though the assets and liabilities had been acquired directly by the parent, provides useful information for investment decisions and for users generally. For example, is it an entirely accurate view of the economic relations between a subsidiary and parent that the transactions of the subsidiary are seen as relating only to the parent and not having their economic basis in the activities of the subsidiary itself?

The answer to that question must depend to a large degree on the facts in any particular case. For example, if a British manufacturing company sets up a Spanish subsidiary whose sole purpose is the marketing of the finished goods manufactured in Britain, there is a strong case for treating the Spanish subsidiary as nothing other than part of the parent's distribution costs. The separate legal status can be seen merely as a convenience, and the entity has no independent existence outside its marketing function. Translation of its statement of financial position (consisting perhaps of a warehouse, inventory of finished goods and receivables, with its main creditor being the UK manufacturing company), as though the transactions were those of the parent, would probably reflect the economic substance.

However, what if the Spanish subsidiary were a rather more complex business that manufactured its own finished goods (under the group brand name perhaps), sold these independently throughout the world (perhaps using other group subsidiaries in countries where these existed) and also sold products manufactured in other countries by other members of the group (a structure used by Philips, for example)? What if, as is often the case, there were local Spanish minority shareholders in the company and if, in order to finance its operations, the Spanish company also borrowed on the local capital market? The situation here is rather more complex, since the Spanish subsidiary is arguably a complete and independent trading entity in its own right and to account for its transactions as though they were carried out by the parent is a denial of that. It would not reflect the economic reality of the situation.

Looking at the mechanics of translation, we can argue a case that the assets and liabilities of the complex subsidiary have an economic relationship with each other, rather than with those of the parent. For example, the inventory does not derive from external manufacturing operations; the manufacturing plant is not an extension of an operation by the parent; the long-term loans borrowed on the Spanish market relate to the Spanish operation and its assets, not to the parent's global financing needs. If we translate the assets at the rate ruling when they were acquired, but the long-term liabilities at the closing rate ruling on reporting date, we are using different rates to translate two items whose economic existence is interdependent. We are arguably distorting the economic relationships and therefore it is questionable whether such an approach does give some approximation of the economic relationship. There seems a good reason here for using the same rate for both assets and liabilities to preserve their interrelationship.

In practical terms, the 'independent' subsidiary could be recognized as a set of interrelated assets and liabilities which were translated for consolidation purposes at the closing rate ruling at the reporting date when consolidation is taking place. In other words, the value used would merely represent a mathematical conversion from one currency to another to enable the group financial statements to be stated in a single currency.

Critics point out, though, that there is a major conceptual flaw in this approach: by consolidating the subsidiary using the current exchange rate, one is importing current values into historical cost accounts and this represents some form of hidden revaluation. According to purchasing power parity theory, exchange rates move in response to inflation, and the use of current rates for fixed assets would mean that an inflation adjustment was automatically being built into the group financial statements. This is not acceptable within the context of pure historical cost, but also it would be inconsistent to revalue some assets and not others; revaluation should be worked out systematically and not on the haphazard basis of currency and differential inflation. The correct rate must be the historical rate.

To illustrate the effect of this, suppose that a German subsidiary of a UK parent bought plant for €300,000 on 1 January 20X1 when £1 = €1.5; at that point the asset, if translated, would be worth £200,000. During 20X1 inflation is 10 per cent in the UK and 5 per cent in Germany. According to purchasing power parity theory, the exchange rate at the end of the year should be £1 × 1.1 = €1.5 × 1.05, or £1 = €1.43. If the asset were translated at the current rate at the year-end, it would appear in the group financial statements as £209,790.

Alternative accounting methods for secondary translation

Over the years, regulatory regimes converged towards a motivated choice of two methods, based largely on the rationale we have considered above. Typically, two methods are allowed, depending on the actual conditions under which the foreign subsidiary operates. The method that takes the subsidiary as an extension of the parent is known as the *temporal method*, while that taking the subsidiary as a whole is known as the *net investment method* (also the *current* or *closing rate method*). These methods figure in the EU Accounting Directive, US GAAP and, historically, in IFRS Standards.

In order to demonstrate the implications of the choice of method on the picture presented in the group financial statements, we shall now translate the financial statements of a foreign subsidiary using each of these methods.

Temporal method

The temporal method is based on the assumption that the best way of translating the statement of financial position and income statement of a foreign subsidiary is by treating the transactions as though they were carried out by the parent, and thus using rates which relate to the time when the transaction took place (hence 'temporal'). Assets which are carried in the books at historical values are translated at the rate ruling when the asset was acquired, while assets having a current or nominal value (i.e. receivables, cash) are translated at the current rate. The broad lines used are shown in Table 13.3.

Current monetary assets will be received after the reporting date, while current liabilities and long-term liabilities will be payable after the reporting date, so all are stated at the closing or current rate as being the best approximation. Other assets are translated at the historical rate that was obtained at the time of acquisition. Revenue and expenses are translated at the exchange rates prevailing when the underlying transactions took place. However, in practice, the average rate will be used, except for the inventory component of cost of sales and depreciation cost which are translated at historical rates to keep the link with the statement of financial position intact.

Table 13.3 Exchange rates – temporal method

Financial position component	Exchange rate
Non-current assets	
Property, plant and equipment	Historical
Accumulated depreciation	Historical
Current assets	
Inventory	Historical
Monetary assets	Current
Liabilities	
Current liabilities	Current
Non-current liabilities	Current
Equity	
Share capital	Historical
Retained earnings	Historical/Average

Worked example

The European Trading Co. plc invests CHF3m in a Swiss subsidiary. The subsidiary borrows a further CHF2m locally and buys a factory for CHF5m. At the time the subsidiary was set up (1 January 20X1) the exchange rate was £1 = CHF4.00, so the European Trading Co. plc invested £750,000 in the share capital of its new subsidiary. During 20X1 the Swiss company traded successfully and achieved profits of CHF500,000. The exchange rate had been slipping against the pound during the year and at the end of the year had reached £1 = CHF3.00. The average rate during the year was £1 = CHF3.50. The statements of financial position of the Swiss subsidiary (as expressed in local currency) are shown below:

	1 Jan 20X1 CHF'000		31 Dec 20X1 CHF'000	
Property, plant and equipment		5,000		5,000
less Accumulated depreciation		—		−250
Net current assets				
Inventory	—		500	
Monetary assets	—		750	
Current liabilities	—		−500	
				750
		5,000		5,500
Long-term liabilities		−2,000		−2,000
Total net assets		3,000		3,500
Financed by equity				
Share capital		3,000		3,000
Retained earnings		—		500
Total equity		3,000		3,500

During the year the net asset value of the Swiss subsidiary has risen from CHF3m to CHF3.5m. If we now take the financial position of the subsidiary at the beginning and end of the year and use the temporal method to translate it into sterling in order to prepare consolidated financial statements, the relationship of assets and liabilities within the subsidiary will change as shown below:

	1 Jan 20X1 £'000	31 Dec 20X1 £'000	Rate used £ =
Property, plant and equipment	1,250	1,250.00	4.0
less Accumulated depreciation	—	−62.50	4.0
Net current assets			
Inventory[1]		142.86	3.5
Monetary assets		250.00	3.0
Current liabilities		−166.67	3.0
		226.19	
	1,250	1,413.69	
Long-term liabilities	−500	−666.67	3.0
Total net assets	750	747.02	
Equity			
Share capital	750	750.00	4.0
Retained earnings[2]	—	142.85	3.5
Translation adjustment[3]	—	−145.83	
Total equity	750	747.02	

Notes:
1. This rate is assumed: the temporal method requires use of the actual rate at the time the inventory was acquired. For simplicity the example assumes that inventory was acquired uniformly throughout the year.
2. Again to simplify, the depreciation cost in retained earnings is translated at the average rate and not at the historical rate.
3. Under the temporal method the translation adjustment is charged against net income and is only shown separately in this example in order to highlight its existence.

In applying the temporal method, different exchange rates are used for different elements of the statement of financial position, and in this case we can see clearly the dilemma which emerges: in Swiss franc terms the subsidiary has grown by 16.67 per cent in value, but when translated back to sterling using this method the net asset value has fallen slightly. Which is the more useful picture from the point of view of users?

Probably your immediate reaction will be that this translation method must be wrong – but you need to think carefully about it. The major difference between the sterling result and the Swiss franc result derives from the fact that the long-term liability is translated at the current rate, while the major asset is translated at a historic rate. As in this example, the rate has moved against sterling, the liability has risen considerably in sterling terms while the asset has remained at its historic sterling value. This is exactly what would happen if the parent had borrowed in Switzerland for repayment ultimately from sterling resources.

The dilemma arises from the fact that the assets and liabilities are being viewed from the parent company standpoint, and the application of the prudence principle requires that the growth in current value of the liability is recognized while the assets are at historical cost. So the question arises as to whether one should ignore the prudence principle and state the liability also at a historical cost, or whether the asset might be revalued. Revaluation of the asset, however, would be inconsistent if other assets owned by the group were not revalued as well.

The strict application of accounting rules designed for accounting within one country and one currency to a multicurrency problem leads to this situation, and one should consider whether such rules can reasonably be extended in that way. The application of the rules ignores the economic reality, which is that the Swiss franc loan was negotiated in order to purchase a Swiss franc asset, and it is expected that the loan will be repaid out of Swiss franc earnings derived from the use of that asset. Does this have anything to do with the parent company other than to the extent of its investment?

This use, in the example, of a local loan to back up the purchase of a local asset is a classic technique in international business. If the parent company had not borrowed any capital but had invested CHF5m, its economic exposure to rate changes would obviously be much greater than for the investment of CHF3m. In effect, it has acquired an asset of CHF5m with a currency risk of CHF3m. Economically the loan element is balanced by the asset, since a rate change affects both asset and liability in the same way. This is known as a currency 'hedge'. The major difficulty with the temporal method is that it fails to recognize the economic existence of the hedge – the rate change is reflected in the financial statements only in so far as it affects the liability and not where it affects the asset.

	1 Jan 20X1 £' 000	31 Dec 20X1 £' 000
Property, plant and equipment	1,250	1,666.67
less Accumulated depreciation	—	−83.33
Net current assets		
Inventory	—	166.67
Monetary assets	—	250.00
Current liabilities	—	−166.67
	—	250.00
	1,250	**1,833.34**
Long-term liabilities	−500	−666.67
Total net assets	750	1,166.67
Equity		
Share capital (initial)	750	750.00
(Translation difference)	—	273.82
Retained earnings	—	142.85
Total equity	750	1,166.67

Note: The original share capital has been translated at the historical rate, with the difference between that and the closing rate being part of a translation adjustment. The average rate has been used for retained earnings.

Net investment method

The net investment method (or closing rate method) approximates to the alternative view of the parent/subsidiary relationship. It assumes that the subsidiary should be considered as an entity and the assets and liabilities translated at the same rate, thereby in effect showing the results of rate changes on the parent company's net investment in the subsidiary.

If we apply the net investment approach to the same Swiss subsidiary, the translation would be made at the rate ruling on reporting date (i.e. closing rate on the date of the statement of financial position): in this case therefore the opening statement of financial position would be translated at £1 = CHF4.00, while the closing statement of financial position would be translated at £1 = CHF3.00. Retained earnings are translated at the average rate £1 = CHF3.50.

Use of the net investment method ties in the rate change to both assets and liabilities, reflecting a current exchange value for both. The precise differences in the results of the two methods may perhaps best be viewed if we now compare the sterling translation of the closing statement of financial position under each method.

The difference in result between the two methods is quite dramatic and emphasizes a point we hope you have now fully realized: that the measurement of profit is subject to all kinds of quite subjective decisions on accounting principles. The essential difference in result derives from the fact that the net investment method has recognized the increase in sterling value of the asset as a result of a rate change, while the temporal method has not done so. Either view of the sterling result of the subsidiary is justifiable, depending on how you interpret the economic relationship between the parent and the subsidiary:

	Temporal method 31 Dec 20X1 £'000		Net investment method 31 Dec 20X1 £'000	
Property, plant and equipment		1,250.00		1,666.67
less Accumulated depreciation		−62.50		−83.33
Net current assets				
Inventory	142.86		166.67	
Monetary assets	250.00		250.00	
Current liabilities	−166.67		−166.67	
		226.19		250.00
		1,413.69		**1,833.34**
Long-term liability		−666.67		−666.67
Total net assets		747.02		1,166.67
Equity				
Share capital		750.00		750.00
Retained earnings		−145.84		142.85
Translation adjustment		142.86		273.82
Total equity		747.02		1,166.67

In the example chosen, the rates of exchange used presented a picture where sterling was weakening against the foreign currency, and the effect of that on the translation was to show up an increased liability under the temporal method.

If the rate movements had been the opposite, however, the picture would have been the exact reverse. Under the temporal method, the asset would have remained at its old sterling value while the liability would have diminished, thereby showing a positive translation adjustment. Under the net investment method both asset and liability would have declined, giving a negative translation adjustment. Do not fall into the trap of supposing that the net investment method always gives a more profitable result.

One implication of the differences thrown up by translation methods is that when assessing the performance of a subsidiary from a parent company viewpoint, care must be taken to distinguish the currency effects in the sterling results from the real underlying operating results. Using the relationship which profit bears to the investment in an operation as a yardstick (return on equity), the results for the Swiss operation could be interpreted three different ways:

	Growth in equity	*Opening equity*	*Percentage growth in year*
CHF financial statements	500	3,000	16.67%
Temporal method	−2.98	750	−0.40%
Net investment method	416.67	750	55.56%

Precisely the same economic situation can yield three different measures of success or failure, depending on the perspective chosen. This is clearly a problem for the analyst. The effect of translation differences can be highlighted in two ways. First, it will be reflected to an extent in the analysis of non-current assets – when the net investment method is used (and this is standard practice under IFRS Standards – see next section) the translated value of assets will change, as we discussed above. The amount of this change will be reflected in the non-current assets notes, and the analyst can check whether this is material in relation to total assets or whether a portfolio effect applies (what accountants call 'swings and roundabouts') and translation gains on some items are balanced by losses on others.

For example, Agfa-Gevaert (see Company report) shows a negative effect of exchange differences on the cost of all property, plant and equipment items in 2017, indicating that, on average, the euro got stronger in 2017 relative to the functional currencies of its foreign operations. Second, the analyst should look at the translation difference taken to equity ('OCI' accumulated in a separate component of equity) – is this material? If possible, a five-year or more time series should be constructed (back copies of the financial statements would be required) in order to see whether there is a definite trend.

Functional currency and type of foreign operation

IAS 21 *The Effects of Changes in Foreign Exchange Rates* avoids the difficult choice between alternative secondary translation methods through its guidance for determining the functional currency of a foreign operation. The standard-setter starts from the premise that the functional currency of a foreign operation that is integral to the reporting unit and the functional currency of the parent will always be the same, because they share the same primary economic environment.

It follows that there is no need for specific accounting rules to translate the financial statements of an integral foreign operation for consolidation purposes, as they will already be measured in the parent's functional currency. Consequently, translating a subsidiary's financial statements (in its functional currency) into a different group presentation currency according to IFRS Standards basically follows the net investment method. IAS 21 specifies these basic secondary translation rules in paragraph 39 (see IAS 21 extracts).

COMPANY REPORT

AGFA-GEVAERT

Notes to the consolidated financial statements (extract)

Exchange differences in Note 14 – Property, plant and equipment

Million euro	Land, buildings and infrastructure	Machinery and technical equipment	Furniture fixtures and other equipment	Construction in progress and advance payments to vendors and contractors	Total
Cost at December 31, 2016	358	1 479	213	15	2,065
Exchange differences	(11)	(27)	(6)	(1)	(45)
Change in consolidation scope	—	—	—	—	—
Capital expenditures	2	14	12	16	44
Retirements	(4)	(29)	(5)	(1)	(39)
Transfers	1	2	3	(10)	(4)
Cost at December 31, 2017	346	1,439	217	19	2,021
Accumulated depreciation and impairment losses December 31, 2016	281	1,406	186	—	1,867
Exchange differences	(7)	(25)	(5)	—	(37)
Change in consolidation scope	—	—	—	—	—
Depreciation during the year	7	19	13	—	39
Impairment loss during the year	—	—	—	—	—
Retirements	(2)	(28)	(5)	—	(35)
Transfers	—	(5)	1	1	(3)
Accumulated depreciation and impairment losses December 31, 2017	279	1,361	190	1	1,831
Carrying amount December 31, 2016	77	80	26	15	198
Carrying amount December 31, 2017	67	78	27	13	190

Source: Agfa, Annual Report, 2017

If, for example for regulatory purposes, a company keeps its accounting records and presents its individual financial statements in a currency which is different from its functional currency, the temporal method would, however, still be relevant. For consolidation purposes all amounts would have to be remeasured into the functional currency using the historical rate on initial recognition. Subsequent to this, only monetary items denominated in a foreign currency should be remeasured. This (temporal method-like) procedure produces the same amounts as would have occurred had all transactions been recorded initially in the functional currency.

Consistent with the translation logic of the net investment method, secondary translation differences do not affect profit or loss on initial recognition, but are recognized as OCI as accumulated in a separate component of equity. They will, however, eventually affect profit or loss on (partial) disposal of the foreign operation. On the disposal of a foreign operation, the cumulative amount of the exchange differences relating to that foreign operation have to be recycled (reclassified) from equity to profit or loss when the corresponding disposal gain (or loss) is recognized (IAS 21, para. 48).

With respect to the consolidation process, IAS 21 requires goodwill and fair value adjustments to assets and liabilities that arise on the acquisition of a foreign entity, to be treated as part of the assets and liabilities of the acquired entity. As such, they have to be translated at the closing rate.

Both primary and secondary exchange differences must be disclosed, including the amount of exchange differences recognized in profit and loss and the net exchange differences recognized in OCI and accumulated in a separate component of equity. For the secondary exchange differences, a reconciliation of the net amount at the beginning and end of the period has to be provided.

Hedging a net investment in a foreign operation

There is, however, a major loophole in IAS 21, which concerns dealing with currency hedges. A multinational company has investments in many countries that are therefore denominated in many currencies. This potentially creates many exchange exposures and a multinational usually tries to minimize this by borrowing in foreign currencies.

So if a British company wants to buy a US subsidiary for $100m it will try to borrow US dollars to finance the deal, rather than sterling. The investment will yield a dollar cash flow that can be used to pay interest and ultimately repay the debt. With a US dollar loan, any move in exchange rates has no effect on this closed circuit; a sterling loan would have fluctuating results.

Companies therefore hedge their investments and borrow in currencies that reflect the currencies of their future expected cash flows. These debts have to be translated into functional currency at reporting date at the closing rate notwithstanding, while the underlying investment is held in the parent at the historical rate. Following normal rules this would mean that the two were not balanced, but IFRS 9 *Financial Instruments* allows that translation gains and losses on loans which are hedges of investments may be taken directly to equity, without flowing through the statement of profit or loss. This is very rational, but has a flaw in that complex multinationals tend not to hedge individual investments, but rather take out a basket of currency loans to hedge a basket of investments, so one cannot tie down individual assets to individual debts. Consequently, it is rather in the hands of the treasury department at year-end to say which items are *trading debts* (gains and losses to profit or loss) and which are *hedges* (have no effect on profit), and one does not have to be unduly suspicious to see that this system is open to abuse.

IAS 21 – THE EFFECTS OF CHANGES IN FOREIGN EXCHANGE RATES *(extracts)*

Translation to the presentation currency

39. The results and financial position of an entity whose functional currency is not the currency of a hyperinflationary economy shall be translated into a different presentation currency using the following procedures:

(a) assets and liabilities for each statement of financial position presented (i.e. including comparatives) shall be translated at the closing rate at the date of that statement of financial position;

(b) income and expenses for each statement of profit or loss and OCI or separate statement of profit or loss presented (i.e. including comparatives) shall be translated at exchange rates at the dates of the transactions; and

(c) all resulting exchange differences shall be recognised in OCI.

40. For practical reasons, a rate that approximates the exchange rates at the dates of the transactions, for example an average rate for the period, is often used to translate income and expense items. However, if exchange rates fluctuate significantly, the use of the average rate for a period is inappropriate.

Source: IAS 21, The Effects of Changes in Foreign Exchange Rates

Summary

The analysis of multinational operations faces problems of highly aggregated data and of financial statements denominated in many currencies. Companies are required to provide some analysis of business and geographical segments to help the analyst.

Fluctuating exchange rates pose a major accounting problem when it comes to recognizing transactions denominated in foreign currencies and preparing consolidated financial statements which include foreign subsidiaries.

The notion of functional currency plays a key role in the accounting rules on foreign currency translation. The functional currency of a company is the currency of the primary economic environment in which the company operates. The functional currency is determined separately for each individual entity within a group and each entity has to prepare its individual financial statements in the functional currency.

Business transactions denominated in foreign currency are recorded in the functional currency by applying the spot exchange rate between the functional currency and the foreign currency at transaction date. Subsequently, monetary assets and liabilities must be translated at the rate ruling on each successive reporting date, as providing the best approximation of their ultimate settlement value. Differences arising from translation of such items, whether gains or losses, are taken to the statement of profit or loss.

Accounting regulation has traditionally put forward two methods for translating financial statements of foreign subsidiaries for consolidation purposes. If the subsidiary is translated as though the transactions were those of the parent, its accounts are translated at different rates appropriate to the category of asset or liability concerned. This is known as the *temporal method*. The translation difference is seen as either income or expense for inclusion in the consolidated statement of profit or loss. Alternatively, if the subsidiary is considered to be economically a whole entity in its own right, its financial statements are translated at the rate ruling on reporting date. This is known as the *net investment* (or *closing rate* or *current rate*) *method*. The use of this method preserves the relationships between assets and liabilities within the subsidiary's statement of financial position. It does, however, risk including assets which have, in effect, been revalued, within a historical cost oriented statement of financial position on an unsystematic basis.

IAS 21 sets the functional currency of a foreign subsidiary, which is heavily integrated with the operations of the parent and for which the temporal method is more appropriate, equal to the functional currency of the parent. As such, it only refers to the net investment method as the method to be used when translating foreign financial statements to the presentation currency of the group. The translation difference arising on consolidation is not recognized in profit or loss, but is treated as a direct adjustment to shareholders' equity (OCI accumulated in a separate component of equity).

Discussion questions

1. Discuss why it is important to complement consolidated financial statements with segment reporting.
2. A central issue in applying IFRS 8 *Operating Segments* is the determination of which operating segments should be reported. Explain the tests to determine whether or not an operating segment is a reportable segment.
3. Explain the difference between primary and secondary translation issues.
4. In what circumstances can a company's local (national) currency be different from its functional currency? If different, what are the accounting implications?
5. Explain why secondary translation differences are not recognized in profit and loss and deferred (as part of equity) under the net investment method.
6. Discuss the purpose and accounting consequences of currency hedges.

Assignments

The following assignments have answers on the lecturer side of the digital support resources for the book.

1. Norwood Ltd contracts to buy a new machine tool from Illinois Tools Inc. at a price of $85,000 on the following terms of payment: 10 per cent on delivery, 50 per cent after one month and the balance after a further two months. The machine is ordered on 1 September 20X1, leaves the Illinois factory on 1 October and reaches Norwood on 30 November. Norwood makes its payments on 1 December 20X1, 1 January 20X2 and 1 February 20X2. The £/$ exchange rates during this period were:

Date	Exchange rate
1 Sept. 20X1	£1 = $1.20
1 Oct. 20X1	£1 = $1.25
30 Nov. 20X1	£1 = $1.20
1 Dec. 20X1	£1 = $1.20
31 Dec. 20X1	£1 = $1.15
1 Jan. 20X2	£1 = $1.15
1 Feb. 20X2	£1 = $1.10

Required:

(a) On the assumption that the invoice was denominated in US dollars, show the balance sheet entries for Norwood at 31 December 20X1 and the income statement items for 20X1 and 20X2 which relate to this transaction.

(b) On the assumption that the invoice was agreed in sterling at £70,000, show the same financial statement items for Illinois Tools Inc.

2. Continental Holdings borrows CHF20m on 1 July 20X1 for a five-year term, at a time when £1 = CHF4.00. Show the relevant statement of financial position and profit or loss items relating to this loan for the years 20X1 to 20X6 inclusive, given the following exchange rate information:

Date	Exchange rate
31 Dec. 20X1	£1 = CHF4.25
31 Dec. 20X2	£1 = CHF4.10
31 Dec. 20X3	£1 = CHF3.50
31 Dec. 20X4	£1 = CHF3.25
31 Dec. 20X5	£1 = CHF3.60
30 June 20X6	£1 = CHF4.10

3. Voltaire Industries SA set up a UK subsidiary, Candide Ltd, on 1 July 20X1 with an investment of €17m. The subsidiary borrowed £500,000 on the UK market and purchased a leasehold factory for £300,000 and plant for £1.0m. The draft statements of financial position of the two companies as at 30 June 20X2 are given below. The exchange rates which applied during the year were:

Date	£ = €
1 July 20X1	1.7
30 June 20X2	1.5
Average for year	1.6

Candide purchased its closing inventories at a time when £1 = €1.55.

Required:

(a) Apply IAS 21's secondary translation requirements in order to prepare consolidated financial statements for Voltaire Industries as at 30 June 20X2.

(b) Comment on how the use of the temporal method (secondary translation) would affect the consolidated financial statements.

	Voltaire		Candide	
	€'000	€'000	£'000	£'000
Non-current assets				
Leaseholds	315,000		3,000	
Accumulated depreciation	−75,000	240,000	−300	2,700
Plant	850,000		10,000	
Accumulated depreciation	−375,000	475,000	−2,000	8,000
Investment in Candide		17,000		
		732,000		10,700
Current assets (A)				
Inventories	85,000		1,750	
Receivables	120,000		2,500	
Cash	163,000		2,500	
	368,000		*6,750*	
Creditors due in less than 1 year (B)	−250,000		−1,250	
Net current assets (A − B)		*118,000*		*5,500*
Creditors due in more than 1 year (C)		−100,000		−5,000
Total net assets		750,000		11,200
Financed by equity				
Share capital		400,000		10,000
Reserves		250,000		—
Profit for the year		100,000		1,200
Total equity		750,000		11,200

On 1 January 20X1 Flubdub Company set up Yabber Company with a share capital of LC200m (LC = local currency) and acquired 100 per cent of the outstanding shares of Yabber. At that date the exchange rate was LC1 = €4, so the acquisition cost of the investment in the books of Flubdub amounts to €800m. LC is Yabber's functional currency.

During 20X3 Flubdub grants a loan of €600m to Yabber, refundable at nominal value in € after a period of 10 years. On granting date, the exchange rate was LC1 = €3. At the end of 20X5 the exchange rate amounts to 1LC = €2. The average rate for 20X5 is LC1 = €2.5.

The condensed statement of financial position and statement of profit or loss of Yabber at the end of 20X5 are as follows (all amounts in LC million):

Statement of financial position at 31 December 20X5	*Yabber*
	(LC million)
Assets	
Property, plant and equipment (net)	560
Non-current financial assets	40
Inventories	300
Trade receivables	300
Cash and cash equivalents	200
	1,400
Equity and liabilities	
Share capital	200
Reserves	280
Profit for the year	40
Provisions	40
Long-term liabilities – Flubdub	300
Long-term liabilities – others	200
Short-term liabilities	340
	1,400

Statement of profit or loss of 20X5 – Yabber	
Revenue	1,800
Raw materials and consumables used	−600
	1,200
Staff costs	−800
Depreciation and amortization expense	−80
Profit from operations	320
Other expenses	−280
Profit for the year	40

Yabber's property, plant and equipment were acquired at foundation date and have been financed by the share capital funds and short-term liabilities. These short-term liabilities have been replaced by Flubdub's long-term loan in 20X3. Yabber's non-current financial assets were acquired at the beginning of 20X4, when the exchange rate was LC1 = €3. The historical cost of inventories acquired and used during 20X4 follows the year-average pattern. The reserves reflect the accumulation of retained profits. The historical exchange rate of the reserves corresponds to LC1 = €3 for 20X1 until 20X4.

Required:

Translate the statement of financial position and the statement of profit or loss of Yabber into euro according to the:

(a) Net investment method (as in IAS 21).

(b) Temporal method.

CHAPTER 14

Issues in financial reporting by multinationals

The object of this chapter is to review what are currently considered to be problems either in understanding corporate reports or in the quality of the information given in them. A financial analyst is likely to encounter some of these in looking at different companies. The subjects are not necessarily related to each other, and you might regard this as a reference section for advanced problems in financial reporting.

Chapter structure

- Introduction
- Values in accounting
- Expanding measurement attributes
- Mixed-attribute model
- Financial instruments
- Investment property and agriculture
- Pension obligations
- Provisions
- Post-reporting period events
- Discontinued operations
- Environmental disclosures
- Intellectual capital
- Summary
- Discussion questions
- Assignments

Introduction

The object of this chapter is to provide a few bridges towards further study of measurement and disclosure in financial reporting. It explores some basic notions of value and how they are related to measurement attributes of assets and liabilities and to the International Accounting Standards Board's (the Board's) mixed-attribute model.

Historical cost accounting has been perceived to be inadequate in reporting some transactions and circumstances and has been significantly modified in specific reporting domains . . . the boundaries of the traditional accounting model are moving. Similarly, supplementary disclosures in the notes to the accounts have been expanding considerably. We will review a number of significant disclosure domains such as contingent liabilities, discontinued operations, pension benefits, and environmental and intellectual capital disclosures. A financial analyst is likely to encounter some of these in looking at different companies. The disclosure items are not necessarily related to each other, and you might regard this as a reference section for advanced topics in financial reporting.

Values in accounting

We think it is useful first to remind you that the value of anything cannot be stated without some sort of qualification as to the context. For example, what is the value of your computer? First, we have to specify: are we looking at its value to you as a tool? As a fashion accessory? As a social symbol? Or some form of economic value? In management, we are usually looking at the economic value of an asset and trying to put a financial measurement on that. But even that needs further qualification: is the relevant value what it cost you to buy the computer originally? Or what it would cost you to buy a new one now? Or how much you could sell it for? (Another way of looking at that is to ask in which market you are making the valuation.)

In thinking about values, it is useful in the first place to distinguish between entry value, exit value and value in use. Recall that we touched upon these value concepts in Chapter 3 when we introduced the measurement bases that are common in IFRS Standards.

Entry value, exit value and value in use

Entry values are those that relate to acquiring something (how much can you buy it for?), exit values are those that relate to selling or liquidating something, whereas value in use is the incremental firm value from continuing use of the item (which can be seen as a variant of the exit value – an asset can disappear either through being sold, or through being used up within the company). Entry and exit values are both market values, i.e. all similar assets have the same value, whereas value in use is a value specific to the company that uses the item – it is an *entity-specific value*. The distinction between market values and entity-specific values is quite significant. In financial markets it is assumed that there is information asymmetry between the market and the management of the company. Market values contain less information, but are more reliable. Entity-specific values contain more information relative to that business, but are less reliable because they are usually subjective.

An entry value represents a market buying price, while an exit value is a market selling price. When market values are used, they provide comparable information between companies. Value in use, however, incorporates information about management intent and is therefore subjective and unique to the particular asset. In fact, when measuring value in use the company is asked to estimate the future net cash flows expected to arise from the continuing use and ultimate disposal of the asset and then discount these to present value. Different people have different views as to whether the user of financial statements finds the comparable market measure more useful than the unique entity-specific measure.

An investor is looking at a company and asking whether the price of the security is justified in the light of the cash flows that will accrue to the owner of the securities. In effect, this is the assessment which the analyst is making – what are the future cash flows that the investment will generate (what is the exit value?; what is the value in use?) and do these justify paying the purchase price of the security (entry value)?

The traditional accounting model is concerned above all with *entry values*. Under the historical cost model, the gross value of an asset in the statement of financial position is what it cost to acquire it. This is usually the market value at the time it was acquired (initial measurement) and if there is no subsequent remeasurement, this is called *historical cost*. However, in more sophisticated accounting, one may also consider whether it could provide more useful information to remeasure the value of assets at subsequent reporting dates. We then enter the realm of *current value* measurement. If subsequent remeasurement were desirable, one would have to prescribe a value principle: decide on what basis a new value was to be derived.

Measurement could be a revised entry cost – what would it cost to acquire now an asset in the same age and condition as an existing asset? This is known as *current cost*. Someone who is trying to value a company might approach it on the basis of what it would cost to acquire a similar bundle of assets at today's prices. That might be a current entry value. In an economy where there is rapid inflation, historical cost values soon become irrelevant, and current cost might be a more useful measurement approach in some circumstances. It is a problem for analysts when making comparisons between companies that historical cost values are not comparable because of different acquisition dates and subsequent inflation.

Value in use is based on what benefits can be generated from owning and using the asset. As an entity-specific value, it probably will differ from company to company. Estimating value in use comes down to estimating and discounting the net cash flows that the asset can generate. Financial accounting uses value in use as a *control measure* only. Recall that IAS 36 *Impairment of Assets* demands the calculation of value in use as a threshold value to arrive at an estimate of the recoverable amount of an asset. Long-term assets which are held for use rather than resale are held at cost unless the cash flows which are expected to be generated by their use and later disposal are lower than cost.

Financial accounting uses exit values both as a control and as a measurement base for subsequent measurement after initial recognition of a specific set of balance sheet items. Recall that inventories must be held at the lower of cost (normal convention) or net realizable value (the exit value of the inventories). The exit value provides a ceiling for the carrying value of the inventory. However, market exit values could also be used for subsequent measurement of any asset, not just those held for resale.

Boundaries of the accounting model

Value concepts are key to the debate on how the financial accounting model should work. In the nineteenth century annual income was defined as the change in wealth from the beginning to the end of the year, which could be translated in accounting terms into using the statement of financial position as the measurement focus instead of the statement of profit or loss. As discussed earlier, much of European regulation derives from a seventeenth-century requirement for businesses to prepare an annual 'inventory' of their worth. There was a period of experimentation as financial reporting evolved in the nineteenth century when the statement of financial position was the focus of corporate reporting in a number of countries, where, to put it in a simple form, a railway company might have had the following statements of financial position:

	1 Jan 1870	31 Dec 1870
Current value of track, buildings, rolling stock	100,000	135,000
Net current assets	20,000	30,000
Loans	−40,000	−50,000
Net worth	80,000	115,000

Difference in net worth = 35,000 = Profit for year

This approach uses remeasurement of assets and is consistent with a definition of income which is grounded in economic theory: that a company's income can be objectively determined from the change in its wealth plus what is consumed during the period (see Hicks, 1946). Under this approach, the measurement issue becomes the valuation of assets and liabilities at a given moment with market exit values as the measurement attribute. However, financial reporting as it evolved in the twentieth century has been oriented around reporting completed transactions, using entry measurement values, without any subsequent remeasurement or much acknowledgement of possible changes in the economic status of assets other than through depreciation.

There are a couple of points to bear in mind here. The most important is that in accounting the statement of profit or loss (income statement) *articulates* (as the jargon puts it) with the statement of financial position (balance sheet). The statement of profit or loss is an explanation of changes in the internal value of equity as a result of operations; it explains a change in equity, but it is also directly linked, through accruals, depreciation and provisions, to the balance sheet value of assets and liabilities. Balance sheet values and values in the statement of profit or loss are not derived independently of one another. Either you measure balance sheet values independently on different dates and the difference is the profit or loss for the intervening period, or you measure income, and the statement of financial position represents unabsorbed costs (assets) and anticipated expenditure (current liabilities) and financing.

The following question then arises: Is the analyst trying to measure future cash flows from the company's operations or the value of the company's assets? We would say that the investor is interested in the future cash flows that he or she is going to receive (dividends plus growth in the market value of the company) and that the company's ability to deliver (increasing) annual profits is the surrogate that is used (it is assumed that if the company produces increasing profits these will generate positive cash flows that will be used for dividends and investment in capacity, which will be reflected in higher market value). The current stock exchange value of a listed company is held, therefore, to represent the present value of the expected future cash flows of the company.

There is a *general belief that current accrual-based earnings measures are a better predictor of future cash flows than are current cash flows*. The logic behind this is that in making accrual adjustments, management build in their view of the long-term likely outcomes. This lends to the earnings figures more predictive value than is in the current cash flow figures, which include random events. In fact, this general belief is supported by empirical accounting research that shows that current accrual earnings outperform current cash flows in forecasting future cash flows. Moreover, market returns of shares are empirically better correlated with accrual earnings than with actual cash flow measures. These arguments support an analyst's measurement focus on the statement of profit or loss.

Expanding measurement attributes

Evolution of the accounting Standards of both the IASB and FASB (Financial Accounting Standards Board) has had the effect of challenging the twentieth century accounting model and its historical cost base. The standard-setters have been expanding the boundaries of the accounting model with the idea that economically significant changes may take place ahead of a completed transaction, sometimes many years ahead, and that more of these changes should be recognized than was previously the case. This is accompanied by the use of economic measurement techniques. This does not change what is ultimately recognized as profit or loss, but rather changes in which accounting periods something is recognized. Some would argue that it is a sufficiently substantial change to imply quite a radical reorientation of financial reporting, to give much more emphasis on representing the current economic status of the entity's assets and liabilities in addition to its completed transactions.

The recognition and measurement rules inherent in any accounting model impose artificial boundaries on what is reported in financial statements. It is a commonplace in teaching accounting to acknowledge that there are many aspects of the company, especially intangibles such as customer loyalty, acquired knowledge of a particular business, etc., which are not included as they have no clearly identifiable historical cost or their value cannot be measured with sufficient reliability. In recent years, it has become apparent that the information (economic facts and circumstances) that escapes the historical cost model (based on completed transactions) is more economically important than in the past. This discovered economic significance may derive from changes in circumstances or from changes in understanding of business and business measurement. The effect of the change in perceptions is to drive towards earlier recognition of (changes in) assets and liabilities than takes place under the completed transaction approach.

The most obvious example of a shift in circumstances is the growth in the use of *derivatives* (such as futures contracts) to manage currency and interest rate exposures and sometimes commodity prices. The rapid rise in this kind of economic activity brought about a situation where companies (and sometimes municipalities) were engaged in contracts whose outcomes were uncertain and which were largely unrepresented in the statement of financial position, because they were incomplete transactions which escaped the measurement model and there was no historical cost to begin with.

Executory contracts

The recognition issue here is the accounting treatment of *executory contracts*: binding contracts between two parties where performance is not complete. The traditional accounting model largely ignores executory contracts, except in the context of accounting for long-term contracts (and only if the percentage-of-completion method is applied). The problems with financial instruments are that the executory contract has potential value (positive and negative) for the business and challenged accounting to move the boundaries of its measurement model to acknowledge this.

IAS 37 *Provisions, Contingent Liabilities and Contingent Assets* has the notion of an *onerous contract* ('the unavoidable costs of meeting the obligations under the contract exceed the economic benefits expected to be received from it', IAS 37 para. 10), and represents a first step towards bringing executory contracts within the boundaries of financial reporting. The scope of IAS 37 excludes contracts for financial instruments and all executory contracts other than onerous ones. IAS 37 reflects the prudent bias of the traditional model, recognizing executory contracts as significant but addressing only those that are liabilities and not those that are assets. IFRS 9 *Financial Instruments* goes much further, however, by recognizing both assets and liabilities that arise from executory contracts that are financial instruments.

IFRS 15 *Revenue from Contracts with Customers* also goes in this direction. Where a company has contracts that are fulfilled over time, the Standard will require them to recognize the value of these executory contracts. However, the company has to measure at the same time the *performance obligation*, which is the delivery of goods or services to satisfy the contract (see also Chapter 4). Since the performance obligation is measured as an allocation of the contract price across different elements of the contract, the net effect on the statement of financial position is nil. However, the acknowledgement of executory contracts is a significant shift in the boundaries of financial reporting.

Closely related to this is the issue of recognizing changes in economic value in general (value changes both on the downside and on the upside through the revaluation of assets and liabilities). IFRS Standards have been equivocal about revaluation. The 1998 crop of Standards produced IAS 36 *Impairment of Assets*, which calls for assets to be reassessed in the event that some indicator suggests that they might be impaired. Recognition of negative changes in value, not linked to any transaction, was therefore brought into the IASB® measurement model. The model was then extended on the upside in 2000 with two industry-specific Standards: both IAS 40 *Investment Property* and IAS 41 *Agriculture* allow for assets to be remeasured at subsequent reporting dates.

Fair value measurement

The change in the boundary of what should be measured has been accompanied by a change in the boundary of how one might measure. This appears to be partly as a result of better measurement models, and partly as a result of established techniques in economics being more fully exploited in accounting. In this vein, recent IASB® rules have sometimes required companies to carry assets and liabilities in the statement of financial position at *fair value*. The Board defines 'fair value' as 'the price that would be received to sell an asset or paid to transfer a liability in an orderly transaction between market participants at the measurement date' (IFRS 13 *Fair Value Measurement*, para. 9). This fair value definition is essentially current market value.

Fair value has been introduced either as a *means of putting a value on an incomplete transaction* (i.e. simulating a completed transaction by asking what would be the exit value if one quit the transaction at that point) or as the *measurement attribute for subsequent measurement* in a number of significant accounting Standards. In some ways, the use of fair value can be seen as a logical extension of the traditional transaction model: if one wanted to value an executory contract or other asset or liability because the information is necessary ahead of the transaction being complete, fair value in effect simulates a transaction at reporting date. In other words, if the asset were sold or the liability settled, this would be done in the market, so by going to the market for a price, one is staying with the transaction model but applying it in a notional sense.

Fair value measurement hierarchy

Conceptually, fair value is a market-based measurement and as such is not affected by factors specific to a particular company. In that sense, it can be considered to be an unbiased measurement that is consistent from period to period and across companies. Many standard-setters believe that this makes it a superior reporting basis to historical cost.

If available, an observable market price in an active market is the best evidence of fair value and should be used wherever possible as the fair value measurement. In an efficient market, the market price of an asset or liability at any point in time reflects all available information and represents the market's assessment of all relevant economic factors and events . . . a perfect fair value.

The difficulties that present themselves for accountants in arriving at fair value are what to do when:

a. There is more than one market price

b. The market is (very) illiquid

c. There are no recent prices

d. There is no market for the specific asset or liability one is trying to measure.

Clearly as soon as you move away from a current, liquid market in exactly the same kind of asset or liability, the extent to which the value ascertained can be relied on starts to diminish, and the usefulness of the measurement becomes questionable.

IFRS 13 *Fair Value Measurement* (converged with US Standards) provides the rules for arriving at a fair value when another Standard stipulates that fair value should be used as the measurement basis. It identifies a *measurement hierarchy* with three levels of fair value measurement (see Figure 14.1).

Figure 14.1   Fair value measurement hierarchy

Level 1 is where exactly the same transactions (identical assets/liabilities) can be seen in an active market (using this is sometimes described as 'marking to market'). *Level 2* fair value is based on similar but not exactly the same transactions (similar assets/liabilities) being observable in an active market which can be adjusted reasonably. *Level 3*, however, is where there are no market transactions and the company must use a financial model to estimate market values (some people refer to this as 'marking to model'). IFRS 13 discusses various accounting models that are available. Since the market price is believed to reflect the market's estimate of expected future cash flows, discounted to present value, then this is an obvious model to use. Clearly Level 3 valuations are more uncertain since they are based on estimates. The Standard responds to this by requiring disclosures of assumptions and sensitivities to variations in those.

IFRS 13 specifies that fair value should be an exit price, but also that both entry and exit price are the same. Many people find this peculiar, since they think the price at which you bought something is not the same as that at which you could subsequently sell it. The explanation is that the standard-setters consider these as two different markets. If you buy a new car, the price you pay is the same as the price the dealer will receive (his exit price is the same as your entry price). If you immediately decide to sell it, you enter a different market, that of second-hand cars, which, in turn, can be segmented into the market at which a dealer might buy a second-hand car, and also the market in which a private individual sells to another private individual. The Standard says you have to correctly identify what is the *principal market* for the asset or liability whose fair value you are calculating. In the absence of a principal market, you use the *most advantageous market*.

Linked to this is the notion of *highest and best use*. Fair value of non-financial assets, under IFRS 13, is not necessarily the value of the asset in its current use. If there is a use that the market values more highly, then this is the fair value. For example, if you were operating a cinema on a town centre site, it might be that the highest and best use for the asset would be to sell it to a property developer.

A continuing debate on innovation

Standard-setters claim that fair value is the most relevant measure for some balance sheet categories, especially financial instruments, and that a market-based value is capable of being both objective and consistent. However, critics argue that market prices fluctuate rapidly, and reflecting day-to-day movements in the accounts just creates gratuitous instability rather than reflecting long-term economic value.

Given that analysts are trying to value the individual entity, one might have thought that entity-specific values were more useful, but analysts frequently say that they want to make their own entity-specific estimates, based on objective information, so market values are useful and also allow more direct interfirm comparisons, a mainstay of stock selection.

Mixed-attribute model

The IASB *Conceptual Framework* has a measurement section which discusses the allowable measurement bases (see also Chapter 3). It further elaborates that the factors to be considered in selecting a measurement basis should be in line with the fundamental qualitative characteristics of useful information – relevance and faithful representation.

Significant factors to take into account in determining which is the most relevant measurement basis are:

a. the characteristics of the asset or liability (for example, the nature or extent of the variability in the item's cash flows, the sensitivity of the value of the item to changes in market factors or other risks inherent in the item); and

b. how the asset or liability will contribute to future cash flows.

The nature of the business activities being conducted is likely to determine whether an asset generates cash flows on its own or whether it needs to be used in conjunction with other inputs to do so. When an asset such as an investment property generates rental income independent of other assets, or when a financial instrument generates interest without any need to participate in a process, the item's future cash flows can be directly assessed and a current exit value may give the most relevant information. A retail shop, on the other hand, needs inventory to be displayed and staff to service customers, and therefore is part of a process and does not earn cash flows directly. Its cash flows are earned as a component of a cash generating unit, and a different measurement basis is probably more appropriate, such as an entry cost.

Faithful representation of information provided by a measurement basis would be affected by measurement inconsistency and the level of uncertainty associated with the measurement. The latter factor resonates with concerns that have been expressed about the reliability of fair value measurements, limiting its applicability to a number of circumstances. Cost will also constrain the selection of a measurement basis.

The standard-setter acknowledges that consideration of all these factors is likely to result in the selection of different measurement bases for different assets, liabilities, income and expenses, resulting in a *mixed-attribute model*.

An area where mixed attributes are quite common and fair value accounting has proved to provide useful information is the domain of financial instruments: IFRS 9 *Financial Instruments*.

Financial instruments

A specific problem that has become increasingly important is the ability of companies to enter into forward deals to buy or sell, to borrow or lend, to issue shares or buy back shares, etc. This is the world of financial instruments where the markets are in theory being used to reduce risk because they enable companies to match their risk with a company that has an opposite risk.

For example, your company has a US dollar loan to repay in five years, and has revenues in euros. The market matches that with another company which has a euro loan to repay in five years and has revenues in US dollars – you agree an acceptable rate and swap the obligation to repay. This enables both companies to cancel the risk of the exchange rates moving against them. Certainly they lose the potential for gain at the same time, but this is normal – the lower the risk, the lower the potential gain (and the lower the potential loss).

However, this idyllic scenario is an oversimplification and the markets do not always work out the problems correctly. As far as commercial operating companies are concerned, sometimes they receive bad advice and make losses. Sometimes executives look at the upside potential of the currency or commodity markets and are tempted to think they could be making money for their company. They stop trying simply to reduce the company's risk and start trying to bet against the market, occasionally with disastrous results. This happened in the 1990s with Sumitomo Corporation and its copper trader, which tried to influence the copper markets by taking major positions, and lost the company millions of dollars in the end (as well as conducting various frauds to obtain the cash resources to pay for the trading).

The position is much more serious with banks, although these are (fortunately) outside the scope of this book. The banks are often the intermediaries in the marketplace and sometimes take on risks expecting to be able to find a counter-risk and not doing so, or occasionally just betting on the way the market is moving (e.g. Nick Leeson and the collapse of Barings Bank, or more recently Société Générale).

Fortunately, most commercial companies are not heavily involved in financial instruments, but the publicity given to the major losses that have been run up in this sort of area have caused investors and analysts to call for much more information about company involvement. Unfortunately, this has proved very difficult to regulate, not least because companies which make widespread use of commodity markets, for example, see it as unnecessarily onerous and potentially damaging in competitive terms, to disclose their dealings. Equally, there are problems about (a) how to value futures contracts; and (b) whether a relevant current valuation should be brought into historical cost accounts. Preparers argue that the final settlement value of a futures contract cannot be known until settlement because the markets are volatile. Consequently, potential losses recognized prior to settlement may never be realized and are misleading. The current value of a contract is not necessarily any guide to its future value. But efficient market theorists say that the current price embodies everything known about the future at that point.

Another problem in this area is the question of whether a *financial instrument* has been entered into *as a hedge for another transaction*. For example, if a company has to pay a US dollar sum in two years, it could enter into a forward contract to buy US dollars. This would in effect be a hedge of its exchange rate risk and would enable it to lock into the exchange rate guaranteed by the forward contract. The economic argument is that transactions and their related hedges should be accounted for the same way and balancing gains and losses be offset against each other.

This means that in regulating accounting for financial instruments one should potentially have one rule for financial instruments that are either entered into for speculative reasons or as part of general trading policy and another rule for those that are entered into as hedges of specific transactions. Regulators do not like rules that enable corporates to defer accounting for losses, even if there is a related profit due at the end of the contract, but corporates resent recognizing 'paper losses' when the overall arrangement is neutral in profit and loss terms.

IFRS 9 *Financial Instruments* addresses financial assets, financial liabilities and some commodity contracts (contracts to buy and sell non-financial items like oil, corn, electricity, etc.). Financial instruments include cash, receivables, payables, equity and debt securities as well as financial derivatives. The Standard establishes principles for recognizing and measuring financial instruments, whereas IFRS 7 *Financial Instruments: Disclosures* deals with supplementary information disclosure requirements.

More specifically, IFRS 9 provides recognition and measurement rules for derivative instruments, such as foreign currency options and forwards, commodity futures or interest rate swaps, which were mainly kept off balance under the historical cost model as their initial cost is often zero or very small. *Derivatives* are defined as financial instruments exhibiting three characteristics:

1. Their value changes in response to a change in some market-related underlying variable, such as an interest rate, a commodity price or a foreign exchange rate.

2. They require no or a relatively small initial investment.

3. They are settled at a future date.

These characteristics make derivatives risky contracts with potentially significant future cash flow consequences. The potential cash flow effects imply future economic benefits or sacrifices and bring derivative contracts within the scope of the asset and liability definitions. Fair value is generally considered to be the most relevant measurement attribute of derivatives.

IFRS 9 also contains an option for companies to designate a qualified financial instrument (asset or liability) on initial recognition as one to be measured at fair value with fair value changes in profit or loss (the *fair value option*). IFRS 9 has a basic model where there are three classifications of financial instruments, (see Figure 14.2) and *three measurement approaches*:

- The *default* measurement basis is *fair value* with subsequent changes in fair value flowing *through profit or loss*. The other two bases are treated as exceptions.

- To be measured at *amortized cost* (i.e. historical cost), the company's business model must be to hold the asset to collect contractual cash flows, and these cash flows can only be principal and interest.

- The third category is those instruments which are held to collect contractual cash flows, but which may also be sold. Many financial institutions hold a relatively fluid category of asset whose function is to earn interest, but instruments may be sold or bought to rebalance the risk of the portfolio on a periodic basis. Where the company's business model includes this kind of area, the instruments are measured at *fair value with subsequent changes flowing through Other Comprehensive Income (OCI)*.

Figure 14.2   IFRS 9 – Measurement bases of financial assets

Hedge accounting rules will apply if the financial instrument (usually a derivative) qualifies as an effective hedging instrument. The hedge accounting rules will try to match any gain or loss that arises due to movements in the hedged item (the result of a hedged risk) with corresponding (but opposite) movements in the hedging instrument.

Investment property and agriculture

IAS 40 *Investment Property* covers tangible non-current assets of property that are held as an investment for the purpose of earning rental or for capital appreciation (expected increase in value). IAS 40 requires a company to choose between a fair value model and a historical cost model and to apply the chosen model consistently across all investment properties. Under the fair value model, investment property should be periodically remeasured at fair value and the changes in the fair value should be recognized in profit or loss. Where the historical cost model is chosen, the fair value of the investment property has still to be established and disclosed in the notes to the accounts.

STANDARDS

 IFRS 7 – FINANCIAL INSTRUMENTS: DISCLOSURES *(extract)*

1. The objective of this IFRS is to require entities to provide disclosures in their financial statements that enable users to evaluate:

    (a) the significance of financial instruments for the entity's financial position and performance; and

    (b) the nature and extent of risks arising from financial instruments to which the entity is exposed during the period and at the end of the reporting period, and how the entity manages those risks.

Source: IFRS 7, Financial Instruments: Disclosures

IAS 41 *Agriculture* is an industry-specific Standard and covers valuation of biological assets and agricultural produce at the point of harvest, but does not apply to products that are the result of processing after harvest. IAS 41 requires measurement at *fair value less estimated point-of-sale costs* from initial recognition up to the point of harvest. The change in the fair value of the biological assets must be included in the net profit or loss of the period up to harvest. There is a general presumption that the fair value of a biological asset can be measured reliably. If not, the company should apply cost minus accumulated depreciation and minus any impairment losses. Some people view this as controversial because the company has to estimate the eventual sale value of a biological product, and then allocate that back across the years where it is being grown, less an allowance for spoilage. The Standard contains a recent modification to the effect that plants which are held exclusively to grow crops (e.g. rubber trees, or vines) can be measured at historical cost under IAS 16 *Property, Plant and Equipment*.

Pension obligations

Another issue related to financial instruments is that of a company's obligations to pay pensions to former employees. Pension arrangements differ widely between countries and companies. In some countries, such as France, ultimate pension provision is largely in the hands of the government and is funded by social security charges. Private pension pools are paid out proportionately to those with an interest and there are no guaranteed payments. However, in many countries employers have played a significant role in the past in providing pensions in excess of state benefits. Typically such pension schemes are funded by the company putting money into a separate fund (which accumulates pension assets or plan assets), and the fund pays out the pension. The pension schemes are generally classified as either defined contribution plans or defined benefit plans. Under a *defined contribution plan*, the company pays fixed contributions to the fund and has no obligation to pay further contributions if the fund does not hold sufficient plan assets to pay the pension benefits. The kind of scheme that gives the most difficulty is the defined benefit pension scheme. *Defined benefit plans* were very common in Europe and North America. The pension scheme guarantees to provide a pension to the retired employee that is a proportion of their final salary or some average of their later years working at the company. The employee accumulates rights to a bigger and bigger proportion with each year of work.

IAS 19 *Employee Benefits* sets the rules for pension plan accounting. Defined contribution plans are relatively easy to account for: contributions payable to the plan are recognized as an expense as the employee provides services. For defined benefit plans, IAS 19 requires the company to make an estimate of the pension obligation at reporting date (the present value of its defined benefit obligations (DBOs) for current and past service of employees) and to recognize a defined benefit liability (a kind of provision), net of the fair value of the funded plan assets. As for the statement of profit or loss effect (pension cost), the underlying principle of IAS 19 is that the cost of providing retirement benefits should be recognized in the period when the benefit is earned, not when it is paid. Broadly, the pension cost for the current year is determined as the change in the defined benefit liability for the year and charged to the statement of profit or loss. Pension plans need not be fully funded; they may even be unfunded. The funding rate does affect the defined benefit liability as recognized in the statement of financial position (through the fair value of the plan assets), but not the DBO.

There are a number of problems with defined benefit schemes. The central problem is that the *defined benefit obligation* is estimated based on a set of actuarial assumptions. The company (or its actuaries) have to forecast how long employees will work for the company, what their final salary will be and how long they will live after retirement. In assessing how much funding to put aside for this, they similarly have to forecast what the return will be on investments (plan assets) over the expected life of the employee.

Obviously, both these areas of forecasting involve some quite distant time horizons and some very significant unknowns, even if the law of large numbers does reduce the forecast risk. The actuarial assumptions encompass demographic and financial assumptions: demographic assumptions about future characteristics of current and former employees (and their dependents), such as mortality during and after employment, rates of employee turnover and early retirement, and financial assumptions dealing with items such as the discount rate (to calculate present value over a relatively long period of time), future salary and benefit levels (defining the target pension) and the expected rate of return on plan assets. Defined benefit calculations are quite sensitive for these actuarial assumptions, meaning that if the assumptions prove to be wrong, current shareholders may find themselves making extra provision for employees who stopped work years before.

Recent years have proved to be very difficult for companies with defined benefit schemes, precisely because their calculation of the funding requirements has been seriously wrong, leaving a number of schemes acutely underfunded. The primary reasons for this are (a) a considerable increase in life expectancy (50 years ago a European man retiring at 65 would very likely die before reaching the age of 67, whereas he would now probably live to about 75 or 80 years old); (b) the volatile performance of the stock markets in recent years; and (c) the low rates of interest on loans, affecting the discount rate to be used in the present value calculations. This has left some companies facing considerable deficits.

Actuarial assumptions have to be best estimates and financial assumptions must be based on market expectations at the balance sheet date for the period over which the obligations are to be settled. Changes in actuarial estimates (for example for greater life expectancy) will affect the accumulated benefit obligation. These changes in actuarial assumptions, but also unexpected changes in the fair value of the plan assets, result in *actuarial gains and losses*.

IAS 19 *Employee Benefits* requires service cost and interest to be reported in the statement of profit and loss with *changes in actuarial assumptions being shown as 'remeasurements' in OCI*. The discount rate which is used to calculate the present value should be the market rate on high-quality corporate bonds. Companies must disclose the discount rate, since use of a high rate has the effect of reducing the present value very significantly. Analysts should compare the discount rate used with that used by other companies.

The disclosures also include the fair value of plan assets. This should be the current market value, where there is one. However, if there is no market, then the fair value has to be estimated by discounting forecast future cash flows. The IASB also introduced extra disclosures calling for a breakdown of the investments included in plan assets by class of investment and a note of the expected rate of return. This too is aimed at allowing analysts to gauge the reasonableness of the assumptions behind the figures

Many companies have closed defined benefit schemes as a result of the changes in demographics and new variants of defined contribution schemes are evolving. The key characteristic of the classic defined contribution scheme is that the pensioner takes all the investment risk. A new variant is that the employer might offer some form of guarantee, e.g. that the rate of return on investment is not less than 4 per cent. IAS 19 will eventually be modified to address such schemes.

COMPANY REPORT

STORA ENSO – POST-EMPLOYMENT BENEFITS

Note 20 – Accounting principles (extract)

Employee benefits

The Group operates a number of defined benefit and contribution plans throughout the world, the assets of which are generally held in separate trustee administered funds. Such pension and post-retirement plans are generally funded by payments from employees and by the relevant Group companies, taking into account the recommendations of independent qualified actuaries. Employer contributions to the defined contribution pension plans are charged to the Consolidated Income Statement in the year they relate to.

For defined benefit plans, accounting values are assessed using the projected unit credit method. Under this method, the cost of providing pensions is charged to the Consolidated Income Statement to spread the regular cost over the service lives of employees in accordance with the advice of qualified actuaries who carry out a full valuation of the plan every year. The pension obligation is measured as the present value of estimated future cash outflows using interest rates of highly rated corporate bonds or government securities, as appropriate, that match the currency and expected duration of the related liability.

The Group immediately recognises all actuarial gains and losses arising from defined benefit plans directly in equity, as disclosed in its Statement of Comprehensive Income. Past service costs are identified at the time of any plan amendments and are recognised immediately in its Consolidated Statement of Comprehensive Income regardless of

(Continued)

vesting requirements. In the Group Consolidated Statement of Financial Position, the full liability for all plan deficits is recorded.

Amounts Recognised on the Statement of Financial Position – Defined Benefit Plans

EUR million	As at 31 December					
	2017	2016	2017	2016	2017	2016
	Total Defined Benefit Plans		Defined Benefit Pension Plans		Other Post-Employment Benefits	
Present value of funded obligations	851	909	851	908	—	1
Present value of unfunded obligations	288	314	264	289	24	25
Defined benefit obligations (DBO)	1 139	1 223	1 115	1 197	24	26
Fair value of plan assets	762	787	762	786	—	1
Net Liability in Defined Benefit Plans	377	436	353	411	24	25

Amounts Recognised in the Income Statement

EUR million	Year Ended 31 December					
	2017	2016	2017	2016	2017	2016
	Total Defined Benefit Plans		Defined Benefit Pension Plans		Other Post-Employment Benefits	
Operating costs						
Current service cost	13	12	12	12	1	—
Finance cost						
Net interest on net defined benefit liability	6	8	6	7		1
Cost recognised in income statement	19	20	18	19	1	1

Statement of Actuarial Gains and Losses

EUR million	Year ended 31 December	
	2017	2016
Gain/loss on pension scheme assets	24	37
Gain/loss arising on pension scheme liabilities	37	−99
Total Gain/loss	61	−62

Defined Benefit Plans: Country Assumptions Used in Calculating Benefit Obligations

| | Year Ended 31 December | | | | | |
| | Finland | | Germany | | Sweden | |
	2017	2016	2017	2016	2017	2016
Discount rate %	1.4	1.2	1.5	1.2	2.5	2.2
Future salary increase %	2.5	2.6	2.5.	2.5	2.7	2.5
Future pension increase %	1.8	1.5	1.8	1.8	1.8	1.6
Average current retirement age	64.0	63.9	63.0	63.0	65.0	65.0
Weighted average life expectancy	87.0	89.0	86.0	85.0	89.3	89.3

Source: Stora Enso, Annual Report, 2017

Provisions

Provisions and related issues are covered in IAS 37 *Provisions, Contingent Liabilities and Contingent Assets*. IAS 37 refers to a contingency as a condition or situation, the ultimate outcome of which, gain or loss, 'will be confirmed only by the occurrence, or non-occurrence, of one or more uncertain future events not wholly within the control of the entity' (see box on IAS 37, definitions). In a sense, all provisions are contingent because they are uncertain in timing or amount. We have already dealt with the borderline between provisions and contingent liabilities in Chapter 6. Recall that IAS 37 retains a specific distinction between provisions and contingent liabilities. Provisions imply a *present obligation* where an outflow of resources is probable, whereas a contingent liability reflects a *possible obligation* or a present obligation where the outflow of resources is not probable or cannot be measured with sufficient reliability.

Generally speaking, any company has an ongoing bundle of obligations, contracts and operations. It is the fact that the company is a continuing business that makes the annual profit of necessity an estimate based on a number of assumptions about the future. IAS 37, in effect, says that as long as future foreseeable events are expected to be profitable there is no need to reflect them in the financial statements, and indeed prudence requires that future profits are not recognized in advance. However, future losses are another matter entirely.

If a company has a loss-making division, this would not generally qualify as requiring a contingency note disclosure, but one would expect that the chairman's statement or management's review of operations would make clear that this is the case and would outline what action is being taken to deal with it. However, the outcome of a legal case such as being pursued for anti-competitive behaviour by the European Commission would certainly qualify as something that needs treatment in the financial statements. The question that next arises is, if there is a foreseeable future loss, should we disclose it in the financial statements or do we need actually to recognize the amount of the loss in the accounts?

IAS 37 explicitly states that *future operating losses* cannot be provided for. Such losses do not meet the IASB definition of liability and, consequently, the recognition criteria set out for provisions in IAS 37. Future operating losses have to be reported in the future in the same way as future operating profits. An expectation of future operating losses constitutes, however, a primary indication that certain operating assets might be impaired and thus could trigger extensive impairment testing of assets. An exception is made for *onerous contracts*, which could be executory contracts.

IAS 37 – PROVISIONS, CONTINGENT LIABILITIES AND CONTINGENT ASSETS (extracts)

Definitions

10. A *contingent liability* is:

(a) a possible obligation that arises from past events and whose existence will be confirmed only by the occurrence or non-occurrence of one or more uncertain future events not wholly within the control of the entity; or

(b) a present obligation that arises from past events but is not recognised because:

(i) it is not probable that an outflow of resources embodying economic benefits will be required to settle the obligation; or

(ii) the amount of the obligation cannot be measured with sufficient reliability.

A *contingent asset* is a possible asset that arises from past events and whose existence will be confirmed only by the occurrence or non-occurrence of one or more uncertain future events not wholly within the control of the entity.

Source: IAS 37, Provisions, Contingent Liabilities and Contingent Assets

An executory contract, as discussed above, is a contract where the company has entered into an agreement but fulfilment of the terms has not been completed (and perhaps not even started). Most businesses have many of these and, if the business is continuing, you might expect at any given moment that there would be sales agreements, supplier purchase contracts, capital commitments, etc. at varying stages of completion. IAS 37 says that these contracts need no special treatment except if such a contract is particularly 'onerous' – i.e. where the expected unavoidable costs of meeting the contract are greater than the benefits expected to be received from it. In general, if a contract is onerous, the company should recognize the present obligation under the contract as a provision in the balance sheet. An example of an onerous contract could be a non-cancellable operating lease for office space which is no longer needed by the company.

Recall that IAS 37 *Provisions, Contingent Liabilities and Contingent Assets* acknowledges the following categories of (potential) obligations:

1. *Present obligation* but where the amount and/or timing of future expenditure is uncertain. Here the company should make a *provision* – expense an estimated figure in the statement of profit or loss and carry forward a provision in the balance sheet, against which the expense will be offset when it arises.

2. *Possible obligation* arising from past events whose existence will be confirmed only by the occurrence of uncertain future events not wholly within the company's control. The company should *disclose* a *contingent liability* in the notes to the accounts. The same would apply for a present obligation where the amount involved is so uncertain as to make a reliable estimate impossible or where future expenditure is not probable (more likely than not).

3. *Possible obligation* for which the possibility of *future expenditure* is only *remote*. This is a *contingent liability* unlikely to cause an outflow of resources and, therefore, *no disclosure* is required.

On the one hand, related information is clearly important to the analyst in forming an opinion about the future profitability of the business. At the same time, it is sometimes quite sensitive information whose disclosure may have wider consequences for the company than simply influencing analysts' forecasts. A disclosure that the company is being pursued in the courts for causing environmental damage or infringing other company patents would have a considerable negative public relations impact.

Contingent assets, on the other hand, arise where events give rise to the possibility of an inflow of economic benefits to the company. Suppose, for example, that the company pursues a claim through legal processes, but the outcome is still uncertain. Prudence considerations prohibit in this case the recognition of an asset in the financial statements since it would probably result in the recognition of income that may never be realized. However, when the inflow of economic resources is probable, the contingent asset (material contingent gains) should be disclosed in the notes. If the inflow of resources is either possible or remote, the contingent asset is not even disclosed. Qualification for disclosure is thus tighter for contingent liabilities than for contingent assets.

The approach with regard to contingent assets and contingent liabilities may, however, change drastically in the future. In working on the conceptual framework the IASB has suggested removing the requirement for *probable* cash flows, leaving a threshold of relevance to the financial statements.

Post-reporting period events

A more specialist disclosure is events occurring after the reporting period (also referred to as events after the balance sheet date). While multinationals try to publish their financial statements as quickly as possible after the financial year-end, it is difficult to finalize the financial statements of all subsidiaries, obtain auditor approval and then consolidate the statements in under two months. Potentially, this means that events may take place between the financial year-end and the publication date of the financial statements that have a significant bearing on the future of the company. IAS 10 *Events after the Reporting Period* addresses more specifically events (both favourable and unfavourable) occurring between the end of the reporting period and the date when the financial statements are authorized for issue.

STANDARDS

 IAS 10 – EVENTS AFTER THE REPORTING PERIOD *(extract)*

Definitions

3. *Events after the reporting period* are those events, favourable and unfavourable, that occur between the end of the reporting period and the date when the financial statements are authorised for issue. Two types of event can be identified:

   (a) those that provide evidence of conditions that existed at the end of the reporting period (*adjusting events after the reporting period*); and
   (b) those that are indicative of conditions that arose after the reporting period (*non-adjusting events after the reporting period*).

Source: IAS 10, Events after the Reporting Period

IAS 10 distinguishes between *adjusting* and *non-adjusting events* after the reporting period. Adjusting events after the reporting period are those that provide evidence of conditions that existed at the end of the reporting period. These events should be reflected in the financial statements by adjusting the amounts recognized in the financial statements. Examples are:

- After the reporting period a court decision confirms that the entity had a present obligation at reporting date – in this case a new provision will be recognized or an existing one will be adjusted.
- The discovery of fraud that shows that the financial statements are incorrect.
- The bankruptcy of a current customer after the end of the reporting period probably confirms an impairment loss on a trade receivable at reporting date – in this case the company will have to adjust the carrying amount of the trade receivable.

Non-adjusting events after the reporting period will not affect the amounts recognized in the statement of financial position or statement of profit or loss but, if material, their nature and an estimate of their financial effect should be disclosed. Examples of such events might be that after the reporting period a fire destroys a major production plant or a restructuring plan is announced. These events could influence the economic decisions of users taken on the basis of the financial statements and thus have to be disclosed. IAS 10 also explicitly states that dividends declared after the reporting period are not recognized as a liability because at the end of the reporting period they do not constitute a present obligation. They should, however, be disclosed in the notes.

Discontinued operations

Multinational companies are in effect usually a bundle of businesses that are not necessarily related to each other except by ownership. Often they will sell off parts of the group that they have decided are no longer 'strategic', or they will buy another group and hive off some of its businesses. IFRS 5 requires that information about a major line of business that either has already been discontinued or is about to be sold should be shown separately in the financial statements as *discontinued operations*.

STANDARDS

 IFRS 5 – NON-CURRENT ASSETS HELD FOR SALE AND DISCONTINUED OPERATIONS *(extract)*

32. A discontinued operation is a component of an entity that either has been disposed of, or is classified as held for sale, and:

    (a) represents a separate major line of business or geographical area of operations;

    (b) is part of a single co-ordinated plan to dispose of a separate major line of business or geographical area of operations; or

    (c) is a subsidiary acquired exclusively with a view to resale.

31. A *component of an entity* comprises operations and cash flows that can be clearly distinguished, operationally and for financial reporting purposes, from the rest of the entity. In other words, a component of an entity will have been a cash-generating unit (CGU) or a group of CGUs while being held for use.

33. An entity shall disclose:

(a) a single amount in the statement of comprehensive income comprising the total of:
   (i)   the post-tax profit or loss of discontinued operations; and
   (ii) the post-tax gain or loss recognised on the measurement to fair value less costs to sell or on the disposal of the assets or disposal group(s) constituting the discontinued operation.

(b) an analysis of the single amount in (a) into:
   (iii) the revenue, expenses and pretax profit or loss of discontinued operations;
   (iv) the related income tax expense as required by paragraph 81(h) of IAS 12;
   (v)   the gain or loss recognised on the measurement to fair value less costs to sell or on the disposal of the assets or disposal group(s) constituting the discontinued operation; and
   (vi) the related income tax expense as required by paragraph 81(h) of IAS 12.
         The analysis may be presented in the notes or in the statement of comprehensive income. If it is presented in the statement of comprehensive income it shall be presented in a section identified as relating to discontinued operations, i.e. separately from continuing operations. (...)

(c) the net cash flows attributable to the operating, investing and financing activities of discontinued operations. These disclosures may be presented either in the notes or in the financial statements. (...)

(d) the amount of income from continuing operations and from discontinuing operations. These disclosures may be presented either in the notes or in the financial statements. (...)

Source: IFRS 5, Non-current Assets Held for Sale and Discontinued Operations

It is very useful for analysts who are trying to predict future profits, to have the profits or losses from businesses that are being sold, or have been sold, stripped out of the statement of profit or loss. When that has been done, they can see what the profits from the continuing business are. The same applies to the information presented in the statement of cash flows. IFRS 5 *Non-current Assets Held for Sale and Discontinued Operations* therefore requires a separate presentation of this (as set out in the extracts from IFRS 5).

The Standard also requires that non-current assets that are being sold (*non-current assets held for sale*), should be separately identified in the statement of financial position and measured at an exit value (fair value less costs to sell) if the exit value is lower than book value (in most cases depreciated historical cost). This measurement and presentation approach also extends to what is called a *disposal group*: a bundle of assets and liabilities representing a business to be sold.

The accounting for this (measurement at a lower exit value) is another case where prudence is applied. When the multinational has decided to sell a disposal group (a business), it must work out what is the fair value (less costs of disposal). If this is lower than the book value, then an impairment loss has to be taken, and the disposal group shown in the statement of financial position at fair value less costs to sell. However, if fair value is higher than book value, no gain is recognized at this point.

Once non-current assets are classified as held for sale, further depreciation of the asset is no longer allowed: the asset is now available for immediate sale and its service potential will no longer be consumed through the use of the asset in the company's operations.

Note that the remeasurement of assets held for sale (or of disposal groups) according to IFRS 5 differs somewhat from the main impairment rules set out in IAS 36 *Impairment of Assets*.

BETWEEN THE LINES

NON-CURRENT ASSETS HELD FOR SALE

Classification of non-current assets as held for sale is subject to some limitative conditions. In general, the following conditions must be met for an asset (or 'disposal group') to be classified as held for sale:

- Management is committed to a plan to sell.
- The asset is available for immediate sale.
- An active programme to locate a buyer is initiated.
- The sale is highly probable, within 12 months of classification as held for sale.
- The asset is being actively marketed for sale at a sales price reasonable in relation to its fair value.
- Actions required to complete the plan indicate that it is unlikely that plan will be significantly changed or withdrawn.

The assets have to be disposed of through sale. Assets that are abandoned because operations cease, would not meet the classification criteria (although they may be classified as discontinued once they are put out of service).

Environmental disclosures

Companies are under pressure to discuss their relationship with society in general and in particular how the company impacts on the physical environment. The European Commission is becoming more active in requiring disclosures beyond the financial statements. The International Integrated Reporting Council is a prestigious non-governmental organization promoting *Integrated Reporting* (www.theiirc.org) that encourages discussion of the network of interrelationships between the company and the society in which it operates.

Environmental disclosures by companies are still at an early stage, but very few large companies do not make reference somewhere to their environmental policies. Companies exhibit a range of different strategies in pursuing environmental disclosure: from adapting reactive positions in debates on environmentally damaging issues to taking proactive positions, mainly in relatively less sensitive sectors. The less discretionary part of environmental reporting relates to environmental costs being brought into the financial statements.

Accounting standard-setters as such have so far not addressed the broader issue of corporate environmental reporting, but a number of professional accounting bodies have produced guidelines and the United Nations Intergovernmental Working Group of Experts on International Standards of Accounting and Reporting (ISAR) published detailed recommendations in 1998 which remain the most thorough review of the area but have no regulatory authority. In the EU, environmental accountability and reporting has increased through new initiatives of the European Commission.

The absence of comprehensive regulation leaves companies with a free hand in determining what they publish, with the consequence that information is generally quite specific to the reporting company and is not audited. The majority of the environmental disclosures appear in the directors' report or an equivalent management commentary section of the annual report. Alternatives are a stand-alone report or a stand-alone environmental section in the annual report. Financially oriented environmental disclosures figure primarily in the notes to the accounts and deal mainly with environmental liabilities and contingencies in compliance with financial reporting requirements. The bulk of the environmental reporting is, however, voluntary. The aspects of environmental management that are reported most often include capital expenditures for anti-pollution equipment, recycling and conservation policy, environmental management and audit practices, and the costs of complying with governmental emissions standards.

Should analysts be interested in this information? Well, yes, because viewed from a strictly capitalist standpoint, we are moving further into a political environment in which governments are insisting that 'the polluter pays'. This means that any company that has caused pollution, intentionally or otherwise, may become liable to clean up the countryside and compensate people who are badly affected. Hidden pollution is therefore, aside from social considerations, very bad from an investor's point of view because it may mean a severe drain on future earnings. The case of Volkswagen's diesel engines and their level of pollution in the USA and elsewhere which came to light in 2015 is an example of how an environmental issue may damage a company's share price and cause a continuing stream of costs.

Decommissioning liabilities

This brings us back to formal accounting. A potential clean-up or compensation liability should be addressed in compiling the financial statements as either the object of a provision or disclosure of a contingent liability. At a more advanced level, it is worth looking at how companies have to account for decommissioning costs.

Decommissioning liabilities arise if a company, when it purchases or constructs an asset, takes on a contractual or statutory obligation to decommission the asset or restore the asset site to certain minimum standards or both, at the end of the asset's life. For nuclear power plants, for example, there usually exists a statutory obligation to dismantle the operational facilities at the end of their useful life. Such future dismantling expenditure and accompanying site restoration costs can be profound. Also oil companies now provide for decommissioning costs alongside the depreciation of mineral resources. In other words, they now recognize that they cannot just close down a well and go away, they need to make good the land as far as possible. Since this cost of using the mineral resource can be estimated, it should be spread over the period when the asset is used. Increasingly, we should expect this approach to be applied to factories as well.

There has been some disagreement as to how such *decommissioning provisions* should be applied. Previous practice was to charge an amount each year to the statement of profit or loss and build up the required provision year on year over the life of the operational facility. However, IAS 37 *Provisions, Contingent Liabilities and Contingent Assets* says that if there is a dismantling obligation, a full provision should be recognized as soon as the obligation exists, usually at construction date or commencement of operations. Additionally, the IASB considers these decommissioning and site restoration costs necessary expenditure in order to access the economic benefits expected to flow from the asset. Therefore, these costs have to be *capitalized* as part of the acquisition cost of the asset at the date on which the company becomes obligated to incur them (cfr. IAS 16 *Property, Plant and Equipment*).

BP - DECOMMISSIONING OBLIGATION AND ASSET COST

Extract from Note 1 – Accounting policies
Property, plant and equipment
Property, plant and equipment is stated at cost, less accumulated depreciation and accumulated impairment losses. The initial cost of an asset comprises its purchase price or construction cost, any costs directly attributable to bringing the asset into the location and condition necessary for it to be capable of operating in the manner intended by management, the initial estimate of any decommissioning obligation, if any, and, for assets that necessarily take a substantial period of time to get ready for their intended use, directly attributable finance costs. The purchase price or construction cost is the aggregate amount paid and the fair value of any other consideration given to acquire the asset. The capitalized value of a finance lease is also included within property, plant and equipment.

Source: BP Plc, Annual Report, 2017

However, one of the key differences between decommissioning costs and other costs of acquisition is the timing of the related expenditures. Decommissioning costs will not become payable until some future date, possibly several decades in the future. Consequently, there is likely to be uncertainty over the amount of costs that will be incurred and the issue of the time value of money undoubtedly will be very significant. Management should record its best estimate of the company's obligations and will have to use discounting to address the impact of the delayed cash flows. The amount capitalized as part of the asset's cost will be the amount estimated to be paid, discounted to the date of initial recognition. The related counterpart is recognized in provisions. Thereafter, the asset (capitalized decommissioning costs included) is depreciated over its useful life, while the discounted provision is progressively unwound. With the passage of time the increase in the decommissioning provision is recognized as a borrowing cost. From this, it should be clear that accounting for decommissioning costs will have a profound impact on the statement of financial position and statement of profit or loss as it affects long-term assets, provisions, operating and finance expenses over a long period of time.

If we look further than the financially oriented disclosures on environmental liabilities it becomes, however, apparent that the content and quality of environmental reports varies widely across companies. The heterogeneity of environmental disclosures makes them not comparable.

Intellectual capital

One of the issues the analyst needs to review in addition to assets and liabilities that appear in the statement of financial position is the existence and relevance of the 'intellectual capital' of a group. Essentially the argument is that, while physical assets (such as a city centre sales location or an efficient factory) may be important for the group, intellectual assets (patents, brands, staff know-how, research and development, customer loyalty) are possibly even more so: you can build a new factory in a few months for a finite amount of money, but a brand takes years and the cost cannot be forecast reliably. Intellectual capital is even more important, obviously, in a service industry in which it relates to the quality and nature of the service, which, in turn, is the product you are selling. Increasingly there is a perception that business now changes rapidly, and the ability to develop new products or adapt methods quickly is considered to be part of the intellectual capital of the group. Intellectual capital fits into the framework of analyst's concerns about assessing the quality of the management and the quality of the assets under their control.

How do companies convey this information? We discussed the difficulties of measuring intangible assets in a historical cost framework in Chapter 5. There are several problems. First, a company incurs costs often over several years in product research, staff development and related areas, without being able to tie these costs to an identifiable asset (source of future cash flows) until towards the end of the process, so these costs are taken directly to the statement of profit or loss. Second, where staff development is concerned, the company does not 'control' the asset: a trained person usually has the right to leave the company, so money spent training them cannot be regarded as an asset in accounting terms. Third, a company may hire people who have the skills needed (who have themselves invested in their personal development by doing an MBA) and so there is no acquisition cost available to be capitalized.

Clearly, traditional accounting does not provide the techniques for this kind of asset, and that is not surprising when you remember that corporate financial reporting was developed in the nineteenth century. So far there is therefore no way of reflecting this through recognition in the annual report. However, it is an issue which some companies address internally and where some discussion should be expected somewhere in the annual report.

BETWEEN THE LINES

The measurement and management of intellectual capital: an introduction

It is recognized that the intellectual capital of a firm plays a significant role in creating competitive advantage, and thus managers and other stakeholders in organizations are asking, with increasing frequency, that its value be measured and reported for planning, control, reporting and evaluation purposes. However, at this point, there is still a great deal of room for experimentation in quantifying and reporting on the intellectual capital of the firm.

Source: IFAC Handbook 1999, extract from summary of study published by the International Federation of Accountants, New York, October 1998

Summary

In this chapter, we have looked at more advanced measurement issues and at a number of domains of supplementary disclosures. An overview of the IASB's requirements makes clear that the boundaries of the traditional accounting model are moving, if slowly. It seems that the age of financial instruments has ushered in incremental changes which tend in the direction of earlier recognition of assets and liabilities in the transaction cycle, as well as remeasurement within the cycle. When it happens, this does not change the amount of profit in an absolute sense – the lifetime profits of the business will still be the same in total – but it does change the period in which profits are recognized.

We also noted that the trend has been for more and more disclosures, although there has been some pushback and a growing emphasis on the need to communicate in the annual report, rather than just publish lists of compliance-driven disclosures. In particular, we have looked at the problem of anticipating future costs, both in a general sense as provisions or disclosure of contingencies, and explored the reporting headlines of financial instruments, pension benefits, post-reporting period events and discontinued operations. Moreover, we noted that environmental disclosure and intellectual capital reporting has increased over time, but remains largely fragmentary and lacks comparability across companies.

Discussion questions

1. Explain the differences between the following value concepts: exit value, value-in-use and fair value.
2. What is meant by an executory contract? Do executory contracts affect financial statements?
3. Provide examples of adjusting events after the reporting period and explain how these would affect a company's financial statements.
4. Discuss why the existence of contingencies is important to the financial statement analyst, making reference to environmental issues and financial instruments.
5. Explain what is meant by intellectual capital and discuss what an analyst can do to make an assessment of the intellectual capital of a particular group.

Assignments

The following questions have answers on the lecturer side of the digital support resources for the book.

1. On 31 December 20X8 (fiscal year-end), Bruinzee NV is in the process of defending a legal case brought against it for damages caused by the use of some of its products. Bruinzee's legal advisors provided the following estimates of the likely outcome of the litigation:

    ■ 60 per cent probability of defending the case successfully
    ■ 30 per cent probability of being required to pay €4m in damages
    ■ 10 per cent probability of being required to pay €6m in damages.

    Given these estimates, a provision of €1.8m (60 per cent × nil + 30 per cent × €4m + 10 per cent × €6m) has been recognized in the 20X8 financial statements. Moreover, the Board of Directors of Bruinzee NV estimate that total legal costs of defending the case will amount to €300,000 (of which €200,000 has already been invoiced by the legal advisors covering fees up to and including 31 December 20X8). The legal fees of €200,000 have been expensed but the remaining expected future legal costs have not yet been provided for at the end of 20X8.

    In the event of successfully defending the litigation case, the legal costs will be recovered, but this has not yet been reflected in the 20X8 financial statements of Bruinzee NV.

Required:

(a) Evaluate the accounting treatment applied by Bruinzee NV. If you do not agree, propose and explain appropriate adjustments.

(b) Idem, considering the following revised estimates of Bruinzee's legal advisors and provision amount: '30 per cent probability of defending the case successfully – 60 per cent probability of being required to pay €4 million in damages – 10 per cent probability of being required to pay €6 million in damages'. Given these estimates, a provision of €3m (30 per cent × nil + 60 per cent × €4m + 10 per cent × €6m) has been recognized in the 20X8 financial statements.

2. On 2 January 20X0, Philippo Tist Corporation brought into use an industrial site that had been constructed at a total cost of €50m. The company has the legal right to use the site for a 10-year period, at the end of which the site has to be returned to the legal owner in its original condition. The directors of Philippo Tist estimate that the cost of restoring the site on 31 December 20X9 will be €15m (in 20X9 prices). The construction cost includes the right to use the site without further payment for the 10-year period. The rate to use in any discounting calculations is 8 per cent. The present value of €1,000 receivable in 10 years when the cost of capital is 8 per cent is €463.

Required:

(a) Show the amounts that will appear in the statement of financial position of Philippo Tist Corporation as at 31 December 20X0 in respect of the site and the amounts that will appear in the statement of profit or loss for the year ended 31 December 20X0.

(b) Indicate where in the statement of financial position and where in the statement of profit or loss the relevant amounts should be presented.

(ACCA adapted)

3. Omega Company follows the cost model when measuring its property, plant and equipment. One of its properties was carried in the statement of financial position at 31 March 20X7 at $6m. The depreciable amount of this property was estimated at $3.6m at 31 March 20X7 and the estimated future economic life of the property at 31 March 20X7 was 18 years. Omega depreciates its properties on a monthly basis. On 1 January 20X8, Omega decided to dispose of the property as it was surplus to requirements and began to actively seek a buyer. On 1 January 20X8, Omega estimated that the market value of the property was $7.1m and that the costs of selling the property would be $80,000. These estimates remained appropriate at 31 March 20X8. The property was sold on 1 June 20X8 for net proceeds of $7m.

Required:

Explain, with relevant calculations, how the property would be treated in the financial statements of Omega Company for the year ended 31 March 20X8 and the year ending 31 March 20X9.

(ACCA adapted)

4. On 31 October 20X7, Power Company decided to dispose of Theta Company, a 100 per cent owned subsidiary. The business activities of Theta are substantially different from those of the rest of the group and represent a major line of business. Theta has been followed as a separate CGU for internal reporting purposes. The net assets of Theta at 31 October 20X7 were included in the consolidated financial statements of Power Company at a net carrying amount of €200m, made up as follows:

	€m
Unimpaired goodwill	40
Other assets	260
Liabilities	(100)
	200

On 31 October 20X7, Power Company immediately began to seek a buyer and initial expectations were that the sale price (net of incremental selling costs) would be €170m. None of the identifiable assets of Theta had suffered obvious impairment at 31 October 20X7. The carrying value of the identifiable net assets of Theta in the consolidated statement of financial position at 31 December 20X7 was approximately the same as their carrying amount on 31 October 20X7.

The latest position is that negotiations are at a relatively advanced stage with a buyer who is expected to pay €170m (net of selling costs). Completion of the transaction is expected in the second quarter of 20X8.

Required:

Explain how the prospective sale of Theta Company will affect the consolidated financial statements of Power Company at 31 December 20X7.

(ACCA adapted)

CHAPTER 15

International taxation

The object of this chapter is to give you a working overview of taxation. Generally speaking, governments have a bigger stake in companies than do shareholders (in terms of receiving cash flows from the company), and yet not all companies pay as much attention to tax minimization as they might; neither do company executives have a clear idea of where tax bites in a company's cost structure.

This chapter will first look at the different kinds of tax and how they are levied within a single jurisdiction and then focus on corporate income taxes and the allocation of income tax expense to accounting periods. The chapter ends with a specific look at tax issues that concern multinationals and cross-border activities.

Chapter structure

Introduction

The number of taxes to which a company is subject varies considerably from country to country and depends partly on political structure and partly on historical precedent. The way in which taxes are collected varies widely as well. From a company perspective, we can identify the main types of taxation that are 'costs' to the company, as follows:

1. Social security charges
2. Local/regional taxes
3. National corporate income taxes.

Some accountants would say that corporate income-based taxes are not a cost as such because they are not made in exchange of goods and services specific to the company and are only levied when there is profit, so they are a distribution of profit to the government as a priority stakeholder in the success of the company.

However, assuming that we expect a company to be profitable to shareholders, we should try to maximize after-tax cash flows for them, and tax represents a negative flow. In practice, accounting standard-setters do not adhere to the distribution view of corporate income taxation and deal with income-based taxes as a business expense.

Within the European Union (EU), value-added tax (VAT) is a major source of tax income and companies collect this for the government, but, technically speaking, this is a tax on the consumer, not on the company, in the same way as sales taxes are in the USA and other countries:

■ *Social security charges*. Here, there is a great difference between countries in the extent to which they levy contributions from employers and employees based on the amount of pay. In Switzerland, for example, the deductions are relatively low but the employee is obliged to take out compulsory private medical insurance, whereas in France, the deductions are high and relatively little is left to the individual. There is also a great variation in contributions to pension schemes, with some countries preferring a system in which the State plays a major role and others preferring to participate in private sector schemes. This means that in some countries, payroll-based charges can amount to an additional 50 per cent on top of gross salaries, whereas in others, the employee expects to pay more – and may expect a higher salary. Payroll-based taxes and contributions to pension schemes are generally accounted for in the financial statements as part of personnel cost, and are therefore invisible both to the external analyst and often the internal manager.

■ *Local/regional taxes*. Here again, there is a wide variety of taxes and methods of collecting them. In federations, such as Germany or Switzerland, regional political units (Länder, cantons) are able to levy taxes on corporate profits, as also are municipalities. This means that corporate income taxes may be split three ways: local municipality, regional political unit and federal government (and they are not necessarily calculated off the same profit base). All of these taxes, since they are profit based, will appear in the financial statements as a deduction from shareholder profit.

However, in other countries, there are different ways of channelling money to municipalities. In France, they receive the proceeds from annual vehicle taxes, and also levy a tax that is based on the capital structure of the company. In the UK, municipalities receive tax based on the value of property occupied by people in their jurisdiction. These are not income taxes as such and do not therefore normally appear in the statement of profit or loss as a tax but as a cost of property or of running motor vehicles, etc.

■ *National corporate income taxes*. These are the most visible part of company taxation. Governments use this kind of taxation both to raise funds and to encourage (or to penalize) particular kinds of behaviour by companies. The calculation of taxable profit is done according to tax rules, rather than accounting rules, but one of the most important shaping forces in accounting is the relationship between these and, in particular, the degree to which in any jurisdiction, the calculation of taxable profit is limited by what is in the published accounts.

■ *Value-added tax* is applied throughout the EU and the European Commission, in fact, receives a small proportion (less than 2 per cent) of the proceeds of the national rate. VAT is imposed on customers at each stage of a product's value-added chain, based on the value added at that point. For example, suppose that in a country with a 20 per cent VAT rate, a manufacturer sells its product for €1,000 to a retailer. If the seller's cost to manufacture the product is €800, the VAT is 20 per cent of (€1,000 – €800) or €40. In practice, companies do not charge the net VAT amount, but charge VAT to their customers on the full amount of the sales and are themselves charged VAT on their purchases. Afterwards, the company separates out VAT received from customers and VAT paid to suppliers in its accounting and every month (or three months depending on jurisdiction) pays the difference between the two to the tax authorities. Consequently, a company's accounts exclude VAT for income reporting purposes, both inside and outside the company. In general, where taxes are simply collected from customers on behalf of a third party, they are not part of the company's revenue and, by implication, are not an expense of the company paying the taxes to its suppliers.

VAT is therefore not a tax as such on companies, but it does bear on them to an extent. First, there is the administration of VAT, which involves elaborate accounting systems to measure and control VAT payments. Second, there is the cost of maintaining the knowledge of staff and using outside experts to deal with changes and complex transactions. And, third, there is the cash flow problem. A company that sells on credit and is obliged to settle monthly with the VAT authorities will be in effect paying to the authorities VAT from customers that has been invoiced but which the customer has *at that time* not paid. There is a disguised cash flow effect which can increase a company's capital requirements considerably.

In the remainder of this chapter, we will focus on how taxes levied on corporate profits are accounted for and reported in the financial statements. IAS 12 *Income Taxes* covers the requirements on this within the context of IFRS Standards.

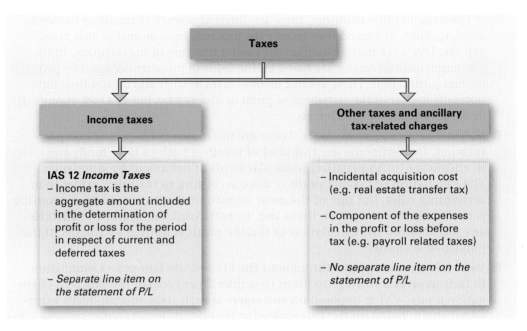

Figure 15.1 Overview of taxes

Corporate income tax and dividends

In most countries, even those such as Germany or France which are reputed to have a very close relationship between accounting profit and tax profit, the calculation of taxes on profits is based on an approach where there is a *reconciliation statement between accounting profit and taxable profit*:

Accounting profit before tax:

Add back: Disallowed expenses such as entertaining, fines, excess depreciation, excess provisions

Deduct: Special allowances for capital investment, environmental protection, etc., non-taxable income

= Taxable profit

A particular problem in corporate taxation is that of the potential *double taxation of dividends*. Double taxation arises from concurrent corporate and personal income taxation.

Suppose a country levies 30 per cent corporate income tax and then the company pays what is left as dividend to its shareholders. Suppose further that personal income tax is 50 per cent. That means that the dividend (70 per cent of the original pre-tax profit) will be subject to a supplementary 50 per cent personal income tax, which amounts to another 35 per cent of the original profit. The pre-tax profit has therefore been taxed in total at 65 per cent. This is a major disincentive to investors and different countries find different solutions to the problem. One way is to tax profits that are to be paid to shareholders at a lower rate than those retained in the company. Another way is to give shareholders a tax credit with their dividend.

A *dividend tax credit* is intended to remove double taxation and to ensure that only personal income is taxed. Suppose in the above example that the company earns a pre-tax profit of €200,000 and decides that the whole post-tax profit will be made payable to shareholders as a dividend. The government first collects €60,000 as corporate income tax, but gives the shareholders a full tax credit for the same amount. The €60,000 tax credit allows the shareholders to pay no more than an additional €40,000 to comply with their tax obligation of a 50 per cent personal tax rate on €200,000 pre-tax income. In practice, governments will often grant tax rebates equivalent to a partial tax credit and therefore only partially remove double taxation of dividends.

The objectives of determining (accounting) profit for financial reporting purposes are quite different from the basic tax raising motives of measuring taxable profit. Consequently, the income tax expense reported in the statement of profit or loss will probably not be equal to the amount that is actually paid. The topic of *deferred taxation* arises from these differences. In general, deferred taxation rules will require companies to account for the future tax consequences of transactions when the transactions are recognized in the financial statements.

Deferred taxation

The more advanced sets of accounting rules require that the tax effects of transactions are recognized in the financial statements in the same period as the transactions themselves. Deferred taxes (*deferred tax expense* and/or *deferred tax income*) arise in the statement of profit or loss when the amount of taxes payable in the current period (*current tax expense*) does not correspond with the amount of tax expense for the period based on the pre-tax profit reported in the financial statements. In the statement of profit or loss, deferred tax expense and deferred tax income will adjust current tax expense to arrive at the income tax expense for the period. Evidently, deferred taxation will also affect the statement of financial position: *deferred tax assets* and *deferred tax liabilities* will reflect the future tax consequences of transactions that were not treated identically for taxation and financial reporting purposes.

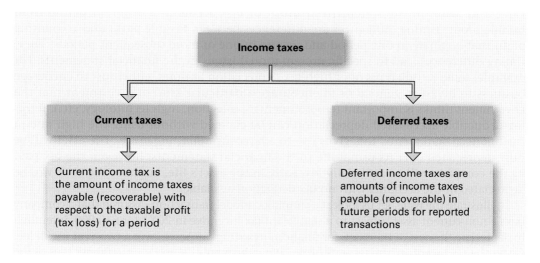

Figure 15.2 Current versus deferred taxes

Over the years, different sets of rules for accounting for deferred taxation have evolved. The earlier sets of rules were grounded in a statement of profit or loss perspective on deferred taxes. They focused on *timing differences* or differences between the timing of the recognition of items of income and expense for financial reporting purposes (in the statement of profit or loss) and tax purposes. Inconsistencies with the conceptual framework of the International Accounting Standards Board (the Board) and US Generally Accepted Accounting Principles (GAAP) led in the 1990s to the development of a *temporary differences* approach where the deferred taxation reasoning starts from an analysis of the tax consequences of balance sheet components and not from a tax reconciliation of statement of profit or loss items.

A statement of profit or loss view on deferred taxes

The intuitively most appealing way to illustrate the concept of deferred taxes is, however, still the statement of profit or loss approach. Later we will comment on the balance sheet perspective of deferred taxation that underlies current international reporting rules on income taxes.

Starting from the statement of profit or loss, there are in effect two kinds of difference between the accounting measure of profit and the tax authorities' measure:

1. Permanent differences
2. Reversing timing differences.

Permanent differences arise because the tax authorities do not accept some expenses as a deduction from taxable profits. Examples of this would be fines (in some countries), bribes, sometimes entertaining or what the authorities consider to be unnecessarily expensive consumption such as supplying managers with luxury cars or holding board meetings in holiday resorts. These are simply 'disallowed', they cause taxable profit for the year to be higher than accounting profit and do not call for any special accounting. Permanent differences can also work in the opposite direction, for example when items of income recognized in the financial statements will never be taxable or where items are recognized as deductible for tax purposes but will never enter the statement of profit or loss as expenses.

Timing differences arise because the timing of the recognition of revenue, expenses, gains and losses in the statement of profit or loss occurs in a different period from taxable profit. Timing differences are differences between taxable profit and accounting profit that originate in one period and reverse in one or more subsequent periods. These timing differences lead to specific presentational issues in the financial statements. For example, some jurisdictions offer high tax depreciation at times, either just to encourage business to invest in general or to encourage a particular kind of investment that the government thinks is important (environmental protection, high technology, etc.). If this tax-deductible accelerated depreciation can be claimed without using the high rate in the financial statements, this gives rise to a *reversing timing difference*. The asset will be fully depreciated over its useful life in the financial statements; however, the tax paid by the company will be artificially low early in the asset's life, but later the asset will be depreciated in the accounts with no tax deduction available.

To illustrate the issue, let us look at a simplified model transaction. Assume that a company buys a non-current asset subject to a significant tax incentive in 20X1 for €10,000, intending to depreciate the cost of the asset, for financial reporting purposes, over a two-year useful life. Given the tax incentive, the tax authorities allow the whole depreciation (100 per cent of the asset cost) in the first year.

COMPANY REPORT

PHILIPS – INCOME TAX EXPENSE

Income taxes
The income tax expense of continuing operations amounted to EUR 349 million (2016: EUR 203 million).
The components of income before taxes and income tax expense are as follows:

Philips Group
Income tax expense in millions of EUR
2016–2017

	2016	2017
Netherlands	137	929
Foreign	886	451
Income before taxes of continuing operations	1,023	1,381
Netherlands:		
Current tax (expense) benefit	10	(15)
Deferred tax (expense) benefit	(95)	(150)
Total tax (expense) benefit of continuing operations (Netherlands)	(85)	(165)
Foreign:		
Current tax (expense) benefit	(155)	(258)
Deferred tax (expense) benefit	37	73
Total tax (expense) benefit of continuing operations (foreign)	(118)	(184)
Income tax expense of continuing operations	(203)	(349)

Income tax expense of continuing operations excludes the tax expense of the discontinued operations of EUR 182 million (2016: EUR 181 million).

Source: Philips, Annual Report, 2017, Reproduced by Courtesy of Royal Philips

If the company's profit before depreciation is €25,000 in each year, the pre-tax accounting profit in both years (20X1 and 20X2) would be €20,000 (€25,000 less €5,000 depreciation on asset). However, the tax computations would be:

20X1	€	€
Profit before tax	20,000	
add back Depreciation	5,000	
deduct Capital allowance	−10,000	
Taxable profit		15,000
Tax due at 50 per cent		*7,500*

20X2	€	€
Profit before tax	20,000	
add back Depreciation	5,000	
deduct Capital allowance	0	
Taxable profit		25,000
Tax due at 50 per cent		12,500

Returning to the statement of profit or loss, the unadjusted figures would be:

	20X1	20X2
Profit before tax	20,000	20,000
Corporate income tax	−7,500	−12,500
Net profit after tax	12,500	7,500

The result of the timing difference is that the same net profit before tax yields quite different results over the two years. So the issue is: should that be reported in the financial statements as given above, or should the tax saving in year 20X1 (€2,500 or 50 per cent of the depreciation difference) be set aside and carried forward to year 20X2 to offset against the year 20X2 tax charge and equalize the accounting charge for tax?

Deferred tax accounting rules require that the future tax consequences of this difference are recognized in the financial statements. So, in the case above, the statement of profit or loss for 20X1 should be constructed:

Profit before tax		20,000
Taxes due (Current tax expense)	7,500	
Deferred tax expense	2,500	
Total tax expense		−10,000
Net profit after tax		10,000

The €2,500 deferred tax expense will appear in the balance sheet at the end of 20X1 as a deferred tax liability. The following year the timing difference reverses and the deferred tax liability is released to the statement of profit or loss:

Profit before tax		20,000
Taxes due (Current tax expense)	12,500	
Deferred tax expense	−2,500	
Total tax expense		−10,000
Net profit after tax		10,000

For analytical purposes, all you need to know is that a deferred tax liability in the statement of financial position represents the fact that accounting profit for financial reporting purposes has in the past been higher than that for tax purposes and the liability is there to compensate for future taxation on that difference. The tax liability reflects, in fact, the postponement of tax payments to future accounting periods.

Deferred taxes will normally arise in individual company accounts in jurisdictions where the relationship between accounting profit and taxable profit is reasonably loose. It should also normally appear in consolidated financial statements prepared according to IFRS Standards. Companies based in jurisdictions such as Germany or France, where there is a close relationship between accounting profit and taxable profit, should restate the individual company accounts for consolidation purposes. Excess depreciation or provisions that have been introduced for tax minimization purposes should normally be corrected during the consolidation process, and deferred tax liabilities introduced if appropriate.

A balance sheet perspective on deferred taxes

IAS 12 *Income Taxes* deals with the current set of accounting rules for deferred taxation. Although, originally, IAS 12 required a company to account for deferred taxes using the statement of profit or loss approach, the current (revised) IAS 12 (and the corresponding US GAAP rules for that matter) applies a method that is known as *the asset–liability approach* to deferred taxation: it is balance sheet oriented.

Essentially, the reasoning of IAS 12 on deferred taxes starts from the company's balance sheet and addresses what it calls *temporary differences* between the carrying value of assets and liabilities and their tax value. Every asset or liability is assumed to have a *tax base*, the amount at which the asset or liability concerned is recognized for tax purposes. Temporary differences are differences between the tax base of an asset or liability and its carrying amount in the statement of financial position. Broadly, the company's deferred tax position is calculated, based on these temporary differences, as the taxes that would be paid (or received) if the assets of the company were to be realized and its liabilities settled at their current book value.

It is important to note that the timing differences between pre-tax accounting profit and taxable profit do result in assets and liabilities having different valuation bases for financial reporting purposes than for taxation purposes at the end of a given accounting period. Therefore, timing differences will probably be the major source of temporary differences. But the point is that IAS 12 starts from an analysis of carrying values of assets and liabilities to identify temporary differences and not from a detailed review of the eligibility of revenues and expenses for tax purposes.

Additional temporary differences may occur because specific tax law rules create different tax bases for taxation purposes to those used for financial reporting purposes. Many of these additional temporary differences, however, relate to more complex taxation issues and are outside the scope of this course. Under the asset–liability approach there is no such thing as a permanent difference. Any difference between the book value of an item in the statement of financial position and its tax base is a temporary difference.

IAS 12 acknowledges two types of temporary difference:

1. *Taxable temporary differences* that result in deferred tax liabilities (i.e. taxable amounts in determining taxable profit of future periods)

2. *Deductible temporary differences* that will result in deferred tax assets (i.e. amounts that are deductible in determining taxable profit in future periods).

Figure 15.3 illustrates how temporary differences are qualified as taxable or deductible.

A difference between the **carrying amount** of an asset or liability on the statement of financial position and its **tax base** may be **taxable** or **deductible**

	For assets	For liabilities
Carrying amount **>** **Tax base**	**Taxable** temporary difference – deferred tax liability	**Deductible** temporary difference – deferred tax asset
Carrying amount **<** **Tax base**	**Deductible** temporary difference – deffered tax asset	**Taxable** temporary difference – deferred tax liability

Figure 15.3 Temporary differences

STANDARDS

IAS 12 – INCOME TAXES – DEFINITIONS (extracts)

5. The following terms are used in this Standard with the meanings specified:
Accounting profit is profit or loss for a period before deducting tax expense. *Taxable profit (tax loss)* is the profit (loss) for a period, determined in accordance with the rules established by the taxation authorities, upon which income taxes are payable (recoverable).
Tax expense (tax income) is the aggregate amount included in the determination of profit or loss for the period in respect of current tax and deferred tax.
Current tax is the amount of income taxes payable (recoverable) in respect of the taxable profit (tax loss) for a period.
Deferred tax liabilities are the amounts of income taxes payable in future periods in respect of taxable temporary differences.
Deferred tax assets are the amounts of income taxes recoverable in future periods in respect of:

(a) deductible temporary differences;
(b) the carry forward of unused tax losses; and
(c) the carry forward of unused tax credits.

Temporary differences are differences between the carrying amount of an asset or liability in the statement of financial position and its tax base. Temporary differences may be either:

(a) *taxable temporary differences*, which are temporary differences that will result in taxable amounts in determining taxable profit (tax loss) of future periods when the carrying amount of the asset or liability is recovered or settled; or
(b) *deductible temporary differences*, which are temporary differences that will result in amounts that are deductible in determining taxable profit (tax loss) of future periods when the carrying amount of the asset or liability is recovered or settled.

The *tax base* of an asset or liability is the amount attributed to that asset or liability for tax purposes.

Source: IAS 12, Income Taxes

The recognition criteria for deferred tax assets are, however, somewhat tougher than for deferred tax liabilities. A deferred tax asset should only be recognized for all deductible temporary differences to the extent that it is probable that taxable profit will be available against which the deductible temporary difference can be utilized, i.e. there should be a valid expectation of sufficient future taxable profits against which the deductions can be offset.

The deferred tax asset or deferred tax liability is measured as the temporary difference multiplied by the tax rate (see Figure 15.4). The tax rate to be used is the rate that is expected to apply when the asset is realized or the liability is settled, based on tax rates that have been enacted by the end of the reporting period.

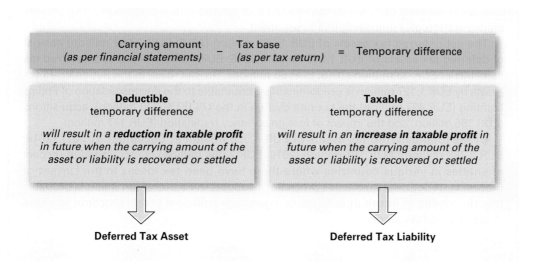

Figure 15.4 Deferred tax assets and liabilities

Returning to the previous accelerated tax depreciation model, we can apply the temporary differences approach as follows:

	20X1	20X2
(a) *Accounting balances*		
Asset carrying amount at 1 January	—	5,000
Additions	10,000	0
Accounting depreciation	−5,000	−5,000
Asset carrying amount 31 December	*5,000*	*0*
(b) *Tax values*		
Asset tax base at 1 January	—	0
Additions	10,000	0
Tax depreciation	−10,000	0
Asset tax base 31 December	*0*	*0*
(c) *Temporary differences*	*5,000*	*0*
(d) Deferred tax balance (50 per cent tax rate)	2,500	0

PHILIPS - OVERVIEW OF DEFERRED TAX ASSETS AND LIABILITIES

Deferred tax assets and liabilities

Deferred tax assets are recognized for temporary differences, unused tax losses and unused tax credits to the extent that realization of the related tax benefits is probable. The ultimate realization of deferred tax assets is dependent upon the generation of future taxable income in the countries where the deferred tax assets originated and during the periods when the deferred tax assets become deductible. Management considers the scheduled reversal of deferred tax liabilities, projected future taxable income, and tax planning strategies in making this assessment.

The net deferred tax assets of EUR 1,565 million (2016: EUR 2,692 million) consist of deferred tax assets of EUR 1,598 million (2016: EUR 2,758 million) and deferred tax liabilities of EUR 33 million (2016: EUR 66 million). The decrease in the net deferred tax assets by EUR 1,127 million is predominantly attributable to the deconsolidation of Philips Lighting (EUR 437 million) the tax rate change in the US (EUR 200 million), acquisitions (EUR 186 million) and the impact of foreign currency translation (EUR 177 million).

Of the total deferred tax assets of EUR 1,598 million at December 31 2017 (2016: EUR 2,758 million), EUR 161 million (2016: EUR 2,054 million) is recognized in respect of entities in various countries where there have been tax losses in the current or preceding period. Management's projections support the assumption that it is probable that the results of future operations will generate sufficient taxable income to utilize these deferred tax assets.

Philips Group
Deferred tax assets and liabilities in millions of EUR
2017

	Balance as of January 1, 2017	Recognized in income statement	Transfer to assets held for sale	other[1]	Balance as of December 31, 2017	Assets	Liabilities
Intangible assets	(676)	549	(28)	(228)	(383)	423	(806)
Property, plant and equipment	10	15		(2)	23	39	(16)
Inventories	347	(34)	(52)	(29)	231	235	(4)
Other assets	138	7	(82)	12	74	96	(22)
Pension and other employee benefits	597	(126)	(149)	(57)	265	265	—
Other liabilities	989	(388)	(8)	(158)	536	596	(61)
Deferred tax assets on tax loss carryforwards.	1,288	(201)	(125)	(144)	819	819	—
Set-off-deferred tax positions			—	—		(876)	876
Net deferred tax assets	2,692	(77)	(444)	(606)	1,565	1,598	(33)

1) Other includes the movements of assets and liabilities recognized in OCI, which includes foreign currency translation differences and acquisitions, as well as the effects of US Tax Cuts and Jobs Act.

Source: Philips, Annual Report, 2017, Reproduced by Courtesy of Royal Philips

In 20X1, the accounting depreciation is €5,000 (50 per cent of the asset's historical cost or €10,000). The tax depreciation amounts to the full historical cost (€10,000). At the end of 20X1, the temporary difference between carrying amount of the asset in the financial statements and its tax value is €5,000, and the asset has a carrying value that is greater than its tax base. At that time the tax authorities have allowed a bigger tax deduction than recognized for financial reporting purposes. In 20X2, this situation will reverse when the accounting deduction becomes greater than the tax deduction.

This means that it is a *taxable temporary difference*, and therefore this will give rise to a *deferred tax liability*. The deferred tax liability amounts to €2,500, being 50 per cent (tax rate) of the temporary difference. Recognizing the deferred tax liability requires a *deferred tax expense* in the statement of profit or loss of 20X1. In 20X2, the temporary difference disappears (accumulated accounting depreciation equals accumulated tax depreciation) and the *deferred tax liability will be released*, implying a *deferred tax income* (or negative deferred tax expense) of €2,500 in 20X2.

This brings us back to essentially the same statement of profit or loss effect as under the statement of profit or loss approach to deferred taxes. It would, however, be wrong to conclude that the statement of profit or loss approach and the asset–liability approach will always produce the same result. In more complex multinational group structures, and when we consider the instances where temporary differences are not timing differences, the two approaches can produce quite different results.

The asset–liability approach also implies that every time there is a subsequent change in tax rates, the deferred tax asset/liability will change.

Tax loss carryforwards

A *tax loss carryforward* is a tax rule that allows a company to carry over a loss to future years to offset a profit. The tax loss carryforward can be claimed by a company in order to reduce any future tax payments. So, tax losses are not necessarily all bad news as they may be a tool for creating future tax relief. The carryforward can be valid for several years, but the number of years tends to vary by jurisdiction.

The tax effect of a loss carryforward represents *future tax savings*. These can be quite significant for start-up companies that tend to accumulate losses when establishing their business and expanding market share, hoping to generate profitable economies of scale later on. It can also be an incentive in business combinations, when a profitable company acquires a business with large accumulated losses that would allow the acquirer to shield its future profits against taxation (but some jurisdictions have anti-avoidance rules to prevent this).

IAS 12 *Income Taxes* allows the recognition of a *deferred tax asset* for a tax loss carryforward (similar criteria as for deductible temporary differences) and a corresponding deferred tax income when a company incurs the tax loss. Realization of the future tax savings depends however on future profits and is thus uncertain. Therefore, recognition of the deferred tax asset is contingent on evidence that sufficient future taxable profits will be available against which the unused tax losses can be utilized by the company.

To illustrate the issue, let us consider a company that incurs a tax loss of 500 in 20X1, but expects a pre-tax accounting profit of 200 in 20X2 and a pre-tax accounting profit of 900 in 20X3. Applicable tax rules allow tax loss compensation for future taxable profits up to five years and set a tax rate of 50 per cent.

Without deferred taxation, the statement of profit or loss would show the following:

	20X1	20X2	20X3
Pre-tax accounting profit	−500	+200	+900
Tax loss carried forward		−200	−300
Taxable profit	0	0	600
Taxes due (50%)	0	0	−300
Net profit/loss (after tax)	−500	+200	+600

No taxes are due on losses in 20X1, while the tax loss compensation (tax loss carried forward) results to zero taxable profit in 20X2 and reduces taxable profit in 20X3 to 600. This leads to an income tax expense of 0 in 20X2 and of 300 (33.33 per cent of profit before tax) in 20X3.

Accounting for the future tax consequences of the tax loss in 20X1, would bring about a deferred tax asset and corresponding deferred tax income of 250 (50 per cent of the tax loss) in 20X1. Subsequently applying tax loss compensation in 20X2 and 20X3 will gradually decrease the deferred tax asset and create a deferred tax expense. So, with deferred taxation the statement of profit or loss will be the following:

	20X1	20X2	20X3
Pre-tax accounting profit	−500	+200	+900
Tax loss carried forward		−200	−300
Taxable profit	0	0	600
• Current tax expense (50%)	0	0	−300
• Deferred tax income/expense	+250	−100	−150
Net profit/loss (after tax)	−250	+100	+450

In both 20X2 and 20X3 the total tax charge (current plus deferred) amounts to 50 per cent of profit before tax.

In some jurisdictions (although very rare) tax rules also allow a *tax loss carryback*, whereby a tax loss of one period can be carried back to offset profits made in earlier periods. A tax loss carryback does, however, not create a deferred tax asset, but calls for a tax refund. For accounting purposes, it creates a claim to receive refunds for income taxes already paid in previous years and only affects the current tax charge.

Presentation of deferred taxes in the financial statements

Deferred tax assets and *deferred tax liabilities* are presented separately from all other assets and liabilities in the statement of financial position. They are classified as *non-current items*.

Income tax expense related to profit or loss from ordinary activities should be presented on the face of the *statement of profit or loss*. The income tax expense figure presented in the statement is usually the aggregate of current tax expense and deferred tax expense (income), with details on its components to be found in the notes to the accounts.

Dividing the income tax figure in the statement of profit or loss by pre-tax accounting profit leads to the *effective tax rate*, which is commonly different from the *theoretical tax rate* as set by the tax authorities. Permanent differences (see above) will be the major source of difference between the effective and the theoretical tax rate.

Additionally, a set of supplementary information on deferred taxes is to be disclosed in the notes to the accounts, such as details on the major components (and changes) of temporary differences and related deferred tax assets and liabilities. A prominent disclosure will be an explanation of the relationship between tax expense and accounting profit as a numerical reconciliation between the effective and the (average) theoretical tax rate. In practice, these disclosures can be quite extensive, although not always easily accessible for a multinational group due to aggregation of tax information related to divergent taxation regimes.

COMPANY REPORT

PHILIPS – RECONCILIATION OF THEORETICAL TAX RATE TO EFFECTIVE TAX RATE

Philips' operations are subject to income taxes in various foreign jurisdictions. The statutory income tax rates varies up to 40.0%, which results in a difference between the weighted average statutory income tax rate and the Netherlands' statutory income tax rate of 25.0% (2016: 25.0%).

A reconciliation of the weighted average statutory income tax rate to the effective income tax rate of continuing operations is as follows:

Philips Group
Effective Income tax rate in %
2016–2017

	2016	2017
Weighted average statutory income tax rate in %	23.3	24.5
Recognition of previously unrecognized tax loss and credit carryforwards	(1.9)	(2.3)
Unrecognized tax loss and credit carryforwards	5.5	0.6
Unrecognized (recognition of) temporary differences	(3.1)	(2.6)
Non-taxable income and tax incentives	(8.2)	(9.8)
Non-deductible expense	9.3	6.4
Withholding and other taxes	1.2	4.0
Tax rate changes	(0.5)	5.2
Prior year tax	(1.8)	(0.6)
Tax expense (benefit) due to other tax liabilities	(2.6)	(1.7)
Others, net	(1.3)	1.5
Effective income tax rate	19.9	25.3

The effective income tax rate was higher than the weighted average statutory income tax rate in 2017, largely due to a tax charge recorded for the re-measurement of Philips' US deferred tax assets as a result of the enactment of the US Tax Cuts and Jobs Act in December 2017. This effect was partly offset by tax benefits from the recognition of deferred tax assets which were previously unrecognized.

Source: Philips, Annual Report, 2017, Reproduced by Courtesy of Royal Philips

International taxation

The general rule in taxation is that a profit is taxed in the country where the transaction takes place, although this is obviously more complicated for cross-border trading and internet sales. Generally, it is then the country in which the buyer resides that determines tax, even if for the moment internet sales are largely untaxed. From a corporate perspective, tax is administered on a company-by-company basis, and calculated on individual subsidiaries' accounts, not on the group accounts as a whole.

This is sometimes an issue that MBA students find bizarre. While the whole point of consolidated financial statements is to look at the company as an economic whole, and from a management perspective one should never lose sight of the overall group, from a tax perspective, the focus is exactly the opposite: tax sees the group as a collection of more or less unconnected activities and deals with it subsidiary by subsidiary.

Consequently, it is useful for a multinational to try to compartmentalize its activities within each tax jurisdiction by forming separate companies and retaining clear records of transactions for discussion with different tax authorities. As noted earlier, many corporations use worldwide systems for uniform internal accounting but then retain local specialists in each country to recalculate the figures in line with local measurement rules and tax needs.

International business presents both threats and opportunities as far as tax is concerned. On the one hand, the fact that national tax authorities cannot go outside their jurisdiction enables the corporation to structure international transactions in the most tax efficient way. On the other hand, mishandling can cause a revenue to be taxed in two different countries, or an expense not to be accepted as a deduction from profit.

Leaving aside tax havens, most countries have entered into *double tax treaties* with main trading partner nations. These deal with issues like the taxation of international transactions, the rules for withholding taxes on royalties, interest and dividends and similar items. So, if a company is thinking about doing business in a country other than its main base, one of the first things to do is check whether there is a double tax treaty and what its content is.

Transfer pricing

The double tax treaty will normally have a section dealing with *transfer prices*. These are the prices, often very difficult to calculate, at which goods and services change hands between subsidiaries of the same group. Artificially fixing the transfer prices is a way of determining where profits are taxed.

Supposing a company makes a machine in country A (corporate income tax rate of 50 per cent) for a cost of €10,000 and sells it to a fellow subsidiary in country B (tax rate 25 per cent) for €11,000. This subsidiary sells it in turn to a subsidiary in country C (tax rate 40 per cent) for €18,000 and that subsidiary sells it to the customer for €20,000. The taxable profit will be distributed over the three countries:

	Taxable profit	*Rate*	*Income tax*
Country A	1,000	50	500
Country B	7,000	25	1,750
Country C	2,000	40	800
Total	10,000	30.5	3,050

The group has been able to reduce consolidated tax by artificially fixing the transfer prices and flowing the transaction through a low-tax country. Of course, the tax authorities are well aware of this possibility, so the double tax treaty usually states that transfer prices must be 'at arms' length' (i.e. what an independent buyer would have to pay) or at market rates. It is not always easy to prove these prices and companies are well advised to reflect carefully on these issues because most tax jurisdictions can go back many years in a tax investigation and levy penal rates of tax if they do not agree the basis of the transfer price. It remains, for all that, an interesting corner of profit management.

Related to this is the issue of what expenses can be charged by head office or other corporate service centres against subsidiaries. Typically, a multinational has regional management centres that are not themselves revenue generating. Equally, it has research and development activities that probably involve costs being incurred in one jurisdiction and subsequently a new product or process being exploited in other jurisdictions. The same is true of advertising – maintaining a worldwide brand is expensive and has effects everywhere. If your company takes advertising at (say) the World Cup in Dubai, which is televised all over the world, does the Dubai subsidiary pay that, or head office, or who?

This is a problem for internal management purposes in terms of relating costs to revenues, but it is also a problem with the tax authorities. If your R&D is based in the UK but exploited in the USA, the UK tax authorities are not likely to accept that the cost should all be offset against UK tax. But the US authority may refuse to accept any expenses either, in the sense that the costs were not incurred in the USA.

Basically, flows between subsidiaries in different countries are easiest when structured according to the tax treaty: transfer prices for goods and services (but may be subject to justification, which is not always easy), royalties for use of intellectual property (brands, product manufacturing processes) and interest (in relation to financing). All of these are, however, with the proviso that the company may need to persuade the tax authorities that the level of charge is justified.

Tax havens

Tax havens have a small place in the corporate world, but they may well be expensive to use (you usually need to work through a local lawyer or accountant) and other tax jurisdictions usually have extensive powers to stop you sheltering profits in a haven. For example, if the UK considers that you have a controlled foreign corporation (CFC) in a jurisdiction that is on its list of havens, it will feel free to tax you in the UK on the profits of that CFC. If you do not provide accounts for the CFC, it will simply estimate the profits and tax accordingly. Tax havens do not generally benefit from double tax treaties with other countries.

Tax havens typically offer low tax or flat rate tax for companies that are resident there but whose activities are external to the haven (hence 'offshore' companies). These can be used legitimately and effectively by a multinational to provide international services such as finance or insurance to itself. For example, an offshore finance vehicle will borrow on the international markets (guaranteed by the group) and then lend to fellow subsidiaries.

The tax haven lends itself also to the internet business and it is surprising that more companies such as internet sales companies or those with international transactions such as tour operators do not site themselves in tax havens. The costs are not negligible and therefore the throughput needs to be substantial to create a saving on tax after professional costs.

In recent years a new kind of tax minimization opportunity has appeared – what are known as 'offshore financial centres'. These are a near relative of the tax haven, but with the difference that they have double tax treaties with major trading countries – they have a foot in both camps, as it were. Like a tax haven, their object is to attract corporate business whose operations take place outside the financial centre. Unlike the tax haven, they levy corporate taxes on income, but these are at a level that is sufficiently high for developed countries not to treat the financial centre as a haven, but sufficiently low so as to still be attractive to companies. Dublin is a financial centre in this sense, as is Botswana.

Summary

This has been a short tour through the rather strange land of corporate taxation. The principal points to retain are that individual companies pay taxes to governments in a number of different ways. These can impact substantially on business costs and need to be thoroughly reviewed at the project stage, not left until a new operation is up and running. Corporate income tax is calculated in quite a complicated way and is linked to accounting profit through a reconciliation exercise. Where accounting profit and taxable profit differ, deferred taxes arise. Deferred taxation for financial reporting purposes can be looked at using a statement of profit or loss perspective or a balance sheet perspective. Deferred tax rules as set by IAS 12 *Income Taxes* are based on the balance sheet view, which is consistent with asset–liability approach of the IASB *Conceptual Framework*.

Tax is levied on a country-by-country basis, which calls for a good deal of expenditure of resources to compile tax data. The fact that multinationals usually have transactions that run through several subsidiaries and different countries, presents tax planning opportunities and some risks in that national tax authorities do not necessarily agree with the company's way of calculating profits, or with that of other tax authorities. Multinationals can make a limited use of tax havens and offshore financial centres to reduce their taxation.

Discussion questions

1. Is all the tax that a group pays visible in the financial statements?
2. Explain how VAT is accounted for in a wholesale company. Use an example of a sales invoice and of a purchase invoice to illustrate your reasoning. Refer to the definitions of elements of financial statements as provided by the IASB *Conceptual Framework* to back up your case.
3. Contrast the deferred tax concepts of 'timing differences' and 'temporary differences'.
4. For what purposes may a tax haven be profitably used by a multinational group?
5. ZZ consultants have won a contract from the Russian government to advise on small company accounting regulation and to provide training for government officials and educators. Some of the contract will be performed by staff in ZZ's Moscow office, but they will be helped by staff transferred from their offices in Germany, the UK and Switzerland. If the rate of corporate income tax in Russia is 80 per cent, in Germany

60 per cent, in the UK 35 per cent and in Switzerland 25 per cent, how would you advise them to structure their internal transactions? Should all the staff to be used be transferred to the Moscow office or should Moscow be invoiced from other locations with staff flown in and out to meet specific assignments?

Assignments

The following questions have answers on the lecturer side of the digital support resources for the book.

1. On 3 January 20X1, Foldet SA purchased specialized equipment for €1.4m. The equipment has a useful life of four years and will be depreciated using the straight-line method for financial reporting purposes. The residual value is estimated at €200,000. For tax purposes the following tax depreciation amounts are allowed: 450,000 (20X1), 350,000 (20X2), 250,000 (20X3) and 150,000 (20X4). The enacted income tax rate is 20 per cent for 20X1 and thereafter.

    Required:

    Explain how you would account for this transaction from a deferred taxation perspective.

2. Company Deftax purchases an item of heavy machinery on 1 January 20X1 at a cost of €20,000. The machinery has an expected useful life of four years and the company applies straight-line depreciation. Tax authorities allow a regime of accelerated depreciation resulting in the following amounts: 8,000 (20X1), 6,000 (20X2), 4,000 (20X3) and 2,000 (20X4). The financial year of Deftax ends at 31 December and the applicable tax rate is 30 per cent.

    Assume that profit before depreciation of the new machinery is €15,000 each year and there are no disallowed expenses or other adjustments in calculating taxable profit.

    Required:

    (a) Calculate current and deferred taxes of Deftax for the years 20X1 to 20X4.

    (b) Prepare a simplified statement of profit or loss of Deftax for the years 20X1 to 20X4.

3. Company T-Haven purchases production line equipment on 1 January 20X1. The acquisition cost of the equipment amounts to $2,000. T-Haven depreciates the equipment over 10 years for statutory reporting and tax purposes, but for IFRS® reporting purposes it depreciates the asset straight-line over an estimated useful life of 20 years. Statutory reporting does not take into account deferred taxes. T-Haven's financial year ends at 31 December and the applicable tax rate is 34 per cent.

    On 1 January 20X6, the company decides to sell the production equipment and finds a buyer who pays $1,600.

    Assume that profit before tax (after taking into account depreciation on the equipment) is $300 for statutory purposes and $400 for IFRS reporting (for all years until 20X5) and there are no disallowed expenses or other adjustments in calculating taxable profit.

    In 20X6, T-Haven's profit before recognizing the sale of the production line equipment amounts to $1,000 (both for tax/statutory purposes and IFRS reporting).

Required:

(a) Calculate and account for current and deferred taxes of T-Haven at the end of 20X1, 20X2 and 20X5, taking into account the purchase of the equipment.

(b) Prepare a simplified statement of profit or loss for 20X1 (both for statutory and IFRS reporting) and calculate the effective tax rate.

(c) Prepare a simplified statement of profit or loss for 20X6 (both for statutory and IFRS reporting) and calculate the effective tax rate.

CHAPTER 16

Auditing and corporate governance

The subject of auditing and auditors was covered in Chapter 2 of this book. The object of this chapter is to set out a little more background information concerning external audit and the framework of corporate governance as they impact on multinational groups. The chapter does not bear directly on the techniques of financial statement analysis, but is intended to broaden the knowledge base of analysts in respect of the financial statements and the constraints on corporate reporting. It will deal first with the subject of corporate governance, then the audit of group financial statements and related issues of independence, audit committees and finally internal control and risk management.

Chapter structure

- Corporate governance
- Statutory audit
- Issues in international audit
- Auditor independence
- Internal control and risk management
- Audit committee
- Summary
- Discussion questions

Corporate governance

In a small or medium-sized business, the owners are very often also the managers of the business and prior to the Industrial Revolution most businesses were run this way. It was only in the nineteenth century that a major change took place, as a result of the Industrial Revolution, and businesses started to become much larger. This had two consequences: large companies were financed by larger numbers of shareholders and so were less and less dominated by individual or family shareholders, and the 'professional manager' started to appear. This gave rise to what is known as an 'agency problem' – the owners of the business (*principals* in the jargon) had to find means to ensure that those whom they appointed to run the business (*agents*) did so in a way that matched with shareholders' needs.

There are a number of ways of addressing this problem. One of the most frequent in the Anglo-Saxon world is to give top managers contracts under which their salaries vary according to how well they meet key shareholder objectives, such as increase in share price or return on equity. However, accounting and audit also play a highly significant role. Historically, the accounting statements were a means through which professional managers reported to shareholders on what they had done with the company over a 12-month period, and in many countries audit was introduced as a means whereby a representative of the shareholders checked the accuracy of the financial statements on behalf of the shareholders. It is not clear that this was originally a very effective way of checking on managers, and the evolution of accounting regulation and the audit profession has, in part, been a response to the need to create transparency in the financial statements and confidence in their accuracy.

In current times the agency problem has been broadened out into the concept of corporate governance. On the one hand, the corporate governance debate puts increased emphasis on the effectiveness and accountability of corporate boards of directors, while, on the other hand, it tends to extend the shareholder perspective to wider stakeholder concerns.

The latter is an important shift in focus and involves a cultural change in what is expected of companies and their management. What it means is that the company can no longer be seen as an isolated unit whose central task is to make money for shareholders and whose other obligations can be summarized as simply to meet legal requirements in all other areas, if they cannot be got round. Increasingly, society is saying that multinationals are extremely powerful and rich entities, many of them more so than the governments of the world's smaller or economically weak states, and they are able to escape control because their structure is international while law is basically restricted to national boundaries. Such companies must be constrained to take into consideration the public interest as well as that of their shareholders, and there must be transparent systems of corporate governance to see that this is done.

Since the beginning of the 1990s many countries have been revising national corporate governance rules or endorsed corporate governance guidance after extensive public consultation and debate (Viénot I and II in France, the Cromme Report in Germany, the Cardon Report in Belgium, the Peters Report in the Netherlands, the early Cadbury Report of 1992 and the Higgs Report of 2003 in the UK and many others). On the international level, the Organisation for Economic Co-operation and Development (OECD) has been particularly active in the debate with its report of 2004 on principles of corporate governance. The OECD Principles of Corporate Governance have been widely adopted as a benchmark for achieving good corporate governance in OECD countries and elsewhere.

BETWEEN THE LINES

Defining corporate governance – OECD Principles of Corporate Governance (extract)

Corporate governance involves a set of relationships between a company's management, its board, its shareholders and other stakeholders. Corporate governance also provides the structure through which the objectives of the company are set, and the means of attaining those objectives and monitoring performance are determined. Good corporate governance should provide proper incentives for the board and management to pursue objectives that are in the interests of the company and its shareholders and should facilitate effective monitoring. The presence of an effective corporate governance system, within an individual company and across an economy as a whole, helps to provide a degree of confidence that is necessary for the proper functioning of a market economy. As a result, the cost of capital is lower and firms are encouraged to use resources more efficiently, thereby underpinning growth.

Source: OECD Principles of Corporate Governance, 2004

They are intended to assist governments in their efforts to evaluate and improve the regulatory framework for corporate governance, and to provide guidance and suggestions for stock exchanges, investors, corporations and other parties that have a role in the process of developing good corporate governance.

Corporate governance regimes

Different countries have different views about corporate governance. Governance regimes are heavily influenced by the institutional environment. The Anglo-Saxon environment, characterized by large liquid capital markets, a growing concentration of power within institutional investors and an active market for corporate takeovers, has been generally supportive of the development of strong investor protection and of shareholder primacy in the corporate governance debate. In contrast, for example, the continental European institutional environment is characterized by less liquid markets and greater concentration of power with banks, employees and governments, and stronger family ties. For example, in German companies with their two-tier board system, banks are often represented on the supervisory boards and own large shareholdings in many listed companies. Employee organizations play a significant role in corporate governance through their direct involvement with works councils and, indirectly, in supervisory boards. The stakeholder model of corporate governance in continental Europe tends to give greater attention to the social dimension and the longer term effect of corporate governance issues.

Although those differences in the governance environment and structures have a significant effect on governance practices at company level, economic globalization tendencies and pressures from cross-border investment with investors increasingly seeking opportunities outside their domestic markets, seem to weaken the distinction between governance models and promote convergence, especially on the issue of the effectiveness and accountability of corporate boards.

Reporting on internal control

An effective system of internal control is generally seen as crucial for good governance. The US Sarbanes–Oxley Act (2002) made executive management responsible not just for establishing, evaluating and assessing over time the effectiveness of internal control over financial reporting and disclosure, but also for periodically asserting its effectiveness. To this effect, each annual report filed with the Securities and Exchange Commission (SEC) has to include an internal control report. In this report, management should state its responsibility for establishing and maintaining an adequate internal control structure and procedures for financial reporting and assess, as of the end of the company's fiscal year, the effectiveness of the internal control system with regard to financial reporting. Moreover, the company's independent auditors must attest to and report on the assessments made by company management. In this context, the Committee of Sponsoring Organizations of the Treadway Commission (COSO) framework is considered to offer an established set of control criteria to assess the effectiveness of internal control over financial reporting. Related guidance on internal control can be found in the Turnbull (UK) and the CoCo (Canada) frameworks which build on the COSO framework of internal control.

STANDARDS

 OUTLINE OF THE SARBANES–OXLEY ACT OF 2002

The Sarbanes–Oxley Act (SOX) affects corporate managers, independent auditors and other players who are integral to capital formation in the USA. This omnibus regulation will forever alter the face of corporate reporting and auditing. SOX titles and key sections are outlined herein:

1. *Title I – Public Company Accounting Oversight Board:* Section 101 establishes an independent board to oversee public company audits. Section 107 authorizes oversight and enforcement of the board to the SEC.

2. *Title II – Auditor Independence:* Section 201 prohibits a CPA Firm that audits a public company to engage in certain non-audit services with the same client. Most relevant to accounting information systems is the prohibition of financial information systems' design and implementation services to audit clients. Section 203 requires audit partner rotation in their fifth, sixth or seventh year, depending on the partner's role in the audit.

3. *Title III – Corporate Responsibility:* Section 302 requires a company's chief executive officer (CEO) and chief financial officer (CFO) to certify quarterly and annual reports. They are certifying the following: they reviewed the reports; the reports are not materially untruthful or misleading; the financial statements fairly reflect in all material respects the financial position of the company; and they are responsible for designing, establishing, maintaining, and monitoring corporate disclosures, controls and procedures. Section 303 makes it unlawful for corporate officers or directors to fraudulently influence, coerce, manipulate or mislead any independent auditors who are engaged in auditing the firm's financial statements.

4. *Title IV – Enhanced Financial Disclosures:* Section 404 requires each annual report filed with the SEC to include an internal control report. The report shall: state the responsibility of management for establishing and maintaining an adequate internal control structure and procedures for financial reporting and assess, as of the end of the company's fiscal year, the effectiveness of the internal control structure and procedures of the company for financial reporting. The company's independent auditors must attest to and report on the assessments made by company management.

5. *Title V – Analysts' Conflicts of Interests:* Requires financial analysts to properly disclose in research reports any conflicts of interest they might hold with the companies they recommend.

6. *Title VI – Commission Resources and Authority:* Authorizes the SEC to censure or deny any person the privilege of appearing or practicing before the SEC if that person is deemed to: be unqualified, have acted in an unethical manner, or have aided and abetted a violation of federal securities laws.

7. *Title VII – Studies and Reports:* Authorizes the General Accounting Office (GAO) to study the consolidation of public accounting firms since 1989 and offer solutions to any recognized problems.

8. *Title VIII – Corporate and Criminal Fraud Accountability:* Section 802 makes it a felony to knowingly destroy, alter or create records and/or documents with the intent to impede, obstruct or influence an on going or contemplated federal investigation. Section 806 offers legal protection to whistle-blowers who provide evidence of fraud.

9. *Title IX – White-Collar Crime Penalty Enhancements:* Section 906 sets forth criminal penalties applicable to CEOs and CFOs of up to $5m and up to 20 years in prison if they certify and file false and/or misleading financial statements with the SEC.

10. *Title X – Corporate Tax Returns:* Section 1001 conveys a 'sense of the Senate' that the corporate federal income tax returns are signed by the CEO.

11. *Title XI – Corporate Fraud and Accountability:* Section 1102 provides for fines and imprisonment of up to 20 years to individuals who corruptly alter, destroy, mutilate or conceal documents with the intent to impair the document's integrity or availability for use in an official proceeding, or to otherwise obstruct, influence or impede any official proceeding. Section 1105 authorizes the SEC to prohibit anyone from serving as an officer or director if the person has committed securities fraud.

Source: Sarbanes–Oxley Act, 107 P. L. 204, § 1, 116 Stat. 745, 30 July 2002

With the passage of the Sarbanes–Oxley Act, company executives in the USA must now personally certify the accuracy of the financial statements as well as to the related controls. This requirement has produced a strong incentive for top management to familiarize themselves with the processes underlying financial reporting and to give priority to internal control issues. Applying section 404 – 'Management assessment of internal controls' – of the Sarbanes–Oxley Act of 2002 has proved to be a challenging experience. Section 404 calls on companies filing with the SEC to identify financial reporting risks, ascertain related controls, assess their effectiveness, fix and control deficiencies, rework documentation and ensure continued monitoring of the controls. This has been a daunting task, especially for companies with complex organizational structures and extensive foreign operations. Practical experience showed that internal control-related roles and responsibilities were often poorly defined and not well incorporated into daily business routines. Risk assessment (although an essential component of a system of internal control according to the COSO framework) was generally underdeveloped with the effect that it becomes quite difficult to prioritize control activities: without proper risk assessment control goals remain vague and criteria to assess the effectiveness of control measures arbitrary. Without proper risk assessment, it is impossible to discern obsolete or redundant controls from those that mitigate true financial reporting risks. In practice, applying section 404 of SOX has had the effect of dramatically increasing the responsibilities of the average line manager engaged in the processing of transactions that feed the financial statements.

In the European Union (EU), no equivalent of the SOX requirements on internal control currently exists, but the European Commission tightened audit requirements in 2014 and moved to the use of International Standards of Auditing, which include assessment of and reliance on internal control.

Independent directors

The role of independent non-executive directors features prominently in recent corporate governance codes. The presence of independent representatives on the board, capable of challenging the decisions of the management, is widely considered as a means of protecting the interests of shareholders and, where appropriate, other stakeholders.

Good corporate governance practices are considered to involve the presence in the central decision-making unit of the company of a number of external or independent directors. In a system such as that of Germany, where large companies have two boards, an executive or management board and a supervisory board, this function already exists, with the supervisory board exercising oversight over what the executive directors are doing. In countries where a unitary board is the norm, such as France, Belgium and Italy, the recommendation is that a board should include a proportion of non-executive or independent directors whose function is simply to attend board meetings on a regular basis and monitor corporate behaviour. A mixture of executive and non-executive directors has the advantage of combining the executives' in-depth knowledge of the daily operations of the company with the wider experience of non-executive directors. In the best companies, the monitoring function of non-executive directors offers an opportunity for the company to emphasize its ethical behaviour by appointing high-profile figures who are completely independent of the business. Independent directors should be selected on their merits and for the greater good of the company as a whole, not to represent concerns of specific interest groups.

However, neither the dual board system nor the unitary board with independent directors is foolproof. Famously, the supervisory board of Metallgesellschaft in Germany was unaware of the dealings of its US subsidiary in oil futures, which cost it many millions of dollars to unwind. The supervisory board of Ahold in the Netherlands was not informed on the specifics of revenue dealings of its US operations, leading to the embarrassment of very significant revenue restatements in Ahold's financial statements in 2002/2003. A report on accounting frauds by SEC-registered companies identifies what it calls 'grey' directors, defined as independent directors who have a business connection with either the company or its executive directors. Although independence is a matter of judgement, it is reasonable to expect that independent directors are free of personal and business connections with the companies of which they are a director. In that sense, former executive (or employee) status, close family relationships with an executive director or representation of a major shareholder would be an indication of an absence of independence.

BETWEEN THE LINES

Fraudulent financial reporting: 1998–2007 (extract)

A large body of academic research finds that board and audit committee independence affects the effectiveness of board and audit committee oversight. We examined the relation between board independence and fraud. In analyzing board member independence, the following definitions were used to categorize individual members of the board of directors into one of three categories:

- *Inside director* – A director who was also an officer or employee of the company or a subsidiary or an officer of an affiliated company.

- *Grey director* – A director who was a former officer or employee of the company, a subsidiary or an affiliate; relative of management; professional advisor to the company; officer or owner of a significant supplier or customer of the company; interlocking director; officer or employee of another company controlled by the CEO or the company's majority owner; owner of an affiliate company; or creditor of the company.

- *Outside director* – A director who had no disclosed relationship (other than stock ownership) between the director and the company or its officers.

The average percentage of inside directors on the board for fraud firms was 30 per cent as compared to 25 per cent for no-fraud firms. This difference was statistically significant (p-value $= 0.010$). There was no significant difference in the percentage of outside directors for fraud firms (60 per cent of the board) versus no-fraud firms (63 per cent of the board). There was no statistical difference between the two groups in the average percentage of grey directors. We were able to analyze the types of grey director serving on the board of directors for 63 fraud and 63 no-fraud firms. The most common types of grey director were former company officers, consultants and outside legal counsel. Differences in types of grey director serving on fraud and no-fraud firms were not statistically significant, except for the difference in the percentage of grey directors who were relatives of management. Seven per cent of fraud firm grey directors were relatives of management as compared to 18 per cent for no-fraud firms (p-value $= 0.086$).

Source: Fraudulent Financial Reporting 1998–2007. An Analysis of US Public Companies, published by the Committee of Sponsoring Organizations of the Treadway Commission (COSO), 2010

Aside from generally monitoring what the company is doing, the independent directors are increasingly asked to participate in subcommittees to deal with particular tasks. The most important are the *remuneration committee* and the *audit committee*. The idea of the remuneration committee is that executive directors should not be in a position to fix their own salaries; this should be done by independent directors who make comparisons with other companies and ensure that the package offered is in line with the market and the good of the shareholders and others. It is not clear how well this works either, and the existence of remuneration committees has not stopped major shareholder criticisms of some pay proposals.

The audit committee is responsible for overseeing the financial reporting process and increasingly for monitoring the effectiveness of the system of internal control as well. It acts as an intermediary between the board and the external auditors (and possibly internal auditors as well) on the basis that auditors should not be reporting management failings directly to the managers potentially concerned. The audit committee may need to challenge management decisions or take a position that is not in concert with that of executive directors. That is why independence is an essential quality for audit committee members. We will look at audit committees in more detail later in this chapter.

Chairman of the board and chief executive officer

Most corporate governance codes recommend a clear division of responsibilities at the top of the company between the chairman of the board of directors and the CEO to ensure a balance of power and authority. The running of the board of directors (the chairman's role) should be separated from the executive responsibility of running the company's business (the CEO's role). Concentration of both functions within one person is seen as undermining the accountability of corporate boards.

In two-tier boards (as in Germany and in the Netherlands) the concentration of power issue is less acute. In two-tier boards, the management board is responsible for management of the company while the supervisory board is responsible for overseeing the management board.

Institutional shareholders

It has been argued that part of the need for formal corporate governance frameworks arises from the fact that the major shareholders in large multinationals are typically financial institutions (banks, insurance companies, fund managers, pension funds, etc.). In the USA, institutional investors hold more than 50 per cent of all listed corporate shares (about 60 per cent in the largest 1,000 corporations), while the largest 25 pension funds accounted for 42 per cent of the foreign equity held by all US investors. Historically this kind of shareholder has considered that they should not intervene in the management of the company directly. They have taken the view that they are making an investment to get a return; if that return is not delivered, they take their investment elsewhere. This kind of passive shareholder approach is blamed for creating an environment where company management felt they could do what they liked as long as the share price held up.

However, this situation is changing, partly because the investment industry has wanted to respond to the criticisms and partly because the individuals who invest in pension funds and collective investment vehicles are increasingly wanting an assurance that their money is not being used to invest in companies with whose behaviour they do not agree. The personal finance press is increasingly vociferous in raising these issues and individuals are increasingly demanding that their money goes into 'ethical' investments. As a consequence, institutional investors are drawing up codes of conduct for companies, and some are now asking company boards to sign up to a code of conduct before the investment fund will buy any shares. This is, of course, another sign of the change in society's values and increases the pressure on companies to address these issues.

Statutory audit

The independent auditor has always had a role to play in corporate governance, and never more so than now when the multinational has subsidiaries all over the world and only the Big Four audit firms have similar organizations that can check on the existence and activities of these vast networks. Essentially, the signature of a Big Four audit firm on a multinational's audit report is taken to be the guarantee of the accuracy and validity of the financial statements, and an assurance that there is nothing nasty hidden behind the bland comments of the chairman. The investment market places a very heavy reliance on the auditor's assurance – the analyst may modify the figures to compare with other companies, may make all sorts of adjustments for forecasting purposes, but the very existence of all the company's assets, its activities and their legality, and the main board's control over these is attested to by the auditor.

In fact, the audit of a multinational group is a very difficult task and one which carries with it a great deal of legal and moral responsibility. In essence, the audit of a multinational is no different from that of an individual company, since the consolidated accounts are simply a reworking of the financial statements of all the individual companies that make up the group. However, it is more complicated in that the subsidiaries are working in different legal environments, and the more complex the accounting web, the easier it is to 'lose' transactions. The auditor of the group accounts is responsible for any error in the group audit, even if such an error has arisen because of a mistake by the auditor of a subsidiary. Equally, multinationals are under pressure to publish their results as soon as possible after the year-end, which means that the process of auditing and agreeing the accounts of the individual subsidiaries may have to take place within two months of the year-end, leaving a further month to consolidate and agree the consolidation adjustments.

This leads to a situation where the large audit firms like to be the exclusive auditor of a multinational and all its subsidiaries. Critics say this is simply to build up their fee base, which may be true, but it is also true that using several different firms of auditors is necessarily more expensive because they need to have meetings to liaise with one another and necessarily more risky because there is no one with an overview of the whole group. The Bank of Credit and Commerce International (BCCI) is a famous example of a group that operated as two separate but related networks, each network audited by a different Big Four auditor. After the collapse of BCCI it became apparent that there had been a 'black hole' between the two networks that was used to conceal fraudulent or illegal transactions.

Typically, the audit of a multinational is a continuing operation where one year's audit leads into the next, and if doubtful issues are identified one year, they may well be subjected to a more intensive scrutiny the following year and so on. The auditor will attempt to identify the areas of the group that have the highest audit risk (operations in a difficult trading and credit environment, such as Russia, high volume of cash transactions, poor control environment, poor local accounting systems, high volume of foreign currency transactions, etc.) and devote most resources to checking these. The auditor will also each year select particular areas for special investigation. These might be selected in response to worries expressed by the group's internal audit or accounting units, or may be selected more or less at random so that even a low-risk part of the group is occasionally subject to an intense scrutiny.

Fortunately, the rules for the conduct of an international audit are less likely to be radically different from country to country than for accounting. While audit rules may differ quite radically even between developed countries, there is a set of international audit rules put out by the International Federation of Accountants (IFAC – see Chapter 2), which are often used for multinational audits, and in particular when the accounting rules used are those of the International Accounting Standards Board (the Board). Analysts should check the audit report carefully, however, to see what rules have been applied. The standard audit report should specify both what accounting rules have been applied by the company and what auditing rules have been used by the auditor in conducting the audit. Beware terms such as 'have been prepared subject to professional standards' that do not specify which professional standards. While auditing standards are much the same in developed countries, they are not uniform and in developing countries may be fairly rudimentary.

Issues in international audit

That brings us to a delicate subject in international audit – how much reliance should you place on the financial statements of companies headquartered in developing or newly industrialized countries? These have been the subject of quite a lot of criticism, mostly as a consequence of the financial crisis in South-East Asia in the late 1990s. Here it became apparent that a number of companies had had their financial statements audited by Big Four firms, but had either used local accounting standards with a low degree of transparency or used International Accounting Standards while not complying fully with their requirements – using what is known as 'IAS-lite' in the trade.

It became clear that many relevant bits of information had not been disclosed to investors – in particular, issues such as unhedged loans in strong currencies to finance investments that would generate cash flows in weak currencies. This was an important cause of a flight from the Asian markets and the economic depression and collapse of many companies that followed. These deficiencies in reporting and auditing raised a number of questions. First, should the Big Four sign clean audit reports of financial statements which do not conform to high-quality international standards? The Big Four pointed out that the accounts made it clear that local standards had been followed and analysts should be reminded that the first thing to do when looking at a company report is indeed to check what rules have been applied. However, the market sentiment was rather that the Big Four should maintain certain minimum standards. More recently the SEC has pursued Chinese companies with activities in the USA where it had concerns that they did not understand the reporting infrastructure.

This in turn raises another issue – to what extent is an audit by the same Big Four firms the same the world over? Or, put another way, are the Big Four firms uniformly run and directed? In fact, the firms are not multinational companies with pyramid-style reporting and authority chains. They are networks of national partnerships or similar structures which work together through varying mechanisms, but which lack any formal or legal means whereby an international board, as it were, can impose its will on a national partnership on all questions. It is rather like running a franchise operation such as McDonald's where some outlets are directly owned by head office and some are franchises, both regional and local, but without the right to specify in detail what is sold or how it is prepared.

Auditor independence

A perpetual policy issue in audit is the independence of the auditor. Of course, the value of the modern audit depends partly on the technical skills of the auditor and partly on the independence and ethical qualities of the auditor. Without the competence and the distance from the management of the company, the audit report is worthless.

In some countries, such as Germany and France, the governments take the view that independence can only be obtained if the auditor performs only audit for the client and has no other relationship with the management. However, in many other countries, including Switzerland, the UK and the Netherlands, the auditor is free to sell other services to the same client, although in the UK the company must publish details of how much it paid for the audit and what other fees it paid the auditor.

There is a good deal of discussion about the effect of this on independence. Audit firms say that independence is a state of mind and does not vary directly with the commercial relationship. The Big Four also point out that they are bigger than many of their clients, and independence is much more a problem for a single partner firm than one with thousands of partners. However, there is also evidence that over time, audit partners come to identify fairly closely with their clients, and in this connection, the old firm of Coopers & Lybrand, for example, were sanctioned for having been too ready to listen to Robert Maxwell, whose companies they audited for many years.

In France, the audit appointment is for six years, and a listed company must appoint two auditors. In Italy, the appointment is for three years and may only be renewed twice, leading to a maximum of nine years for the audit engagement. However, auditors point out that statistically the most likely time for a fraud is when there is a new auditor – it takes time for a new firm to understand thoroughly the workings of a large multinational. There is clearly no magic solution to the independence problem.

Following the requirements of the Sarbanes–Oxley Act of 2002, SEC rules further restrict (but do not completely eliminate) the types of non-audit service that an auditor is allowed to provide to audit clients, and the employment of former audit firm employees by the audit client, and provide for audit partner rotation after a period of five years. If an audit firm provides non-audit services that are not prohibited for public company audit clients, such as tax services, these must be pre-approved by the company's audit committee. The EU 2014 Auditing Regulation has circumscribed further the supply of non-audit services to audit clients.

Internal control and risk management

The new corporate governance framework generally stresses the role and implications of an effective system of internal control. It sees internal control as part of the accountability of a company's board of directors and management to stakeholders and extends the internal control logic to enterprise-wide risk management. Profitable corporate performance is more and more recognized as the result of successful risk-taking. Corporate activity necessarily involves taking risks and corporate returns are expected to reflect rewards for considered risk-taking. In that sense, effective risk management is essential as good business practice to enable companies to take risks with more confidence and in a rational and informed manner.

Those charged with governance of a company are expected to systematically identify, evaluate and respond to the company's risks. These risks relate to strategy and business operations as well as to compliance with laws and regulations and financial reporting. Stakeholders, and shareholders in particular, expect those charged with governance of the company to inform them about the risks the company faces and also to put the necessary controls in place to deal with these risks. This emphasis on risk control and risk accountability was the result of a number of recent corporate failures where investors were not informed about disproportionate levels of risks incurred by corporate management.

Enterprise-wide risk management and control is particularly important in large multinational groups. In such groups, there are many parts that senior executives never see. Decisions are passed up and down the management pyramid, but only an effective internal financial reporting system shows that those decisions are carried out, and only an effective risk management and internal control environment ensures that the risks being taken by the company are being clearly identified, measured and monitored.

In September 2004, COSO published its *Enterprise Risk Management – Integrated Framework*, which, in fact, extends its internal control framework to risk management and strategic risks. COSO's definition of enterprise risk management (ERM) is as follows:

> Enterprise risk management is a process, effected by an entity's board of directors, management and other personnel, applied in strategy setting and across the enterprise, designed to identify potential events that may affect the entity, and manage risk to be within its risk appetite, to provide reasonable assurance regarding the achievement of entity objectives.

The COSO ERM *Integrated Framework* sees internal control as a subset of risk management. Risk management extends the scope of internal control as it is concerned with wider external and internal risks relevant to the determination and execution of a company's strategy to reach the company's objectives, than the set of risks focused on within the internal control framework. Nevertheless, internal control is seen as highly instrumental in achieving these objectives. As we have observed before, it is the absence of good internal controls which permits executives to carry out transactions against company policy and without the financial consequences being immediately visible, as Ahold, Parmalat, Enron and others can testify, and hence its importance in corporate governance discussions. There is no point in central management having the right policies in place if they are unable to monitor their application. Internal control is, however, only one of the means to manage risk exposures. Other devices include transferring risk to third parties, risk-sharing, contingency planning and consciously excluding activities deemed too risky.

A good system of risk management provides the means for central management to effectively deal with uncertainty and associated opportunities, with the ultimate goal of achieving the company's objectives. The ERM framework provides integrated ERM principles, common risk-related terminology and practical implementation guidance to help companies develop and benchmark risk management practices. An effective risk management system will be beneficial to external auditors also as they assess the company's business risks.

In the UK, the Turnbull Report has been quite influential in this respect. It reinforced the awareness of disciplined risk management as being crucial to good corporate governance and UK boards are nowadays significantly more involved in risk management than before.

A logical extension of a governance perspective on risk management is the development of a set of risk disclosure requirements empowering shareholders to use disclosures to bring companies to adopt more elaborate risk management standards. Currently, however, there exist no EU disclosure requirements regarding risk management and internal control. European directives do require disclosure of a company's principal risks, but not how they are managed or controlled. Further risk disclosures could relate to the overall process of risk management and internal control, the management of specific risks and information on the assessment of the effectiveness of risk management and internal control. Moreover, in the EU there is no equivalent to the Sarbanes–Oxley requirements on effectiveness disclosures. Recall, however, that the Sarbanes–Oxley Act only requires the disclosure of opinions about the effectiveness of internal control over financial reporting. It contains no disclosure requirements on compliance risks and operational/strategic risks, although the SEC asks for disclosures of specific risks faced by a company in the management discussion and analysis (MD&A) section of the mandatory filings.

The board of directors is expected to provide oversight of enterprise risk management, but they tend to delegate responsibility and accountability on these matters to one or more committees. The audit committee is a likely candidate. With its focus on internal control over financial reporting, the audit committee is already well positioned to assume this task. Some companies have however established a specific risk committee to focus directly on enterprise risk management.

LUFTHANSA – RISK MANAGEMENT SYSTEM

Opportunity and risk management (extracts)

Risk management in the Lufthansa Group

As an international aviation company, the Lufthansa Group is exposed to a number of macroeconomic, sector-specific, financial and Company-specific opportunities and risks. The Lufthansa Group defines opportunities and risks as the possible positive or negative deviations from a forecast figure or a defined objective for possible future developments or events. Opportunities and risks are an ever present part of doing business; their active management is deliberately integrated into business processes.

The Supervisory Board's Audit Committee monitors the existence and the effectiveness of the Lufthansa Group's risk management.

The Risk Management Committee ensures, on behalf of the Executive Board, that business risks are always identified at an early stage, evaluated and managed across all functions and processes. It is also responsible for ensuring that the risk management system is always up to date and for making improvements to its effectiveness and efficiency. Appointments to and the responsibilities of the committee are defined in internal regulations.

The 'Risk Management, Internal Control System and Data Protection' staff unit has functional responsibility for ensuring that the risk management system is standardised across the Group. It reports directly to the Chief Financial Officer and is responsible for implementing Group-wide standards and methods for the coordination and ongoing development of the risk management process.

The managing directors or management boards of all the companies covered by the risk management system also appoint risk managers. They are responsible for implementing the Group guidelines within their own companies and are in close,

(Continued)

regular contact with the Lufthansa Group's risk management function. In addition, they ensure that risk-relevant information is agreed with the planning and forecasting processes in their company (risk controlling).

As risk owners, managers with budgetary and/or disciplinary responsibility are obliged to implement risk management at a segment level. The identification, evaluation, monitoring and management of risks are therefore fundamental aspects of every management role.

The Internal Audit department carries out internal, independent system audits focusing on the effectiveness, appropriateness and cost-effectiveness of the risk management system practised in the Lufthansa Group.

During its annual audit of the financial statements, the auditor examines the system for the early identification of risks in place at Deutsche Lufthansa AG with regard to statutory requirements. In 2017, the review came to the conclusion that all statutory requirements were met in full.

Source: Lufthansa Annual Report, 2017, extract from Combined Management Report

Audit committee

This brings us back to the question of the audit committee. The idea of an audit committee originated in the USA in the last century and initially spread only slowly to Europe. Companies listed on US exchanges were obliged to have an audit committee, and this, of itself, meant that European companies listed in the USA needed to have one. However, as the corporate governance movement has gathered pace, the European Commission has also required listed companies to have an audit committee.

Where an audit committee functions effectively, it has the potential not only to improve the quality of financial reporting as such, but also to reinforce the quality of the control environment and strengthen the position of both the internal audit function and of the external auditor. Essentially, the idea is that the audit committee should provide a quasi-independent forum where those concerned with checking the effectiveness and quality of the company's accounting and control should be able to meet and discuss with shareholder representatives (independent directors) and raise issues of concern. In theory, this is a fine idea, and helps encourage an open discussion about the group's effectiveness and protects the 'whistle-blower' from inside the company who is concerned about management fraud, ecological damage, tax fraud or whatever. It also helps preserve the independence of the external auditors from management. However, it depends on the independent directors being willing to listen and to take action where they think this is necessary. Clearly, in practice, there is a risk that the audit committee will think it is there to defend the executives, or that it will not follow up the issues raised with the executives. In other words, the success of the audit committee is not guaranteed at all – it depends very much on the quality of the people concerned.

In the EU, the Statutory Audit Directive (2006) requires all public interest entities, essentially companies whose securities are trading on a regulated market, to have an audit committee composed of non-executive directors or supervisory directors and/or members appointed by the general meeting of shareholders. At least one of the members of the audit committee should be independent and have competence in accounting and/or auditing. The 2013 Accounting Directive includes a requirement for all public interest entities in the EU to provide a corporate governance statement in their management report which contains a description of the company's internal control and risk management systems.

Meanwhile in the USA, the Sarbanes–Oxley Act has increased the role and independence of the audit committee. It made the audit committee explicitly and directly responsible for the appointment, compensation and oversight of the work of the external auditor, including resolution of disagreements concerning financial reporting issues between management and the external auditor. Moreover, the audit committee must pre-approve all audit and non-audit services of the auditor.

COMPANY REPORT

NOKIA – AUDIT COMMITTEE

Committees of the Board of Directors (extracts)

The Audit Committee consists of a minimum of three members of the Board who meet all applicable independence, financial literacy and other requirements as stipulated by Finnish law, the rules of NASDAQ Helsinki and the NYSE. From May 23, 2017, the Audit Committee consisted of the following five members of the Board: Elizabeth Nelson (Chair), Jeanette Horan, Louis Hughes, Edward Kozel and Carla Smits-Nusteling.

The Audit Committee is established by the Board primarily for the purpose of oversight of the accounting and financial reporting processes of Nokia and the audits of its financial statements. The Committee is responsible for assisting the Board in the oversight of:

■ the quality and integrity of the company's financial statements and related disclosures;
■ the statutory audit of the company's financial statements;
■ the external auditor's qualifications and independence;
■ the performance of the external auditor subject to the requirements of Finnish law;
■ the performance of the company's internal controls and risk management and assurance function;
■ the performance of the internal audit function; and
■ the company's compliance with legal and regulatory requirements, including the performance of its ethics and compliance program.

Audit Committee also maintains procedures for the receipt, retention and treatment of complaints received by the company regarding accounting, internal controls, or auditing matters and for the confidential, anonymous submission by our employees of concerns relating to accounting or auditing matters. Nokia's disclosure controls and procedures, which are reviewed by the Audit Committee and approved by the President and CEO and the Chief Financial Officer, as well as the internal controls over financial reporting, are designed to provide reasonable assurance regarding the quality and integrity of the company's financial statements and related disclosures.

Under Finnish law, an external auditor is elected by shareholders by a simple majority vote at the Annual General Meeting for one year at a time. The Audit Committee prepares the proposal to the shareholders, upon its evaluation of the qualifications and independence of the external auditor, of the nominee for election or re-election. Under Finnish law, the fees of the external auditor are also approved by the shareholders by a simple majority vote at the Annual General Meeting. The Committee prepares the proposal to the shareholders in respect of the fees of the external auditor, and approves the external auditor's annual audit fees under the guidance given by the Annual General Meeting.

(Continued)

In discharging its oversight role, the Audit Committee has full access to all company books, records, facilities and personnel. The Committee may appoint counsel, auditors or other advisors in its sole discretion, and must receive appropriate funding, as determined by the Audit Committee, from Nokia for the payment of compensation to such outside advisors.

The Audit Committee meets a minimum of four times a year based on a schedule established at the first meeting following the appointment of the Committee. The Committee meets separately with the representatives of Nokia's management, heads of the internal audit, and ethics and compliance functions, and the external auditor in connection with each regularly scheduled meeting. The head of the internal audit function has, at all times, direct access to the Audit Committee, without the involvement of management.

The Audit Committee held nine meetings in 2017. Attendance at the meetings was 100%. Additionally, any director who so wishes may attend meetings of the Audit Committee as a non-voting observer.

Source: NOKIA, Annual Report, 2017

Summary

The object of this chapter was to give you a certain amount of background information on current corporate governance issues and their relationship with, in particular, the effectiveness and accountability of corporate boards, internal control and external audit. The tenets of recent corporate governance developments are that good governance and internal control must become integrated into the mission, culture and daily operations of the company. This background information should serve to make you better understand the context within which the financial statements have been prepared and some of the information that is published in the annual report. If, as an analyst, you have the opportunity to attend company investor briefings, you should not hesitate to ask companies about the independent directors, the composition and mandate of the audit committee and the functioning and effectiveness of the internal control and risk management system. These are all indications of the transparency of company management and their effectiveness.

Discussion questions

1. What is the current state of the corporate governance debate in the country in which you are based? Try to identify from the different sources of regulation (stock exchange, government, accounting profession, etc.) current guidance in your country.
2. Compare the audit committee disclosures of a US corporation (see SEC EDGAR database) with that of a company based in your country.
3. Do you think that the independence of auditors is an issue about which you should be concerned? What are the rules in your country?
4. Explain the relationship between enterprise risk management and internal control.

PART 5

Advanced financial statement analysis

This last section consists of one chapter. Chapter 17 takes up from Chapters 8 and 9 and goes further into the art of financial statement analysis.

Financial statement analysis II

This is the second chapter to look at how users draw information from financial statements. The first part of the chapter reviews the relationship between the company and its investors, and how information flows from the company to the investors. The second part extends the work done in Chapter 9 on the tools and methods of financial statement analysis.

Chapter structure

- Introduction
- Investor relations
- Earnings management
- Professional analysts
- Quality of earnings
- Analytical techniques
- Strategic ratio analysis
- Shareholder value
- Summary
- Assignments

Introduction

In this chapter, we intend to take your analytical skills a stage further, introducing some more analytical concepts and tools that provide further insights into a company's financial statements. By the end of it, you should know what other inputs are used by analysts to arrive at their opinions about companies. You should have considered what is implied by the quality of a company's earnings, and learned new methods to use ratios dynamically as a clue to the strategic positioning of a company.

Investor relations

A problem for the financial markets is that, although stock exchanges require companies to publish widely any information that is likely to affect the market price of a share (this is often done by sending a release to the stock exchange itself), in practice, not all investors have access to the same information. The bulk of investment in the market comes from collective investment vehicles and not directly from private individuals. Many people save for retirement by buying shares in a unit trust or investing in a life assurance policy or an independent pension scheme. Employer schemes are frequently handed over to professional managers. Consequently, the individual rarely intervenes directly in the market and the vast majority of investment is channelled through different institutional investors. This means that a company seeking investors can address most of the market in effect by talking with professional fund managers and analysts.

This has given rise to the *investor relations function*. Large companies maintain a department whose job is to communicate, often on a one-to-one basis, with investment organizations. This department is somewhere between a public relations unit and a financial reporting unit. Their job is to maintain continuing relations with market professionals, to respond to their questions and to organize 'road shows': visits to different cities around the world to explain results and usually to enable investors to meet the chief financial officer or chief executive and talk about the company. Company websites often provide their financial data via a link on the home page entitled 'investor relations', rather than (say) financial statements. Analysts are invited to contact the 'corporate communications director', not the finance director.

At the same time, professional analysts will follow individual companies very closely and aim to become a specialist in that company. They will attend company presentations but also make visits to company sites and will constantly be updating their knowledge of the company and their future expectations. Evidently, such analysts have a much more detailed knowledge of the company than the average private individual and this creates an imbalance of knowledge in the market.

That said, the internet has modified that a little. Nowadays more and more brokers sell shares to private individuals on the internet and a market is developing where TV companies will screen business reports early in the morning, often with soundbites from well-known analysts. Private investors then turn to their computer and buy and sell on the basis of that morning's comments. They then check the market regularly through the day to see how their gamble is paying off – all the excitement of betting on horse races or whatever, with the added psychological boost that what you are doing is seriously managing your finances, not amusing yourself. Private investors are coming back to direct buying and selling, but they are taking advice from professional brokers and others. In some ways, this is likely to bring further complications to regulating the market because most effort currently goes into ensuring quality information to the professional investor and regulators may yet feel they have to step in to regulate the advice being given to private individuals in order to protect them and preserve confidence in the market.

INVESTOR RELATIONS MEETINGS

The analysts sought to make the best qualitative judgement on the company. Factors of particular interest about the company which were said to make a strong contribution to this qualitative judgement may be summarized as:

- quality of management
- performance indicators
- quality of assets
- verification and assurance.

What was clear from the analysts' comments was that relatively little of this information came directly from the annual report. Company meetings were the key source of qualitative information and the annual report was the confirmation in terms of financial outcomes.

Source: ICAS, Corporate Communications: Views of Institutional Investors and Lenders

(Research Committee, Institute of Chartered Accountants of Scotland, 1999)

Earnings management

There is a basic problem in financial reporting that the net earnings of a company are likely to vary from year to year because they are the result of many different factors, whereas the financial markets want earnings to increase progressively from year to year. This means that company financial executives are under some pressure to 'manage' the reported earnings so that they meet analysts' expectations.

Let us look at the issue of *earnings management* in more detail. First, why are earnings important to analysts? Second, why do they fluctuate? Third, how are they managed?

Earnings and analyst forecasts

We talked in Chapter 9 about the *price/earnings (P/E) ratio*. This is a ratio that reflects the degree of risk which the market considers inherent to a particular company within a particular business sector. The relationship is expressed:

$$\text{P/E ratio} = \frac{\text{Market price of share}}{\text{Earnings per share}}$$

This relationship is fundamental to the stock market. When investment managers are looking for shares to buy, what they are seeking is a share which is undervalued, i.e. whose market price is below its real value. The current market price is determined by analysts as a function of the historic P/E for that company, multiplied by forecast earnings per share. If the share is undervalued, that means that the market is either underestimating future earnings or overestimating the riskiness of the company (the higher the risk, the higher the return necessary to compensate investors for running the risk, and so the lower the P/E and price).

BETWEEN THE LINES

The accounts are now so complex that most users need someone else to explain them. But financial analysts are only interested in earnings per share and the price/earnings ratio. Les Cullen, a director of Inchcape, said: 'Standard-setters must realize there is a limit to the complexity which preparers can put up with.' He added: 'The City is not using the more complex information. It is still seeing the company as a sort of annuity.' He explained that the markets are more interested in stable earnings patterns and this creates a pressure on preparers to smooth earnings, even though in the modern economy earnings are becoming more volatile. 'There is a disconnection at present between accounting principles and the financial market.'

Source: Accounting & Business, July/August 1999, p.20

The P/E ratios for the sector often fluctuate together (many aspects of risk will affect all companies in the same sector similarly), but the P/E for the individual company within that tends to be fairly stable in relation to other companies in the same sector.

It is changes in expected earnings that are the more frequent cause of fluctuations in price affecting individual companies. During the accounting year, professional analysts will visit the company and will try to obtain information that will give them as good as possible an idea of the likely outcome for the year's earnings. A forecast increase in earnings will cause them to buy more shares (market currently undervalues shares) whereas a drop in forecast earnings will cause them to sell shares (market overvalues the company at current price). There is therefore a direct link between accounting earnings and the market price.

Why earnings fluctuate

The net profit after tax of a multinational is subject to an enormous number of different variables – temporary changes in turnover as a result of local conditions, the arrival of competing products on the market, unexpected losses as a result of, for example, civil unrest, tax changes and so on. A multinational may well be operating in over 100 countries and selling many different types of product, so the number of factors that contribute to the shape of the consolidated statement of profit or loss is inevitably substantial. While there may be a portfolio effect (i.e. if you have enough different risk factors they may cancel each other out), there are many circumstances that can influence the final outcome.

Another issue is that net profit after tax is a small percentage of revenues. For example, if you take the results of Volkswagen for 2014, sales were €202,458m and profit attributable to shareholders €10,784m – a net profit margin of 5.38 per cent. The previous year sales were €197,007m and profit €9,066m – a net profit margin of 4.6 per cent. In effect, a 2.77 per cent increase in sales has generated an 18.95 per cent increase in profit.

You can see that a small shift in costs has a major effect on profits. This has two consequences: first, profits are likely to move up and down, year on year, in an apparently arbitrary fashion but, second, that management can influence profits by relatively small manipulations of costs. If management wants the share price to rise steadily year on year, it has to ensure, given the market's dependence on P/E ratios, that profits rise steadily year on year.

How do managers manipulate profits?

There are a number of classic ways in which this can be done legally and they are all difficult for the analyst to recognize. The most difficult to detect is the management of what are sometimes called *discretionary costs*. These are costs that the group can stop incurring without having any immediate effect on profitability, such as research and development, staff training and advertising. Of course, it is suicide for the company in the medium to long term and also has a bad effect on company morale in the short term, but it is frequently practised. Most groups operate an internal monthly reporting system that compares actual performance with budget and many add to that a forecast for the year-end profit, which is updated every month. If this forecast shows that the target profit for the year is unlikely to be achieved, it is possible that the call will go out from head office to abandon advertising campaigns, halt product development or simply defer these until the start of the next accounting year. Any of these tactics will increase short-term profits and there is little or nothing visible on the outside to warn the analyst. Where a company discloses its annual research and development expenditure, this may show a decrease. But even here, the classification as to what is development expenditure and what ordinary running costs is not that clear, and a little creative redefinition could hold the figure up even when real expenditure has dropped.

A second area of action is *closure of loss-making divisions*. Suppose that a company has five divisions with forecast results as follows:

Division	Profit €m
A	140
B	−120
C	80
D	75
E	50
Group	225

If you close division B, group profit jumps immediately from €225m to €345m. This may or may not be a good idea. It may just hasten the demise of a division that had no future – the product was near the end of its life cycle and could no longer make an adequate contribution. By the same token, it may cause the company to close a unit which is in a start-up situation. Many operations lose money in their early days – you have only to look at companies such as Amazon and other very visible internet start-ups to see that. The very difficult trick for central management is to decide how long to continue to nurse a start-up (potentially up to five years) and when to decide to cut one's losses and stop the experiment. In this situation, pressure to help the group profit can result in a start-up being abandoned too early because its losses are causing aggregate group profit to suffer. This tactic is usually not all that difficult to spot because there is likely to be some mention of the closure in the notes to the accounts or the management report, but there may be only hints which require interpretation.

A variant on this involves an *accounting manipulation*: consolidated accounting rules may allow the group to exclude from the consolidation any subsidiary which is to be disposed of. Flagging division B as a disposal would mean that it could be held out of the group result without even closing it down. IFRS 5 *Non-current Assets Held for Sale and Discontinued Operations* provides for operations that are to be sold to be shown separately as discontinued operations in the profit or loss statement and as a disposal group in the balance sheet.

The third way of managing profits is what the Securities and Exchange Commission (SEC) has called 'cookie jar accounting'. This involves using unrealistic assumptions to estimate liabilities for such items as sales returns, litigation costs, product warranty costs, etc. In doing so, they accumulate accruals (or sometimes unearned revenues) in 'cookie jars' during the good times and reach into them when needed in bad times. Making provisions when profits are higher than expected and releasing them when times are difficult is a classic example. The basic tactic is to create a provision by making a charge against profits and carrying forward a credit in the statement of financial position (go back to Chapter 6 if you want to review the basic technique). This charge will generally not be accepted for tax purposes, but that does not matter since its function is to deceive the market not the taxman. The more difficult problem is to convince the group auditors.

The way this would work might be:

Year 1	Market expectations of profit	150
	Actual revenues	3,400
	Actual expenses	−3,200
	Actual profit	200
	Create provision	−45
	Reported profit	155

When the results are announced, the slight increase against analysts' forecasts would generate a slight increase in share prices.

Year 2	Market expectations of profit	170
	Actual revenues	3,450
	Actual expenses	−3,300
	Actual profit	150
	Release part of provision	+20
	Reported profit	170

Had the group reported the actual result for Year 1 of €200m and, a year later, the actual result of €150m, the share price would first have rocketed, and the market might have expected profits of €250m in Year 2, leading to a steep decline in the share price once the actual result was announced.

Is this manipulation visible to the analyst? Well, up to a point. In the statement of financial position, the manipulation would show up as a change in the balance for provisions. Provided this is well enough analyzed in the notes to the accounts, the analyst can see whether there has been a net increase or decrease in provisions, without necessarily having enough information to know what exactly has happened – but an analyst attending a roadshow could ask questions. Equally, the statement of cash flows usually includes a reconciliation between accounting net profit and operating cash flows. The effect on the statement of profit or loss of changes in provisions will also be visible here, because they do not affect cash flows and have therefore to be highlighted in the reconciliation between profit and operating cash flow.

A variant on this technique is known as *'big bath' accounting*. This is most frequently applied when a group takes over a new subsidiary but may also occur when there is a change of chief executive. Typically, the company sets up large charges associated with a restructuring operation. These charges help the company to 'clean up' the balance sheet – giving it a so-called 'big bath'. The idea is that the acquiring group or the new chief executive identifies overvalued assets (and undervalued liabilities) and makes a once and for all adjustment for these. This involves major charges and tends to put a crater in the year's profit, but is explained to analysts as an exceptional year where a major cleaning-up exercise (big bath) has been done.

BETWEEN THE LINES

Cookie jar reserves

One of the accounting 'hot spots' that we are considering this morning is accounting for restructuring charges and restructuring reserves. A better title would be accounting for general reserves, contingency reserves, rainy day reserves or cookie jar reserves.

Accounting for so-called restructurings has become an art form. Some companies like the idea so much that they establish restructuring reserves every year. Why not? Analysts seem to like the idea of recognizing as a liability today, a budget of expenditures planned for the next year or next several years in down-sizing, right-sizing, or improving operations, and portraying that amount as a special, below-the-line charge in the current period's statement of profit or loss. This year's earnings are happily reported in press releases as 'before charges'. CNBC analysts and commentators talk about earnings 'before charges'. The financial press talks about earnings before 'special charges'. (Funny, no one talks about earnings before credits – only charges.) It's as if special charges are not real. Out of sight, out of mind …

The occasion of a merger also spawns the wholesale establishment of restructuring or merger reserves. The ingredients of the merger reserves and merger charges look like the makings of a sausage. In the Enforcement Division, I have seen all manner and kind of things that ordinarily would be charged to operating earnings instead of being charged 'below the line'. Write-offs of the carrying amounts of bad receivables. Write-offs of cost of obsolete inventory. Write-downs of plant and equipment costs, which, miraculously at the date of the merger, become non-recoverable, whereas those same costs were considered recoverable the day before the merger. Write-offs of previously capitalized costs such as goodwill, which all of a sudden are not recoverable because of a merger. Adjustments to bring warranty liabilities up to snuff. Adjustments to bring claim liabilities in line with management's new view of settling or litigating cases. Adjustments to bring environmental liabilities up to snuff or in line with management's new view of the manner in which the company's obligations to comply with Environmental Protection Agency (EPA) will be satisfied. Recognition of liabilities to pay for future services by investment bankers, accountants and lawyers. Recognition of liabilities for officers' special bonuses. Recognition of liabilities for moving people. For training people. For training people not yet hired. For retraining people. Recognition of liabilities for moving costs and refurbishing costs. Recognition of liabilities for new software that may be acquired or written, for ultimate sale to others. Or some liabilities that go by the title 'other'.

It is no wonder that investors and analysts are complaining about the credibility of the numbers.

Source: Speech by Walter P. Schuetze, Chief Accountant, Enforcement Division,
US Securities and Exchange Commission, 22 April 1999 (www.sec.gov/news/speech/speecharchive/1999/spch276.htm)

The advantage of this is that future depreciation charges will be lower (and therefore future profits higher) or that excess provisions are available to boost future profits, but, at the same time, the current share price is often not affected. In fact, if analysts accept the argument they have been given, they tend to look beyond the one-time loss and focus on future earnings. The share price may even rise despite the disastrous immediate effect on profit or loss of the write-offs or accrued expenses, because the market expects even better results in the future.

Is earnings management a good thing or a bad thing?

This is difficult to say. On the positive side, theorists argue that *clean surplus accounting* (profits after earnings smoothing) is a very good guide to long-term profitability, even if the year-on-year result has been managed. They say that the management has the best grasp of the real underlying capabilities of the group, and it will manipulate the profits to fit into their view of the long-term growth of the group. Consequently, the 'managed' profits are a reliable indicator of long-term performance.

On the negative side, people point out that the markets are misled by income smoothing. They claim that often when a company goes broke or is taken over in disastrous circumstances, this follows on a period of profit manipulation that built up market expectations well beyond the capabilities of the company. Some standard-setters work to correct this, saying that the market should have as much information as possible and be allowed to make up its own mind.

Professional analysts

Accounting numbers are not the only input into the assessment of a company's prospects. Analysts use many other factors, mostly economic, about the state of the economies where the company operates, the state of the industry, etc. to help predict future performance. An example of this type of information is provided by Moody's.

Moody's is one of a number of firms that offer a *bond rating service* – it assesses the riskiness of individual companies and then publishes its risk rating, which in turn impacts on a company's cost of borrowing. Moody's uses inputs from the following areas (not given in any priority ranking) in order to determine their risk rating:

- Industry
- Company
- Capital structure
- Sovereign risk
- Bond instrument
- Financial flexibility
- Capital expenditure
- Internal cash flow
- Competitors
- Use of debt capacity
- Customers
- Management risk appetite.

Not all the information comes from financial statements! Moody's talks to company management and since it provides ratings for all large companies, talks to all the competing managements too, and therefore has a broad picture of competition and patterns of development. Moody's offers the 'rating pyramid' (Figure 17.1) which shows how it approaches the rating decision.

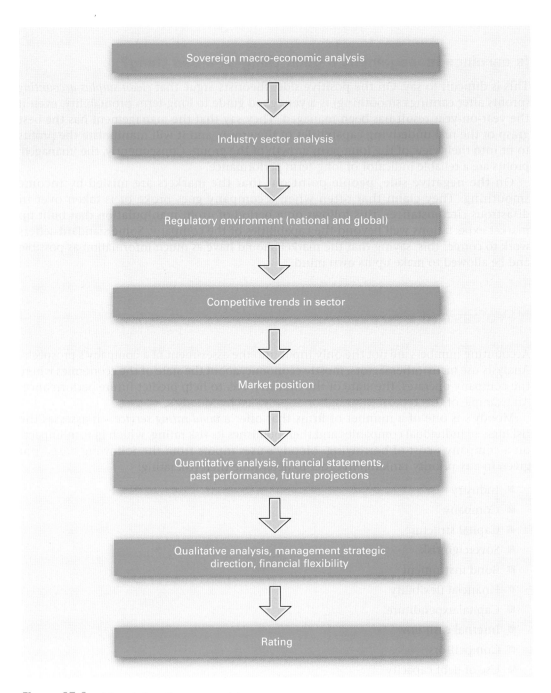

Figure 17.1 Moody's rating pyramid

It is our intention within this book to provide some of the skills necessary for quantitative analysis, and you will draw from other books and courses insights into economics, finance, business strategy, etc. that can be used to refine your analysis.

BETWEEN THE LINES

All expert users showed a clear desire to identify what drove cash flow and profits, together with the expert users' application of a mixture of systematic search and intuition for the likely answer. The systematic search followed the route of considering:

- the economy
- product market
- industry
- the business of the company
- quality of management, and
- quality of assets.

Source: ICAS, Corporate Communications: Views of Institutional Investors and Lenders
(Research Committee, Institute of Chartered Accountants of Scotland, 1999)

As far as accounting analysis goes, however, you should note the increasing use of investor briefings by companies as a means of obtaining explanations. Investor relations departments in large companies are generally also willing to respond to individual queries, provided that they know the analyst. In this context, the analyst carries out a series of technical measures, calculating ratios and so on, and uses the ratios to form a view about what is going on in the company or to recognize that the expected patterns do not emerge and further information is necessary to explain this anomaly. For example, if sales are increasing, you would expect the level of inventories and receivables to increase as well. If this is not the case, you should ask the investor relations department to comment.

Another point is that analysis frequently involves comparing companies in the same industrial sector. As a consequence, the analyst gains insights into what are the typical financial structures and operating margins in the industry.

Quality of earnings

An analyst is looking for sustainable profit and growth of that profit. So a key question to start with is to assess the extent to which the current earnings are subject to short-term influences or accounting manipulations. You should check for such things as:

a. Changes of accounting policies or accounting estimates
b. Pension holidays
c. Unusual asset disposals
d. Distortions caused by buying and selling business segments

e. Changes in the consolidation scope and of the interest percentages in associates and joint ventures

f. Anything else which suggests that short-term results will not be replicated in the long term.

This kind of subjective assessment of earnings is generally referred to as *quality of earnings* and involves posing the question (as far as it is possible to tell) as to what extent the earnings revealed by the financial statements are sustainable in future years. Some analysts will compare, in a longitudinal fashion, operating profit to net operating cash flow to identify and analyze the effect of accruals games on operating earnings. This is computed as follows:

$$\text{Quality of operating earnings} = \frac{\text{Net operating cash flow}}{\text{Net operating profit}}$$

A ratio of higher than 1 means that each currency unit of operating profit is supported by one currency unit or more of positive cash flow and can be considered to reflect high-quality operating earnings.

Non-recurrent items and transactions

Increasingly, accounting standards try to restrict and regulate what information companies should provide about unusual transactions or changes in the components of the group. This information is important in helping analysts forecast future earnings, but in the past has been manipulated by some companies to try to mislead analysts. IAS 1 *Presentation of Financial Statements* prohibits the distinction of ordinary activities and extraordinary items on the face of the statement of profit or loss. The International Accounting Standards Board (the Board) reasoned that extraordinary items are not that special in the sense that they result from the normal business risks faced by the company and, thus, do not warrant presentation in a separate caption of the statement of profit or loss. In line with this, the EU Accounting Directive also prohibits (from 2016) the use of a separate extraordinary results category on the face of the profit and loss account.

Disclosures in the notes to the accounts (and even on the statement of profit or loss) may, however, hold significant information to identify and analyze the effect of special and non-recurrent items and transactions. Indeed, IAS 1 requires that when items of income and expense are material, their nature and amount should be disclosed separately.

STANDARDS

 IAS 1 – PRESENTATION OF FINANCIAL STATEMENTS *(extracts)*

Separate disclosure of material items of income and expense
97. When items of income and expense are material, an entity shall disclose their nature and amount separately.
98. Circumstances that would give rise to the separate disclosure of items of income and expense include:

(a) write-downs of inventories to net realisable value or of property, plant and equipment to recoverable amount, as well as reversals of such write-downs;

(b) restructurings of the activities of an entity and reversals of any provisions for the costs of restructuring;

(c) disposals of items of property, plant and equipment;

(d) disposals of investments;

(e) discontinued operations;

(f) litigation settlements; and

(g) other reversals of provisions.

7. Material. Omissions or misstatements of items are material if they could, individually or collectively, influence the economic decisions that users make on the basis of the financial statements. Materiality depends on the size and nature of the omission or misstatement judged in the surrounding circumstances. The size or nature of the item, or a combination of both, could be the determining factor.

Source: IAS 1, Presentation of Financial Statements

Critical accounting judgements and estimates

IAS 1 *Presentation of Financial Statements* also requires that companies explain critical judgements and estimates that impact the financial statements significantly (see Standards box).

STANDARDS

 IAS 1 – PRESENTATION OF FINANCIAL STATEMENTS *(extracts)*

Judgements and sources of estimation uncertainty

122. An entity shall disclose, in the summary of significant accounting policies or other notes, the judgements, apart from those involving estimations (see para. 125), that management has made in the process of applying the entity's accounting policies and that have the most significant effect on the amounts recognised in the financial statements.

125. An entity shall disclose information about the assumptions it makes about the future, and other major sources of estimation uncertainty at the end of the reporting period, that have a significant risk of resulting in a material adjustment to the carrying amounts of assets and liabilities within the next financial year. In respect of those assets and liabilities, the notes shall include details of:

(a) their nature; and

(b) their carrying amount as at the end of the reporting period.

Source: IAS 1, Presentation of Financial Statements

This is very useful information for analysts, assuming that the company has correctly identified and discussed these. The nature of the expenses of each company and those that are subject to major uncertainties will vary considerably, so this is a helpful note pointing the analyst to issues that may help in assessing the quality of earnings and in forecasting future earnings.

RYANAIR – USE OF ESTIMATES AND JUDGEMENTS

Critical accounting policies (extracts)

The preparation of financial statements in conformity with IFRS requires management to make judgements, estimates and assumptions that affect the application of policies and reported amounts of assets and liabilities, income and expenses. These estimates and associated assumptions are based on historical experience and various other factors believed to be reasonable under the circumstances, and the results of such estimates form the basis of judgements about carrying values of assets and liabilities that are not readily apparent from other sources. Actual results could differ materially from these estimates. These underlying assumptions are reviewed on an ongoing basis. A revision to an accounting estimate is recognised in the period in which the estimate is revised if the revision only affects that period or in the period of the revision and future periods if these are also affected. Principal sources of estimation uncertainty have been set forth in the critical accounting policies section below. Actual results may differ from estimates.

The Company believes that its critical accounting policies, which are those that require management's most difficult, subjective and complex judgements, are those described in this section. These critical accounting policies, the judgements and other uncertainties affecting application of these policies and the sensitivity of reported results to changes in conditions and assumptions are factors to be considered in reviewing the consolidated financial statements.

Long-lived Assets

As of March 31, 2018, Ryanair had €8.1 billion of property, plant and equipment long-lived assets, virtually all of which consisted of aircraft. In accounting for long-lived assets, Ryanair must make estimates about the expected useful lives of the assets, the expected residual values of the assets, and the potential for impairment based on the fair value of the assets and the cash flows they generate.

In estimating the lives and expected residual values of its aircraft, Ryanair has primarily relied on its own and industry experience, recommendations from Boeing, the manufacturer of all of the Company's aircraft, and other data available in the marketplace. Subsequent revisions to these estimates, which can be significant, could be caused by changes to Ryanair's maintenance program, changes in utilisation of the aircraft, changes to governmental regulations on aging of aircraft, and changing market prices for new and used aircraft of the same or similar types. Ryanair evaluates its estimates and assumptions in each reporting period, and, when warranted, adjusts these assumptions. Generally, these adjustments are accounted for on a prospective basis, through depreciation expense.

Ryanair periodically evaluates its long-lived assets for impairment. Factors that would indicate potential impairment would include, but are not limited to, significant decreases in the market value of an aircraft, a significant change in an aircraft's physical condition and operating or cash flow losses associated with the use of the aircraft. While the airline industry as a whole has experienced many of these factors from time to time, Ryanair has not yet been seriously impacted and continues to record positive cash flows from these long-lived assets. Consequently, Ryanair has not yet identified any impairments related to its existing aircraft fleet. The Company will continue to monitor its long-lived assets and the general airline operating environment.

The Company's estimate of the recoverable amount of aircraft residual values is 15% of current market value of new aircraft, determined periodically, based on independent valuations and actual aircraft disposals during prior periods. Aircraft are depreciated over a useful life of 23 years from the date of manufacture to residual value.

Source: Ryanair, Annual Report, 2018

Analytical techniques

Common accounting base

Moving on to the techniques used to analyze the accounting data, when comparing two or more companies it may be necessary to adjust the statements because of accounting differences. Of course, there are often elements for which the analyst is unable to adjust because insufficient information is available, but the more one is comparing like with like, the more useful is the analysis. Many analysts try, when carrying out cross-sectional analysis, to eliminate any major accounting differences between companies or, for that matter, convert all companies to a common accounting base. The most obvious examples of this are reducing all revalued assets back to historical cost or writing off goodwill instead of treating it as an asset. As discussed before, the first thing to do when analyzing a company is to look at the notes to the accounts dealing with accounting policies. When comparing two different companies, you should compare their policies on major issues such as accounting for goodwill, depreciation rules, accounting for R&D costs, and valuation generally. You should also look at their provisions to see whether they are comparable.

The analyst can often usefully put pro-forma statements on to a spreadsheet, using an adjusted, common accounting base to make comparisons. Indeed, this is a technique which is virtually essential when analyzing the financial statements of companies which are based in different countries. This is a subject that is beyond the scope of this book, but it is easy to see that common assumptions – or as near as the analyst can get – are essential to make valid comparisons.

Common size

Ratios have the characteristic that they do away with size considerations so that quite different companies may be compared. You will remember that this may also be done by the preparation of *common-size financial statements* – these consist of a statement of profit or loss and a statement of financial position expressed in percentages (i.e. profit or loss items expressed as a percentage of sales, balance sheet items as a percentage of total assets). Common-size financial statements are usually a good starting point in the financial statement analysis process. They allow a straightforward internal or structural analysis of the company's financial position and performance and can be easily used for comparisons in time or in space (industry comparisons).

EBITDA and free cash flow

EBITDA sounds like some strange mantra, and certainly some analysts can be heard chanting it at times, but this is simply a rough proxy for the net operating cash flow. EBITDA stands for *earnings before interest, taxation, depreciation and amortization.*

While multinational companies have largely harmonized their cash flow reporting and produce statements of cash flows in line with IAS 7 *Statement of Cash Flows* and therefore provide operating cash flow data, some analysts prefer a measure drawn directly from the statement of profit or loss. The idea is that the analyst is trying to assess operating cash flows before non-cash accounting allocations of cost (depreciation, provisions and amortization) and before returns to lenders and taxation. How much cash is the business generating on a day-to-day basis? This measure may be subject to technical criticism, but it has the advantage that it strips out – as far as possible – subjective accounting adjustments from the income measure and enables a more robust comparison of performance year on year or company to company.

Based on this, analysts like to elaborate on *free cash flow,* commonly computed as:

$$\text{Free cash flow} = \text{Operating cash flow}$$
$$\textit{Less } \text{Capital expenditures}$$
$$\textit{Less } \text{Dividends}$$

The metric of free cash flow is interpreted as an indicator of a company's *financial flexibility.* It stands for the amount of *discretionary cash flow* that the company has available to expand its long-term investments and resources (beyond capital spending needed to maintain its competitive position), retire debt, repurchase its own shares or simply enhance its liquidity.

Normal capital expenditures (normal investing cash flows) and dividends are deducted from the net operating cash flow as they are seen as the least discretionary. Normal capital expenditure is needed to maintain and enhance current operating infrastructure and cannot be cut without endangering the company's current competitive position. Cutting dividends is also seen as a measure of last resort (see Chapter 8 on a company's dividend policy). Some analysts will also deduct scheduled debt repayments to arrive at their free cash flow metric. Analysts tend to calculate and evaluate a company's share price as a multiple of its free cash flow and compare it in time and cross-sectionally.

Additionally, analysts will use cash flow information to construct some extra liquidity and solvency ratios, such as net operating cash flow (or EBITDA) to current liabilities (as an additional liquidity test) or net operating cash flow (or EBITDA) to current liabilities plus long-term debt (as a solvency test). This last ratio is typically used by credit officers in evaluating a company's creditworthiness for long-term debt.

Objectives of analysis

As we have discussed, there are many potential uses and users of annual financial statements, but for the immediate purpose of financial statement analysis we are addressing only the needs of the two main groups for whom the financial statements are formally prepared: investors and creditors. These two groups are concerned with similar but different investment decisions about the company.

Investors (whether actual or potential) face a buy/sell/hold decision. They receive a return on their investment in the form of a flow of dividends and the difference between buying and selling price of the shareholding. There is no established pattern of behaviour among long-term shareholders as to whether they prefer income by way of dividends or by way of holding gain. (Clearly short-term holders are only interested in a speculative holding gain.) Finance theory suggests that shareholders should be indifferent, on the assumption that if a company restricts its dividend payments the share price will rise, so shareholders wanting cash flow can realize this by selling a part of their holding.

The evidence suggests that some companies pay high dividends in the belief that their shareholders want this, while others believe that shareholders prefer capital gains and restrict dividends. The way in which unit trusts are sold suggests that fund managers believe these are different markets. Some companies attempt to satisfy both types of shareholder and offer the option of taking the dividend in the form of new shares.

Professional investors have varying points of view. US pension funds often look at dividend flows (over as much as a 50-year time horizon) while many UK brokers sell to institutional investors on the basis of expected holding gains. For example, Ian Hay Davison, then chairman of Alexander Lang & Cruikshank, wrote the following:

> At 8.15 each weekday morning the security salesmen and analysts in my firm meet to consider the ideas that will be put to our 300 or so institutional customers during the day. Analysts responsible for following companies in various sectors of the market give their recommendations for specific shares: buy, hold or sell. It is these recommendations, together with similar conclusions reached at 20 or so other security houses, that collectively drive prices in the market. The single most important figure affecting the analyst's – and hence the market's – view is forecasted earnings per share. I know that accountants deplore the fact that judgements about the worth of a share turn largely on one number. Nonetheless that is what happens, and you and I know that it is accounting rules that determine earnings per share.

The way this works is that brokers expect the price/earnings (P/E) ratio of a company to be stable (subject to economic changes, management changes, etc.) and the market price to be a function of the forecast earnings and the P/E ratio (as discussed earlier on in this chapter).

For example, if a hotel company is forecast to have earnings per share of €4 and a P/E of 12, its market price should be €48. If an analyst who follows the hotel sector believes that the company is actually going to achieve significantly better than €4, say €5, this would mean that he or she would expect the price to rise to €60, and the securities house would issue a buy recommendation to its clients. These recommendations can themselves move the market.

The professional investor will look at indicators that are predictors of future performance on the assumption that growth in profits will lead to high dividends or high share price rises. Clearly, these indicators may be to do with the state of the economy or may be based on some inside information (stock exchange regulations prohibit companies from providing information to only part of the market, but investor relations departments of large companies hold special briefings for brokers and institutional shareholders that are available on the internet to satisfy regulators, but are often not viewed by retail investors) about new products etc. However, this course is concerned directly only with the information that can be gleaned from the published financial statements, so while acknowledging that investors use many different information sources, we will concentrate on financial statement information.

Growth in profits may be predicted from the financial statements based on a number of factors such as evidence of management skill, or evidence of high investment. Other factors such as a high debt/equity ratio will provide indicators of some aspects of the degree of risk in investing in the company.

The investor wishes (a) to predict the level of future returns and (b) to evaluate these against competing investment opportunities in the light of the riskiness of the investment (the higher the risk, the higher the expected return to compensate for the investment).

The creditor (the supplier of loans rather than short-term trade credit) is also concerned with predicting performance but from a slightly different angle. The creditor's main risk is default risk but ordinarily the creditor will also be concerned to assure himself that the company's likely future cash flows will be sufficient to meet interest payments and finally repay the debt. The creditor will have more interest in the financial structure and prospective cash flows of the company. But then again, it is earnings that ultimately generate cash flows, bringing us back to earning power or profitability as a fundamental concern for both (prospective) shareholders and creditors.

Broadly, both investor and creditor will use much the same indicators, but the relative importance of specific indicators will be different. The indicators may also serve different purposes at different times. The investor may use indicators which lead to a buy decision. Having already bought a holding, the release of new accounting data will prompt a hold/sell decision. In making this decision the investor will look not only for the indicators of the future, but will also look for feedback into his or her own decision-making process. He or she will examine how the company actually performed during the period an investment was held, as compared with the predictions made at the time of making the investment, to improve future predictions.

Strategic ratio analysis

A further development in financial statement analysis has been the attempt to develop (combinations of) ratios that will give insights to a company's strategic positioning in terms of the kind of analysis proposed by authors such as Porter or Peters. These authors introduced a strategic analysis framework centred around ideas such as the life cycle phases of products and firms, whether the company operates in a market where entry is difficult (margins should be large) or entry is easy (margins are tight), whether its products are specialist, niche products (low volume, high margin) or bulk (high volume, low margin) and many other considerations. Again, detailed discussions of business strategy should be looked for in specialist publications or courses, but our point is that proper analysis of financial statements can provide significant inputs for strategy analysis.

Sustainable growth

Most analysts will start their analysis by looking at growth of key items of financial statements, such as sales, net fixed assets, net profit and earnings per share (EPS). Trend analysis will automatically deliver the necessary data to determine a year-to-year growth rate or an average growth rate over a longer period. Growth rates are often compared with the rate of inflation to determine 'real' growth. The point of departure usually is sales growth, with the co-variation of sales and net working capital, net long-term assets, operating margins, net profit and operating cash flows being primary material for further analysis. It makes sense to try to differentiate organic growth and acquired growth as they tend to have quite different implications for further analysis. *Organic growth* is fuelled by the company's own operations, whereas *acquired growth* is the result of buying the assets and operations of other companies (through mergers and acquisitions). Sales growth is not always an indicator of successful performance and its relationship with operating efficiency and liquidity concerns needs careful attention.

The concept of sustainable growth looks at growth from an overall shareholder profitability perspective and measures the rate at which a company can grow while keeping its profitability and financing structure unchanged. The *sustainable growth rate ratio* is calculated as:

$$\text{Sustainable growth rate} = \text{Return on equity} \times (1 - \text{Dividend payout ratio})$$

The dividend payout ratio is:

$$\frac{\text{Dividend}}{\text{Profit attributable to shareholders}}$$

Sustainable growth stands for the internally generated growth potential if the company's profitability, dividend payout policy and level of debt financing are kept constant. Equity is, of course, equal to the net worth of a company, so the return on equity (ROE) ratio would tell you by what proportion the company would grow if it retained its profits and reinvested them. This is then reduced by the dividend payout, since clearly the dividend involves returning cash to shareholders, to show the proportion of net worth retained in the company each year out of that year's earnings. This is described as 'sustainable growth'. It ignores the fact that depreciation has been charged in arriving at this figure because that is regarded as a surrogate for the cash outflow required to sustain the company at its present size.

Put another way, a company that is breaking even after depreciation charges (which reflect the economic life of the assets) should be able to replace its assets and stay the same size; a company that makes a profit (i.e. makes a positive return on equity) but pays it all out to shareholders by way of dividend will similarly stay the same size; but to the extent that a company has profits that are greater than the dividend, it will have internal growth potential.

This potential growth rate can be used as one basis of comparison. Clearly, companies can also borrow, but ultimately that increases risk and is subject to fairly finite limits linking back to the company's equity base and the growth of that equity base. It is therefore a useful growth indicator to compare companies. If comparing companies within the same industry, one might predict that a company with a higher than average sustainable growth rate would be able to increase its market share.

ROI decomposition

There is a conventional relationship between management performance ratios that links return on investment (ROI), profit margin and asset turnover as follows:

$$\text{Profit margin} \times \text{Asset turnover} = \text{ROI}$$

A ROI ratio can be analyzed as a combination of two factors: overall profitability of sales and asset utilization.

If we apply this reasoning to the return on assets (ROA) ratio, we arrive at the following algebraic equality:

$$\frac{\text{Profit before interest}}{\text{Sales}} \times \frac{\text{Sales}}{\text{Total assets}} = \frac{\text{Profit before interest}}{\text{Total assets}}$$

Each of the terms on the right-hand side of the equation has its own meaning. Profit before interest divided by sales is a variant of the net profit margin (an overall profitability measure). Sales divided by total assets is the total asset turnover ratio. In fact, we decompose the ROA ratio into other financial characteristics that can be examined individually.

The ROA decomposition suggests two ways to improve the ROA: by increasing either the net profit margin or the turnover of total assets (or both). The net profit margin will increase by earning more profit per currency unit of sales. The total asset turnover will increase in either of two ways: (a) by generating more sales volume with the same amount of assets; or (b) by reducing the amount of assets required for a given volume of sales (for example, by disposing of or decreasing less productive assets). The total asset turnover ratio can be analyzed further through the component measures of total assets turnover (inventory turnover, fixed asset turnover, receivables turnover, etc.). Profit margins will improve by (a) reducing cost of sales and other operating costs for a given volume of sales; or (b) increasing unit sales prices.

The ROI decomposition logic underscores the fact that an overall ROI measure is the combined effect of a large number of factors and responsibilities. It can be used by external analysts as a guide to drill down to specific policy areas and identify areas of concern.

To a certain extent the relationships among the decomposed ratios/factors are industry specific. Industries that are capital intensive are likely to have a low asset turnover ratio. However, such an industry is also usually characterized by high margins because it is difficult for new companies to enter the market. A company that is capital intensive but also has low margins will be on a declining trend in its life cycle. Industries that have little capital involved will have higher asset turnover ratios. However, they will normally be highly competitive because of the lack of barriers to entry into the market and will therefore show lower margins.

Financial leverage

Taking the analysis one step further, the ROE can be analytically linked to the return on assets ratio with the introduction of the concept of financial leverage:

$$\text{ROA} \times \text{Financial leverage} = \text{ROE}$$

Starting with the ROA ratio, we arrive at the following algebraic equality:

$$\frac{\text{Profit before interest}}{\text{Total assets}} \times \frac{\text{Total assets}}{\text{Equity}} = \frac{\text{Profit before interest}}{\text{Equity}}$$

Alternatively, we can start from the original ROE definition and get the following:

$$\frac{\text{Net profit for the period}}{\text{Total assets}} \times \frac{\text{Total assets}}{\text{Equity}} = \frac{\text{Net profit for the period}}{\text{Equity}}$$

In both formulae, financial leverage is defined as the proportion of total assets acquired with funds supplied by the shareholders. It measures how many euro of assets are employed for each euro invested by shareholders. Financial leverage will increase if debt financing increases or if part of the shares outstanding are repurchased. The essential message of the ROE decomposition is that both financial leverage and ROA are drivers of the return to shareholders: debt financing can be used to lever shareholder profitability.

A related, but somewhat different, concept is the *financial leverage coefficient* ratio, defined as ROE divided by ROA:

$$\text{Financial leverage coefficient} = \text{ROE\%} / \text{ROA\%}$$

Leverage is positive (or financial leverage coefficient greater than one) if the company's rate of return on total assets exceeds the average after-tax interest rate on its debt. In that case, the company lends money at one rate and uses that money productively at a higher rate of return. The excess of the after-tax rate of return on assets and the after-tax interest rate on the borrowed funds, accrues to the benefit of the shareholders. Note that financial leverage can be a disadvantage, too: if the company does not succeed in earning a rate of return on assets that is higher than the after-tax cost of debt, the shareholders will have to support the deficit.

Debt financing will increase the financial leverage effect. If leverage is positive, the financial leverage coefficient will increase with gearing. We illustrate this effect in Table 17.1 under three different gearing assumptions with total assets, ROA and after-tax cost of debt being held constant.

The higher the debt/equity ratio, the higher the effect (positive or negative) of debt financing on the ROE. Note that in this scenario analysis we kept the cost of debt constant. In practice, however, increasing gearing will undoubtedly have an effect on the cost of debt too. Increased debt financing will bring lenders to demand a higher risk premium and, thus, a higher interest rate, possibly up to the level where leverage becomes negative (financial leverage coefficient 1).

Table 17.1 Financial leverage effect at different debt/equity ratios

Total assets = 1,000
ROA = 10%
After-tax cost of debt = 7%

Debt/Equity	100%	150%	300%
Profit before interest	100	100	100
Cost of debt	35	42	52.5
Net profit	65	58	47.5
ROE	13%	14.5%	19%
Financial leverage coefficient	13%/10% = 1.30	1.45	1.90

Combining ROI decomposition and financial leverage brings us to the following overall model (also called the DuPont model):

$$\text{ROE} = \text{Net profit margin} \times \text{Asset turnover} \times \text{Financial leverage}$$

or:

$$\frac{\text{Net profit for the period}}{\text{Equity}} = \frac{\text{Net profit for the period}}{\text{Sales}} \times \frac{\text{Sales}}{\text{Total assets}} \times \frac{\text{Total assets}}{\text{Equity}}$$

This model allows an integrated profitability analysis with the three factors as profit drivers and by linking these to underlying competitive mechanisms and managerial coping behaviour.

Segment data analysis

The analysis of the consolidated financial statements, using ratio analysis and related techniques, is important to evaluate company performance through time and relative to its peers. However, it does not shed light on the inner dynamics of the company's performance. In that sense, examining the performance of the company's operating segments through an analysis of the segment reporting data may deepen the understanding of the factors and operations that drive the group's consolidated performance.

Given the nature of the operating segment information provided, a number of segment ratios can be computed, such as:

$$\text{Segment profit margin} = \frac{\text{Segment result}}{\text{Segment revenue}}$$

$$\text{Segment operating cash flow (EBITDA) margin} = \frac{(\text{Segment operating result} + \text{Depreciation and amortization expense})}{\text{Segment revenue}}$$

$$\text{Segment asset turnover} = \frac{\text{Segment revenue}}{\text{Segment assets}}$$

$$\text{Segment ROA} = \frac{\text{Segment result}}{\text{Segment assets}}$$

$$\text{Segment gearing} = \frac{\text{Segment liabilities}}{\text{Segment assets}}$$

Comparing these ratios through time and across segments will increase the understanding of the factors driving overall company performance. They are useful in comparing risks and returns of different operations within a company and among investment alternatives.

The segment ROA can be further analyzed by performing a DuPont type of analysis in the following way:

$$\text{Segment ROA} = \text{Segment profit margin} \times \text{Segment asset turnover}$$

Taking into account intercompany differences in segment reporting formats, segment data analysis could also be used to analyze and benchmark comparable segments of peer companies within the same industry. This type of comparison probably makes more sense than comparing high-level, aggregated data of peer companies where similarities are usually much less evident than at operating segment level. But then again, one should keep in mind that segment reporting according to IFRS 8 *Operating Segments* is entity specific, not only with regard to information items reported, but also in respect of the measurement bases used.

Operational gearing

Another aspect of a company's competitive position is the flexibility of its cost structure: companies with high fixed costs cannot react easily to downturns and generally need to seek high market share to maximize their fixed capacity. Companies in the same industry but that organize themselves with higher variable costs are more flexible, but may need to site themselves in a high price niche rather than look for large market share.

This can be illustrated graphically. The convention in management accounting is that a company's costs are either fixed or variable in the short to medium term (this is an oversimplification, but useful for analytical purposes). Thus a company with high fixed costs would have the relationship between volume and profit shown in Figure 17.2.

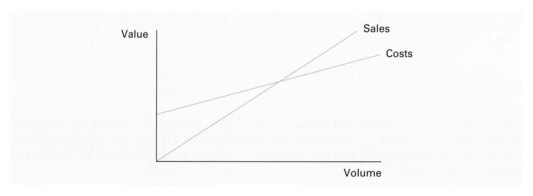

Figure 17.2   The relationship between volume and profit in a company with high fixed costs

Clearly, the higher the volume, the more the profit, and such a company has some interest in reducing prices to gain market share, because that will lead to more than proportionately higher profits. Conversely, a company with low fixed costs and high variable costs is not very sensitive to volume changes and has much more interest in increasing prices. Such a company should therefore seek niche products, or highly differentiated products, where a small volume can be sold at high price.

Analytically, the concept of *operational gearing* refers to the volatility of profit as a function of changes in sales while taking into account the company's cost structure.

Operational gearing can be interpreted as the percentage change in profit as sales changes 1 per cent. It can be measured as follows:

$$\text{Operational gearing} = \frac{\text{Sales} - \text{Variable costs}}{\text{Profit before tax}}$$

or:

$$\text{Operational gearing} = \frac{\text{Profit before taxes} + \text{Fixed costs}}{\text{Profit before tax}}$$

Let us look at the following illustration with two companies (Company A and Company B) with identical sales and total costs, but with a different cost structure (mix of fixed and variable costs):

	Sales	Fixed costs	Variable costs	Profit before tax	Operational gearing
Company A	100	20	70	10	3:1
Company B	100	70	20	10	8:1

If sales increase by 10 per cent, net profit of Company A will increase by 30 per cent (increase in sales minus proportionate increase of variable costs, or 10 minus 7), while net profit of Company B would increase by 80 per cent. Conversely, if sales decline, this would have a much more dramatic impact on the profitability of the company with high operational gearing (Company B).

Unfortunately, the split between fixed and variable costs is not transparent from financial statements and the external analyst will have to settle with a rough proxy for operational gearing (a proxy for fixed costs to total costs), or the ratio:

$$\frac{\text{Long-term assets}}{\text{Total asset}} \quad \text{or} \quad \frac{\text{Long-term assets}}{\text{Current assets}}$$

This assumes that the fixed cost element comes from plant costs (labour and materials being relatively variable). The high variable cost operator will buy semi-finished goods, for example, rather than process raw materials in house, so variable costs are higher and the asset base is lower.

Z scores

Some analysts like to use computerized models for assessing company performance. The best known authors in this kind of area are Altman in the USA and Tafler in the UK. Essentially, their technique consists of comparing the past financial statements of successful companies with those of similar but unsuccessful companies from which they derive a model against which to assess other companies. To give a simplified example, such a model typically works on a weighted series of ratios such as:

$$0.2 \text{ ROE} + 0.5 \text{ Debt/equity} + 0.25 \text{ Current ratio} \geq 1$$

If a company scores below a certain value, it is deemed to be at risk. These models are known generically as 'Z scores' after Altman's original work. Declining profitability and liquidity ratios typically have a significant effect in business failure models.

Such models may well be useful to audit firms and to banks to assess the viability of clients, and have the merit that they are an objective test. Critics, by way of contrast, point out that the models are derived from statistical relationships that existed between particular companies in the past in particular industry sectors and particular economies and there is no guarantee that other companies at other times and in other circumstances will replicate the same relationships. The method does not, as it were, attempt to harness together data about actual economic circumstances as such.

It is a complex technique that is beyond the scope of this book. A number of proprietary versions are available on the market and there is an extensive research literature.

Shareholder value

An alternative approach to analyzing financial statements is the concept of shareholder value, which appeared in the USA during the 1980s, but does not really have a generally agreed rationale or working methodology. Our intention here is to provide an introduction to the subject, which students can take forward when they study the related material in the finance literature. The underlying idea is that instead of looking at earnings per share and the P/E ratio to arrive at the value of a company, the analyst should look at the discounted present value of forecast earnings.

In principle, the idea is excellent and in effect simply uses the definition of income which is used in economics. However, in practice the idea is more difficult because it involves forecasting future earnings over at least a 10-year horizon and determining the appropriate discount rate to use.

The basis normally used for imputing value in economics is the discounted value of the future cash flows that a project presents. You will normally cover the concepts of discounting and present values in the context of a finance or business statistics course. The essence is covered below.

BETWEEN THE LINES

Present value

Present value calculations are used in economics, finance and financial management to assign a value to future cash flows after adjusting for the time value of money. The essence of present value is that a rational person will prefer to have a receipt sooner rather than later because the money can be used to generate more money.

For example, if a company has a choice of receiving $1,000 now or $1,000 in a year's time, it would prefer to have the cash now because it could be invested and earn a return. If the money were put into risk-free securities where it could earn 5 per cent, then $1,000 now would be worth $1,050 in a year's time.

Extending that, the $1,000 to be received after a year is worth $1,000/1.05 (or $952) today, because $952 invested today at 5 per cent would yield $1,000 in a year's time. Similarly, $1,000 to be received in two years' time is worth $1,000/(1.05 × 1.05) $907 at present (i.e. compound interest at 5 per cent for two years would be $93).

By way of a simplified example, supposing that a listed company was forecast to have a life cycle of five years, the cost of capital for a company at that level of risk is 10 per cent and it is forecast to generate the following cash flows after meeting its operating costs:

	1 €m	2 €m	3 €m	4 €m	5 €m
Net cash flows	100	250	250	200	50
Discount factor:	0.909	0.826	0.751	0.683	0.621
Present values	90.9	206.6	187.8	136.6	31.0

The present value of the company – or the shareholder value – is €652.9m. Supposing that it has 200m shares in issue, the share price should be (€652.9/200) = €3.26. If the actual share price is €2.70, then the investor should buy or hold, whereas if the actual market price was €3.50, the investor should sell (if holding shares) or simply not buy, on the basis in both cases that the share price will be likely to move towards €3.26.

If the management of the company is performing well, it will be increasing the future net cash flows of the company and therefore increasing shareholder value. The concept of shareholder value as a means of evaluating investments is very useful; however, the methodology involves a considerable amount of subjective inputs. These revolve around two key points: (1) the forecast cash flows of the company; and (2) the discount rate.

Forecast cash flows

The cash flow forecast needs to consider both the likely cash flows from existing operations and the capital expenditure necessary to renew existing equipment and expand capacity. The cash flow statement gives cash flows both from operations and outflows to pay interest and tax (the dividend stream is part of shareholder value, since this is being directed to the shareholder), the net after these is in effect the cash available for the shareholder or for reinvestment. In forecasting the future, it is necessary to make assumptions about the rate of inflation and the rate of real growth (which derive partly from observation of economic indicators and partly from an estimate of management's performance).

Estimating the capital expenditure rate is even more difficult. In the future, given a long time series of cash flow statements, it will be possible to produce a long-term average correlation between profit growth and investment growth. At this time, the analyst could take annual depreciation as a surrogate for maintaining existing equipment, and add to that a year-on-year change in net fixed assets and net working capital. The longer the time series, the more reliable an average figure would be.

Discount rate

There is an extensive literature on this subject. The discount rate should reflect the cost of capital as adjusted for inflation and the risk associated with the particular activities of that company. Alternatively, the analyst might use the weighted average cost of capital for the individual company.

There are many different formulations that might be used, both to forecast cash inflows (e.g. starting from forecast sales and using profit margins) and cash outflows, and the question of discount rate is contentious, since a small difference in discount rate usually gives a large difference in present value. However, it is a valuation model that best approximates the real cash flows of the company and is particularly useful in cross-sectional analysis of companies in the same industry, since the same basic assumptions can be used.

equipment itself in an attempt to strengthen its position in that particular market as well as increase the profitability of that activity segment. As a result, Cleaney now on longer

Summary

In this chapter, we have aimed to expand your knowledge of financial statement analysis and put it in closer touch with the actual practices of securities houses. We have looked at the evaluation model that examines the surrounding economic environment and we have quality of earnings considerations and accounting adjustments that should be considered in making financial information more directly comparable. We have seen that the analyst's forecast of earnings and the market P/E ratio are used to forecast the future share price and make buy/sell/hold decisions by investors.

We then went on to look at how financial statement analysis can give inputs into the strategic analysis of a company. We looked at a ratio for sustainable growth, ROE decomposition as well as indicators of how capital intensive an industry is and its operating gearing. Finally, we looked also at the evolving concept of shareholder value.

Assignments

The following questions have answers on the lecturer side of the digital support resources for the book.

1. Cleaney Inc.

   You are an analyst working for the American venture capital firm Docker Warden (DW). DW has received a request from a company called Cleaney Inc. to provide the latter with additional venture capital. Should DW accept to do so, then Cleaney will issue new shares to which DW will subscribe.

   However, before discussing the terms of the potential transaction, the board of DW wishes to obtain an objective image of Cleaney Inc. Thus, it is your assignment to conduct a preliminary analysis on the basis of the available financial data (including segment information). The board of DW has asked you to prepare a report that includes:

   (a) an analysis of Cleaney's investment and financing policy

   (b) a review of Cleaney's management as evidenced by the financial statements

   (c) an executive summary, including your assessment of the situation and recommendations.

To complete this task, you are provided with the company's annual financial statements from 20X4 to 20X8, as well as with the following additional information: the principal activity of Cleaney, incorporated at the start of 20X0, consists of the production of card and coin-operated washing machines. These are subsequently sold or leased out either to commercial launderettes or to laundry rooms on the multi-housing market. The latter consists of apartments, condominium units, colleges and universities. Since 20X1, Cleaney has been generating additional revenue from the selling and leasing out of card and coin-operated reprographics equipment (i.e. mainly photocopiers) to schools, colleges, universities, libraries and government institutions. Up until the end of 20X5, Cleaney simply traded in such reprographics equipment. At the beginning of 20X6, Cleaney's management decided, however, that the company would manufacture the equipment itself in an attempt to strengthen its position in that particular market as well as increase the profitability of that activity segment. As a result, Cleaney now no longer purchases any finished photocopiers from other manufacturers: all the reprographics equipment that it sells or leases out is own manufacture:

Annual financial statements: Cleaney Inc. (in US$'000)

Income statements

	20X8	20X7	20X6	20X5	20X4
Sales	158,268	150,260	134,200	81,400	64,400
Cost of sales	-120,345	-114,926	-102,400	-61,200	-48,600
Gross operating margin	37,923	35,334	31,800	20,200	15,800
Distribution costs	-17,100	-16,863	-10,200	-6,500	-5,300
Administration expenses	-9,230	-8,607	-7,100	-3,400	-2,500
Operating income	11,593	9,864	14,500	10,300	8,000
Interest expense	-8,270	-7,085	-4,000	-2,300	-2,100
Income before tax	3,323	2,779	10,500	8,000	5,900
Taxation	-1,662	-1,727	-5,400	-2,700	-500
Net income	1,661	1,052	5,100	5,300	5,400
Dividends proposed	-332	-0	-1,020	-1,060	-0

Statements of financial position

	20X8	20X7	20X6	20X5	20X4
Non-current assets					
Tangible assets	82,435	78,440	67,382	35,300	33,250
Intangible assets	59,840	61,516	60,482	22,500	12,850
Current assets					
Inventories	3,391	6,521	3,800	2,900	1,500
Receivables	7,992	8,551	6,500	4,300	1,600
Cash and cash equivalent	13,559	6,047	8,506	7,576	9,700
Total assets	167,217	161,075	146,670	72,576	58,900
Current liabilities					
Loans (interest-bearing)	17,840	9,454	0	0	0
Trade payables	13,932	16,840	15,330	9,776	13,600
Taxes payable	1,662	1,727	5,400	2,700	500
Non-current liabilities					
Long-term debt	88,550	89,482	82,400	20,600	25,300

Equity
  Ordinary shares

($1 nominal value)	2,000	2,000	2,000	2,000	1,300
Share premium	25,400	25,400	25,400	25,400	11,400
Dividend (proposed)	332	0	1,020	1,060	0
Retained earnings	17,501	16,172	15,120	11,040	6,800
Total liabilities and equity	167,217	161,075	146,670	72,576	58,900

Analysis of non-current assets

	20X8	20X7	20X6	20X5	20X4
Acquisition cost					
Balance 1 January	185,470	157,450	78,380	62,260	62,470
Additions	22,710	29,660	89,640	16,970	130
Disposals	−2,630	−1,640	−10,570	−850	−340
Balance 31 December	205,550	185,470	157,450	78,380	62,260
Accumulated depreciation					
Balance 1 January	45,514	29,586	20,580	16,160	13,820
Disposals	−1,769	−1,120	−7,334	−600	−240
Depreciation expense	19,530	17,048	16,340	5,020	2,580
Balance 31 December	63,275	45,514	29,586	20,580	16,160
Net book value					
31 December	142,275	139,956	127,864	57,800	46,100

Segment information

	20X8	20X7	20X6	20X5	20X4
Sales					
Laundry services	114,251	114,186	105,822	72,015	58,965
Reprographics services	44,017	36,074	28,378	9,385	5,435
Gross operating margin					
Laundry services	27,490	26,210	23,580	16,470	13,240
Reprographics services	10,433	9,124	8,220	3,730	2,560
NBV of non-current assets					
Laundry services	93,659	95,367	85,516	46,166	40,128
Reprographics services	44,327	40,825	38,479	9,691	4,492
Distribution and	4,289	3,764	3,869	1,943	1,480
administration					

2. Gloucester Gardens plc.

You are an analyst working for an American investment bank, Insecurity International (II). You are called in by a junior associate in the mergers and acquisitions department to comment on a particular case.

II has been approached by a venture capital firm, Kindly Keep Repaying (KKR), which wants to dispose of a small investment in a company (Gloucester Gardens), which runs a chain of garden centres in southwest England. Gloucester Gardens (GG) started out as a nursery growing plants for direct sale to the public and also selling to the trade. Over a period of 20 years it first expanded its retail activities to sell a wide range of garden products beyond its own plants, and then took on more and more new retail units, supplied partly from its own nursery.

The company is now operated as two divisions: nursery and retail. All the output from the nursery is sold through the GG retail division, although for internal control purposes, it is sold at market prices by the nursery division to retail.

The KKR representative says that GG is family run but the founder is nearing retirement and is quite interested in selling out, although his daughter is also involved in managing the business and would like to stay on and participate in the expansion of the business, assuming that some satisfactory package could be worked out. The family knows that KKR is making this approach.

KKR thinks that the GG operation has potential as the basis of establishing a national chain of such centres, but thinks that the existing family management do not have the necessary expertise to grow any further. KKR would like to see their stake bought out by a major national retailer, possibly with the potential to slot the GG operation alongside a chain of out-of-town DIY or similar stores. KKR itself paid £1,400,000 for a 25 per cent stake in GG early in 20X8 and is looking for upwards of £3,000,000 for its stake.

The M&A associate wants you to prepare an analysis of the figures for the last five years for GG for presentation to a potential client.

When the KKR representative has left, the M&A associate provides the attached figures and asks you to prepare a report for her to include:

(a) an analysis of the company's investment and financing policy

(b) a review of its management as evidenced by the financial statements (including segment information)

(c) an executive summary, including your assessment of the situation and recommendations.

£'000	20X5	20X6	20X7	20X8	20X9
Statements of profit or loss					
Sales	2,220.0	2,941.3	3,537.8	4,573.0	5,584.0
Cost of sales	−1,344.7	−1,766.8	−2,105.0	−2,697.4	−3,262.5
Gross margin	*875.3*	*1,174.5*	*1,432.8*	*1,875.6*	*2,321.6*
Distribution expense	−116.0	−130.0	−147.0	−160.0	−171.0
Administration expense	−245.0	−268.0	−304.0	−337.0	−383.0
	514.3	*776.5*	*981.8*	*1,378.6*	*1,767.6*
Interest expense	−83.0	−146.0	−232.3	−269.0	−332.6
Disposal income	0.0	2.0	−4.0	0.0	3.6
Profit before tax	*431.3*	*632.5*	*745.5*	*1,110.6*	*1,438.6*
Taxation	−125.1	−202.4	−246.0	−388.7	−517.9
Profit after tax	306.2	430.1	499.5	721.9	920.7
Dividends declared	−75.0	−100.0	−140.0	−190.0	−240.0

£'000	20X5	20X6	20X7	20X8	20X9
Statements of financial position					
Non-current assets (A)					
Retail premises	2,086.0	3,006.0	4,478.0	5,847.0	6,774.0
Accumulated depreciation	−208.8	−284.0	−395.9	−542.1	−711.4
Nurseries	3,200.0	3,200.0	3,200.0	4,400.0	4,400.0
Accumulated depreciation	−624.2	−730.9	−837.6	−984.3	−1,131.0
Plant and equipment	91.0	109.0	158.0	296.0	278.0
Accumulated depreciation	−56.4	−68.0	−82.8	−142.0	−146.4
Vehicles	49.0	65.0	122.0	176.0	194.0
Accumulated depreciation	−19.7	28.6	246.9	290.9	296.3
	4,516.9	**5,268.5**	**6,594.8**	**8,959.7**	**9,560.9**
Current assets (B)					
Inventories – retail	139.4	233.2	350.3	546.5	799.0
– nurseries	440.0	530.0	588.6	699.8	761.6
Receivables	111.0	147.1	212.3	320.1	446.7
Cash at bank	56.3	101.7	108.4	15.2	13.1
	746.7	**1,012.0**	**1,259.6**	**1,581.6**	**2,020.4**
Short-term liabilities (C)					
Trade payables	−269.0	−353.4	−484.1	−701.3	−880.9
Taxes payable	−125.1	−202.4	−246.0	−388.7	−517.9
Overdraft	0.0	0.0	0.0	−182.2	−182.8
	−394.1	**−555.8**	**−730.2**	**−1,272.2**	**−1,581.6**
Sub-total (A+B−C)	**4,794.5**	**5,624.7**	**6,984.2**	**9,079.1**	**9,759.7**
Long-term liabilities (D)	−1,500.0	−2,000.0	−3,000.0	−3,200.0	−3,200.0
Net Assets (A+B−C−D)	3,369.5	3,724.7	4,124.2	6,069.1	6,799.7
Equity					
Ordinary shares	1,800.0	1,800.0	1,800.0	2,400.0	2,400.0
Share premium	784.0	784.0	784.0	1,547.0	1,547.0
Retained profit	785.5	1,140.7	1,540.2	2,122.1	2,852.7
Total equity	3,369.5	3,724.7	4,124.2	6,069.1	6,799.7

(Continued)

Analysis of non-current assets

20X5

	Retail premises £'000	Nursery premises £'000	Plant and equipment £'000	Motor vehicles £'000	Total £'000
Cost					
Cost: 1 Jan	1,369.0	3,200.0	82.0	26.0	4,677.0
Additions	717.0	0.0	24.0	31.0	772.0
Disposals	0.0	0.0	−15.0	−8.0	−23.0
Cost: 31 Dec	*2,086.0*	*3,200.0*	*91.0*	*49.0*	*5,426.0*
Depreciation					
Balance 1 Jan	156.7	517.5	49.2	13.5	736.9
Disposals	0.0	0.0	−11.0	−6.0	−17.0
Additions	52.1	106.7	18.2	12.2	189.2
Balance 31 Dec	*208.8*	*624.8*	*56.4*	*19.7*	*909.1*
Net book value 31 Dec	*1,877.2*	*2,575.8*	*34.6*	*29.3*	*4,516.9*

20X6

	Retail premises £'000	Nursery premises £'000	Plant and equipment £'000	Motor vehicles £'000	Total £'000
Cost					
Cost: 1 Jan	2,086.0	3,200.0	91.0	49.0	5,426.0
Additions	920.0	0.0	32.0	28.0	980.0
Disposals	0.0	0.0	−14.0	−12.0	−26.0
Cost: 31 Dec	*3,006.0*	*3,200.0*	*109.0*	*65.0*	*6,380.0*
Depreciation					
Balance 1 Jan	208.8	624.2	56.4	19.7	909.1
Disposals	0.0	0.0	−10.2	−7.4	−17.6
Additions	75.2	106.7	21.8	16.3	220.0
Balance 31 Dec	*284.0*	*730.9*	*68.0*	*28.6*	*1,111.5*
Net book value 31 Dec	*2,722.0*	*2,469.1*	*41.0*	*36.4*	*5,268.5*

20X7

	Retail premises £'000	Nursery premises £'000	Plant and equipment £'000	Motor vehicles £'000	Total £'000
Cost					
Cost: 1 Jan	3,006.0	3,200.0	109.0	65.0	6,380.0
Additions	1,472.0	0.0	83.0	72.0	1,627.0
Disposals	0.0	0.0	−34.0	−15.0	−49.0
Cost: 31 Dec	*4,478.0*	*3,200.0*	*158.0*	*122.0*	*7,958.0*

20X7

	Retail premises £'000	Nursery premises £'000	Plant and equipment £'000	Motor vehicles £'000	Total £'000
Accumulated depreciation					
Balance 1 Jan	284.0	730.9	68.0	28.6	1,111.5
Disposals	0.0	0.0	−16.8	−12.2	−29.0
Additions	111.9	106.7	31.6	30.5	280.7
Balance 31 Dec	395.9	837.6	82.8	46.9	1,363.2
Net book value 31 Dec	4,082.1	2,362.4	75.2	75.1	6,594.8

20X8

	Retail premises £'000	Nursery premises £'000	Plant and equipment £'000	Motor vehicles £'000	Total £'000
Cost					
Cost: 1 Jan	4,478.0	3,200.0	158.0	122.0	7,958.0
Additions	1,369.0	1,200.0	138.0	54.0	2,761.0
Disposals	0.0	0.0	0.0	0.0	0.0
Cost: 31 Dec	5,847.0	4,400.0	296.0	176.0	10,719.0
Accumulated depreciation					
Balance 1 Jan	395.9	837.6	82.8	46.9	1,363.2
Disposals	0.0	0.0	0.0	0.0	0.0
Additions	146.2	146.7	59.2	44.0	396.1
Balance 31 Dec	542.1	984.3	142.0	90.9	1,759.3
Net book value 31 Dec	5,304.9	3,415.7	154.0	85.1	8,959.7

20X9

	Retail premises £'000	Nursery premises £'000	Plant and equipment £'000	Motor vehicles £'000	Total £'000
Cost					
Cost: 1 Jan	5,847.0	4,400.0	296.0	176.0	10,719.0
Additions	927.0	0.0	46.0	56.0	1,029.0
Disposals	0.0	0.0	−64.0	−38.0	−102.0
Cost: 31 Dec	6,774.0	4,400.0	278.0	194.0	11,646.0
Accumulated depreciation					
Balance 1 Jan	542.1	984.3	142.0	90.9	1,759.3
Disposals	0.0	0.0	−51.2	−33.4	−84.6
Additions	169.3	146.7	55.6	38.8	410.4
Balance 31 Dec	711.4	1,131.0	146.4	96.3	2,085.1
Net book value 31 Dec	6,062.6	3,269.0	131.6	97.7	9,560.9

(Continued)

Segment information					
	20X5	*20X6*	*20X7*	*20X8*	*20X9*
	£'000	*£'000*	*£'000*	*£'000*	*£'000*
Sales					
Nursery	1,100.0	1,325.0	1,415.0	1,620.0	1,700.0
Retail	2,220.0	2,941.3	3,537.8	4,573.0	5,584.0
Gross margin					
Nursery	220.0	265.0	283.0	324.0	340.0
Retail	655.3	909.5	1,149.8	1,551.6	1,981.6

3. Who is who?

The following eight ratio sets refer to real-life-listed companies (consolidated financial statements). These are:

1) A supermarket chain (selling food and non-food)
2) A manufacturer of chemical products (capital-intensive production processes)
3) A provider of catering services (onsite catering services for business clients)
4) A pizza restaurant chain with delivery services
5) A real estate renting company (rents out office buildings that it owns and tailored office space)
6) A producer and distributor of luxury products (luxury clothing, jewels, wines and champagne)
7) A temporary employment agency
8) An internet retailer of fashion clothing.

	A	*B*	*C*	*D*	*E*	*F*	*G*	*H*
Current ratio	2.59	1.03	1.31	0.66	1.41	0.95	1.49	0.61
Acid test ratio	1.65	0.99	1.31	0.66	0.54	0.89	0.71	0.44
Inventory turnover	6.80	68.15	n.a.	n.a.	6.06	61.45	3.23	17.85
Credit given (days)	48.83	63.21	93.82	34.54	2.82	3.00	26.72	2.00
Credit obtained (days)	22.86	35.24	7.02	13.29	10.08	18.79	42.36	32.88
Fixed assets turnover	1.90	2.64	25.01	1.23	8.20	3.28	1.16	1.72
Return on assets (%)	7.70	3.38	8.02	3.59	9.63	25.87	10.58	1.93
Gross profit margin (%)	27.06	16.87	20.32	22.89	49.88	37.74	68.59	3.54
Net operating margin (%)	9.60	5.20	3.77	6.22	4.77	18.60	17.72	2.12

Required:

Identify which company is represented in columns A to H.

FURTHER READING

Abela, M. and Mora, A. (2012) 'Understanding the consequences of Accounting Standards in Europe: The role of EFRAG', *Accounting in Europe* 9(1): 147–170.

Adams, C. A. (2004) 'The ethical, social and environmental reporting-performance portrayal gap', *Accounting, Auditing and Accountability Journal* 17(5): 731–57.

Aerts, W. (2015) 'Narrative accounting disclosures', in C. L. Cooper (ed.) *Wiley Encyclopedia of Management, Volume I - Accounting*, 3rd ed. (pp. 311–317), Oxford: John Wiley & Sons.

Aerts, W. and Cormier, D. (2009) 'Media legitimacy and corporate environmental communication', *Accounting, Organizations and Society* 34(1), 1–27.

Aerts, W. and Tarca, A. (2010) 'Financial performance explanations and institutional setting', *Accounting and Business Research* 40(5): 421–450.

Aerts, W. and Cheng, P. (2012) 'Self-serving causal disclosures on earnings and short-term IPO valuation – Evidence from Chinese initial public offerings', *Accounting and Business Research* 42(1): 49–75.

Alexander, D. and Jermakowicz, E. (2006) 'A true and fair view of the principles/rules debate', *Abacus* 42(2): 132–64.

Armitage, S. and Marston, C. (2008) 'Corporate disclosure, cost of capital and reputation: Evidence from finance directors', *British Accounting Review* 40(4): 314–366.

Bamber, M. and McMeeking, K. (2016) 'An examination of international accounting standard-setting due process and the implications for legitimacy', *The British Accounting Review* 48(1): 59–73.

Barker, R. (2015) 'Conservatism, prudence and the IASB's conceptual framework', *Accounting and Business Research* 45(4): 514–538.

Barth, M. E. and Landsman, W. R. (2010) 'How did financial reporting contribute to the financial crisis?', *European Accounting Review* 19(3): 399–423.

Barth, M., Nobes, C. and Tarca, A. (2015) 'Conceptual framework for financial reporting: An introduction to the special issue', *Accounting and Business Research* 45(5): 543–544.

Baudot, L. (2014) 'GAAP convergence or convergence Gap: Unfolding ten years of accounting change', *Accounting, Auditing & Accountability Journal* 27(6): 956–994.

Bay, W. and Bruns, H-G. (2003) 'Multinational companies and international capital markets', in P. Walton, A. Haller and B. Raffournier (eds) *International Accounting*, 2nd edn (pp. 385–403), London: Thomson Learning.

Beattie, V. and Davison, J. (2015) 'Accounting narratives: Storytelling, philosophising and quantification', *Accounting and Business Research* 45(6–7): 655–660.

Bocqueraz, C. and Walton, P. (2006) 'Creating a supranational institution: The role of the individual and the mood of the times', *Accounting History* 11(3): 271–88.

Boerner, H. (2005) 'Are corporate accounting systems out-of-date?', *Corporate Finance Review* 10(2): 35–41.

Botosan, C. and Huffman, A. (2015) 'Decision-useful asset measurement from a business valuation perspective', *Accounting Horizons* 29(4): 757–776.

Bradbury, M. (2007) 'An anatomy of an IFRIC Interpretation', *Accounting in Europe* 4: 109–22.

Brown, P. (2011) 'International Financial Reporting Standards: What are the benefits?', *Accounting and Business Research* 41(3): 269–285.

Camfferman, K. and Zeff, S. (2007) *Financial Reporting and Global Capital Markets: A History of the International Accounting Standards Committee, 1973–2000*, Oxford: Oxford University Press.

Cammferman, K. and Zeff, S. (2015) *Aiming for Global Standards – the International Accounting Standards Board 2001-2011*, Oxford: Oxford University Press.

Cascino, S., Clatworthy, M., García Osma, B., Gassen, J., Imam, S. and Jeanjean, T. (2016) *'Professional investors and the decision usefulness of financial reporting'*, Report prepared for ICAS (The Institute of Chartered Accountants of Scotland) and EFRAG (European Financial Reporting Advisory Group), 77 pages.

Chen, J. J. and Zhang, H. (2010) 'The impact of regulatory enforcement and audit upon IFRS compliance – evidence from China', *European Accounting Review* 19(4): 665–692.

Coates, J. and Srinivasan, S. (2014) 'SOX after ten years: A multidisciplinary review', *Accounting Horizons* 28(3): 627–671.

Colley, J. L. Jr, Doyle, J. L., Logan, G. W. and Stettinuis, W. (2005) *What is Corporate Governance?* New York: McGraw-Hill.

Cooper, S. (2007) 'Performance measurement for equity analysis and valuation', *Accounting in Europe* 4: 1–50.

Cormier, D., Ledoux, M. J., Aerts, W. and Magnan, M. (2010) 'Corporate governance and information asymmetry between managers and investors', *Corporate Governance* 10(5): 574–589.

Dellaportas, S., Gibson, K., Alagiah, R., Hutchinson, M., Leung, P. and Homrigh, D. V. (2005) *Ethics, Governance and Accountability: A Professional Perspective*, Brisbane: John Wiley & Sons.

Denning, B. (2004) 'Adopting International Financial Reporting Standards: The tax implications', *Accountancy Ireland* 36(4): 19–22.

Detzen, D. (2016), 'From compromise to concept? – A review of "other comprehensive income"', *Accounting and Business Research,* DOI: 10.1080/00014788.2015.1135783.

Erchinger, H. and Melcher, W. (2007) 'Convergence between US GAAP and IFRS: Acceptance of IFRS by the US Securities and Exchange Commission', *Accounting in Europe* 4: 123–40.

Faux, J. and Wise, V. (2005) 'Financial reporting policy in a dynamic environment', *International Review of Business Research Papers* 1(2): 1–9.

Gélard, G. (2004) 'What can be expected from accounting standards?', *Accounting in Europe* 1: 17–20.

Haller, A. (2003) 'Segmental reporting', in P. Walton, A. Haller and B. Raffournier (eds) *International Accounting*, 2nd edn, London: Thomson Learning.

Henderson, S., Peirson, G., Herbohn, K., Artiach, T. and Ramsay, A. (2006) *Issues in Financial Accounting*, 12th edn, Sydney: Pearson-Prentice Hall.

Hooghiemstra, R. (2012) 'What determines the informativeness of firms' explanations for deviations from the Dutch corporate governance code?', *Accounting and Business Research* 42(1): 1–27.

Hunter, L., Webster, E. and Wyatt, A. (2005) 'Measuring intangible capital: A review of current practice', *Australian Accounting Review* 15(2): 4–21.

James, S. and Nobes, C. (2006) *The Economics of Taxation*, Harlow: Prentice Hall.

Johnson, L. T. and Petrone, K. R. (1998) 'Is goodwill an asset?', *Accounting Horizons* (September): 293–304.

Kvaal, E. and Nobes, C. (2010) 'International differences in IFRS policy choice: A research note', *Accounting and Business Research* 40(2): 173–187.

Lamb, M. (1995) 'When is a group a group? Convergence of concepts of "group" in European Union corporation tax', *European Accounting Review* 4(1): 33–78.

Larson, K. (2007) 'Constituent participation and the IASB's International Financial Reporting Interpretations Committee', *Accounting in Europe* 4: 207–54.

Leuz, C. (2010) 'Different approaches to corporate reporting regulation: How jurisdictions differ and why', *Accounting and Business Research* 40(3): 229–256.

Morris, R., Gray, S., Pickering, J. and Aisbitt S. (2014) 'Preparers' perceptions of the costs and benefits of IFRS: Evidence from Australia's implementation experience', *Accounting Horizons* 28(1): 143–173.

Nielsen, C. and Roslender, R. (2015) 'Enhancing financial reporting: The contribution of business models', *The British Accounting Review* 47(3): 262–274.

Nobes, C. W. and Schwencke, H. R. (2006) 'Modelling the links between tax and financial reporting: A longitudinal examination of Norway over 30 years up to IFRS adoption', *European Accounting Review* 15(1): 63–87.

Nobes, C. (2015) 'Accounting for capital: The evolution of an idea', *Accounting and Business Research* 45(4): 413–441.

Penman, S. H. (2003) 'The quality of financial statements: Perspectives from the recent stock market bubble', *Accounting Horizons* 17 (supplement): 77–96.

Pope, P.F. and McLeay, S.J. (2011) 'The European IFRS experiment: Objectives, research challenges and some early evidence', *Accounting and Business Research* 41(3): 233–266.

Power; M. (2010) 'Fair value accounting, financial economics and the transformation of reliability', *Accounting and Business Research* 40(3): 197–210.

Previts, G., Walton, P. and Wolnizer, P. (eds) (2010) *A Global History of Accounting, Financial Reporting and Public Policy: Europe*, Bingley: Emerald.

Richard, J. (2004) 'The secret past of fair value: Lessons from history applied to the French case', *Accounting in Europe* 1: 95–108.

Rowbottom, N. and Locke, J. (2016) 'The emergence of <IR>', *Accounting and Business Research* 46(1): 83–115.

Sarens, G., De Beelde, I. and Everaert, P. (2009) 'Internal audit: A comfort provider to the audit committee', *British Accounting Review* 41(2): 90–106.

Schmidt, M. (2013) 'Equity and liabilities – A discussion of IAS 12 and a critique of the classification', *Accounting in Europe* 10(2) 201–222.

Shortridge, R. T. and Myring, M. (2004) 'Defining principles-based accounting standards', *The CPA Journal* 74(8): 34–8.

Sloan, R. G. (2001) 'Financial accounting and corporate governance: A discussion', *Journal of Accounting and Economics* 32: 335–47.

Soderstrom, N. and Sun, K. J. (2007) 'IFRS adoption and accounting quality', *European Accounting Review* 16: 675–702.

Stanton, P. A. and Stanton, P. J. (2002) 'Corporate annual reports: Research perspectives used', *Accounting, Auditing and Accountability Journal* 15(4): 478–500.

Sunder, S. (2011) 'IFRS monopoly: The Pied Piper of financial reporting', *Accounting and Business Research* 41(3): 291–306.

Tarca, A., Street, D.L. and Aerts, W. (2010) 'Improving MD&A: A national necessity', *Financial Executive* 26(10): 53–56.

Tarca, A., Street, D.L. and Aerts, W. (2011) 'Factors affecting MD&A disclosures by SEC registrants: Views of practitioners', *Journal of International Accounting, Auditing and Taxation* 20(1): 45–59.

Taylor, P. A (2003) 'Foreign currency translation', in P. Walton, A. Haller and B. Raffournier (eds) *International Accounting*, 2nd edn (pp. 405–442), London: Thomson Learning.

Teixeira, A. (2014) 'The International Accounting Standards Board and evidence-informed standard-setting', *Accounting in Europe* 11(1): 5–12.

Tokar, M. (2005) 'Convergence and the implementation of a single set of global standards: The real life challenge', *Accounting in Europe* 2: 47–68.

Van den Bogaerd, M. and Aerts, W. (2015) 'Does media reputation affect properties of accounts payable?', *European Management Journal* 33(1): 19–29.

Van Caneghem, T. and Aerts, W. (2011) 'Intra-industry conformity in dividend policy', *Managerial Finance* 37(6): 492–516.

Van Mourik, C. and Walton, P., (eds) (2014) *The Routledge Companion to Accounting, Reporting and Regulation*, Abingdon: Routledge.

Van Mourik, C. (2014) 'The equity theories and the IASB Conceptual Framework', *Accounting in Europe* 11(2): 219–234.

Van Mourik, C. and Walton, P. (2018) 'The European IFRS Endorsement Process – in Search of a Single Voice', *Accounting in Europe* 15(1): 1–32.

Vasarhelyi, M., Kogan, A. and Tuttle, B. (2015) 'Big data in accounting: An overview', *Accounting Horizons* 29(2): 381–396.

Walton, P. (1993) 'The true and fair view in British accounting', *European Accounting Review* 2: 49–58.

Walton, P. (2004) 'IAS 39: Where different accounting models collide', *Accounting in Europe* 1: 5–16.

Walton, P. (2006) 'Fair value and executory contracts: Moving the boundaries in international financial reporting', *Accounting and Business Research* 36(4): 337–43.

Walton, P. (ed.) (2007) *The Routledge Guide to Fair Value and Financial Reporting*, Abingdon: Routledge.

Walton, P. (2015) 'IFRS in Europe – An observer's perspective of the next ten years', *Accounting in Europe* 12(2): 135–151.

Wheeler Spencer, A. and Webb, T. (2015) 'Leases: A review of contemporary academic literature relating to lessees', *Accounting Horizons* 29(4): 997–1023.

Whittington, G. (2005) 'The adoption of International Accounting Standards in the European Union', *European Accounting Review* 14(1): 127–53.

Zhang, S. and Aerts, W. (2015) 'Management's performance justification and failure to meet earnings thresholds', *Accounting and Business Research* 45(6–7): 841–868.

CREDITS

Chapter	Details	Item	Page number	Sourceline
Ch 1	Box feature	Standards box – IASB Conceptual Framework *(extracts)*	6	Source: IASB, *Conceptual Framework for Financial Reporting*
Ch 1	Box feature	Standards box – IASB Conceptual Framework *(extracts)*	7	Source: IASB, *Conceptual Framework for Financial Reporting*
Ch 1	Table	Table 1.1 List of IASB pronouncements as of January 2019	17	Source: IASB
Ch 1	Figure	Figure 1.1 The structure of the Board	19	Source: IASB
Ch 1	Table	Table 1.3 Effects of the IAS Regulation (EU)	23	Source: IAS
Ch 1	Box feature	Standards box – IASB Conceptual Framework *(extracts)*	25	Source: IASB, *Conceptual Framework for Financial Reporting*
Ch 2	Box feature	Standards box – COSO – Components of a system of internal control *(extracts)*	41	Source: COSO, Internal Control – Integrated Framework, Executive Summary
Ch 2	Box feature	Standards box – Defining internal auditing	47	Source: Institute of Internal Auditors (www.theiia.org)
Ch 2	Box feature	Standards box – Institute of Internal Auditors: Standards for the professional practice of auditing	47	Source: Institute of Internal Auditors, 2016 (www.theiia.org)
Ch 2	Box feature	Company report – Nestlé	50	Source: Nestlé, Financial Statements, 2017
Ch 3	Box feature	Standard practice box – Why global financial reporting standards for small and medium-size enterprises? *(extracts)*	62	Source: IASB, IFRS for SMEs® Standard, Basis for Conclusions, July 2009
Ch 3	Box feature	Standards box – IAS 1 – *Presentation of Financial Statements (extracts)*	73	Source: IAS 1, *Presentation of Financial Statements*

Chapter	Details	Item	Page number	Sourceline
Ch 4	Main text	Accrual accounting depicts the effects of transactions ....during that period.	103	IASB, *Conceptual Framework for Financial Reporting*, para. 1.17
Ch 4	Box feature	Standards Box – IFRS 15 – *Revenue from Contracts with Customers* – Customer contracts *(extracts)*	111	Source: IFRS 15, *Revenue from Contracts with Customers*
Ch 4	Box feature	IAS 2 – *Inventories* – Cost of inventories *(extracts)*	120	Source: IAS 2, *Inventories*
Ch 4	Box feature	IAS 2 – *Inventories* – Net realisable value *(extracts)*	125	Source: IAS 2, *Inventories*
Ch 4	Box feature	Company report – Nokia – Inventories *(extracts)*	127	Source: Nokia, Annual Report, 2017
Ch 5	Box feature	Standards box IAS 16 – *Property, Plant and Equipment* – Elements of acquisition cost *(extracts)*	145	Source: IAS 16, *Property, Plant and Equipment*
Ch 5	Box feature	Standards box – *Property, Plant and Equipment* – Depreciation accounting *(extracts)*	147	Source: IAS 16, *Property, Plant and Equipment*
Ch 5	Box feature	Company report – Lufthansa – Tangible assets *(extract)*	150	Lufthansa Group Annual Report, 2017
Ch 5	Box feature	Company report – Nestlé – Reconciliation details on net carrying amount of property, plant and equipment *(extracts)*	156	Consolidated Financial Statements of the Nestlé Group 2017
Ch 5	Box feature	Standards box – IAS 38 – *Intangible Assets* – Definition *(extracts)*	160	Source: IAS 38, *Intangible Assets*
Ch 5	Box feature	Standards box – IAS 38 – *Intangible Assets* – Research and development *(extracts)*	162	Source: IAS 38, *Intangible Assets*
Ch 5	Box feature	Standards box – IAS 38 – *Intangible Assets* – Exclusions *(extract)*	164	Source: IAS 38, *Intangible Assets*
Ch 5	Box feature	Company report – TomTom – Intangible assets	165	Source: TomTom International BV, © 2017 Annual Report
Ch 5	Box feature	Company report – Bekaert – Leases *(extract)*	169	Source: Bekaert, Annual Report, 2017
Ch 6	Box feature	Company report – Vodafone – Accrued and deferred revenue *(extracts)*	181	Source: Vodafone, Annual Report, 2018
Ch 6	Box feature	Standards box – IAS 37 – *Provisions, Contingent Liabilities and Contingent Assets (extract)*	184	Source: IAS 37, *Provisions, Contingent Liabilities and Contingent Assets*
Ch 6	Box feature	Company report – Novartis – Provisions for product liabilities, government investigations and other legal matters *(extracts)*	186	Source: Novartis, Annual Report, 2017
Ch 6	Box feature	Company report – Philips – Contingent liabilities *(extracts)*	187	Source: Philips, Annual Report, 2017, Reproduced by Courtesy of Royal Philips

Chapter	Details	Item	Page number	Sourceline
Ch 6	Box feature	Company report – Novartis – Impairment of goodwill and intangible assets *(extracts)*	188	Source: Novartis, Annual Report, 2017
Ch 6	Box feature	Standards box – Value in use – Calculation headlines	190	Source: Adapted from IAS 36, *Impairment of Assets*, paras 30–57
Ch 6	Box feature	Standards box – Impairment rules – Individual assets versus cash-generating units *(examples)*	192	Source: IAS 36, *Impairment of Assets*, paras 67 and 68
Ch 6	Box feature	Standards box – Illustration – Identification of a cash-generating unit in a retail store chain	193	Source: Adapted from IAS 36 – Illustrative Examples
Ch 6	Box feature	Standards box – Illustration – Identification of a cash-generating unit in a single product company	193	Source: Adapted from IAS 36 – Illustrative Examples
Ch 6	Box feature	Company report – BP – Significant accounting policies, judgements, estimates and assumptions *(extract)*	195	Source: BP Annual Report, 2017
Ch 6	Box feature	Company report – Siemens – Allowance for doubtful trade receivables *(extract)*	198	Source: Siemens, Annual Report, 2018
Ch 9	Box feature	Company report – Ericsson	251	Source: Ericsson, Annual Report, 2017
Ch 9	Box feature	Standards box – IAS 33 – *Earnings per share (extract)*	256	Source: IAS 33, *Earnings per Share*
Ch 10	Box feature	Standards box – IAS 7 – Cash and cash equivalents *(extracts)*	278	Source: IAS 7, *Statement of Cash Flows*
Ch 10	Box feature	Standards box – IAS 7 – Investing and financing activities *(extracts)*	280	Source: IAS 7, *Statement of Cash Flows*
Ch 10	Box feature	Company report – Capgemini – Consolidated statement of cash flows	281	Source: Capgemini Group, Consolidated Financial Statements, 2017
Ch 10	Box feature	Standards box – IAS 7 – Direct method statement of cash flows *(extract)*	287	Source: IAS 7, *Statement of Cash Flows* – Illustrative examples
Ch 10	Box feature	Standards box – IAS 7 – Indirect method statement of cash flows *(extract)*	288	Source: IAS 7, *Statement of Cash Flows* – Illustrative examples
Ch 11	Box feature	Standards box – Other comprehensive income – Definition	314	Source: IAS 1, *Presentation of Financial Statements*, Extract from para. 7
Ch 11	Box feature	Standards box – Presentation of profit or loss and other comprehensive income in one statement	314	Source: IAS 1, *Presentation of Financial Statements*, Extracts from Implementation Guidance
Ch 11	Box feature	Standards box – Presentation of profit or loss and other comprehensive income in two statements	316	Source: IAS 1, *Presentation of Financial Statements*, Extracts from Implementation Guidance

Chapter	Details	Item	Page number	Sourceline
Ch 12	Box Feature	Company report – The acquisition of Regal Cinemas by Cineworld Group	322	Source: Cineworld Group announcement, 5 December 2017
Ch 12	Box feature	Company report – Roche – Accounting policies *(extract)*	325	Source: Roche Group, Finance Report, 2018
Ch 12	Box feature	Standards box – IFRS 3 – Definition of a business *(extract)*	331	Source: IFRS 3, *Business Combinations*
Ch 12	Box feature	Standards box – IFRS 3 – The acquisition method *(extracts)*	332	Source: IFRS 3, *Business Combinations*
Ch 12	Box feature	Standards box – IFRS 3 – *Business Combinations (extract)*	339	Source: IFRS 3, *Business Combinations*
Ch 12	Box feature	Company report – Roche – Consolidation *(extract)*	344	Source: Roche Group, Finance Report, 2018
Ch 12	Box feature	Standards box – IAS 28 – *Investments in Associates and Joint Ventures (extracts)*	347	Source: IAS 28, *Investments in Associates and Joint Ventures*
Ch 12	Box feature	Standards box – IFRS 12 – *Disclosure of Interests in Other Entities (extracts)*	349	Source: IFRS 12, *Disclosure of Interests in Other Entities*
Ch13	Box feature	Company report – Groupe PSA (Peugeot Citroën/Opel Vauxhall) – Segment information	361	Source: Groupe PSA Annual Report, 2018
Ch 13	Box feature	Company report – Nestlé Group	364	Source: Nestlé Group, Annual Report, 2017
Ch 13	Box feature	Standards box – IFRS 8 – *Operating Segments (extracts)*	366	Source: IFRS 8, *Operating Segments*
Ch 13	Box feature	Standard box – IFRS 8 – *Operating Segments (extracts)*	368	Source: IFRS 8, *Operating Segments*
Ch 13	Box feature	Standards box – IFRS 8 – *Operating Segments (extracts)*	369	Source: IFRS 8, *Operating Segments*
Ch 13	Box feature	Standards box – IAS 21 – *The Effects of Changes in Foreign Exchange Rates (extracts)*	373	Source: IAS 21, *The Effects of Changes in Foreign Exchange Rates*
Ch 13	Box feature	Company report – AngloGold Ashanti – Foreign currency translation	376	Source: Extract from 'Summary of significant accounting policies', AngloGold Ashanti, Notes on Financial Statements, 2017
Ch 13	Box feature	Company report – Agfa-Gevaert	385	Source: Agfa, Annual Report, 2017
Ch 13	Box feature	Standards box – IAS 21 – *The Effect of Changes in Foreign Exchange Rates (extracts)*	387	Source: IAS 21, *The Effects of Changes in Foreign Exchange Rates*
Ch 14	Box feature	Standards box – IFRS 7 – *Financial Instruments: Disclosures (extract)*	403	Source: IFRS 7, *Financial Instruments: Disclosures*
Ch 14	Box feature	Company report – Stora Enso – Post-employment benefits	405	Source: Stora Enso, Annual Report, 2017
Ch 14	Box feature	Standards box – IAS 37 – *Provisions, Contingent Liabilities and Contingent Assets (extracts)*	408	Source: IAS 37, *Provisions, Contingent Liabilities and Contingent Assets*

Chapter	Details	Item	Page number	Sourceline
Ch 14	Box feature	Standards box – IAS 10 – *Events after the Reporting Period (extract)*	409	Source: IAS 10, *Events after the Reporting Period*
Ch 14	Box feature	Standards box – IFRS 5 – *Non-current Assets Held for Sales and Discontinued Operations (extract)*	410	Source: IFRS 5, *Non-current Assets Held for Sale and Discontinued Operations*
Ch 14	Box feature	Company report box – BP – Decommissioning obligation and asset cost	414	Source: BP Plc, Annual Report, 2017
Ch 14	Box feature	Between the lines box – The measurement and management of intellectual capital: an introduction	415	Source: IFAC Handbook 1999, extract from summary of study published by the International Federation of accountants, New York, October 1998
Ch 15	Box feature	Company report – Philips – Income tax expense	425	Source: Philips, Annual Report, 2017, Reproduced by Courtesy of Royal Philips
Ch 15	Box feature	Standards box – IAS 12 – *Income Taxes – Definitions (extracts)*	428	Source: IAS 12, *Income Taxes*
Ch 15	Box feature	Company report – Philips – Overview of deferred tax assets and liabilities	430	Source: Philips, Annual Report, 2017, Reproduced by Courtesy of Royal Philips
Ch 15	Box feature	Company report – Philips – Reconciliation of theoretical tax rate to effective tax rate	433	Source: Philips, Annual Report, 2017, Reproduced by Courtesy of Royal Philips
Ch 16	Box feature	Between the lines box – Defining corporate governance – OECD Principles of Corporate Governance (extract)	441	Source: OECD Principles of Corporate Governance, 2004
Ch 16	Box feature	Standards box – Outline of the Sarbanes–Oxley Act of 2002	442	Source: Sarbanes–Oxley Act, 107 P. L. 204, § 1, 116 Stat. 745, July 30, 2002
Ch 16	Box feature	Between the lines box – Fraudulent financial reporting – 1998–2007	445	Source: Fraudulent Financial Reporting 1998–2007. An Analysis of US Public Companies, published by the Committee of Sponsoring Organizations of the Treadway Commission (COSO), 2010
Ch 16	Box feature	Company report – Lufthansa – Risk management system	451	Source: Lufthansa Annual Report, 2017, extract from Combined Management Report
Ch 16	Box feature	Company report – Nokia – Audit committee	453	Source: NOKIA, Annual Report, 2017
Ch 17	Box feature	Between the lines box – Investor relations meetings	458	Source: ICAS, Corporate Communications: Views of Institutional Investors and Lenders (Research Committee, Institute of Chartered Accountants of Scotland, 1999)

Chapter	Details	Item	Page number	Sourceline
Ch 17	Box feature	Between the lines box	459	Source: Accounting & Business, July/August 1999, p.20
Ch 17	Box feature	Between the lines box – Cookie jar reserves	462	Source: Speech by Walter P. Schuetze, Chief Accountant, Enforcement Division, US Securities and Exchange Commission, 22 April 1999 (www.sec.gov/news/speech/speecharchive/1999/spch276.htm)
Ch 17	Box feature	Between the lines box	465	Source: ICAS, Corporate Communications: Views of Institutional Investors and Lenders (Research Committee, Institute of Chartered Accountants of Scotland, 1999)
Ch 17	Box feature	Standards box – IAS 1 – *Presentation of Financial Statements (extracts)*	466	Source: IAS 1, *Presentation of Financial Statements*
Ch 17	Box feature	Standards box – IAS 1 – *Presentation of Financial Statements (extracts)*	467	Source: IAS 1, *Presentation of Financial Statements*
Ch 17	Box feature	Company report – Ryanair – Use of estimates and judgements	468	Source: Ryanair, Annual Report, 2018

INDEX